Adolphe-Napoléon Didron

a French archaeologist (1806-1867) of wide interests and learning, was inspired to study the antiquities of the Middle Ages after reading Hugo's *Notre Dame de Paris*. His theological ideas and his knowledge of Scripture and the legends of the saints led him further to the study of iconography. He was highly instrumental in reviving Christian art in his native France; he constructed a glass manufactory in 1849, and established a goldsmiths' workshop in 1858, both of which produced some notable work. Didron was also the founder of a library of archeological literature. Foremost among his other writings are the accounts of his travels and studies in iconography published in the review *Annales archeologiques* (1844-1881).

CHRISTIAN ICONOGRAPHY

CHRISTIAN ICONOGRAPHY

The History of Christian Art in the Middle Ages

ADOLPHE NAPOLEON DIDRON

VOLUME I

Translated from the French by
E. J. MILLINGTON

With numerous illustrations

FREDERICK UNGAR PUBLISHING CO.
NEW YORK

Republished 1965

Reprinted from the first edition, 1851

Printed in the United States of America

Library of Congress Catalog Card No. 65-23577

TRANSLATOR'S PREFACE.

M. Didron's work on Christian Iconography is well known to the Archæological world; but as it has never appeared in an English form, and the original volume is not very accessible to general readers, the present publication will, it is believed, prove an acceptable contribution to Archæological literature.

The subject of which it treats has never yet been adequately investigated, although the various sketches which have occasionally appeared prove that its importance has been duly appreciated. The ensuing pages will be found to contain much valuable information, available equally to the artist and the architect, and to every votary of Archæological science. In the chapter on the nimbus, many curious facts are elicited in reference to the form and decoration of that symbolic ornament, which cannot fail to be materially useful in marking correctly the distinct character of different figures in early subjects, whether of painting or sculpture. As, unhappily, it is of too common occurrence in this country, to find figures mutilated and partially destroyed, every additional characteristic that may aid in setting a distinctive mark upon the persons represented, is an acquisition of no trifling importance. For this object, the form of the nimbus, and the distinct signification of cruciform, triangular, and decorated nimbi, present most invaluable data which have never, it is believed, been so clearly set before the reader as in the work of M. Didron.

The history of the various gradations by which the art advanced to its most perfect and glorious conceptions of the Deity, under a human form, and the influence of popular feeling, as exemplified in the manner of representing God the Father, form a most interesting portion of this work. It embraces the whole range of Iconography, in its relation to the Divine persons of the Blessed Trinity; first treating of each individually, and lastly, as of the three persons united in one. Many contending elements grew up, even in the bosom of the Christian Church; men's minds were subjected to opposing influences, and the faintest shadow that darkened or the lightest breath that disturbed, the internal harmony of the Church, was immediately reflected by the pencil of the artist and the chisel of the sculptor. Almost every ancient edifice, therefore, becomes as it were to the eye of the Christian student a hieroglyphic record of the changes which the Church has undergone during successive ages, whether produced by external influences, or by heresies generated within herself. In some countries, too, even local feelings and jealousies have occasionally been perpetuated, as is exemplified by certain sculptures in the porch of the church at Rouen.

Neither time nor labour has been spared in rendering the present translation as perfect as possible. In many instances the books and sculptures mentioned by M. Didron have been examined by the *Editor* of the present volume, who availed himself of the opportunity afforded by a stay of some months in Paris to investigate several MSS. in the Bibliothèque Royale and elsewhere. To his fine taste and knowledge of the subject the Translator is, indeed, most deeply indebted; and she gladly takes this opportunity of expressing her lively sense of the advantages she has derived from his friendship and assistance.

The value of the translation is considerably enhanced by the fact that the engravings are the identical ones used by M. Didron; they are in no respect inferior to those in the French work, and their perfect accuracy as illustrations of the text may be most confidently relied on.

At page 437 will be found an extract from the translation of the third book of Durandus—the *Rat. Div. Off.*, and the correction of a singular error committed by the translators of that work, published by the Cambridge Camden (now the Ecclesiological) Society. The word "rotuli," by them translated *wheels*, is clearly shown to be incorrect, *rolls* being the proper term. And taken in this sense, the passage, which is at present unintelligible (none of the Old Testament prophets having, I believe, ever been represented with *wheels*), becomes simple and highly interesting. The different signification of the *roll* and *open volume*, the one prophetic and shadowy, the other an open and perfect revelation, is well known and generally recognised.

Little more need be said in reference to the original work, which will, doubtless, commend itself by its title to all who are interested in this peculiar branch of Art, and by whom the want of the aid which it affords, has no doubt been frequently experienced. We have not at this moment any work in our own language to which the student could apply for a knowledge of the leading principles of sacred Archæology. Treatises there are; some on one important branch; some on another. Sketches, too, there are of the science of Iconography, but they are mere silhouettes; the outline of a painted window with the contours only; the minor details, the colours, and all that gives warmth and animation to the subject, omitted. What has principally been required is a grammar of the science, containing its fundamental principles clearly set forth, systematically arranged, and illustrated by choice examples and copious authorities. Each subject should be traced through the various changes which have taken place since Christian artists first commenced their labours of love, and should be compared with the holy texts from which they were originally derived.

All this M. Didron has done, and the evidence of his success is before us. If it be objected that the same facts and deductions are too frequently reiterated, it may be replied, that his work being intended as a medium of instruction, the plan pursued in it, has not been adopted without a due consideration.

Every student will, we are convinced, feel satisfied, before he has closed the book, that he has really gained a new intelligence, and imbibed the leading principles, at least, of a science, previously but very dimly comprehended. With a full knowledge of the sacred texts, he will find no difficulty in determining any of the usual subjects met with in sacred edifices, and M. Didron's lucid explanation of the various modes of treating them at different eras, and in different countries, will make it a comparatively easy task to decide on the age which ought to be assigned to them.

The field, however, is as yet only opening before us, and much remains to be investigated, many theories to be confirmed or set aside, many opinions to be qualified or more strongly asserted; while the investigation itself may be carried on from the Divine Persons, with whom it commences, through all the hierarchical gradations of angels,—good and evil,—saints and martyrs, not forgetting the Virgin Mary, whose Iconographic history would furnish a volume in itself. All these the Author proposes to treat, at some future, and, we trust, not very distant period. The original of the present work has been favourably noticed in several of our leading Reviews, and although, in the translation, some technical difficulties have presented themselves, the utmost care has been taken to give the Author's sense as clearly and precisely as possible; and the Translator earnestly hopes the work will not be found to have deteriorated in her hands, either in interest or importance.

E. J. MILLINGTON.

SEPT. 1851.

CONTENTS.

PART II.

LIST OF ILLUSTRATIONS.

CHRISTIAN ICONOGRAPHY.

INTRODUCTION.

Christianity was the all-powerful influence which, during the centuries intervening between the ninth and seventeenth of our era, produced in cathedrals, parish churches, and private chapels; in colleges, abbeys, and priories; a profusion almost incredible of figures, images, and sacred subjects, sculptured, carved, painted, engraved, and even woven into tapestries and costly hangings.

Some large churches, such as those of Chartres, Rheims, Paris, and Amiens, are adorned with no fewer than two, three, or even four thousand statues of stone; or, as is the case in that of Chartres, and in those of Bourges and Mans, with three, four, or five thousand figures painted on glass. Formerly, there was not a church, however small its dimensions, that did not possess thirty, forty, or perhaps a hundred figures either in sculpture or painting.

If, then, we take a mean number between the largest and smallest amounts, and multiply that number by the quantity of religious edifices known to have existed in France, whether before the fanatical devastation of the sixteenth, or the political destruction of the eighteenth century, we shall be able to judge of the vast importance that had been given by Christianity to the imitative arts.

Owing to the ravages of the weather, the changes of the seasons, the course of ages, and the revolutions to which mankind have been exposed, the number of such figures now existing, whether executed in sculpture, carving, or painting, is singularly diminished. The entire series of personages represented at Chartres and at Bourges, are, however, yet in existence, and at least three-fourths of those at Lyons. More than half the original number still remain at Rheims and at Strasbourg. The great cathedrals, those which were most thronged with worshippers, have suffered less than churches of the second or third rank, so that France is even now incredibly rich in statues and stained glass. The single city of Troyes contains no less than nine churches, into which the light is still admitted through windows of stained glass, on which are painted historical subjects, memorials extending from the thirteenth to the seventeenth centuries.

With a few exceptions, nearly all the figures sculptured or painted in churches are religious or biblical, and we must seek an explanation of them either in the Scriptures or in the Golden Legend; occasionally, perhaps, in Fabliaux and other popular poems and fictions, but never in serious history, and very rarely even in the early chronicles. We should carry with us these two volumes, the Bible and the *Legenda Aurea*, when we study the monuments of sculpture to be found in our cathedrals; the "Monuments de la monarchie Française," by Montfaucon, must, on the contrary, be discarded altogether, as his theories are calculated to involve us in most serious errors.

The instruction of the people, and the edification of the faithful, were the paramount objects proposed to itself by Christianity in adopting this singular system of historical embellishment. Writers of every epoch bear witness that this idea prompted the execution and arrangement of the numerous statues and figures which crowd our earlier religious edifices. Quotations might be multiplied to excess; but we shall be content to mention a few only, beginning with one inscription, the most recent of all, which might, not long since, have been read in the church of St Nizier, at Troyes, but which has now disappeared, together with the painted window, filled with historic figures, beneath which it was inscribed. A curé of St. Nizier, in the sixteenth century, directed the principal themes of the Gospel, the Legenda, and the Dogma, to be painted on glass, and had them placed in the windows of the nave, the choir, the apse, and the side-aisles, where they are still to be seen. Below the eastern window he inscribed, "SANCTA PLEBI DEI." At a very different epoch, in the year 433, Pope Sixtus, in the same manner, dedicated to the "people of God," the mosaics in Santa Maria Maggiore, at Rome; and beneath the sacred persons whom he had caused to be pourtrayed, he placed the following inscription: "Xistus episcopus plebi Dei."* Thus, at the two extreme points of the middle ages, viz. the fifth and sixteenth centuries, the same idea prevailed, and even found expression in the same words. Between those two limits it was propounded in detail, and often commented upon with eloquence. So, at the close of the seventh century, Benedict Biscop, Abbot of Wearmouth, in England, adorned a church, which he had erected, with paintings brought from Italy for that purpose. He wished that all, on entering the House of God, especially those who knew not how to read, should have before their eyes the ever-beloved image of Christ and his saints. They were thus stimulated to meditation upon the blessings of the Divine incarnation, and reminded, by the sight of the Last Judgment, of the duty and necessity of strict self-examination.†

St. John Damascenus, in the eighth century, employed the same reasoning in defence of images. "Images speak," cries the eloquent apologist; "they are neither mute, nor lifeless blocks, like the idols of the Pagans. Every painting that meets our gaze in a church, relates, as if in words, the humiliation of Christ for his people, the miracles of the Mother of God, the deeds and conflicts of the Saints. Images open the heart and awake the intellect, and, in a marvellous and indescribable manner, engage us to imitate the persons they represent." ‡

* Ciampini *Vetera Monumenta*, p. 49, pars prima.

† "Quatenus intrantes ecclesiam omnes, etiam litterarum ignari, quaquaversum intenderent, vel semper amabilem Christi sanctorumque ejus, quamvis in imagine, contemplarentur adspectum; vel Dominicæ incarnationis gratiam vigilantiore mente recolerent; vel extremi discrimen examinis, quasi coram oculis habentes, districtius se ipsi examinare meminissent."—(*Act. SS. ord. S. Bened.* 2e Vol., où IIe *Siècle Bénédictin*,) Life of St. Benedict Biscop, first Abbot of Wearmouth, written by the Venerable Bede, his disciple.

‡ "Etiam loquuntur (imagines) nec mutæ prorsus sunt omnisve sensus expertes, uti gentium idola. Omnis enim pictura, quam in ecclesia LEGIMUS, aut Christi ad nos demissionem, aut Dei genitricis miracula, aut sanctorum certamina et res gestas, velut imagine loquente, enarrat; sensumque ac mentem aperit, ut miris eos infandisque modis æmulemur."— (Opera S. Johannis Damasceni, *Adversus Constantinum Cabalinum oratio*, vol. i., p. 619, edition of 1712, in fol.)

The Synod of Arras, in 1025, declared, as Benedict Biscop had done, that the illiterate contemplated in the lineaments of painting what they, having never learned to read, could not discern in writing.* An ecclesiastical chronicler of Auxerre supports, in an interesting passage, the texts which precede and confirm the religious dogma concerning images. It is stated in his "Histoire des évêques d'Auxerre," that under Bishop Geoffrey, son of Hugh, Count of Nevers, in the time of Henry I., the cathedral of Auxerre was partly destroyed by a conflagration. The bishop, in the space of one year, caused it to be repaired, the stained glass replaced, and the whole covered with a roof of timber and tiles. He commanded the circular wall of the inclosure, surrounding the altar, to be filled with fresco portraits of the holy bishops, his predecessors. He desired, by this means, not only to direct the eye of the officiating priests from the contemplation of all vain and profane objects, but, above all, to assist those who were likely to be distracted by vanity or weariness; thus, in the presence of these images, and at the recollection of all those pious persons, disinterred, as it were, by painting, the mind of each was recalled, as by a living counsellor, to the courage of piety.† To this explicit passage, belonging, like the Council of Arras, to the eleventh century, we shall add the testimony of St. Paulinus, Bishop of Nola, near Naples, written at the commencement of the fifth, and, consequently, much earlier than the quotations inserted above. St. Paulinus, after having described the pictures which he had had executed in the basilica of St. Felix, built by him at Fondi, says:—"If any should inquire why, contrary to

* "Illiterati, quod per scripturam non possunt intueri, hoc per quædam picturæ lineamenta contemplantur." Suger (*de Administratione suâ*, ap. Félibien, *Histoire de l'Abbaye de St. Denis*, Pièces justificatives), uses precisely the same language, 115 years later than the Council of Arras.

† "Neque de corona muri claudentis altare, sanctorumque præsulum pictas habentis effigies sileıo justum est, quem canentium oculis sacerdotum non solum ideo opposuit ut ab eis visus inanes et illicitos excluderet, verum et idcirco, ut si quis vanitate vel tædio gravatus extra se duceretur, sicut sæpe contingere ex nostræ fragilitatis vitio solet, illa præsenti visione et aperta tot bonorum per picturam memoria mentem et omnium quasi vivo revocatus consilio ad fortitudinem pietatis relevaret."—(*Nova Bibliotheca Manuscriptorum librorum*, par le P. Labbe, tom i., p. 452; *Historia episcoporum Autissiodorensium*. Paris, 1652, in fol.)

common usage, I have given personal representations of holy people in this sacred dwelling, I answer: 'Among the crowds attracted hither by the fame of St. Felix, there are peasants recently converted, who cannot read, and who, before embracing the faith of Christ, had long been the slaves of profane usages, and had obeyed their senses as gods. They arrive here from afar, and from all parts of the country. Glowing with faith, they despise the chilling frosts; they pass the entire night in joyous watchings; they drive away slumber by gaiety, and darkness by torches. But they mingle festivities with their prayers, and, after singing hymns to God, abandon themselves to good cheer; they joyously stain with odoriferous wine the tombs of the Saints. They sing in the midst of their cups, and, by their drunken lips, the demon insults St. Felix. I have, therefore, thought it expedient to enliven with paintings the entire habitation of the Holy Saint. Images thus traced and coloured will perhaps inspire those rude minds with astonishment. Inscriptions are placed above the pictures, in order that the letter may explain what the hand has depicted. While showing them to each other, and reading thus by turns these pictured objects, they do not think of eating until later than before,—their eyes aid them to endure fasting. Painting beguiles their hunger, better habits govern these wondering men, and studying these holy histories, chastity and virtue are engendered by such examples of piety. These sober gazers are intoxicated with excitement, though they have ceased to indulge in wine. A great part of the time being spent in looking at these pictures, they drink much less, for there remain only a few short minutes for their repast.' "*

* "Forte requiratur quanam ratione gerendi
Sederit hæc nobis sententia pingere sanctas,
Raro more, domos animantibus adsimulatis
Accipite, et paucis tentabo exponere causas."
*   *   *   *   *
*   * "Visum nobis opus utile, totis
Felicis domibus pictura illudere sancta;
Si forte attonitas hæc per spectacula mentes,
Agrestem caperet fucata coloribus umbra.
Quæ super exprimitur titulis, ut littera monstret
Quod manus explicuit. Dumque omnes picta vicissim,
Ostendunt releguntque sibi, vel tardius escæ

Thus, then, for those men of the middle ages, for those Christians of lively susceptibility, but who yet knew not how to read, the clergy provided rondes-bosses, bas-reliefs, and pictures, where science on the one hand and doctrine on the other were personified. A sculptured arch in the porch of a church, or an historical glass painting in the nave presented the ignorant with a lesson, the believer with a sermon,—a lesson and a sermon which reached the heart through the eyes instead of entering at the ears. The impression, besides, was infinitely deeper; for it is acknowledged, that a picture sways the soul far more powerfully than any discourse or description in words.*

The dramatic art also aimed at similar results. The representation of mysteries and miracles served to put in action the persons painted on glass windows, sculptured on the capitals, or encrusted in the vaultings of cathedrals.

In these same cathedrals were performed the Miracles of St. Martin and of St. Nicholas, the Mysteries of the Annunciation, and of the Nativity, which had already been represented by the hand of art, in sculpture and in painting. Words and gestures interpreted what outline and colouring had expressed, and the intention which actuated both was the same; in short, the graphic and dramatic arts became a book to those who could read no other.† It is in this light that they must be regarded; in this character

Sint memores, dum grata oculis jejunia pascunt,
Atque ita se melior stupefactis inserat usus,
Dum fallit pictura famem; sanctasque legenti
Historias, castorum operum subrepit honestas,
Exemplis inducta piis. Potatur hianti
Sobrietas; nimii subeunt oblivia vini.
Dumque diem ducunt spatio majore tuentes,
Pocula rarescunt, quia, per miracula tracto
Tempore, jam paucæ superant epulantibus horæ."

—(Divi Paulini episcopi Nolani opera, *poema* XXVI., *de Felice natal. carm.* ix., v., 541—594, p. 642 et 643 de l'edit. de Muratori. Verone, 1736, fol.)

* Horace (*de Arte Poeticâ*) expresses this idea in the two following verses:—

"Segnius irritant animos demissa per aurem
Quam quæ sunt oculis subjecta fidelibus."

† "Ejus (Dei) porro formam, sensibili expressam modo, omni in loco statuimus ac per eam sensum primum sanctificamus—inter sensus enim primas tenet visus—quemadmodum et per sermones auditum. Imago siquidem monimentum quoddam est; ac quidquid liber est iis qui litteras didicerunt, hoc

we must seek a clue to the interpretation of the figures —true hieroglyphics of the middle ages, which Christian archæology, although at present only in its infancy, already begins to decipher and comprehend.

The imitative art as practised in cathedrals, performed the combined offices of a lesson for the purpose of instruction, of a sermon for morality, and an example for edification; like the religious drama, it gave individual forms to the whole range of Christian science and its dogmas. Assisted by such material objects, by statues, images, and scenic games, the most feeble intelligence might rise to the conception of truth, and a soul plunged in the lowest abyss of darkness might soar upwards in the light displayed by art before its eyes.

> "Mens hebes ad verum per materialia surgit
> Et, demersa prius, hac visa luce resurgit." *

It was in order to attain the twofold object of instruction and edification that writers selected their doctrinal texts from the sacred Scriptures, and texts referring to science from the didactic writers of the age. The book composed by the first class, the Theologians, was the "Bible Historiale," in which both the Old and New Testament were melted into one; that of the other party, the Savants, bore divers names, but all are comprised in the general appellation of "livres de clergie"—"clergie" signifying science. From these two works, one sacred and doctrinal, the other civil and scientific, were framed general Encyclopædias, called also by various names, the most popular of which were the "Hortus Deliciarum," or "le Vergier de Solas;"

imago est illiteratis et rudibus; et quod auditui præstat oratio, hoc visui confert imago."—(Opp. S. Johannis Damasceni, *Oratio prima de Imaginibus*, tom. i., p. 314, 315.)

* These two verses, more beautiful in idea and expression than those of Horace quoted above, and which express an analogous idea, were written by the Abbé Suger, the great artist of the Cathedral of St. Denis. They were inscribed, by his command, on the western portal central entrance, upon the bronze folding-doors of which were the "Passion," the "Resurrection," and the "Ascension," and beneath the carvings representing the "Last Judgment." These verses, which still exist, serve as an explanation of the door-posts, vaultings, and tympanum, which are completely covered with illustrious personages.—(Suger, *de Administratione suâ*, in Félibien, *Histoire de l'Abbaye de St. Denis*, Pièces justificatives, p. clxxii. Paris, 1706, fol.)

the "Summa Theologiæ," by Thomas Aquinas; the "Miroir Universel," by Vincent de Beauvais;* the "Image du Monde,"† the "Propriétaire des Choses,"‡ and the "Lucidaire." §

In the eleventh, twelfth, and thirteenth centuries learned men and philosophers thought only of making encyclopædias. The number of facts relating to nature or to mankind, accumulated by the Greeks, the Romans, the Byzantines and Alexandrians, had become a chaos, and unparalleled exertions were made in order to carry light into this night of intelligence, in which all was disjoined, incoherent, or misapplied. Before proceeding to investigate new facts, before calling other ideas into existence, it was indispensably necessary to pause for a while to reflect, to arrange an inventory of the treasures already acquired, and classify as in a museum or library those disorderly heaps of information which had hitherto been thrown together pell-mell in all the confusion and disorder of a storehouse or magazine. It was thought desirable to glance back at the past before proceeding onwards.

A feeling of the necessity of, and a prepossession for, classification, prevails in all works of the middle ages, whether literary or scientific. To give some few examples only. Innumerable legends existed, scattered throughout a host of volumes. An Archbishop of Genoa, Jacques de Voragine, collected all in one single volume, to which he gave the name of "Légende dorée," or *Legenda Aurea.* ||

* Vincentii Bellovacensis *Speculum Quadruplex, Naturale, Doctrinale, Morale, Historiale,* 7 vols. folio. Argent. Mentelin, 1473-76. Frequently reprinted. The first French translation was published at Paris by Verard in 1495-6, in 5 vols. folio.

† Two English editions were printed by Caxton, both in 1487, under the title of "Thymage or Myrrour of the World."

‡ Originally written in Latin by Bartholemæus Anglicus (Glanville) and supposed to be printed at Cologne by Caxton, about 1470. The many early editions, and the several translations into French and English, bespeak its great popularity. Shakespeare is shown by Mr. Douce to have been familiar with its contents.

§ An English translation was printed by Caxton, in small 4to, under the title of "A lytel treatise, intytuled or named, The Lucidarye."

|| One ought to say "Légende d'or," as one would say "Livre d'or," since the word is "aurea," not "aurata," but "dorée" has prevailed.

Theological science was diffused throughout a multitude of treatises: St. Thomas concentrated all in one grand work, entitled the "Summa Theologiæ." Even the books of Holy Scripture had been hitherto separated, the Old Testament from the New, and in the New Testament the Acts of the Apostles from the Four Gospels. The Acts were now united with the Gospels, the Old Testament with the New, and the single volume thus produced was entitled "Scholastic History."* The plan adopted was similar to that pursued in natural science, in which several species collected form a genus, several genuses a family, several families a kingdom. The *Legenda Aurea*, a combination of all the different families of legends, and the "Scholastic History," or "Bible Historiale," a combination of the various families of the Holy Books of Scripture, may aptly be compared to the several families forming the kingdom of Nature. Vincent de Beauvais, a man of profound learning, went still farther, and, under the name of "Miroir Universel," (*Speculum Universale*,) comprised in one book all the different facts and ideas then current in the Christian world.

Classification became almost a mania. In narrating a history, or reciting a fact, it was always contrived, however unnecessary and irrelevant, to introduce a catalogue of objects, more or less analogous with, or foreign to, the subject under consideration.

Jacques de Voragine tells us, that at the feast of the Nativity, all created nature acknowledged and celebrated the Birth of the Saviour, and he eagerly seizes the opportunity thus afforded him, of explaining into how many families and kingdoms, natural objects, the beings created by God, ought to be divided. "There are," says he, "beings which exist, but do not live, as the stars; which exist and live, but do not feel, as plants; which exist, live, and feel, but do not think, as the animals; which exist, live, feel, and think, but are without prescience, as men; and, lastly, beings in whom all the preceding qualities are united and combined with perfect intelligence, as the angels." In the Legend of St. Catherine, who was herself a philosopher,

* The *Historica Scholastica* was the work of Peter Comestor, or Pierre Mangeur, and was written in the latter half of the twelfth century.—*Trans.*

the same Genoese encyclopædist takes occasion to explain the meaning of the term philosophy. He insists that this science must be divided into theory, practice, and logic; then he proceeds to subdivide each of these divisions: Theory into intellectual, natural, and mathematical; Practice into ethics, economy, and politics; Logic into demonstration, supposition, and sophistry.*

Fashion and Necessity inspired in everything a taste for classification and encyclopædias.

Since the philosophers, who originated ideas, and the learned men, who scrutinised facts, together, fixed at that time the arrangement of both, artists, whose office it is to give a special and peculiar form to the impulses of the age in which they live, bowed to the prevailing influence; they could not breathe this encyclopædic atmosphere without imbibing the predominant ideas and rendering them after their manner.

Consequently, the object of art being to instruct, the plan of instruction was intended to be encyclopædic, and effectively it became so.

Among the numerous different encyclopædias composed at this epoch, that of Vincent de Beauvais, was the latest, and consequently the most complete; it was also the most remarkable, having been produced by one whose mind was clear and well organised. This work bears, as has been said, the title of "Speculum Universale," or "Miroir Universel."

Vincent de Beauvais, the preceptor of the children of St. Louis, was a man of extraordinary erudition; he was as deeply learned as Pliny the Elder, and knew all that could be known at the close of the thirteenth century, and he classified all human knowledge according to a plan which has never yet been surpassed. In this arrangement, the chronology, carried down from the earliest period, agrees admirably with the clearest method, the most rigid analysis.

He follows the course of time from year to year and from age to age, interweaving logically, and as if of necessity, all those facts pertaining to nature or to mankind, of which he had, by careful analysis, traced the distinction or the connection.

* *Légende dorée*, de Nativitate Domini—De sanctâ Katarinâ virgine.

He commences by classifying all objects with which we are acquainted, according to the nature of those objects, and the system adopted in Botanical works; that, for example, in which plants are arranged according to their organic structure. This plan is immutable as nature herself, and far superior to that of the French encyclopædists of the eighteenth century, who divided all branches of knowledge according to the order and imaginary affiliation of our faculties. The classification of the French philosophers is artificial and arbitrary: it is a classification that must vary with every change in the psychological system.

Vincent de Beauvais established, besides, four orders of science; Historical, Moral, Abstract or Mechanical, and Natural science. These divisions, determined by analysis, are arranged in their chronological order. First, Nature, next Science, then Ethics, and lastly History. It is not a pure dry classification, nor a picture merely, but a framework filled up by degrees; for each title is followed by its appropriate chapter, and the first mention of the science is immediately succeeded by the scientific treatise.

According to the teaching of Vincent de Beauvais, before the creation of the universe, God alone existed, in solitary grandeur and immensity: but, desiring to see himself reflected in his works, and to make himself adored, beloved, and comprehended by his creatures, the Supreme Being determined to call the angels into existence. At this point, the Christian encyclopædist explains what God is; considers whether there are one, two, several, or none; and details the nature and attributes of divinity. Then he passes to the celestial spirits—to the Angel, the Spirit of Good, and the Demon, or Spirit of Evil, who were the first of all created beings.

God afterwards created heaven and earth: and then comes a treatise on geography and mineralogy; the creation of the sun, moon, and stars, serves to introduce astronomy and astrology. On the day on which the earth is said to bring forth and bud, a treatise on botany is subjoined, together with its application to agriculture and horticulture. The day of the creation of birds, fishes, and terrestrial animals, is followed by an entire system of zoology. At length, man is created, and to the scriptural account is appended an anthropology or disquisition on the structure of the human frame and intellect, and on the anatomy and physiology of the various families of the human race, which, considering the period in which it was written, is wonderfully lucid and complete. Then God rested; and Vincent pauses to examine and discuss the harmony and beauty displayed in the economy of the universe.

This harmony is too soon interrupted by the Fall of Man; and the beautiful cosmical drama which had opened in such perfect symmetry, becomes broken and confused; then the elements break their bonds, and ravage the physical creation, while human passions shake the foundations of the moral world: hence volcanoes, hurricanes, and crime. At the fall of Adam, the first series of natural and physical science is brought to a close.

Man had fallen; but he had still the power to rise. He might, says Vincent de Beauvais, repair by science his lost perfection. Consequently, the indefatigable encyclopædist resumes his discourse, and proceeds to teach man to speak, to reason, and, last of all, to think. He gives treatises on grammar, logic, rhetoric, geometry, mathematics, music, and astronomy. Then follow the other sciences; their application to domestic life being exhibited in economy, and to public life in politics; while their employment in the mechanical arts is shown in architecture, navigation, the chase, commerce, and medicine.

The second division, the class of sciences, properly so called—those which Vincent terms doctrinal, is thus brought to a conclusion.

It is well for man to know, but it is no less necessary for him to act. The stream of science flows onward, but it must flow restrained within due limits, without overwhelming the intellect or laying waste the reason. The moral sciences therefore are next invoked to point out to man that it is his duty to walk in a certain straight line, called the law, and which is both divine and human, both ancient and new. The law teaches man his duties by instructing him in the nature of virtue. Vincent de Beauvais wrote as many treatises as there are distinct and particular virtues. Men must have faith, hope, and love; must be chaste, humble, meek, patient, temperate, courageous, and prudent: thus they will be meet for happiness in heaven, and the bliss of heaven is detailed at length, as an incentive to good works. If men relax ever so little in their onward progress, or turn aside voluntarily from the right path, they become liable to purgatory: and purgatory is, therefore, described, and the different sorts of sin enumerated, and defined either as mortal or venial. Those who go entirely astray will be cast into hell, where pride, envy, blasphemy, sloth, and simony, are punished with peculiar rigour. Not a single moral treatise of any real importance, is forgotten in this framework, which forms the third division of the Encyclopædia.

Man is born, he is endowed with knowledge and the power of action; science has been placed as a buckler in his left hand; morality, as an instrument of action, in his right. He may then live in the world, and work out his own history. Thenceforth all the different epochs of the universal history of our species, from the period when Adam, driven from the terrestrial Paradise, was condemned to constant labour, form themselves into groups around him. Vincent passes in review, and relates the history of, all nations and people; he pauses at the year 1244, that in which he lived; but he has almost divined (if I may be allowed the expression) the events that would succeed. Besides, he was far too catholic, too universal in his ideas, to leave a vacancy. He tells us when time will be accomplished; when the universe shall perish; how mankind shall be judged; and when eternity without end shall recommence, as if it had not been interrupted for a season by the creation and by history; how the world will end, whether by water or by fire. He predicts all the phenomena that will precede the Last Judgment; and the fourth and last portion of this work closes with the end of the world.

I must again repeat that this analytical and chronological arrangement, at once historical and natural, is most remarkable. I am myself disposed to consider it superior to that adopted by Bacon, or by the encyclopædists of the eighteenth century; and even to that of Marie Ampère, whose classification is almost the latest, and seems, perhaps, preferable to any that has been attempted up to the present time.

This order is precisely that in which the statues decorating the exterior of Chartres Cathedral are arranged. The sculptures here open with the creation of the world, to the illustration of which thirty-six tableaux and seventy-five statues are devoted, beginning with the moment when God leaves his repose to create the heavens and the earth, and continued to that in which Adam and Eve, having been guilty of disobedience, are driven from Paradise, to pass the remainder of their lives in tears and in labour. This is made by the encyclopædist, the first groundwork of his subject; it is the Genesis of organic and inorganic nature—of living creatures and reasoning beings; that in which the biblical cosmogony is developed, and which leads to that terrible event, the fearful malediction pronounced upon man by his God. This first section, called by Beauvais the "*Miroir Naturel,*" is sculptured on the central arch of the north porch.

But although man, by the guilt of Adam, had incurred the penalty of death to the body, and torment to the soul, he might yet redeem himself by labour. Even while expelling them from Paradise, God still had compassion on our first parents: he gave them skins of beasts for garments, and taught them how to clothe themselves; and the sculptor hence took occasion to instruct the Beaucerons how to labour with the hands, and with the mind. On the right of the Fall of Man, he sculptured, under the eyes of all men, and for their perpetual instruction, first, a calendar of stone, describing all the labours of the country in their seasons; then a catechism of the mechanical arts practised by the dwellers in towns; and, finally, for the benefit of those engaged in intellectual occupations, a manual of the liberal arts, personified, preferably, under the figures of a philosopher, a geometrician, and a magician. The entire subject is developed in a series of 103 figures, in the north porch, and more especially in the arch on the right hand. Such is the second division, exhibiting at once an historical and allegorical representation of agricultural and manufacturing industry—of commerce, and of art.

It is not, however, enough for man to labour only; his muscular powers and intellectual energy must be exerted for a worthy object; he must make a good employment of the faculties with which he is endowed by God, and of the riches acquired by his own industry. To walk is not enough: we must walk in a straight path, nor is it enough to act, unless we act well and virtuously. Thus, for moral and religious purposes, the porches of Nôtre Dame de Chartres were encrusted with 148 effigies, representing the virtues which it is our duty to embrace—the vices that we ought to overcome.

Man, created by God, has duties to fulfil towards his Maker from whom he is derived, towards society in the bosom of which he lives, towards the family in which he was brought up, and the household over which he, in his turn, presides; lastly, he has duties towards himself, possessing, as he does, a physical organisation to be preserved, a heart to be softened and warmed, and a mind to be enlightened. Thence arise four orders of virtues, the theological, political, domestic, and personal; all placed in opposition to their contrary vices, as light is to darkness. Personifications of all these virtues are sculptured in the different bands or courses of the vaulting. Theological and political virtues, the influence of which is external, and suitable for the public arena, are placed without; domestic and personal virtues, which affect the individual and his family, are made to retire within the porch, where they find shelter, in stillness and comparative obscurity. Such is the third part, the "*Miroir Moral*," which occupies the left archway, and the north porch generally.

Now that man is created; that he has learned to labour, and to guide his actions aright; that he takes toil with the one hand for his support, and virtue with the other for his guide and protectress, he may advance without fear of going astray: he may live, and become the architect of his own history; and, after a certain period, he will reach the point he has had in view. Man's career is then continued from the Creation to the Last Judgment, just as the sun pursues his course from east to west, and the remaining statues are, therefore, devoted to exhibiting the history of the world, from the period of Adam and Eve, whom we left digging and spinning without the gates of Paradise, down to the end of time. The inspired sculptor has, indeed, by the aid of the Prophets and of the Apocalypse, divined the future fate of man, long after (poor mortal!) his own earthly existence should hàve terminated. No less than 1488 statues were employed, and still remain, to set forth a history comprising so many ages, so many events, and so many human beings. This is the fourth and last division; it fills three recesses of the north porch, as well as the entire porch and the three bays of the southern entrance.

These sculptures, then, are, in the fullest sense of the word, what, in the language of the middle ages, was called the "Image or Mirror of the Universe." They form an entire poem, in the first canto of which we see reflected the image of Nature, organic and inorganic; in the second, that of science; that of the moral sense in the third; of man in the fourth; and in the whole, lastly, the entire world. Such is the intellectual framework of this stone Encyclopædia; such its plan and moral unity. It remains for us now to examine its material unity and physical arrangement.

The history of religion resolves itself for the Christian into two distinct periods; the first, precedes the coming of our Saviour, and is occupied by the history of the Hebrew nation, the people of God; the second, commencing at the birth of Christ, comprehends the history of all Christian people, the Law and the Gospel, the Old and New Testament. As the Jews did not in their social life consort with Christians, and as in the thirteenth century the Old Testament, represented by tables, with circular tops, differed from the New, which was always represented in the form of a square book, so in Nôtre Dame de Chartres the history of the Jewish people is actually separated from that of Christians by the entire breadth of the church, or, we should rather say, by the whole length of the transepts. The effigies illustrating Old Testament history, from the creation of the world to the death of the Virgin, are ranged in the north porch; and those of the New, from the moment in which Christ first bade his Apostles who were around him, "Go teach and baptise all nations,"* even to and including the Last Judgment, in the south. In stained glass of the thirteenth century, and sculpture of the fourteenth, Christ is represented enthroned on clouds, and his back supported by a

* "Go ye therefore, and teach all nations, baptising them."—Matt., xxvii. 19.

rainbow; the Tables of the Law are placed upon the Ark of the Covenant on his left hand, the Book of the Evangelists* is lying open upon an altar on his right. In every epoch the Old Testament has had its position on the left, and the New Testament on the right hand. This is as it should be; for Christians regard the Old Testament as the pedestal or groundwork of the Gospel. The Old Testament is an anticipatory portrait, of which the New presents the after-model. The New Testament is the fulfilment, the Old the metaphorical or prophetic type. Now, in all times, even at the present day, in civil customs as well as in military manœuvres and religious ceremonies, the left is held inferior to the right; the right hand is given invariably to those who are most honourable. The artists at Chartres, therefore, placed the Bible on the north, or the left hand (when we face the east), and the Gospel on the south, or the right hand. Thus, too, the Northumbrian bishop, Benedict Biscop, commanded that the southern portion of the church should be entirely filled with pictures from the Gospel.†

The 1814 statues which people the exterior of the church of Nôtre Dame de Chartres, are arranged on the same principle.

Many encyclopædias of the middle ages are far less complete than that of Vincent de Beauvais. Some writers have selected one particular portion, or one "Miroir" only, in preference to another, instead of combining the four several branches into one united work. Others have preserved the unity of each branch of the four divisions; but in one or other of the "Mirrors" they have omitted either entirely or in part some particular branch of science, or passed it over with slight notice, in order to exaggerate the dimensions of some other science connected with it. In the same manner, many, one might even say the majority of the French cathedrals, are incomplete in comparison with that of Chartres. Some one branch of the Encyclopædia is treated too fully, to the neglect of one, two, or sometimes of the three other branches. Thus, in the Cathedral of Rheims,

* *Missale abbatiæ Sancti Maglorii parisiensis.* *Bib. Arsen. Thèol. Lat.* 188, fol. 214, recto. XV. century.

† "Detulit .... imagines evangelicæ historiæ quibus australem ecclesiæ parietem decoraret." (*Life of Benedict Biscop*, cited above, p. 3.)

what we may call the "Historical Mirror," comprising more especially the Life of Christ, and the end of the world, or the Apocalypse, is extended beyond all due proportion; while the "Mirror of Nature" is greatly abridged, and that of "Doctrine" seems almost forgotten. Still, in each of these cathedrals the principal chapters of the "Universal Mirror" are represented by eight or ten figures at least. Even that of Laon, which is in this respect more exclusive and less complete than most others, gives the argument or summary of the book, which is treated in full detail at Chartres. It has, for these reasons, been thought expedient to adhere in the following work to the classification adopted by Vincent de Beauvais, and reproduced in the Cathedral of Beauce.

The order of this arrangement is of the highest importance; and should be constantly borne in mind and diligently followed, while examining or describing sculptured statues or painted effigies. Many a statue which, isolated, appears uninteresting and unintelligible, takes a new meaning when connected with the others which ought properly to precede and follow it. Either from negligence in the person appointed to superintend the building, or ignorance in the sculptor, transpositions frequently occur in regard to the places occupied by certain figures; or the displacement may have been occasioned by the architectural form of the building; by its exaggerated or limited dimensions; by the limited surface of the area appointed for decoration, or by the preponderance of that from which ornaments were excluded. In every occasion of difficulty, or when there is reason to suspect that such alterations have been made, it will be expedient to have recourse to the arrangement of Vincent de Beauvais. In the Cathedral of Chartres, for instance, one vaulting of the eastern porch is devoted to the signs of the zodiac and the labours of the different seasons. As, however, there was space for ten signs only, it was necessary to remove the two signs, Pisces and Gemini, which could find no place in the first vaulting, to another; and thus, banished from their proper sphere, they seem devoid of meaning or intention. Similar examples are numerous, and must be regarded with scrupulous attention.

As the statues and effigies with which our churches are decorated are all arranged according to the system of Vincent de Beauvais, it has been found necessary to adhere closely to that arrangement in the following treatise. The subject opens, therefore, by speaking, firstly, of God; secondly, of the creation of the first divine beings; and proceeds thus in order, through the four encyclopædic divisions mentioned above, down to the end of the world. It commences, before the "Genesis," that is, before the Creation, and will not terminate till it reaches the "Apocalypse," after the end of the world. It begins with God, because God existed before all things; from God, the fountain of universal existence, it descends to the final judgment, that point in which the several streams of facts and ideas terminate their course.

The first part of the "Instructions for Iconography" contains the Archæological History or Iconography of God; then follows that of the Angel, a Being immortal, if not eternal, and who ranks next to the Deity, both in the hierarchy and in chronology; next, the Iconography of the Devil—that fallen angel who was precipitated from heaven, crushed and overwhelmed, at some period subsequent to the creation of angels, and before the birth of man.

In a future work I propose to treat upon the seven days of Creation so often represented in our churches, the Birth and Fall of Man, the archæological history of Death, and of the "Dance of Death." As man, though doomed to death, may yet regain something of his original virtue by the labour of his hands, the cultivation of his mind, the practice of what is good, and the avoiding of evil; personifications of the labours of the country and the city, of the liberal arts, of the Virtues and Vices, will be given, and their intention and signification fully explained.

The History of the Patriarchs, Judges, Prophets, and Kings of Judah, will occupy the succeeding portion; next to this will come the Life of the Virgin Mary, and that of Christ—admirable subjects, well worthy of being treated at length. We must afterwards pass in review the figures of Apostles, Martyrs, Confessors, the most distinguished saints, and those whose effigies are most frequently seen on our portals and painted windows. The concluding portion of the work, of which this is only a preliminary sketch, will contain a description of such figures as are borrowed from the Apocalypse.

The principal types will be shown in engravings, and the text will be little more than the legend of the figures represented. The designs will all be outlines from authentic monuments, and the date and origin of each will be given with the greatest possible precision. They will be selected principally from illuminated manuscripts, statues, or paintings on glass; but frescoes, mosaics, tapestry, enamellings, and carvings will also be laid under contribution.

The drawings, like those in the present volume, will be executed by M. Paul Durand, Correspondent of the Historical Society of Arts and Monuments, a patient antiquary, who examines, with most scrupulous attention, every archæological character likely to afford either indispensable or merely useful information. M. Durand accompanied me, with the greatest zeal and disinterestedness, during my visit into Greece and Turkey, in July, 1839, and February, 1840, to the city of Athens, to the Morea, Sparta, Salamis, Thebes, Delphi, the Meteora of Thessaly, Macedonia, Salonica, M. Athos, and Constantinople. He made drawings of every monument, whether in architecture, sculpture, or painting, which I had proposed to myself to describe: several Byzantine types of God, Angels, and the Evil Spirits, reproduced by his pencil, are inserted in the work now before the reader.

All the drawings here given have, with some few exceptions, been either copied or outlined by M. Durand. A few subjects only were copied from the designs of MM. Lassus and E. Boeswilwald, architects at Paris; Duthoit, sculptor at Amiens; Ch. Fichot, designer at Troyes; Amable Crapilot, architect at Auxerre; Klein, painter at Strasbourg, and Hippolyte Durand, formerly an architect at Rheims. These artists, skilful, learned, and obliging, placed their time and talents at my entire disposal, in order to procure for me the subjects I required, and which are dispersed throughout the cathedrals of Amiens, Auxerre, Rheims, Troyes, and Strasbourg. M. E. Boeswilwald gleaned for me among the beautiful paintings of the Campo Santo at Pisa.

The designs were all engraved, with studious care, by

MM. Andrew, Best, and Leloir, who are entitled to my warmest thanks.

The text of the work was read before a special committee, selected from the Historical Society of Arts and Monuments. It was composed of MM. Delécluze, Baron Taylor, Comte de Montalembert, Comte Auguste de Bastard, Du Sommerard, Auguste Leprévost, Schmit, and Albert Lenoir. Several doubtful points were discussed and decided, several suggestions were made and adopted. The work was ordered and approved by the Committee, but the arrangement and appreciation of the facts was left entirely to the author's discretion. M. Villemain, Minister of Public Instruction, was induced, at the request of the committee, to authorise the printing and publishing of the work.

M. Chabaille, Correcteur to the Comités Historiques revised the proofs of my work with great attention—I may almost say, with peculiar affection. He did not confine himself to the mere correction of typography; but, being well versed in the dramatic art of the Middle Ages, and the literature of the Mysteries and Miracles, he advised me occasionally to draw a parallel between the *imitative*, and the spoken or *mimetic* arts; and to consider scenic representations in their connexion with effigies and statues: and I gratefully accepted suggestions so judicious, offered, too, with so much candour and politeness.

Finally, and to acquit myself, in some degree, of my numerous obligations, I must express my gratitude to MM. the Conservators of the Bibliothèque Royale; to MM. the Librarians of St. Geneviève; and to M. Amyot, of the Library of the Arsenal, who placed at my disposition the finest illuminated MSS., from which I copied several miniatures. MM. le Comte Auguste de Bastard and Du Sommerard entrusted me with, or described to me, many valuable specimens of carving in ivory, glass painting, and painting in enamel or on vellum. I shall always retain a grateful remembrance of the kindness which aided and encouraged my efforts, and conferred personal honour on myself.

DIDRON.

Paris, *May*, 1841.

PART I.

THE NIMBUS, OR GLORY.

Before entering on the subject of Iconography generally, it may be advisable to devote a few pages to the examination of an attribute which is of very frequent occurrence in Christian Archæology, and which alone will often be found sufficiently expressive to enable us to determine the dignity and character of the personage invested with it. This peculiar ornament is usually designated the Nimbus, or Glory.

The Glory is constantly adopted by artists, both in painting and sculpture, as a characteristic ornament: it either encircles the head alone or the entire figure. As an attribute it serves to denote a holy person, in the same manner as the crosier or the sceptre distinguishes a bishop or a king. When this attribute enriches the head only it is called a nimbus. In this case it is analogous in signification to a crown, from which, however, it differs essentially in position if not in form. Both the crown and the nimbus are circular, but the former is placed horizontally on the head, the position of the latter is vertical.

The nimbus may sometimes be almost microscopic in dimensions, but its importance ought never to be overlooked. Every sculptor occupied in making or re-modelling Gothic statues, every painter engaged in the restoration of ancient frescoes, or of early stained glass, each antiquary whose time and energies are devoted to researches in Christian Iconography, will find this characteristic to be of the highest practical importance, and one, too, which requires to be studied with scrupulous attention, since the omission of it may transform a saint into an ordinary mortal, or an incorrect application elevate the mere mortal into a divinity. Errors of this description are frequently committed by artists of the present day in their representations of religious themes. Some years since, for example, a painting on glass, representing Christ and a few saints,

Fig. 1.—CHARLEMAGNE CROWNED, AND WITH THE NIMBUS.
Painting on Glass from the Cathedral of Strasbourg, XII and XIV centuries.*

was exhibited. One of the saints, a bishop only, was adorned with that form of nimbus, which is appropriated to the Deity alone, and the figure of Christ was entirely destitute of the insignia which Christian artists have universally employed as the symbol of his divinity. Consequently the saint was represented as divine, while

* This head of Charlemagne occupies the upper part of a beautiful stained glass window in the left aisle (*collateral gauche*) of Strasbourg Cathedral. Charlemagne is represented with a crown and nimbus. On the circumference of the nimbus the following legend is inscribed: KAROLVS MAGNVS REX. This glass painting, as well as the series of fifteen Kings or Emperors, in the same side aisle (*bas côté*) belongs to the eleventh or twelfth century, but was restored in the fourteenth. The floriations on the crown and the inscription on the nimbus belong to the period of that restoration.

our Saviour appeared but as a man. The nimbus, therefore, in Iconography is of equal importance with the fingers and the mammals in zoology, and although its form may

Fig. 2.—CHRIST IN AN ELLIPTICAL AUREOLE.
Miniature in the Bibliothèque Royale, XIV cent.*

be by no means striking to the eye, the idea it should convey is often of the highest importance.

In some instances, not the head alone but the entire person is encircled by a nimbus; in this latter case, it ought to be designated by another name, in order that two

* This drawing is taken from the *Speculum Humanæ Salvationis*, a beautiful Italian MS. of the fourteenth century, belonging to the Bibliothèque Royale. The elliptical figure within which the Saviour is represented is an

ornaments, varying so much in size and nearly always in form, may not be confounded one with another. The nimbus encircling the body will for the present be distinguished by the term aureole, and the propriety of this denomination will be justified hereafter. The aureole is of less universal application than the nimbus, or ornament of the head, properly so called; it is very rarely seen in Pagan Iconography, and in Christian art is restricted almost exclusively to the Divine persons, to the Virgin Mary, or to the souls of saints, exalted after the death of the body into the kingdom of heaven.

The nimbus of the head and the aureole of the body differ in a remarkable degree, yet both are sometimes figured in the same manner, and both usually impart the same idea, that of apotheosis, glorification, or deification. It seems, therefore, desirable that one single word should be employed as a generic term to include both species of nimbus, and express the union of the two ornaments.

In speaking of the combination of the nimbus and aureole, I shall in future employ the term *glory*: *nimbus* will be applied peculiarly to that encircling the head, *aureole* to that of the body, and *glory* to the union of both.*

DEFINITION OF THE NIMBUS.

The Latin word nimbus appears to agree in signification with the Greek *νιφάς*, of which *νίφω* is the original root. The verb *νίφω νίφειν* signifies to snow, to water, to wet; *νιφάς* is used to express snow, shower, dew, a raindrop, and even, by extension, hail.

The meaning of nimbus is the same as that of the Greek noun *νιφάς*; and it also signifies cloud, that is to say, the place in which are formed rain, hail, or snow, either of which

aureole; the transverse line, intersecting this ellipsis in the centre, is the rainbow, or, perhaps, clouds, as they were usually drawn by Italians at that epoch. This line seems, also, to form a support for the Saviour in his ascension to Heaven.

* In fig. 2, the figure of Christ has the nimbus around the head, and the aureole encircling the body, and is consequently enveloped in a complete glory.

may be intended by the Greek word. Nimbus may also be understood to signify the aerial car, the cloud, which, according to Virgil, serves as a chariot for the gods; in a metaphorical sense it means also the veil worn by women, a fine and transparent covering, air, consolidated as it were into substance, woven wind, a cloud of gauze, as the ancient Greeks would have said.

Isidore of Seville, in his "Origines," describes the nimbus to be a transverse bandeau of gold, sewed on the veil and worn by women on their forehead.*

The Romans employed the expressions, *nimbus florum—nimbus saxorum—nimbus sagittarum, nimbus equitum—nimbus numismatum*—to indicate a shower of blossoms shaken from the trees, the odoriferous snows of spring, as

* "Nimbus est fasciola transversa ex auro, assuta linteo, quod est in fronte fœminarum."—(*Orig.*, lib. XIX., cap. xxxi.)

It seems, nevertheless, probable that the learned Bishop of Seville was mistaken in his explanation of the terms *nimbus* and *nimbatus*. He was probably misled by that passage of Plautus, in the Pœnulus, scene 2, in which the servant, speaking of a lady beloved by his master, says,

"Quam magis aspecto, tam magis est nimbata,"

and thence concluded that *nimbata* signified wearing a coquettish head-dress. Comparing the passage in Plautus, with one in the Satire of Petronius, where, in enumerating the charms of a Roman lady, he particularly notices the lowness of her forehead (*frons minima*), with another, in which Horace declares that his dear Lycoris was distinguished by her low forehead (*insignis fronte tenui*), and with a third, in which Arnobius, in his Treatise on the Nature of Man (ch. viii.), asserts that women who desired to possess this charm, then valued as a sign of intellectual endowments, lessened the forehead by concealing it with bandeaux, Isidore de Seville imagined the term *nimbata*, used by Plautus, to refer to a woman who attempted, by wearing an elegant head-dress placed low upon the brow, to make her forehead appear lower; hence he drew his definition of *nimbus*. I imagine that the text of Plautus should rather be translated as follows:—"The more I look at her the more radiant (*nimbée*) she appears;" that is to say, bright, dazzling, or beautiful; for the nimbus, as will hereafter be shown, is an emanation of light, the rays of which are rendered visible in sculpture or painting. In fact, Isidore himself says, "Lumen quod circa angelorum capita pingitur nimbus vocatur; licet et nimbus sit densitas nubis." *Nimbata* must, then, be considered in the light of a metaphor serving to express an ideal beauty, and is well rendered in our language by the word "radiant." It is not a word properly applicable to any peculiar ornament for the head; besides, had the word been properly understood in the latter sense, as a woman's veil or bandeau, its derivation would probably have been found in the transparent delicacy of the tissue.

an illustrious French poet of our time has happily termed them; also the hail of stones or arrows with which an enemy is pierced and crushed; the cloud of soldiers who darken the air with the dust raised by the galloping of their horses; the handfuls of largesse or showers of money thrown to the people on occasions of public rejoicings.* This "rain," "snow," "hail," or "cloud," are but metaphors which serve to explain and elucidate the signification of nimbus, and of *νιφάς*.

It has thus been shown that the analogy between these two words, the one Greek and the other Latin, approaches almost to an identity of meaning.

With regard to the pronunciation, if the Latin *b* be changed into the Greek *φ*, that is to say, if the soft labial be transformed into the labial-aspirate, and the *b* pronounced like a *v*, as is the practice among the modern Greeks, the resemblance between the two words will become even more remarkable. There can thus be little doubt, that nimbus is derived from *νιφάς*.

The etymology of the word has been little regarded by artists, for the nimbus, which ought always to have the character of a cloud, a vapour, or flakes of snow, frequently assumes the form of a circular disk, sometimes opaque, sometimes luminous, and sometimes transparent. It has the shape of a triangle or a square; that of several jets of flame; of a star, with six, eight, twelve, or sometimes even a countless number of rays. There is scarcely, perhaps, a single instance in which the shape of the nimbus agrees entirely with the idea which that word seems intended to convey.

* *Monarchie françoise*, par le P. Montfaucon, Discours préliminaire, p. xx. Servius, the commentator on Virgil, in the fourth century, referring to the following verse in the Æneid, book i. *v.* 51:

> "Nimborum in patriam, loca fœta furentibus austris,
> Æoliam venit—"

observes "Nimbus nunc ventos significat; plerumque nubes vel pluvias—Proprie nimbi repentinæ et præcipites pluviæ.—"(Virgil, 4to. édition de Genève, 1636, p. 176.)

FORM OF THE NIMBUS.

The nimbus is almost invariably circular, in the form of a disk, although in some cases the centre of the disk has disappeared and the outer line only is left.*

The centre field of the circular nimbus is either plain or ornamented. When not plain it is striated with foliage, or decorated with countless radiating lines, occasionally with three rays only, narrow or broad, resembling the branches of a Greek cross.

These transverse lines are either plain or adorned with pearls and precious stones (the latter unpolished), or marked with Greek or Latin letters: they are formed either of straight geometrical lines, or of lines resembling the undulating motion of flame.†

The preceding observations may suffice for the description of the lines radiating from the centre and finishing at the circumference of the nimbus; but, besides these, it is frequently divided by concentric circles into several zones; the central zone then becomes the nimbus properly so called; the others are rather prolongations of the first, or radiations from it. Pearls and precious stones, polished or unpolished, are introduced into these zones, which are one, two, or three

* See for the first species of nimbus, figs. 1 and 2, pp. 23, 24, and those which follow. The drawings here given being in outline merely, the nimbus is indicated by the outer line alone; but in the originals the centre is filled up and solid. The transparent nimbus, marked by the line of the circumference alone, was frequent among the Greeks before the thirteenth century, and the Italians after the fifteenth. In the History of God the Father, we shall give a design copied from a Greek MS. in the Bibliothèque Royale, representing the Father conversing with Isaiah, standing between allegorical figures representing Night (*νύξ*) and Day (*ὄρθρος*.) The figure of Night has a nimbus, consisting of the single line of circumference only. Raphael, in the "Dísputa," has adorned with a perfectly transparent nimbus the several personages assembled in council.

† These varieties, and others, will be shown in the various drawings which follow. In the Evangeliaire of Charlemagne, Bib. Roy., St. Matthew wears a nimbus ornamented with a semicircle of rays, in the form of a shell. The Angel who appears to be giving inspiration to the Evangelist has a nimbus, the rays of which diverging from one common centre, each terminate in a pearl, at the line of circumference, resembling needles with pearl heads.

in number. In some cases the name of the personage whose head they surround is inscribed upon them.*

The outer edge of the circumference of the nimbus is usually either plain or indented, that is to say, furnished

Fig. 3.—ST JOHN THE EVANGELIST, WITH A CIRCULAR NIMBUS SURMOUNTED BY TWO SUN-FLOWERS, EMBLEMS OF THE SUN.
Glass Painting of the XII cent. St. Rèmi. Rheims.

with prolongations, formed ordinarily either by straight or wavy lines. Sometimes, as at St. Rèmi of Rheims†, two sunflowers are inserted in the outer circle of the nimbus, this plant being considered in the vegetable kingdom

* The nimbus of Karolus Magnus, fig. 1, p. 23, is composed of three zones: the first and innermost is plain, the second ornamented with figured bands and small crosses of St. Andrew, and on the third, or outer circle, are written the name and title.

† From a stained glass window in the apse in the Tribune, dating from the twelfth century. It represents the Blessed Virgin and St. John the Baptist, standing beside Christ on the Cross, and bewailing the agony of the Redeemer. Both Mary and St. John wear the nimbus, and, from the top of each nimbus, rise two sun-flowers, the stalks crossing each other. The head here given is that of St. John. This idea is curious in itself, and reminds us of those Egyptian figures, from the heads of which two lotus-flowers rise in a similar manner. The great work on Egypt is full of such figures.

as symbolic of the sun or of the light, of which the sun is the source. It here forms a sort of double feather surmounting the symbolic headdress.

The nimbus is sometimes triangular.* This form is

Fig. 4.—GOD THE FATHER, WITH A TRIANGULAR NIMBUS BEARING RAYS.†
Greek Fresco of the XVII. cent.

extremely rare in France: it is frequent enough in Greece and Italy, especially after the fifteenth century.‡

* The figure of God the Father, which follows, is copied from a fresco at Mount Athos. Rays issue from each side of the triangular nimbus.

† It must be observed, that in a mosaic belonging to the close of the eighth or the beginning of the ninth century, in the Cathedral at Capua (see Ciampini, *Vetera Monimenta*, part 2, pl. 54), the Holy Ghost, in the form of a dove, with a triangular nimbus, is represented hovering above the Virgin, who carries the Infant Saviour in her arms. St. Peter, St. Paul, St. Stephen, and St. Agatha, stand around the Virgin. It is possible that this nimbus may be a later restoration; and this opinion is confirmed by the circumstance that the figure of Christ, and that of another divine person in the upper part of the mosaic, are without a cruciform nimbus. Mosaics have been so frequently retouched! Ciampini (*Vet. Mon.*, part 2, p. 168,) says:—"Hujus triangularis formæ aliud antiquius me vidisse minime recordor." He is right; the triangular nimbus is always of recent date, and that at Capua, if genuine, would be unique.

‡ See also a Greek engraving, representing the "Skite du Prodromos," a monastic village situated near Ivirôn, on Mount Athos.

The nimbus is sometimes a double triangle, constructed of two intersecting triangles, which thus form a star of five points.*

Fig. 5.—ST. GREGORY IV. WITH A SQUARE NIMBUS.†
Roman Mosaic in St. Mark, IX cent.

The nimbus is at other times square: a perfect square, with sides either straight or concave.

The nimbus is occasionally a rectangular or oblong square, or, to use the expression of St. John the Deacon, in the

* This bi-triangular nimbus is figured below in the chapter on the Application of the Nimbus, fig. 21, p. 60.

† A Roman mosaic, representing Gregory offering to God the Church of St. Mark, which was built and decorated by his command, about the year 828.—(Ciampini, *Vet. Mon.*, part 2, p. 119, tab. 37.) In Ciampini, the Pope is young, beardless, and smiling; but M. P. Durand, who made this drawing from the mosaic, assures me that the expression of the countenance is melancholy, as it is here represented.

form of a table, as shown in the preceding design. Another kind of nimbus also is often met with in Italian MSS., resembling a volumen of parchment unfolded in the centre, remaining partially rolled at each end, or a roll which has not entirely taken the plane form, or a cylinder not completely flattened, so that the extremities at which the pressure is less powerful, curl inwards on themselves.*

Fig. 6.—THE THREE DIVINE PERSONS, ADORNED WITH THE CRUCIFORM NIMBUS.†

Miniature of the close of the XIII cent. MS. in the Bibliothèque Royale.

The nimbus may sometimes be met with lozenge-shaped, with straight sides, as in the head of God the Father in the "Dísputa;" or the sides are concave, as in an example given below in the History of God, fig. 22.

When the nimbus is circular and belongs to one of the Persons of the Holy Trinity, it is always, unless the omission arises from the ignorance of the artist, divided by two lines, drawn from the outer edges and intersecting each other at right angles in the centre. These lines form four rays, but one of them, the lowest, is concealed by the head.

Sometimes of the entire disk, only the rays or cross lines that divide the field, are retained.

When these intersecting lines have the form of luminous rays, they often spread and approach so nearly as almost to re-compose the disk; the rays, however, that issue from the temples and the summit of the head or brow, are longer

* See Seroux d'Agincourt (*Hist. de l'Art par les monuments, peinture*, pl. 37.) An example of this form is given below, fig. 27.

† This drawing, which is copied from the "Biblia Sacra," No. 6829, represents the persons of the Trinity creating Adam, whom they appear to raise from the ground. The Holy Spirit is in the form of a Dove, and has the cruciform nimbus, as well as the other two persons. This form of nimbus is a valuable archæological characteristic, and the invariable attribute of Divinity.

than those intervening. In this case the circumference being broken into three parts, assumes what we might almost call the form of a Greek cross, broader at the extremities than in the centre.

Besides the circle, either plain or ornamented; besides the simple and the double triangle, or the star; besides the square, the oblong, and the lozenge shape; the nimbus has still other forms, which it may not be useless to describe. It will be shown hereafter that the nimbus is nothing more than a representation of the radiation of light supposed to issue from the head, and there are various ways in which that radiation has been represented.

Sometimes rays of equal number and dimensions emanate from all points, and thus produce a circular nimbus. Sometimes the rays issuing from the temples and the summit of the head, are stronger and more vivid, while those from other points are shorter and more feeble. If in these cases an external line be traced, uniting all those rays of unequal lengths, a sort of lozenge with concave sides, similar to that above mentioned, will be produced. This line is very

Fig. 7.—NIMBUS WITH RAYS OF UNEQUAL LENGTH, WITHOUT ANY CONNECTING LINE. Miniature of the XVI cent. MS. in the Bibliothèque Royale.

seldom supplied, and the nimbus consequently appears as in the above drawing.*

* If these rays were all united by one external line, we should have a lozenge-shaped nimbus with concave sides. This drawing is taken from the MS. 920, in the Bibliothèque Royale. The miniature is of the sixteenth century.

The intermediate space between the three grand luminous points is, in some instances, destitute of rays, and the nimbus is then reduced to three clusters, each consisting in general of three rays only. These three streaks of light are frequently connected by a circle which thus forms the cruciform nimbus so commonly to be met with, but at other times the three luminous clusters of rays pass beyond the line of circumference, as if too strong to be contained within its limits.

Fig. 8.—TRANSVERSE LINES, OR LUMINOUS CLUSTERS OF RAYS PASSING BEYOND THE CIRCUMFERENCE OF THE NIMBUS.*
Miniature of the IX cent. MS. of the Bibliothèque Royale.

It will be remarked that these rays diverge from the centre towards the circumference; that is to say, they are contracted at the base; broader and more open at the extremities.

In Pagan Iconography we particularly observe a nimbus, the rays of which are broad at the base and pointed at the extremity; they are placed at equal distances and appear to emanate equally from all points of the circle of the head.†

* This beautiful head of Christ, beardless, but serious in expression, and of mature age, was given by M. de Bastard in his great work, *Peintures et Ornéments des Manuscrits*, 4th book. The cross-lines of the nimbus are formed of three clusters, each containing three rays; the clusters, it will be observed, emanate from the temples and the upper part of the head.

† Montfaucon (*Antiq. Expliq.*) gives several examples of rays thus sharpened at the points.

This form, resembling that given by artists to the stars, forcibly reminds us of the radiated crowns so frequently seen on Greek and Roman coins. The disposition of these rays is exactly the reverse of those clusters of light of which we have just spoken, and is, it must be added, completely opposed to the physical nature of luminous rays; for light emanating from a centre, becomes, at the circumference, divergent, not convergent. In this design, the rays are linked together, not at their points, but at about half their length, by a circle or thread which appears to confine them. The circumscribing thread is sometimes placed nearer to the head, in which case the rays, instead of emanating from the head itself, start from that circle. The nimbus, as has been already observed, is a disk, the field of which is sometimes streaked with rays: in this case the rays are within the interior of the circumference, covering the interior space within the outer circle, but in the arrangement just described it is exactly the reverse, the line of circumference being within, and the rays without.

Fig. 9.—APOLLO AS THE SUN, ADORNED WITH THE NIMBUS, AND CROWNED WITH SEVEN RAYS.*
Roman Sculpture.

The extent of the nimbus is generally indicated by an

* These seven rays, placed at equal distances, exceed the limits of the nimbus surrounding the head. The head given above is that of the Sun; it is taken from the "Antiquité Expliquée de Montfaucon," tom. i., p. 118, pl. 54. Lucian also observes, that the head of the Syrian Goddess had rays, ἐπὶ τῇ κεφαλῇ ἀκτίνας φέρει. Ciampini (*Vet. Mon.*, part 1.,) says, "Publ. Victor in Colosso Solis, quem Zenodorus Neroni dicavit, de quo Plin., cap. xxiv., lib. 7, SEPTENIS caput ejus radiis coruscâsse tradit, quorum singuli viginti duos pedes et semis in longitudine præstabant." It will be observed that the number of rays surrounding the head of the colossal Sun of Zenodorus are precisely the same as those of the youthful Sun figured in our engraving. Each ray is supposed to dispense its radiance to a planet, and the Sun forms the centre of all. The Star of Julius Cæsar, says Suetonius, shone for seven successive days.—*See below, note*, p. 37.

unbroken line, forming a perfect circle; yet, among the Romans especially,* and also among the Hindoos,† this circle is frequently broken into zigzag lines, which give the edge the appearance of being cut like the teeth of a saw. The points of these teeth may be considered as the extremity of the cloud of rays emanating from the head, and which spread, in one compact body of light, to the circumference, but, when they reach that limit, become broken and divided, extending their points in every direction.

Fig. 10.—NIMBUS BORDERED WITH FOURTEEN RAYS.‡

Engraved gem of the early Christian period.

I shall notice, in the last place, a form which appears to be antique, and constantly occurs in the Iconography of the

* See the coins of the time of the Antonines; they bear on the reverse a bird—the phœnix—symbol of immortality. This bird, which is supposed to be regenerated by fire, has its head encircled by an indented nimbus. On the coins of Faustina, Eternity is represented with a peacock, wearing a similar nimbus. It is a singular fact, that a Christian MS. in the Bib. Roy., 434, St. Germ., has two peacocks wearing the nimbus appropriated to Saints.

† See the symbolism of Creuzer, (*German Atlas*, pl. 31,) among others, and pl. 17 of the French Atlas, accompanying the translation of M. Guignaut. The sun is there placed in the centre of a disk indented interiorly; between the luminous circle surrounding the sun, and an exterior circle containing the signs of the Zodiac, is a narrow space on which eight personified planets are represented: Luna, or rather Lunus—that constellation being masculine amongst the Hindcos—Mars, Mercury, Jupiter, Venus masculine, Saturn, Rahou, and Ketou. The head of each is encircled by a nimbus or aureole, indented like that of the immortal bird of the Romans (*See below*, fig. 12, p. 43. Maya surrounded by a nimbus indented or zigzag). In the fresco paintings of Greece, the Holy Spirit is frequently drawn under the form of a Dove, generally within a nimbus or aureole, with a zigzag circumference, like that of the Pagan Phœnix. An engraving brought from Mount Athos, representing the great Monastery of Iviròn, has a similar figure of the Holy Ghost, descending from Heaven at the time of the Annunciation. Ciampini (*Vet. Mon.*, part 1, pl. 36, fig. 14,) gives an engraving from a coin of Faustina, in which the allegorical figure of Eternity holds a bird, supposed by Ciampini to be a peacock, but which may, possibly, be a phœnix. It is represented with an indented nimbus, like that of the Holy Spirit at Ivirôn.

‡ This outline is taken from an engraved gem called Abraxas, used as

Renaissance: it is that of a tongue of fire placed upon the forehead of genii. At the removal of the remains of Napoleon, on the 15th of December, 1840, this tongue of fire might be seen illumining the brows of the statues of genii placed on the Pont du Carousel, and on the esplanade of the Invalides. The Holy Spirit, descending upon the Apostles at Pentecost, was represented in the seventeenth and eighteenth centuries, by a similar tongue of flame. The Apostles are supposed to have been transformed at that moment, from ordinary mortals, into divinely inspired beings almost genii. This tongue of flame was the star shining on the forehead of the statue of Julius Cæsar.*

Such are the principal varieties of the nimbus. We have yet to notice the different modes of application which have been commonly adopted, and which will be easily defined and understood.

ON THE APPLICATION OF THE NIMBUS.

The nimbus, in Pagan Iconography, is the ordinary attribute of divinity; but it is also given frequently to Roman Emperors, to the Kings of Eastern Europe, and of Asia. It is likewise commonly worn by female magicians and prophetesses, and almost invariably distinguishes personified figures of the constellations, or of the good and evil

an amulet by the Gnostics. It is a species of Panthaic* deity. This genius of the world is shown to be Celestial by the Sun and Moon, introduced into the field on which he is engraved; Terrestrial, by the Lion's head; Aquatic, by the serpent-like tail; Divine, by the nimbus of twice seven luminous rays. See "l'Ant. Exp. de Montfaucon," tom. iv., p. 363.

* "Ludis quos primo consecratos ei (Julio Cæsari) hæres Augustus edebat, stella crinita per SEPTEM dies continuos fulsit, exoriens circa undecimam horam. Creditum est animam esse Cæsaris in cœlum recepti, et hac de causa simulacro ejus in vertice additur stella."—(Suetonius. *Vita Julii Cæsaris.*)

---

* Panthée, nom que les anciens donnaient aux statues qui réunissaient les symboles ou les attributs de differentes divinités.—(*Dictionnaire de l'Académie.*)

powers, which exert their influence on the human soul, on nature, and on society.*

In Christian Iconography, it is worn by the three Holy persons of the Trinity, whether represented together, or apart; it distinguishes the Virgin Mary, the apostles, angels, saints and prophets. Sometimes, but more rarely, it is given to the personifications of the virtues; to allegorical figures of natural or psychological objects; to several of the constellations; and to certain qualities or affections of the soul. Political power, the energies of nature, and the genius of evil, are sometimes dignified with this attribute, but very rarely, and only when Pagan influences have been infused into the symbolism of Christianity.

THE NIMBUS OF GOD.

In representations of the Godhead, the figure of the Divinity, like that of angels and saints, is depicted with the circular nimbus or disk; but that the Creator may be distinguished from his creatures, the field of the divine nimbus is intersected by two bars, which, meeting in the centre, cross at right angles, and thus present the figure of a Greek cross. One of the half bars, that which forms the foot of the cross is concealed by the head, which appears to rest upon it. The three others are visible, and extend vertically from the summit of the head, and horizontally from the extremity of the temples.

It seems doubtful whether it can actually have been intended to decorate the field of the Nimbus of God, with a cross; possibly, the form of the ornament which marks the nimbus of divine persons, is not borrowed, as one might be led to believe, from the instrument of our Saviour's suffering.

The propriety of the Redeemer being represented with a nimbus thus decorated, is sufficiently obvious: but why should it be worn also by the Father and the Holy Spirit? It is as if they wore the badge and insignia of the Son, which would not be very consistent. Besides, the halo

* See page 84, and figs. 9, 44, 45.

encircling the heads of several Buddhist and Hindoo divinities, is marked with a similar cross; and it cannot be

Fig. 11.—THE TRINITY—EACH DIVINE PERSON WEARING THE CRUCIFORM IMBUS.* Miniature taken from the "Heures du Duc d'Anjou."—Bib. Roy. End of XIII. cent.

supposed that, in these instances, any allusion is designed to the Cross of Calvary.

The nimbus, worn as a badge of holiness by an ordinary saint, or a mortal who has received the honour of apotheosis or canonisation, is properly plain; the simple glory; but in a figure of God, this halo should be more distinctly marked. Not only is the entire body encircled by a nimbus, that is, to speak more correctly, by an *aureole*, as will appear hereafter, but the nimbus of the head is marked with a cross, the one limb drawn from the top of the head, and the two

* This miniature of the Trinity belongs to the fourteenth century, or rather to the close of the thirteenth. It is taken from a MS. bearing the name of Louis, Duke of Anjou, and containing an inexhaustible fund of information for iconologists. I shall notice here, with a view to deducing a conclusion hereafter, that it is not possible to distinguish the figure of the Father, in this painting, from that of the Son. *Vide* fo. 183 of the MS. Coté Lavall, 127.

others from the ears or the temples. Rays of light may be seen to emanate from the entire *contour* of the head;* but there are three principal sources of radiance, namely, the three essential parts of the cranium, the region of the brain or cerebrum, and the two temples, where life, defined and concentrated, throbs in the great arteries. The forehead and temples may therefore be termed the three cardinal points of the cerebral sphere.

When the figure of God is surrounded by an aureole, as well as by the nimbus, and the field of both is striated by luminous rays emanating from all parts of the body, these rays are seen to issue in much greater abundance from the head than from the trunk, because the head is the most important part of man. The brow and the temples are still more radiant; for the forehead and the temples bear the same relation to the head as the head does to the body: they are, in fact, the essential organs.

Thus, in the following sketch, the Hindoo goddess, Maya, is represented pressing her breasts, whence flow those copious streams of milk by which all living creatures are nourished and supported. A veil of Ideas, the prototypes of creation, surrounds the richly-attired figure of the goddess. Maya is represented in a semi-aureole, or large Nimbus, the circumference of which is indented with zigzags, and the field striated with luminous sparks. Parallel with the temples and forehead, and stretching beyond the circumference, three clusters of rays dart forth, corresponding exactly with the cross lines in the Divine nimbus of Christian archæology. In fig. 34, an infant Christ may be seen wearing similar jets of light; these rays, on transverse lines, seem therefore intended rather to symbolise the superior power residing in those three regions of the head, than the Divine cross.

Still, it must be acknowledged that in some rare instances, and when Christ alone is represented, the figure behind the head of our Saviour is indeed that of a genuine cross, the instrument of the passion. This is seen clearly on an ivory tablet in the Louvre, belonging to the eleventh century.†

* See in the History of Christ, fig. 67, a figure taken from the Campo Santo, in which the rays of light spread in all directions.

† Armoires du Musée Charles X., Salle Gothique.

The Christ sculptured on this curious monument rests his head upon a cross, the upper limb of which is longer than

Fig. 12.—MAYA, THE HINDOO GODDESS, WITH A CRUCIFORM NIMBUS.*
Hindostan Iconography.

the transverse bars. The three branches are not united by a circular line, and thus their identity with the cross becomes even more striking.

In an ancient sarcophagus preserved in the Vatican, and belonging to a very early period, is a figure of Christ, bearded, and standing on the mystical mountain, whence flow the four streams of the Celestial Paradise. Our Saviour appears to be giving his last instructions to his apostles. He tells them to go forth into all parts of the

* *Réligions de l'Antiquité*, atlas, planche 19, No. 103.

world to preach and to baptise; to preach the Word written in the volume in his right hand, which he extends towards them; to baptise with the water of the sacred streams which roll their waves at his feet. The apostles, of whom six only are represented on the sculpture, three on the left and three on the right hand, are under the form of lambs; Christ himself is accompanied by the symbolic lamb, as the Ferouer, the emblem of man among the Persians, accompanies the individual, whose person he is supposed to inhabit. These lambs have no nimbus, neither has the person of Christ; for the monument belongs to an epoch antecedent to that in which the nimbus was first adopted; but the symbol of Christ, the Divine Lamb, bears on its brow the image of the cross on which our Saviour suffered.* At Arles, in the church of St. Trophemius, chapel of the Sepulchre, a tomb, which was brought hither from the Aliscamps,† presents a figure of Christ, with a beard, teaching the Gospel, and seated within an aureole, the upper part of which is circular. On the head of the Saviour, almost as if implanted in the crown of the skull, is a little cross, perfect in form; a curved line drawn in an angle on the right of the upper part of the cross, forms a P, the *rho*

* See a drawing on this subject, in the History of Christ, fig. 86.

† "Beyond the walls, to the east of the town, is situated the ancient cemetery of Arles, called Aliscamps, a slight variation from the original name (*Elisii Campi*) by which it was known eighteen centuries ago. It was of vast extent, a complete necropolis, and the dead were brought hither from other cities, as far distant as Lyons, for interment. Dante mentions it in the Inferno, IX. 112:—

'Si come ad Arli ove 'l Rodano stagna,
Fauno i sepolcri tutto 'l loco varo:'

and Ariosto alludes to it in the Orlando Furioso,

'Piena di sepolture è la Campagna.'

One portion of the ground was used for burial in Pagan times; another marked off with crosses, was afterwards designated for the interment of Christians. The ground teems with gravestones, sepulchral memorials, and sarcophagi; but the most curious have been removed to the museums of Arles, Toulouse, Marseilles, &c."—*Murray's Hand-Book of France*, page 467, edition 1847.

In a work upon Arles in my possession I met with the following anecdote of a tomb, which I think may be the one alluded to by M. Didron. I shall, I trust, be pardoned for introducing it here:

"Dans un autre chapelle (de St. Trophime), Il y a un tombeau de marbre blanc, orné de trois belles figures, dont celle du milieu représente Jésus

of the Greeks. The cross itself is equivalent to a *chi*, X, and we thus obtain the monogram of Christ, XP (Χριστός). These examples prove more decidedly than those before given, that the rays from the head of God, united by a circle, are designed to represent a cross, more particularly when they adorn the head of Christ.

Fig. 13.—DIVINE LAMB, WITH CRUCIFORM NIMBUS AND THREE SMALLER CROSSES.*
Italian Sculpture of the x cent.

It must also be remarked that the nimbus worn by the Lamb of God, of which a drawing is here given, is not only

Christ, qui, d 'une main, présente l'évangile à Geminus Paulus Gouverneur, et de l'autre, il lui donne sa bénédiction.

" Ce tombeau a été transporté dans la chapelle du Saint Sepulchre de l'église métropolitaine (d 'Arles) en 1804, où il sert d 'autel.

" Voici l 'épitaphe qui est sur le tombeau :—

Vir Agrippinensis Nomine Geminus,
Hic jacet qui post dignitatem Præsidiatus
Administrator rationum qui novem,
Provinciarum dignus est habitus
Hic post annos XXXIIX.M.II. Dies sex
Fidelis in fata concessit
Cujus ob insignem gloriam
Cives sepulchralia adornaverunt.

—*Abrége Chronologique de l'Histoire D'Arles*, par M. De Noble Lalausiere, Arles, 1808.—*Trans.*

* Engraved in Bosio. *Roma sotterranea,* in fo., édit. de Rome, 1636 (1632), p. 627.

cruciform, like that borne by several other lambs, but that each cross limb contains a smaller cross.

If, then, these transverse bars be intended, as seems probable, to indicate the divine power or energy, this singular peculiarity of a nimbus, the transverse branches of which also bear crosses, would appear in some sort to elevate that energy into a fourth power. A romanesque fresco, in one of the transepts of the Church of Montoire (Loire-et-Cher), near Vendôme, represents Christ in an oval glory.

Fig. 14.—DIVINE NIMBUS, WITH THE TRANSVERSE BRANCHES OF THE CROSS ELEVATED.* Fresco of the XI cent. in the Church of Montorio (Loire-et-Cher).

The nimbus surrounding the head is divided by rays, but the transverse branch, the centre of which in the

* See the "Musée Egyptien," in the Louvre; the great work on Egypt, the Zodiac of Denderah; and pl. 29, 30, 32, 33, 34, 35, &c., of the "Atlas des Religions de l'Antiquité."

preceding examples is concealed by the head itself, in this is raised above it and entirely visible. This transverse limb, being thus entirely visible, makes the cross-like form of these rays more distinctly evident than in any other of the like kind of nimbus. The form of a cross is, therefore, more distinctly recognised in this nimbus than in any of those hitherto described. Still the upper limb and branches of this cross (the foot, if it exists, is concealed by the Saviour's head) are confined by an external line in such a manner, that the nimbus in its general form resembles that of the terrestrial globe, as it is ordinarily represented in the hand of God. The three bands which form the cross of Montoire exactly resemble the circles drawn upon the representation of the terrestrial globe; Christ would thus appear to support the world upon his head, and this circled sphere carries us back immediately to Egyptian Iconography, in which we meet with numerous personages bearing the world upon their heads in a similar manner.

The arms forming the transverse bar in the divine nimbus, vary considerably in size, and are sometimes broad, more or less; sometimes more or less slender; occasionally they are formed by one line only, a simple thread, and at other times they occupy half of the entire surface. In the latter case they are ordinarily adorned with pearls, precious stones, or other varied ornaments. Among the Greeks each bar of the cross bears a letter, and the three united form *ο ων*, *I am*, or "the Being." The arrangement of these letters varies; sometimes, and most frequently, the omicron is on the left, sometimes at the top, as in the drawing given below.

In the "Guide de la Peinture,"* we find the following directions: "On the cross intersecting the crown (nimbus) of each of the three persons of the Trinity, the Father, Son, and Holy Ghost, let the following letters be inscribed, *ὁ ὤν*, for it is by these words that God was pleased to reveal himself to Moses in the burning bush; '*ἐγὼ ἐιμὶ ὁ ὤν*,' 'I am that I am.' Let the letters be thus arranged: Place

* *ἑρμῆνειά τῆς ζωγραφικῆς*, a MS. which I purchased at Mount Athos, and which my fellow-traveller, M. P. Durand, has recently translated and prepared for the press, with an introduction and notes, written by myself.

the omicron (ο) on the righthand branch of the nimbus,* the omega (ω) on the upper part, and the nu (ν) on the left."

Fig. 15.—A GREEK PAINTING OF CHRIST, WITH A CRUCIFORM NIMBUS, THE TRANSVERSE BRANCHES INSCRIBED WITH ο ὢν, "I AM."†
Fresco des Météores, in Thessaly, XIV cent.

The ο is occasionally placed on the left, but with the ν at the top, and ω on the right, as in the crown of enamelled copper, presented as an offering by the Emperor Frederic Barbarossa, and which is suspended under the dome in the cathedral of Aix-la-Chapelle.‡ Each transverse bar is

* The right of the figure, the left of the spectator.

† Similarly "Jehovah" signifies "He is," or "Being itself." See *Mant's Bible*, Exodus, iii., 14.

‡ It is impossible to give drawings of every monument mentioned in illustration of the facts cited. Of many of these monuments no engravings exist, so that it will be necessary to trust to oral testimony, which is the case in regard to the crown at Aix-la-Chapelle; that crown, however, I have myself seen, and the description of it was written on the spot. Whenever, therefore, any monument is mentioned without either an engraving, or a reference to any, in support of my statements, it may be inferred that I have myself seen and examined it.

formed by two parallel lines, drawn from the centre of the disc to the circumference. The bar is often equal in breadth throughout its entire length, but sometimes increases in width, like a spatula, at the circumference; it is then narrower in the middle of the disk, and at the half of its length considerably narrower and appearing as if forcibly compressed.

Between these transverse bars there are no ornaments, and most frequently the field is plain. Sometimes narrow threads or little rays, in groups of threes, or fours, fill the space intervening between the great rays which compose the cross of the nimbus.

The cruciform nimbus is entirely appropriated to the Deity: it is given more peculiarly to Christ the Saviour, and frequently, as in the Byzantine monuments, as has been already shown, the letters *ο ων*, *I am*, or "He who is," are inscribed on the branches of the cross.*

This idea has sometimes been imitated by the Latins; but instead of ὁ ὢν they inscribe the word REX, also in three letters, one for each visible branch of the cross.†

Both the original artists and the copyists of the middle ages appear to have been often ill-instructed, and either from ignorance or negligence the latter frequently passed over some important word or phrase, and the artists omitted

* The Greeks, who were intimately conversant with the sacred writings, remembered, as we are told in the "Guide de la Peinture," that verse in the book of Exodus, where God announces himself by the words, "I am that I am," (Exod. iii., 14). They wished, by the aid of painting, to embody that sublime expression; and, not content with the divinity of expression conveyed by painting alone, added the letters *ὁ ὢν*, in the halo encircling the head of God. The Christian artists of the West, on the contrary, either less instructed, or relying more implicitly on the omnipotence of art, sought to convey the idea of Deity by the countenance alone. In the cathedral of Athens, now transformed into a public library, a figure of Christ, painted in fresco on the vaulting of the cupola, has a cruciform nimbus, but without the *ὁ ὢν* inscribed upon it; rough precious stones and pearls supply their place. The absence of these three Greek letters is, perhaps, a token of antiquity; the cathedral is certainly the most ancient church in Athens.

† See *Gori Thesaurus Veterum Diptychorum*, vol. iii., p. 79. The drawing represents Christ within an oval aureole, and is sculptured on an ivory tablet, which served as a cover to a book of the Gospels. This singular relic, the date of which is uncertain, is from the Musée of the Camaldules de St. Michel de Mariano, at Venice, and must have been executed by some Latin artist who loved and had studied Byzantine art.

some constant characteristic feature. We must not, therefore, be astonished often to find one of the persons of the Trinity without a nimbus, or with a nimbus plain instead of cruciform. Such errors are, indeed, extremely common, as in the annexed engraving, which represents the Ascension of Christ, and is taken from a carving on wood, executed in Italy about the fourteenth century.*

Fig. 16.—CHRIST WITH A PLAIN NIMBUS, ASCENDING TO HEAVEN IN A CIRCULAR AUREOLE. Carving in wood of the XIV cent.

A contrary error, but much less frequent than the former, is that of representing an ordinary mortal with the cruciform or divine nimbus. An ancient MS. in the Bibliothèque d'Amiens,† contains at the commencement, within an illuminated capital B, adorned with arabesques, a young man, beardless, crowned with a diadem and seated; he holds in

* This carving is the property of M. Paul Durand, who brought it with him from Italy.

† *Liber Psalmorum:* attributed to the ninth century. M. le Docteur Rigollot (*Atlas de l'Essai Historique sur les Arts du dessin en Picardie, depuis l'époque Romaine jusqu'au* XVIe. *siècle*, 8vo, Amiens, 1840,) gives a drawing by M. Duthoit, of this capital B, illuminated with arabesques and miniatures. It is the first letter of the "Beatus Vir," with which the

his left hand an open book, and in the right a pen, which he is in the act of dipping into an inkstand. This young writer wears a cruciform nimbus; he appears to be listening attentively, as if to catch inspiration from a dove hovering near his ear, and breathing into it, we may imagine, the poetry he is about to write. The miniaturist is here undoubtedly in fault; the figure is probably intended for David writing the Psalms, or at the most for St. John the Evangelist, attended and assisted by his eagle; but in either case the figure is that of a mortal, not of a god.

In the Bibliothèque de l'Arsenal a miniature* is preserved, representing a priest officiating and adorned with a cruciform nimbus of gold. It may be that the personage is designed for Christ himself performing the functions of a priest; but it must be remarked, in confutation of this, that the figure here has the head bald, the characteristic of St. Peter, and that our Saviour is never so represented.

Still granting that this be Jesus in person and that no error exists in reality, other unquestionable facts may easily be adduced.

The missal of the Abbey of St. Magloire, at Paris,† belonging to the fifteenth century, contains a picture of the "Nativity of Mary," in which the little virgin is represented wearing a golden nimbus, divided by three black transverse lines. The Virgin has also a large aureole, in which her body is entirely enclosed, exactly like that encircling the figure of God, of which an engraving will be given further on. The Virgin is thus made almost equal with God. The figure may have been designed by one of her enthusiastic votaries, and the error may be one of intention and not

book of Psalms opens. M. Rigollot, without deciding (Essai, &c., p. 36,) the question, considers the young man to be intended either for the Evangelist St. John, or the Psalmist David. I believe it to be David, inspired by the Holy Spirit. The figure of David is frequently thus painted at the head of the book of Psalms; and a similar drawing will be given in the History of the Holy Ghost, in which the Spirit is seen to hover above him, and inspire his sacred songs.

* Evangelarium in fo. Théolo. lat., No. 202. End of the fourteenth century. This miniature is to be found in the Gospel for the Feast of the Holy Trinity, fo. 139, verso.

† Bibliothèque de l' Arsénal, Théol. lat. 188, fo. 307, verso. *In Nativitate beatæ Mariæ.*

simply of fact. But in another MS. of the end of the thirteenth century the mistake is clearly evident, and even involves a double error.* The Prophet Joel is there represented youthful, beardless, with a cruciform nimbus; Joel is listening to the words of inspiration, breathed into his ear by a form, intended to be a personal representation of the Deity; but it is singular that God is drawn with a simple nimbus. The true intention is, in fact, reversed; the cruciform nimbus, the symbol of divinity, is removed from God to a mortal, while the Creator has simply the attributes of the creature. Such errors are of much importance and throw a certain light on the education then received by Christian artists.

The divine nimbus was not immediately cruciform; the earliest Christian monuments found on Sarcophagi are, it will be remarked, generally either without the nimbus, or, if introduced, it is completely simple and undecorated.

I would mention, as instances of the latter style, an old carving on ivory, in the possession of M. le Comte Auguste de Bastard,† the bible of Charles the Bald,‡ and the first and most ancient portion of the MS. of Herrade.§ In this latter work, with the exception of God creating the angels, the other representations of the deity, up to folio 54, have only a plain nimbus without the cruciform divisions.

In the drawing on the following page, taken from a fresco in the Roman catacombs,|| our Saviour is represented beardless, seated between the two apostles St. Peter and St. Paul, who are standing; the nimbus of our Saviour is plain,

* *Officium Ecclesiasticum.* Bib. de l'Arsénal. Théol. lat. 123; fol. 790, verso.

† This carving belongs, probably, to the fourth or fifth century. It represents the paralytic healed by Jesus; the woman touching his garments; the swine rushing into the sea, at the voice of the Incarnate God. Christ is in each scene represented beardless, with a simple nimbus, and sandals on his feet.

‡ In the "Creation," in this beautiful Bible, God the Creator is represented young, beardless, his feet bare, and with a staff in his hand. The nimbus is not cruciform.

§ *Hortus Deliciarum,* MS., filled with splendid miniatures. It is an Encyclopædia, compiled and even painted, it is said, in 1180, by Herrade de Landsberg, Abbess of the convent of Saint Odile, in Alsace. This precious MS. belongs to the Bibliothèque de Strasbourg.

|| *Roma Sotterranea,* p. 475.

Fig. 17.—CHRIST WITHOUT A BEARD, WEARING A PLAIN NIMBUS.
Fresco in the Catacombs. Earliest ages of Christianity.

not cruciform, and exactly resembles those of the two apostles.

The age of this painting is uncertain, but the monument itself belongs to the earliest period of the Church, and this example of the Christian nimbus is certainly the most ancient that can be found. The other representations of God are like that given below without a nimbus: Christ is here represented beardless and with long hair.* (Fig. 18.)

Both angels and saints wear the plain nimbus. Still numerous MSS. contain figures of angels wearing a cruciform nimbus, like that appropriated to the Deity. Various explanations may be given of this singular anomaly; either the artist has been mistaken, as sometimes appears, and inadvertently made the nimbus cruciform when he ought to have left it plain, or, he has here intended to represent that historical scene mentioned in the Old Testament, wherein it is related that Abraham, having met three angels, prostrated himself at the feet of one only and worshipped him. "Tres vidit, unum adoravit:" "Three he saw, one he worshipped."†

Commentators having asserted that these three persons represented the divine Trinity under the angelic form, artists followed the directions of theologians and made the nimbus of the heavenly angel, whom Abraham was said to have adored, cruciform. In the Bible, No. 6 of the "Bibliothèque Royale," even the wings are removed, and the personage before whom Abraham prostrates himself is represented with a beard, in order the more fully to display the characteristics of the Deity.‡ (Fig. 19.)

* Christ is here without a beard, seated on a throne, and his feet supported by a scarf held by a naked female figure, the personification of the Earth; the Earth being thus the "footstool" of Christ, as had been prophesied by Isaiah. ("Ponam terram scabellum pedum tuorum." (See *Roma Sotter.*) In this picture, the allegorical figure sustaining Christ is a woman, probably because it represents the Earth. Elsewhere we generally find an aged man with a beard; this aged man is, perhaps, designed to symbolise the Heavens, and, if so, the idea must have been borrowed from Paganism. Mythological ideas have, in many cases, been adopted by Christian Art; it is not unlikely that these ideas were, in the first instance, borrowed from the Jewish faith; and Christianity, in reclaiming them from the Pagans, merely entered into possession of her own birthright.

† M. Didron's version of this scene is different from that in our Bible. Gen. xviii. 2.

‡ These figures are scrupulously correct as copies, but the original drawing

In the History of the Devil, a drawing taken from the "Emblèmes Bibliques," MS. of the thirteenth century,

Fig. 18.—CHRIST WITHOUT NIMBUS, AND BEARDLESS.
Sculpture from one of the Sarcophagi in the Vatican. First ages of Christianity.

in the Bibliothèque Royale, will be given. It represents three angels engaged in combat with Behemoth and Leviathan;* one only of the three has the cruciform nimbus; he is engaged in single conflict with Behemoth, while the other

is bad. The MS. from which they are taken is no less ugly, in an æsthetic point of view, than it is valuable as an archæological treasure.

* Vide *infra*, fig. 132.

two, who attack Leviathan, have only a plain nimbus and appear to be angels. Was there intention in this fact, or is it an inadvertence? Was it the artist's design to represent the Triune god united in one person, and attack-

Fig. 19.—THE THREE HEAVENLY BEINGS WHO APPEARED TO THE PATRIARCH ABRAHAM, ONE WEARING A CRUCIFORM NIMBUS, OR NIMBUS STAMPED WITH A CROSS.
Miniature of the x cent. Bible No. 6. Bibliothèque Royale.

ing the Genius of Evil under the form of that Behemoth, who exerts his evil influence upon Earth, even as Leviathan holds dominion over the waters?

The nimbus, as has already been observed, by established usage encircles the head: it is a species of religious crown;

but there is in this respect one singular exception, referring only to God the Father. Artists, for various reasons which will hereafter be explained in the Archæological History of God, have sometimes thought fit to represent the Divinity by one portion only of his body; by the hand, for instance, which is seen extended from the clouds, while the entire body remains concealed in the heavens. In these instances the *hand* is distinctly shown to be the emblem of Deity by being encircled with a cruciform nimbus.

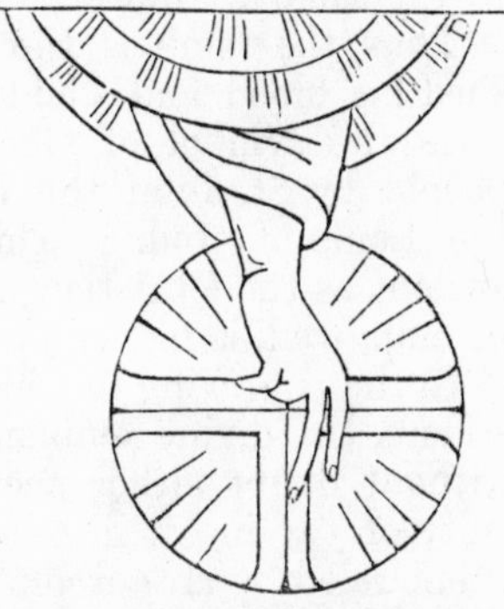

Fig.20.—THE DIVINE HAND, WITH A CRUCIFORM NIMBUS.
Miniature of the IX cent. Bib. Roy.

Hands thus decorated with the nimbus formed the earliest symbolic representation of the Father; the example subjoined, which belongs to the ninth century,* is interesting on account of the peculiar direction given to the branches of the cross, and of the rays which seem attached in groups of four to the line of circumference. Either from a feeling of reverence, in compliance with some religious dogma, or even, as will be subsequently explained, from an ill-feeling towards the supreme Being, nothing more was shown of the Father than the hand extended to bless, at first destitute of any nimbus,† and subsequently with the cruciform nimbus.

* Bib. Roy. *Liber Precum.* The miniature represents the Martyrdom of St. Stephen, who appears to be gazing into the opening Heaven, from which the hand of God is extended towards him.

† See (*Peintures et Ornements des Manuscrits*) a Divine Hand without the nimbus, belonging to the first half of the eleventh century, in a collection of Treatises on various subjects. (*MS. de la Bibliothèque Royale fonds de St. Germain.*) Another hand, without a nimbus, appearing to St. Stephen at his Martyrdom, may be seen in a missal of St. Denis, of the middle of the eleventh century, Latin MS., supplement. In the frescoes of St. Savin, twelfth century, the hand of God, without a nimbus, is extended from the clouds in the act of blessing Melchizedeck. In the cathedral of Chartres is a painting on glass, representing the History of Charlemagne and the Death of Roland. The hand of God, without a nimbus, is seen extended from the

Not merely the countenance of God, but even his hand, when the hand alone is shown, is decorated with the cruciform nimbus; not only the actual figure or person of Divinity, but even the Ideal of Divinity itself, the symbol under which that idea is sometimes conveyed, is distinguished by the same attribute.

Thus, the lamb is the symbol of our Saviour, for Jesus shed his blood and yielded up his life without a murmur; it is the symbol of Christ, who was pointed out to the people by St. John the Baptist with these words, "Behold the Lamb of God." This symbol, the use of which is as ancient as the Christian faith, and which still continues to be employed, is likewise invested with the cruciform nimbus.

In the engraving in which St. John is represented holding a lamb, the divine emblem has no nimbus; the omission is without doubt either accidental or occasioned by the difficulty of carving it in so small a space: the lamb, however, is encircled by an aureole.*

In the History of Christ, an engraving copied from a sculpture in the Catacombs, will be found belonging to a period prior to that in which the nimbus was universally adopted among Christians, and for this reason, the Divine Lamb is distinguished from the Apostolical Lambs around by the cross upon its brow.

In fig. 13, the Lamb has a cruciform nimbus, and each branch is again marked by a lesser cross.

The lamb is the most common, and generally popular, symbol of our Saviour; still it is far from being the only one in use. The lion is the type of the tribe of Judah,† and Christ is descended by David from that tribe;‡ Christ,

clouds, appearing to Roland, who, in his distress, sounds the oliphant, and cleaves a rock with his good sword Durandal. This painting belongs to the thirteenth century. The hand of God, represented on sarcophagi of the first Christian ages, as presenting to Moses the Tables of the Law, never has a nimbus; still, notwithstanding these and similar exceptions, the hand of the Eternal is very frequently decorated with a circular nimbus, divided by the cross-bars. We shall meet with many more examples.

* This figure is given in the History of Christ. It represents a colossal statue placed against one division of the north porch in the cathedral of Chartres. See fig. 83.

† "*Catulus leonis Juda.*" Genesis, xlix. 9.

‡ St. Matt., i. 1, 2.; Rev. v. 5. "*Ecce vicit leo de tribu Juda, radix David.*"

like the lion of St. Mark, filled the deserts with the voice of his Gospel;* as Christ lived in the tomb,† so likewise the lion sleeps with unclosed eyes. In short, since the lamb, the personification of gentleness, was the accepted emblem of the Son of God, Art, which delights itself in contrasts, completed the symbolism by the introduction of the lion, the type of strength and energy. In fact, the Bible of Charles le Chauve‡ contains a sacred lamb, adorned with the cruciform nimbus, and gazing on a lion, with a glory divided in the same manner by the cross. The combined symbols are significative of Christ in his fulness of perfection, ready to break the seals of the mysterious volume placed near him.

The Abbé Suger § confirms this explanation. In a large painting on glass which he commanded to be executed for the western window of St. Denis, among other symbolic themes, the lion and the lamb are introduced breaking the seven seals of the book of the Apocalypse. The two verses subjoined, which are from his pen and placed by his command upon the window, explain the allusion:

"Qui Deus est magnus, librum Leo solvit et Agnus;
Agnus sive Leo fit caro juncta Deo."

It is probable that this lion and lamb, both of which unhappily are destroyed, had the cruciform nimbus like those in the Bible of Charles le Chauve.

The nimbus represents the radiation of light from the head, and the head being spherical, this radiation ought

* "*Marcus ut alta fremit vox per deserta leonis.*" Inscription in Saint Paul hors-les-Murs (*S. Paoli di fuori*), copied or repeated in several MS. Gospels, particularly in the *Quatuor Evangelia,* Theol. Lat., 33; Bib. de l'Arsénal.

† Alciatus thus explains the presence of the sculptured lions who frequently guard the entrance of churches:—

"Est Leo, sed custos oculis quia dormit apertis;
Templorum idcirco ponitur ante fores."

‡ This Bible is in the Bib. Roy. M. de Bastard (*Peintures et Ornements des Manuscrits*) has given the miniature of the Lion and Lamb, each with the cruciform nimbus, standing face to face, the book of the Apocalypse lying between them.

§ *De Administratione Suâ,* ap. Félibien. *Histoire de l'Abbaye Royale de St. Denis.*

necessarily to be of the same form, and the nimbus in consequence is almost always round.

Still there are instances of both the triangular and the square nimbus being applied to the head of Deity. The reason may, probably, be thus explained: the jets of flame from the brow and temples are represented as larger, longer, and more abundant, because there the emanation is supposed to be more energetic. In this case the circular nimbus is intersected by cross lines, or by rays drawn from the centre towards the circumference. At certain epochs, however, and more particularly in the fifteenth century, these jets of flame were made to exceed the limits of the circumference of the disk; and to render this extension less unpleasing to the eye, the line circumscribing the disk was omitted.*

On the other hand, some artists, in certain countries, wishing to re-connect these three rays from the brow and temples, drew a direct line from the extremity of one to that of the other two points, and thus formed a pyramid, the point of which was above; the base was formed by the horizontal line which connected the two jets of flame from the temples, as the two sides of the pyramid connected the temples with the brow; a triangle was thus formed.†

But although first produced by chance, or, at least, without direct design, the triangle has maintained itself, and indeed, been further developed in Iconography, from a much higher cause, for a mystical reason. In all ages, the triangle has been the geometrical emblem of the Divine Trinity. An unbroken area, terminated by three angles, expressed, with wonderful exactitude, the unity of one God in three persons. Consequently, Italy, more ideal and imaginative than France, or any other country of Western Europe, eagerly adopted for the nimbus a figure which thus symbolised the fundamental dogma of Christianity. Greece embraced the same idea, and even heightened it, declaring positively that the triangle was a fitting symbol of the Deity—of the great I AM—by inscribing, in each of the three angles, one of the letters, *ο ων*, THE BEING.‡

* See Fig. 7. † See Fig, 4.

‡ See a Greek engraving of the Annunciation, from Mount Athos, copied rom a fresco there. At Kares, Mount Athos, which is the capital of this province of monks, copper-plate engravings may be purchased, either coloured

The Greeks, more mystical even than the Italians, were not content with one triangle only; they made the nimbus to consist of two triangles intersecting one another, and thus forming five angles instead of three. If a single triangle express the perfect divinity, two would seem to indicate the infinity of the Godhead. This idea is analogous to that of the cruciform nimbus, in which each limb further bears a cross, and is an ingenious manner of figuring the omnipotence of the Divinity.

It should be remarked that it has always been the practice to indicate the divine attributes by means of the nimbus.* The Supreme Being is designated by the three Greek letters; the Trinity by the triangle; the infinity of God by the double triangle; eternity by a circle; life by a square, and the eternity of existence by a square within a circle.

A nimbus, of triangular form, is thus seen to be the exclusive attribute of Deity, and is most frequently restricted to the Father Eternal. The other persons of the Trinity sometimes wear the triangle, but only in representations of the Trinity, and because the Father is with them. Still, even then, beside the Father, who has a triangle, the Son and the Holy Ghost are often drawn with a circular nimbus only; but in all cases these two persons of the Trinity, like the first, are alone honoured with the triangular nimbus of divinity. A copy of Dante, printed in the sixteenth century, and ornamented with engravings, contains, amongst others, a Trinity of three heads on one single body; this Trinity has one triangular nimbus only for the three heads.† In some instances, both the Father and the Son have a triangular

or plain, representing all the monasteries and the different villages (*skites*) of the mountain. These drawings, moreover, analogous to those made at Epinal, present to us the chief Saints, and the principal Legends of Christianity. We thus obtain the entire Greek Iconography. I brought back with me a complete series of these engravings, which, although sufficiently rude, yet possess much interest.

* See Fig. 13.

† See this design below, in the History of the Trinity (Fig. 147). Since it has been found necessary, in this Iconographical History to be somewhat sparing of engravings, when any particular fact is enunciated, and not accompanied by a drawing in illustration of it, it will almost invariably be found in some other paragraph to which it more decidedly belongs. The reader is, therefore, requested to look through the engravings, in order to discover the solution of any difficulties, or the explanation of certain facts that may perplex him.

nimbus, while the Holy Spirit is encircled by a circular aureole. The divine persons are thus figured in the

Fig. 21.—GOD THE FATHER, WITH A BI-TRIANGULAR NIMBUS;
GOD THE SON, WITH A CIRCULAR NIMBUS;
GOD THE HOLY GHOST, WITHOUT A NIMBUS, AND WITHIN AN AUREOLE.*
Fresco at Mount Athos.

"Epigonation," with which Greek archbishops and bishops

* This representation of the Trinity is taken from a fresco, in one of the Greek convents of Mount Athos. The Holy Spirit is drawn within a radiating aureole, the flame of which encloses within its light the two other Divine Persons. The Holy Ghost has no nimbus. The Son has a circular nimbus with the cross rays, on which are inscribed the letters *o ων*. The Father has a double triangular nimbus, and the three letters, *o ων*, are traced in the corners of that triangle, the point or apex of which is at the top. See, further, a Greek engraving, representing the Monastery of St. Paul, one of the convents on Mount Athos. The lower portion of this engraving contains a general view of the Monastery; the upper part gives a representation of the Trinity. The Son and the Holy Ghost have each a circular cruciform nimbus; the Father a bi-triangular nimbus. The five points of the triangle are connected by a circle. Another, an engraving of the Convent of Chilandari, also on Mount Athos, contains the Coronation of the Virgin by the Holy Trinity. Mary has a simple circular nimbus, the Holy Ghost a circular radiating nimbus, Christ a circular cruciform nimbus, with the letters *o ων*. The Father alone has the triangular nimbus. Thus, then, from the Virgin up to the three Divine Persons, are different gradations of dignity, as from Saints to Angels. The artist may also have intended, by the various kinds of nimbus, to express the different relations existing between the Divine Persons themselves. The different forms are thus made to indicate the hierarchy of created beings,

are sometimes decorated. The Holy Trinity is represented in the same manner on the "Epigonation," worn by a great image of St. Nicholas, which may be seen in the principal convent of Météora, in Thessaly, near the ancient city of Tricca, now Triccala.* It has thus been clearly shown that the triangle belongs especially to the Father, sometimes to the Son, occasionally, though not often, to the Holy Ghost, and is never given to the Blessed Virgin, nor to the Apostles.

The ancients, the platonists, the neo-platonists, Pythagoras, Plutarch, Pliny, Vitruvius, &c., have dilated on the value of the triangle in its geometric and symbolic properties. In the traditions of India, and, indeed, of the whole of Asia, the Triad is a mystic number; it is symbolic of the attributes of the Supreme Being, uniting in itself the properties of the two first numbers of the unity, and the dual.† These discussions on numbers were echoed by the West, resounding and increasing in vehemence throughout the entire course of the Middle Ages. St. Angilbert, the father of Nithard and the companion of Charlemagne, constructed the Abbey of Centula, or St. Riquier, in the form of a triangle. The cloisters formed a triangle, and a church was erected at each angle; the number three, shone on the altar, chandeliers and ciborium in each. One hundred monks were devoted to the service of each of these churches, amounting altogether to three hundred; and thirty-three children formed the choir of each. It is expressly stated that all was thus arranged in honour of the Holy Trinity.‡ Even in our

and the relative position of the different persons of the Trinity. The same fact may be noticed in the fresco paintings of the Greek Church; the engravings alluded to are a reproduction or *calque* of these paintings. We cite the drawings in preference to the frescos, because the engravings may easily be obtained in confirmation of the assertions here advanced.

* The "Epigonation," ἐπιγονάτιον, is a lozenge-shaped ornament depending over the right knee, whence it derives its name (ἐπὶ and γονυ), and which, like the stole amongst ourselves, forms a part of the Pontifical costume. The Epigonation is embroidered with ornaments and figures. Among the latter the Trinity is frequently conspicuous.

† M. le Baron di Gerando, *Vie de Pythagore,* in "la Biographie Universelle."

‡ "Claustrum monachorum triangulum factum est. Sic que sit, ut dum hic inde parietes sibi invicem concurrunt, medium spatium sub divo triangulum habeatur.—Quia igitur omnis plebs fidelium sanctissimum atque inseparabilem Trinitatem confiteri, venerari, et mente colere, firmiterque credere debet,

time, Cambry, in his "Monuments Celtiques," asserts that the triangle expressed three of the inseparable attributes of Deity—to be; to think; to speak.* The triangle, having thus been, at all periods, the geometrical expression of the Trinity, it may easily be conceived that the triangular nimbus would be peculiarly appropriate to God the Father.

In France, nevertheless, although the divine nimbus, that is to say, the circular nimbus, with three rays, is often omitted, when applied, its figure is never altered, nor is it ever brought back to that of the triangle. This change was effected in Italy, in which country the nimbus assumes a diversity of form, distracting to the antiquary, and sub-

secundum hujus fidei rationem in omnipotentis Dei nomine tres ecclesias principales, cum membris ad se pertinentibus, in hoc sancto loco, Domino cooperante, et prædicto domino Augusto [he alludes to Charlemagne] juvante, fundere studuimus [here Angilbert himself speaks] in ecclesia sancti Benedicti, altaria parata tria; in ecclesiis vero sanctorum angelorum Gabrielis, Michaëlis et Raphaëlis, altaria tria, quæ simul fiunt altaria triginta, et ciboria tria, et lectoria tria.—Quapropter trecentos monachos in hoc sancto loco regulariter victuros, Deo auxiliante, constituimus.—Centum etiam pueros scholis erudiendos sub eodem habitu et victu statuimus, qui fratribus per tres choros divisis in auxilium psallendi et canendi intersint: ita ut chorus Sancti-Salvatoris centenos monachos cum quatuor et triginta pueris habeat; chorus Sancti-Richarii centenos monachos, tresque et triginta pueros jugiter habeat; chorus psallens ante Sanctam-Passionem centenos monachos, triginta tribus adjunctis pueris, similiter habeat. Ea autem ratione chori tres in divinis laudibus personabunt, ut omnes horas canonicas in commune simul omnes decantent. Quibus decenter expletis, uniuscujusque chori pars tertia ecclesiam exeat, et corporeis necessitatibus vel aliis utilitatibus ad tempus inserviat, certo temporis spatio interveniente ad divinæ laudis munia celebranda denuo redeuntes. In unoquoque etiam choro id jugiter observetur, ut sacerdotum ac levitarum reliquorumque sacrorum ordinum æqualis numerus teneatur. Cantorum nihilominus et lectorum æquali mensura divisio ordinetur, qualiter chorus à choro invicem non gravetur." (*Acta SS. ord. S. Benedicti*, IVe. Siècle Bénédictin, 1re. partie, Vie de St. Angilbert.) It has been thought advisable to transcribe a portion of the text of this work, which, in regard to the history of symbolic monuments, is one of the most interesting works we possess on Christian Archæology. This triangular cloister is unfortunately no longer in existence, and the loss is irreparable, as we know of no other monastery thus appropriating the symbolic form of the triangle.

* He might have substituted "to act," in the place of "to speak," since speech is but one of the thousand varieties of action, merely a simple phase of that intellectual activity which is multiplied to infinity. Still, God created all things by His word; and, in this sense, Cambry would be right. (*Monuments Celtiques*, par Cambry, in 8o., Paris, 1805, p. 157.)

verting every fixed rule which one might attempt to assign to it. A similar change was made in the Greek Church, which adopts many ideas of religion completely at variance with ours; it was introduced also at the period of the Renaissance, when the laws of previous epochs became the sport of fancy, and rules were abandoned to caprice. France has been less variable, and is still content with the circle, a form which, indeed, is better suited to the head. The few examples of the triangular nimbus, which are to be found amongst us, deserve to be carefully noted; they will always be found to be exceptions, indicating, probably, either a Greek or Latin influence.

It is easy to understand why the triangle should be an attribute of God, since the Godhead is tri-une (DEUS TRINUS UNUS, says Lactantius); but the application of the square is more difficult to comprehend. In fact the square, in the opinion of neo-platonists and pythagoreans, symbolises the earth; and the earth, in symbolism as well as in reality, is inferior to heaven, of which, according to ancient ideas, it can at most be only the pedestal. The square nimbus has nevertheless sometimes been given to God, and to God the Father; a circumstance which it is difficult to explain, especially when we remember that, in Italy, the square nimbus is frequently granted to virtuous mortals, but only when they are painted during their lifetime, in order to distinguish them from figures of saints or holy persons departed; a living personage, however holy, being always held inferior to a dead saint, however inferior may be the reputation he enjoys: the living is still but human; the canonised dead, almost a god. For this reason the square, a geometrical symbol of the earth, adorns the heads of the living; and the circle, a celestial figure, decorates the heads of saints in Paradise.* Wherefore, then, should the Creator of all these

* The Bollandists (*Acta SS. Maii*, tom. i., p. 62, in the introduction to the Saints of that month,) have had engravings made from a painting at Mount-Cassin. It represents St. Benedict giving the rules of his order to the Abbé Jean. St. Benedict has a circular nimbus, as well as the Angel who stands behind to aid him with his counsel; the Abbé Jean, on the contrary, has a square nimbus. The Bollandists observe, in reference to this subject:—Vides gemmatum utrique circa caput ornatum, cum hac diversitate quod S. Benedicto, ut æternitatem felicem adepto, caput ambiat circulus, æternitatis

beings, whether living or dead, have an attribute which lowers him to the condition of his creatures—and of his creatures, too, while still living, and, as yet, unglorified? It must be observed that the square nimbus, as worn by God, is generally concave, not straight at the sides; while the sides of that of living created beings are right lines, not rounded into an arc; it must be especially noticed that the nimbus of God is almost invariably placed upon an angle, in the manner of a lozenge, and not, like that of his creatures, on the side.*

Fig. 22.—GOD THE FATHER WEARING A LOZENGE-SHAPED NIMBUS.
Miniature of the XIV cent. Italian Manuscript in the Bibliothèque Royale.

Raphael also, has represented God the Father, with a lozenge-shaped nimbus, but with straight sides.† Pos-

symbolum; Johanni vero, ut adhuc viventi, quadratum quid post caput sit, quo creditur firmitas fidei, velut quadro lapide immobiliter nixæ, repræsentari." If the square nimbus indicates the energy of faith, why give it to God, who is himself the object of faith?

* In a Mosaic, in the Church of San Giovanni in Laterano, is a representation of God, with a square nimbus, resting on the sides, not angularly.

† The nimbus, with concave sides, is from the MS. entitled *Speculum Humanæ Salvationis;* that with straight sides is taken from the "Disputà" of Raphael.

sibly, this lozenge may have been regarded by artists as a purely mystical emblem, a symbol unencumbered by any material signification. In this case, the lozenge-shaped nimbus would imply only an idea analogous to that which is conveyed by a triangular nimbus. In fact, in the Apse of S. Giovanni-in-Lateran, at Rome, there exists a mosaic, executed between the years 1288 and 1294, under Pope Nicholas IV., in which God the Father is seen, under the figure of Christ, the upper part of the body only issuing from the clouds; below him is the Holy Spirit, and, lower still, the Cross, richly decorated; a Cross of gems. The nimbus of the Father is no longer a lozenge, as in the preceding examples, but square, like those of the Popes Gregory and Pascal: God is living. The square nimbus is, however, inscribed within a circular nimbus; the circle is the common symbol of eternity: God is, therefore, eternally living.* I AM, and I SHALL BE, are words used by the Eternal in several passages of the Sacred Books.† Such may, probably, be the signification of the square nimbus contained within the area of a circle; for life is comprehended in eternity.

The field of the divine nimbus is generally more highly ornamented than that of the nimbus worn by angels, mortals, or allegorical beings. The divine head, the centre of all light, almost invariably has rays or jets of light thrown out on the field of the nimbus. Prior to the fifteenth century, these rays or jets of light terminated at the line of circumference, by which they were bound together; but about that period they first became separated one from another. The line of circumference disappears, the rays alone remain. These rays are generally straight, and of equal lengths; sometimes those on the forehead and temples are gathered into a sheaf, and extend beyond the intermediate rays; sometimes all are flamboyant, or alternately straight and flamboyant.

* M. Tournal gives the above explanation of this figure, and I accept it with pleasure. I am indebted to the kindness of the learned antiquary of Narbonne for a copy of this curious mosaic, recently taken in Rome by himself.

† The term of duration is even more complete, embracing not only the present and future, but also the past: "Ego sum . . qui est, et qui erat, et qui venturus est." (*Apocalyp.* i. 8.)

During the primitive ages of Christianity, when Christ was often, indeed almost invariably, represented under the form of a lamb; this lamb was generally without any nimbus, but frequently also with a circular nimbus. At a somewhat later period, the field of the nimbus became crossed. From that time (although rarely, it is true) the field was sometimes marked by the monogram of the divine person whom the lamb was designed to symbolise, the X and P, two Greek letters, with which the name of ΧΡΙΣΤΟΣ commences. Lastly, the A and Ω, signifying the beginning and the end, a monogram pertaining equally to each of the three persons, accompanies the special monogram of Christ, as in the opposite drawing.*

THE NIMBUS OF ANGELS AND SAINTS.

The angel has a circular nimbus, but with the field plain.† Sometimes, however, in Italy especially, and in Greece,‡ in the fourteenth, fifteenth, sixteenth, and seventeenth centuries, the field is striated or adorned with an arcature, or with strings of pearls, or even with rays; but it must be observed that, in the latter case, the rays are dispersed without regard to number, and not limited to three, as in the nimbus of God. It seems to be the same with the rays of the nimbus, as with the *fleurs-de-lys* in heraldry; an indefinite number of *fleurs-de-lys*, indicate noble, but not royal,

* This Lamb was taken from *Roma Soterranea*, p. 591. He stands on the mystical mountain, whence descend the four streams of Paradise—the Pison, Gihon, Tigris, and Euphrates.

† See in the Hist. of Angels various delineations of these celestial beings.

‡ In Greek frescoes the nimbus is not merely painted, but is also sculptured or modelled. Before painting this insignia, a matrix of wood is impressed upon the soft coating, which gives the ornaments hollow and in relief. On the plaster thus modelled the painter spreads his colours; the same plan was adopted among us also, particularly in the thirteenth century. The nimbus executed in this manner, first modelled and afterwards painted, is to be seen on the basement in the interior of the Sainte Chapelle, at Paris (Chapelle Haute). Similar hollows and projections of nimbi, which I remarked in the year 1836, led me to suspect the existence of fresco painting concealed under several layers of whitewash in an apsidal chapel of St. Julien de Brioude. These paintings are now, probably, exposed to view.

birth, while three *fleurs-de-lys* characterise royalty, at least starting from a certain period. So, also, a nimbus of three rays indicates divinity; a greater number of rays are attributes of created beings, and more especially of angels, the most noble of all creatures. Thus, then, no angel ever wears the cruciform nimbus, unless, as amongst the Greeks, that angel is a personification of the Deity. In Greece, Christ is called the Angel of the Great Will (ὁ ἄγγελος τῆς μεγάλης βουλῆς), and he is often represented, at the back of the apse of the left aisle, under the form of a great angel, winged and beardless. This divine angel, this messenger of God (ἄγγελος), an admirable creation peculiar to Greece, wears the divine nimbus. In the scene in which Abraham, seeing three angels, prostrates himself in adoration at the feet of one, the angel whom he adores, frequently wears a cruciform nimbus, to signify his being the representative of Deity.*

Fig. 23.—DIVINE LAMB, WITH A CIRCULAR NIMBUS, NOT CRUCIFORM, MARKED WITH THE MONOGRAM OF CHRIST, AND THE A AND Ω.

Sculptured on a Sarcophagus in the Vatican.
The earliest ages of Christianity.

The exceptions to this rule are very numerous, and most frequently these three angels differ in no respect from other creatures of the celestial hierarchy, and like them wear a simple nimbus, or at least, one not divided by a cross.

The persons of the Old Testament, particularly in the East, have all a nimbus, like the saints of the New Testament.

* See Fig. 19, p. 54, in which one of the three persons appearing to Abraham has a cruciform nimbus, while the other two, who are simply angels, have the nimbus plain.

In the West the Jewish kings, patriarchs, judges, and prophets are far less honoured. Jacques de Voragine, in the "Legenda Aurea," says that none of the festivals of the Old Testament saints are observed, except that of the Holy Innocents, who suffered for Christ; of the Maccabees, whose patience and courage under torture and suffering are proposed as examples for Christians; and lastly, of St. John the Baptist, because he forms a link between the Old Testament and the Gospel.* No festivals are kept for Adam, Abel, Noah, or Abraham, nor for Moses, Samuel, David, or Isaiah; they are not called saints, they do not act as patrons, and their names are seldom selected for baptismal names. In Litanies, where the saints of Christendom are enumerated one by one, the people of the West are content to mention the Old Testament saints *en masse.* "All ye patriarchs, all ye prophets, pray for us!" It is not thus in the East, either in Greece or in Asia; there they say St. Abraham, St. Isaac, St. Jacob, St. David, St. Solomon, and St. Isaiah. When an infant is baptised, biblical names are as frequently given as evangelical; it may even be affirmed that biblical names are held in greater favour in the East, and frequently preferred to others.

Churches are dedicated to St. Abraham, St. Isaac, and St. David. These personages are painted at full length in the interior; they are invoked singly by name in litanies; regarded thenceforth as saints, and by the same title as apostles, martyrs, and confessors; their heads are encircled with a nimbus, sometimes circular, sometimes with a striated field. A fresco painting of Adam, drawn in this manner, with a nimbus, and honoured with the title of (ἅγιος) saint, is to be seen in the pretty church of the monastery of Kaiçariani, concealed in a vale or dip on the south-east of Mount Hymettus at the distance of one myriamêtre from Athens.

* "Notandum quod Ecclesia orientalis facit festa de sanctis utriusque Testamenti, occidentalis autem non facit festa de sanctis Veteris Testamenti, eo quod ad inferos descenderunt, præterquam de Innocentibus, eo quod in ipsis singulis occisus est Christus, et de Machabæis. De Machabæis, propter quatuor rationes, &c." *Legenda aurea* de sanctis Machabæis. He ought also to have included St. Joseph and St. Elizabeth, both of whom are alike worshipped.

In certain localities, where the Oriental and Byzantine spirit has showed itself among us, as at Rheims, Troyes, St. Savin near Poictiers, and Chartres, the nimbus is seen more particularly on prophets; it is less frequently given to patriarchs and judges, and more rarely still to kings; amongst the kings, those most preferred and most frequently decorated with the nimbus, are David and Solomon; in Greece the nimbus is also given to Hezekiah and to Manasseh, holy kings, more especially revered than the others. In the church of St. Savin, among the curious frescoes which the "Comité des arts et monuments" are about to publish, is one which represents Cain and Abel offering their sacrifice to God.

Cain, the accursed, has no nimbus; Abel, the righteous, has a gold coloured nimbus.

Further on, when Cain, after having killed his brother, replies to God, who enquires for Abel, that he knows nothing of him, and that he had not been charged to keep guard over him, the head of the fatricide is encircled by a nimbus, possibly intended for the sign with which God marked Cain, that he might not be slain like a wild beast.* Further still, in the scene in which Abraham, after having conquered the five kings of the Pentapolis, receives the bread and wine, presented by Melchizedeck, the royal priest is crowned as a king, and has a nimbus of the colour of gold, like a Christian saint. At Chartres, in the north side porch, is a colossal statue of Melchizedeck, with a nimbus, and crowned in addition with the tiara, like that worn by a pope. A few similar examples will be mentioned, which may be observed in certain towns of France, particularly at Bourges, where Jacob and Elias are represented on stained glass, each with the nimbus.† But it may be

* "Posuitque Dominus Cain SIGNUM, ut non interficeret eum omnis qui invenisset eum." (*Genesis*, iv. 15.)

† See the "Monographie," on the painted windows of Saint Etienne, the cathedral of Bourges, which the Abbés Cahier and Martin have in preparation. On the very same window are representations of Abraham about to sacrifice Isaac; Moses causing water to flow from the rock; and a personification of the Christian Religion attending at the death of Christ; neither of whom have the nimbus. Still, the Church, the personification of the Christian Religion, is rarely seen thus destitute of the nimbus.

observed generally, that amongst ourselves and in the entire West, the nimbus is generally denied to saints of the Old Testament and restricted to those of the New. In the East, on the contrary, it is lavished equally on both.

St. John the Baptist is always honoured with the nimbus, even in Western Europe, where, indeed not only the day of his death, but the Festival of his Nativity also is observed; he loses this attribute only at the same period at which other saints of the New Testament are deprived of it.

Fig. 24.—ST. JOHN THE BAPTIST, WITH A NIMBUS.
Fresco from the Convent of Kaiçariani, Mount Hymettus.

St. John the Baptist, the Precursor, who, although himself belonging to the circumcision, yet already baptises: he who points out the Lamb of God, who is the preparation for the Gospel, who (to employ the words of the Church on the day of his festival) is the link or "Fibula" between the Old and New Testament, St. John the Baptist, is certainly entitled to the nimbus. The engraving subjoined is an oriental representation of St. John the Baptist, with his name written in Greek characters, "ὁ ἅγιος Ἰοάννης ὁ Πρόδρομος," St. John the Precursor.*

St. Joseph, the foster-father of Christ, usually has the nimbus;† still he is, in some instances, represented without it;‡ in the cloister of the choir of Notre Dame de Paris, for instance, and on a glass painting in Notre Dame de Chartres, at the extreme end of the apse. The Virgin Mary has a circular nimbus, frequently too, magnificently ornamented.§ The Virgin, the mother of God, that created being who in the worship of the middle ages, was assimilated as closely as possible with the supreme Creator and the divine Son, has rays, emanating not only from the head but also from the body and hands. She has not a cruciform nimbus, the cross rays being reserved solely to Divinity,||

* St. John is here represented bearing his head in a vase. He is clad in a camel's skin, with a leathern girdle, and hair dishevelled, in the manner of a penitent; he wears a circular nimbus. The Greek Church translates literally these words of St. Mark: "Behold, I send my angel [messenger] before thy face," (i. 2,) and constantly attach angel's wings to the shoulders of St. John the Baptist. In the West, where the spirit is more regarded than the letter, St. John has a nimbus, as will be seen below (Fig. 83, 84,), in two examples given in the History of Christ, but the wings are dispensed with.

† In a MS. chronicle, and various treatises, of the eleventh century, belonging to St. Germain, Bibliothèque Royale, St. Joseph being warned by the Angel to take the young child and his mother and flee into Egypt, is represented with a nimbus. In the Benedictional of St. Ethelwold, a MS. of the tenth century, in the possession of the Duke of Devonshire, Joseph, who is present at the birth of the Saviour, has a nimbus.

‡ Joseph has no nimbus in the "Flight into Egypt," in the "Evangiles de Saint Martial," a MS. of the thirteenth century, in the possession of the Comte Auguste de Bastard. Yet the same MS. gives a nimbus to the Magian Kings, and even to Herod. It would seem that the nimbus is here an indication of power, rather than holiness, and, consequently, that the MS. was executed under Byzantine rather than Latin influences, belonging rather to the East than to the West.

§ In the altar-piece of St. Germer, near Beauvais, in the chapel of the Virgin, Mary has a nimbus, splendidly decorated with pearls, and the rainbow. Christ alone has a nimbus rather more richly ornamented. See the work of M. le Baron Taylor, *Voyage dans l'ancienne France*, province of Picardy, which contains a lithograph of this beautiful altar of the thirteenth century, executed by M. Nicolle, from a drawing by M. Lassus. This monument is sculptured and painted. M. Boeswilwald repaired and restored all the paintings, in a drawing prepared for the *Exposition* of 1842.

|| The cruciform nimbus, (quoted above, p. 50,) given to the infant Mary at her entrance into the world, in the missal of St. Magloire, is an isolated instance, and probably an error of the miniaturist.

but with that distinction only her nimbus is as rich as that of God.

She is encircled by the aureole and entire glory; her hands are wrapt in flame; the rainbow is her throne, the moon her footstool; she has the sun for a vestment, and is crowned with stars, equal in all respects to the Saviour Jesus Christ. In the frescoes of St. Savin, the Virgin of the Apocalypse is represented wearing a nimbus, throned upon the sun, and her feet supported by the moon. In speaking of the *glory*, subsequently (Fig. 74), it will be seen, by a drawing, brought from the Campo Santo, that the Blessed Virgin is as glorious, as luminous, as her Son, although He is there represented (Fig. 67) in all his glory as the great judge. Lastly, a medal has been struck, even in these later times, in which Mary is represented diffusing streams of light from the ten fingers of her hands, exactly in the same manner as the colossal figure of Christ sculptured at Vezelay, a town in France (department Yonne), from whose hands floods of grace appear to stream down upon the Apostles. In the effigy of Mary, as well as in that of Christ, these streams take the character of rays.

The Apostles are always, and with propriety, adorned with the nimbus. Like the divine persons, the Apostles are the first to assume the nimbus, and the last to quit it.* In the western porch of Rheims cathedral, the nimbi of St. Peter and of St. John the Evangelist are adorned with pearls; on the windows of the Sanctuary in the same church nearly all the Apostles are represented with nimbi ornamented with precious stones either rough or polished, emeralds, rubies, and sapphires.

All the various orders of Saints, Martyrs, Confessors, and Virgins, have the circular nimbus.†

The field of the disk is more or less ornamented according to the period and the country in which it was produced, and the material on which it is executed. In the first ages of

* See fig. 17, in which St. Peter and St. Paul are represented with nimbi like the youthful Christ, and at as early a period.

† See the vaulting of the cathedrals at Rheims, Paris, and Chartres. The *Hortus Deliciarum*, specimens of Mediæval art, paintings and illuminated ornaments of MSS., present numerous and highly-varied examples of the nimbus.

Christianity, and at the period of the Renaissance,* the nimbus is more richly decorated than during the middle ages properly so called.† The nimbus in Italy and in Greece is much less simple than with us. The Greeks, as has been said, not content with tracing with the brush the ornaments on their frescoes, further contrived to make a sort of relievo on the plaster of their walls. Nimbi executed in goldsmith's work, in ivory, enamel, or painting on glass, are generally more elaborately rich than those sculptured on freestone or granite. The first are executed with more care and costliness; besides, it is more easy, and often necessary, to ornament them.

The beautiful reliquary at Mauzac, in Auvergne, displays the Virgin thus inscribed in an elliptical glory. Mary has a circular nimbus of blue enamel, gemmed with little red flowers.‡

* A painting on glass (*en grisaille* *) of the sixteenth century, belonging to M. Guénebault, represents St. John the Baptist, carrying the Lamb of God, with nimbi charged with ornaments and rays of light. The fine paintings on glass of St. Alpin, at Châlons-sur-Marne; of Ste. Madeleine, at Troyes; and of the Church at Epernay, are filled with richly-decorated nimbi. These windows are all of the time of the Renaissance. The edge of the nimbus is generally a sort of hem worked with pearls, or a ribbon more or less richly embroidered. This edge is extremely rich in the nimbi of Christ and of Mary, represented on the tympanum of the Cathedral at Autun; they belong, however, to the twelfth century. The employment of the decorated nimbus, as an hierarchical distinction, is well exemplified in the Benedictional of St. Ethelwold, Bishop of Winchester. There St. Mary, St. Peter, St. Paul, and St. John, have the nimbus much more highly ornamented than any other Saints or Apostles. This Anglo-Saxon MS. is the work of Godeman, with whose name it is inscribed, and who, in the year 970, was Bishop of Thorney.

† The Evangeliaire of Charlemagne (known under the name of "Evangiles de St. Midard de Soissons," Latin MSS. in the Bibliothèque Royale,) contains fine examples of richly-decorated nimbi. See St. Matthew and his angel, as reproduced in the "Peintures et Ornaments des Manuscrits." The tympanum of the cathedral of Autun, belonging to the twelfth century, and the altar-piece of St. Germer, chapel of the Virgin, thirteenth century, present fine examples of the striated and channelled nimbus. But these two monuments, although of stone, are as rich as if they had been of gold or silver; in the altar-piece of St. Germer the nimbi are not only modelled but also heightened by colouring.

‡ See the work of M. Mallay, architect at Clermont-Ferrand, on the Romanesque Churches of Puy-de-Dôme. Various coffers, relic chests, crosses, and enamelled altar-fronts, given by M. du Sommerard, in "l'Atlas

---

* "En grisaille"—a term used to denote a style of painting in two neutral colours: the one light, the other dark.—*Translator.*

During the fourteenth century, a custom prevailed in Europe, and more especially in Germany, of writing, within the edge of the nimbus, the name of the saint whose head it adorned. The painted windows in the cathedral of Strasburg, for example, representing several kings and emperors, (and which, though originally the work of the eleventh or twelfth century, were restored, particularly the heads and nimbi, about the fourteenth century), have inscribed within each nimbus the name of the person represented; thus, "Karolus-Magnus Rex," "Rex Bippinus pater Karoli," "Rex Henricus Claudus."*

We have seen the first-named of these, Charlemagne;† the annexed Plate represents Henry II. the Lame, who is honoured with the title of king only, as is the case with Charlemagne himself, the titles of king and emperor not bearing at that time the same relative value

et l'Album des Arts au moyen âge," confirm the facts proved by the châsse of Mauzac. See principally, le Paliotto of Milan, la Palla-d'oro of Venice, the golden altar at Basle, and the Romanesque reliquary at Chartres.

* This *Henricus Claudus Rex* is Henry, Duke of Bavaria, who became Emperor after the death of Otho III., in 1002, under the name of Henry II. He died on the 13-14th July, 1024, and was canonised in 1152, by Pope Eugenius III. St. Henry was one of the benefactors of the Cathedral at Strasbourg. In the German Chronicles, the epithet Claudus is translated by "*lahme*" (lame.) The fifteen Kings painted on glass in the north window of the side aisle of the Cathedral at Strasbourg, are all designated as benefactors to the Cathedral, and it was indebted to them for the considerable revenues which not only afforded the necessary means for the erection of that edifice, but are still employed in its preservation. Although none of these emperors and kings, with the exception of Henry II., and, perhaps, of Charlemagne, were ever canonised or recognised as Saints, all are, nevertheless, decorated with the nimbus. This is a curious fact, and well deserving of investigation. M. Klotz, architect to the Cathedral of Strasbourg, will doubtless offer some explanation of it in the work he is now preparing, which is to contain a graphic and literary description of all the monuments of painted glass confided to his care. The important repairs which these paintings on glass underwent in the fourteenth century will facilitate the solution of this difficulty.

† See above, plate 1, p. 23. Raphael, in the "Disputà," has painted several names in the interior of the nimbi decorating the heads of certain Saints, who are contemplating or adoring the Host, in the "ostensoir,"* or

* "Ostensoir," Pièce d'orfévrerie dans laquelle on expose la Sainte Hostie, ou des reliques qu'on y voit à travers une glace.—*Dictre. de' Academie.*

which we attach to them now.

This custom prevailed in Germany even till the close of the sixteenth century.* It is adopted in our time also, as may be seen by the attempts made in Bavaria and the Grand Duchy of the Bas-Rhin to revive the art of painting on glass.

The Greeks invariably follow the same plan; but instead of giving the name at length, they frequently inscribe the monogram only,† as $\overset{\Omega}{\mathrm{IC}}$. $\overset{\Omega}{\mathrm{XC}}$. (Jesus Christ), and $\overset{\Omega}{\mathrm{MP}}$ $\overset{\Omega}{\Theta\Upsilon}$ (the Mother of God)—for Christ

Fig. 25.—THE EMPEROR HENRY II. WITH A CIRCULAR NIMBUS BEARING AN INSCRIPTION.

Painted Glass in the Cathedral at Strasbourg, XII and XIV cent.

radiating sun. In France, during the twelfth and thirteenth centuries, the names of Saints were generally written on the scroll which those holy persons have in their hands; the inscription around the nimbus resembling the legend upon a medal, is far preferable; it seems a happy idea to make the Saints bear their names upon their heads, and even within the nimbus itself, the symbol of their apotheosis.

* See, amongst other examples, the stained glass in the apse of the Cathedral of Freybourg, in Brisgau, and the beautiful paintings on glass attributed to Albert Durer, which adorn the north side aisle (*nef latérale du nord*) of the Cathedral at Cologne.

† See a fresco surmounting the south and side door of the principal

and the Virgin; or simply the initial letters Γ, Μ, Ρ, Μ, Η, Π, for Gabriel, Michael, Raphael, Moses, Elias, Peter.

NIMBUS OF PERSONS LIVING.

Men who had attained an undoubted and recognised degree of sanctity were honoured, during their lifetime, with the nimbus; a fact which is positively asserted by John the Deacon, and repeated, on his authority, by Ciampini; * but, in order to preserve the high position due to departed saints, the nimbus of the living saints was square. †

church at Argos. See also in the "Histoire de Jèsus Christ et de l'Ange," engravings taken from Greek frescoes, in which Christ is represented in the character of Archbishop, with the *Σύναξις*, or assembly of Archangels. See also an engraving of the Transfiguration (*Μεταμόρφωσις*) of Jesus Christ, beneath which is introduced a view of the Monastery of Coutloumoussi, near Karès, on Mount Athos. Michael, Gabriel, and Raphaël, are among the Archangels figured in the drawing above mentioned; each has his name indicated in the nimbus by the monograms Μ, Γ, or Ρ.

* John the Deacon (*Vit. S. Gregorii*, lib. iv., cap. 84,) says, speaking of Gregory the Great, who had commanded his own portrait to be executed during his life-time, "Circa VERTICEM vero, TABULÆ similitudinem quod VIVENTIS insigne est, præferens, non CORONAM. Ex quo, manifestissime declaratur quia Gregorius, dum adhuc viveret, suam similitudinem depingi salubriter voluit." Ciampini, who had at first adopted this opinion, afterwards thought differently (*Veter. Monim.*, pars. 2, p. 140), but without reason; both facts and texts are opposed to him. The square nimbus always implies the person wearing it to have been living when the drawing was made. The rectangular nimbus is frequently seen in Italy. M. du Sommerard has recently cited St. Appollinaire *in classe*, at Ravenna; Ciampini, in the second part of the *Vetera Monimenta*, gives no less than eight examples of it; the Bollandists, in the introduction to the first volume of the *Act. SS.* of the month of May, give an engraving of a square nimbus; Seroux d 'Agincourt in the *Histoire de l'art par les Monuments*, atlas of painting, gives numerous examples of the rectangular nimbus arranged under three different types. Lastly, in *Les Arts au moyen âge*, ninth series of the Album, is a magnificent drawing of the celebrated Altar, called "Paliotto di San Ambrogio," at Milan, and in it the Bishop Angilbert, who, while living, presented this altar to St. Ambrose, is ornamented with a rectangular nimbus, while St. Ambrose himself has the nimbus circular.

† Fig. 26 represents Pope Pascal holding in his arms the Church of St. Cecilia, which he caused to be erected, and in which he was himself represented, during his life-time, in a mosaic. This mosaic belongs to the year 820. The same Pope, still with a square nimbus, may be seen at Rome, on two

The square, as has been already said, was held inferior to the circle by Pythagoras, and the neo-platonists. The square, according to their doctrine, was a geometrical symbolic figure, employed to designate the earth; the circle was the symbol of heaven. The circle is a square perfected, the square in the language of heraldry, a diminished or broken circle. At Rome, in the ancient Basilica of St. Peter, there was a series of Popes, painted originally at a very remote period. In the thirteenth century, this gallery of Roman Pontiffs was repainted by command of the Pope, Nicholas III., who had it placed somewhat lower down. In the new gallery, Pope Liberius was represented with a square nimbus; the painter employed by Pope Nicholas in the work of restoration had scrupulously copied every figure in the ancient gallery, in which the nimbus of Pope Liberius had been rectangular, and appropriately so as regards the ancient work, since that portrait was dated, in all probability, from the time of that very Pope. It could not, however, be applicable to a portrait drawn in the thirteenth century; and the painter, doubtless, imitated the figure of the nimbus without regard to its signification, or considering the important meaning attached

Fig. 26.—POPE PASCAL, WITH A SQUARE NIMBUS.
Mosaic in the Church of St. Cecilia at Rome, IX cent.

other mosaics, executed by his direction: one, in 815, in the Church of S[a]. Maria della Navicella; the other, in 818, in that of S[a]. Prassede. (See Ciampini, *Vet. Mon.*, Pars secunda, tab. 44, 47, and 52.)

to the rectangular form. This peculiarity is, even now, the subject of critical discussion among archæologists and antiquaries. We believe, however, that the signification here given is correct.

The Benedictine monks of Solesmes, who have devoted much attention and research to the study of the square nimbus, give a very different explanation of this circumstance.* "We must take leave to remark," say they, "that the difference in the manner of representing Liberius may possibly have arisen from the fall of that Pope, † and the slighter veneration with which he was, in consequence, regarded by the Roman Catholic Church. It appears that he was never honoured by that Church with particular worship, as was the case with all his predecessors, and a great number of his immediate successors. The inferior estimation in which his memory was held may have been thus expressed by an external sign." This explanation is ingenious, but it does not appear to be strictly archæological. It will serve, however, to confirm the opinion already set forth of the symbolic signification attached to the square nimbus, namely, that that figure is inferior to the circle, and that the square, or rectangle, is a circle broken and diminished. It may have been given to Liberius, as the Benedictines imagine, in order to make a degrading distinction between him and the other popes, who are adorned with a circular nimbus, just as, in heraldry, one abates, ‡ by marks of degradation, the armorial bearings of an attainted noble, or of a noble who has forfeited his rights.

* *Origines de l'Eglise Romaine*, tome i., pp. 167, 168, in-4°. Paris, 1836.

† Liberius had confirmed the condemnation of St. Athanasius, who was persecuted by the Arians.

‡ Writers on Heraldry have given certain figures, which, it is pretended, were formerly added to the coats of arms of such as were to be punished and branded for cowardice, fornication, slander, adultery, treason, or murder, to which they give the name of "Abatements of Honour;" but they have only produced one instance of such whimsical bearings. Arms, being marks of honour, cannot admit of any note of infamy; nor would anybody, now-a-days, bear them if so branded.—*Encyc. Britann.*, Art. "Heraldry."

"'Abatement,' a certain mark of disgrace added to the coat-armoury of certain persons. Abatements are called in Latin *Diminationes vel discernula Armorum*, of which Guillim mentions nine different sorts, as follow:—1. The Delf, exactly a square in the middle of the coat. 2. An Escutcheon reversed, or a small escutcheon turned upside down in the middle of the coat.

The square or rectangular nimbus is found in Italy, on various frescoes, old enamels, ivories, or ancient mosaics, and the miniatures of illuminated MSS. That form of nimbus is peculiar to Italy, and never to be met with either in Greece, Germany, England, or Spain.* In Italy, the square nimbus is most lavishly employed, and under various configurations; sometimes it is simply rectangular, as in the case of the Popes Gregory and Pascal, already mentioned; † at times it is actually in the form of a tablet, with an indication of solidity and thickness, as in the examples given by Ciampini, in the second part of his work. ‡ Occasionally, it assumes the form of a triptych, the head resting on the centre tablet at the back, the two shutters being half opened, as in the models engraved by Seroux d'Agincourt; or it has the form of a square picture, with the field and frame, as is also shown by Seroux d'Agincourt; § or it is in the form of a roll, partially unfolded, as in the example given below. || Possibly, other varieties of this

3. A Point parted dexter, when the upper right corner of the escutcheon is parted from the whole. 4. A Point in Point, when the ends of two arched lines are joined in the middle of the escutcheon so as to part off the base from the rest. 5. A Point Champagne, or a hollow arched line cutting off the base of the escutcheon. 6. A Plain Point, or a straight line parting off the base of the escutcheon. 7. A Gore, or two hollow lines between the sinister chief and the sinister base. 8. A Gusset, a line sloping a little, and then perpendicular from the upper corner to the bottom or base. These eight Abatements, if ever they were used, required to be of a stained colour, *i. e.*, Sanguine or Tenne; but it is supposed by modern heraldic writers, that these distinctions were only imaginary. 9. The ninth and last Abatement is when the whole coat is reversed, which was never done but to a traitor. An instance of this kind occurs in the arms of Sir Andrew de Harcla, knight, who, for his treachery towards his master, King Edward II., by taking a bribe from the Scots, was first degraded, then drawn, hanged, beheaded and quartered, in 1322. He beareth white, a red cross, and in the first quarter a black martlet, as in the annexed cut, the shield being reversed."—Selden. "Tit. of Honour," pp. 337, 338. Guillim, Disp. of Herald.—Extract from Crabb's *Technological Dictionary*, art. "Abatement."—*Trans.*

* This peculiarity deserves consideration. Possibly in Italy, where Christian monuments of every age are so abundant—where individualities have always been more marked and striking than amongst ourselves—a new form was invented with all its concomitant varieties while in our own country, and other people of the west, one uniform type was observed.

† Figs. 5, 26.

‡ *Vetera Monimenta.*

§ *Histoire de l'Art par les Monuments*, peinture, pl. 53.

|| Ibid. pl. 37 and 54. This engraving is taken from a pontifical manuscript

singular species of nimbus may still exist. It would be well to note carefully any that may be met with, and which

Fig. 27—A BISHOP WHILST LIVING, HAVING A RECTANGULAR NIMBUS IN THE FORM OF A VOLUMEN.
Miniature taken from a Latin manuscript of the IX cent.

might hereafter admit of our arriving at a satisfactory

with miniatures, in Latin, of the ninth century, in the "Bibliothèque de la Minerve," at Rome. It contains twelve pictures, representing the Pontiff consecrating Priests, and in each the nimbus of the Bishop resembles a parchment volumen. An "Exultet," several of the miniatures of which have been engraved by d'Agincourt, presents similar examples.

explanation of this singular form of nimbus, instances of which have, as yet, been afforded by Italy alone.

The fact here proved by the quadrature of the nimbus is of extreme importance, as it affords a clue for ascertaining the exact age of mosaics, manuscripts, and other monuments of art, all which may unquestionably be assigned to the period at which any personage, represented in them with a square nimbus, was living. It is a subject of much regret that France has not in this respect imitated Italy, and reserved the square nimbus for the living and the round nimbus for the dead. Had this plan been universally adopted, we should now be enabled to fix with great certainty the date of various monuments of sculpture, painting, and even architecture, the age of which is still matter of discussion and will probably continue so for ever without the possibility of determining their exact epoch. The discovery of a nimbus of this description would produce such important results that I deem it right to call particular attention to the attributes of this form.

The Italians did not confine themselves to the use of the square or rectangular nimbus alone.

They invented also the hexagon which is applied to personifications of the theological and cardinal virtues. The form in these cases is no longer susceptible of a chronological interpretation, since it does not indicate that the individual adorned with it was then living, but it is employed to convey a mystical meaning, and its signification is purely allegorical. The triangular nimbus, when given to God, makes allusion to the divine Trinity; and the hexagon assigned to the personified Virtues, is understood to convey an analogous idea.

But, in truth, I do not clearly see the analogy; for the Virtues are three in number, if we speak of the theological, or four if referring to the cardinal, or twelve, as in the portals of the cathedrals of Paris, Chartres, Amiens, and Rheims; in every case there are either more or less than six. It may perhaps be said, on the other hand, that the hexagon has some reference to the number twelve, of which it is the half. However this may be, the gates of the Baptistery at Florence, executed by Andrea Pisano;

the paintings in the choir of San Francesco, at Pisa, by Taddeo Gaddi; those in the groined vaulting (*voûte d'arrête*)

Fig. 28.—SQUARE NIMBUS WORN BY CHARLEMAGNE AND POPE LEO III.
ST. PETER WITH THE CIRCULAR NIMBUS.
Roman Mosaic.* Triclinium of the Vatican, IX cent.

above the altar of the lower church of Assisi, by Giotto,

* This picture, which has been partly destroyed and very ill restored, represents St. Peter presenting Leo III. with the insignia of the Popedom,

present examples of the personified Virtues with the nimbus of the hexagonal form.*

In France the nimbus is neither square nor polygonal, and with the exception of the single instance mentioned above, invariably circular; it is intended, in fact, to convey the idea of radiation from the head; and the head being round, the nimbus must consequently be circular, or at most slightly elliptical.

THE NIMBUS OF ALLEGORICAL BEINGS.

Those allegorical personages to whom our Saviour, in his parables, gave in some sort a rational existence, are adorned with the nimbus, when they figure either of the Virtues or any holy quality. Such are the wise, and sometimes also the foolish Virgins, and they wear a nimbus, like persons who have actually existed. Virtues, when personified by art, and represented in sculpture or painting, usually have the nimbus; and so also have the theological virtues, Faith, Hope, and Charity, and the cardinal virtues, Justice, Prudence, Temperance, and Strength.† The nimbus worn

and giving the Standard of War to Charlemagne. It is in mosaic, and adorned the *triclinium* of San Giovanni di Laterano, built under Charlemagne, by Pope Leo. Both Leo and Charlemagne have a square nimbus, and that of St. Peter is circular. See Nicolo Alemanni, *De Lateranensibus Parietinis*, Rome, 1625, p. 12. Alemanni, in the same work, gives an engraving from a mosaic which once existed in Ste. Suzanne, at Rome, and was destroyed about 250 years since. In this, also, Leo and Charlemagne have the square nimbus. The Church of Ste. Suzanne had been rebuilt by Leo III., who is represented standing, holding the Church on his chasuble. Charlemagne was also standing, habited like the figure in this mosaic of the *triclinium*, gesticulating and apparently addressing himself to the Pope, who is bare-headed.

* I am indebted for this information to M. Orsel, an artist, most profoundly versed in Christian Iconography, and who is now employed in painting a chapel in Notre Dame de Lorette, at Paris.

† See in the Bibliothèque Royale, the Missal of St. Denis, *Manuscrits Latins*, supplement. This missal is supposed to belong to the first half of the ninth century. The miniature, in which Christ is represented descending from Heaven to administer the Communion to St. Denis, in prison, is enclosed in a frame-work containing the four Cardinal Virtues personified by female figures, whose heads are environed by the circular nimbus. M. de Bastard (*Peintures et Ornements des Manuscrits*) has reproduced this picture. The "Pastoral" of St. Gregory, a very fine ancient manuscript

by the Virtues is in Italy occasionally hexagonal, as has been already been observed, but with us always circular. In the Cathedral of Chartres, among the fourteen virtues public and social, which occupy a cordon, or band of the vaulting in the left entrance of the north porch, is a figure of Liberty. The first rank is assigned, in right of precedence, to the personification of Virtue, in the abstract, as the mother of those that are attending her, just as in Pagan mythology Mnemosyne is regarded as the mother of the Muses. Liberty stands second in rank; she is, consequently, the eldest, and held superior to all those who follow her; the names, which were engraven in the stone, have some of them been effaced by the action of the weather; but amongst those which yet remain we can decipher, in characters of the thirteenth century, the words, "*Libertas, Honor, Velocitas, Fortitudo, Concordia, Amicicia,* (sic) *Majestas, Sanitas, Securitas.*" Three names only are wanting, and possibly they have always been thus deficient. Each Virtue bears a characteristic attribute. Doves dwell peacefully on the bucklers of Concord and Friendship; arrows and a battlemented castle distinguish Swiftness and Security; fishes, a singular and curious fact, adorn the buckler of Health. The annexed plate of Liberty will give an idea of the others, for a resemblance may be traced throughout these Virtues as in children of one family.

Liberty, like her mother, who precedes, and the twelve sister Virtues, who follow her, is decorated with a large nimbus; she is a holy virtue, and well entitled to that honour, as are all the others who accompany her, or rather defile after her.*

Natural beings, personifications of the cardinal points, of the winds, the four elements, the constellations, and of

belonging to the bishopric of Autun, contains the Cardinal Virtues, with similar nimbi.

* The right hand, which is broken, ought properly to hold a standard or a pike. The nimbus is thick and solid, as is evident from the engraving. The word "Libertas" is distinctly legible, not "Liberalitas," as might be imagined; there is not the slightest sign of abbreviation. Besides, according to the rules of palæography, it is not possible to abridge "Liberalitas" by the omission of the second L. Before making the above drawing of Liberty, I took the precaution of getting an impression of the inscription; the correctness of the form, and of the number of the letters, may, therefore, be relied on.

day and night, sometimes have the nimbus. The Christian religion, or the Church, is personified by a female figure,

Fig. 29.—LIBERTY WITH A NIMBUS.
Sculpture of the XIII cent. Cathedral of Chartres.

crowned and with a nimbus, holding in one hand a chalice, in the other a cross;* this was one of the most frequent

* See particularly a fine Champenois Manuscript of the end of the thirteenth

personifications throughout the middle ages. A Greek MS., preserved in the Vatican,* contains the city of Gabaon (πὸλις Γάβαων) under the figure of a tall woman, wearing on her head a mural crown, her feet bare, and a long staff in her hand; the personified city, wears, besides the crown, a large circular nimbus. The sun and moon often have a nimbus in imitation of the Pagan custom: this is easily accounted for, the nimbus being a radiation of light, and the sun and moon, which divide time into day and night, being the two pre-eminently luminous objects in creation, at least to the inhabitants of our world. In our own country where the nimbus is less prodigally given than in Greece, instead of encircling with that insignia the heads of the sun and moon, a torch or a flambeau is frequently placed in the hands of those stars, as may be remarked in the north porch of the cathedral of Chartres.

Fig. 30.—DIANA, THE MOON, WITH A CIRCULAR NIMBUS.
Roman Sculpture.†

Christians bestow the nimbus on saints, exactly in the same manner in which the ancients gave it to the sun and moon; thus in the annexed example, the head of Diana, or the Moon has a circular nimbus, but in order to distinguish her by some peculiar attribute, the crescent is placed upon her head.‡

century, in the Bibliothèque de l'Arsenal. The Christian Church and the Synagogue are both present at the Crucifixion of our Blessed Saviour. The Church, the personification of Christianity, has a nimbus; the Synagogue, personifying the Jewish religion, whose existence terminated at the death of Christ, is without. The MS. of Gulielmus Durandus (*Racional des offices*) "Theol." fr. No. 24, close of the fifteenth century, in the same library, also contains a personified figure of the Church with a nimbus. The celebrated MS. of Drogon (Bib. Roy.) *Supplément Latin*, 645, contains a personification of the Church, similarly adorned with a golden nimbus.

* See Seroux d'Agincourt, *Histoire de l'Art par les Monuments*, p. 28. This MS. belongs to the seventh or eighth century.

† Montfaucon, *Antiquité Expliquée*, tom. ii., p. 414. The Sun, in the next example, is in the first vol., pl. 53, p. 106. Observe here, also, as above, the astronomical and planetary number of the seven rays.

‡ See below in The History of God, fig. 52, a very fine design, taken from a Greek MS., giving a personification of Night, represented with a nimbus like that of the Prophet Isaiah, near whom she is stationed. The MS. of Drogon,

The following engraving represents the sun. The nimbus is formed by the seven rays issuing from his head, together with the material representation of the sun in the form of a wheel, which forms his characteristic attribute.

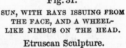

Fig. 31.
SUN, WITH RAYS ISSUING FROM THE FACE, AND A WHEEL-LIKE NIMBUS ON THE HEAD.
Etruscan Sculpture.

The sun and moon are frequently represented in works of Christian art, as present at the death of Christ, and weeping at the sacrifice of the Deity. In the thirteenth century this sun and moon were figured under the form of stars, held by two angels, who seem, as it were, the genii of those orbs: but in the eleventh and twelfth the two stars are personified and placed, in half lengths only, on the field of the nimbus, which is bordered by undulating lines, in imitation of clouds or flame.* Upon a crown of gilded copper, presented by Barbarossa to the Cathedral of Aix-la-Chapelle, Christ is represented bound to the cross. The sun and moon are half figures, the moon is a woman bearing a crescent on her head; the sun a young man with a nimbus of sunbeams. In several manuscripts with miniatures belonging to the eighth or ninth centuries, these two stars, the sun and moon, are represented quite after the antique type; they have a circular nimbus, and are mounted on a car drawn by four horses.

The four attributes of the Evangelists, the Angel of St. Matthew, the Eagle of St. John, the Lion of St. Mark, and the Ox of St. Luke, wear a nimbus like that of the saints and apostles themselves.† A manuscript in the

quoted above, also presents a miniature of the Crucifixion, in which the Moon is personified by a tall, white female figure, with a crescent on her head. The Sun is personified by a red coloured youth, with a radiated crown; both are inscribed within a medallion.

* See below, in The History of God the Son, fig. 68, a Sun and Moon thus represented, mourning the death of Christ.

† See, in "The History of the Trinity and of Jesus Christ," several designs representing the symbolic animals wearing the circular nimbus. Below, in the description of the aureole, a representation is given (No. 36) of the romanesque fresco in the Cathedral of Auxerre; both the Eagle of St. John, and the Ox of St. Luke, have the nimbus. On the tympanum of the central

Bibliothèque Royale, a kind of encyclopædia or "livre de clergie," of the eleventh century, furnishes one instance of a singular peculiarity.* Two peacocks looking at and apparently advancing towards each other, climb up the rampe of a circular arch, the tympanum of which contains a figure adorned with a cruciform nimbus and holding a book. The triple aigrette of light rises like a plume from the heads of the peacocks, which are also girt by a broad circular thread, forming, in fact, a nimbus. These peacocks are unquestionably symbolic and ought to express some idea analogous to that conveyed by the animals of the Evangelists. A manuscript psalter† in the library at Amiens, contains at the eighty-second psalm a figure of the lamb of God, painted and inscribed within the D, which is the initial letter of the first verse. The lamb has a plain nimbus without a cross, the first peculiarity to be remarked; but the head of the D is in the form of a bird, which appears to seize a serpent by the throat with its beak. This bird, resembling an eagle, and which is unquestionably intended to symbolise courage or virtue triumphant over vice, has a nimbus resembling that of the lamb; a plain nimbus of the colour of parchment, and the form designed by one simple black line.

Finally, Satan, the Genius of Evil, is sometimes drawn with a nimbus: it will at this point be necessary to make a few observations concerning the importance of the nimbus, and the idea intended to be expressed by it.

door, in the west porch of the Cathedral of Chartres, is a sculpture representing Christ surrounded by the symbolic animals; of these, the Eagle alone has a nimbus, the heads of the other three being so completely detached from the ground, that the nimbus would be more difficult of execution.

* "Fonds de St. Germain," lat. No. 434, olim 547. See *Peintures et Ornements des Manuscrits*, 8ième. livraison.

† *Liber Psalmorum*, ninth century. The 82nd Psalm begins with these words: *Deus, quis similis erit tibi?*

SIGNIFICATION OF THE NIMBUS.

The nimbus, in the West more especially, is regarded as an attribute of holiness; a king, according to our ideas, should be adorned with a crown, a nimbus marks the saint.*

It is not thus in the East: the nimbus is there a characteristic of physical energy no less than of moral strength, of civil or political power, as well as of religious authority. A king is equally entitled to the nimbus with a saint. In a Turkish manuscript, preserved in the Bibliothèque Royale, is a figure of Aurungzebe mounted on horseback and reading. The aged descendant of Timour is preceded and followed by an escort of persons on foot. The Grand Mogul alone, among all the persons there, is represented wearing a circular or radiating nimbus on the head. This example may serve to illustrate its application to civil power; in proof of its use in expressing religious domination, we may cite an oriental picture, brought by General Allard from the kingdom of Lahore, representing Gourou-Sing and Baba-Nanck, founders of the Sikh religion. Baba-Nanck, its first revealer, has a radiating nimbus; Gourou-Sing, a reformer only and a warrior reformer, has a simple luminous circle of unradiating light by way of nimbus. Thus then we discover that the nimbus is given in the East, to all who govern by civil power alone, by military and religious authority combined, or by purely religious authority. It is awarded in the East to everything powerful, not only to kings and saints, but to good and evil genii, to devils and false gods; it is, on the contrary, withheld from all beings destitute of power or deficient in virtue. The distinction is most easily established. Any creature, supposed to be infirm, conquered, or ready to yield, will be drawn without a nimbus; it is an insignia borne by the mighty and powerful alone.

* See, amongst other examples, a copy of a beautiful miniature, presented in the grand work of M. le Comte Auguste de Bastard, *Peintures et Ornements des Manuscrits*.

In the western world, and in countries wholly uncontaminated by contact with eastern opinions, the nimbus, except in the few instances noticed above, is given only to the heads of God, angels, saints, and the personification of holy ideas. A king, or an emperor, a bishop, a priest, a *religieux*, or a magistrate, is, notwithstanding his power and authority, without a nimbus, unless, indeed, he be something higher than either king, emperor, bishop, clerk, or citizen. To be entitled to a nimbus, he must, like St. Louis, St. Charlemagne, St. Remi, St. Victor, St. Bernard, Ste. Regina, have been canonised, or be esteemed as a saint. For yet more weighty reasons, the nimbus is not given to a serf, a vicious man, or a demon, however great may be his reputation in other respects; yet, on the other hand, a poor and holy woman, like St. Geneviève; a poor beggar, like St. Alexis; a poor boatman, like St. Julian; a poor shoemaker, like St. Crispin, will all have the nimbus, because they, in their lifetime, loved God, mortified the flesh, prayed for others, and succoured the unfortunate. If any have performed the six works of mercy, have nourished the hungry, refreshed the thirsty, entertained strangers and sick persons, clothed the naked, visited those in prison,* they will be honoured with the nimbus; they are greater in heaven than the King Clovis, the Emperor Otho, the famous Pope Sylvester II., and the great Archbishop Hincmar.

We must, however, guard against misconceptions; as, for example, when statues, or sculptured figures, are without the nimbus, as is the case in the grand porch of the Cathedral of Amiens, it must not be too hastily concluded that the persons they represent were non-canonised; for, at Amiens, the figures are, in fact, very holy saints, apostles, and martyrs; and, although without a nimbus, the deficiency arises from the difficulty of sculpturing that insignia, in a permanent manner, around the head, and from their being too far distant from the wall, against which alone the nimbus could possibly have been applied; and, in fact, on the vaultings, and in the tympanum, where its execution was more easy and practicable, that attribute will be found to exist.

On the other hand, it must not be imagined, in conse-

* St. Matthew, xxv., 35, 36.

quence of what has been now said, that any personage, whose head is not adorned with the nimbus, may, nevertheless, be a saint; and that, although deprived of the nimbus, it is only because that attribute was forgotten, or found difficult of execution. That it may have been forgotten, is possible and is known to be frequently the case. But although errors of this description abound in miniatures, and in illuminated manuscripts, they are seldom found in statuary, in which greater correctness is observed. Besides, if the persons in question be surrounded by other figures, in the same position, and all wearing the nimbus, it must be concluded that the person without it is not canonised, but that the others, on the contrary, are all saints. Thus, in the tympanum of the right hand door, at the grand entrance of the Cathedral of Paris, a king is seen on his knees, and a bishop standing beside him, both figures destitute of the nimbus, while the other persons have it; it is because the bishop is Maurice of Sully, and the king is Philip Augustus, neither of whom were saints.

In short, neither the absence nor the presence of the nimbus must be assumed to be an unquestionable proof of sanctity or its reverse, except during the period preceding, and inclusive of, the fourteenth century. After that time, the important signification of the nimbus disappears; it is given, or withheld, in a somewhat arbitrary manner. But, during the thirteenth century, especially in certain edifices where the true signification of the nimbus is observed, we may affirm that the nimbus, when encircling the head of any figure, proves the person represented to have been a saint. A figure of an ecclesiastic placed erect against the side of the left doorway, in the south porch of the Cathedral at Chartres, has the nimbus: this man must, consequently, have been a saint; he cannot, therefore, be intended for Fulbert, Bishop of Chartres, who was never canonised, but rather for the Pope St. Clement, who may, besides, be recognised by his crown, which is a tiara, not a mitre, and by the little building surrounded with water, on which he rests his feet, and which is not intended, as has been asserted, to figure the destruction of the Cathedral of Chartres by fire.

Still, notwithstanding the above observations, the only

certain guides in such investigations are sound judgment, and the habit of examining and studying ancient monuments.

HISTORY OF THE NIMBUS.

It is the object of the nimbus, forcibly and at a glance, to express the distinctive character of the person decorated with it. It is placed like a crown on the head, the head being the noblest portion of the human being, and the loftiest and most conspicuous part of the person.

The head has, indeed, been invariably selected as the peculiar point of attraction, whenever men have desired to excite attention, or to command respect.

In all ages, and among all people, the head has been regarded as the noblest portion of man. It is to the head that the lion owes his title of monarch of the brute creation. It is from carrying his head erect, and thus directing his gaze freely and naturally towards heaven, that man himself derives his rank, as the chief of all created beings.* The head is to man what the flower is to the plant—the pediment to the portico; it is, if we may be permitted the expression, the material soul of the body—the outer covering—the seat and temple of the immortal spirit. To the head belong the faculties of taste, sight, smell, and, above all, of thought; in the brain, the source and fountain of ideas, the motions of the senses, and their peculiar organs and affluents, are found to terminate. Properties, which are dispersed irregularly throughout the body, are united and concentrated in the head; beauty itself, although it has for its development the varied surface of the entire person,—beauty itself is most vividly displayed, most powerfully concentrated, in the head. A fine head gives beauty to an ugly form; but there can be no true beauty in a noble person, with a commonplace or vulgar head and countenance.

Thus, in the material economy, both anatomical and physiological, the entire man is concentrated in the head; and in æsthetics, also, we find the head to be the seat of

* "Pronaque cum spectent cætera animalia terram,
Os homini *sublime* dedit (Opifex rerum) cœlumque tueri
Jussit, et *erectos* ad sidera tollere vultus."

Ovid, *Metamorphoses,* lib. i.

supreme beauty and intelligence. In psychology, the body is of little consequence; the head is everything. The body, divested of the head, is a plant without a flower, a column without a capital, a nameless and formless object. But, on the other hand, a rose taken from the plant, a capital separated from the shaft, may, each respectively, become a graceful ornament, either for a woman or a monument; in short, the human head, apart from the trunk, has been exalted into the purest of all celestial intelligences, the Seraphim, who are, solely and entirely, love.

The Christian Church and religion thought but lightly of the human body; but the head was held in high estimation. "Any spot may be chosen for the interment of the trunk, when separated from the head," say the ancient liturgists, Gulielmus Durandus and John Beleth; "but the head may not be buried except in holy and consecrated ground—in the church or the cemetery." The body, without the head, does not consecrate the place in which it rests; the head, without the body, sanctifies the spot immediately.*

Of all the millions of martyrs belonging to the Theban legion, who repose at Cologne in the church dedicated to St. Gereon, their companion and one of their chiefs, the heads in particular are preserved, ranged in cabinets with glass doors, like costly books in a library. So in the church of St. Ursula, also at Cologne, what are the memorials there preserved of the eleven thousand virgins? still, the heads; enclosed in reliquaries of gold, silver, or precious woods.

* Durandus, Bishop of Mende, writes thus (*Rationale Divin. Offic.*, lib. i., cap. v., de cimeterio et aliis, &c.):—"Religiosa sunt ubi cadaver hominis integrum vel etiam caput tantum sepelitur, quia nemo potest duas sepulturas habere. Corpus vero vel aliquod aliud membrum, absque capite sepultum, non facit locum religiosum." John Beleth (*Rationale Divin. Offic.*, cap. ii., de loco,) says, in his turn:—"Postremo locus religiosus ille dicitur in quo integrum hominis cadaver sepultum est, vel tantum etiam caput. Corpus enim obtruncatum, nisi et caput adsit, locum religiosum facere non potest." "*Religious* places within which the entire body of a man, or, at least, his head, is buried, because no man can have two sepulchres. But the body, or any member without the head, doth not make the place wherein it is buried religious." In these quotations we see the working of that spirit of Christianity which gives every honour to the head, the especial seat of the soul. M. l'Abbé Pascal, correspondent of the "Comité des Arts et Monuments," is about to publish a Liturgical Dictionary, in which the question of the preference of the head over the body will be treated at length.

There is a large chamber entirely occupied by these rich and curious relics. How much have people contended for the head of John the Baptist! five or six different churches pretended, and do still pretend, to possess it; has his body ever been the subject of the slightest contention? Has any one ever sought to discover in whose possession it might be, or where it was laid?

The head being thus invested with such pecular importance, the insignia employed to distinguish or classify various ranks of men, was naturally enough attached to the head. Some men are born to command, others to obey; some march first, direct, command; others follow and execute. The former are chiefs, the latter workmen.

The chiefs wear on their heads a distinctive sign; the king is recognised by his crown, the pope by his tiara, the bishop by his mitre; even the distinction of sex is marked amongst us by a difference in the head-tire, which is fixed upon women and moveable on men.

The crowns or head-tire of civil and military chiefs are extremely varied; but amongst all nations, whether highly civilised or in the lowest state of barbarism, the crown has been and still is the insignia of supreme power.

The diadem amongst the Greeks, the open crown of the Romans, the cone or cylinder amongst Eastern nations, the cupola of the Byzantines, and the close crown worn by Christian sovereigns, are but the principal types of a host of varieties. The crown, in the middle ages, was a hierarchical symbol, and used like the escutcheon, as a token of recognition amongst nobles. The escutcheon distinguishes families, the crown marks different orders of rank. The crown of an emperor is closed; a king's crown is arched but open; a prince's crown is of *fleurs-de-lis* and *feuilles-d'ache.*

As the crown descends step by step in the scale it becomes diminished in proportion to the rank of the wearer; it loses its *fleurs-de-lis*, and is first formed simply of *feuilles-d'ache*; or secondly, of *feuilles-d'ache* intermingled with pearls; or thirdly, of eighteen large pearls without leaves; or fourthly, of four large pearls intermingled with lesser ones; or fifthly, and finally, of small pearls alone, arranged in a simple thread or twist. Crowns thus diminished are worn, the first by dukes, the second by marquises, the third by counts, the fourth by viscounts; the fifth is the baronial crown; and the knight's crown is formed by the helmet only.

The crown may be likened in its use to a standard, borne aloft in the air by the leader to serve as a guide to those who follow. At the battle of Ivry, Henry IV. exclaimed, "Follow my plume, you will always find it in the path of honour." It may possibly be from a similar motive and as a decorative mark of honour, that kings of savage nations crown themselves with lofty and brilliant plumes.

When any man has rendered himself illustrious by brilliant actions, a crown is generally awarded to him as a recompense; the mark of homage being invariably appropriate to the head.* The mural crown, crowns of oak, olive, and laurel† were granted by the ancient Romans to those who headed the assault of a city, gained a victory, or performed any other illustrious deed, and crowns were given by the Greeks to those gods whom they desired especially to honour. The great poets and philosophers of ancient times were distinguished by various crowns, and we find them often thus decorated in their Iconography.

When, with the first rise of Christianity, a mode of becoming illustrious before unknown, was as it were revealed to the world; when martyrs shed their blood in witness of the faith which they proclaimed, preached and propagated, God himself consecrated the system adopted by profane policy, and these heroic deeds were recompensed by crowns bestowed upon those who had performed them. The earliest monuments of Christian art represent either divine hands, extended from the highest Heaven, proffering crowns to the martyrs,‡ or angels descending in like manner from Heaven, bringing crowns by the command of

* It may be said that with us that mark of homage has descended from the head to the shoulders, with the epaulettes, and been removed with the cross from the shoulders to the breast.

† At Notre Dame de Brou is a statue of St. John the Evangelist of carved wood, a work of the sixteenth century. It belonged originally to the ancient sculptured pulpit, and is now placed in a niche in one of the stalls. St. John is young, beardless, represented like a Roman Emperor; he wears on his head a crown of laurel, like an ancient conqueror. This crown appears to be a species of nimbus borrowed from Pagan antiquity.

‡ See, in the History of God, a hand thus holding forth a crown (fig. 55), taken from the *Vetera Monimenta,* secunda pars, pl. 53.

God to all, who, by their death, had borne witness to their faith.*

The entire basement of the Sainte Chapelle at Paris is decorated with a system of arches. The deaths of various martyrs are represented in the tympanum of the arcades; amongst others the martyrdom of St. Stephen, and of Thomas of Canterbury. Above the mortal suffering appears the celestial reward, for angels descend from Heaven bearing crowns, which they bestow upon those glorious martyrs.†

Another method, however, if not invented, was at least very widely adopted among the Christians and awarded as a mark of honour and distinction to saints and martyrs. The crown is a material ornament, encircling the head like a sort of head-tire. This new mark of honour, more ideal and differently placed, although also encircling the head, took another name, and was called the *nimbus*.

The crown is an insignia of civil power, borne by the laity; the nimbus is ecclesiastic and religious; but the nimbus, like the crown, is applied to the head. It might, therefore, be desirable, in treating of archæological subjects referring especially to the head, to give a history of these two modes of conferring honour on different personages, and which, although diverse, are yet analogous in form and treatment. But as the present work is devoted to religious archæology, we are called upon solely to speak of the nimbus without in any way noticing the crown.

The Pagans, as has been already said, were familiar with the use of the nimbus, but it has been most frequently and constantly employed by Christians, and with the most varied and significant application. From the fifth or sixth century of the Christian era down to the present time the

* See, in The History of the Angels,* one of these celestial beings, in a design taken from the "Roma Sotterranea." The angel bears in one hand a palm, in the other a martyr's crown.

† M. de Sommerard has in his possession a valuable manuscript covered with plates of ivory; these plates are fixed in a framework adorned with filagree work, and rich precious stones, unpolished. The Crucifixion is sculptured on one of these plates of ivory, and above it is seen a hand issuing from the clouds; it is the hand of God the Father presenting a crown to the divine martyr.

* This history has not yet appeared.

nimbus has never ceased, except in some few instances of casual omission, to be painted or sculptured around the heads of various statues and figures, to indicate their dignity and their hierarchical rank and degree.

The history of the nimbus is, therefore, marked by several distinct phases, the principal among which will now be enumerated and explained.

The nimbus is little seen during the four first centuries of the Christian era, for that distracted period was one of strife, persecution, and contention. The Church was established, but having as yet no form of art peculiarly her own, had recourse in her need to the arts of antiquity. She constantly adopted from the Jewish religion whatever belonged to her by anticipation, and did but borrow doubtfully from Pagan art such themes as it was in her power to sanctify to her use. She might well transform by the aid of lustral water* the Roman Basilica into a church, because constrained by wants and imperative necessity so to do; but it was possible for her to dispense for some time with the Pagan nimbus, which would have recalled the emperors by whom she had been persecuted, and the false gods whom she had abjured; most frequently, therefore, it was omitted altogether. The nimbus rarely occurs in the catacombs, either on frescoes or sarcophagi.

Not only are apostles and saints drawn without that distinctive mark, but the Virgin, and even Christ himself are without it. The annexed plate is taken from an antique sarcophagus preserved in the Vatican.

Here, as in the greater number of similar monuments, God is represented beardless and without a nimbus; He is

* "It would be instructive to trace the rites and customs adopted by the Roman Church from Pagan ceremonies; for instance, the *Aqua lustralis* was a species of holy water, since it was that in which a torch from the altar, during the offering of a sacrifice, had been extinguished. Thus sanctified, it was put in a vase at the entrance of the temples, and into it every one dipped his fingers at ingress or egress; and, to make the analogy between the Roman Catholics and the Pagans, in this respect, more complete, we may observe that light brooms being dipped in it by the officiating priest, it was scattered in the form of dew over those who were present.

"'Idem ter socias purâ circumtulit undâ
Spergens rore levi.'"

—Lardner's Cabinet Cyclopædia, "Greeks and Romans," vol. ii., p. 59.

sentencing Adam to till the ground, that it may bring forth corn, of which He offers him a little sheaf, and commanding Eve to spin the wool of the lamb, which He presents to her.

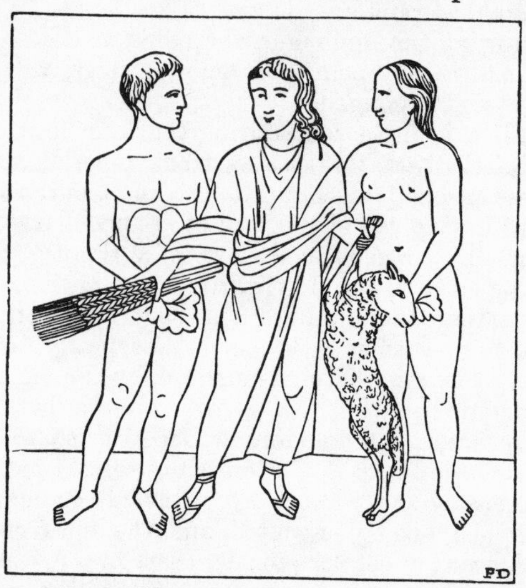

Fig. 32.—GOD THE FATHER, WITHOUT A NIMBUS AND BEARDLESS, CONDEMNING ADAM TO TILL THE GROUND AND EVE TO SPIN WOOL.

Sarcophagus in the Vatican—earliest ages of Christianity.

Thus, in the most ancient monuments of France and Italy, divine and sacred persons are constantly represented without the nimbus.*

* This engraving is taken from the work of Bosio, "Roma Sotterranea," p. 295. See, in the "History of Jesus Christ," two other designs, also copied from early Christian sarcophagi now in the Museum of the Vatican. One represents Christ, beardless (Fig. 66), seated on a throne, his feet resting on a figure personifying the Heavens; in the other, Jesus Christ is represented with a beard, standing on a mountain, whence flow the four rivers of Paradise. Both these figures represent the Saviour preaching the Gospel. In the last mentioned, he addresses his Apostles, who stand round under the form of sheep. None of these personages have the nimbus, not even the Lamb of God, who is distinguished only by the cross which rises above his head. On the sarcophagi at Arles are several figures of Christ, without beard or nimbus. I am indebted to the kindness of M. H. Clair, correspondent of the "Comité des Arts et Monuments," and author of "Arles, Ancien et Moderne," for two drawings representing Jesus, without a beard or nimbus. These drawings, executed by M. Dumas, were taken from the sarcophagi of the Aliscamps.

In later times, towards the fifth and sixth centuries, the Church, powerful at Rome, in Europe, in Asia, and even in Africa, was but rarely exposed to contradiction or opposition. She had, in those days, to contend with heretics, rather than with heathens. At that period, she distributed, into groups, all her personalities, laic and ecclesiastical; she had attained power, and it became her, therefore, to assume its attributes.

Feudalism was just about to rise; everything was becoming hierarchical; men and things were all disposed in regular order. The Church had herself founded a hierarchy on earth as well as in heaven; she arranged, in categorical order, the multitude of saints triumphant in Paradise, and of Christians militant on earth: she assigned, to all, their chiefs. As in the army the distinction of grade of the various officers commanding battalions and companies, is marked by the epaulette, so the saints who command in heaven are distinguished by the varied forms of the nimbus.

The supreme head of all, God the Father, or the Son, or the Holy Ghost, had a circular nimbus, a disk precisely resembling that of the saints; but the nimbus of the divine persons was, as a mark of special distinction, divided diagonally by two intersecting lines, in the form of a cross, as has been said and shown above.

When the nimbus had once been adopted among Christians as a characteristic of holiness, and to mark the distinction of rank, it was constantly employed nearly to the period of the Renaissance; still it was subject to certain modifications, which supply the materials of its archæological history, and of which it is now time to speak.

The nimbus is not constantly figured around the heads of saints, in monuments belonging to a period earlier than the eleventh century. The Christian nimbus is not found on well authenticated monuments anterior to the sixth century. The transition from the complete absence to the constant presence of the nimbus, was effected during the seventh, eighth, and ninth centuries. During that period, figures, even on the same monument, are represented sometimes with, and sometimes without, that attribute. Thus, at the conclusion of a manuscript in the "Bibliothèque Royale,"* we find a figure of St. Daria without a nimbus, and St. Chrisant with a nimbus formed of a simple thread; while, elsewhere, in the body of the manuscript, Jesus Christ bears a nimbus marked with the cross, while that of the apostles has a simple edge or hem, and other saints have it of a disk-like form. It is evident, therefore, that, at that epoch, the nimbus was not constant, and, further, that it varied considerably in form.

The nimbus, up to the twelfth century, was in the form of a disk, but fine and attenuate. A very beautiful Greek manuscript, of the tenth century, belonging to the "Bibliothèque Royale," and which has been already mentioned, contains a personification of Night, under the figure of a woman, clad in black robes. Her head is encircled by a luminous and transparent nimbus, through which, as through the glass of a telescope, the stars of heaven are discernible.† Even if the nimbus be not, in all cases, equally diaphanous, it is always so lightly traced as to suggest the idea of transparency, and of the artist's desire to figure it as a luminous atmosphere.

During the twelfth, thirteenth, and fourteenth centuries, the nimbus became more dense, narrower, and extending less beyond the head; it had, till then, been transparent, but now became opaque. It was nothing more thenceforth than a rude disk, a kind of plate, a sort of circular pillow painted or sculptured behind the head. It no longer, as in the preceding periods, permitted the sky and the surrounding landscape to be seen through it. It was a thick wall, not transparent glass. Such is the nimbus given to God, his saints and angels, in the cathedrals of Paris and of Chartres.‡ In the admirably carved basement decorating the Sainte Chapelle at Paris, both saints and angels are represented; and the nimbus worn by them is luminous, very elegant, and painted in brilliant colours. But the Sainte Chapelle, as a monument, is an exception; it is a

* *Liber Precum,* suppl. lat. 641. This curious MS. may belong to the ninth century; it has generally been assigned to the eleventh.

† See the "History of God," Fig. 52.

‡ See Fig. 29, representing Liberty.

royal edifice, in which one might imagine the genius of the East to have found a place of rest.

During the whole of the fifteenth, and the opening of the sixteenth century, Gothic art was on the decline, and finally expired; the elegance by which it had been characterised during the thirteenth and fourteenth centuries, was lost; it became heavy and materialised, sculpture degenerated into vulgarity in its choice of types, and architecture into coarseness of outline.

Simultaneously the nimbus also became materialised; till that time it had continued to be of large dimensions, but thenceforth it became narrower, more confined, and, above all, more solid. Previous to that epoch, and even throughout the fourteenth century, it had been regarded as an aureole, a light emanating from the head. This idea was most clearly defined up to the twelfth century, it continued to be expressed, but more clumsily, till the fifteenth; nevertheless the intention of figuring a light was clearly manifest. In the fifteenth century, on the contrary, the form of the nimbus only was preserved; its signification was entirely lost, and it seemed rather to be regarded as a head-dress. The aureole became gradually more and more condensed; the light solidified and extinguished; and the nimbus itself transformed into a large cockade, or a sort of casquette, placed upon the head of a saint, or of God himself, and inclining sometimes to the right ear, sometimes to the left. The nimbus of God or of the saints was worn precisely as some persons, our villagers more especially, affect to wear their head-tire. The stained glass of the latter part of the fifteenth century, several windows for example in the churches of Troyes and Châlons-sur-Marne, present nimbi, which are in reality nothing more than a sort of tire for the head.

In the Cathedral of Amiens, on the stalls which were erected in 1508 (the date is there given), is a youthful figure of our Saviour teaching in the Temple, and wearing above the ear one of those solid nimbi, worked, and resembling an embroidered cap (casquette). The annexed plate is taken from the same stalls, and represents Christ ascending to the Temple, whither he is conducted by St. Joseph and St. Mary. The nimbus, as may be seen, is actually a head-dress, the exterior plate ornamented like that of a casquette of cloth.*

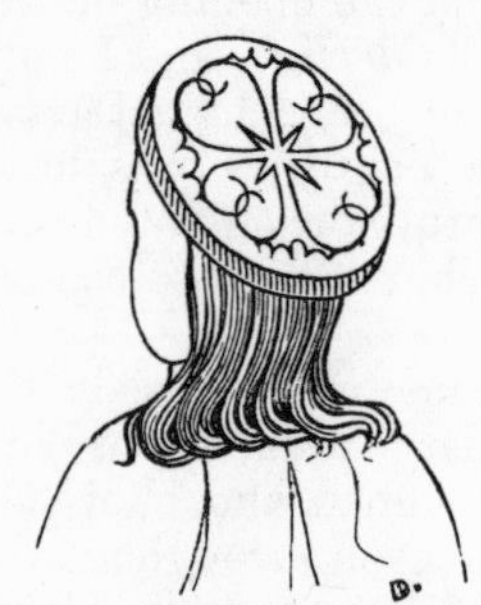

Fig. 33.—CHRIST, WITH A NIMBUS RESEMBLING A FLAT CAP, OR CASQUETTE.

From a carving on wood in the stalls of Notre Dame d'Amiens. XVI cent.

Not one among all the angels sculptured or painted in the church of Notre Dame de Brou, at Bourg, has a nimbus; nor is there a single nimbus on either of the stone statues.

A small wooden statuette, representing Christ teaching in the Temple, has indeed a nimbus, but it is of the casquette form, similar to that in the stalls at Amiens Cathedral. A few nimbi may, however, be remarked in the painted windows.

On one window is a painting of the Assumption of the Virgin, in which the apostles are decorated with a nimbus, resembling, with the exception of the barbes† and cylinder, the hat of the Bressane peasant girls. This nimbus is even ornamented on the plane, and at the outer edge.

All these examples belong to the first half of the sixteenth century; the nimbus after that period either disappeared altogether in France, or was changed into an actual head-dress. I say in France, because in Italy, at that period, and even for more than a century previous, the nimbus was correctly represented.‡

At the Renaissance, notwithstanding the reverse has been asserted to be the fact, the delicate idea and the elegant manner of depicting the nimbus prevalent in earlier times was revived; the Italian Renaissance was 100 or 150 years earlier than the French Renaissance. The nimbus,

* This drawing represents our Saviour, seen from behind, ascending the steps of the Temple.

† "'Barbes,' des bandes de toile ou de dentelle, qui pendent aux cornettes des femmes."—Dict. de l 'Academie.

‡ See below, in the "History of the Glory," a plate of the Virgin, taken from Orcagna's magnificent picture of "The Last Judgment." Mary, seated like her Son, Jesus Christ, in an elliptical aureole, is represented with her

which had fallen so low, and become so materialised and degraded, began again to rise; it succeeded in obtaining once more that ethereal subtlety, which, towards the end of the fourteenth century, it had aspired to reach in vain. At Brou, where the nimbus is, in general, so completely material, there is on one of the painted windows a figure of Mary Magdalene at the feet of her risen Lord, who commands her not to touch him (*Noli me tangere*). The figure of Christ is illumined by a nimbus formed of clusters of flame.

From that period the ingenuity of the artist is exerted to make the nimbus completely expressive of the idea which it was originally intended to convey.

It is reduced to an outer circle only, the field of the disk is altogether omitted or suppressed, as amongst the Pagans and during the first ages of Christianity, and thenceforth it becomes transparent like that of the Byzantine "Night" above mentioned.

The circle is regular and firm like the edge of a vase, or perhaps it is merely an uncertain wavering line, resembling a circle of light.*

On the other hand, this circular line often disappears, the frame or circumference of the entire disk is removed and the internal field alone retained; the framework being considered too coarse, too thick, and, as it were, unworthy to enclose the electric light emanating from the head. It is a shadow of flame, circular in form, but not permitting itself to be circumscribed. In a plate†, which will be given in the History of the Holy Ghost, and which represents God pronouncing a blessing on the world, at the moment when the Holy Dove moves upon the face of the waters, the outer circle of the divine nimbus has disappeared,

head surrounded by a host of rays, extending even beyond the circumference of the glory. The head of the Virgin diffuses on all sides a brilliant radiance. Figs. 67 and 74.

* See, for Italy, the "Disputá;" for France, the magnificent manuscript of "Anne de Bretagne," in the Bibliothèque Royale. Few of the nimbi in this MS. are in the form of a disk; circular nimbi, on the contrary, with a firmly marked outer line, are seen in abundance, and several with trembling uncertain lines resembling a misty light.

† Fig. 112. The Holy Ghost as a Dove; it is worthy of remark that the nimbus of the Dove is still solid and cruciform. Trans.

although the rays are of equal length, and terminate in the form of a circle.

On other monuments these rays are long or short, disposed either alternately or irregularly. In the beautiful paintings on wood at Amiens, called "Tableaux du puys de la confrérie de Notre Dame," the Virgin Mary is represented with a nimbus of luminous rays, some long and others short. The infant Christ himself is similarly nimbed, but with the addition of the rays being longer and floriated at the extremity, and which thus form the cross. The circumference of the nimbus, which serves in other instances to unite the rays, is here altogether omitted.*

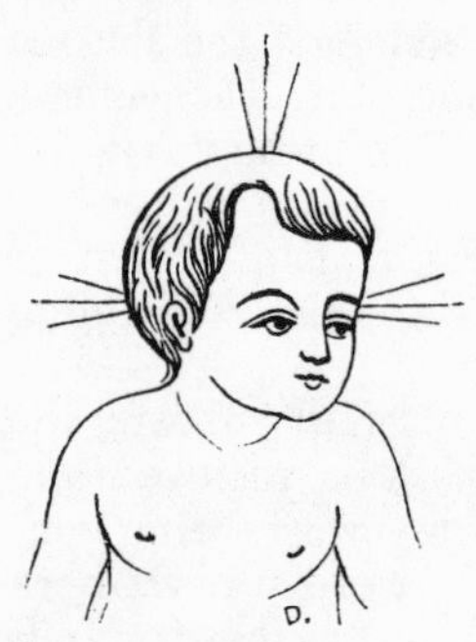

Fig. 34.
CHRIST, WITH A NIMBUS OF THREE CLUSTERS OF RAYS.
Miniature of the XVI cent. MS. of the Bib. Royale.

Both the circle and the disk are often omitted in the nimbus of Christ, and nothing is retained except the cross, which marks his divinity.

The cross is formed of three plumes or jets of light, rising from the summit of the head, and the temples, as in the charming infant Christ, subjoined, which is taken from a MS. of the sixteenth century. †

At that period also, luminous circles, drawn in perspective, first appear,—transparent nimbi, that adapt themselves to the movements of the head. The "Disputá" affords several very fine examples; the following is a form that occurs frequently in Italy in the sixteenth century. The subject is a head of St. Peter.

The monuments which afford instances of these and other varieties of the nimbus, are within reach of all the world. The churches of Paris for example, from Saint-Germain-

* See *l'Atlas et l'Album des Arts au Moyen Age.* M. du Sommerard, who possesses one of the Amiens Pictures, has produced with success admirable copies of those celebrated paintings, which tend to prove that the *Renaissance* in France took place earlier than the sixteenth century; and that our style of oil painting on wood is national, not exotic. The Amiens Pictures, which are of the fifteenth century, preceded the irruption of Italian artists into France.

† See MS. 920, Bib. Roy.

des-Prés, to Saint-Sulpice, including the cathedral, the Sainte-Chapelle, Saint-Germain-l'Auxerrois, Saint-Eustache, and Saint-Etienne-du-Mont, afford the most satisfactory evidence on all these points. Every form and variety of the nimbus may be found in abundance upon the sculptures and painted windows which decorate these edifices, and which embrace a period of seven, or perhaps, nine centuries.

Fig. 35.
A NIMBUS DRAWN IN PERSPECTIVE, FORMED BY A SIMPLE THREAD OF LIGHT.
The "Disputá" of Raphael.

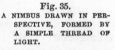

At length, following the common course of all things, the nimbus vanished. At the close of the sixteenth century, not only Saints, the Virgin and the Apostles, but the angels, God the Father, and even Jesus Christ, were despoiled of that characteristic attribute. If the nimbus was still casually seen to illumine some statue or effigy, it was simply because the artist, struggling against fashion, attempted a return to ancient usages. A host of monuments dating from that period, and extending down to our own, exhibit divine personages, whether angelical or canonised, without any nimbus* Thus, the close of the middle ages was marked by a repetition of the same peculiarity which had attended their commencement: God and the Saints were alike destitute of the nimbus.

In the first centuries of the Christian era, it had not yet sprung into existence: in the latter part of the fifteenth century its existence had already terminated.† Take, for instance, the angel, and apply the same example to God and

* See, in the "History of Jesus Christ and of the Trinity," an example (Fig. 126) of the Divine Persons, taken from a stone sculpture in the environs of Troyes. This bas-relief belongs to the end of the sixteenth century, and represents the Trinity crowning the Virgin Mary after her Assumption. Neither Mary, the two Angels who have carried her to Heaven, nor the three Persons by whom she is crowned, present the slightest appearance either of the nimbus or the glory. Nothing could be more completely human, more coldly real.

† The Breviary of Salisbury, in the Bibliothèque Royale, and of the year 1434, illustrates the indifference with which the nimbus was regarded at that period. In the picture of "The Lord's Supper," Christ has a nimbus, but it

all the saints. In the "History of the Angel" a design is given, taken from a Sarcophagus, belonging to the earliest ages of Christianity; it represents two creatures of human form with wings, supporting books, upon a frieze, the centre of which is filled by a cross patée; another design is from a MS. of the sixteenth century, and gives two angels, supporting the armorial bearings of the Cardinal of Lorraine, Archbishop of Rheims. In the first, the angels are not as yet invested with the nimbus; in the second, it is no longer applied; but in both examples the angels resemble the genii of the ancients, of whom indeed they appear to exercise nearly all the functions.

In the present day, however, when Christianity is better understood, and studied with more intelligence than formerly, the use of the nimbus has been revived. But the present age is one of eclecticism, and anterior forms and ideas are adopted, without regard to the confusion attendant upon the amalgamation of incongruous elements induced by this spirit of universal and arbitrary adaptation.

Our artists employ the circular or triangular nimbus, the disk and the aureole, almost at pleasure; being little versed in archæology, they place the cross in the nimbus of ordinary saints not entitled to such an honour, or, on the other hand, represent the Deity with a plain nimbus, destitute of the divine symbol of the cross. Thus in pictures of the Holy Family, St. Joseph frequently has a cross in the nimbus, while that of the infant Saviour is without. The artist, with one stroke of the pencil, robs Christ of his Divinity, and bestows the symbol of Deity upon one who is but an ordinary mortal.

is not cruciform. In that of "The Annunciation," the Holy Ghost also has a nimbus, without a cross. There are numerous angels in this manuscript, which is, in truth, peculiarly rich in miniatures; but not one amongst them has a nimbus of any description.

THE AUREOLE.

The aureole, as has been said above, is a nimbus of the entire body, in the same manner as the nimbus is the aureole of the head. The word aureole is derived from the Latin *aureola*, the diminutive of *aura*, a breeze, zephyr, breath; *aura* also means day and light, because the rising light of day is ushered in by the morning breeze, or perhaps bright rays and flame, which are as it were the efflorescence of light and day. Horace employs that word to signify, a sweet odour, or slight perfume.

Aura, comes from the Greek *αὖρα*, a gentle wind, zephyr, exhalation, vapour, *aurora* in short. These meanings may all be reduced to one only, luminous breath—indicating precisely the nature of the aureole, which is itself a flame, and expressed, in Iconography, by undulations surrounding the body, or by lines, intended to represent rays of light. The aureole and the nimbus are identical in their nature, which is that of a transparent cloud or a solid light. The luminous atmosphere, described by Virgil as encircling the goddess Minerva, and which he expresses by the words "nimbo effulgens," was undoubtedly an aureole, rather than a nimbus.*

The aureole is an enlarged nimbus; the nimbus, a diminished aureole. The nimbus cinctures the head; the aureole surrounds the entire body. The aureole seems like a drapery, a mantle of light, enveloping the entire body from the feet to the crown of the head. The word aureole is much in use in Christian Iconography, but its signification is vague and undefined, and it is applied sometimes to the

* Æneid, book ii., v. 615:—

"Jam summas arces Tritonia, respice, Pallas
Insedit, nimbo effulgens et Gorgone sæva."

"*Nimbo effulgens.* Nube divina. Est enim fulvidum lumen quod deorum capita tinguit (*sic*)." Such are the expressions of Servius, the commentator of Virgil, who lived in the fourth century. (See edition of Virgil, 4°. Geneva, 1636, p. 260.)

ornament of the head, sometimes to that of the body. In the present work it will be employed in a more limited sense, and will refer only to that large nimbus which usually enframes the entire body of Christ, and sometimes also of the Virgin. This kind of nimbus has, by some antiquaries, been termed the "Vesica Piscis," but a term so gross deserves to be expunged from every refined system of terminology; it was invented and employed even to abuse, by English antiquaries. This term, in other respects also, is faulty and incorrect, for the aureole as will presently be shown, often varies greatly in form. It has some-

Fig. 36.—GOD IN AN AUREOLE OF QUATREFOILS.
Fresco, from the apse in the crypt of the Cathedral of Auxerre, end of the XII cent.

times been called the "divine oval" or "mystical almond;" the word "mystical" would seem at the first glance to intimate a symbolic intention, the correctness of which, one may reasonably venture to doubt. Besides, the aureole is very frequently neither an oval, nor an almond, but simply a nimbus like that of the head. The head is round, the nimbus round; the human figure when erect forms a kind of elongated oval, and the aureole is usually elongated, somewhat in the form of an oval. But when the person is represented sitting, the oval is contracted into a circle,* and sometimes into a quatrefoil, in which case the four salient or projecting parts of the body, the head, the legs, and the two arms, have each their particular lobe, or section of the nimbus, and the torso is enclosed within a frame in the centre of the quatrefoil.

The above engraving is taken from a fresco placed at the back of the great crypt which extends beneath the choir and sanctuary of the Cathedral of Auxerre. Two candlesticks of seven branches shine within the aureole of God: without it, are painted two angels, bearing censers, and the four symbols or attributes of the Evangelists, one of which, however, the lion, is destroyed. In the centre of the western rose of the Cathedral of Chartres, Christ is painted, seated in a similar manner, within an aureole of quatrefoils, and judging the human race. Each lobe of the quatrefoil is better filled, and the intention is even more clearly marked, than at Auxerre; because Christ, instead of holding in his left hand the book, which rests upon his knees, and raising the right hand in the air, as in the fresco at Auxerre, extends both hands horizontally to show his wounds to the sinners whom he condemns. The hands being thus extended, the two lateral lobes of the aureole become imperatively necessary.

The name of Byzantine nimbus has also been given to the aureole; and this denomination is much better suited to its nature, which, in fact, is that of a true nimbus; but the epithet Byzantine is open to one serious objection, as seeming to attribute to the Greek school and the Byzantine style, as if it had issued from thence, or had been there most frequently employed, a form which is neither peculiar to that school nor to the style, and which belongs quite as justly to the Latin Church and the Western style. We

* At St. Savin, near Poitiers, in the porch and the crypt of the church, God is painted in fresco. He is seated, inscribed within an aureole, an entire circle, the field of which is greenish. In the nave is a figure of God, represented standing, and, therefore, in an oval aureole.

shall therefore restrict ourselves to the term aureole, in preference to any other, and we venture to hope that it may henceforth be generally employed in the terminology of Christian Archæology.

THE FORM OF THE AUREOLE

The form of the aureole, as has been seen, is very varied; that most commonly to be met with is ovoïdal at the base and pointed at the summit; not blunted as in a true oval. This form seems well fitted to encircle a figure in an erect position. The aureole is either a vestment of light,* or a radiation of light from the body. In the first case the aureole clings closely to the form of the body, which it clothes as with a garment; in the second it also assimilates itself to the form of the body, but is detached from it like rays drawn outwards from a centre. The points of the ovoïd are general acute, but in some instances obtuse, in order that they may adapt themselves more perfectly to the outline of the head and feet; or, perhaps, the oval, shortened from the summit to the base, envelopes the trunk only, being elongated above by a vaulted lobe and below by a lobe of a similar form, both of which are intersected by the oval of the trunk. In the following example, taken from a MS. of St. Sever, of which we have already spoken, a cloud with four undulating lines encircles Jesus, who is descending from heaven. This cloud takes exactly the form of the feet, the trunk, and the head. It adapts itself in a remarkable manner to the shape of the head, which might almost be said to be incrusted with it, the aureole resembling a sort of mould from whence the entire body seems to have received its form.

The external edge, confining the entire field of the aureole, is, amongst the Italians, regular and geometrical, like all the lines adopted by Christian art in Italy. It might be compared to a frame, cut out by a workman with a plane, in proof of which see the plate of the "Ascension," taken from an Italian Manuscript, see *ante*, fig. 2.

* "Deus . . . . . amictus lumine sicut vestimento." Psalm ciii., v. 2.

Amongst ourselves, as has been shown by the Manuscript of Saint Sever, the aureole is generally an undulating line,

Fig. 37.

THE LORD IN AN AUREOLE OF CLOUDS, WHICH TAKE THE FORM OF THE BODY.
Miniature of the x cent.; MS. de St. Sever, *Bibliothèque Royale.*

figuring the clouds or aërial vapour;* for the field of the aureole is nothing more than the heaven itself, the abode of God. It is in fact to God that the aureole is usually

* Christian artists represent water and vapour, fire and clouds, in the same manner.

restricted; to God the Father, the Son, and sometimes to the Holy Ghost.

But in this latter case, and especially before the fourteenth century, the Holy Ghost belongs to the Trinity, and necessarily accompanies the other two Divine persons. In the fifteenth century the edge of the nimbus is frequently filled with angels, just as the frame of a picture is ornamented with arabesques. Thus a painting on wood, in the church of the abbey of Saint Riquier, representing the Assumption, shows in the upper part of the picture, or, as it were in heaven, the Trinity preparing to receive Mary, who is lifted up by angels and borne away into heaven. The Holy Trinity appear in the bosom of an almost circular aureole, and a cordon of angels glitters in the band of the circle. The magnificent "Cité de Dieu," translated by Raoul de Presles, and now in the Bibliothèque de Sainte Geneviève, presents several examples of similar aureoles surrounding the Deity, and carpeted with cherubim and seraphim of azure, flame-colour, and gold.

When God is represented sitting within an aureole, his feet are frequently placed upon the rainbow; a second rainbow supports his back, and a third forms a pillow for his head. This is a fine idea, especially when the field of the aureole is blue, studded with golden stars; and the frame greyish and undulating, like clouds.

The two rainbows of the head and back are often suppressed, for the Deity needs no support; in this case the rainbow of the feet is sometimes replaced by a carpet of gold, starred with silver. See a fresco belonging to the commencement of the thirteenth century, and which still exists in the tower of Baugency, representing Christ holding a book in the left hand, and in the act of blessing with the right.*

This conception is less exalted than the preceding; still it is grand, for the carpet may be intended for heaven, with a ground of gold, gemmed with silver stars; in most instances, instead of a carpet, we have a stool, as at Chartres,

* This fresco, now half ruined, and which ought to be restored by Government, has been copied by a young artist of Orleans. The drawing is in the possession of M. A. Duchalais.

on the tympanum of the Porte Royale.* We here recognise the third motive, or manner of treating this subject, the most material of all; it is merely a rude literal translation of that passage in the prophet Isaiah; CŒLUM SEDES MEA; TERRA AUTEM SCABELLUM PEDUM MEORUM.† At St. Denis, in the tympanum of the central door of the western porch, the feet of Christ rest upon a stool; the lower part of the body is circumscribed by an aureole, but a cross is planted in the interior of the aureole, against which the Sovereign Judge is leaning; this design is very good, and very rare in this part of the twelfth century.

The stool supporting the feet of God, who is represented seated on a throne, and surrounded by an aureole, is very frequent. Thus in the frescos of St. Savin, near Poitiers, God is three times represented surrounded by an oval or circular aureole, and three times his feet rest upon a stool. This stool, more or less ornamented *en creux*, and in relief, is not a "chauffoir" as has been asserted. Nothing is to be found in Holy Writ, which could countenance the adoption of so vulgar an idea, while the footstool (scabellum) is very clearly indicated. Besides, the form prevents any mistake of this kind. The design given below, Fig. 38, is taken from a fresco, in the west wall of the great church of the convent of Salamis, known under the name of Panagia Phanéroméni. It exhibits Christ, descending from heaven, to judge the world; the aureole surrounding him is circular, a variety already presented in Fig. 16, and it is upheld by four cherubim, at the four cardinal points. The field of the aureole is divided by symbolic squares with concave sides, intersecting each other; the feet of the divine Judge rest on a circular line, intended to represent a rainbow; a second rainbow forms his seat. This painting is of the eighteenth century; in France it would probably belong to the thirteenth, for the Greeks have made no progress in art during the last five or six hundred years. The explanation of the design, from this remarkable fresco, is to be found in the words of David: "He bowed the heavens also, and came down; and darkness was under his feet. And he rode upon

* Monography of the Cath. of Chartres; drawing of M. Amaury Duval.
† Chap. vi., v. 1.

a cherub, and did fly; yea, he did fly upon the wings of the wind."* "O Lord my God, thou art very great, thou art clothed with honour and majesty. Who coverest thyself with light as with a garment; who stretchest out the heavens like a curtain. Who layeth the beams of his chambers in the waters; who maketh the clouds his chariot; who walketh upon the wings of the wind; who maketh his angels spirits, and his ministers a flaming fire."†

Fig. 38.—GOD, IN A CIRCULAR AUREOLE, RADIATING WITHIN, AND INTERSECTED BY SYMBOLIC SQUARES WITH CONCAVE SIDES. GOD IS SITTING ON A RAINBOW; HIS FEET RESTING ON ANOTHER.

Fresco in the great Convent of Salamis; XVIII cent.

The field of the aureole is sometimes lighted by two stars, shining near the head of the divine person whom it incloses; one is on the right, the other on the left. When the field of the aureole is narrow, and the sitting figure in the act of

* Psalm xviii. 9, 10.

† Psalm civ. 1—4.

blessing with the right hand, that hand occupies the place of one star, and both are necessarily placed on the left. The entire field is sometimes gemmed with stars, like the sky on a clear night,* but this is not common. The number of the rays or points of the stars, varies; some being four in number,† some five, six, seven,‡ or even eight.§ The left-hand star sometimes has fewer rays than that on the right. When this is the case the left star is intended for the moon, and the right for the sun,|| although both are represented under the same form. The sun and moon are almost invariably introduced into representations of Christ's ascension into heaven, and of his descending upon the earth at the last judgment; the stars also are sometimes seen. The sun, moon, and stars, presiding over the scene of Christ's ascension, have already been distinctly shown in Fig. 16; the magnificent tympanum of the Cathedral of Autun, sculptured in the twelfth century, represents the Last Judgment, in a similar manner, with the sun on the right, and the moon on the left hand of Christ, the Judge of the world, who is inscribed within an elliptical aureole.¶

In Byzantine, and modern Greek paintings of the Transfiguration, the aureole surrounding the Saviour offers a singular peculiarity of construction. It is in the form of a wheel; six rays, diverging from the centre, or nave of the wheel, extend to the felloe at the circumference; but instead of terminating there, as in an ordinary wheel, they are

* "*Histoire de l'Art par les Monuments,*" by Seroux d'Agincourt; sculpture; plate 2. This design represents an altar-front of the Cathedral of Città-di-Castello, in Italy, and which was presented, in 1143 or 1144, by Pope Celestin II. In the centre, within an oval aureole, appears Christ with the cruciform nimbus; on his left, the Moon's crescent; on his right, the Sun spreads his glistening rays; and, in the field of the aureole, shine Stars, either with five points, or five lobes, or in the form of a rose.

† See the altar of St. Guillaume, at Saint-Guilhem-du-Désert, described and designed by M. R. Thomassy, in the "Mémoires de la Société Royale des Antiquaires de France," tom. xiv., p. 222.

‡ See the personification of the Air, or of Music, a drawing of the thirteenth century, in a Pontifical, MS. in the Bibliothèque de Reims.

§ Witness a Virgin of silver repoussé in my possession.

|| See the personification of the Air, MS. de Reims.

¶ See a very fine drawing of this tympanum, executed by M. Victor Petit, which forms part of "L'Atlas des Arts au Moyen Age," of M. du Sommerard. It is one of the most valuable engravings in that rich collection.

prolonged so as to reach, one as far as Moses, the other to Elias, the third to St. Peter, the fourth to St. John, and the fifth to St. James. These persons alone, according to the Greek Fathers, were present at the transfiguration or metamorphosis. The sixth ray is absorbed and concealed by the body of Christ himself. The figure of Christ is affixed to this wheel-like glory, and might be supposed to be nailed to an instrument of torture; for the martyrdom of St. George, who suffered death upon the wheel, is thus represented.* This singular arrangement is very rare in the west;† it is seen only in buildings, which seem to betray at least an indirect Byzantine influence; as for example, the church of Notre Dame de Chartres, whence the following drawing is taken, and which was copied from one of the three great Romanesque windows of the western porch.

In Sicily, on the contrary, and in that portion of ancient Magna Græcia where the rites and religious offices of the Greek Church are still observed, as well as in several other localities, the transfiguration is constantly treated in this manner; we may notice particularly, in illustration, the fresco paintings in the Chapel Royal at Palermo. The aureole there is elliptical, not circular, but its rays are equal in number to those at Chartres, and fall or rise in a similar manner, as they issue from the divine person of the transfigured Saviour.

Besides the circles, the oval, and the quatrefoil, of which we have just spoken, the form of the aureole presents several other varieties. Being a sort of luminous shadow, it embraces the form of the person, and is frequently divided into two; the upper section being smaller in diameter, confines the head and bust, reaching to the waist, where it is intersected by the lower division, which is somewhat

* See, in the Cathedral of Chartres, the Martyrdom of the warrior St. George, painted on a window in the nave of that church; and the same martyrdom, sculptured on the south porch, on the basement or pedestal of a statue representing that Saint.

† The manuscript of Herrade, *Hortus Deliciarum*, in which the influence of the Byzantine school is clearly discernible, contains a miniature painting of the Transfiguration. Rays of silver issue from the body of Christ; they are sixteen in number, eight on each side. But these rays are not connected by a circular line; they form a wheel without the felloe. The pure Byzantine type is not strictly observed.

broader, and descends from the waist to the feet. This aureole is composed of two superimposed intersecting circles,

Fig. 39.—THE TRANSFIGURATION; CHRIST IN A WHEEL-SHAPED AUREOLE. Painted Glass of the XII cent.; Chartres Cathedral.

cut away at the point of intersection, and resembling in form the vertical cup of the gourd carried by pilgrims. It is from this configuration in particular, that antiquaries have derived the name of "Vesica Piscis," but it is far less common than the elliptical or ovoïdal form. The term alluded to has, therefore, in addition to its impropriety, the disadvantage of expressing only one unimportant variety; a double reason for rejecting it altogether.

The circle below is sometimes narrower, that above wider; it is then a gourd reversed; the upper circle is sometimes open, the lower closed, the feet resting on the closed circle, while the head appears at liberty to move to the right or left, unchecked by a frame. At other times, the lower circle is open, and that above closed; or, both the upper and lower portions are open, and the aureole composed of parallel lines more or less irregularly placed, but which never touch, just like the asymptotes, in geometry, which never meet the curves to which they belong.

These varieties, and some others, are still more distinctly illustrated in a Psalter preserved in the Bibliothèque Royale, and belonging to the close of the twelfth century.* The miniatures adorning the conclusion of this Manuscript appear to have been executed in Italy during the fourteenth century. This great variety of aureoles would be one more argument added to the treatment, colouring, design, costume, and general tournure of the persons represented, in confirmation of the opinion that the manuscript in question is Italian.†

Persons who suppose the aureole to be a symbolic representation of certain natural forms, a kind of maternal bosom, in which the Deity appears to float, will find an insuperable difficulty in accounting for these varied and heterogeneous forms. For it will be necessary to explain for what reason God the Father, who is born of none, who begets, but was not begotten, should be inclosed in that aureole as well as the Son and the Holy Ghost.

The aureole, when in the form of a circle, or an almond, may remind Pagan antiquaries, of the IMAGINES CLYPEATÆ, so common amongst the Romans, and even with the Greeks also.‡

In a manuscript belonging to the Bibliothèque Royale there is a figure of God armed with a sword and carrying arrows; it is a half-length, in relief, and within a circle like a buckler, resembling in every point those figures on bucklers which are constantly seen upon Roman sarcophagi.

* Suppl. fr. No. 1132, *bis*.

† See frescos 27, 58, 80, and others. Italy is the country of archæological variation; that is to say, of movement. The art is, with us, more uniform, and the imagination less active.

‡ In the "Greek Iconography" of Visconti, the poets Sophocles and Menander project thus in *imagines clypeatæ* from a disk pierced like a dormer window. In the sixteenth century, at the time of the Renaissance, this motive was singularly in favour, and very frequently employed in decoration.

An engraving * given below, in the History of God the Father, represents the Deity within a medallion, and like a Pagan God holding a bow, arrows, and a sword. He is personified as the God of strength and of battle. The drawing is copied from the Psalter of the twelfth century mentioned above. It becomes easy, therefore, to trace one source of the aureole in Roman Archæology, if it be remembered that busts of Christ are frequently placed in the front of basilicas of Pagan form; precisely in the same spot where the rose-window was afterwards pierced by Gothic architects; or where Romanesque architects, before the time of Gothic art, opened an "oculum;" or, at an earlier period still, the place of the open *oculum* was occupied by a blank *oculum* containing a figure of Christ and the four evangelical attributes. Notre Dame de Poitiers, built in the twelfth century, still bears traces of this early custom; Christ is there seen surrounded by the evangelical symbols, and inclosed in a kind of oval, an *oculum*, or blank rose-window.†

S. Paoli fuori delle Mura, before the disastrous conflagration of 1823, and St. Peter's at Rome, before its destruction by Paul V., when it gave place to the St. Peter's of the present day, both contained a series of Roman pontiffs painted in fresco, at very ancient epochs. The portraits were all half-lengths, framed in a circular field, and resembled the embossed figures upon the old Roman bucklers.

The aureole is most frequently oval in form; but the oval is sometimes formed by intersecting branches of trees, which open and leave a vacant space, and then, crossing again, form a sort of double ogive, one above, the other below or reversed.

Nearly all genealogical trees, particularly those of the

* Fig. 51.

† See the numerous designs in the porch of Notre Dame de Poitiers. "With regard to this mode of representing Christ in half-length," says M Raoul-Rochette (*Discours sur l'Art du Christianisme*, note 2, p. 25), "copied from the images on a buckler, see Buonarotti, who cites, in illustration, a mosaic, now destroyed, but then in the grand arch of S. Paolo fuori delle Mura (*Dittico sacro*, &c., p. 262). This custom continued in vogue till the seventh century, as is proved by the paintings in the Oratory of Santa Felicità, discovered in the Baths of Titus, in the year 1812, in the upper part of which a similar half-length figure of our Saviour was discovered."—Guattani, *Memorie Enciclopediche*, &c., t. i. tav. xxi.

twelfth and thirteenth centuries, in which the ancestors of Christ and of the Virgin are ranged in order, one above the other, are thus disposed.*

Each oval contains an ancestor, a king. Christ seated on a throne and blessing the world with his extended right hand, is placed at the summit. The following design is taken from the Psalter of St. Louis.† One entire page of the manuscript is occupied by a genealogical tree of this description.

Fig. 40.—CHRIST IN AN ELLIPTICAL AUREOLE FORMED OF BRANCHES
Miniature of the XIII cent.; Psalter of St. Louis.

The summit alone is here given, with the highest oval, in which Christ is enframed. The Holy Spirit is seven times

* See St. Cuthbert's Church, Wells.
† The MS. belongs to the Bibliothèque de l'Arsenal.

repeated in the outer edge of the oval, because on Christ were conferred the seven gifts of the Holy Ghost. Each of these spiritual gifts is represented under the form of a dove, and inclosed within a circular aureole. The superior Spirit—he who commands the others, and who is placed at the top—is not only inclosed within an aureole, but has also a nimbus encircling the head. Still the nimbus of this chief Spirit is not cruciform, which must be either an error of the artist, or an imperfection in the miniature. The doves ought each to have a cruciform nimbus, as personifying the divine qualities of the Holy Ghost. This fault has been avoided in a painted window on the left of the nave of the Cathedral of Chartres.

It gives a representation of the Virgin with the infant Saviour in her arms. The gifts of the Holy Ghost, under the form of doves, and borne upon rays of flame-like red, converge towards the head of the divine child. The doves have each a cruciform nimbus.

THE APPLICATION OF THE AUREOLE.

The aureole cannot be said to belong exclusively to God; still, except in the instances about to be considered, and of which an explanation will be given, the aureole is an attribute especially characteristic of divinity. It is in fact the symbolic token of supreme power, of energy, exalted to the highest possible degree. It ought, therefore, to be given before all to God, who in himself is properly and intrinsically, the centre of omnipotence, while his creatures, however lofty may be their rank and degree, hold it only from him, like the moon, which shines but with the borrowed radiance of the sun.

The Virgin, however, the first in honour among pure human creatures, ranking immediately after God himself; Mary, rendered superior to saints and angels by the functions she performed, and the homage that has been rendered her, is frequently, and most appropriately, invested with the glory.

In this drawing the aureole is oval, with obtuse points. Elsewhere the point is sharp, and formed by intersecting branches, as in genealogical trees; or it is a cloud, enveloping

Mary in an oval, which takes the form of her body, and seems to carry her to heaven as in the Assumption.* In

Fig. 41.—MARY, IN AN OVAL AUREOLE, INTERSECTED BY ANOTHER, ALSO OVAL, BUT OF SMALLER SIZE.
Miniature of the x cent.; *Liber Precum*, Bib. Roy.

the Last Judgment, painted in the Campo Santo by Andrea and Bernardo Orcagna, the Virgin, like Christ, is depicted sitting upon a rainbow, within an elliptical aureole; the

* See in Notre Dame de Paris, a bas-relief affixed to the north side wall, representing the Virgin carried by angels up to heaven; the Virgin is framed

mother is no less honoured than the son, who is at her side. In the sixteenth century, the aureole is generally freed from its edge or framework of clouds. The field alone remains, and is formed of flamboyant rays,* or of rays alternately straight and flamboyant, emanating in every direction from the body of the Virgin. Thus it is seen that Mary is invested with the aureole under four particular conditions. Firstly, when she holds the divine infant in her arms; secondly, at the Assumption, when carried by angels into heaven; thirdly, at the last judgment, when she implores the clemency of Christ for man; fourthly, when represented with the attributes of the woman of the Apocalypse—a prophetic symbol, of which she is the reality. In the first instance, of which Fig. 43 furnishes an example, we may suppose the aureole to be given in honour of her son rather than herself; in the second the aureole appertains entirely to herself; in the last judgment she is sometimes without an aureole, but this attribute is invariably given, and is most perfect, when to her is applied that passage in the Apocalpyse,—"A woman clothed with the sun, and the moon under her feet, and upon her head a crown of twelve stars."†

Sometimes, in the thirteenth and fourteenth centuries, and in the fifteenth and sixteenth more especially, at which time ancient traditions became degraded, and were finally lost, the aureole degenerated into a mere symbol of the apotheosis of holy persons. Thus, a glass painting at Chartres, of the close of the thirteenth century, represents St. Martin, Archbishop of Tours, carried up to heaven by two angels, in

in an oval of clouds. In the Campo Santo at Pisa, in the Last Judgment, the Virgin, like her Son Jesus Christ, is sitting on a rainbow, and surrounded by an aureole. See Fig. 74.

* See the bas-relief on the tympanum of the south gable of the Cathedral of Reims. In Fig. 43, the aureole is composed of rays alternately straight and flamboyant.

† *Apocalypse*, xii. 1. The following inscription is found on a painted window of the sixteenth century, in the Church of Notre Dame de Moulins: "Hæc est illa de qua sacra canunt eulogia; sole amicta, lunam habens sub pedibus, stellis meruit coronari duodenis." The window on which this inscription is painted represents Mary holding in her arms the Infant Jesus, which clearly proves the woman in the Apocalypse to be the emblem of the Holy Virgin, as the bleeding lamb is of Christ.

an aureole of fire. In illuminated manuscripts of about the time of the Renaissance, Mary Magdalene is represented in a state of divine ecstasy supported in the arms of angels, above the holy ointment or "Sainte Baume," and in a similar manner encircled by the divine aureole. We must, therefore, be careful not to confound pictures of the Magdalene with those of the mother of God — the exaltation of

Fig. 42.—SOUL OF SAINT MARTIN IN AN ELLIPTICAL AUREOLE.
Painted Glass Window of the XIII cent., Cathedral of Chartres.*

Mary Magdalene with the assumption of the Virgin. The grotto, the age of the saint, and other characteristic

* Saint Martin, in the above engraving, is naked, according to the customary mode of depicting souls; but elsewhere, even at Chartres, in the glass window

features, will sufficiently mark the distinction between them.* The honour of the aureole had, it appears, been decreed to an ordinary saint, long before the thirteenth century. We read, in fact, in the Life of St. Benedict, who died in 590, that he one day saw the soul of Germanus, Bishop of Capua, carried up to heaven by angels in a globe of fire.† The globe of fire, is in fact an aureole, although it no longer enveloped the living body, but the soul of the saint; and in truth, such a soul seems to assimilate itself in some measure to the Deity. The soul of St. Martin, in the representation of his apotheosis at Chartres, is also carried up in an oval aureole, red, or the colour of fire.‡

The aureole is so completely the attribute of supreme power or divine omnipotence, that the angels themselves, which of all God's creatures seem most nearly allied to the Creator, are yet not invested with this mark of dignity. In some cases, of which the miniatures of illuminated MSS. offer numerous examples, the angels are comprehended within the aureole of God, when they attend him either at the Creation, on mount Sinai, or at the last judgment; but the aureole does not properly belong to them; it is the attribute of God, and the angels seem as if absorbed in the resplendent luminous atmosphere, radiating from His glorious person. One curious and remarkable coincidence may, however, be noticed in a painted window in the south transept of the cathedral of Chartres.

representing the History of St. Remi, the soul of the Bishop of Reims is completely clothed. We are told, in the Life of Saint Francis Romaine (*Acta SS.* des Bollandistes, 2nd vol. of Mars), that the soul of St. Ambrose of Sienna ascended to heaven clad in pontifical robes.

* See the "Poetry of Sacred and Legendary Art." Translator.

† "Vidit Germani, Capuani Episcopi, animam in *sphera ignea* ab angelis in cœlum deferri." (*Acts SS. ord., S. Bened.*, 1 vol., Vie de Saint Benoît.) It is in this manner that Saint Ouen (Vie de Saint Eloi, dans d 'Achery *Spicilegium*, tom ii., p. 113,) relates the death of Saint Eloi, his friend; and he thus describes the resplendent aureole, the spherical light, the pharos surrounding the soul of the Saint as he ascends to Heaven: "Inter verba orationis flagitatum à superis emisit (Eligius) spiritum. Statim vero cum esset hora prima noctis, visus est subito velut *pharus* magnus ingenti claritate resplendens ex eadem domo coruscando conscendere, atque inter mirantium obtutus *sphæra ignea* crucis in se similitudinem præferens, velocique cursu densitatem nubium præteriens, cœli altitudinem penetrare."

‡ See painted window in one of the chapels in the apse, on the south side.

On this window, belonging to the thirteenth century, is a painting of the celestial hierarchy, or the distribution of the angels into nine choirs. Each choir of angels is characterised by a peculiar attribute; the Thrones, represented by two great angels with green wings and sceptres in their hands, and enclosed in a crimson aureole of elliptical form, are the first and most elevated of the three groups. The Thrones alone are honoured with this badge; now these angels, as their name indicates, are the depositories of Almighty power. This fact affords further confirmation of the assertion that the aureole is the peculiar attribute of God, for the Deity in delegating his authority to thrones delegates to them at the same time a portion of his Majesty and glory.*

THE HISTORY OF THE AUREOLE.

The nimbus, as has been said above is frequently wanting. It seems scarcely to have existed among the early Christians, and is not observable on the sarcophagi and frescos of the catacombs; it disappears altogether at the close of the middle ages.

The aureole, which is, in fact, only a larger form of the nimbus, is naturally subject to the same historic changes; nor is it found on any of the earliest Christian monuments. The reader may refer to the drawing, Fig. 32, *ante*, taken from the Christian sarcophagi found in the catacombs. This engraving represents God the Father, beardless, condemning Adam to till the ground, and Eve to spin wool; to the one

* St. Dionysius, the Areopagite (*De Celesti Hierarchiâ*, cap. xv., p. 198), says, that the angels are sometimes robed in clouds. The aureole surrounding the thrones at Chartres may be intended to figure the clouds. In fact, the aureole encircling God, the Virgin, and the souls of the saints, is nothing more than the cloud on which these divine and holy persons ascend and descend. At Aix-la-Chapelle, in the centre of the crown given by Barbarossa to the Cathedral there, and still suspended above the tomb of Charlemagne, the Archangel Michael is seen, enclosed in an aureole of quatrefoils, like the figure of Christ at Auxerre, given above (Fig. 36.) The Archangel is descending from heaven, to combat the enemies of Peace; for, in singular contrast to the warlike spirit of Charlemagne, and of Barbarossa, the legend on the crown proclaims the blessedness of the peaceful: "Beati pacifici, quoniam filii Dei vocabuntur," are the words of the inscription, taken from the Sermon on the Mount, (Gospel of St. Matthew, v. 9.)

he offers a lamb, the fleece of which she is to spin into garments; to the other, ears of corn, imaging those which man is to cultivate by the sweat of his brow. God is not invested either with the nimbus of the head or the aureole of the body. Fig. 18 is equally remarkable for the absence of that characteristic attribute.

The aureole is even later in its appearance than the nimbus, which was adopted, in most of its varieties, before the aureole had been introduced; the latter was discontinued, also, before the nimbus fell into disuse, so that its existence was but of limited duration. Even in the middle ages, when the nimbus, unless accidentally forgotten, was constantly employed, the aureole was not invariably added. It is therefore undoubtedly a rarer form, and of more brief existence than that around the head. See, in the History of the Trinity, a drawing, Fig. 144, taken from the Manuscript of the Duc d'Anjou, Bibliothèque Royale, thirteenth century: the Trinity has a cruciform nimbus, but the aureole has already disappeared.

About the fifteenth and sixteenth centuries, the nimbus loses its exterior border; the outer line also, uniting the rays, is often abridged. The same may be said of the aureole; the circumference disappears and the field alone remains. The field is striated with simple or flamboyant rays, and sometimes with rays alternately straight and flamboyant.

A drawing, Fig. 150, given below in the History of the Trinity, taken from a manuscript in the Bibliothèque Royale, of the end of the fifteenth century,* represents the Trinity under three figures of human form; the Father, like a pope, holding in his hand the globe; Christ, as the crucified, bearing his cross; the Holy Ghost, under the figure of a young man, with the divine Dove, his appropriate symbol, resting on his head. All the three have the cruciform nimbus; even the dove is glorified with that mark of honour. Flamboyant rays, or in other words, the aureole, emanate in streams of light from the three divine persons. These rays are not united, but escape freely, unconfined by any line of circumference. The same may be observed in the following figure.

* *L'Aiguillon de l'Amour Divin*, in 4°., Nos. 5094 and 7275.

This drawing represents Mary with the infant Christ in her arms. The Virgin and Child are both within a

FIG. 43.—MARY AND JESUS IN AN AUREOLE OF STRAIGHT AND FLAMBOYANT RAYS. Miniature of the XVI cent. Bibliothèque de Sainte Geneviève.

white ovoïdal aureole, the circumference of which is fringed with rays, some straight and others flamboyant. Christ and his mother rise from the mystical Lily of the tribe of Judah.*

* This engraving is copied from a miniature of the sixteenth century, manuscript No. 460, in the Bibliothèque de Sainte Geneviève. It will be seen that the Mother and Divine Infant both wear the circular nimbus, but that of Jesus is not cruciform. Errors of this kind are of frequent occurrence in the sixteenth century.

THE GLORY.

The term Glory, as we have said, is employed to express the union of the nimbus and the aureole, as the word hand implies the union of the fingers which compose it. It seemed absolutely necessary to find some generic word comprehending both species combined, and this word we shall borrow from the vocabulary of Iconography, first giving a precise definition of its meaning.

The word "Gloria" is, according to our definition, formed of an onomatopœia, or of the two sounds or exclamations expressed by the two principal vowels, which in combination with the three consonants form the word "Gloria." This word in ordinary language implies an extraordinary splendour surrounding every individual, who has rendered himself illustrious by noble deeds, lofty ideas, or sublime works. Alexander, the conqueror of Asia; Cæsar, who subdued Europe; Aristotle and Plato, rulers of the intellectual world; Homer and Virgil, who still excite all imaginations; St. Vincent de Paul, who inflamed all hearts with love, and worked prodigies of charity; Phidias and Raphael, who produced masterpieces of sculpture and painting; these, with many others in every station and sphere of human activity and genius, are men of brilliant reputation, and crowned with glory.

In the earliest ages of the world, when language was in its infancy, and ideas were expressed chiefly by gestures and exclamations, the appearance of genius such as that above named was hailed by an enthusiastic people, with cries of admiration, with those sounds which grammarians call vowels, and such especially as are most sonorous, most noisy, and therefore, most in accordance with the predominant feeling of those by whom they were uttered. Now amongst vowels, the *o* and *a* are the two most sonorous; if uttered successively and repeated several times without interruption they become blended together, and modified. The modifying link is furnished by the consonants *g* and *l* which precede the *o*; and for the same reason an *r* is introduced before the *a*, and coupled with the vowel *i*—a mute vowel, employed to facilitate the enunciation of the resonant *a*.

It is possible that the word *gloria*, like *bravo*, in which the *o* follows the *a*, is merely a forcible exclamation expressive of the homage addressed to men of genius.

But, whatever may have been its first origin, the word itself distinctly expresses the splendour, or moral light, surrounding every illustrious individual. When it was first thought desirable to give this radiance a material form through the medium of painting or sculpture, to render it visible to the eye and sensible to the touch, it was represented by a circular line enclosing the entire body, and by another circle, forming the nimbus of the head.

We give the name of glory to this combination of the nimbus and aureole, because it is a word which perfectly conveys the signification, and has by long use become almost consecrated, in ordinary language, to the idea of the nimbus. In fact, the word glory, is still popularly applied to that form; it is given to those great suns displayed in the eastern end of churches, that is to say to those radiations of gilded wood, with which the back of the Sanctuary is sometimes decorated.* Besides the word glory is often applied in Holy Writ, to the rays of light escaping from the body of God, or to clouds surrounding Him on his descent to earth. Thus Ezekiel says, "Then I beheld, and lo, a likeness as the appearance of fire; from the appearance of his loins even downward fire; and from his loins even upward, as the appearance of brightness, as the colour of amber. . . . And behold the glory of the God of Israel was there." † . . . . . "And the glory of the God of Israel was gone up from the cherub whereupon he was." ‡ "Then the glory of the Lord went up from the cherub, and stood over the threshold of the house; and the house was filled with the cloud, and the court was full of the brightness of the Lord's glory." §

Thus David in the Psalms, says that God shows himself in his glory, and it is even declared that the glory of God resembles flame. ||

* See the sanctuary of the Cathedral of Amiens, and that of St. Roch, at Paris. † *Ezekiel*, viii., 2, 3. ‡ *Ezekiel*, ix., 3.

§ *Ezekiel*, x., 4. "Et elevata est *Gloria* Domini desuper Cherub ad limen domus; et repleta est domus nube, et atrium repletum est splendore Gloriæ Domini."

|| *Exodus*, xxiv, 17. "Erat autem species Gloriæ Domini quasi ignis ardens."

In a number of scriptural texts, Jesus is spoken of as descending in glory and majesty at the end of the world to judge the quick and dead. Whenever the scenes referred to in these texts are depicted in sculptures, stained glass, or the miniatures of manuscripts, at all times when God is represented as the centre of a radiating light, or surrounded by clouds, those radiations, or clouds, assume precisely the circular form to which we give the name of glory. It is by encircling the Deity with similar undulating or geometrical lines to which we give this name of glory, that Christian artists have sought to mark the Divinity revealing himself to Christ and his prophets,* at the last judgment. The design, Fig. 37, shows Christ thus descending from heaven to earth; he is surrounded by clouds, and, within them, by the glory. The inscription, "*Dominus in nubibus, et vident eum inimici ejus et qui pupugerunt*," leaves no doubt on this point.† The miniature belongs probably to the ninth or tenth century. It is taken from a manuscript now in the Bibliothèque Royale, but belonging originally to the Abbey of Saint Sever in Gascony.

THE NATURE OF THE GLORY.

There can be no doubt that the nature of the nimbus, and of the aureole is the same; or that the element constituting both is fire, or flame, which may be termed the efflorescence of fire. The last design (Fig. 43), proves this most decisively with regard to the aureole, and two engravings (Figs. 67 and 74) given below, taken from the paintings in the Campo Santo, are equally conclusive in regard to the nimbus.

* Ezekiel, in his prophetic visions, employs the most decisive expressions. Read and compare the different verses of the first chapter. These extraordinary texts, explain most vividly the Glory of God; the waving character and circular form of that Glory; the mysterious wheels and the symbolic animals by which they are accompanied, have been constantly rendered in sculpture and painting, at every period of Christian art.

† *Rev.* i., 7. "Behold He cometh with clouds, and every eye shall see Him, and they also which pierced Him." The text of the manuscript differs slightly from that of the Apocalypse. David, Psalm xviii., 2, says, "His pavilion round about Him were dark waters, and thick clouds of the skies;" a literal explanation of the Glory in the manuscript of Saint Sever.

The aureole of the head and that of the body, encircling the deities of the Hindoos, is represented under the form of luminous rays, or wavy plumes. At the birth of Zoroaster, that pure emanation of the divinity of the ancient Persians, his body emitted so brilliant a light, that the entire chamber was illuminated by its radiance.* Krishna also, when being nursed by Devaki, his mother, lighted up the room in which he passed his infancy by the rays emitted from his head, and which were rendered more brilliant still by others emanating from the head of his mother. †

Fire sparkles on the head, and is emitted from the body of Maya, at the moment when the sea of milk flows in two rich streams from her bosom.‡ In the Buddhist books in the Bibliothèque Royale, pious Buddhist saints are often encircled by an oval or circular aureole, from the circumference of which, straight or flamboyant rays extend on every side.§ Amongst the Greeks, Romans, and Etruscans, all the constellations, the sun, the moon, and the planets when represented under the humanform are surrounded either by rays or by luminous circles, exactly resembling our nimbi and aureoles. || We have already seen the sun and moon; the plate annexed is a head of Mercury, who may be recognised by his little wings and his caduceus; his nimbus resembles that of a Christian saint.¶

Fig. 44.
MERCURY WITH A CIRCULAR NIMBUS.
Roman sculpture.

These rays and circles are the emblem, or, to speak more

* *Religions de l'Antiquité;* par M. J. D. Guigniaut; vol. i., p. 317.

† *Ibid.*, pl. cah. i., No. 61.

‡ *Ibid.*, pl. cah. i., No. 103. The drawing of this Goddess is given above (Fig. 12).

§ I owe my information respecting these valuable works to the kindness of M. Stanislas Julien.

|| See the Planisphère of Bianchini, in the Musée of the Louvre; "L'Antiquité expliquée," de Montfaucon, *passim*, &c.

¶ *Antiq. Expliquée,* tom. ii., pl. 224, p. 414.

correctly, the image of light; for when these constellations, instead of being personified are represented in their natural character, they are equally surrounded by them. Paintings have been recently discovered in Egypt, in which the sun is depicted shedding forth rays, to the extremity of which a hand is attached;* thus with the exception of the hands the Holy Ghost is represented on our monuments, when at Pentecost he descended in the form of tongues of flame upon the heads of the apostles.†

Fig. 45.
A PERSIAN KING, ADORNED WITH A PYRAMIDAL FLAMBOYANT NIMBUS.
Persian manuscript, Bibliothèque Royale.

Among the modern Persians, the Arabs, and the Turks, the heads of all superhuman personages whether good or evil, whether akin to Mahomet or to Eblis, are surmounted by pyramids of flame, rising, according to the nature of fire, with the points in the air, as may be remarked in the annexed example. The subject, a king crowned with flame, is taken from a fine Persian manuscript in the Bibliothèque Royale.‡

There can be no doubt that it is a flame which appears to surround the head of this king, for in another Hindoo manu-

* *Journal des Savants,* numéro d' Octobre, 1840; article de M. Letronne.

† Cloister of St. Trophimus, at Arles; capitals, in St. Madelaine de Vezelay; several miniatures in illuminated manuscripts, in the Bib. Roy. The grand cupola of St. Mark's, at Venice, contains one of the most remarkable instances of these tongues of flame, attached to the point of a luminous ray, and resting on the brow of the Apostles. The magnificent mosaic with which this cupola is lined, represents the Descent of the Holy Spirit on the Apostles. In the Acts of the Apostles, (i. 3,) we read: "Apparuerunt illis dispertitæ linguæ tanquam ignis."

‡ See also a Persian manuscript of the Bibliothèque Saint Geneviève, entitled, *Medgialis;* and the "Livre des Augures," a Turkish manuscript

script, in the Bibliothèque Royale, a widow is represented burning herself upon the funeral pile of her husband, and the flames of the funeral pyre are exactly similar to those rising from the head of the Persian king above-mentioned.

The "*lambere flamma comas*" of Virgil comes next in support of our theory; then the *sphere of fire* enveloping the soul of Germain, Bishop of Capua, and the soul of Saint Eloi; the face of Moses and the luminous horns which lighted his brow when he descended from Mount Sinai, after having conversed with God; God himself, who is like a furnace, and makes Sinai smoke and tremble at his presence;* and a number of texts, from which I quote the following:—"On a sudden the blessed Egidius was ravished in spirit, and he saw the soul of Consalvus, freed from its fleshy encumbrance, and shining with a dazzling radiance; it was carried away by the ministry of angels, across the immensity of space."†

Thus on the châsse of Mauzac, in Auvergne, the soul of St. Calminius, under the form of a naked infant, is borne away by two angels. The soul is inscribed within a perfect circle, cut into four lobes, two of which adapt themselves to the form of the shoulders, and two to that of the hips. A hand, the hand of God, appearing against a cruciform nimbus, is extended from the clouds to receive the approaching soul.

"On the side of the wall, within which repose the conse-

in the Bibliothèque Royale, and which was written and illuminated for an Ottoman princess. The *Medgialis*, contains a picture of a Holy Man with a nimbus of golden flame, with green and red threads, giving audience to two Demons. The "Livre des Augures," which is rich in pictures of Demons, contains one which will be given below, with a nimbus of flame like the Persian King, and the Holy Man in the *Medgialis*. These flame-formed nimbi resemble the peculiar configuration of the Turkish capitals; the same principle of decorative ornament is applied, but in the capitals, the base of the pyramid or the cone is truncated and reversed, in compliance with the law of construction. May not a Turkish column be said to resemble an immense torch, ignited at its capital?

* *Exodus*, xix., 18. "And Mount Sinai was altogether on a smoke, because the Lord descended upon it in fire; and the smoke thereof ascended as the smoke of a furnace, and the whole mount quaked greatly."

† "Vidit Consalvi animam, terrena mole jam deposita, fulgentissima luce radiantem, per immensi aeris hujus spatia angelorum manibus sursum ferri." (Bollandistes *Act. SS.* 3 vol. de Mai, p. 412. Vie du B. Egidius, prêcheur, né en Portugal, en 1190.)

crated remains of St. Anthony, a painter had traced the image of that saint. He was preparing to adorn the head of the figure with a crown of gold, and in the act of hollowing out the wall for that purpose,* when behold, through the openings he had made, there shone on a sudden an ineffable and precious light; it flashed upon the face of the painter. Unable to endure the intolerable radiance reflected in his eyes, he was on the point of falling to the ground; but, sustained by devotion, he persevered, and was enabled quickly to complete his work."† The radiation of the nimbus is here distinctly alluded to.

In Flodoard‡ we are told, "A ray of light descended from heaven to crown St. Remi, while a divine liquor shed itself upon his head, embalming it with celestial perfume. At this sight, the assembly of the bishops of the province proclaimed him without hesitation, and he was consecrated Bishop of Rheims." It would seem as if the Christian historian had borrowed from the text of Virgil, who informs us that the hair of the youthful Ascanius was caressed by a flame. In both instances the light prefigured a glorious destiny: royalty to Iülus (Ascanius), and almost the ecclesiastical dominion to St. Remi. Light descended from heaven in a similar manner upon the head of St. Léger, a celebrated bishop, who was martyred by the orders of Ebroïn, shining upon his forehead as in the centre of a circle.§

Glories reserved especially to God and to the Virgin

* This practice of modelling the nimbus before painting it is ancient and well attested, as is proved by the above extract. It is invariable in Greece and Italy, and may be seen in the Sainte-Chapelle, at Paris, on the reredos of St. Germer, and in the Church of St. Julien de Brioude.

† "In latere muri ubi sanctæ ejus (S. Antonini Abbatis Surrentini) reliquiæ continentur, in imagine ipsius designata, cum pictor coronam inauratam capiti circumponere pararet, parietem, prout necesse fuit, cavabat. Et ecce per rimas factus lux inæstimabilis et inenarrabilis subito emicans vultum dolantis faciebat. Quam per intolerabiles radios oculorum acie reverberata non sustinens, ruinam dare in terra minabatur, sed tamen pro devotionis intentione confirmatus, opus festinanter consummavit." (*Acta SS. Or. S. Bened.*, 5 vol., Vie de St. Antonin, Abbé de Sorrento, ver. 820; written by an anonymous writer of Sorrento.)

‡ *Histoire de l'Eglise de Reims*, liv. i.

§ Vie de St. Léger, évêque d'Autun, by an anonymous cotemporary, a monk. Translated by M. Guizot, *Collection des Historiens de France.*

derive their origin from two texts of the Apocalypse. The first relates to Christ descending to judge the world: "Behold he cometh with clouds: and every eye shall behold him, and they also that pierced him," exclaims St. John. "And in the midst of the seven candlesticks, one like unto the Son of Man, clothed with a garment down to the foot, and girt about the paps with a golden girdle. His head and his hairs were white like wool, as white as snow; and his eyes were as a flame of fire; and his feet like unto fine brass, as if they burned in a furnace; and his voice was as the sound of many waters. And he had in his right hand seven stars; and out of his mouth went a sharp two-edged sword; and his countenance was as the sun shineth in his strength." *

With regard to the Virgin Mary, of whom the woman of the Apocalypse, persecuted by the dragon, has been considered as a symbol, we have already seen that she had the sun for her garment, the moon for a footstool, and was crowned with the twelve stars.† Not the Apocalypse alone, but the Apocryphal books also, have furnished artists with the idea of the nimbus or aureole, that glorious radiance encircling the face and form of the Virgin. One of the most important of these books thus relates the particulars of her death and interment. Angels having placed in her coffin the mother of their Lord, the Apostles raised the precious burden upon their shoulders, and transported

* *Rev.* i., 7, 12—16.

† "Amicta sole, et luna sub pedibus et in capite ejus corona stellarum duodecim." *Apocalypse*, xii., 1. Amongst the charming figures representing the history of the Virgin, in the Church of Solesmes, an Eulogium of Mary is inscribed, beside the beast with seven heads. The termination of the panegyric is as follows:—"O tu mystica a Johanne visa mulier amicta sole, habens sub pedibus lunam, id est affectionibus per vanitatum contemptum dominari; et in capite tuo coronam stellarum duodecim moralium, seu omnium virtutum perfectionem, habensque in utero tum mentis, tum corporis, quasi speculo et rorida nube, sapientiam Dei se in eis efformantem." The woman of the Apocalypse is certainly employed to symbolise the Virgin Mary, as has been already pointed out in describing the painted window at Moulins. The manuscript of Herrade (*Hortus Deliciarum*) contains a most beautiful example of this mystical woman, against whom the beast vomits forth a stream. The woman is standing on the crescent of the moon, and her figure seems resting against the disk of the Sun; a smaller disk, a nimbus, cinctures her head, and she wears a Byzantine crown. This diadem is adorned with twelve stars, in the manner of diamonds. (*Peintures et Ornements des Manuscrits.*)

it to the tomb in the Valley of Gethsemane.* "Before the bier of the Virgin Mary was borne the miraculous palm, which diffused a brilliant light around. All nature seemed attentive to the spectacle. At the moment when the body was removed from the house, a brilliant cloud appeared in the air and placed itself before the Virgin, forming on her brow a transparent crown, resembling the aureole, or halo, which surrounds the rising moon."†

Nothing can be more resplendent than the descriptions contained in the texts quoted above; nothing can more decisively prove that the glory is light embodied in painting or sculpture. Nothing in created nature is more brilliant than the sun, the moon, the stars, white wool, snow, gold, polished steel, brass or gold melted in a furnace. For this reason the monuments themselves display aureoles, channelled by streaks of flame, within which God and the Virgin are enclosed. Sometimes the entire glory is formed of flame, and rays emanate from every point as from a common centre.‡

The eucharist in our churches appears luminous in the bosom of those sacred vessels (ostensoirs) of gold which are displayed on high festival days. From the circumference of these metallic aureoles, called also suns, innumerable rays are seen to emanate, in precisely the same manner as from the aureoles already given, surrounding images of God and the Virgin. Even the cross, painted on a gold ground, as in the mosaics of Italy and Greece, sheds light on all sides, being formed of rays of precious stones, or of stars, whence its name, "crux gemmata," "crux stellata." Dante gives the following description of the living cross and the crucified, whom he had seen in paradise:—

Qui vince la memoria mia lo 'ngegno;
 Che 'n quella Croce lampeggiava Cristo
 Sì ch 'io non so trovare esemplo degno.

---

* See the bas-reliefs enchased in the north side wall of Notre Dame de Paris. The Death, Funeral, Assumption, and Coronation of the Virgin, are there sculptured in detail. It is a translation into stone of the Apocryphal book above mentioned.

† "De Transitu B. Mariæ Virginis, ap. Fabricium *Codex Apocryphorum Novi Testamenti.*" See also the Apocryphal books collected by Thilo.

‡ "And the sight of the glory of the Lord was like devouring fire." *Exodus*, xxiv., 17.

Ma chi prende sua croce e segue Cristo
  Ancor mi scuserà di quel ch'io lasso,
  Vedendo in quell' albor balenar Cristo.
Di corno in corno, e tra la cima e'l basso
  Si movean lumi scintillando forte
  Nel congiungersi insieme e nel trapasso.
Così si veggion qui diritte e torte
  Veloci e tarde rinnovando vista
  Le minuzie de' corpi lunghe e corte
Muoversi per lo raggio, onde si lista
  Tal volta l'ombra, che per sua difesa,
  La gente con ingegno ed arte acquista.*

Having named Dante, whose writings comprehend the entire written art of Christendom, just as the imitative art seems concentrated in the cathedral of Rheims, it will be well to make such further extracts from his sublime poem, as will further illustrate the subject under consideration. The Paradiso is replete with light, encircling every saint, precisely in the same manner as on earth; the soul is enveloped by the material frame, or rather, all those saints, the blessed Virgin, and the Apostles; confessors and martyrs are but lights reciprocally kindled and inflamed. The great poet says, for example:

Quale ne' plenilunii, e ne' sereni
  Trivia ride tra le Ninfe eterne
  Che dipingono 'l ciel per tutti i seni.
Vid' io sopra migliaia di lucerne
  Un Sol che tutte quante l'accendea
  Come fa 'l nostro le viste superne;

---

* "Here memory mocks the toil of genius. Christ
Beamed on that cross; and pattern fails me now.
But whoso takes his cross, and follows Christ,
Will pardon me for that I leave untold;
When in the fleckered dawning he shall spy
The glitterance of Christ. From horn to horn,
And 'tween the summit and the base did move
Lights, scintillating, as they met and pass'd.
Thus oft are seen with ever-changeful glance,
Straight or athwart, now rapid and now slow,
The atomies of bodies, long or short,
To move along the sunbeam, whose slant line
Checkers the shadow interposed by art
Against the noontide heat."

Cary's Dante, Paradise, c°. xiv., l. 103.

E per la viva luce trasparea,
La lucente sustanzia tanto chiaro
Che lo mio viso non la sostenea.*

Dante had already said, (in the preceding canto), speaking of various saints,

* * Vidi cento sperule che'nsieme
Più s'abbellivan con mutui rai.
* * * * * * *
E la maggiore, e la più luculenta,
Di quelle margherite innanzi fessi
Per far di se la voglia mia contenta.†

If we turn from poetry to history, we shall there find, that Jesus at his transfiguration was surrounded by a glory; this glory was formed of light, and has been so represented by Christian artists in paintings of that subject. What says the Evangelist? "Jesus taketh with him Peter, James, and John his brother, and bringeth them up into a high mountain apart; and was transfigured before them; and his face did shine as the sun, and his raiment was white as the light. And, behold, there appeared unto them Moses and Elias talking with him." (Matt. xvii. 1—3.)

"But Peter and they that were with him were heavy with sleep; and when they were awake they saw his glory, and the two men that stood with him."‡ (Luke ix. 32.)

* "As in the calm, full moon, when Trivia smiles
In peerless beauty, 'mid the eternal nymphs,
That paint through all its gulfs the blue profound;
In bright pre-eminence so saw I there
O'er million lamps a sun, from whom all drew
Their radiance, as from ours the starry train;
And through the living light, so lustrous glowed
The substance, that my ken endured it not."
Cary's Dante, Paradise, c°. xxiii., l. 25.

† ——————— "I saw
A hundred little spheres, that fairer grew
By interchange of splendour. I remain'd
As one, who fearful of o'er much presuming
Abates in him the keenness of desire,
Nor dares to question; when, amid those pearls,
One largest and most lustrous onward drew,
That it might yield contentment to my wish."
Cary's Dante, Paradise, c°. xxii., l. 23.

‡ The face and brow are illumined by the nimbus, the vestments are

This transfiguration, changing the Son of Man into a resplendent Deity, recals to the mind those words of Solomon, which indeed have already been applied to Christ by all the fathers of the Church, beginning with St. Paul: "For she [wisdom] is the breath of the power of God, and a pure influence flowing from the glory of the Almighty; therefore can no defiled thing fall into her. For she is the brightness of the everlasting light, the unspotted mirror of the power of God and the image of his goodness." (Book of Wisdom, vii. 25, 26.)

St. Paul, in allusion to this passage, calls Jesus "the brightness of His glory." * Combining all the facts here quoted, with the monuments, of which engravings have been given, in which Christ is seen shining in the midst of an aureole, whether circular, oval, elliptical, or of the quatrefoil form, we can no longer doubt the nature of the aureole to be igneous, and that the flame, which under various forms surrounds the head or the entire person, is a special attribute, expressive of the divinity of the Creator, the sanctity of angels, the virtue of the Virgin, and of innocent souls, creatures who, more than any other created beings, assimilate with the Deity. I am, therefore, justified in my assertion, that the nature of both the nimbus and the aureole is that of light; that the nimbus forms a luminous adornment for the head; and the aureole is the dazzling garment of the body. It seems a fine idea, to have selected fire, as the chosen attribute of human power; the sign of apotheosis, and the symbol of divine omnipotence. Fire is the strongest, the most mysterious and irresistible of all elements; it is thus defined by Dionysius the Areopagite:

"Fire exists in everything, penetrates into everything, is received by everything. Although it sheds a full light, still it is at the same time hidden. Its presence is unknown, unless some material be given to induce the exertion of its power. It is invisible, as well as unquenchable, and it has the faculty of transforming into itself everything it touches. It renovates everything by its vital heat; it illu-

embraced within the aureole, and the whole forms a complete glory. See St. Matthew, xvii.; St. Mark ix. 3, and St. Luke, ix. 29—32.

* *Hebrews*, i. 3: "Splendor gloriæ."

mines everything by its flashing beams; it can neither be confined nor intermingled; it divides, and yet it is immutable. It always ascends . . . it is constantly in motion . . . . it moves by its own will and power, and sets in motion everything around it. It has the power of seizing, but cannot itself be taken. It needs no aid. It increases silently, and breaks forth in majesty upon all. It generates, it is powerful, invisible, and omnipresent. If neglected, its existence might be forgotten; but on friction being applied to certain substances it flashes out again, like the sword from its scabbard, shines resplendent by its own natural properties, and soars into the air. . . . .

"Many other powers may yet be noticed as belonging to it. For this reason theologians have asserted that celestial substances were formed of fire, and thus created as nearly as possible in the image of God."*

The Deity would thus seem to be only an immense furnace, breathing upon Adam, and infusing into his body a soul, or divine ray; an emanation from his holy light descended in tongues of flame upon the Apostles. He is a brasier of living fire shedding forth upon all his saints an aureole, which seems as it were to be a breathing from himself. The sun, in short, becomes the finite and visible image of that infinite and invisible flame which constitutes the divine essence. Power, therefore, a member severed as it were from the divinity, ought to be expressed materially by a flame, the composition of the divine substance.

A few words must be added in explanation of the last mentioned idea.

God has no material body: the Deity is purely spiritual. Whenever men have desired to give a sensible or palpable existence to Him, who is immaterial and invisible, it has been thought fitting to invest Him with a body, formed of the most subtle and etherial elements. If this body of man be animated clay, his soul, made in the image of God, and in truth the very breathing of divinity, participates in the nature of fire and flame. Fire, which is one of the visible manifestations of electricity, enters into the formation of the body of God, as bones and sinews do into that of man. For this reason God, in the Bible, in the gospel, and

* *De Cœlesti Hierarchia,* xv. 193, 194, édition d 'Anvers, 1634, vol. i.

in Dante's "Divina Commedia," is constantly described as surrounded by fire, flame, or rays issuing from his body, as water is thrown upwards by a fountain. Under his visible form God is a light: his most constant natural symbol, that under which he is in the East most frequently adored, is the sun, the centre, to mankind of all light and radiance. When our Saviour says, "I am the light of the world," (St. John viii., 12; xii., 46,)* the words are to be taken as much in the literal as in the figurative sense.

In the East, kings, emperors, and prophets are considered, not merely as delegates of Divinity, in which light they are regarded amongst us, but as emanations from the Deity, as the immediate sons of God, and almost as being themselves incarnate gods. Carrying out this idea, the sun being adored as the visible symbol of God, these same kings, emperors, and prophets are hence regarded as descendants of the sun. Such are Zoroaster among the Persians, Manou among the Indians, Confucius among the Chinese, and Hermes among the Egyptians.

In those royal scrolls with which the temples and obelisks of Egypt are covered, and which have been correctly deciphered, the Pharaohs are styled sons of the sun, sons of God. Such also are the Persian Magi.

God being light, and the sun His image, the sons of God, or of the sun, the kings of Persia and Egypt, the emperors of China, and possibly even the emperors of Constantinople, might be supposed to inherit from God their Father some share of that light of which He is himself composed. God and the sun both shed forth rays, and their children may be expected to do so likewise, and therefore wear the nimbus, the material form of that radiation.

Amongst the colder people of the West, kings do indeed reign by the grace of God, but they are not regarded as the sons of God, and their heads are therefore rarely adorned by the nimbus.† Saints, on the contrary, being considered, from their virtues and actions, as immediate emanations from Divinity, are appropriately decorated with a nimbus,

* "Ego sum lux mundi. Ego lux in mundum veni, ut omnis qui credit in me in tenebris non maneat."

† It must be observed that in a gallery of kings (from which we have extracted figures of Charlemagne and Henry the Lame), painted on glass, and

although it is always less luminous, less rich, than that of God himself. In addition to this, they are often also enveloped in the glory of God, which lights them up with dazzling radiance. Thus in our own cathedrals, the western porch is frequently pierced by an immense circular opening, to which is given the name of rose window. The bay of the window is filled with coloured glass, arranged in four, five, or six concentric circles, diminishing in extent in proportion to their proximity to the centre. God, seated on his throne, or the Virgin holding in her arms the infant Saviour, shines resplendent in the central circle. A cordon of angels surrounds the central group; then the patriarchs; after them apostles, martyrs, and confessors, each in separate rings or "cordons; lastly the external cordon or outer edge of the circumference is filled by virgins. All these persons are framed in medallions of glass, as transparent and luminous as the saints themselves, and resembling circles of rubies, emeralds, or sapphires, studded with diamonds. These rose windows are glories, embracing an entire world, encircling a multitude instead of girdling a single individual. The same may be observed of sculptures: the vaultings of porches are divided into several concentric semi-circles, into several rings or cordons, each restricted to one particular body of saints. Dante has himself given the name of "rose" to those circular expansions of light, in which the saints are represented ranged in a divine effulgence, emanating from

in the north side aisle of the Cathedral of Strasbourg, all these kings, without exception, have the nimbus. It seems fitting that Henry, who was a Saint, should wear the nimbus; it may also be correct for Charlemagne himself, who was canonised (although by an anti-Pope, it is true), to be thus distinguished; but the nimbus cannot be given, as a symbol of holiness, to Charles Martel, who lavished the wealth and offices of the clergy on his brutal and libertine soldiery. The legend relates, that for these his ewil deeds, Martel, after death, was devoured in his tomb by the devil. It cannot certainly be held to be symbolic of holiness when worn by the terrible Frederic Barbarossa, who was excommunicated, who created anti-Popes, led a scandalous life, and is said to have been the author of an impious, if not atheistical work. Yet both Charles Martel and Barbarossa, in the painted glass at Strasbourg, are represented with very large rich nimbi; they must, therefore, have been decorated with that mark of honour rather as political chiefs, delegates of God, emanations of the eternal sun, than in the character of Saints. This curious circumstance would alone suffice to prove these windows to be Byzantine, even were not that fact distinctly proved by the costume of these emperors and kings, from the crown of the head down to the very sandals.

the centre, which is filled by the splendour and brilliancy of God himself. I must claim permission to close this paragraph with an extract from the "Paradiso" of Dante, which will suffice to prove that the nimbus, aureole, and glory are images of light reduced to form by the pencil:—

"E vidi lume in forma di riviera
Fulvido di fulgori, intra due rive
Dipinte di mirabil primavera
Di tal fiumana uscian faville vive
E d'ogni parte si mettean ne' fiori
Quasi rubini ch' oro circonscrive;
"Poi come inebriate dagli odori
Riprofondavan se nel miro gurge
E s'una entrava, un' altra usciane fuori.
* * * * *
* * * "Il fiume e li topazii
Ch' entrano ed escono, e'l rider dell' erbe.
Son di lor vero ombriferi prefazii;

says Beatrice to Dante. The poet adds:—

* * * "Chinandomi all' onda,
E sì come di lei bevve la gronda
Delle palpebre mie, così mi parve
Di sua lunghezza divenuta tonda.
Por come gente stata sotto larve
Che pare altro che prima se si sveste
La sembianza non sua, in che disparve;
Cosi mi si cambiaro in maggior feste
Li fiori e le faville, sì ch' io vidi
Ambo le corti del Ciel manifeste."*

The stream having thus become round, and the surface, which at first was long, having been gathered up into a disk,

* ——— ——— "I look'd,
And in the likeness of a river, saw
Light flowing, from whose amber-seeming waves
Flash'd up effulgence, as they glided on
'Twixt banks, on either side, painted with spring,
Incredible how fair; and from the tide
There ever and anon outstarting flew
Sparkles instinct with life; and in the flowers
Did set them, like to rubies chased in gold;
Then, as if drunk with odours, plunged again
Into the wondrous flood, from which as one
Re-entered, still another rose.
* * * *
This stream; and these, forth issuing from its gulf
And diving back, a living topaz each;

the poet goes on to relate what he perceived in the *Rose*, and continues :—

"In forma dunque di candida rosa
  Mi si mostrava la milizia santa
  Che nel suo sangue Cristo fece sposa;
Ma l'altra, che volando vede e canta
  La gloria di Colui che l'innamora,
  E la bontà, che la fece cotanta;
Sì come schiera d'api, che s'infiora
  Una fiata, ed altra si ritorna
  Là dove il suo lavoro s'insapora,
Nel gran fior discendeva, che s'adorna
  Di tante foglie, e quindi risaliva,
  Là, dove il suo amor sempre soggiorna
Le facce tutte avean di fiamma viva,
  E l'ali d'oro, e l'altro tanto bianco
  Che nulla neve a quel termine arriva.
Quando scendean nel fior, di banco in banco
  Porgevan della pace e dell' ardore
  Ch' egli acquistavan, ventilando il fianco.
Nè 'l interporsi tra 'l disopra e 'l fiore,
  Di tanta moltitudine volante
  Impediva la vista e lo splendore;
Che la luce divina è penetrante
  Per l'universo, secondo ch' è degno
  Sì che nulla le puote essere ostante." *

With all this laughter on its bloomy shores,
Are but a preface, shadowy of the truth
They emblem; not that in themselves, the things
Are crude ; but on thy part is the defect,
For that thy views not yet aspire so high,
  * * * *
——————— bending me
To make the better mirrors of mine eyes
In the refining wave; and as the eaves
Of mine eyelids did drink of it, forthwith
Seem'd it unto me turn'd from length to round.
Then as a troop of maskers when they put
Their vizors off, look other than before;
The counterfeited semblance thrown aside ;
So into greater jubilee were changed
Those flowers and sparkles, and distinct I saw
Before me, either court of Heaven displayed."
Cary's Dante, Paradise, canto xxx., l. 61, 58.

* "In fashion as a snow-white rose, lay then
Before my view the saintly multitude,

OF THE GLORY: ITS ORIGIN AND NATIVE COUNTRY.

Nothing now remains to be inquired into but the origin of the glory, and the place and exact period of its birth.

It is impossible to speak with certainty of the epoch at which the use of the glory was first introduced; but it appears to be at least as ancient as the most ancient system of religion. Both the nimbus and aureole are found represented on those primitive Hindoo monuments, which are considered to be among the earliest existing in the world.

The Egyptians were not strangers to the use of the glory; for the large lenticular disk surmounting the heads of several Egyptian divinities, certainly resembles a nimbus: * it is usually painted either in white or red (the most luminous of all colours), and is peculiarly well

Which in his own blood Christ espoused. Meanwhile
That other host that soar aloft to gaze
And celebrate his glory, whom they love
Hover'd around; and like a troop of bees,
Amid the vernal sweets alighting now,
Now, clustering, where their fragrant labour glows,
Flew downward to the mighty flower, or rose
From the redundant petals, streaming back
Unto the stedfast dwelling of their joy.
Faces had they of flame, and wings of gold;
The rest was whiter than the driven snow;
And, as they flitted down into the flower,
From range to range, fanning their plumy loins,
Whisper'd the peace and ardour, which they won
From that soft winnowing. Shadow none, the vast
Interposition of such numerous flights
Cast, from above, upon the flower, or view,
Obstructed aught. For, through the universe
Wherever merited, celestial light
Glides freely and no obstacle presents."

Cary's Dante, Paradise, c°. xxxi, l. i.

* Ciampini (*Vetera Monimenta*, pars 2). "Hunc orbem Egyptii in summo capite simulacrorum suorum locabant . . . . . ab illis Romanos sumpsisse licet suspicari, et variasse, habita decoris ratione, quod capiti cui divinum quid inesse putabant, eo situ corona aptaretur." The Romans have thus transformed a globe into a disk.

defined, and well coloured, on an Egyptian painting in the Musée of the Louvre.*

It has been remarked above, that in a fresco in the Church at Montoire (Fig. 14), the Saviour bears on his head a sort of sphere, or Egyptian disk, divided into circles, like those on the globe of the world. The Egyptian Harpocrates is constantly figured with a nimbus.†

The nimbus was in frequent use, also, among the Greeks and Romans. In fact, in the paintings found at Herculaneum, Circe, appearing to Ulysses, is depicted wearing a nimbus precisely as the Virgin Mary and saints are usually represented in Christian art. The sorceress is thus drawn, adorned with the glory, at the moment when Ulysses, sword in hand, attempts to force her to restore his companions, who had been transformed by her sorceries into hogs, to their proper form. A Cassandra and a Priam; three guests seated at a table, in a triclinium,‡ all of which are painted in the Virgil of the Vatican; § a woman on a Greek vase, engraved in the "Antiquité Expliquée" of Montfaucon; various personages painted on Greek vases, in the collection of the Louvre; the bust of the Emperor Claudius;|| the Emperor Trajan sculptured¶ on the arch of Constantine,

* Musée Charles X., salles Égyptiennes.

† *Antiquité Expliquée*, tom. iv.

‡ *Antiquité Expliquée*, tom. v., p. 113.

§ Montfaucon (*Antiquité Expliquée*, tom. xiii., pl. 35, p. 84,) takes this woman for Proserpine; everything concurs to prove that she is intended for Diana, or, rather, for the Moon, the Goddess of Night. See, in fact, Seroux d'Agincourt (*Recueil de Fragments de Sculpture antique en terre cuite*, pl. 28); and in *L' Atlas Allemand de la Symbolique de Creuzer*, pl. 44, a representation of the Sun and Moon, each in a car drawn by four horses, and rising from the sea, to give light to the world. The Moon, whose horses are guided by the winged genius of Sleep, has the same nimbus, the same tournure and costume, and is of the same age as the Proserpine of Montfaucon. The Sun has a nimbus like the Moon, and a profusion of short rays emanate in the form of elongated pearls, from several circular cordons or rings. See, again, in the Musée Charles X., salles Étrusques, one of the large Greek vases placed on a marble table in the centre of the hall.

|| *Antiquité Expliquée*, tom. v. p. 162.

¶ The arch of Constantine is enriched with the spoils of that of Trajan, who is represented in bas-relief offering a sacrifice to Apollo. Trajan has around his head a circle of luminous gold, such as was formerly placed by painters on the heads of our own Saints. The Romans also gave it to their gods and

in three different places; the Valentinian, found in the eighteenth century in the bed of the Arve; * the Emperors Maurice and Phocas, engraved upon their medals; an immense number of figures, both Greek and Roman, representing the sun, under the form of a young man, and the moon under that of a woman; the different constellations; the Apollo on the medals of Rhodes; the radiating sun upon the Roman "as;" † the astronomical divinities of the planisphere of Bianchini; ‡ the other gods of the ancient Pantheon; and Pan, the chief of those gods, leading on the Satyrs in their dance, and who is called the luminous Pan; §—all the figures just enumerated, whether belonging to history, allegory, or religious myths, have a nimbus exactly resembling that which adorns the head of John the Baptist, of angels, and of Christ. Lastly, Servius, as has been seen above, asserts the nimbus to be a luminous fluid, surrounding the head or person of the gods. Virgil himself referred to the nimbus, when he spoke of the flame

emperors; this circle was called nimbus. Pliny says, with respect to this nimbus, that Trajan deserved, but that Caligula had usurped it. (*Antiquité Expliquée*, vol. vi., pl. 179 and 183.)

* On a discus of silver found in the ancient bed of the Arve, near Geneva, in 1721, Valentinian is depicted with a nimbus: he is making largesses to his soldiers, and holds in his hand a figure of Victory, winged, and with the feet resting on a globe. (*Antiquité Expliquée*, tom. xiv., pl. 28, p. 51.)

† *Antiquité Expliquée*, vol. xiii., pl. 47.

‡ Musée du Louvre, salle de la Melpomène. This relic was found upon the Aventine Mount, in 1705; it is called the planisphere of Bianchini, because first published by that learned Italian astronomer. The Pagan gods engraved upon it have their heads encircled by the nimbus. It presents Egyptian figures of the Décans, subaltern deities, to each of whom Egyptian astrology assigned the government of ten days in each month: thus placing three Décans under the influence of each of the twelve signs, they obtain thirty-six Décans. The Zodiac, in the Cathedral of Athens, has thirty-five figures only; one is wanting, and, what is more worthy of remark, the others have no nimbus. It is singular, that the Egyptian deities in the planisphere of Bianchini have no nimbus, while it is given to the corresponding Greek deities. Can it be possible, that notwithstanding the presence of the globe of which we have spoken, the nimbus was unknown to the Egyptians, and in use only amongst the Greeks, who must, in that case, have derived it from the Hindoos? Every form of the nimbus is found in India; the aureole also is there seen, at least in its rudimentary state.

§ *Antiquité Expliquée*, vol. xi., pl. 55, p. 166. The Pan has two horns on his brow, and wears a nimbus, formed of numerous short rays, arranged in a circle. All the Roman nimbi vary greatly in form.

descending from heaven upon the head of the little Iülus, as if to caress and kiss his hair. We subjoin the passage of Virgil to which allusion has already been made; it perfectly explains the nature of the aureole, and recals the two luminous horns which Moses had upon his brow,* and that resplendent countenance by which the Hebrews were dazzled and alarmed, when their lawgiver descended from Mount Sinai after his long conference with the Deity :—

> "Ecce levis summo de vertice visus Iüli
> Fundere lumen apex, tactuque innoxia molli
> Lambere flamma comas, et circum tempora pasci.
> Nos pavidi trepidare metu, crinemque flagrantem
> Excutere, et sanctos restinguere fontibus ignes.†

The aged Anchises, who was versed in Egyptian lore and oriental symbolism, far from being alarmed at the sight, like the other persons who were present, was filled with great joy. He raises his eyes and hands to heaven, imploring Jupiter to grant that the happy fortune presaged by this augury may be realised. Anchises well knew that that aureole of light, or terrestrial apotheosis, announced that his grandson should be the future sovereign of a great kingdom and the founder of a potent empire.‡

The native country of the glory will be found in the East;

* "Videbant faciem egredientis Moysis esse CORNUTAM." *Exodus*, xxxiv., 35.

† *Æneid*, book 2nd. In the manuscript Virgil, in the Vatican, from which Seroux d'Agincourt (*Histoire de l' Art par les Monuments*, pl. 23, de l'Atlas de la Peinture,) has had several miniatures engraved: the head of Ascanius is represented as surrounded with flames, and the terrified domestics are endeavouring to extinguish with water the miraculous conflagration, while old Anchises, on the contrary, is seen filled with joy, addressing to Jupiter his fervent prayers and thanksgivings. There is in the same manuscript a miniature of the Sun, rising to light the toils of the husbandmen and shepherds. The Sun is in the form of a young man, beardless. From the head of that personified star rise pencilled streaks of light, linked together by a circular line, the circle of the nimbus; but these luminous plumes are powerful, and dart beyond the circle. The figure of the Sun is similar in every respect to that of Christ (Fig. 8); the only difference is in the number of the rays, the nimbus of the Sun projecting five clusters of light, that of Christ only three. (*Histoire de l' Art par les Monuments, Peintures*, pl. 20.)

‡ It would seem that Virgil borrowed his poetical fiction from the pages of history; for the future elevation of the young slave, who subsequently

the glory comes from the East, where light also has its birth; *ex Oriente lux*. Not only because the glory is a material image of light, but more especially because it shows itself there much earlier than with us, and is also much more frequently employed there than in the West.

Both the nimbus and the aureole appeared in the East long before the rise of Christianity;* they rose with the religions of India, Persia, and Egypt; with Brama, Siva, and Vishnoo; with Maya, Sacti, and Devaki, and all the male and female pantheon of India, with Ormuzd and Zoroaster; with Iris, Horus, and Osiris; and with the astronomical decans of Egypt and of Greece. The Christian religion did not invent, but appropriated that symbolic figure. Thus much for the period of antiquity, properly so called. In more recent times, in the period dating from our own era, the earliest and most constant use of the nimbus may still be traced to the East, to Asia, and Constantinople.

M. de Saulcy gives an engraving of a silver medal of the Emperor Anastasius, who reigned from the year 491 to 518.† The emperor is standing, holding a globe in his left hand, and with a nimbus. Before and after Anastasius is a con-

became king, under the name of Servius Tullius, was announced in a similar manner by a flame encircling his head. Servius, the commentator, makes the following curious observation upon the "lambere flamma comas" of Virgil: "Item hoc quoque de igni [*sic*] ad Servium Tullium pertinet. Nam cum Tarquinius cepisset Vericulanam civitatem, ex captiva quadam in domo ejus natus est Servius Tullius Hostilius; qui cum obdormisset, caput ejus subito flamma corripuit. Quam cum vellent restinguere, Tanaquil regis uxor, auguriorum perita, intelligens augurium, prohibuit. Flamma puerum cum somno deseruit. Unde intellexit eum clarum fore usque ad ultimam vitam." (Servius, *Commentaire sur le Livre* 11 *de Virgile*, p. 263 of the 4°. edition, printed at Geneva, 1636.)

Compare the Roman poet and Eastern historian with the Western tradition of St. Remi and St. Leger, whose future fate was in like manner foretold by flame descending upon their heads; the stories are identical. Remark also the expressions employed by Servius, the commentator, who says that the light with which the head of the young slave was encircled announced that his whole life should be brilliant (clarum) and illustrious. The material radiance was a presage of the ideal splendour, and the nimbus became actually the image of an illustrious destiny and the emblem of light.

* See "L 'Antiquité Expliquée," "Les Religions de l 'Antiquité," "Le Planisphère du Louvre," "L 'Atlas Allemand de la Symbolique de Creuzer," &c.

† *Essai de Classification des Suites monétaires Byzantines*. Metz, 1838, pl. 1, fig. 3.

tinued series, not only of emperors, but also of empresses, all adorned with the nimbus.* The nimbus is found in all modern antiquities of the East, if that expression may be used.† It is never seen in the West, and in Italy, upon the sarcophagi, which are the most ancient of all Christian monuments. On them, neither God nor the apostles, nor any of the saints have the nimbus; and yet at that very period it was given to Constantine and Helena, to Anastasius and Justina, to Justinian and Theodora, Tiberius Constantine, and his wife Anastasia. In the most ancient frescos, and even the earliest mosaics, the nimbus is not ordinarily given to divine or holy persons.‡ If ever seen on mosaics which appear to date from the sixth century, as on those in the churches of San Vitale, and Santo Appollinario-in-Classe at Ravenna, § its appearance may be accounted for by the fact that those mosaics were executed by eastern, or rather Byzantine artists, and that they represent Justinian and Theodora, who reigned in Constantinople.

Historical facts and ancient monuments concur in demonstrating the nimbus to be of Eastern origin. This assertion, supported as it is by history and archæology, may be yet further confirmed by physical facts and observations founded on the nature of the soil in those regions.

That the nimbus is a luminous fluid has been abundantly proved. In the fifteenth century, with us, this mystic headtire, adorning the heads of the saints, appears, in the monuments cited, like an expansion or unfolding of flamboyant rays, or the beams of a glowing sun. Now every image, allegory, symbol, or metaphor even, must be borrowed from the imagery, or, to speak more correctly, from the reality of nature. The ideal is transformed into the cor-

* The Emperors of Constantinople were always figured with a nimbus, up to the taking of that city by Mahomet II., 1453. (*Monuments de la Monarch. Franc.* discours préliminaire.)

† *Constantinopolis Christiana,* by Du Cange; *Vetera Monimenta,* by Ciampini.

‡ See Bosio, *Roma Sotter.*; *Vetera Monimenta,* by Ciampini, *Thesaurus Veterum Diptychorum,* Gori; *Vasi Antichi di Vitro,* by Buonarotti, *passim.* An exception in the case of frescos has been noticed above.

§ See M. de Sommerard, *Album des Arts au Moyen Age.*

poreal. I feel therefore convinced, that the nimbus was first attached to the heads of intelligent and virtuous persons, from its analogy with that radiation which we may observe to be exhaled by natural objects in the most mature and energetic periods of the year. In summer, during the hours of noon-tide heat, everything radiates in the fields; all nature emits light; a brilliant vapour rises from the earth, floating around the ears of corn, and the topmost branches of the trees. This flame plays around plants, like that which caressed the hair of the youthful Iülus, or the young Servius Tullius, or which descended on the heads of Saint Remi, and Saint Léger. Every branch and flower, every group of trees, the summit of each distant hill, or rocky eminence, seems gilded by an aureole—a kind of natural, and universal nimbus. Now what with us is but an accidental appearance,—what in our climate is seen but rarely, at certain seasons, and on certain sultry days of intense heat, is in the East of habitual occurrence.

Summer, in the East, is, comparatively speaking, eternal; and the heat during every period of the year is intense. Consequently, objects emit light at all times; plants and animals, houses and men, all are encompassed by a flickering flame-like luminosity of atmosphere.

"Aderbijan, a large country in Persia, is famous for its sources of naphtha, and the soil is charged with resinous substances. Bitumen there floats upon the surface of the lakes, and frequently when, in the midst of a gloomy night it becomes ignited, is seen to escape suddenly in brilliant flame, and the spectacle thus afforded is well calculated to exalt the imagination. Men who were still in a state of semi-barbarism, and little capable of tracing to physical causes the origin of that flame, naturally saw in it an immediate manifestation of divinity.*" In Arabia Petræa, God appointed a column of fire to guide the Israelites into the promised land, where Sodom and Gomorrah had, at an earlier period, been engulfed in a lake of fire. In Egypt, and in Africa, the desert is transformed into pools of fire; the sand boils in the plains, like water in a cauldron; and the Saracens of Tunis when fighting against St. Louis flung handfuls of

* *Religions de l' Antiquité*, vol. i., p. 319.

earth into the faces of the crusaders, just as in our own times red-hot balls and shells are used. Fire and light are in the East what humid vapours and fogs are to us—a permanent phenomenon, endowed with a fearful power.

It is not then surprising that the idea of illumining with a nimbus the heads of distinguished persons, of strong men, of men of genius, or of holiness, should have arisen in that country earlier than in the West. It seems very natural that a phenomenon so usual and constant should have been honoured by art, and that a reality of every day should, in the East, have been invested with a metaphorical signification.

THE CHARACTER OF THE GLORY.

Not only was the nimbus adopted at a much earlier period in the East than in the West, but it was also much more lavishly given there than with us; in fact, except in the few rare instances about to be noticed, its use here is restricted entirely to God and the saints; in the East few heads are without it. Every emperor, every king, prince, and even their consorts, are dignified with this glorious attribute: it seems inherent in the persons themselves. Justinian, who is not a saint, has a nimbus. In the Musée of the Louvre* there is a carved cup of Arabic workmanship, which was formerly kept in the chapel of the Chateau de Vincennes. The figures on this vase represent hunters, in pursuit of stags and wild beasts; all these huntsmen without exception are invested with the nimbus, and what is even more remarkable, those who appear to be the chiefs amongst them are encircled, together with their horses, by a large circular aureole. The beautiful vases, procured from China and Japan, which we see exposed for sale in old curiosity shops, often exhibit figures of persons of secular character adorned with the nimbus.

It sometimes even surrounds the head of those monstrous and fantastic beasts, which seem to growl at us from our brilliant porcelain, and bear so strong a resemblance to Christian devils, or the open-mouthed gurgoyles of our

* Salle des Bijoux.

cathedrals. In the Buddhist volumes belonging to the Bibliothèque Royale, some good and even evil genii, are honoured with the nimbus. A Greek psalter with many curious and beautiful miniatures (No. 139 in the Bibliothèque Royale) contains a number of different figures, all adorned with the nimbus. First come the prophets, Isaiah, Jonah, Nathan, Samuel, Moses, and the prophetess Anna. There is little in this to excite astonishment, for the same individuals frequently have a nimbus in the West also,* and although not generally styled saints by the Latin Church, yet possess all the attributes of true holiness; but each historical subject in the manuscript is accompanied by allegorical personages, serving to explain the history related. Thus beside King David stand figures of Wisdom and Prophecy (Σοφια, Προφητια), personified by two tall genii, clad like women, giving inspiration to the Poet and Prophet-King.† In the same manner, David repentant is attended by the genius of Repentance; when killing the lion who had attacked his lambs, he is assisted by the powerful genius of Strength. Prayer assists Hezekiah in his entreaties for a prolonged life, and Night watches the disasters of Pharaoh, who is being drowned in his passage through the Red Sea. All these genii, who in other respects have the antique form, are adorned with a nimbus—blue, yellow, red, or rose-colour. The kings themselves, both David and Hezekiah, wear the nimbus; so even has Saul, a king who was guilty of suicide; and, what is still more surprising,

* The Cathedral of St. Nizier de Troyes; the beautiful Church of St. Urbain, in the same city; the north porch of the Cathedral of Chartres; and some other churches, contain figures of Prophets and Prophetesses executed in painting and sculpture, all invested with the nimbus. At Chartres, Aaron, Moses, and Melchizedek may be observed with the nimbus. A proof still more convincing is furnished by the painted glass window in the same cathedral, representing the History of Roland and the expedition of Charlemagne into Spain, in which both Charlemagne and Roland are invested with the nimbus. It is true that Sarius, "Vitæ Sanctorum," enrols Roland and Oliver among the saints, and consecrates to them one chapter of his book, under the title of "De Sanctis Rolando et Oliviero, e sociis eorum." Yet St. Roland is not named in the Martyrology. The Cathedral of Chartres presents many ascertained and singular points of affinity with the East, which well deserve to be examined.

† See an engraving of this subject in the History of the Holy Ghost, Fig. 110.

Pharaoh,—the impious king of Egypt, at the moment when he is engulfed in the abysses of the Red Sea,—has a nimbus, and even a golden nimbus resembling that of David himself, or Hezekiah; finally the terrible King Herod, that monster by whose command all the young children in his dominions who had been born at the same time with our Saviour were slain, is invested with a nimbus in a mosaic in the church of Santa Maria Maggiore, the work of a Greek artist. And the scene in which he is introduced is precisely that of the massacre of the innocents! It cannot therefore be denied that the nimbus is most prodigally given by the Byzantines,* and indeed in every region of the East.

The nimbus is not there, as amongst us, exclusively the symbol of holiness; it is also, and more particularly, an attribute of power generally, or of virtue, taking that word in its most enlarged signification, which, properly speaking, is that of strength. The nimbus is not there confined to the qualities of the soul, but is also extended to express physical strength and vigour, intellectual power, and authority, however acquired, and whether employed for good or evil purposes. This assertion is supported in a very curious manner by several monuments of western art, those most especially in which we trace any influence of Byzantine or oriental genius. Take for example the parable of the wise and the foolish virgins, sculptured in the Cathedral of Rheims. The wise virgins have the nimbus, to which they seem justly entitled, and they are contantly figured with that attribute, as having been admitted by Christ into paradise: but at Rheims, the foolish virgins also have the nimbus—a singular circumstance, and very rarely to be observed elsewhere.† It

* In the Illuminated Bible of San Paoli fuori-le-Mura, which dates from the ninth century, we find Joshua, at the passage of Jordan, drawn with a nimbus. Balaam, an infidel and prevaricating prophet, has a nimbus, even at the moment when his ass is stopped by the angel of God, who commands the Prophet, instead of cursing, to bless the people of Israel.—(*Hist. de l' Art par les Monuments*, Pl. 43 and 44; "Atlas de la Peinture.")

† These virgins are in the north porch, in the vaulting of the left entrance. In the vaulting of the west porch in the Cathedral of Laon, the series of Virgins are represented in a similar manner, the five foolish having a nimbus as well as the five wise. The Cathedral of Laon is the parent of that at Rheims, and I am not aware that this singular peculiarity exists anywhere except at Rheims and Laon. It may possibly be there owing to Byzantine influence, and this idea is supported by several other facts analogous to these.

cannot of course be their folly which is thus honoured and canonised, but rather their virginity; for these unhappy women, however foolish they might be, were not the less virgins; and virginity, in the East especially, is a peculiarly sublime virtue.

Notre Dame de Rheims, in most of its sculptures and throughout its painted glass, exhales, as it were, a Byzantine spirit, replete with grace and ideality. A manuscript in the Bibliothèque Royale contains a miniature of the taking of Christ, at the precise moment of his betrayal by the kiss of the traitor Judas; our Saviour's nimbus is cruciform; St. Peter, who is cutting off the ear of Malchus, has the nimbus, and most appropriately, for Peter is a hero and a saint. Judas, too, has a nimbus, although every devout Christian would recoil with horror if the title of saint were applied to Judas Iscariot.

But Judas it should be remarked is not merely a covetous person, a traitor, and an apostate: with all this, but, which is here more important far, he is an apostle. Now the apostleship being a sublime office, emanating immediately from God, the nimbus—which we must remember, is in the East an attribute of dignity and power, whether exerted for good or evil—ought, unquestionably, to illumine the brow of Judas. In the West it is the ordinary attribute of sanctity alone, and Judas, even at the Last Supper, and with still greater justice, on the Mount of Olives, is destitute of the nimbus.*

* Yet M. le Comte Auguste de Bastard (*Peintures et Ornemens des Manuscrits*) gives several examples of western design in which Judas is invested with the nimbus. M. de Bastard has made outlines of several beautiful miniatures of a manuscript of the thirteenth century, known under the name of "Manuscrit de Limoges," because brought from St. Martial. In the Last Supper, Judas has a golden nimbus, exactly like that of Christ. Herod, too, has a golden nimbus, at the very moment when he is represented as in great perplexity, and making contemptible grimaces, while the Magi inquire where the new-born King of the Jews is to be found. It would be interesting to know whether this manuscript, belonging as it does to a province bordering on countries covered with churches that are unquestionably of Greek and Byzantine origin, may not have been executed under the influence of certain Byzantine or oriental ideas. When one sees in Périgueux, Angoulême, Saintes, Cahors and Le Puy, at Solignac, Souillac, and Bourdeille, cathedrals, abbeys and parish churches with vaulted cupolas like St. Mark's

The manuscript in the "Bibliothèque Royale" may have been painted by a miniaturist either of Byzantine origin, affection, or education.

In the apse of one of the numerous small churches with which the city of Athens is crowded,* is a fresco painting of the Last Supper. All the apostles have the nimbus, Judas not excepted; but those of the good apostles are of some bright, glorious colour, white, green, or golden yellow, while that of Judas is black. Judas is an apostle, and, therefore, has a nimbus; but his heart is black, and the nimbus appears clad in mourning.

The Byzantines, however, go farther still; and even Satan is represented with a nimbus. An old illuminated Bible, containing miniatures of the ninth and tenth centuries, has a picture of Job,† sitting mournfully upon the

at Venice and St. Sophia's at Constantinople, we easily admit the possibility of certain Byzantine principles having been infused into Limousin. About the year 977, or 987, when Venice was entirely Byzantine, a colony of Venetian merchants established themselves at Limoges, and kept up a constant communication with their native country. One of the streets in Limoges is still called "Rue des Venitiens," from having been the residence of these merchants. Excavations recently made at St. Martial, at Limoges, have led to the discovery of Venetian coins, having on one side "*Sanctus Marcus*," and on the reverse ". . *olo*." Can this have been Dandolo, as is sometimes imagined; orr ather Orséolo, a Doge who, at the close of the tenth century, abdicated and retired into France, to the monastery of Saint Michel de Cusan, in the diocese of Perpignan? The Abbey of St. Martin, at Limoges, was rebuilt by Bishop Hilduin in 1010; the Venetians assisted him in this work, and supplied him with money. In the latter years of the eleventh century, Mark and Sebastian, an uncle and nephew, both of a noble Venetian family, founded the convent of l'Artige, distant two *myriamètres* from Limoges.—(Labbe, *Nova Bibliotheca MSS. Latino*, tom. ii., p. 278.) Lastly, in 1421, a woman, Jeanne Aldier, employed a Venetian artist to construct a Holy Sepulchre, or monument, in St. Pierre de Limoges. M. Felix de Verneille is about to publish a valuable work on the existing Cathedral of Perigueux, the ancient Abbey-church of St. Front. As his researches are to comprise all the churches with domes now existing in France, it is to be hoped that some light will be thrown on the Byzantine School in the West, and on the influence of oriental ideas in our own country. The question is one of the most complicated in our national archæology, and has hitherto been one of the least considered.

* Athens, in the month of August, 1839, contained at least eighty-one churches; I visited and counted them myself: since that period, two or three which had been greatly injured during the War of Independence, and which were then in a ruinous condition, have been completely demolished.

† Bibliothèque Royale, Bibl. MS., No. 6. See next Illustration, Fig. 46.

ruins of his house, while Satan stands before him exulting in the destruction he has caused. In another miniature, the infernal being is seen burning Job with a red-hot goad, which renders the body of the patient one immense wound. The Satan dancing on the ruined house, and the Satan wounding Job, have each a nimbus like that ordinarily given to a guardian angel, or consoling spirit.*

Fig. 46.—SATAN, WITH A CIRCULAR NIMBUS, TORMENTING JOB. Miniature of the x cent.; Bible No. 6, Bib. Roy.

The example here given represents Satan standing before Job, who is seated sadly on the ruins of his house. The

* Satan does, in fact, resemble an angel—those angels, more especially, who are painted in other parts of the same manuscript. Thus, in a miniature representing Elijah carried up to heaven in a chariot drawn by horses of fire,

demon is nimbed, and holds in his hand a brazier, wherewith to set on fire the habitations he has overthrown.

Lastly, a manuscript Apocalypse,* with miniatures belonging to the close of the twelfth century, represents the Dragon with seven heads, conquered by St. Michael; the serpent with seven heads, pursuing the woman into the desert; and the monster of the sea shaking seven heads above his frightful body. The heads all have nimbi of yellow or green, as would be the case with the most renowned saints in Paradise. That the Apocalypse was certainly painted either by a Byzantine artist or by one who had visited Byzantium, is sufficiently proved by the crescents emblazoned on the angelic bucklers, and the Arabic cupolas surmounting the buildings represented.†

an angel stands behind the car, like a pilot on the poop of a vessel. That angel exactly resembles the Satan in Fig. 46; like the evil genius, he has bird-like wings, and a nimbus of a simple circular thread; he is almost naked, clothed only with a short petticoat, covering the hips and loins. The only perceptible difference is, that the angel has nails on his feet, and Satan has claws.

* Bibliothèque Royale, No. 7013.

† Crescents and cupolas are neither Arabic nor of Mussulman origin, as has been supposed. The Turks who took Constantinople, in the fifteenth century, found in that city the crescent surmounting various buildings; it had been introduced as blazon into what may be called the arms of Constantinople, as early as the time of Philip, the father of Alexander the Great, that is to say, about the fourth century B. C. They found there also the beautiful domes of St. Sophia, of the Church of the Holy Apostles, and of several other churches. Copyists rather than inventors, the Mussulman conquerors appropriated to their own use both the domes and the crescent; one became a principal characteristic feature in the architecture of their mosques, the other the sole figure of their blazonry, exactly as had been the case in Byzantium. For this reason, a Byzantine miniaturist, or one who had visited Byzantium, in the twelfth century represented crescents and cupolas, long before Byzantium had fallen into the hands of the Mahometans. Constantinople having been conquered, the crescent and the cupola were adopted by the Turks, and soon became general among other Mussulman nations; besides, it is probable that Mahometans, whether in Egypt or in Syria, had long before copied the Christian cupolas of Alexandria and Damascus. Many ideas and facts have been vulgarised by Mahometan nations, and by the Arabs amongst others, but very few have been by them created. They certainly owe us far more than we have received from them. Five-and-twenty years ago it was the fashion to assert that Christendom and the West had been constantly under the dominion of the same Mussulman nations who subjugated Spain. According to that theory, Gothic Architecture, the ogive arch, chivalry, mathematics, physics, alchemy—in a word, arts, manners, and science, descended to us

The engraving given below is taken from a fine manuscript with miniatures, in the Bibliothèque Royale.* It represents the seven-headed monster of the Apocalypse, the leopard, with claws like a bear. His heads have a nimbus of blue, and one—that in the centre, the smallest in reality, but unquestionably the greatest in its hierarchical importance, and sovereign of the others—has a crimson nimbus of the colour of fire.

One of the heads is without a nimbus: it is undoubtedly intended for that, which, as we are told in the Apocalypse, was wounded to death.†

The nimbus being recognised amongst oriental nations as symbolic of power and dominion, a head in the last agonies of death is of course destitute of that symbol. When any individual is in full vigour he is appropriately honoured with the nimbus, but when enfeebled, unable to resist an attack —when overpowered by sickness or death—he is then considered to be degraded and consequently despoiled of the aureole. This seems very reasonable. In the romanesque frescos of St. Savin, near Poictiers, many instances of Byzantine influence are to be discovered: principally, amongst others, the great Dragon of the Apocalypse, represented at the moment of his attacking the woman, who had brought forth a man child destined to rule all nations (Rev. xii., 13, 15); then the same monster, when he in his turn is assailed by St. Michael and his angels

from the Arabs. At present, all such errors have been refuted. The proofs in regard to architecture are most abundant. Our ogive style is completely different, and was probably of earlier date than that of the Arabs; the horseshoe arch, the invention of which was formerly attributed to the Arabs, has lately been discovered in Asia, by M. le Vicomte Léon de Laborde and M. Ch. Texier, in Christian monuments, bearing dates engraven on stone, earlier than the seventh century. The minaret even, which is as indispensable a feature in Mahometan as the bell-tower is in Christian temples, may possibly not belong to Islamism; it is found in churches on the banks of the Rhine,—churches which derived their plan and inspiration from St. Sophia, and which may easily have borrowed staircase-towers and minarets, as indispensable parts of their plan and decoration. As to our chivalry, M. J. J. Ampère, in his Lectures on French Literature, has satisfactorily proved it to be indigenous, and quite unconnected with Arabic chivalry.

* *Psalterium cum Figuris,* Suppl. fr. 1132.

† "And I saw one of his heads as it were wounded to death."—*Rev.,* xiii., 3.

(Rev. xii., 7, 8, 9). In the first picture this red dragon is full of strength and power; it vomits forth from its jaws a flood of water to engulf the woman. There, of course, he is, and ought to be, nimbed; he has a yellow nimbus, a nimbus of the colour of gold, exactly like that of the angel who snatches the infant from the fury of the monster: but in the second picture, when attacked by angels, and on the point of being thrown to the ground and finally subdued, his head is already divested of its nimbus, his brow no longer emits rays of light, because his power is at an end. The western rose window in the Sainte Chapelle, at Paris, presents the same peculiarities. The beast with seven heads, loaded with horns and crowns, is there repeatedly figured. Each head has a nimbus, because the monster is adored by infidels, and because with his tail he draws down a third part of the stars from heaven. He is here all powerful, in the very zenith of his might and triumphant daring; but when conquered by the angel who has the key of the bottomless pit—when chained and sealed for a thousand years, vanquished, imprisoned, and degraded—he is despoiled of the nimbus and bears on his heads only the royal crown.*

It has now been fully shown that in the East the nimbus is constantly symbolic of power, whether of good or evil—whether vested in a fiend or an archangel, in guilt or virtue—whether the individual represented be a God, or the Arch-Traitor himself; if powerful and famous he is unquestionably entitled to the nimbus. The same idea passed into the West at the time of its intercourse with Constantinople, but it never became naturalised, and the inclination to employ the nimbus merely as a mark of personal holiness and moral virtue finally gained the ascendant. We have been more sparing in our use of an attribute which we had borrowed, not created; and in truth, the riches most prodigally lavished are usually those which flow for us immediately from the fountain head. Still at Troyes, Rheims, and throughout the entire province of Champagne, from the days of Ville-Hardouin and Joinville, down to our own, a breeze from Byzantium and the East has been felt

* This painted window dates from the era of Charles VIII., whose cipher is inscribed upon it, surmounted by a yellow crown, in imitation of gold.

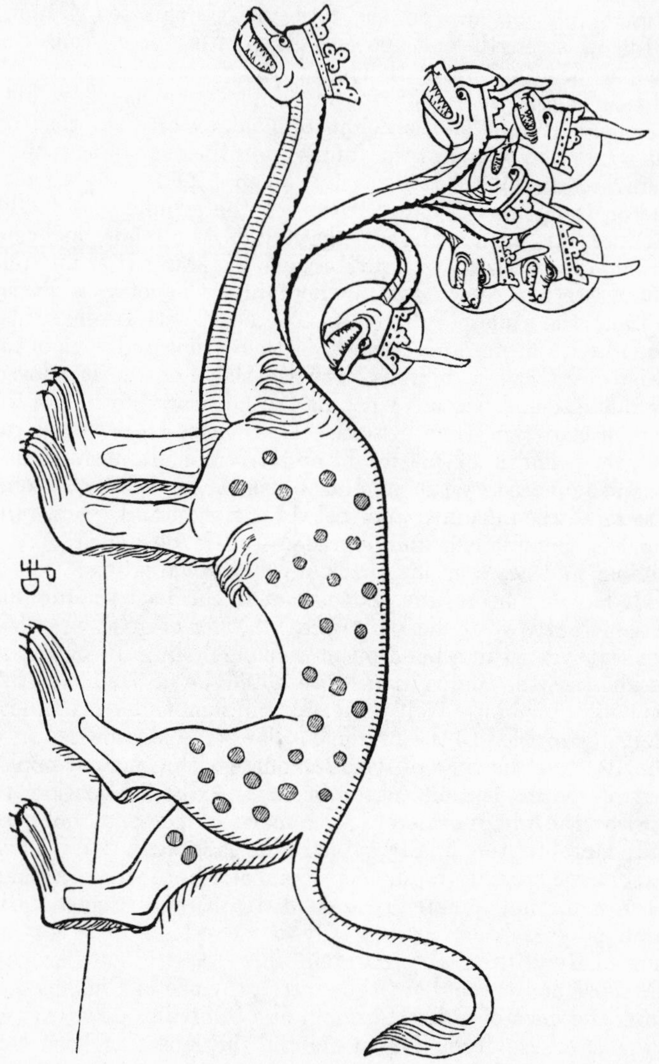

Fig. 47.—THE BEAST WITH SEVEN HEADS; SIX HAVE THE NIMBUS, AND THE SEVENTH, BEING WOUNDED TO DEATH, IS WITHOUT.

From a Miniature of the XII cent. "Psalterium cum figuris." Bibliothèque royale.

awakening and nurturing a host of oriental ideas and imagery. It will be sufficient to mention a painted glass window of the sixteenth century, which lights the nave of the cathedral of St. Nizier de Troyes. The beast with seven heads and ten horns is there also represented, and the nimbus, the oriental attribute of power, encircles each of those heads. An engraving of it will be given in the History of the Devil.

ON THE COLOUR OF THE AUREOLE.

Both the nimbus and the aureole being designed to convey the idea of a luminous efflorescence, investing the head and the person generally, its colouring in carved or painted monuments ought to be that of light itself. This then we should expect to find would be the case in the mosaics, frescos, coloured glass, miniatures of manuscripts, and historical tapestries. But the hues of light are ever varying; like water, it becomes tinged with various colours, according to those of the different objects reflected in it, or its own peculiar intensity. Stars, the most brilliant sources of light, emit scintillations of blue, violet, red and white; cerise-red and white-red are gradations of light highly valued by natural philosophers. Light, when decomposed in the prism, presents seven principal elements, which, when combined, form an infinite number of tints or gradations. The glory, possessing as it does all the properties of light, will consequently vary like it in colour from a deep blue to the most brilliant white. Thus the aureole and the nimbus are sometimes coloured blue, violet, red, yellow or white; but yellow, the colour of gold, has ever been esteemed the most precious and costly, and frequently also the most radiant of all colours: gold, of which it is a type or imitation, was regarded as light consolidated. Consequently the nimbus and aureole, those of the Deity more especially, are most commonly yellow or gold colour. Hence representations, whether ancient or modern, of the sun, are coloured yellow. The sun, too, is generally yellow, except indeed when painted red with any particular view. Homer describes Apollo as having hair of gold, and the blond (golden) or yellow-haired Phœbus seems no less popular than the blonde or golden Ceres.

The colour of the nimbus is occasionally symbolical,—a fact which is proved by the black nimbus, the "nimbe en deuil" given to the traitor Judas: still, in numerous instances, it is purely hierarchical. The form therefore of the nimbus having been ingeniously rendered the vehicle of a strongly marked hierarchical distinction, it seems appropriate that the intention of the form should be heightened and still further carried out by the colouring. To cite an example in illustration. The public library of Strasbourg contains a magnificent manuscript, to which reference has already been made.* If tradition may be credited, this great work was written and painted by Herrade, Abbess of the Convent of Sainte Odile, in Alsace. It is an Encyclopedia of all the sciences known and practised in the middle ages, and appears to be the precursor of the admirable work of Vincent de Beauvais, entitled "Speculum Universale" ("Miroir Universel.") Towards the conclusion of the manuscript is a painting of the celestial courts, of Paradise in short. Christ is drawn above, in the highest place, with a nimbus and crown of gold; then come the nine orders of saints intermingled with angels, and disposed in the following order:—Virgins,† apostles, martyrs, confessors, prophets, patriarchs, the chaste, the married, and lastly the penitent.

The four first orders, the most exalted of all, have the nimbus of gold. Prophets and patriarchs, the saints of the Old Testament, and who knew the truth imperfectly only, through the veil of metaphor and allegory, have a nimbus of silver. The nimbus of the chaste is red; that of the married green; and that of the penitents, yellowish, but slightly tinted. Colour is evidently employed, in these instances, as

* See *Ante*, Page 50, also Page 116, note.

† Observe, that Virgins, elsewhere generally the last, as in the Cathedrals of Paris, Rheims, and Chartres, are here at the head of the celestial hierarchy, immediately succeeding God, and above the Apostles and martyrs. We feel persuaded that the manuscript was the work of a nun, and for the use of a convent. So, in the portal of the Cathedral of Paris, the principal church of a city in which pre-eminence of place has ever been assigned to superiority of intellect, confessors rank above martyrs, which is, in fact, an anachronism, as well as a singular exception to the invariable practice of Christian Art. These irregularities in the sacred hierarchy, these artistic heresies, so to speak, should be noticed with care; for they may possibly lead to important moral and historical results.

an hierarchical medium; it loses its brilliancy in proportion as it descends from a lofty to an inferior grade, after which point the title of saint is no longer awarded, and the persons represented are regarded only as ordinary mortals.

It may be observed, in conclusion, that the hierarchy of colours might easily, in ideas of the middle ages, have allied itself with symbolism. Gold is the most radiant of all colours, and it is here awarded to saints of the highest eminence. Silver, the colour of the moon, which, though inferior to the sun, is ever his constant attendant, stands next in rank; then red, or fire colour, the attribute of those who struggle against passion, which is inferior to the two metals of gold and silver, to the sun and the moon, being merely an emanation from the former; then green, the colour of hope, appropriately assigned to married persons; lastly, a sort of yellow, an equivocal tint, partly white and partly yellow, a mixed colour given to saints who had formerly been sinners, but, by prayer and penitence, had again become acceptable in the sight of God. Such is the hierarchy of symbolism; it might be styled a materialised system of the Hindoo doctrine of emanation.

It has already been observed that the colour of the nimbus and aureole is sometimes, but not invariably, symbolic. It will not indeed be correct, constantly to seek a meaning in the colour; nor must we form an exaggerated idea of the importance to be attached to it: for, in numerous instances, it may easily be proved to be without signification. Take, for example, the frescos of St. Savin. In them the Deity is repeatedly drawn, either with the nimbus only, or with the nimbus and aureole combined. The field of the nimbus is sometimes red, with white cross-lines; red, with yellow cross-lines; yellow, with green lines; yellow, with red lines across; yellow, with blue; or dark blue, with cross-lines of a lighter shade of the same colour. The field of the aureole is, in one instance, yellow; in two others, greenish. To seek a mystical meaning in each of these various colours, would be an useless labour; it may possibly be decided at the most, that yellow and red predominate in the colouring of aureoles, that the yellow is gold colour, and the red that of the sun or of fire; but nothing further can be elicited.

PART II.

THE HISTORY OF GOD.

God is a pure spirit, invisible, but everywhere present. God is eternal and immeasurable; infinite in duration as in immensity. He is supreme in power—supreme in goodness—supreme in intelligence. Single in essence—triple in person: God is the creator, master, and disposer of all things.

Such, according to the doctrines of Christianity, is the true definition of the supreme Being, the great first cause of all existence. This invisible Being, art has attempted to exhibit, through the medium of paintings and statues; this infinite Being has been reduced by art to certain finite proportions: at the command of man, this spirit has assumed a visible body; this eternal Being has seemed to have an existence in time. The various representations of God, painted, carved, or sculptured by Christian artists at different periods of our era, will now be described, together with the various portraits, through the medium of which sculptors and painters have transmitted to us their ideal conception of the Godhead.

One in substance, indivisible in nature, God, nevertheless is, as we have said, threefold in person. It is the union of these three persons or "hypostases" which constitutes the perfect fulness of Divinity. "Deus trinus unus," says Lactantius, in his concise and orthodox language.*

* Ancient philosophy had already said, by the mouth of Plato in the Timæus, "Unity is divided into three, and the trinity is united in one." Dante says also—

> "Quell' uno e due e tre che sempre vive,
> E regna sempre in tre e due ed uno,
> Non circonscritto e tutto circonscrive." [1]

[1] "Him who lives ever, and for ever reigns,
In mystic union of the Three in One,
Unbounded, bounding all."

Cary's Dante. Paradise, Canto xiv., l. 28.

The Christian religion gives to each divine person in the Trinity a different name and a separate office: art on its part has invested each name with an appropriate and special form, and represented each person, and characterised each office, by distinct attributes.

The first person of the Divine Trinity is called the Father; the second the Son; and the third the Holy Ghost. They have all three been represented by artists either singly or conjoined. It will therefore be expedient to study them at first, one by one, and trace their iconography separately, and then to unite them under one head, and in the same chapter, under the appellation of the Holy Trinity.

GOD THE FATHER.

God the Father, as is recorded in history, frequently made himself manifest in his intercourse with mankind. It is true, nevertheless, that the Father in revealing himself, at the same time revealed the Son and the Holy Ghost; still certain actions are attributed more particularly to the Father, than to the other two persons. Every action in which that divine energy, which corresponds to what we call strength and power, is principally manifested, is performed by the Father; the other two energies, corresponding to love and intelligence, seem to belong preferably to the Son and the Holy Ghost.

Historically considered, the Father is the most frequently manifested in the Old Testament, the Bible * properly so called, while the Son is especially present in the Gospel, and the Holy Ghost appears sometimes in one and sometimes in the other. It might be said that the Bible refers more especially to the history of God the Father, and the Gospel to that of the Son.

Thus, the Father was the creator of heaven and earth—

* Throughout the present work, as has been already seen, we have distinguished the Old Testament by the name of the Bible, and have given that of Gospel to the New. The word Bible ought strictly to mean a collection of all the sacred books, of those of the New Testament as well as of the Old; but we have preferred adopting the language most commonly in use, and have restricted the name of Bible to the canonical books of the Old Testament.

of plants, animals, and men. He it was who accepted the offering of Abel and rejected that of Cain—who punished mankind by the deluge—who over-turned the projects of the builders of Babel—who called Abraham to faith in him —who gave to Moses the tables of the law—who guided the Hebrews in the desert and led them towards Canaan— —who fought with the enemies of his chosen people—inspired prophets and judges—gave wisdom to Solomon and goodness to Hezekiah. It was he who brought the Jews into captivity and afterwards restored them to liberty. Lastly, He it was who sent the Archangel Gabriel to the Virgin Mary, and commanded him to announce to her that she had been elected as the chosen mother of his Son.

The Old Testament appears indeed to be the theatre in which God the Father chiefly displays his power. Jehovah is declared to be the Creator of the world, and the two other persons of the Trinity are scarcely mentioned. Their presence is intimated in several passages, particularly in the "Faciamus hominem ad imaginem et similitudinem nostrum." * Still these expressions are quite open to controversy. Besides, in a multitude of very clear and explicit passages, the Father, and the Father alone, is named. In the Old Testament, the Father reigns almost indivisible: He speaks, He shows himself to man, acts, punishes, and rewards: He converses with Adam, Cain, Noah, Abraham, and Moses, with kings and prophets; He is with them, in the midst of them: He is felt, seen, and heard everywhere; each verse speaks of Him.

In the New Testament, on the contrary, God the Father almost completely disappears, and retires to the second rank: He is rarely seen, and seldom heard. The arena seems entirely occupied by the Son. Twice the voice of the Father is heard in the distance; at the Baptism and the Transfiguration of Christ he speaks, saying, "This is my beloved Son, in whom I am well pleased;" † but he immediately appears to resume his impenetrable silence. When Christ in his agony of blood cried to him for succour, exclaiming, "Abba, Father, take away this cup from me" (St. Mark xiv., 36),

* Liber Genesis, i., 26.

† St. Matthew, iii., 17; xvii., 4, 5.

it is not God but an angel who appears unto him strengthening him. When nailed to the cross, the divine victim exclaims, "My God, my God, why hast thou forsaken me?" (St. Mark xv., 34.) Not one word of consolation descends to him from heaven. God the Father is silent, and even the angels hold their peace. Such is the lesson derived from the first reading of the sacred text; such the literal rendering of Holy Scripture.

Artists, guided rather by history than by abstract and logical dogmas of theology, understood Scripture in this literal sense, at least at the end of the Gothic period; and in every scene of the Old Testament, God the Father is figured to the exclusion in some measure of the Son and the Holy Ghost. Still it was not till the end of the fourteenth century, and principally in the fifteenth and sixteenth, that God the Father was thus depicted by painters and sculptors. Another singular fact which marked the earlier ages well deserves consideration, and is confirmed by various archæological examples.

It is easy to understand how the Son, the Father, and the Holy Ghost might concur in the same actions, and manifest themselves at the same time in the various histories of the Old Testament, because the Trinity is doctrinally indivisible, and every work done by one of the three persons is performed collectively by the three at once. From the moment, however, that one single person is represented, it would seem fit that the Father only should be shown at the Creation,* as the Son should appear at the Passion, and the Holy Ghost at Pentecost. It seems an extraordinary thing to represent the Son alone creating Adam and Eve. Historically speaking, it is an anachronism, for the Son, Jesus Christ, had not then been born in his human nature. Still, nothing is more common than to see Jesus taking the place of his Father, and creating the world alone, commanding Noah to construct the ark, arresting the hand of Abraham when on the point of sacrificing Isaac, and speaking to Moses from the midst of the burning bush.

* The question is here considered under its historical bearings alone; for it will instantly be proved by theology that the Son ought to occupy the place which artists of the fifteenth century and of the Renaissance assigned to the Father.

Further, it would seem that when artists designed to represent God the Father as conversing * with Abraham, Moses, the prophets, and the kings, fear and awe restrained them from a delineation of the whole person, and a small part only has been represented; the hand, for instance, or sometimes even the face; but more rarely the bust, and scarcely ever the entire person. Thus the figure of the Son either supplants that of the Father, in representations of works recorded to have been performed by the latter, or the smallest possible portion of the Father's person is shown, or he is altogether absent or almost entirely veiled; one might perhaps say, superseded. These two facts are parallel, and, indeed, almost identical. But before entering upon any explanation, it will be well to prove them by Iconography, and to demonstrate first, that Christ is represented instead of the Father in works of which the latter is more especially the author, and, secondly, that the Father, if it be He whom the artists designed to represent, reveals his presence only by a hand, an arm, or a face, the remainder of the person being concealed.

In the first place then, Christ is represented instead of the Father.

In a subsequent chapter, which will be devoted to the history of the Son of God, an enumeration will be made of the characteristic features of age, physiognomy, costume, attitude and attributes, by which he may be recognised.

It will be sufficient to mention here, that Christ shows himself under two perfectly distinct forms. Either, as on ancient sarcophagi, on certain Greek frescos, and in some sculptures of our own country, executed under the influence of Byzantine genius, he is youthful, beardless, an adolescent of from fifteen to eighteen years of age, the feet sandalled, seldom bare, with long hair descending upon the shoulders, and no nimbus; † or, as is more commonly the case, par-

* On the sarcophagi in the Vatican, and the frescos of the Catacombs, the earliest figured monuments of Christianity, nothing is shown of the Father Eternal except a hand issuing from the clouds. See *Rom. Sotter.* passim, particularly, pp. 45, 59, 73, 231, 339, 363, 367 of the Italian edition. Rome, 1633.

† See Figs. 17, 18, two portraits of the Saviour, both beardless; in the first, the feet are sandalled.

ticularly in the countries of Western Europe, he is about thirty or thirty-three years of age, as at the period of the crucifixion, with a long face, a fine short beard, hair of moderate length and parted over the forehead, the countenance sweet but melancholy, the nimbus divided by a cross, the feet bare, and the robe and mantle long. On seeing either of these two figures, both of which are consecrated to the Saviour, it is impossible to mistake or to confound them with any other person.

Besides, not only is the expression of the face sufficiently characteristic to distinguish him, but his name is frequently written at his feet, or around his head, sometimes at full length, at others, abridged or contracted into a monogram.

Now in a number of monuments representing the creation, and all those biblical scenes in which God the Father is the chief actor and author, it is not the Father who is pourtrayed, but the Son, who may easily be recognised by the hieratical type or character of his physiognomy, and the name, painted or graven. Christ, as has just been said, is thus represented youthful and beardless, on a multitude of white marble sarcophagi belonging to the first epochs of Christianity from the fourth down to the eighth century. There can be no doubt that the figure is intended for that of Christ, for among the subjects depicted on those sarcophagi we find the raising of Lazarus, the cure of the man born blind, and the paralytic, the multiplication of the bread, the conversation with the Samaritan woman, the triumphant entry into Jerusalem, the appearance before Pilate, and the preaching to the apostles; now the person represented as thus raising the dead, healing the blind, multiplying the loaves and fishes, speaking, triumphing, standing before Pilate in the judgment-hall, and preaching, is the same beardless youth of whom we have spoken;—it is Christ in his adolescence. Sculptured on the same monuments, however, and generally on the left side, are subjects parallel with the above, which are then on the right; God is here seen condemning Eve and Adam to labour, speaking to Noah, arresting the hand of Abraham, giving the law to Moses; and God is invariably represented by the same young beardless adolescent, who, in the opposite compartments raises Lazarus from the dead, and sends his apostles to preach throughout the world. It is God the Son who here takes the place of the Father.

In Fig. 32, (God, beardless, giving to Eve and Adam a lamb and some ears of corn,) is a figure precisely resembling the divine youth, without a beard, with long hair descending upon his shoulders, and sandalled feet; in this picture God is condemning Adam to till the ground, which will bring forth ears of corn similar to those of which he presents him a sheaf; and Eve is to spin into wool the fleece of the lamb which he presents to her.

This drawing is taken from a sarcophagus in the Vatican.

One might perhaps imagine the God speaking to Adam and Eve, to be intended for God the Father, although it may appear singular to see the "Ancient of Days," as he is called in the Bible, and by the Greeks (ὁ παλαιὸς τῶν ἡμερῶν) scarcely past the age of infancy; and it might possibly be thought that, adhering in this respect to the practice of the ancient Greeks, the early Christians had represented God the Father, or Jehovah, youthful and beardless in order to indicate the unchangeableness of the Deity, who never becomes old, but lives on in perpetual youth. But the plate annexed * leaves no doubt that it is indeed Christ who is represented presiding over the work of creation, and throughout the entire cycle of Genetical history; for God is there represented creating Adam, the first born (Ἀδὰμ ὁ προτόπλαστος), and this God is no other than Christ, as is proved by his name IC, XC, inscribed in the field of the circular aureole whence he appears to spring.†

The manuscript of Panselinos ‡ is if possible even more explicit and decisive. In the instructions given in that work to artists, on the proper method of representing Moses before the burning bush, the following features are

* The painting was originally copied from an ivory, carved probably in the twelfth or thirteenth centuries. It is given by Gori in his *Thesaurus veterum diptychorum*, vol. ii., p. 160.

† Seroux d'Agincourt (*Histoire de l'Art par les Monuments*) produces another example similar to that here given by Gori.

‡ Ἑρμηνεία τῆς Ζωγραφικῆς. Second part.

indicated, and the picture is drawn in words as follows:—"Moses loosing his sandal; around him, sheep. Before Moses is the burning bush, in the midst and on the summit of which the Virgin and Child shine resplendent. Beside

Fig 48.—THE CREATOR UNDER THE FIGURE OF CHRIST, NOT OF THE FATHER.

Fresco painting, IX century. Gravé en ivoire XII ou XIII siècle.

Mary is an angel, looking towards Moses. On another side of the bush, Moses is again represented standing, with one hand extended, and holding a rod in the other." The Greeks not only substitute Christ for God the Father, but even the Virgin, and that, too, more than eleven hundred years before her birth. Our western art, has more than once followed the direction of Byzantine art, or at least appears to agree with it. To cite but two examples;—at Rheims, on some tapestry of the sixteenth century, and at Saint Saviour of Aix, on a picture attributed to King René, Moses is seen prostrating himself before a green bush, whence issue tongues of flame. On the tapestry in the

Cathedral of Rheims, we read, in verses woven into the wool:—

> Comment Moyse fut tres fort esbahi
> Quant aperceut le vert buisson ardant
> Dessus le mont de Horeb ou Synaï,
> Et n'estoit rien de sa verdeur perdant.*

Lastly a manuscript belonging to the latter portion of the fourteenth century, and which is now in the Bibliothèque Royale,† contains a picture of God appearing to Moses in the midst of lightning on Mount Sinai, and another of God, with the head emerging from the clouds at the moment when Moses raises his hands to him, imploring aid against the Amalekites. In both miniatures God is young and completely beardless. In the frescos of St. Savin, near Poictiers, God is seen giving the tables of the law to Moses on Mount Sinai, or speaking to Noah, or creating the world; God in each of these pictures has the figure of Christ; his age from thirty to thirty-five, the hair young and fair, the countenance full of sweetness. This God is Christ, no longer beardless as in the manuscript of which we have just spoken, but having reached the age of his ministry and public life; it is certainly not intended for God the Father.

On hearing the name of the Almighty, the idea one forms of the person so designated is that of the entire Trinity, in whom resides the fulness of divine power, or that of God the Father, to whom the attribute of strength and energy seems more peculiarly to belong; but that title does not suggest the idea of Christ, the incarnation rather of self-devotion and charity. Yet, the Greeks, within those great cupolas which are raised above the central portion of their churches, delineate a gigantic figure of the Almighty or Pantocrator, as they style the Father, painted in fresco, or in mosaic gold ground. God, from the summit of the artistic heaven, appears to bless the faithful with his

> * How Moses was very greatly astonished
> When he saw the green bush burning
> On the Mount of Horeb or Sinai,
> And yet of its verdure nothing losing.

† Biblia 6829, Cf. Bible 6. *Bibl. roy.* Observe also the miniature representing Shadrach, Meschach, and Abednego, in the fiery furnace.

extended right hand, while in the left he holds a book. The figure, if intended for that of the Father, the "Ancient of Days" appears rather youthful; yet from the words "ὁ παντοκράτωρ," written in large characters, one is tempted for a moment to imagine, notwithstanding the cross with which the nimbus is adorned, that it is indeed "ὁ παλαιὸς τῶν ἡμερῶν." But we are speedily undeceived, for below the first inscription, and just above the shoulders of the figure, shine in still larger letters, ΙC ΧC (Ἰησοῦς Χριστὸς), Jesus Christ. Then, on the open book in his hand, we read what Jesus said himself in the Gospel. "I am the light of the world." For other reasons, too, the figure, even if it were not so fully characterised by the name and inscription, would evidently represent Christ, not God the Father.*

In the Cathedral of Chartres (north porch, central arch) the Creation, as related in the Book of Genesis, is sculptured in minute detail. Now, in Genesis, as has been said, the Father, the Creator, is Jehovah: neither the Son nor the Holy Ghost are mentioned unless they are signified in the words, "*Faciamus hominem ad imaginem et similitudinem nostram,*" "Let us make man in our image, after our likeness;" "*Et spiritus Dei ferebatur super aquas,*" "And the spirit of God moved upon the face of the waters." (Gen. i., 26, 45.) The Father it is who speaks—who approves his own work—who creates man, and from him fashions woman†—who pronounces the prohibition and addresses the reproof. In the history of the Creation sculptured at Chartres, God is represented thirteen times, and in thirteen different bas-reliefs. The God represented in each, is not the Father; it is not Jehovah, but the Son, about thirty years of age, adorned as has been before

* The following engraving was taken from a fresco painting in the principal church of the convent of the Isle of Salamis. At Mistra, and in the Cathedral of Athens; at Meteora, in Thessaly; at Mount Athos, in Macedonia; at Daphne, near Athens, and on the road to Eleusis; at Saint Luke, in Livadia, at the foot of Mount Parnassus, the same thing is constantly to be seen. Now the paintings in these different localities comprise a period of thirteen centuries, from the days of Justinian down to our own. In 1839, in the month of November, I saw, on Mount Athos, one of these very figures of Christ, painted as *Pantocrator*.

† "Et ædificavit Dominus Deus costam, quam tulerat de Adam, in mulierem."—*Gen.* i., 22.

described with the beautiful glossy hair overshadowing his shoulders and with the delicately shaped double-forked beard

Fig. 49.—JESUS CHRIST (NOT THE FATHER), AS THE ALMIGHTY. Fresco Painting at Salamis, of the XVIII cent.

descending from the chin. The Creator here is in every point similar to the Pantocrator described above.

The Bible of Charles le Chauve contains illuminated miniatures, delineating the entire creation. The Creator is there represented not more than twenty years of age; he is beardless, and already appears with the nimbus, though the nimbus is not as yet cruciform. The feet are bare, the sandals usually seen upon the sarcophagi having already disappeared. In the hand is a long staff. The figure is clearly intended for God the Son, and not the Father.

The Nicene Creed, it is well-known, declares all things to have been created by the Word, the Son of God, and art, as we shall find, has remained dutifully faithful to that dogma. But in other subjects where the presence of God the Father is clearly pointed out, or at most, the Word not yet made flesh, it is still the person of Christ that we see represented. In the time of Isaiah the prophet, Christ the incarnate God was not yet born; consequently, whenever in the Old Testament, God is described as appearing to or addressing him or other prophets, it is Jehovah or God the Father who appears and speaks,—and historically considered, it can be no other person of the divine Trinity.

Still in the Cathedral of Chartres, God is not merely removed from the work of Creation, which the Son is represented as accomplishing, but Jesus, not the Father, is also expressly delineated, appearing to the prophets, and conversing with them. Thus, on the basement of one of the pillars supporting the vaulting of the north porch, the prophet Samuel is represented standing; God is in the act of revealing to the youthful prophet his intentions with regard to the house of Eli, and the judgments he is about to bring upon the high priest and his children. (1 Kings, iii., 11, 14.) In the Cathedral of Rheims, God is represented giving to Isaiah his mission, to announce the principal revolutions which were to disturb the kingdoms of Judah and Israel, and to proclaim the birth of the Messiah and the deliverance of the children of Jacob. The figure should have been that of Jehovah, since it was he who conversed with Isaiah on the future birth of the Messiah, his son,* and it was he, also, who spoke to Samuel, a prophet who was never permitted to see Christ on earth. Still, the age, the features, and countenance, clearly prove it to be intended, not for the Father but the Son; but the possibility of any mistake is precluded, and the intention of the sculptor at Chartres clearly testified by the word XPITVS deeply graven in the stone beneath the figure not intended for Samuel.†

* Isaiah. See the prophecies *passim,* especially chapters vi., vii., xi., xiv.

† The name is written as above; the three first letters are Greek, the last three Latin, and the S which should have divided the Greek from the Latin letters is forgotten entirely. This may have been occasioned by custom, symbolism, or ignorance, but I feel inclined to attribute it rather to habit, or

Not only is it God the Son, who according to Christian faith and the doctrines of theology, might indeed have revealed himself to Samuel; but it is the Christ, it is God made man, who seems thus to have appeared on earth more than a thousand years before his human birth.

The Greek manuscript of Panselinos (Ἑρμηνεία τῆς Ζωγραφικῆς) agrees completely with the western sculptures at Rheims and Chartres, for we there find under the title of "The Vision of Isaiah," the following description of the composition and the treatment of it, enjoined to Byzantine painters.

"A grotto;—within it clouds and a brilliant light; Christ in the midst, seated like a king on a lofty throne. His right hand is in the act of benediction, in the left, he holds a scroll, on which is written 'Whom shall I send, and who will go amongst this people?'" (Isaiah vi., 8.) It cannot therefore be doubted that the name of Christ, is inscribed in that book, as well as in the porch of Chartres Cathedral, in which place the subject seems imperatively to require the presence of the Father, or at least of the Eternal Word.

Amongst the Greeks, not only is the Son substituted for the Omnipotence, but also for the Wisdom of the Father. The Greeks of the lower empire, dedicated to the Deity, under the name of Saint Sophia, the most beautiful, the richest and greatest of their temples; the parent indeed of all the Byzantine Churches. It might have been supposed that this epithet was intended to apply to the entire Trinity united, and not to one single person, or in the latter case, that it would belong rightfully to God the Father, and to the Holy Ghost especially, but less peculiarly to God the Son. The very reverse appears to be the case. At Lyons, in the library of the palace of St. Peter, is a very curious manuscript, enriched with miniatures of the twelfth, or perhaps even of the eleventh century. The first of these

even to ignorance, many proofs of which are given by sculptors, and by those of Chartres among the rest. In the "Creation of Heaven and Earth," sculptured in the same porch, the artists or workers in stone have written *terrem* instead of *terram*. Must this be regarded as an error, or does it prove that at the time when Chartres Cathedral was built, the *a* was pronounced like an *e*, as is still the case in certain provinces of France?

miniatures, is an allegorical representation of the Encyclopedia of the middle ages. The principal sciences are personified by women, whom God, St. Sophia, inspires with intelligence and science by a breath, just as by a breath he gave life to the clay of which he had formed the figure of Adam. Saint Sophia is a youthful personification of the Deity, about thirty years of age, slightly bearded, and with a cruciform nimbus. The figure is unquestionably intended for the Christ. To avert the possibility of mistake, the painter, like the sculptor of Chartres, would have done well to engrave the name of Jesus above that of Sancta Sophia.*

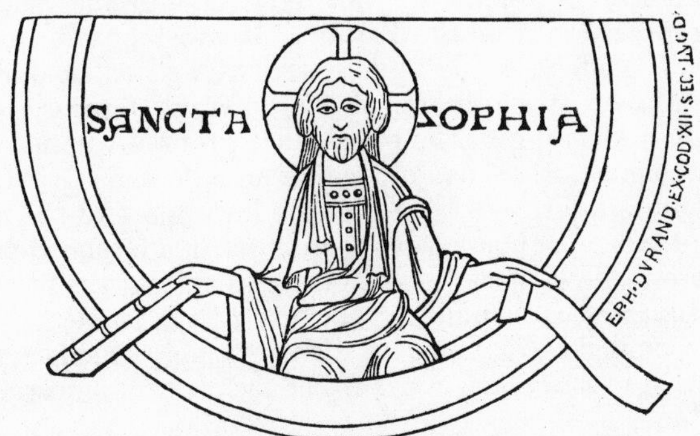

Fig. 50.—JESUS CHRIST AS SAINT SOPHIA.
Miniature of Lyons; XII cent.†

We not only find the Father, to be in many instances supplanted as it were by the Son, but even when depicted,

* This manuscript is the "Psychomachie" of Prudentius; it contains a great number of miniatures representing the Vices and Virtues. The taste of the middle ages inclined to allegorical pictures in which science and morality were so figured as to exhibit their mutual dependence. The alliance between the good and true was often perfected by the addition of the beautiful, and art was then summoned to crown Instruction and Virtue.—(See the Porches of Notre Dame de Chartres.) Andrea Pisano sculptured the Arts and Sciences in the Campanile of Santa Maria del Fiore at Florence, and Giotto completed them by the addition of the figures of Apelles and Phidias, the personifications of Painting and Sculpture. To these Luca della Robbia added the personifications of Grammar, Philosophy, Music, Astronomy, aad Geometry.

† This figure of St. Sophia is represented dispensing complete science and

a trifling portion only of his person is seen. Christ is painted and sculptured at full length, in every attitude, of every age, and under every possible aspect; but the Father is either absent, or his presence revealed only by a small portion of his person. Sometimes a hand only is seen, sometimes the hand and the forepart of the arm; then the entire hand and arm, afterwards the face is attempted, and lastly the bust; but many years elapsed before a full-length figure of Jehovah was ever attempted. I do not pause here to dwell upon a fact so singular, as it will be treated at length in a separate paragraph.

The rank assigned to God the Father, in early Christian monuments, is frequently not very honourable, the Son taking precedence of the Father. It must be remembered that in the ideas of the middle ages as well as in our own, the rank, or place occupied by different figures, is not without a meaning. The precedence granted to one person rather than another, has a peculiar signification. Thus the left hand is inferior to the right, the lower part to the upper, the centre is more honourable than the circumference. A word or two on this subject may be of use in calling the attention of antiquaries, and inducing them to notice particularly the place occupied by any objects, men or things, which they may meet with in their researches. The fact is of unquestionable importance.

wisdom under the symbol of the two different kinds of manuscripts which formed the only medium through which knowledge was then imparted. The two forms were that of the rouleau, which the figure appears to hold in the left hand, and the book, properly so called, which is in the right. The book, being of greater importance in size, and also capable of containing more matter, was regarded as symbolic of the loftiest wisdom. Gulielmus Durandus, a famous liturgist,* asserts that the roll only, was placed in the hands of the Old Testament Prophets, because they saw the truth but imperfectly, and through the veil of metaphor, while the Apostles, to whom the truth was fully revealed, carry books. The remark is of the highest importance in regard to Christian Iconography, although there exist many exceptions to the fact, and many Apostles, even the Evangelists, hold only rolls, while the Prophets on the contrary have large books; another proof, in confirmation of others already quoted, that we must not always rely implicitly on the mediæval writers on symbolism, Durandus, John Beleth, Jean d'Avranches, and Hugues de St. Victor.

---

* Rat. div. off., lib. i., cap. 3.

The left hand is inferior to the right. In stained glass windows, or in sculptures, Christ is often represented enthroned on clouds, his back supported by the rainbow. On his left, we find the tables of the law, resting on the ark of the covenant; on his right, upon an altar, the books, written by his apostles. In fact the Bible has always been placed on the left, and the Gospel on the right. An early English abbot, who caused the church of his Convent to be decorated with paintings, selected for the north, or the left hand, scenes from the Old Testament; and for the south, or the right hand, scenes from the New. The subjects sculptured on the two side-porches at Chartres comprehend the entire cycle of religious themes. On the north porch, which is on the left hand looking towards the apse, are placed figures taken from the Old Testament; on the south or right-hand porch, characters belonging the Gospel, from the advent of the New and Christian world, down to the Last Judgment.* Lastly, according to the Psalm, God, to do honour to the conqueror, Jesus, who had subdued Satan and redeemed the world, desires him to sit down at his right hand. The lower part is less honourable than the upper. A king, a pope, or conqueror, is elevated on a buckler, a throne, or a chariot. Below, on the compartments of the basement, are figures of saints, represented as living, militant, performing the actions recorded of them, and accomplishing their work upon earth; while in the vaulting above, the same saints are seen after death, triumphant, and admitted into paradise. In the lower part they are simply men, above, they are glorified beings or saints. Lastly, at Chartres, completely at the summit of the great western gable, elevated no less than fifty metres above the ground, Christ is represented, with extended hands, blessing the world outspread beneath his feet.

* See Introduction, p. 16. Vasari, *Vies des Peintres,* translated by MM. Leclouché et Jeanron, in the life of Giovanni Cimabue, vol. i. p. 41, says as follows: "Cimabue adorned with fresco paintings the upper part of the walls of the church of San Francisco d'Assisi. On the left of the altar he placed sixteen subjects taken from the Old Testament, and on the right, opposite to them, sixteen taken from the lives of the Virgin and of Christ." Tradition appears to have been invariable on this point, from the period of Benedict Biscop down to that of the sculptors of Notre Dame de Chartres and the great Italian master, Cimabue.

The centre, again, is more honourable than the circumference. In the vaulting of a cathedral, or the field of a rose-window filled with stained glass, the centre is always assigned either to God, the Creator and Judge, or the Virgin Mary, the first of all created beings. Then follow the different orders of angels, commencing with the seraphim, who hold the highest rank of all, and closing with angels, the lowest in degree of the whole heavenly hierarchy; then apostles, martyrs, confessors, and lastly virgins, who being women, and less eminent in virtue than the saintly orders who precede them, are placed in the exterior cordon of the circumference. It is thus shown that in proportion to the distance between God or the centre, and the person represented, the essence of the latter becomes less subtle, the materiality predominates, and virtue grows more attenuate. The hierarchy thus figured in rose-windows, and sculptured on the vaulted roofs of cathedrals, exhibits in a palpable form, as has been before observed,* the system of ethics and cosmogony embodied in the Hindu doctrine of emanation.

There are exceptions to this Christian hierarchical arrangement, but they rather confirm, than disprove, the truth of my assertion. Thus in the central door of the western porch of the cathedral at Paris, the different orders of persons supposed to be in the enjoyment of paradise, are arranged in hierarchical order. God is in the centre—his fitting place; next him are the angels, then follow the apostles; but instead of martyrs, who ought properly to stand next in rank to the apostles, confessors are seen to present themselves; the martyrs are consequently lowered, and confessors elevated by one degree; and, probably for the following reason:—At Paris the capital of intellect, a man, whose mind is enlightened by intelligence, is considered superior even to one who has given his life for the faith. A saint who diffuses his belief throughout the world, is more frequently beloved than the martyr, whose faith is watered by his blood. A similar fact occurs in the Manuscript of Herrade, Abbess of Sainte Odile, which was referred to in giving the history of the aureole. Virgins, who everywhere else, at Paris, Rheims, and at Chartres,

* Chapter on the Glory, p. 143.

hold the lowest rank, are here placed at the head of the celestial hierarchy, immediately after God and before apostles, martyrs, or confessors, the latter of whom, at Notre Dame de Paris, rank first. The manuscript was written and the illuminations executed by a woman, a religieuse, and for the use of women, the sisters of her convent. These women, being nuns and virgins, thought to pay themselves honour, by assigning to their patronesses so noble a rank, and thus to become the artisans of their own glory.

It has thus been shown that the left, the lower parts and the circumference are less honourable than the right, the top, or the centre. This being determined, the following facts have been observed, relating either to the place occupied by God the Father, and the Son in sculptured monuments, or to the manner in which they have been represented. Notre Dame de Paris, a building which is open to the inspection of the world, will furnish us with a type for all other such monuments.

In the north porch of Notre Dame de Paris, of which the period is about the end of the thirteenth century, the presence of God the Father is intimated only by his hand displayed in one of the bands or cordons of the vaulting at the point of the junction (*brisure*) or apex of the arch, while in an interior cordon the sun is placed before him. In the south porch, the head of the Father is given, but on the exterior cordon of the vaulting, where it is exposed to all the injuries of rain and wind, while mere angels are placed in the inner cordons and sheltered from the action of the weather. On the left door of the west porch, the Father is altogether omitted, while the figure of the Son is full length, and the size of life.

At the central door, the face only of the Father is shown, and seems almost strangled between the intersecting points of the cordons of the vaulting, within which cordons are, respectively, the canopies which over-crown the martyrs and patriarchs. The head appears to have been placed in that spot merely to fill up a vacancy, and because owing to a miscalculation of the space to be filled up, a certain portion remained blank. In the door on the right, the figure of the Creator is completely banished to the exterior and least honourable cordon, and even there placed in a narrow and inconvenient situation just at the intersection of the pointed arch; God the Son, on the contrary, is placed in the interior, carefully protected from the effects of rain and wind: he is represented under the figure of a lamb, two angels bear him triumphantly in their arms, and raise him, as it were, upon a throne of clouds. Ample space might have been found in a lower cordon for the Holy Ghost, but the Holy Ghost also has been sacrificed by the artist, who has filled the vacancy in preference, with a large angel, holding in each hand a napkin, on which two little naked souls are seen standing.

In the sculptures of Notre Dame de Paris, we can indeed discover but little reverence for the Father Eternal; but, on the other hand, a thousand tendernesses are lavished on the Son; His are all the honours, His the glory of the triumph. He is represented of colossal size, not merely the bust, but the entire person; seated on a throne in the central door, judging the world at the end of time.

On the right door, He is represented as a child, at His mother's knee. On the left He is a man, standing, attending the death-bed of his mother, whom, in an upper compartment, He is afterwards seen crowning. The events of the life of Christ down to the flight into Egypt, are represented on the tympanum of the north porch, while on the pier between, Mary is seen, presenting the Saviour to the adoration of the faithful. In the south porch, He is seen in the clouds, appearing to St. Stephen, who is being stoned to death,* He receives upon His knees the precious mantle which St. Martin divided in order to give half to the beggar of Amiens. At the Porte Rouge He is crowning His mother; He crowns her again on the bas-reliefs, enchased in the side wall on the north; on the same side He is again seen judging the world. The screen inclosing the choir, in the

* We are told in the Acts of the Apostles, vii. 55, that St. Stephen saw the divine glory and Jesus standing on the right hand of God; "Vidit gloriam Dei, et Jesum stantem a dextris Dei;" and again; "Ecce video cœlos apertos, et Filium hominis stantem a dextris Dei." In the portal of Notre Dame de Paris, where this scene is represented, the Father ought certainly to be present as well as the Son; as the figure of Jesus alone appears, we must again conclude that the Father is superseded.

interior of the church, offers at one view all the principal incidents in the life of Christ, from His birth to the resurrection. In the alto-rilievos, which have not been broken down tc make way for the modern screen or "grille," Christ is represented thirteen times, at every period of His life. He is ever the polar star, towards which all other sculptured figures turn, as the needle to the pole. The Father, on the other hand, is seen but once in the entire series, and then the face only is seen, with the arm extended at the moment when Jesus exclaims, "Take away this cup from me."

Finally, when the figure of God the Father is actually brought upon the scene, the part assigned to him is frequently ridiculous, rude, hateful, and even cruel. Thus, on the capital of a pillar, in Notre Dame du Port, at Clermont, God is represented striking the guilty Adam with his clenched hand; a strange and most improper manner of reproving him for the crime he had committed; while an angel at the same time seizes our poor first father by the beard and plucks it out. The actions, both of God and of the angel, are marked by extreme brutality. In the Bibliothèque Royale is a Latin manuscript, adorned probably with Italian miniatures, and in one of these, God is represented as himself expelling Adam and Eve from paradise, and driving them before him with blows of an arrow, precisely as in the Iliad, Apollo is represented pursuing the Greeks! Such a part might be well suited to Apollo, a man rather than a God, and full of human rage and passion; but we feel indignant that any artist should dare to attribute such a character to Jehovah. A Psalter in the Bibliothèque Royale, belonging to the close of the twelfth century, contains several figures, representing God, holding in his hand a bow and arrows, a spear, and a sword: he appears, indeed, to be the mighty God, the God of armies, the God of battles, the Jehovah of the Hebrews, but not the God of Christians. One of these figures is given on the next page.*

* It belongs to the eighteenth Psalm, in which the Divine wrath is spoken of as red like burning coal, and dark and cloudy as a fall of hail; it is also said that God breathes out his indignation in smoke and flames, and that, after having crushed his enemies with the thunderbolts, he kills them with arrows. "Ascendit fumus in ira ejus, et ignis a facie ejus exarsit; carbones succensi

God Almighty is represented in this miniature with the countenance of the Son, no portrait of the Father having at that period been attempted. The figure, however, is undoubtedly intended for Jehovah, slaying his enemies with arrows, judging all flesh with the sword, according to the words of the Psalmist given below. With a peculiar refinement, and as if to impart to the figure of the Deity, an expression more than ordinarily warlike, he is inscribed within a medallion, and forms one of those "imagines clypeatæ" of which we have already spoken in the history of the aureole.†

Fig. 51.—JEHOVAH, AS THE GOD OF BATTLES.

Italian Miniature; close of the XII cent.*

The art has made Jehovah thus awful, as if with the design of rendering the contemplation uninviting to the mystical taste of the middle ages, and to attract all hearts in preference to Jesus Christ the God of charity and love. Self-sacrifice, and devotedness, are fundamental doctrines of Christianity, but strength, whether from a reaction of the mind in opposition to the Pagan doctrines, or from a feeling of aversion to the feudal system, and the power of the nobility, has always inspired repugnance. It seems, conse-

sunt ab eo. Et misit sagittas suas et dissipavit eos ; fulgura multiplicavit, et conturbavit eos." "There went up a smoke out of his nostrils, and fire out of his mouth devoured ; coals were kindled by it."—Ps. xviii., 8. "Yea, he sent out his arrows and scattered them, he shot out lightnings and discomfited them."—Ps. xviii., 14.

* The engraving is taken from a MS. Psalter in the Bib. Roy. suppl. fr. 1132, *bis.*

† P. 118 and 119. The circle within which God is painted is not only regarded by Christian artists as a buckler, an idea borrowed by them from Greek and Roman artists, but the nimbus itself was by them regarded as a buckler, defending the head. The Manuscript of Herrade, *Hortus Deliciarum*, is explicit on that point, as will be seen by the extract given below. The nimbus thus appears to be a kind of religious casque, or helmet. It is so defined by Gulielmus Durandus, the liturgist, in his *Rat. Div. Off.*

quently, as if artists had been deficient in the respect to which the Father is properly entitled, or in other words, had not held in due reverence that part of the Divine nature, which we regard as the representation of strength and omnipotence.

God the Father, in short, is either entirely absent from sculptured monuments, or if introduced, some insignificant portion only of his figure is exhibited, and that small portion even, is either not honourably placed, or is made to act an incongruous and undignified part. The Son, on the contrary, is constantly present, even in scenes in which he ought not properly, to be represented; he is always worthily depicted and honourably placed. These facts may be explained by several concurring causes, all of which will be here given, as forming an integral part of the Archæological history of God the Father.

The first of these causes was probably the hatred felt by the Gnostics for God the Father; the second, the dread which prevailed amongst the followers of Christ lest they should appear to recal the idea of Jupiter, or to offer a pagan idol to the adoration of ignorant Christians; the third, that identical resemblance between the Father and the Son, which various texts of Holy Scripture appear to intimate; the fourth, the incarnation of the Son, who is the speech or Word of the Father; the fifth, the absence of any visible manifestation of Jehovah, a fact which is confirmed by various texts of Scripture; the sixth and last, the difficulty all artists must have felt in imagining or executing so awful and sublime an image.

We notice in the first place, the hatred borne by the Gnostics to Jehovah; which would most naturally prejudice the iconographic representations of the Father.

In the first centuries of the Christian era there arose a violent heresy against God the Father, or Jehovah. Sectarians, taking up the study of the Old Testament rather like men whose minds were blinded, than those who were endued with the full light of intelligence, discovered, that for having transgressed one prohibition, Adam and all his race had been condemned to death; that for crimes, the magnitude of which they refused to acknowledge, mankind had perished in the deluge; that the Israelites, to expiate their murmuring in the desert, had died by the envenomed bites of fiery serpents; that twenty-four thousand men had perished on one occasion by the command of Jehovah, as a punishment for having been seduced by the beauty of the daughters of Moab, and offering incense with them to their gods; that the people, to atone for the pride of David, his chosen king, had been visited by a plague, which destroyed in a brief period, no less than seventy thousand of them.

Misled by the outward, literal signification of these facts, the Gnostics instead of seeking to comprehend the imperious political reasons, or the profound mystical dogmas which prompted them, became irritated against Jehovah. The new sect rose in revolt against a god who had commanded Samuel to cut in pieces the king of the Amalekites, Agag, whom Saul had spared—they were indignant against that servant of the Lord, the aged Elisha, at whose command, bears, sent by God, devoured the children who had insulted the prophet, and mocked him for his baldness. Passing from facts to ideas, from history to prophecy, the Gnostics inflamed their rebellious feeling against Jehovah by the perusal of that passage of Isaiah, in which the Lord, promising deliverance to Israel, bids the prophet exclaim: "I will feed them that oppress thee with their own flesh; and they shall be drunken with their blood as with sweet wine." (Isaiah, xlix. 26.)* They were irritated to exasperation by another text, in which the same prophet announces that God would descend from heaven in his anger, to slay all mankind.

The Gnostics rejected every explanation of these texts—obstinately determined not to understand that justice, so terrible and rigorous, was imposed by the character of the Jews, not by that of God himself, they closed their eyes to those passages of Deuteronomy in which Moses, before dying, gave his final instructions to the Jewish people, and recapitulated the crimes of which they had been guilty,

‡ "Et cibabo hostes tuos carnibus suis; et quasi musto, sanguine suo inebriabuntur."—Ibid., lxvi., 15, 16. "Quia ecce Dominus in igne veniet, et quasi turbo quadrigæ ejus, reddere in indignatione furorem suum, et increpationem suam in flamma ignis. Quia in igne Dominus dijudicabit, et in gladio suo ad omnem carnem, et multiplicabuntur interfecti a Domino."

contrasting their hardness of heart, ingratitude, infidelity and murmuring, with the patience, equity, and long-suffering of God. They read again the verses in which it is said, "A fire is kindled in mine anger, and shall burn unto the lowest hell" (Deut. xxxii. 22); "The sword without and terror within, shall destroy both the young man and the virgin, the suckling also, and the man of grey hairs" (Deut. xxxii. 25); but they erased from the same chapters, the verses in which Moses reminds the Hebrews that God had "kept them as the apple of his eye," that "as an eagle stirreth up her nest, fluttereth over her young, spreadeth abroad her wings, taketh them, beareth them on her wings: So the Lord alone did lead him, and there was no strange God with him." (Deut. xxxii. 10—12). The dying lawgiver seems as if he would have addressed the Gnostics, when he exclaims: "Oh that they were wise! that they understood this, that they would consider their latter end" (Deut. xxxii. 29). But the Gnostic heretics hardened their hearts, they refused to comprehend; they held in execration God the Father, and the severe justice inculcated in the Old Testament. That insensate sect denied Jehovah to be God, but regarded him as a fearful tyrant, thirsting for blood and eager for the death of his creatures; as a father, jealous of his son, and condemning him to the humiliating punishment of the cross. They broke down his images, and placed in their stead those of Christ, their favourite deity, and forbade that any representation of God the Father, should in future be attempted, either in sculpture or in painting. M. J. J. Ampère, in his "Literary History of France," makes the following observations: *—"There are certain Gnostics who seem to ally themselves with Judaism, but their Judaism is hellenised, platonised, if I may so speak, by Philo.† The opinions of Cerinthus, one of the most ancient Gnostics, resemble in many points those of the old Jewish theology. Still Gnosticism was continually becoming farther estranged from Judaism, and ended by proclaiming a violent opposition and furious hatred against Jehovah. Struck with the

* *Hist. Litt. de la France,* vol. i., pp. 178-180.

† The germs of Gnosticism may be recognised in Philo; he speaks of Ofons, and amongst them of Sophia, Wisdom, whom the Gnostics made the mother of all creatures, but Philo's language is purely metaphysical.

difference between the Old and New Testament, unable to reconcile the exclusive and merciless God of the Jews, with the benevolent and universal God of the Christians, Marcion supposed Jehovah to be an inferior and evil demi-god, the enemy of good, the enemy of the Word, the enemy of Christ, inciting Judas to betray him, and finally causing his crucifixion.

"The Ophites, another Gnostic sect, influenced by similar feelings of aversion, considered the God of the Jews not only as a wicked, but as an unintelligent being; that God, whom they called Jaldabaoth, expected according to them, the advent of a carnal Messiah, and when the true Messiah appeared did not recognise him. The Messiah went to seat himself on his right hand, still without being recognised, and thence attracts to himself the principle of life inherent in all created beings, with the intention of destroying the vicious creation of Jaldabaoth, and making everything return into the bosom of infinite unity. The Ophites gave a strange interpretation of the fall of man through the temptation of the serpent; according to their account, Jaldabaoth, the wicked demi-god adored by the Jews under the name of Jehovah, was jealous of man, and wished to prevent the progress of knowledge; but the serpent, the agent of superior wisdom, came to teach man what course he ought to pursue, and by what means he might regain the knowledge of good and evil: the Ophites consequently adored the serpent, and cursed the true God, Jehovah. It seems probable that the part here assigned to the serpent, was prompted by certain reminiscences of the Phœnician and Egyptian religions, in which the serpent was reverenced as a beneficent being. Another sect had the name of Cainites, because, influenced by the same spirit, they reverenced Cain, and indeed all those who had been reproved in the Old Testament, and even held in honour the cities which were struck with the thunderbolts of heaven, and overwhelmed by the rain of fire."

Sooth to say, the art appears to have imbibed these heretical opinions, for even in its earliest works, on sarcophagi, frescos, mosaics, consecrated glass, and old ivories, the figure of God the Father is rarely seen, or if seen it is imperfect, and sometimes actually degraded. The art seems long to have preserved an ill feeling towards Jehovah, nor was it until a much later period, and by very slow degrees, that she decided on making a fitting representation of the Father.

We cannot be astonished to find that Gnosticism should have penetrated into Christian arts, and exercised a powerful influence, even on our western Cathedrals. M. Raoul Rochette has, in fact, proved the most ancient images of Christ, the Virgin, and the chief Apostles, to have been of Gnostic fabrication, and from that source, impure as it was, we probably derived the portrait of Christ, of his mother, and of the disciples.* It must no longer be supposed that the art has always been perfectly orthodox; one simple observation will suffice to prove the contrary. From the time when the apocryphal books were first condemned by Pope Gelasius I. in the fifth century, down to the sixteenth, when that condemnation was repealed by Pope Paul IV., all, without exception, have been frequently condemned; during the entire course of the middle ages, the pontifical authority was constantly exerted against the apocryphal books. The judgment of the Popes was supported by the the most holy and enlightened minds in Christendom. Saint Athanasius, Saint Cyril of Jerusalem, Saint Augustine, Eusebius of Cesaræa, and Tertullian amongst others, and the ecclesiastical writers Baronius, Bellarmine, Ellies du Pin, Le Nain de Tillemont, seem at a loss for expressions sufficiently severe to be employed in stigmatising this legendary poetry. A compilation of apocryphal works, made by Fabricius, is headed by a collection of all the judgments and censures which had invariably, and at various times, from the third century down to the seventeenth, inclusive, been levelled against the apocryphal books. Pope Gelasius affirms Leuticius, or Leucius, the most prolific of legendary writers, to have been a disciple of the devil; Eusebius of Cesaræa, declares the Apocrypha to be absurd and impious; Saint Athanasius requires them to be rejected as "spurii;" Paul IV. proclaims them unworthy of faith, and rejects them with other condemned writings. Le Nain de Tillemont asserts Abdias the first Bishop of Babylon,

* *Discours sur les types imitatifs qui constituent l'Art du Christianisme;* in 8vo., Paris, 1834, pp. 17 and 18 amongst others.

and author of the "Combat of the Apostles," one of the principal apocryphal books, to have been a mere inventor, a fabulist. Ellies du Pin concurs in opinion with Tillemont, and pronounces the apocryphal legends unworthy of belief, filled with follies, tales and fables. The apocryphal legends have been repeatedly condemned, anathematised, declared to be uncanonical, and yet most of the subjects painted on the stained glass windows, or sculptured in the portals of our Cathedrals, are taken literally from the apocryphal books, and even from the most celebrated amongst them, from those which are most distinctly named in the Anathemas; as, for example,—"l'Evangile de l'Enfance," "La Petite Genèse," the "Combat des Apôtres," and "l'Evangile de Nicodème." At Chartres, the life of Saint John the Evangelist, painted in the south-side aisle, the lives of Saint Thomas, Saint James, and Saint Simon, of Saint Jude, Saint Peter, and Saint Paul, which decorate so brilliantly the windows of the apse, are all extracted from the "Combat des Apôtres," a work which has been condemned as a mere collection of fables.

St. Augustine rejects the cruelty of St. Thomas, as recorded in the Apocrypha, and yet it is sculptured in the Church of Sémur, and painted in Bourges' Cathedral.* It must be acknowledged that subjects taken from heretical books, anathematised by the Church, and originally composed by Gnostics, were, and are still, painted on glass, or carved in stone, in the most sacred part of our grandest and most Catholic edifices.

It is therefore easy to believe that the hatred of the Gnostics to God the Father, may long have survived and have been propagated in the hearts of Christian artists; and if Jehovah appears to have been ill treated by the art, it may be accounted for by the fact, that she was animated, although perhaps unconsciously, by a Gnostic impulse.

To this first reason may be added the great dread then prevalent of making an Idol.

Jehovah, God the Father, is the God of strength, the God of armies and of battles;† the God who spreads terror,

* *Legenda aurea,* "De Sancto Thomo apostolo."

† See in the Bible, and more especially in the Psalms, the warlike and violent epithets given to Jehovah.

and before whom mankind must always tremble.* Jupiter, who dethroned his father, overthrew the Titans, and proposed to the assembled gods to carry them suspended from the end of a chain, is also called the god of strength and of battles.

The analogy between their attributes was so obvious, that to make a portrait of God the Father, was almost like making one of Jupiter, and would have seemed like soliciting the adoration of Christians for an image that would remind them of the great Olympic Idol, held in so much veneration by the Pagans. The inclination to represent God under the character of Jupiter was so strong that, in the earliest ages of the Church, attempts were sometimes made to give the physiognomy of Jupiter even to Christ himself, to that mystic Lamb, who is the personification of the Divine attributes of gentleness and charity,† not that of strength. We are told, in fact, that a Christian artist once attempted to draw a head of Christ after that of an image of Jupiter, but his hand became suddenly withered, and could not be restored to its natural state, except by the prayers and miraculous intervention of Gennadios, Archbishop of Constantinople.‡ There was consequently some-

* "In thy fear will I worship towards thy holy temple."—Ps. v., 8. "Adorabo ad templum sanctum tuum in timore tuo." "Pavete ad sanctuarium meum," is the Judaic inscription sculptured on the pier of the central door of the western porch at St. Germain l'Auxerrois.

† "Jesus cum dilexisset suos qui erant in mundo, in finem dilexit eos."—"Sicut dilexit me pater et ego dilexi vos. Manete in dilectione meâ." "Having loved his own that were in the world, he loved them unto the end."—St. John, xiii. 1. "As the Father hath loved me, so have I loved you; continue ye in my love."—St. John, xv. 9.

‡ Theod. *Hist. Eccles.*, lib. i., cap. 15; S. Joan. Damas. *De imaginibus*, orat. iii., p. 386, 387. The text of Theodoret is as follows: "Pictori cuidam, qui Christi Domini pinxerat imaginem, manus ambæ exaruerunt. Ferebatur autem Gentilis cujuspiam hominis jussu hoc opus, sub nomine Salvatoris specie ita pinxisse, ut capillis ex utraque oris parte discretis facies nullatenus tegeretur (ea utique forma qua pagani Jovem pingunt), ut ab iis qui ipsum viderent Salvatori adorationem offerre existimaretur." Dante, in the fourteenth century, calls Jesus, Sovereign Jupiter.—*Purgat.* Canto vi.

"O summo Giove,
Che fosti 'n terra per noi crocifisso."

At the chronological extremity opposed to that of Theodoret, and almost at our own era, the ideal of Jesus Christ is still sought in the features of Jupiter. In

thing of danger in fixing the genius of artists and the devotion of the faithful on a figure like that of the first person of the Trinity, who would undoubtedly have been invested with the features and attributes of the Father of the Pagan deities; there was less danger as regarded Jesus, whose life, attributes and physiognomy were so far removed from any resemblance with those of Heathen divinities. And when an artist forgot himself, as did he of whom Theodoret speaks, justice was inflicted upon him suddenly and miraculously.

Still that circumstance did not prevent artists from adopting and repeating a type with which the ancients were unacquainted; that of a God-Man, dying for the salvation of mankind. It was scarcely possible to confound the Redeemer with any Pagan deity, and there was comparatively little danger in attempting to depict him.

Even the most rigid of the Iconoclasts, could not maintain, against representations of Christ, the same arguments, which they urged so vehemently against those of the Father, and thus it becomes easy to account for the few existing pictures of Jehovah, and the great number of those of Jesus Christ.

The third reason is the supposed identity and resemblances of the Father and the Son, inferred from various texts of Holy Scripture. "He that seeth me, seeth him that sent me."* "I and my father are one."† "The father is in me, and I in him."‡

fact, Poussin, who had made for a noviciate of Jesuits a picture of St. Francis Xavier, and was reproached with having given the Saviour the character of Jupiter Tonans, replied that he could form no conception of Christ with the visage of a hypocritical devotee, or like the Père Douillet (*Collection des Lettres du Poussin*, Paris, 1824, p. 95). If then, in our time, (and the "Last Judgment" by Michelangelo is an additional proof of the fact,) artists have so far forgotten themselves as to represent the lowly Jesus under the figure of Jupiter, we have so much the stronger reason for supposing that, in the earliest ages of Christianity, at a time when the art was still struggling against the types of Pagan deities, the inclination to represent Christ as Jupiter Tonans was more difficult to resist. It must have been, as I imagine, with a view to avoiding this danger, that early Christian artists were forbidden to attempt any representation of God the Father.

* "Qui videt me videt Eum qui misit me."—St. John, xii. 45.

† "Ego et Pater unum sumus."—St. John, x. 30.

‡ "Pater in me est et ego in Patre."—St. John, x. 38.

Artists, applying these texts in their literal meaning, constantly represented God the Father under the figure of the Son. When in the sculptures at Chartres, in the fresco paintings of Saint Savin, near Poitiers, in the frescos of the Campo Santo, in a number of manuscripts, and even on the early Christian sarcophagi, Jesus is seen creating Adam and Eve, speaking to Noah, to Moses, or to Isaiah, the person is probably intended for God the Father, under the form of the Son, because, in seeing the Son, we see the Father also; because the one who took upon him a human form and was seen amongst men, is the image of the other whom men have never seen. "Who is the image of the invisible God, the first-born of every creature." (Colossians, i. 15.) *

Another text, founded on one of the most strictly fundamental doctrines of Christianity, still further encouraged the substitution of the Son for the Father in figured representations. St. John in the first chapter of his Gospel, declares that Jesus, the divine person who became incarnate, is the Word, the Word of God. "And the word was made flesh."† (St. John, i., 14.)

Consequently, in every religious theme, in which the Deity is described as speaking, the person to be represented is not that of the Father, but of the Son. The Father, may indeed, act, but it is by the Son that he speaks. We are, consequently, less astonished to recognise the features of Jesus, and not Jehovah, in the Divine person who is represented talking with Isaiah in the Cathedral of Chartres, and who on our gothic windows and in old illuminated manuscripts, is seen conversing with the prophets, reproaching our first parents with their disobedience, or accusing Cain of the fratricidal crime he had committed, scenes which are so constantly repeated in ancient sculptures and on sarcophagi, for in all those subjects the Deity speaks, and Jesus is the Word of God made flesh. Besides, in the book of Genesis, we are told that God created all things by his word; God, in fact, does not confine himself to thinking merely, he speaks; when creating the light, the firmament, the luminaries, plants, animals, and man, God says: "Let there be

* "Qui est imago Dei invisibilis, primogenitus omnis creaturæ," in the words of St. Paul.

† "Verbum caro factum est."

light, and there was light" (Gen. i. 3); "Let us make man in our image, after our likeness" (Gen. i. 26). Theologians consequently affirm, that as Jesus according to St. John was the divine Word, therefore Jesus created the world, because the world was formed out of nothing, at the word of God. So Gregory of Tours, at the opening of his "History of the Franks," says, "In the beginning God created in his Christ, who is the beginning of all things; that is to say, God in his Son created the heaven and the earth.*

Thus the Nicene Creed, which is said or sung daily at mass, declares that all things were created by the only Son of God.† The entire Trinity did most assuredly concur in the work of creation, but the Son was the especial agent, the chief actor: and to him the work is chiefly, if not solely attributed. Thus when we find artists, rigorously theological like the sculptors of Chartres Cathedral or the painter of the Church of St. Savin, instead of representing the entire Trinity, exhibiting one divine person only as engaged in the work of creation, that person ought to be Christ, not God the Father, nor the Holy Spirit. In the fifteenth century, and at the Renaissance more especially, theological principles were losing their influence, and at that period, consequently, the Father is most frequently represented creating the world, and not the Son or the Word.

Besides, theology became at that time subordinate to history, and the incarnation of the Son of Man, being chronologically later than the creation, scruples seem to have arisen with regard to the propriety of representing him in that and similar subjects, and the father was substituted in his place. Till at length, art grown bolder and more daring, was not sorry to have an opportunity of attempting the imposing figure of Jehovah; and sought to realise its conception of that sublime and ideal type. In the paintings of Raphael, the God who creates the world, and brings order out of Chaos, is not the Son, but God, the venerable Father, with snow-white beard, and a countenance fraught with power

* *Hist. Ecclesiast. Franc.*, lib. i., No. 1. "Dominus cœlum terramque in Christo suo . . . in filio suo formavit."

† "Jesum Christum, Filium Dei, unigenitum . . . per quem omnia facta sunt."

and energy. When once a figure of the Father had been achieved, it was represented in every biblical scene. Men no longer cared to ascertain whether the Son had or had not created the world, and spoken in the character of the Word of God, to the persons named in the Old Testament; they confounded the Word which is eternal, with the incarnate Jesus who was born in time; they said to themselves that the Old Testament history preceded the birth of Christ, and that whenever in that history God is spoken of, the Father, not the Son, is intended; and consequently, the Father, not the Son, ought to be represented. This reasoning was in conformity with chronological, or rather historical truth in its human sense, but theological truth was thereby completely set aside. Raphael was the first, who in painting for the Popes subjects from the Old Testament, the Creation for example, and other scenes in which God is present, departed from the true Christian doctrine, by representing the Father. Every painter or sculptor, who in our days would represent the work of Creation, ought, rightly, to intimate the presence of the entire Trinity; but were he to select one person only, instead of the whole Trinity, that person ought certainly to be the Word—the Son of God. The heresy of the Gnostics, and the peculiar dogmas of Christian theology, have had greater influence than any other causes on Christian Iconography, in occasioning the rarity of portraits of Jehovah, and the great number of those of Christ.

An additional reason, too, but purely æsthetic, has assisted to produce the same result. It is possible that this result may have been influenced by a motive diametrically opposed to that of the Gnostics.

The idea of a God, creator of the universe and sovereign master of all created beings; a God, whom the most daring imagination can but very imperfectly picture to itself; a God, who by one ray from his eyes kindled the light of day, and with one breath from his mouth called animals and plants into existence;* the idea of such a God, and of attempting to frame his image, might well cause the earlier Christian artists to shrink from the task, since even Raphael himself interpreted it but imperfectly, and the greatest poets of the

* "Qui cœlum palmo metitur, ac terram manu continet et pugillo aquam claudit."—*Opp. S. Joh. Damas.*

present day are dazzled by its grandeur and sublimity. But Jesus Christ had been seen by man, his countenance had been described at length, and even his portrait achieved, and the temerity of representing him seemed therefore less appalling. Whether, then, from the difficulty of representing God the Father, or from a feeling of religious dread and respect of his awful majesty, artists dared not grapple boldly with that subject, till many years had elapsed, and numerous preliminary trials had been made.

It must however be acknowledged in conclusion, that the early Christians, until the fifth and sixth centuries, were rather ill disposed towards images in general; all were in a measure iconoclasts, some in a greater, others in a less degree. They had but recently abandoned Paganism, the religious system of which consisted almost entirely in fabricating and adoring images and statues; besides which, Christianity owed its origin to Judaism, a religion by which every representation or image, whether of God or man, was rigidly proscribed; we must not, therefore, be astonished to find that in order to separate Christians more determinately from idolaters, and to approach a little nearer to that ancient law of God, which was not destroyed but fulfilled in Christ, the Church resolved to restrain the zeal of Christian artists and to prevent them from representing the Divinity in sculpture or in painting as often as they might otherwise have desired.

A singular circumstance may be cited in confirmation of this fact. St. John Damascenus was certainly far from being an iconoclast, since his discourses against the iconoclasts and Leo the Isaurian have been compared to those of Demosthenes against Philip. Yet even he positively declares that the essence of the Divine nature ought not to be represented, since it hath never been revealed to human eye.* But he permits the Son of God only to be figured, because "He, in His ineffable goodness, became flesh, appeared upon earth under a human form, conversed with

* God said to Moses, "Non poteris videre faciem meam; non enim videbit me homo, et vivet."—Exodus, xxxiii. 20. "Thou canst not see my face, for there shall no man see my face and live." Moses in his turn says to the Hebrews: "Locutusque est Dominus ad vos de medio ignis. Vocem verborum ejus audistis, et formam penitus non vidistis."—Deut. iv. 12.

men, took upon Him our nature, our heavy, material body, the form and colour of our flesh. We are not therefore in error," adds he, "when we represent His image, for we desire to see His face, and we thus behold it enigmatically, and as it were through a glass."*

Thus, even Damascenus, so bold, so eloquent, in defending the images of Christ, is restrictive with regard to those of the Father.

If artists venture to represent the Father, it must be under the aspect of the Son, for the Father and the Son are one, and he who hath seen one, hath seen the other also. Christ, in the Gospel of Saint John, speaks thus of himself:—"I and my Father are one." (John, v. 30.) "I am in the Father, and the Father in me." (Saint John, xiv. 11.)

These different texts were supposed, during the middle ages, to refer, not to the divinity of the Father, which is identical with that of the Son, but also, and more particularly, to his form and features. Until the close of the thirteenth century, God is represented as assuming the form of his Son, in order to manifest himself to the world.

Such are the principal reasons to be adduced in explanation of a fact, so singular and interesting to the student of Christian Iconography: such the circumstances by which we would account for the rarity of portraits of the Father, and the numerous existing representations of the Son; together

* The following extracts are from St. John Damascenus:—"In errore quidem versaremur si vel invisibilis Dei conficeremus imaginem; quoniam id quod incorporeum non est, nec visibile, nec circumscriptum nec figuratum, pingi omnino non potest. Impie rursum ageremus si efformatas a nobis hominum imagines Deos esse arbitraremur, iisque tanquam diis divinos honores tribueremus. At nihil horum prorsus admittimus. Sed posteaquam Deus, pro ineffabili bonitate sua, assumpta carne, in terris carne visus est, et cum hominibus conversatus est; ex quo naturam nostram corpulentamque crassitiem, figuram item et colorem carnis suscepit, nequaquam aberramus cum ejus imaginem exprimimus.—Ex quo Verbum incarnatum est, ejus imaginem pingere licet." The great theologian permits the "Word" to be depicted, because the Word was made flesh; but, as God the Father has been seen by no man, it is forbidden to attempt a representation of him: "Dei qui est incorporeus, invisibilis, a materia remotissimus, figuræ expers, incircumscriptus et incomprehensibilis, imago nulla fieri potest. Nam quomodo illud quod in aspectum non cadit imago representarit?" (See the works of St. J. Damas., Paris edition, 1712, fol. vol. i. *Oratio secundo, De imaginibus.*)

with the substitution, in numerous instances, of Christ for Jehovah, and the honour and reverence apparently taken from the Father to be lavished on the Son. Although there can be no doubt that artists felt considerable difficulty in forming an adequate conception of the figure of the Father; still it was rather a feeling of resentment, a sentiment of hostility to strength and violence, by which the art was deterred from attempting any representation of God the Father, and not so much as might be imagined from the fact that God the Father, having never openly manifested himself to the world, the art dared not represent him, and knew not what form to attribute to him. The latter was indeed rather a pretext than a reason. In the first place God the Father had more than once showed himself visibly in the history of the Old Testament: he was seen by Moses in the burning bush: he appeared to the Patriarch Abraham, under the form of an angel, more majestic than the other who accompanied him: and to the Prophet Ezekiel, he appeared under the figure of a man, seated on a throne, and encompassed with glorious light.*

Besides Christian art would not have shrunk from the task of creating a visible form as the interpretation or symbol of an invisible substance; such a theme presented on the contrary, a magnificent opportunity for the exercise of its glowing imagination, in investing with materiality the most elevated, the most sublime of all existing ideas, in clothing the divinity with form and substance. Such a theme would unquestionably have been appropriated by the art with joyous alacrity, ever ready as it has been to give a body to impalpable ideas, and to invest with life so many visionary and metaphysical abstractions.

How many beautiful allegories have been created by the art-sculptured forms of men and women, personifications of liberty, promptitude, courage, faith, hope, charity, cowardice, avarice, the liberal arts, the Jewish religion, the Christian religion, the rivers of the terrestrial paradise, and an infinite

* Ezek., i. 26, 27. "And upon the likeness of a throne was the likeness as the appearance of a man above upon it." "Et super similitudinem throni, similitudo quasi aspectus HOMINIS desuper." In xliii. 3, Ezekiel says again that he saw God under the same form. "Species secundum aspectum quem videram juxta fluvium Chobar."

number of others. If, then, art has given us no representation of Jehovah, it is probably because she wanted the will to attempt it, not the power.

In short, Gnosticism on the one hand, and theological dogmas on the other, had far more potent influence than any other causes, in occasioning the extreme rarity of portraits of God the Father.

The Archæological History of the first person of the Trinity, is necessarily very limited. We now proceed to trace it through its different periods.

PORTRAITS OF GOD THE FATHER.

During the first centuries of Christianity, even as late as the twelfth century, no portraits of God the Father are to be seen. His presence is intimated only by a hand issuing from the clouds, or from heaven.

The hand is sometimes entirely open, and darting rays from each finger, as though it were, if we may be allowed the expression, a living sun. These rays are symbolic of the grace and favour shed forth by God upon the earth. The hand is most frequently seen in the act of blessing, the three first fingers being extended, while the little finger and that adjoining it are closed.* In the annexed engraving the hand is represented as blessing and emitting rays at the same moment.

This engraving is taken from a Greek manuscript, and the form of benediction is Greek,† being given, not with the

* The position of the fingers ought always to be carefully noted. The Greek benediction differs in certain points from the Latin ; consequently, the Greek form of benediction, if observed on a Latin figure, or the reverse, would be of great historical interest.

† Bibliothèque Royale. *Psalterium cum figuris*, Greek, No. 139. In the History of the Nimbus, p. 100 and p. 28, note, we made mention of the transparent nimbus of this beautiful figure of Night (ΝΥΞ), of which the style is completely antique, or rather classical; the veil gemmed with stars, which she raises like a canopy above her head, and the torch reversed, which shows her to be the enemy of the day, complete the allegory. The Prophet Isaiah stands between this personification of Night and that of the dawn. Aurora, or daybreak (Ὄρθρος), is a little genius, a child of about four years old, almost naked, holding a lighted torch, erect, and not reversed. The Prophet

Fig. 52.—THE DIVINE HAND, EMITTING RAYS OF LIGHT, BUT WITHOUT A NIMBUS.
Greek Miniature of the x cent.

three first fingers open, as in the benediction of the Latin

being supposed to be at the close of night and the opening of the day, Night is full-grown, and the day small and in its infancy. Night, which shines

church, but with the forefinger extended, the middle and little finger bent, while the thumb is crossed upon the third finger so as to form a chi (X).

The hand is undoubtedly intended for that of the Father, since a similar hand is seen presenting to Moses the tables of the Law, arresting the arm of Abraham, when he is about to sacrifice Isaac, and appearing in the sky at the moment when Christ is baptised, and also at the transfiguration, when a voice is heard from heaven, saying, "This is my beloved Son, in whom I am well pleased." The historical nature of the subject, and not any characteristic attribute, must therefore be our guide in determining whether the hand be that of God the Father, or whether it belongs to either of the other divine persons of the Trinity, or even to an angel or a saint.

Still a distinctive characteristic is very frequently added to that drawn from the historical subject, in order to prevent the hand of God from being confounded with that of an angel or a saint, or with that of the Son or the Holy Ghost.

It has, in fact, been fully shown in the Introductory Chapter,* that the cruciform nimbus was employed to distinguish God from any of his creatures; any personage adorned with that attribute, may, without hesitation, be infallibly affirmed to represent one of the three Divine

with a borrowed light, has less energy than Day, which gains light and warmth by the immediate agency of the sun; Night is here, therefore, feminine, and Day masculine, and so also the gender of the names which distinguish them is feminine for the one, and masculine for the other. This singular miniature is an interpretation, by painting, of the numerous passages in which Isaiah describes the power of God, and the mission with which he had been charged by Him. "Ecce Dominus Deus in fortitudine veniet, et brachium ejus dominabitur."—Isa. xl. 10. "Dabo in solitudinem cedrum et spinam, et myrtum, lignum olivæ; ponam in deserto abietem, ulmum et buxum simul."—Isa., xli. 19. "Ut sciant hi, qui ab ortu solis, et qui ab occidente, quoniam absque me non est; ego Dominus et non alter. Formans lucem et creans tenebras." —Is., xlv. 6, 7. "Behold the Lord God will come with strong hand, and his arm shall rule for him."—Isa., xl. 10. "I will plant in the wilderness the cedar, the shittah tree, the myrtle, and the oil tree: I will set in the desert the fir-tree, and the pine, and the box-tree together."—Isa., xli. 19. "That they may know, from the rising of the sun, and from the west, that there is none beside me. I am the Lord, and there is none else. I form the light, and create darkness."—Isa., xlv. 6, 7.

* Nimbus, *ante*, p. 38—66.

Persons, except in the few rare instances already noted, and which will generally be found to originate either in the ignorance or negligence of the artist. Thus the hand is often seen, resting against a nimbus, divided by a Greek cross, and it then indicates one of the three persons of the Trinity. If the Son and the Holy Ghost be also present, there can be no doubt that the hand is intended to symbolise the presence of the Father. The following engraving repre-

Fig. 53.—THE HAND OF GOD THE FATHER, NEITHER EMITTING RAYS, NOR ENCIRCLED WITH THE NIMBUS, BUT ENTIRELY OPEN.

Latin Miniature of the IX cent.

sents the baptism of our Saviour.* Christ is standing in the water, and the Holy Spirit, in the form of a dove, descending upon his head; the right hand of God is extended

* This engraving is taken from the *Liber Precum*, Bibliothèque Royale, suppl. lat. 641.

from the starry heaven, interpreting to the eye, the words recorded in the Gospel: "This is my beloved Son." There is no room for hesitation—the hand is, and can be, no other than that of God the Father.

Reasoning therefore from analogy, whenever a hand is seen extended from heaven, whether emitting rays, or in the act of blessing, even should the other persons of the Trinity be absent, which is frequently the case, we may be sure that the hand is really that of God the Father, even though it be not marked with the cruciform nimbus. Thus, then, as the name of Christ is contracted into one or two letters, J. C., so the entire person of Jehovah is contained in one single member, in the hand. The hand is a kind of monogram, employed by sculptors and painters.

The hand, up to the twelfth century, represents the Father exclusively; still, in the second and third periods of Christian art, during the Gothic epoch and that of the Renaissance, even at the time when the Father is represented in half length, or full length, the hand is occasionally seen, and continues to maintain its ground, even till the seventeenth century. It is seen with several varieties, all rather archæological, than chronological, most of them having appeared nearly at the same period.

Fig. 54.—THE DIVINE HAND, RESTING ON A CRUCIFORM NIMBUS.

Italian Sculpture of the XII cent.; in the porch of the Cathedral of Ferrara.

The hand is either in the act of blessing, with two or three fingers only extended, as in Figs. 20 and 52; or it is bestowing (*Donatrice*), that is to say, entirely open, and shedding from each finger rays of light, signifying favour and acceptance, as in Fig. 22, and in other and more complete varieties, to be given hereafter in the History of God the Son; or it is at the same time blessing and bestowing (*Donatrice*), half open, and emitting rays, as at Fig. 52. The hand is sometimes without any attribute, particularly at those epochs distinguished by the absence or rarity of the nimbus: or it is surrounded by a nimbus, usually intersected with cross lines, like the nimbus of the head; or occasionally, either from ignorance or forgetfulness, the cross lines on the nimbus are omitted. In the frescos of the catacombs, on the ancient sarcophagi, and in the earliest mosaics, the nimbus of the hand is invariably absent. Figure 52, given above, contains a hand without a nimbus; in the preceding engraving, the hand will be seen to rest upon a cruciform nimbus.*

In the series of mosaics, we not unfrequently find the fore part of the arm attached to the hand. This is what is termed in heraldry, dextral or sinistral, according to whether the hand, attached to the arm, be the right or the left hand.

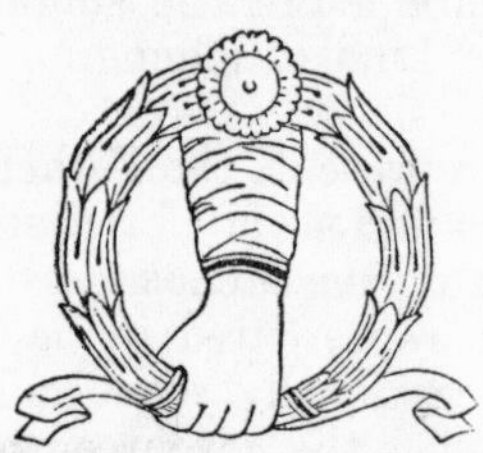

Fig. 55.—THE DIVINE HAND, PRESENTING A CROWN TO THE INFANT JESUS.

Latin Mosaic of the IX century.

The annexed drawing represents the Divine hand, inscribed within a crown, which it seems to offer to our Saviour; the Holy Child is in His mother's arms.†

The crown here offered by the Father to the Son, is still the distinction awarded by God to virtuous men; it is that crown of life which he makes the recompense of virtue.

* The hand in this plate is giving the Latin not the Greek benediction. The position of the fingers does not appear to be intended in our church to be symbolic; but with the Greeks the forefinger extended is designed to resemble an I, the middle finger is bent into the form of C, the ancient *sigma* of the Greeks; the thumb and third finger being crossed make an X, and the little finger is rounded into a C: thus forming IC—XC, the Greek monogram of Jesus Christ (ΙησουC ΧριστουC). This hand is sculptured in the tympanum of the Cathedral of Ferrara, and appears, from its position, to belong to some person on earth, who, standing in an exalted altitude, blesses the individuals placed beneath him. In Fig. 20, a hand is given, in a very different position, descending apparently from Heaven, instead of being raised from earth. In the western gate of the Cathedral of Sens is a Divine hand applied upon a cruciform nimbus; it appears to descend from Heaven, and from the summit of the vaulting, blesses a whole cordon of martyrs, who ascend on the right and left, along the branches of the ogive.

† *Vetera Monimenta*, 2nd part, Fig. 53. A mosaic in the Church of Santa Maria Nova, which dates from 848. Bosio (*Rom. Sott.*, p. 133) gives an engraving of God offering a crown with each hand to two saints.

In the Manuscript of Herrade is figured a moral ladder, reaching from earth to heaven; at the summit, on the highest step, the hand of God, issuing from the clouds, presents a triumphal crown to Virtue, or Charity, which having surmounted all obstacles, has gained the threshold of heaven. In the book of Herrade, God appears to be granting a reward to human virtue; in the Latin mosaic, he does homage to the holy self-devotion of the sacrifice of Jesus.

From the time of the birth of Christ to his return to heaven after the resurrection, the hand of the Father was constantly near to direct, bless, and sustain the steps of the Son.

When, at the baptism of Jesus by St. John, a voice is heard from heaven, saying, "This is my beloved Son," a hand, the hand of the Father, is seen to issue from the clouds, as if, by the aid of art, to interpret to the eyes the words just uttered.* When, in the Garden of Olives, the Saviour, weighed down by unutterable sorrow, exclaims, "My Father, take away this cup from me," (Mark xiv. 36,) a hand, the hand of the Father, is extended from heaven to bless and to console his Son.†

When, at the crucifixion, Jesus in his death agony calls on the Father in these despairing words,—"My God, my God, why hast thou forsaken me:" we discover, traced upon the summit of the cross, a hand, the hand of the Father in the act of benediction.‡

Lastly, when Jesus re-ascends to heaven after His death and

* See Fig. 53.

† The subject is usually represented thus; but on the stone screen enclosing the choir of Notre Dame de Paris, the entire head and the hand of the Father are visible.

‡ See, amongst other examples, a painting on glass of the twelfth, or perhaps even the eleventh century, adorning the apsidal gallery of St. Remi de Rheims. The head of St. John, with a nimbus surmounted by two heliotrope flowers (Fig. 3), is taken from that window. M. du Sommerard is in possession of an enamel belonging to the twelfth century, in which Christ is represented crucified; above the cross a hand appears, as in the window at Rheims—the hand of the Father—whose being present at the death of his Son is thus indicated. The hand has neither rays nor a nimbus. The presence of God is more distinctly manifested in a miniature taken from a copy of Latin Hours, belonging to the fourteenth century—*MS.* 459 of the Bibliothèque St. Geneviève. At the crucifixion there given, the Father is seen in the clouds; a half-length figure of an aged man, with long beard and hair—he is entirely blue, like the clouds and sky surrounding him, from whence he is looking down upon the sacrifice of his Son.

passion, holding in His hand the cross of the resurrection, the Father extends to Him his right hand, and seems in a manner to assist Him to rise; this latter subject is frequently seen in illuminated manuscripts,* and may be explained by the two verses of Alcuin, subjoined, and which were placed immediately under a painting of the Ascension:—

> "DEXTERA quæ Patris mundum ditione gubernat,
> Et Natum cœlos proprium transvexit in altos."†

These Divine hands play an important part, not only in figured monuments, but in the text itself. St. Mark of Athens, a hermit of Lybia, died in the fourth century, and his beatified soul was carried up to heaven on a white napkin, and there received by the great hand of God, who placed it in Paradise.‡

Saint Eucher, Bishop of Lyons, in the fifth century, says, that by the hand of God, the divine power is implied.§ The regal power is indicated by the hand of justice, || and thus the same idea reigns in the religious and the civil systems.

St. Prosper of Aquitaine also speaks of the hand of God, which forms and models *Jod* as a sculptor does a statue.¶ It seems, in fact, as if this motive originated with the Old Testament, for a number of biblical passages make mention of the hand by which all things were made, and which is

* A manuscript in the Bibliothèque Royale, suppl. lat. 648, of the eleventh century, contains a picture of Christ flying up to heaven with extended hands and arms. Jesus, who has a cruciform nimbus, is looking towards the right hand of the Father, who blesses him by opening the three first fingers. Below are the Apostles and the Virgin Mary, whom two angels, hovering between heaven and earth, undoubtedly address in these words: "Viri Galilæi, quid statis aspicientes in cœlum? Hic Jesus qui assumptus est a vobis in cœlum, sic veniet quemadmodum vidistis eum euntem in cœlum." "Ye men of Galilee, why stand ye gazing up into heaven? This same Jesus, which is taken up from you into heaven, shall so come in like manner, as ye have seen him go into heaven." Acts, i. 11.

† See in Baluze (*Miscellanea*, vol. iv.) the different verses composed by Alcuin, to explain the miniatures in a Carlovingian manuscript.

‡ Bolland. Mars, vol. iii., *Vie de St. Marc.*

§ *Liber Formularum Spiritualium*, cap. i. "Per manum Domini ipsius potestas demonstratur."

|| See Mabillon, p. 421. Hugues Capet holds in his right hand a "hand of Justice,"—this hand is in the act of blessing, Latin form, in every respect like the hand of God, Fig. 54.—Trans.

¶ *Exposition des Pseaumes*, ps. cxviii., at the word Jod.

symbolic of that Supreme power* which fashioneth man as a potter doth clay.†

In the opening of his vision, Ezekiel says, "And when I looked, an hand was sent unto me; and lo, a roll of a book was therein; and he spread it before me; and it was written within and without,"‡ Lastly, in the sublime hymn of the *Libera*, the last final prayer of the Church for those who are no more, the departed exclaims, "Oh! my brethren, do ye at least, have pity upon me, for the hand of God hath touched me."§ For the same reason, and by analogous principles of symbolism, the arm, which is the emblem of God, is also made to figure the divine power collectively. When the arm is seen therefore upon our windows, in miniatures of manuscripts, and on the summits of our ogival arches, we are reminded of a passage of the Canticle sung by the Virgin Mary on meeting her cousin Elizabeth: "He hath showed strength with his arm: He hath scattered the proud in the imaginations of their hearts: He hath put down the mighty from their seats, and exalted them of low degree."‖ In short, all the numerous texts contained in the Old and New Testaments, seem to be condensed into the one motive so often adopted among Greek Christians, and which represents the souls of the just, little naked human beings, praying with joined hands in the great hand of God; this hand issues from the clouds, whence it appears to have descended

* "Omnia hæc manus mea fecit et facta sunt omnia, cujus summa potestas." "For all those things hath mine hand made, and all those things have been, saith the Lord." Isaiah, lxvi. 2.

† "Sicut lutum in manu figuli, sic vos in manu meâ, domus Israel." "Behold, as the clay is in the potter's hand, so are ye in mine hand, O house of Israel." Jeremiah, xviii. 6.

‡ Ezekiel, ii. 9: "Et vidi, et ecce manus missa ad me, in quâ erat involutus liber et expandit coram me qui erat scriptus intus et foris." Ezekiel says again, viii. 1-3, "Et cecidit ibi super me manus Domini Dei. * * * Et emissa similitudo manus apprehendit me in cincinno capitis mei; et elevavit me spiritus inter terram et cœlum." "The hand of the Lord God fell there upon me. * * * And he put forth the form of an hand and took me by a lock of mine head; and the Spirit lifted me up between the earth and the heaven."

§ "Miseremini mei, vos saltem amici mei, quia manus Domini tetigit me."

‖ "Fecit potentiam in *brachio* suo; dispersit superbos mente cordis sui, Deposuit potentes de sede et exaltavit humiles." St. Luke, i. 51, 52.

to earth to take the souls of the righteous, and return with them to heaven and Paradise.*

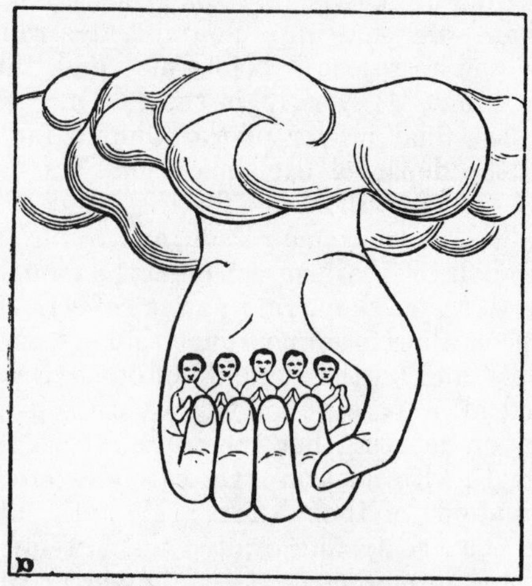

Fig. 56.—THE SOULS OF THE RIGHTEOUS IN THE HAND OF GOD.
From a Greek Fresco of the XVIII cent.

In the thirteenth and fourteenth centuries, God the Father, is no longer content to show merely an arm or a hand; he displays first his face, then the bust, and at length the entire person. In the annexed engraving the face of God is seen, issuing from the clouds.†

* The above plate is taken from a fresco in the church of the great Convent at Salamis. "Animæ justorum in dextra Domini." These paintings have furnished several drawings for the present work, for although they date only from 1735, they exemplify perfectly the system of Byzantine compositions. In Greece, indeed, the art has remained stationary ever since the eleventh and twelfth centuries, so that paintings executed even in the eighteenth century are still of immense archæological value. An inscription which I copied, states that the paintings mentioned above were executed by Georges Marc, of the city of Argos, assisted by three of his pupils, in the year 1735. The school of Argos is now extinct, and nearly all Greek Christian artists have taken refuge in Mount Athos.

† From a manuscript of the fourteenth century, in the Bibliothèque Royale, *Heures du Duc de Berri*, folio 65. The scene represented is that of Christ in the garden of Gethsemane; God the Father looks down from the clouds, and appears to console the Divine victim.

Still the Father has as yet no countenance peculiarly his own, no features appropriate to himself; an inscription is

Fig. 57.—THE FACE OF GOD THE FATHER, WITH THE FEATURES OF THE SON. From a French Miniature of the XIV cent.

required, unless the subject itself clearly points out that the figure must be designed for Jehovah, rather than Jesus. Otherwise, and for the reasons cited above, the figure of the Father might be mistaken for that of the Son: for the age, costume, attitude and expression of both are alike. Like the Son, but with less propriety, the Father wears the cruciform nimbus, a nimbus marked by the cross on which Jesus died. In the church of St. Saturnin at Toulouse, is a marble bas-relief on the basement of the sanctuary, representing the Father Eternal enclosed in an oval aureole, with a pearled edge. The figure is certainly intended for the Father, for he is attended by a cherub, around whom is engraven the following inscription,—"Ad dextram PATRIS cherubin stat cuncta potentis." Now this figure of God the Father, with the cherub on his right hand, is completely beardless, like the figures of the Son, of which examples* have been already given. His head is encircled by a cruciform nimbus, on the transverse branch of which the letters *a*, *ω*, are inscribed.† The features are soft: the expression of

* See Figs. 8, 17, and 18.

† I am indebted for these particulars to M. Ferdinand de Guilhermy. As a pendant to the cherub on the right hand of the Father, a seraph is placed on the left. The two angels are precisely similar; it would be impossible to distinguish them without the inscription. Round the seraph is written, "*Possidet inde sacram seraphin sine fine sinistram.*"

the countenance, benevolent. He is surrounded by the four attributes or symbols of the Evangelists, and holds an open book, on which are inscribed certain words of the Gospel; the salutation in fact, addressed by Christ to his Apostles, "Pax vobis." The figure is similar in every point to that of Christ, as represented on ancient sarcophagi, on the early frescos in the catacombs, and the most ancient illuminated manuscripts.

How then can these attributes and characteristics be reconciled with the inscription declaring the figure to be that of God the Father, not the Son? The Divine person at St. Saturnin bears a striking resemblance to the youthful image of God, given below, and which we can not affirm with certainty to be intended for the Father rather than the Son.

Fig. 58.—GOD, BEARDLESS; EITHER THE SON OR THE FATHER.
French Miniature of the XI cent.

If intended for God the Father, it would have been proper to represent him with a beard: if for the Son, the Resurrection Cross, or the Book of the Gospels ought to have been substituted for the globe. This drawing is taken from a manuscript at Beauvais, containing a treatise on the Genesis, written by St. Augustine. Now in this treatise, the Son is not mentioned, but the Father only, the Almighty God, who, according to the Apostle's Creed, was in an especial manner, the Creator of heaven and earth.*

It seems, therefore, fair to believe, that the figure is intended for that of God the Father: yet hidden as it were under the aspect of the Son, the Father as yet having no peculiar countenance or physiognomy.

Nevertheless, as early as the fourteenth century, in miniatures of manuscripts, more especially, we can detect the tendency, strongly prevalent amongst artists, to give to Jehovah a special form and character. Nothing can be more curious than to observe the timid and progressive efforts of an art which, till then, had either felt no desire to attempt the representation of God, or had been incapable of delineating the Omnipotent Divinity, God the Father, the Creator. There is a constant struggle to mark his charactesistics more distinctly, and to separate them more entirely from those of the Son. It is like being present at the birth, and watching the development of the semblance of the Father Eternal. First, as has been shown, the figures of the Father and Son are identical; it is impossible to distinguish between them. The similitude is as perfect as that between two copies of the same work. Thus in Fig. 6, where the creation of Adam is represented as performed by the co-operation of the three Divine persons, it is absolutely impossible to decide which is intended for the Father, and which for the Son. In the preceding plate, the Father is beardless, as is commonly the case in representations of the Son; in that subjoined, both are bearded, and cannot be distinguished one from the other. Is it the Father who is seated, and receiving the Son? but he holds in his hand the Resurrection Cross, the invariable attribute of the Saviour.

* The treatise of St. Augustine is entitled *de Genesi ad litteram.* M. l'abbè Barraud, Professor of Christian Archæology, in the grand seminary of Beauvais, is decidedly of opinion that the person represented in the vignette is intended for God the Father. The frame-work around the figure forms an O, the first letter in the treatise, which opens thus: "Omnis divina Scriptura."

Is it then the Son who is seated? but this would place him on the left of the standing figure, and, according to Scripture,* the Son's place is on the right of the Father. Besides, the age and aspect of both figures are the same.†

Fig. 59.—GOD THE FATHER, AND GOD THE SON, WITH FEATURES EXACTLY IDENTICAL.
French Miniature, of the commencement of the XIII cent.

In the succeeding period a slight difference becomes perceptible; the two persons are still of the same age, the same complexion, and the outline of the features is similar, but

* "Sede a dextris meis."

† This drawing, rather smaller in size, is contained within the letter D, in the Psalm, "Dixit Dominus Domino meo;" it forms part of a MS. Psalter in the bibl. de Chartres.

in the one they are more strongly marked, as indicating greater energy; in the other they are more delicate, and have an expression of greater gentleness. They might be termed twins, and to them may appropriately be applied

Fig. 60.—THE FATHER, REPRESENTED AS SLIGHTLY DIFFERENT TO THE SON. French Miniature of the close of the XIII cent.

those words of Ovid, "Non facies una nec diversa tamen." In the above engraving, taken from a manuscript, dating from the latter years of the thirteenth century,* the Father

* Bibl. roy. *Heures du duc d'Anjou.* The drawing represents the Trinity; the Father and Son are united by the Holy Ghost, who connects one with the other by touching them with the tips of his extended wings.

may be recognised by the globe in his hand, and the Son by the book. Besides which, the position of the Father on the left hand, while the Son is on the right, tends still further to mark their individual character. In the face itself, very little difference is perceptible; yet the figure of the Son seems perhaps more slender, that of the father stronger and more powerful; the head of Christ may possibly be rather more elongated, that of the Father rounder.

The shades of difference are, as yet, extremely difficult to seize; nevertheless, it is possible to define them with greater precision than formerly: the figures are still those of brothers, but no longer of twins; a year, or perhaps more, intervene between them; the contrast next begins to show itself. The beard and hair of the Father are longer and less abundant; the receding muscles give prominence to the cheek-bones, and the face is marked with numerous lines and furrows; the Son continues of the same age, which he had reached in the thirteenth century, that is to say about thirty or thirty-three years of age.

All these singular iconographic changes were made in the course of the fourteenth century, but about 1360, the idea of paternity and filiation became irrevocably fixed, and shows itself more and more clearly down to our own time, where it has received its most complete development. There is no longer any possibility of mistake. Jehovah is clearly the Father of Jesus, and as such is supposed to be more aged than his Son, by twenty-five, thirty, or even forty years. At the commencement of the fourteenth century, the figure of the Father is still too youthful to permit the idea of any appropriate distance of age between him and the Son, but in the sixteenth, and particularly at the Renaissance, the relative proportion of age is natural, and correctly preserved. In the following engraving, taken from a manuscript belonging to the close of the fourteenth century,* the characteristic features of the Father are well marked. Like the head of a family between his two children, the Son is seated on his right, the Holy Ghost on his left; the Father is twenty or twenty-five years older than Christ, and forty or forty-five more than the Holy Ghost. Besides, the

* *Roman des trois Pélerinages*, folio, 226 verso. Bibl. Sainte Geneviève.

Father seems still further exalted above the other persons by the royal crown upon his head; and the place of honour which he occupies, together with the globe which, like an Emperor, he holds in the right hand, confirm the superior dignity already indicated by his age and the dimensions of the head.

Fig. 61.—GOD THE FATHER, DISTINCT FROM THE SON AND HOLY GHOST. French Miniature; end of the XIV cent.

From this time forward, God the Father appears to have a face and figure peculiarly his own, and of which he is never after deprived. The theological idea succumbs, overpowered by historical truth and human realities. We have reached the period of materialism. The dogma, asserting the Father and Son to be co-eternal; absolutely, mathematically, of the same age, was discarded; the artist looked out into actual nature, and observing every father to be twenty or five-and-twenty years older than his son, chose to depict the Son of God as twenty or five-and-twenty years younger than God himself. In the design which follows, where God the Creator is seen creating Eve from the rib of Adam,* the Father, and not the Son, is plainly intended.

Fig. 62.—GOD THE FATHER, THE CREATOR, AS AN OLD MAN AND A POPE. From a French stained glass window of the XVI cent.

Thenceforth, in pictures of the Creation, we shall always

* Painted window of the sixteenth century, in Ste. Madeleine de Troyes. The Father is in papal robes, and wears a tiara encircled by three royal crowns, like that of the Roman Pontiff.

trace the same Divine figure; aged, sometimes even extremely old; the "Ancient of Days," as we find him constantly represented. Art has at length succeeded in delineating the figure of God the Father.

But it must also be observed that, before the fifteenth century, the principle of the equality of the three persons constantly predominates in representations of the Trinity.

The equality of the three persons of the Trinity is as strikingly marked as possible. The Father, Son, and Holy Ghost, as will be seen in the Chapter on the Trinity, are exactly of the same age; they wear the same robes, are adorned with the same kind of nimbus, and have sometimes the same attributes.

In the fifteenth century, and with still greater reason in the sixteenth, artists aimed more particularly at displaying the difference between them. Thus the three persons are either distinct, and represented separately, as in the Manuscript of "l'Aiguillon de l'Amour divin" or they are blended and incorporated one with the other, as in a copy of Dante, printed at Florence in 1491. In the first case, and this may be remarked as early as the end of the fourteenth century, the Father is an old man of from sixty to eighty years of age; the Son a man of thirty or thirty-five; the Holy Ghost a youth of from twelve to eighteen.* In the second case, the three persons have one body only and two arms for the three; the right hand is raised in benediction, the left hand bears a large globe, which belongs to the three persons collectively; a single nimbus encircles the head. Equality is distinctly represented: but on this single trunk there are three heads, and the three faces are completely distinct one from another. The Father, for instance, is always aged; the Son a man of mature age; the Holy Ghost is always adolescent.

In the thirteenth century, when the three Persons of the Trinity are treated as equal, the Father cannot be distinguished from the Son, and usually has the same characteristics of age and person, as the Son†. In the fifteenth

* See the *Roman des Trois Pélerinages,* an illuminated manuscript of the fourteenth century, mentioned above, Page 216.

† Several examples have already been given, especially Figs. 6 and 11;

and sixteenth centuries the reverse may be sometimes observed: the Son appears to have grown old, and to assume the age of the Father. The Son follows, the Father appears to lead. Amongst other examples of this, we shall quote a picture of the Trinity, taken from the beautiful folio manuscript in the Bibliothèque de Sainte Geneviève, containing the translation, by Raoul de Presles, of the "*Cité de Dieu.*"

The Father and Son are united by the Holy Ghost, which, under the form of a dove, touches the two Divine persons with the tips of the extended wings. The Father is in the Papal robes, as he is frequently drawn at that period; his countenance that of an aged man, with long hair and flowing beard. Christ, on his right hand, seems almost like a reflection of the Father's image, for his age is nearly the same; the beard may, perhaps, be slightly less in length, but not a shade of dissimilarity can be discovered either in the features or hair; the tiara and nimbus, worn by Christ and the Father, are precisely similar.*

Even the figures of the Holy Ghost, who is almost invariably represented as an adolescent, seldom, as having attained the age of manhood, follow the general movement of the epoch, and are sometimes of the same age as those of the Father.† The middle ages may, therefore, be divided into two periods, with reference to God the Father. In the first, anterior to the fourteenth century, the figure of the Father is confounded with that of the Son; the Son is treated as all-powerful, and the Father is invested with his image and likeness. In the second period, extending from after the thirteenth down to the sixteenth century, Christ loses his ascendancy in iconographic assimilation, he succumbs to the Father, whose form, he in his turn assumes, and becomes like him, aged and wrinkled.

With regard to the Holy Ghost, when invested with the

others will be given below in the "History of the Trinity." Proofs of the fact are most abundant.

* A plate from this miniature will be given in the "History of the Holy Ghost," Fig. 143.

† "City of God." Translated by Raoul de Presles, Bibliothèque St. Geneviève. In the manuscript of the Duc d' Anjou, is a picture of the Trinity, in which the Holy Ghost has the countenance of an old man, like the two other Divine Persons.

human form, he is absorbed in the first period by the Son, in the second by the Father: he experiences, but never influences, the iconographic revolutions which take place around him. The figure of the Holy Ghost is left to the pleasure of the artist.

In conclusion, from the first ages of Christianity down to our own day, the esteem in which the Father is held, appears to have been progressively increasing. His portrait was at first interdicted through the influence of Gnostic heresy; then given cautiously and timidly, disguised as it were under the lineaments of the Son; next, rejecting all extraneous accessories, he appears in his own character, and distinguished by peculiar features and aspect. Raphael, and last of all the Englishman Martin, invested him at length with a solemn and and awe-inspiring physiognomy appropriate only to the Almighty Father and Creator.

Having now arrived at the period in which the Father assumes his own peculiar character and countenance, it next becomes necessary to point out the signs and attributes by which the first Person of the Holy Trinity may be distinguished from the other two.

CHARACTERISTIC ATTRIBUTES OF GOD THE FATHER.

Previous to the eleventh century, the presence of the Father was always intimated by a hand extended from the clouds, either in the act of benediction, or grasping a crown; neither the Son nor the Holy Ghost were ever thus represented.

In the twelfth century, when the face of God is first introduced, it cannot positively be defined as the Father's, nor is it possible so to attribute it with any degree of certainty, unless the Son and the Holy Ghost are also present.

In this latter case, the attributes of the other two persons, serve indirectly to characterise the first; if one holds a cross, and the other a dove, the third, whether with or without any attribute, must undoubtedly be the Father.

But this is not the place in which to dwell on the

distinctive attributes of the three persons of the Trinity united in one scene; they will be reserved for the chapter on the Trinity.

The orb, or globe of the world, although it is sometimes given to the other two persons, rarely indeed to the Holy Ghost and rather more frequently to Christ, is restricted almost exclusively to the Father; probably, because the Father was regarded as the principal agent in the work of Creation, or because power appears to be his peculiar attribute. Still this characteristic is not positive, as it is occasionally bestowed on the other two persons. In the Life of Jeanne d'Arc, it is stated that that heroine bore in her hand a white standard adorned with *fleur-de-lis*, upon which was the figure of God, with the world in his hands; on the right and left were angels, each holding a *fleur-de-lis*.

It is vexatious that this standard cannot be more decisively described or restored by archæology, and the figure of God, proved to be intended for that of the Father, and not the Son. However, notwithstanding the great gentleness of disposition manifested by Jeanne d'Arc, we must suppose the figure to be intended for that of God the Father, as he is more frequently seen with the globe than the Son, and above all, he is the God of armies and of battles.

Neither is the book a characteristic that will serve to distinguish the Father, for it is placed indifferently in the hands either of the Father or the Son, and is even more frequently given to the divine Word, to Him who came to bring the Gospel to mankind.*

The cruciform nimbus and bare feet belong equally to either of the three persons, and not to any one in particular, but the triangular or lozenge-shaped nimbus is reserved ordinarily to the Father; it is seldom worn by the Son, and even more rarely given to the Holy Ghost.†

Everything hitherto therefore, seems vague. Indeed, during the second period, which extends from the twelfth to the fourteenth centuries, whenever God the Father is depicted alone and not in the Trinity, it is almost impossible to decide whether the figure is intended for him or for the Son.

* Fig. 61 represents the Father with a crown, the Son with a book, and the Holy Ghost without any attribute.

† See the Chapter on the Nimbus, pp. 59—65.

In the fourteenth, fifteenth, and sixteenth centuries, on the contrary, the characteristic attributes of the Father become more numerous and precise.

In works carefully executed, the age assists greatly in recognising the Father; the hair and beard are longer in the first person than in either of the other two; the face might be pronounced that of a man of fifty, sixty, or sometimes even eighty years old. The head is much larger than that of the Son, and, more particularly, than that of the Holy Ghost; this latter fact which is very interesting, is not invariable, but it is notwithstanding, tolerably frequent. It seems as if the head, like the body, were made to grow larger with age, even when physically speaking, neither head nor body would in the natural course of physical existence continue to increase, but on the contrary, rather diminish and waste away.

This then, may be considered as a rude and entirely conventional mode of indicating more advanced age. A drawing, taken from a manuscript in the Bibliothèque de Sainte Geneviève, of the end of the fifteenth century, will be given in the chapter on the Trinity; * in it the head of the Father is nearly twice the size of that of the Holy Ghost, and about one-third larger than that of Christ. In Fig 61, we discover the earliest germ of this interesting fact.

Towards the close of the fourteenth century, during the whole course of the fifteenth, and in the first years of the sixteenth, men exerted their ingenuity to discover some method of representing the Deity in a manner worthy of himself. Impossible as it was to interpret by the mere expression of countenance, and the moral sentiment, the creative omnipotence and sovereign power of him, by whom the world was made, and is still governed, they sought in the political world some type best fitted to convey the idea of supreme power, and with this social emblem they invested the Divinity, in order to render his supremacy more sensible to our eyes. In Italy the Pope is the most exalted type of unlimited power: he is in himself infallible, he has absolute sway over the consciences of men, and their bodies and souls are subject to his regal and pontifical power. He is the representative of God on earth, the master of emperors and

* See Fig. 123.

kings. To the Italians, the Pope is the all-powerful griffin described by Dante, who without any effort or movement of the wings, moves onward the car of the Church; he is the energetic animal, partly eagle and partly lion, which draws the world after it: his is the two-fold nature of Priest and King, spiritual as the heavenly eagle, and temporal like the terrestrial lion, to whom all are forced to yield.*

In Germany, the Emperor, not the Pope, possesses supreme authority; there every attempt on the part of the Pope to elect, depose, punish, or reward emperors, is regarded as an usurpation.

The imperial power is in Germany the visible expression of an invisible Providence. In France the Pope is revered, the Emperor enjoys his meed of honour, but the executive power is vested in the King, who is in fact the absolute sovereign in his dominions. Thus, then, in Italy, where the Pope was supreme, God was appropriately represented with the papal attributes; in Germany, where the Emperor is chief, he wears the imperial robes; while in France he is represented as a king.† The same course has been pursued in England and in Spain.

In England, where the Pope has long been held in low esteem, it was impossible to represent God the Father with the insignia of the papacy; in Spain, on the contrary, where the authority of the pontiff was equal at least to that of the king, the Father is as frequently seen in one character as in the other.

It is thus, in fact, that God the Father is usually pourtrayed among the various nations above mentioned; still it must not be supposed that God is never represented in Italy as king or emperor; never as Pope or king in Germany; nor as emperor or Pope in England or in France; but such

* *Purgatorio*, canto xxix. The Pope, as pontiff, has limbs of gold in that part of the body in which he has the form of a bird; in the other, the royal quadruped, he has limbs of mingled white and scarlet. The allegorical triumph of Christ and his Church, so richly described in Dante, and so splendidly painted in the window of Notre Dame de Brou, appears never to have been understood by the translators or annotators of the *Divina Commedia*. The griffin has latterly been understood to mean Christ, but it does not appear to have occurred to the commentators that to make Jesus draw the car of the Church is to impose upon him an office unworthy of God.

† Above, Fig. 61, an example is given of God the Father as king.

instances are not in reality very numerous, and are exceptions to the general rule. Any figure of God the Father, if free from foreign influence, or the mystical ideas generally prevalent at the period, or peculiar to the artist himself, will undoubtedly bear the impress of local differences, and be tinged with the historical colouring referred to above. In France for instance, pictures of God the Father as Pope are occasionally seen; but only in convents subject to ultramontane influence, or at some period when the reigning Pope was highly popular;—perhaps at the time of our wars in Italy, or when the artist himself held the papacy in more than ordinary reverence.

Even at such times, and under such peculiar circumstances, the French invariably protest against the idea of assimilating the Eternal Father with the Pope who is only his vicar, as degrading the Supreme God into a being with delegated authority. Either not daring enough, or incapable of creating a new type, French genius strove at least to elevate the Deity, and raise him far above the papal power. The papal tiara is adorned, according to the period, with one, two, or three crowns, the number of which signify the degree, or, mathematically speaking, the power of the sovereignty. The same idea was adopted by the French, and in figures representing God the Father as Pope, his head is surmounted by a tiara of three crowns, that number being considered symbolic of the plenitude of sovereign power; but, growing bolder, they increased the number of crowns to four or even five, signifying thereby that God was infinitely superior to the Pope.

The stained glass windows of Saint Martin-ès-Vignes, at Troyes, contain several of these curious examples, and the plate annexed, which has been engraved, and which was taken from the Church of St. Martin, presents one of these figures of God the Father holding the Saviour nailed to the cross. The Father is robed in an alb, a tunic, a scarf, and wears a tiara, like the pope; but upon the tiara rise in stages, no longer three crowns only, but five; all decorated with floriations and *fleurs-de-lis*, like those of our French kings.*

* The chaussure of God in this figure is worthy of notice. In Christian Iconography, the feet of God the Father, as well as of the Son and of the

In Champagne, therefore, God is superior, by two crowns, to the Pope.

Fig. 63.—GOD THE FATHER, AS POPE, WITH A TIARA OF FIVE CROWNS.
A French Painted Glass Window of the close of the XVI cent.

In France, God the Father appears habited in the costume of a king, prior to his appearance in that of a pope. The

Apostles, are nearly always bare; in this picture he wears slippers, in order to heighten the resemblance between him and the Pope. A singular peculiarity

Divine King wears the royal crown just as we see it worn by Philip of Valois, John the Good, and Charles the Fifth; like our Emperor Charlemagne, he grasps the golden orb or sphere, and is arrayed in the long robe and mantle; but his head is encircled by a cruciform nimbus, and the feet are bare, because in fact, he is God. It is by this royal crown and orb, combined with the flowing beard which marks his great age, that we may distinguish the Father from the Son. One of these attributes alone would not perhaps be sufficient, because, as has been said, the globe is often given to the Son, and so also is the regal crown. This latter ensign is less common on the head of the Son, for he is generally bare-headed, or else wearing a crown of thorns.

The Father, in the character of king, accompanies us through the whole of the fourteenth century, while during the fifteenth he is most commonly figured as pope. In the latter character he is usually robed in the alb and cope; but the latter is often omitted. As pope, it must be acknowledged that the figure of the Father is sometimes pleasing, but never venerable; it excites contempt rather than respect. In proof of this, I need only mention that effigy of the Father, which commences the series of statues in the inclosure of the choir of Notre Dame, at Chartres.

An artist who was capable of forming statues of men so severe in character, and of women so graceful in form, was certainly not wanting in the power to have given a more worthy representation of God the Father; yet his figure there sculptured, is robed in a garment apparently designed

may be noticed in a MS. in the Bibliothèque Royale (*Biblia Sacra*, No. 6829), belonging to the close of the fourteenth century, and richly adorned with miniatures. In a picture representing Aaron after the purification, by which he is prepared to become a worthy priest of God, the Deity is represented with one foot bare and one covered by a black slipper or sandal. Can this be intentional, or is it an error? I do not feel competent to decide, but should rather conclude it to be an error on the part of the artist. The absence of the Holy Ghost will also be remarked in the picture of the Holy Trinity taken from the window at Troyes; and it will be fully discussed in the chapter specially devoted to the History of the Divine Trinity. The original artists, as well as the copyists of the middle ages, were often liable to error. Copyists omitted or altered a word; sculptors and painters forgot or denaturalised some characteristic attribute; and we rarely find a series of subjects in which the artist has not altogether omitted one or two.

for another, and which is both much too long, and much too ample; his aged head is oppressed with the weight of the tiara; a cope envelopes his shoulders; his body seems imprisoned by the alb; a stole hangs over his meagre thighs, and lastly, the face is furrowed with dry and impotent wrinkles.

Neither fulness of days, nor the experience of years appears to have caused the senility of this figure; but rather an untimely decrepitude and wasting of the muscles. The face is not old; it is simply worn out. The eyes are small, dim, and expressionless. In the picture of the Trinity,* in which the Holy Ghost bears on his head the symbolic dove, the Father whom we find there represented, also in the character of pope, is really painful to behold. He is a feeble old man, with scarcely strength sufficient to hold the globe of the world; and who grasps the hand of the Holy Ghost rather as a support for himself, than as a means of indicating their union. The head is bowed upon the breast, like that of an infirm old man, the cheeks are hollow, the face elongated. In the "*Cité de Dieu*,"† the Father has a long white beard; but like an old man worn out by age, the head is quite bald, with the exception of a single tuft of hair upon the forehead.

It is most curious to observe how profoundly, and yet how lucidly, works of art reflect the ideas of the epoch in which they were executed. When society was governed by the clergy, that is from the fifth to the ninth century, the art is found grave and austere; faces, whether in sculpture or painting, are imprinted with one universal character; and never are they seen to relax into a smile. From the ninth to the thirteenth century, during the period of feudal sway, the attitudes become stiff; something arrogant is remarked in the general bearing, something of audacious daring in the expression; the features throughout bear the impress of courage, but mingled with harshness and severity. Subsequently, from the thirteenth century down to the fifteenth, when the bourgeoisie had taken root, and propagated themselves in the emancipated communes, the art

* The figure is given below (See Fig. 150) in the history of the Holy Ghost, represented in the human form.

† Manuscript in the Bibliothèque de Sainte Genevieve, 10th, 11th, and 21st miniatures.

bent before their influence. The stiffness that had prevailed in the preceding epoch was succeeded by varied action; the savage character degenerated into the familiar, and nobleness of features into vulgarity. The ideal was lost in the real.

Artists then sought in living types models for the representation of God the Father, and by this base anthropomorphism, our monuments became crowded with figures of God, transformed into a mortal, and subject to all the low passions of humanity. Yet the type of man at this period was furnished by the "bourgeois" of the middle classes, striving to imitate the noble, whose rank they aspired to gain, and consequently still wearing some semblance of elevation of mind, and displaying an eager desire for distinction. But between the fifteenth and sixteenth centuries, a nameless crowd, a populace in rags, with garments torn, and marks of poverty in figure and in habiliments, their physiognomy and outward expression invariably common, and too often rude and barbarous in soul, broke loose upon the political and artistic world. The irruption of this vulgar crowd troubled the course of æsthetics, and its dull, heavy countenance intrudes on the most elevated ideal conceptions, even on that of the Blessed Virgin; Mary was represented only as a great, vulgar woman, and as such she may yet be seen in all monuments of that period.

The great Italian artists of the Renaissance, Perugino, Raphael, and Michelangelo, were at last sent into the world commissioned to create that magnificent ideal of Jehovah, the Eternal God, the Divine old man who made the earth tremble at his frown, so admirably superior even to the classic Jupiter. With the Renaissance then, the classic ideal reappeared, and it was in truth much required. The genius of the Renaissance re-ascended to the source of all things, to the original type of Christianity as well as of Paganism, and the fountain-head is ever more limpid and pure than the river's mouth. The æsthetic stream, which, during the two preceding periods had been polluted by the vulgar bourgeoisie was purified by the Renaissance; God the Father was re-juvenised, or rather, like all the other Christian types, underwent a complete transformation. Jehovah was despoiled of the tiara, which gave him the appearance of a pope and made him a vicar of God rather than God himself, and his shoulders were once more covered with long flowing hair, snow-white yet powerful and abundant. When contemplating these figures of God the Father produced by artists of the Renaissance, either in painting or in sculpture, we feel, like Job, a thrill of awe and terror; we confess the imposing and sometimes fearful spell, which binds us, when in the presence of a man of genius, on whom we gaze perhaps for the first time. This glorious divinity, this magnificent old man, so powerful, so serene and unmoved, is in very truth the ancient of days, the Παλαιὸς τῶν ἡμέρων of the Greeks.

The Renaissance may then be regarded as the epoch in which God the Father triumphed over the forgetfulness, insults, heresies, barbarity, and coarseness of preceding ages. The Divine sun had at length gained strength to penetrate the mists of jealousy and vulgarity which during the chronological epochs just enumerated, had been heaped up around him. For nearly three hundred years since the period of the Renaissance, the first person of the Trinity has continued to hold the most elevated rank. This re-action, although somewhat tardy,* has nevertheless, produced monuments of some merit; but as it is not our intention to go beyond the sixteenth century, or the Renaissance, properly so called, it will be enough to notice here the indications by which it was preceded. The "Disputá," as well as other paintings of Raphael's, contains a most beautiful figure of God the Father. Jehovah, as represented by Raphael, forming the great luminaries of our world, and with one hand darting the sun into illimitable space, whilst with the other he throws the moon into her appointed place, is indeed an admirable creation. The painter, Martin, in his Cosmogony, designed from the description given in Milton's

* In Italy, where the art has ever been more prompt in her efforts, an attempt at reaction had already been made in the fourteenth century. Thus a carving on wood, executed at that period, a copy of which will be given below, Fig. 133, gives a figure of the Father half issuing from heaven, to bless the Saviour, who is being baptised by St. John in the river Jordan. God the Father is a finely-conceived old man, and seems already to give promise of the admirable works of great Italian artists in the fifteenth and sixteenth centuries.

"Paradise Lost," has even surpassed Raphael, and I regret that the limits imposed upon this work forbid my giving an engraving of his splendid picture.

The doctrines of theology were thenceforth but lightly regarded. Men were ignorant that no personal representation of God the Father ought properly to be attempted, since, strictly speaking, no man hath seen or can see him; they knew not, or had forgotten, that Jesus being the Word, the speech of God, it would be fitting to represent the Son, whenever God was recorded to have spoken. They clung in preference to historical reality, and introduced the figure of God the Father, in every scene taken from the Old Testament; at the Creation, on Mount Sinai, at the election of kings or judges, and the sending forth of prophets. God the Father is present also in some scenes taken from the New Testament, at the baptism, the passion, the crucifixion and ascension of his Son. Finally, in the sixteenth century, the Deity was figured only by his name, inscribed within a geometrical figure. The triangle, as has been said

Fig. 64.—THE NAME OF JEHOVAH, INSCRIBED WITHIN A RADIATING TRIANGLE. Carving on wood of the XVII cent.

in the chapter on the nimbus, is the linear emblem of God and of the Divine Trinity. The name of God, or Jehovah, was inscribed in Hebrew letters within the triangle, and both the name and the figure were placed in the centre of a radiating circle, symbolic of eternity.

God the Father, or Jehovah, here occupies the field of the triangle, or the Trinity, which is itself contained within the circle of Eternity. This abstract formula became very popular, and in a number of churches even of the present day, these letters, the triangle, and radiating circle, shine in resplendent gold in the centre of those glories which we have already described, or else in the middle of the high altar, on the veil of the chalice, on the apron worn by bishops, the hood of the cope, or the back-hanging of the chasuble.

A most brilliant example of this figure may be seen on some beautiful tapestry of the sixteenth century, preserved in the treasury of the Cathedral at Sens. The engraving given above was taken from the church of Hautvillers near Rheims. In the centre of the glory which adorns the further end of the sanctuary, in the chapel of the Palace at Versailles, shines a divine and luminous triangle, nearly resembling that given above.

After the chapter on the nimbus, the aureole and the glory, little remains to be said of those attributes in reference to God the Father. The nimbus of Jehovah is circular, and stamped with the cross; but Raphael and the Italians sometimes represent the Father with a square nimbus, as the "Ancient of Days;" and sometimes it is lozenge-shaped, triangular or radiating. At other times the nimbus disappears; even the aureole ceases to be seen, and a liquid light, or rather a flood of rays, sometimes straight, sometimes flamboyant, or undulating, emanates from the entire person of Jehovah. We here seem to approach the Holy Scriptures, and the idea which great poets, such as Dante, had formed of the Deity. In the Old Testament, God walks constantly surrounded by fire and flame. When Ezekiel perceived Jehovah, in the likeness of a man, he said, "Then I beheld, and lo a likeness as the appearance of fire; from the appearance of his loins, even downward, fire; and from his loins, even upward, as the appearance of brightness, as the colour of amber." (Ezek. viii. 2.)

Dante gives the following dazzling description of that divine light in which saints and angels are enveloped:—

Lume è lassuso, che visibil face,
  Lo Creatore a quella creatura
  Che solo in lui vedere ha la sua pace.
E si distende in circular figura
  In tanto, che la sua circonferenza
  Sarebbe al Sol troppo larga cintura.
Fassi di raggio tutta sua parvenza,
  Reflesso al sommo del mobile primo,
  Che prende quindi vivere e potenza;
E come clivo in acqua di suo imo
  Si specchia quasi per vedersi adorno
  Quando è nel verde e ne' fioretti opimo;
Sì soprastando al lume intorno intorno
  Vide specchiarsi in più di mille soglie
  Quanto da noi lassù fatto ha ritorno.
E se l' infimo grado in se raccoglie
  Sì grande lume, quant' è la larghezza
  Di questa rosa nell' estreme foglie?
La vista mia nell' ampio e nell' altezza
  Non si smarriva, ma tutto prendeva
  Il quanto e'l quale, di quell' allegrezza.
Presso e lontano lì, nè pon, nè leva;
  Che dove Dio senza mezzo governa.
  La legge natural nulla rilieva
Nel giallo della rosa sempiterna
  Che si dilata rigrada, e redole
  Odor di lode al Sol, che sempre verna,
Qual è colui, che tace e dicer vuole,
  Mi trasse Beatrice.*

---

* There is in heaven a light whose goodly shine
Makes the Creator visible to all
Created, that in seeing him alone
Have peace; and in a circle spreads so far
That the circumference were too loose a zone
To girdle in the sun. All is one beam,
Reflected from the summit of the first,
That moves, which being hence and vigour takes.
And as some cliff that from the bottom eyes
His image mirror'd in the crystal flood,
As if to admire his brave appareling
Of verdure and of flowers; so round about,
Eying the light, on more than million thrones,
Stood eminent, whatever from our earth
Has to the skies return'd. How wide the leaves,
Extended to their utmost, of this rose,
Whose lowest step embosoms such a space
Of ample radiance! Yet nor amplitude
Nor height impeded, but my view with ease

It was in the centre, at the very heart of this luminous eternity that the Deity shone forth. Dante no doubt wished to describe one of those roses with a thousand petals, which light the porches of our noblest cathedrals;* the rose-windows, which were contemporaneous with the Florentine poet, and which he had no doubt seen in his travels in France. There in fact, in the very depth of the chalice of that rose of coloured glass, the divine majesty shines out resplendently.

From every step of the corolla, disposed in the form of an amphitheatre, from each hierarchical cordon of the rose, innumerable hosts of angels, the souls of patriarchs, judges, kings and prophets, and lastly those of apostles, martyrs, confessors, and virgins, seem to rise in successive rings, as if reflected from, and delighted to see their images repeated in, the central source and fountain of light.

GOD THE SON.

If the image of God the Father was exposed throughout the entire course of the middle ages, to the ill-will, and even to the insults of heretics; and suffered from the incapacity and vulgarity of artists, far different was the treatment experienced by the Son. Jesus is the author of Christianity; from Him, and not from the Father, the new religion derived its name. Christians consequently looked up to him with gratitude, as children to a parent. In the affections of men as well as in art, which is but the mirror and material expression of ideas, the Saviour Christ has reigned

---

Took in the full dimensions of that joy.
Near or remote, what there avails where God
Immediate rules, and nature, awed, suspends
Her sway? Into the yellow of the rose
Perennial, which, in bright expansiveness
Lays forth its gradual blooming, redolent
Of praises to the never-wintering sun,
As one, who fain would speak yet holds his peace,
Beatrice led me.

Cary's Dante, Paradise, Canto xxx, l. 100.

* Especially at Paris, Rheims, and Chartres.

gloriously from the era of the catacombs down to the present day. He is the Divine Person to whom the art has ever rendered, and does still render, the highest honours. Not one single Church was ever especially erected by Christians in honour of God the Father, while, on the other hand, a considerable number were early dedicated to Christ under the title of St. Saviour,* Saint Cross, Saint Sepulchre, or Saint Anastasia. The cathedral at Aix is dedicated to Saint Saviour, that at Orleans to Saint Cross. The celebrated church at Florence, in which lie the remains of Dante, Michelangelo, Machiavelli and Galileo, is called Santa Croce. Churches of the Resurrection, or of Saint Anastasia are abundant in the East. Churches of Saint Sepulchre are common in France, where chapels of that title are also very numerous. At Cambridge and at Northampton, in England, are two circular churches, called Saint Sepulchre.

It would even appear that the Church of Saint Sophia at Constantinople, was dedicated rather to the Divine Wisdom of Christ than to that of the Father, or to the Holy Trinity.† At Paris, the Church of Val-de-Grâce is dedicated to the Infant Jesus.

Even at the present day, at the conclusion of each psalm in the service of the Church, two verses are sung, a sort of "refrain," announcing that the psalm is over, and that the "antienne" or completion of it is about to begin. These verses are well known, "Glory be to the Father, and to the Son, and to the Holy Ghost. As it was in the beginning, is now, and ever shall be, world without end."‡

It is a glorifying of the entire Trinity; but in the diocese

* Churches, abbeys, villages, towns, and even cities, bear the name of St. Saviour; a large village in the Department du Nord, near Valenciennes, is called "Saint Saulve." Jeanne d'Arc, when on the point of being burned to death, at Rouen, asked in her last moments, for a cross, and one was brought to her from the neighbouring parish of "Saint Sauveur."—Michelet, *Hist. de France*, vol. v., p. 172. A church dedicated to St. Saviour is still standing at Redon. France formerly contained twenty-three abbeys dedicated to Saint Sauveur, that of Redon included.

† "Jesu nascenti," as we read in the inscription traced upon the frieze of the porch.

‡ Gulielmus Durandus (*Rat. Div. Offi.*, lib. v., c. 2) declares the two verses of the Gloria Patri to have been composed by St. Jerome, and sent by him to Pope Damasus, who commanded them to be sung in the Psalms.

of Rheims, the name of the Father when pronounced is passed over without any special notice. Scarcely, however, has the first syllable of the word "Filio" been uttered than the choristers rise and incline themselves reverentially towards the high altar, the priests and chanters make their obeisance by removing their caps, and the congregation bend devoutly before the Divine name. They rise, reseat themselves, and again cover their heads. Then follows the name of the Holy Ghost, and it is passed over without more attention than that of God the Father.

In the Gloria Patri the name of the Father precedes indeed that of the Son, but the reasons of this precedence are genealogical, not reverential. It serves to express the reciprocal relation of the Divine persons, not any different degree of honour or of worship.

When the name of the Father, or of the Holy Ghost, is heard from the pulpit, not the slightest movement is perceptible amongst the congregation; but when the name of Jesus Christ is pronounced, the men immediately bend their heads to do him honour, and the women sign themselves with the cross from the head to the breast, and from one shoulder to the other.

We are told, as a singular fact with respect to Newton, that he invariably removed his hat when the name of God was mentioned in his presence. No one now uncovers himself at that name only; but whether from the early religious feelings implanted by maternal influence, whether from tradition or reflection, few men, however slight may be their religious feelings, can hear the name of Christ without a thrill of reverence and respect. The sentiment is perhaps involuntary, but that reason alone renders it more powerful. "At the name of Jesus," says St. Paul, "every knee shall bow, of things in heaven, and things in earth, and things under the earth."*

* "Ut in nomine Jesu omne genu flectatur, cœlestium, terrestrium, et infernorum."—Phil. ii., 10. When the Nicene Creed is sung, according to Durandus (*Rat. Div. Off.*, cap. xxv., *de Symbolo*), "ut cum dicitur ibi *et homo factus est*, debemus genua flectere, quia Christum hominem factum et pro nobis crucifixum adoramus." Even at the present day we bend the knee, or, at least, bow profoundly. M. l'Abbé Gaume, who has done me the favour to revise the proofs of my work, bids me observe that the honours paid to

It would appear, as if in Jesus Christ the entire essence of Deity were comprehended.*

The cruciform nimbus was, as has been already said, a sign characterising equally the Son and the other two Persons of the Trinity; but the cross itself is an attribute belonging immediately to Christ, and which the Father and the Holy Ghost have derived from him. Besides, the fulness of being, or omnipotence, ought not properly to belong more to Christ than to the Father and the Holy Ghost, for it resides in the Trinity, and is not the special right of any single person. If either of the three persons were to be regarded as appropriating that attribute in preference to the others, it would assuredly be rather God the Father.† And yet, among the

Jesus are not rendered to him as the second person in the Trinity, or as the Son of God, but rather because he died for our salvation. Christ considered only as the second person of the Trinity, does not receive greater homage than the Father or the Holy Ghost. It is before the name of Jesus only that we prostrate ourselves, for that name reminds us immediately of the author of our redemption. When we name the Son of God, the Word, or even Christ, we do not bend any more than at that of the Father or the Holy Ghost. If in the diocese of Rheims any inclination is made at the *Filio* in the Gloria Patri, it is a singular exception; for in other churches the reverence is made at the conclusion of the Gloria, and in honour of the Trinity, of the three divine persons united. M. l'Abbé Gaume is of opinion, that equal honour has always been paid to each of the three Divine persons, that the Son has never been more highly esteemed, either in worship or in theology, than the Father or the Holy Ghost. I bow respectfully to his opinion, and would willingly have erased from my manuscript what has been already said, and what will in future be stated, in opposition to his decision; but to do this would have been impossible, without re-writing several entire sheets of the impression. Not one or two passages alone would have required modification, but the spirit of the whole chapter must have been transmuted. I have therefore preserved it as originally written, adding merely the observations here made, but I shall reserve what I had intended further to advance on this subject.

* Of the twelve clauses of the Apostles Creed, one only, of four words, relates to the Holy Ghost ("credo in Spiritum Sanctum"); one, of nine words, bears reference to the Father ("credo in Deum patrem omnipotentem, creatorem cœli et terræ); but five entire clauses are devoted to Jesus Christ, comprehending, in fact, more than half of the Creed.

† "Credo in Deum patrem, OMNIPOTENTEM, creatorem cœli et terræ, et in Jesum Christum filium ejus unicum," &c. The Apostles Creed, therefore, especially attributes power to God the Father. All Christian tradition agrees on that point; in the chapter relating to the Trinity, a quotation from Richard de Saint-Victor will be given, which may be considered conclusive on that point. Dante (*Divina Commedia*, canto x. "Paradiso") says also, that the Father created, and still governs the world.

Greeks particularly, the source of being is assigned frequently and almost exclusively to Christ. Thus, in the domes of the lofty Byzantine cupolas, the gigantic figure of the Almighty, the Pantocrator, shines forth from the golden background; the word Almighty, which in our minds calls up the idea of the Father rather than the Son, or of the Holy Ghost, seems somewhat incongruous when connected with a countenance belonging apparently to a man of thirty years of age, with a beard of short fine hair, and features youthful and gentle in expression.

The image may be intended for the Father, under the character of the Son, as a strict observance of theological dogmas would seem to require; but, in addition to the inscription "*ὁ Παντοκράτωρ*," we read also ΙC ΧC.

There is no possibility of mistake. It is Christ represented governing the Greek church, as he sways the world. Besides, on the bars forming the cross of the nimbus, the letters *ὁ ὤν* are inscribed. Christ is therefore at once both "the being" and Almighty power. The beautiful Greek manuscripts in the Bibliothèque Royale, contain numerous miniatures, which might be adduced in verification of the above fact.*

It appears, then, that Christ has been more honoured than the Father. An additional proof is furnished by the language usually employed in speaking of him. God the Father is not spoken of as our king and sovereign, although these titles are constantly used in reference to the Son. Before the name of Christ we prefix the title of "Our Lord," as in speaking of the Virgin Mary, we add that of "Our Lady." It seems, in fact, that there are two persons to whom our hearts owe especial allegiance, the Virgin Mary and Jesus, the Mother and the Son. These are the two living stars, which shed their rays upon Christianity.

The God whose person is more peculiarly esteemed and most frequently figured in Iconography, is unquestionably Jesus. He has been, without a single intermission,

* See amongst others the Greek manuscript of 1128. Gulielmus Durandus, remarks, in the *Rationale*, lib. i, cap. 3, that even in the Latin Church, omnipotence is ascribed to Christ. He says .... "Imago Christi ..... picta ut residens in throno, seu in solio excelso, præsentem indicat majestatem, quasi dicat, Data est ei omnis potestas in cœlo et in terra."

represented at every era, and under every possible form. Works of art are ever the proof and counterpart of religious belief. At the time when the hand of God only is shown, Christ is depicted at full length, and of every age; beard less or with a beard, of the age of eighteen, or that of thirty. It is necessary however to say, that he was almost constantly represented at that period, under the figure of a beautiful and adorable youth of about fifteen or eighteen years of age, beardless, with a sweet expression of countenance, and long and abundant hair flowing in curls over his shoulders: his brow is sometimes encircled by a diadem or a *bandeau*, like a young priest of the pagan gods; this is, in fact, a very favourite figure, and has been frequently treated by the art with partial affection.* At a very different period of time, namely, in the fifteenth century, when the idea of God was disfigured in artistic representation, and degraded to the condition of a pope, worn out with old age and decrepitude, Jesus still preserved all his beauty, his radiance and dignity. Italian art has ever been precocious, and one, or perhaps two hundred years in advance of ours, and the portrait of God the Father was consequently, conceived and executed in Italy one or two centuries earlier than in France. Yet Buffalmacco, in the first half of the fourteenth century, when

* See various sarcophagi drawn in the *Roma Sotterranea*, édition de Rome, 1632, pp. 285, 293, 295. Also many sarcophagi found in the Aliscamps at Arles, and now scattered throughout various cities of the South, particularly at Marseilles and probably also at Toulouse. In the small town of St. Maximin, at Tarascon, and Clermont Ferrand, I have seen sarcophagi, on which the Saviour was sculptured beardless. In a village of the arrondissement of Rheims, and even in the Cathedral of Rheims, are sculptures of the tenth and thirteenth centuries, in which our Saviour, in company with the pilgrims of Emmaus, after the Passion, and in the waters of Jordan at his baptism, is represented under the form of the same graceful youth. On the west wall in the interior of the Cathedral of Rheims, Christ is represented beardless. He is appearing to Moses from the top of the burning bush, youthful and smiling. Beardless still, and invariably serene in aspect, he passes before the crowd to whom St. John points him out, in these words, "Behold the Lamb of God." It seems indeed fitting that that divine lamb in human form should be represented as of tender age. Finally, Jesus is beardless when descending to be baptised in Jordan, by St. John the Baptist. The sculptures above described, and all those covering the western wall of the cathedral, are *chefs-d'œuvre* that will bear comparison with the finest statues of antiquity. In action, expression, and design, they are almost unequalled.

painting the walls of the Campo Santo at Pisa, still depicted Jesus, and not the Father, creating the world from a vacuum. It is impossible, in the figure of the Creator, to discover any of the distinctive attributes of God the Father. The youth, and abundant flowing hair, the small and scanty beard, the sweetness of physiognomy, betray all the characteristic features of Christ.*

Fig. 65.—THE CREATOR, UNDER THE FORM OF JESUS CHRIST.
Italian Miniature of the close of the XIII cent.

In the following drawing, the Divine Person who, by the hand extended, in the Latin form of benediction, and by the

* An engraving of this beautiful picture is given below, in the History of the Trinity, Fig. 148.

breath of his lips calls into existence the nine choirs of angels, is still revealed under the figure of the Son, instead of that of the Father.* The figure of the Deity is thirty or thirty-five years of age only, and bears in his hand a globe, symbolic of the world of his creation.

Thus then, during the entire course of the middle ages, the Son of God was constantly depicted under every possible form and character. We have not space to enter here more fully into the archæological biography of Christ in his human relation; but a separate work will at some future time be devoted to the personal History of Jesus, from his incarnation in the womb of the Blessed Virgin, down to the Ascension.

At present he will be considered solely as God, and as the second person of the Holy Trinity. In the majority of the engravings that follow, he will generally be seen engaged in the exercise of his Divine, not of his human, functions. He will be represented speaking to the Father, near whom he is seated, creating the world, pronouncing sentence upon Adam and Eve; or chaining Death, treading underfoot the lion and the dragon, the asp and the basilisk; or, having completed his earthly vocation, re-ascending into heaven, and shining in the radiance of a glory in the bosom of Paradise with his feet resting on the arch of heaven; or borne on the wings of seraphim through the immensity of space, blessing the world from the highest heaven; or standing on that holy mountain whence descend the four mystical streams of the Gospel, and from the summit of which he gives his law to the universe, and presents his Gospel to the Apostles; or he is judging mankind at the end of time, or lastly, dwelling in the bosom of the Trinity, between the Father and the Holy Ghost. He will also be shown under the form of

* Our engraving is taken from the *Psalterium cum Figuris*, suppl. fr. 1132, Bibliothèque Royale. It will be observed that there are nine choirs of angels, grouped in threes; the arrangement is allegorical, and is explained in the Celestial Hierarchy of St. Dionysius the Areopagite. It will be noticed at length in the History of the Angels. We may remark, however, in anticipation, that the nine choirs are in our engraving identical; it is impossible, from the absence of any special attributes, to distinguish the Seraphim, Cherubim, and Thrones, in the first group; the Dominions, Virtues, and Powers, in the second; the Principalities, Archangels, and Angels, in the third. The Greek artists characterised the different orders of angels with much greater precision.

a lamb, or that of the good shepherd, because the symbolism of such representations divests them of every human characteristic.

In some few designs, however, he will be shown as man, born of the Virgin, plunged into Jordan and baptised by St. John; or, again, nailed to the cross, and expiring in the presence of Mary, his mother, and of St. John, his friend; for each of these various designs will be found to determine some point of Divine Iconography. Several varieties of the Cross will also be given, for the Cross alone, without the crucified Lord, is symbolic like the lamb; still we repeat, that the present inquiry is devoted to the second person of the Trinity, to the Son of God alone, not to the God-Man, the crucified redeemer, Jesus Christ.

HISTORY OF THE PORTRAITS OF GOD THE SON.

The same reasons that were alleged against any material representation of the Father could not be advanced against the representations of the Son. In the first place, the Son had become incarnate; his features had been seen by all mankind; there was nothing to prevent men from representing them.

"Since," says Damascenus, "he who is invisible, has been pleased to assume a material body, and to make himself visible to man, his image may be made. Since a being, who, as God, from the excellence of his nature,* has neither substance, dimensions, nor quality, has condescended to take upon himself the form of a slave, and subjected himself to the conditions of quantity and quality; since he has clothed himself with a corporeal figure; that figure may be represented in paintings by you. Show, therefore, publicly, the God who was pleased thus to manifest himself, paint for us his ineffable humanity, his birth in the womb of the Virgin, his baptism in Jordan, his transfiguration on Mount Tabor, the sufferings by which we were redeemed, the miracles which, while accomplished by the aid of the body,

* This little sentence appears in the Latin text, but is omitted in Didron's.

were the manifestation of his divine nature and power; his sepulture, through which we were saved; his resurrection and ascension into heaven: let them all be described by words or colours, in books or in pictures."* The Gnostic heretics on their part, were no less devoted to God the Son, and lastly, theology declared that all things had been created by the Son, or the Word. All these various causes combined to render the early portraits of Jesus Christ numerous in the extreme.

The Gnostics, in their enmity to God the Father, had proscribed his image, but being favourable to the Son, they painted and sculptured the figure of the Saviour, of all dimensions, and under various forms. It even appears, as M. Raoul Rochette has affirmed, that we are indebted to Gnostics for the earliest portraits of Jesus.† "It was for the use of Gnostics, and by the hand of those sectaries, who attempted at various times, and by a thousand different schemes, to effect a monstrous combination of the doctrines of Christianity with Pagan superstitions, that little images of Christ were first fabricated; the original model of these figures they traced back to Pontius Pilate himself, by a hypothetical train of reasoning, which could scarcely deceive even the most ignorant of their initiated disciples. These little statues were made of gold, or silver, or some other substance, and after the pattern of those of Pythagoras, Plato, Aristotle, and other sages of antiquity, which those sectarians were accustomed to exhibit, crowned with flowers

* "Quando is qui cerni non potest assumpta carne se conspicuum præbuerit, tunc illius deformes imaginem. Quum ille qui in forma Dei existens, ob naturæ suæ excellentiam, quantitatis et qualitatis et magnitudinis est exsors, formâ servi acceptâ, ad quantitatem qualitatemque sese contrahens, corporis figuram induerit, tum in tabellis eum exprime, palamque conspiciendum propone qui conspici voluit. Ineffabilem ipsius demissionem designa, nativitatem ex Virgine, baptismum in Jordane, transfigurationem in Thabor, cruciatus illos, quia cruciatus nos exemerunt; miracula quæ cum carnis ministerio patrarentur, divinam ipsius naturam et efficaciam promerebant. Salutarem Salvatoris sepulturam, resurrectionem, ascensum in cœlum, hoc omnia cum sermone, tum coloribus describe, tum in libris, tum in tabellis." (*Opp. S. Johan. Damasceni*, Oratio tertia de imaginibus, vol. i., p. 349.)

† *Discours sur l'Art du Christianisme*, par R. Rochette, in 8vo. pp. 15, 18. M. R. R. quotes St. Irenæus, St. Epiphanius, St. Augustine, Lampridius, Jablonsky, Fueldner, Heyne, and Bottari. The quotations are all preserved in the extract that follows the *Discours*.

in their Conciliabula, and all of which were honoured with the same degree of worship. Such, indeed, is the positive assertion of St. Iræneus,* confirmed, or at least reiterated by St. Epiphanius.† This superstition, which on the same principle permitted painted images of Christ, was peculiarly in vogue amongst the Gnostics of the sects of Carpocrates; and history has preserved the name of a woman, Marcellina, adopted by that sect, for the propagation of which she removed from the farthest East, to Rome; and who in the little Gnostic church, as it may be called, which was under her direction, exposed to the adoration of her followers images of Christ and of St. Paul, of Homer and Pythagoras. This fact, which is supported by the serious evidence of St. Augustine,‡ is, besides, perfectly in accordance with the celebrated anecdote of the Emperor, Alexander Severus, who placed amongst his Lares, between the images of the most revered philosophers and kings, the portraits of Christ, and of Abraham, opposite those of Orpheus and Apollonius of Tyana, and who paid to all a vague kind of divine worship.§ It cannot, therefore, be doubted, that this strange association originated in the bosom of certain schools of the Neo-Platonists, as well as in several Gnostic sects, and we may thence infer, that the existence of images fabricated by Gnostic hands, induced Christians, as soon as the Church

* *St. Irenæus, Advers. Hæres.* lib. i., cap. xxv., s. 6, édition de Massuet.

† *St. Epiphanius, Hæres.* cap. xxvii., s. 6. See on this subject the dissertation of Jablonsky, "de Origine imaginum Christi Domini in Ecclesia Christiana," s. 10, in his *Opuscul. Philol.* vol. iii., 394-396.

‡ *St. Augustin, de Hæresib.* cap. vii.: "Sectæ ipsius (Carpocratis) fuisse traditur socia quædam Marcellina, quæ colebat imagines Jesu et Pauli, et Homeri et Pythagoræ, adorando incensumque ponendo." (See the dissertation of Fueldner, upon the Carpocratians, in the *Dritte Denkschrift der Hist. Theol. Gesellschaft zu Leipzig.*, p. 267, et seq.)

§ *Æl. Lamprid. in Alexandr. Sever.* cap. xxix. "In larario suo, in quo et divos principes, sed optimos (et) electos et animas sanctiores, in queis et Appollonium, et quantum scriptor suorum temporum dicit. Christum, Abraham et Orpheum, et hujusmodi ceteros, habebat ac majorum effigies, rem divinam faciebat." Such is the lesson proposed by Heyne for the employment of this text. (See the dissertation of Alexandr. Sever. *Imp. religion. miscell. probant.*, &c., in his Opuscul. Academ. vol. vi., p. 169-281; see also on this subject the dissertation of Jablonsky, *De Alexandro Severo, Imperatore Romano, Christianorum sacris per Gnostico initiato,* in his Opuscul. Philol. vol. iv., p. 38-79.

relaxed in its primitive aversion to monuments of idolatry, to adopt them for their own use.* Everything, indeed, countenances the opinion, that from the commencement of the third century, images of Christ were in circulation among the faithful, at least among those of the lower order, and particularly in Rome, where Gnosticism had made many proselytes, and was at this period favourably received."

The miraculous images, those not formed by the hand of man, and therefore called "acheiropoiètes;" the impression, whether real or apocryphal, imprinted on the veil of Saint Veronica; the portraits attributed to Nicodemus, Pilate, or Saint Luke; the portraits current in the time of Eusebius; the statue, said to have been erected to Jesus Christ in the city of Panéas, by the woman whom the Saviour cured of the hemorrhöissis.† All these facts, whether real or imaginary, handed down by written tradition from the earliest centuries of our era, serve at least to prove that even in the dawn of Christianity, the Son of God was often represented both in sculpture and in painting. Saint John Damascenus mentions a tradition, anciently believed, and current even in his time, by which Jesus was himself recognised as the author of one of his own portraits.

Abgarus, king of Edessa, having learnt, says Damascenus, the wonderful things related of our Saviour, became inflamed with Divine love; he sent ambassadors to the Son of God, inviting him to come and visit him, and should the Saviour refuse to grant his request, he charged his ambassadors to employ some artist to make a portrait of our Lord. Jesus, from whom nothing is hidden, and to whom nothing is impossible, being aware of the intention of Abgarus, took a piece of linen, applied it to his face, and depicted thereon his own image. This very portrait, continues Damascenus, is in existence at the present day, and in perfect preservation.‡

* Such, we are told by M. Raoul Rochette, is the inference drawn by the pious and learned Bottari, from the testimony quoted above, *Pitture e Sculture Sacre*, vol i., p. 196; and that his opinion, formed in the bosom of orthodox Catholicism, has been adopted by all Roman antiquaries.

† *Fabricius*, *Codex Apocryphus Novi Testamenti.*

‡ *Opera S. Joh. Damasceni*, vol. i., Oratio Prim. de Imaginibus, p. 320, édit. de Lequien, Paris, 1712. "Antiquitus tradita narratio ad nos usque

At the same epoch, a minute verbal description of the appearance of Christ was in circulation. The following description, which is of great importance, was sent to the Roman Senate by Publius Lentulus, proconsul of Judea, before Herod. Lentulus had seen the Saviour, and had made him sit to him, as it were, that he might give a written description of his features and physiognomy. His portrait, apocryphal though it be, is at least one of the first upon record; it dates from the earliest period of the Church, and has been mentioned by the most ancient fathers. Lentulus writes to the senate as follows:—"At this time appeared a man who is still living and endowed with mighty power; his name is Jesus Christ. His disciples call him the Son of God; others regard him as a powerful prophet. He raises the dead to life, and heals the sick of every description of infirmity and disease. This man is of lofty stature, and well-proportioned; his countenance severe and virtuous, so that he inspires beholders with feelings both of fear and love. The hair of his head is of the colour of wine, and from the top of the head to the ears, straight and without radiance, but it descends from the ears to the shoulders in shining curls. From the shoulders the hair flows down the back, divided into two portions, after the manner of the Nazarenes; his forehead is clear and without wrinkle, his face free from blemish, and slightly tinged with red, his physiognomy noble and gracious. The nose and mouth faultless. His beard is abundant, the same colour as the hair, and forked. His eyes blue and very brilliant. In reproving or censuring he is awe-inspiring; in exhorting and teaching, his speech is gentle and caressing. His countenance is marvellous in

pervenit Abgarum scilicet, Edessæ regem, auditis quæ de Domino ferebantur, divino succensum ardore, legatos misisse, qui eum ad se invisendum invitarent; sin vero abnueret mandat ut pictoris opera imaginem ejus exprimant. Quod cum sciret ille, cui nihil obscurum est, quique omnia potest, accepto panno, suæque faciei admoto, propriam effigiem appinxisse. Quæ ad hæc usque tempora servatur incolumis." Damascenus adds, pp. 631, 632, of the same volume, "Quin et ipse omnium Salvator et Dominus, cum adhuc in terra ageret sancti vultus sui expressam in texto lineo effigiem. Abgaro cuidam magnæ Edessenorum civitatis regulo per Thaddæum apostolum misit. Divino namque sui vultus absterso sudore, cuncta illius lineamenta in linteo servavit. Quam effigiem præmagnifica celeberrimaque Edessenorum civitas ad hunc usque diem, haud secus atque sceptrum regium retinens, præclare gloriatur et exsulsat."

seriousness and grace. He has never once been seen to laugh; but many have seen him weep.* He is slender in person, his hands are straight and long, his arms beautiful. Grave and solemn in his discourse, his language is simple and quiet. He is in appearance the most beautiful of the children of men."†

The Emperor Constantine caused pictures of the Son of God to be painted from this ancient description.

In the eighth century, at the period in which Saint John Damascenus wrote, the lineaments of this remarkable figure continued to be the same as they are to this day.

The hair and the beard, the colour of which is somewhat undetermined in the letter of Lentulus, for wine may be pale, golden, red, or violet colour, is distinctly noted by Damascenus, who also adds the tint of the complexion; moreover, the opinion of Damascenus, like that of Lentulus, is decidedly in favour of the beauty of Christ, and the former severely censures the Manichæans, who entertained a contrary opinion. Thus, then, Christ in taking upon him the form of Adam, assumed features exactly resembling those of

* The Latin text is not sufficiently clear; strict grammatical accuracy would perhaps require it to be thus rendered: "Personne ne l'a vu rire, et pas même pleurer." But the Gospel tells us that Jesus wept for Lazarus and for Jerusalem. One of the tears shed by Christ was peculiarly honoured at Vendôme, where it was preserved. Père Mabillon wrote a celebrated letter upon that tear.

† "Hoc tempore vir apparuit et adhuc vivit, vir præditus potentia magna; nomen ejus Jesus Christus. Homines eum prophetam potentem dicunt; discipuli ejus filium Dei vocant. Mortuos vivificat, et ægros ab omnis generis ægritudinibus et morbis sanat. Vir est altæ staturæ proportionate, et conspectus vultus ejus cum severitate et plenus efficacia, ut spectatores amare eum possint et rursus timere. Pili capitis ejus vinei coloris usque ad fundamentum aurium sine radiatione, et erecti; et a fundamento aurium usque ad humeros contorti ac lucidi; et ab humeris deorsum pendentes, bifido vertice dispositi in morem Nazaræorum. Frons plana et pura; facies ejus sine macula, quam rubor quidam temperatus ornat. Aspectus ejus ingenuus et gratus. Nasus et os ejus nullo modo reprehensibilia. Barba ejus multa, et colore pilorum capitis, bifurcata. Oculi ejus cærulei et extremè lucidi. In reprehendendo et objurgando formidabilis; in docendo et exhortando blandæ linguæ et amabilis. Gratia miranda vultus cum gravitate. Vel semel eum ridentem nemo vidit, sed flentem imo. Protracta statura corporis, manus ejus rectæ et erectæ, brachia ejus delectabilia In loquendo ponderans et gravis, et parcus loquela. Pulcherrimus vultu inter homines satos."—*Codex Apocryphus Nov. Testam. ab Fabricium*, Hamburgi, 1703, 1e pars., pp. 301, 302.

the Virgin Mary. "Lofty stature, thick eyebrows, gentle eyes, well-formed nose, curling hair, figure slightly bent, delicate complexion, black beard, face of the colour of wheat, like that of his mother, long fingers, sonorous voice, and persuasive language. He is most amiable in character, calm, resigned, patient, invested with every virtue that our reason conceives to be appropriate to the Incarnate God." * In the West, a century later than the time of Damascenus, Christ was always thus depicted. S. Anschaire, Archbishop of Hamburgh and Bremen, who beheld Christ [in a vision], described him as "tall, clad in the manner of the Jews, and beautiful in face, the splendour of Divinity darted like a flame from the eyes of the Redeemer, but his voice was full of sweetness.†"

Let us next examine the evidence afforded by authentic monuments. We shall not rely altogether on the Gnostic abraxas, nor the Christian tessera, whether of stone or

* Qui cum impollutis manibus formaverit hominem, homo ipse ex sancta Virgine ac Dei genitrice Maria sine mutatione aut variatione factus, carni communicavit et sanguini, animal ratione, intelligentiæ et scientiæ capax, trium forte cubitorum magnitudine, carnis crassitie circumscriptus, nostræ simili forma conspectus est, maternæ similitudinis proprietates exacte referens, Adamique formam exhibens. Quocirca depingi eum curavit (Constantinus Magnus) quali forma veteres historici descripsere ; præstanti statura, confertis superciliis, venustis oculis, justo naso, crispa cæsarie, sub-curvum, eleganti colore, nigra barba, triticei coloris vultu pro materna similitudine, longis digitis, voce sonora, suavi eloquio, blandissimum, quietum, longanimem, patientem, hisque affines virtutis dotes circumferentem, quibus in proprietatibus Dei virilis ejus ratio repræsentatur; ne qua mutationis obumbratio, aut diversitatis variatio in divina Verbi humanatione deprehenderetur veluti Manichæi delirarunt."—*Opp. S. Joh. Damas.*, vol. i., pp. 630, 631. The beard of Christ, at present generally approaching to red, was at that period black.

† "Ecce vir per ostium veniebat, statura procerus, judaico more vestitus, vultu decorus; ex ejus oculis splendor divinitatis, velut flamma ignis radiabat. Quem intuitus, omni cunctatione postposita, Christum Dominum esse credebat, atque procurrens ad pedes ejus corruit. Cumque prostratus in facie jaceret, ille ut surgeret imperavit. Cumque surgens coram illo reverenter adstaret, atque præ nimio splendore oculis ipsius emicante in faciem ejus intendere non valeret, blanda voce illum allocutus est." (*Act. SS. Ord S. Bened.*, vol. vi., Vie de St. Anschaire.) St. Anschaire died about 864. His life was written by St. Rembert, his disciple and successor. St. Anschaire, as will be observed, mentions the costume in addition to the details contained in the preceding descriptions, and dwells more particularly on the extraordinary brilliancy of the eyes.

metal, nor even on certain pictures in the Roman catacombs, all of which, abraxas, tessera, and paintings, bear the image of Christ; for the date of these monuments has been much contested, and is still doubtful. We propose rather to consider the entire body of the most ancient Christian monuments, as for example, the frescos in the catacombs, the earliest sarcophagi, and most ancient mosaics; thence we shall pass to illuminated manuscripts, the capitals of Romanesque churches and vaultings, and the painted windows of Gothic churches. The following is the result of our investigations:—

In the long series of monuments, two iconographic facts, are seen to develope themselves side by side. The figure of Christ, which had at first been youthful, becomes older from century to century, in proportion as the age of Christianity itself progresses. That of the Virgin, on the contrary, who was originally represented in the catacombs as from forty to fifty years of age, becomes more youthful with every succeeding century, until, at the close of the Gothic epoch, her age appears to be not more than fifteen or twenty. In proportion as the Son grows older, the mother is represented as more youthful. Towards the thirteenth century Jesus and Mary are of the same age, about thirty or thirty-five years. The mother and child, who have thus met, as it were, afterwards separate, and thence continue to diverge still more widely one from the other.* The youthfulness of Christ, which is remarked on the most ancient Christian mouuments, is a predominating and very curious fact. On sculptured sarcophagi, in fresco paintings and mosaics, Christ is represented as a

* In the Church of St. Peter, at Rome, we view with admiration a group of the Virgin and dead Christ, sculptured by Michelangelo; it is the only work to which the great artist has put his sign manual. "This *chef d'œuvre,*" says Vasari, "covered Michelangelo with glory, and extended his fame to far distant countries. Yet there were some fools who pretended that the artist had erred in giving so youthful a countenance to the Virgin. Were these men ignorant that chaste, pure women, retain for a long period the graces of youth? It was of necessity otherwise with the Saviour, who had been called upon to endure all the vicissitudes to which humanity is subject." (Vasari *Vies des Peintres*, Vie de Michelange, trad. et annot. par MM. Leclanché et Jeanron, vol. v.) The explanation given by Vasari of the Virgin's youthful appearance, and of the advanced age of Christ, is certainly curious.

young man of twenty years of age, or a graceful youth of fifteen, without any beard, the shape of his face round, the expression gentle, resplendent with divine youth, just as

Fig. 66.—FIGURE OF CHRIST, BEARDLESS.
Roman Sculpture of the IV cent.*

Apollo was figured by the Pagans, and as angels are drawn by Christians. You find him seated on a curule chair, like a

* This youthful figure of the Saviour is taken from the sculptures decorating the celebrated tomb of Junius Bassus. Bassus died in 359, and the sarcophagus dates apparently from the same epoch. Below the figure of Jesus above described (who appears to be giving instructions to his two chief apostles, St. Peter and St. Paul), is another figure of God, youthful and beardless, riding on a she-ass, and about to make his entry into Jerusalem. His extreme youth is, therefore, symbolic and not natural, for Christ, at the time of his entering Jerusalem, on Palm Sunday, was at least thirty-three years of age; according to St. Irenæus, he was even older. Gulielmus Durandus says: "Et nota quod Christus completis triginta duobus annis et mensibus tribus, vel, secundum Chrysostomum, triginta tribus et dimidio, crucifixus est eadem die qua conceptus est de Virgine, scilicet in sexta feria quæ fuit octavo kalend. Aprilis." (*Rat. Div. Off.*, lib. vi., cap. lxxvii., de die Parasceves, No. 28.)

youthful senator, wearing also the long Roman robe and toga; or else he is standing on the mystic mountain, whence flow the four sacred streams.* On his feet are sandals fastened by little bands; the right arm is extended and the hand open, while, in the left, is the ancient volumen either unfolded or rolled up. The figure is charming, but has no resemblance to those which have since been hallowed by Christian art.

The above picture of Christ might be supposed to represent the Divine child teaching in the temple before he began his ministry, and that the juvenility is natural and not symbolic. But Christ is represented equally youthful; with his feet resting upon heaven whither he has returned after his Ascension; or giving his latest instructions to his apostles; or condemning Adam and Eve to labour: all actions performed either previously to his human birth or subsequent to his death. He may be traced, in like form, performing the miracles of his life; raising Lazarus from the dead; curing the man born blind, the paralytic, and the hemorrdöidal woman; blessing and multiplying the loaves and fishes; and lastly, he is thus seen before Pilate, by whom he is condemned to death. Now all the above events took place during the public ministry of Christ after his baptism, and when he was between thirty and thirty-three years old. There can, therefore, be no room for doubt, that not the child, but the man is intended; yet the man who, according to historical records was more than thirty years of age, is treated by the art as no more than twelve, fifteen, or twenty. The art has, in this manner, interpreted an idea which we shall try to make more distinctly evident; but before going further, we must complete our notice of the portraits of our Saviour.

During the first and second periods of Christian art; that

* "Quatuor Paradisi flumina, quatuor sunt evangelia ad prædicationem cunctis gentibus missa." (St. Eucher, *in Genes.*, lib. i., cap. iii.; Cf. Bede, Isidore of Seville, and G. Durandus.) Bede (*in Genes.* cap. ii.) says, "Quatuor Paradisi flumina, quatuor evangelistæ." In Fig. 23, we see the Lamb of God standing on an eminence, from which the four symbolic streams descend. Below, at Fig. 86, Jesus and his divine lamb are standing together on the mountain of the four springs, and accompanied by six Apostles, also figured by six lambs.

is to say, from the second or third centuries down to the tenth, until the reign of the first Capetian kings, Christ was most generally depicted youthful and beardless. But Lentulus and Damascenus had not declared the Saviour to be a man of mature age, with a thick, forked beard, either black or of the colour of wine, in vain; for beside the beardless figures just noticed, and at the very same period, we find some figures not inconsistent, in any respect, with the description of Lentulus, and representing Christ as a fine man, of from thirty to thirty-five years of age, and with a beard.

The sarcophagi, the paintings in the catacombs, the ancient tombs at Arles, all present similar figures of Christ of that age, and bearded, although they are far less numerous than the others, and strictly speaking, might almost be called exceptions.* One of the sarcophagi in the Vatican presents a highly interesting peculiarity.† Christ is there represented in four different scenes: in one, that in which he heals the hemorrhöidal woman, who throws herself at his feet, he is bearded; but in the other three, in which he gives his law to the apostles,‡ predicts the denial of St. Peter, and is brought before Pilate, he is young and beardless. Down to the time of the Capets, the type of youth, grace, delicate beauty, and charming benevolence, predominates. Hroswitha, the celebrated nun of the convent of Gandersheim in Lower Saxony, still imagines Christ under the form of a young man.§ In the comedy of Callimachus, where she brings on the stage the raising of Drusiana by St. John the Evangelist, that apostle, the friend of Christ, says to Andronicus, the husband of

* *Roma Sotterr*, pp. 61, 63, &c. In the History of the Nimbus, and in that of God the Father, we have given several figures in which Jesus is drawn bearded: we shall meet with others also as we proceed.

† Engraved in the *Roma Sotterr*, pp. 85-87. The sarcophagus, Fig. 63, shows the same fact. There, on Palm Sunday, and when before Pilate, Jesus is beardless; but when giving his law to the Apostles he is bearded. This Christ with a beard, is the same Christ with seven lambs, given below, Fig. 86.

‡ This subject has been given, Fig. 18.

§ See in the *Bibliothèque Mazarine*, "Opera Hrosvite, illustris virginis et monialis germane (*sic*) gentis Saxonia orte, nuper a Conrado Celte inventa." It is a small folio volume, exceedingly rare, with engravings and ornaments on wood of the fifteenth century.

Drusiana, "See, Andronicus! the invisible God appears to you under a visible form. He has assumed the features of a beautiful young man."

Lastly, towards the close of the tenth century, under the Emperior Otho II., Christ is still an adolescent, a beardless young man. But at the approach of the year, 1000, everything looked gloomy and overcast. The belief that the end of the world was approaching was not perhaps so universally prevalent as has been asserted, nor was its influence upon art so great as has been imagined. Still, the events then passing were sufficiently gloomy. Barbarism had scarcely as yet been subdued; manners were rude; ecclesiastical society, overrun by men of arms and exposed to violence, could no longer be content with the young and merciful Deity, who healed all infirmities, comforted all sorrows, and smiled benignly and constantly upon all. A God more severe was needed, to terrify the descendants of those Normans who had ravaged France with blood and fire. In the eleventh century, therefore, and even as early as the tenth, Christ was depicted by artists as a man of severe aspect, and melancholy countenance. In the Last Judgment, Christ, condemning the wicked, appears an inexorable judge. He addresses himself not to the elect, but to the lost; instead of re-assuring the former by his words, he is seen blasting the latter with a glance. Christians seem to have felt a pleasure in representing on sarcophagi, frescos, and even in ancient mosaics, the miracles worked by Christ; the actions of that benevolent life which had been passed in healing diseases of the body, and soothing the anguish of the soul.*

The commencement only of the Passion had been indicated, and even from that commencement, the Lord's Supper, the Agony in the Garden, the Betrayal by Judas, the taking of Christ had been omitted, and nothing more was shown of the condemnation than the moment in which Pilate washes his hands, exclaiming that he is innocent of the death of that just man. But from the tenth to the twelfth century, men were content merely to indicate, to pass lightly over, or even altogether omit, the miracles of

* We may constantly apply to Jesus at this period the "pertransiit benefaciendo" of the Gospel: "he went about doing good."

charity, in order that every episode of the Passion might be fully developed in minute detail from the commencement, even to the Crucifixion. At the Last Judgment, Jesus is no longer beardless, smiling, and sitting upon the symbolic personification of heaven or of the world; but he appears on the contrary, bearded, severe, and inexorable.

One theme which the earlier Christians held in peculiar favour, and which is repeated even to satiety on the paintings and sculptures of the catacombs, disappeared altogether after the commencement of the year 1000; it is that of the Good Shepherd.

Our feelings are touched in the primitive ages by that passage of the Gospel in which Christ is compared to the Good Shepherd, who leaves his flock in the wilderness, to go in search of the one lost sheep, and having found it, lays it across his shoulders, and notwithstanding the weight of the burden, the length and difficulty of the way, brings it back with joy to the fold.*

At that time men studied to represent the scene under every possible variety, and with a thousand modifications, invented chiefly to display more and more clearly the goodness and love of the Saviour. But from the eleventh century down to the sixteenth, no further trace of this consoling parable is to be met with on monuments, either of painting or of sculpture. It would seem as if the heart of Jesus had become hardened by the ingratitude of his sheep, formerly so gentle and so beloved.†

Christianity had indeed passed its spring, the period when everything smiles, and had entered on its summer, when nature is powerful, but stormy; when everything comes to maturity under the burning influence of the sun, and when the rolling of the thunder strikes every imagination with awe.

The end, which artists and the clergy had in view, in making Christ youthful and smiling during the first period of the art, and aged and severe in the second, was in the first place to charm, and in the second to alarm the minds of men;

* Luke xv. 4—6.

† See below, at Fig. 89, a drawing and remarks on the figure of the Good Shepherd.

this is clearly seen from the following interesting history given by Ordericus Vitalis, born in 1075, and who wrote the History of Normandy in the first years of the twelfth century:—

"One day certain idle knights were playing and conversing together in the hall of the Castle of Conches; they talked as is usual in such company on different subjects, in the presence of Madame Elizabeth. At length one among them spoke thus:—'Not long since I had a dream with which I was greatly terrified; I saw our Saviour hanging on the cross, his body was all livid, and he himself tortured by exceeding agony, and he looked upon me with a severe and terrible aspect.' As the knight related these things, those who were there present exclaimed, 'The dream is of serious import, and doubtless sent as a dread warning; it would appear to threaten you, on God's part, with some fearful judgment.' Then Baldwin, son of Eustace, Count of Boulogne, made rejoinder, and said, 'And I also, had recently a dream, in which the Lord Jesus appeared, hanging upon the cross, but looking brilliant and beautiful; he smiled favourably upon me, and blessing me with his right hand, made graciously the sign of the cross upon my head.' Those present answered him and said, 'Such a vision seems intended to announce to you great favour and blessing.' . . . . . Shortly after . . . . . while engaged on a certain expedition, the first knight received a mortal wound, and perished without confession or viaticum. But Baldwin, son-in-law of Raoul de Conches, placed upon his right shoulder the cross of the Lord, and, by the command of Pope Urban, took part in the successful expedition or crusade against the Pagans . . . . . he was made governor of Ragès or Edessa, and some years later, after the death of his brother Godfrey, he possessed for a long period the kingdom of Jerusalem."*

Figures of Christ are at this period more frequently terrible, like that seen by the cavalier who died without viaticum or confession, than brilliant and beautiful like that described by Baldwin. Still there was no sudden transition

* *Orderici Vitalis uticensis monachi, Ecclesiast. Hist.*, lib. viii, ad annum 1090; pp. 688, 689 in *Duchesne Hist. norm. script.* See the excellent edition of *Ordericus Vitalis*, now being published by M. Aug. Leprévost.

from portraits almost invariably young, to those which are constantly aged. In certain localities, more civilised in manners, or more behind the prevailing habits, we sometimes meet with figures of Christ, youthful and smiling. After the twelfth century such exceptions become more and more rare; the figures of Christ take a more gloomy character, and he is more constantly visible in the scenes of the Passion, and in the Last Judgment. He is, then, indeed, terrible; and truly the "Rex tremendæ majestatis" of our DIES IRÆ; he is almost the God of the Jews, willing that fear should be the beginning of wisdom.*

In representations of the Last Judgment, sculptured on the vaulting, or painted on the wheel windows of our cathedrals, Christ appears insensible to the prayers of his mother, who is placed on the right hand; of Saint John the Evangelist, the beloved disciple, and of Saint John the Baptist, the Precursor, who stand on his left. He crushes the wicked while exhibiting to them the wounds in his hands, in his feet, and in his side; he drowns them in the blood flowing from those wounds. The Greeks, more hebraic than the Latins, imagined a Christ even more terrible in aspect. The Byzantine frescos on the western wall, within,† and even on the exterior,‡ of these churches, are usually representations of the Last Judgment. Christ is there represented seated on a throne, while the angels surrounding him tremble in terror on hearing the awful maledictions that he launches against sinners. Not only is God the Son judge, as amongst ourselves, but he himself executes the judgment pronounced. Scarcely has he uttered the sentence of reprobation, when at the sound of his voice a stream of fire issuing from the throne beneath his feet, consumes the guilty. These subjects, treated in general with remarkable talent, are the literal interpretation of a passage from the writings of Saint John Damascenus, which is even at this day received as an authority.§

* "Initium sapientiæ timor Domini."—Ps. cx. 10.

† As in the principal church of the convent of Salamis, called Panagia-Phaneromèni.

‡ As in the great church of the convent of Vatopèdi on M. Athos.

§ The following is the passaage alluded to: "Nam, rogo, ubi repræsentante imagine secundum Christi Dei nostri adventum inspexeris, quando veniat in

Eastern Christianity is far less gentle and benevolent in spirit than that of the West. Thus, in the convent of St. Laura, on Mount Athos, there is a half-length picture of Jesus Christ, on a medallion from which flames are issuing; the Son of God holds in his left hand an open book, in his right a naked sword. When viewing a picture of this description, we seem as if watching the revival of the spirit of Paganism, of the religion of violence, or at least the Judaism of Moses and Isaiah. It seems as if the Christ of Mount Athos offered men the choice of belief or death, the book or the sword. This picture is of the sixteenth century, and seems to betray more especially a Mahometan spirit. The Greeks have borrowed greatly from the Turks, and the Christ of St. Laura affords an interesting confirmation of this fact; one might imagine the Saviour to have assumed the semblance of Mahomet. It was with the Koran in one hand and the scimitar in the other that the mighty religious conquests of Mahomet and his successors were actually achieved. The manuscript of Panselinos, in conformity with Greek taste and the writings of Damascenus, recommends artists to make Christ terrible in aspect, in their paintings of the Last Judgment; the following are the directions there

majestate; angelos item innumera multitudine cum timore et tremore ejus adsistentes throno; IGNEUM FLUMEN quod de throno egrediens peccatores devorat."—Opp. S. Joh. Damas., *Oratio adversus Constantinum Cabalinum*, vol. i., p. 619. In the manuscript of Herrade (*Hort. Delic.*), which dates from 1180, Christ is figured in the Last Judgment sitting on a rainbow; he is encircled by an oval aureole, his pierced and bleeding feet supported by a second rainbow; exhibiting his bleeding hands, and the open, bleeding wound in his side. Under this awful form is written, "Deus manifeste veniet et non silebit; ignis in conspectu ejus exardescet, in circuitu ejus tempestas valida. Ignis ante ipsum precedet et inflammabit in circuitu inimicos ejus." "Our God shall come, and shall not keep silence; a fire shall devour before him, and it shall be very tempestuous round about him."—Ps. l. 3. "A fire goeth before him, and burneth up his enemies round about."—Ps. xcvii. 3. This fire, according to Greek painters, and the quotation from St. John Damascenus, issues from the feet of Christ, to envelope and consume the false prophets, "qui per inspirationem et incantationem immundorum spirituum ventura predixerunt, vel qui vera dixerunt et falsa operati sunt. Omnes superbi et omnes facientes impietates erunt quasi stipula." Everything here is strictly in accordance with the opinions of the East, and Eastern art. The influence of the Byzantine spirit must have been powerfully felt in the convent of St. Odile, for the women and nuns of our country to have chosen so violent a manner of representing the Last Judgment.

given:—"Christ is sitting on a lofty throne of fire; he is clad in white, and darts his thunderbolt over the sun. All the choirs of angels are seized with dread, and tremble before him. With the right hand he bestows his benediction on the saints, but with the left he indicates to sinners the place of torment. . . . A river of fire flows from the feet of Christ, and the wicked are flung by demons into the stream. . . . Prophets, with their rolls, stand on the right and left of the scene of Judgment." Malachi says: "Behold the day cometh that shall burn as an oven; and all the proud, yea, and all that do wickedly shall be stubble; and the day cometh that shall burn them up saith the Lord of Hosts."* (Mal. iv. 1.)

Dating from the second period, that is from the eleventh to the sixteenth century, Christ is always a man in the full vigour of life, from thirty-five to forty years of age; he is invariably bearded, never smiling, and his countenance, when not sad, is serious. It is very rarely that we meet with a figure of Christ beardless, or with a countenance unmarked by deep, and perhaps, melancholy feeling. Still this anomaly may be found in the Cathedral of Rheims, in a sculpture of the close of the thirteenth, or perhaps even the opening of the fourteenth century. The Cathedral of Rheims is, however, an exception to all rules, and filled with peculiarities that seem to contradict every other monument of the same period.

During the thirteenth and fourteenth centuries, we remark the first appearance and frequent adoption of an iconographic theme, which will be noticed at length in the chapter on the Trinity. God is at this period frequently represented sitting in heaven and holding in his arms, the Son affixed to the cross. Thus the crucified is not only seen upon earth, where he expired, in the midst of agonies which distorted his glorious body, but his cruel anguish is even brought to sadden heaven. Thenceforth, the cross, the instrument of his suffering, will rarely be found absent, even when the Saviour is shown triumphant after death. Assuredly the cross in the hand of Christ should be to

* Ἑρμηνεία τῆς ζωγραφικῆς. Christ hurling the thunderbolt, recals the idea of Jupiter Tonans.

Christians what the rainbow in the clouds is to the descendants of Noah, and to the human race; the rainbow announces that there shall be no second deluge, and the Cross that the world, from henceforth, is redeemed. When Noah quitted the ark, and also after the death of his Blessed Son, God made an eternal covenant with man; He saved his body at the deluge, and by the passion of Jesus he redeems his soul. Still the Cross, while it presents a signal of peace to the righteous, is to the wicked a token of wrath; it offers at the same time, a re-assurance and a terrible warning.

In the fifteenth and sixteenth centuries, the sadness of preceding epochs is even more fondly indulged. The Ecce-homo, Crucifixes, exaggerated pictures of the Deposition from the Cross, and of Christ in the Tomb, are really the fashion of the time; but we must pass them over here with but slight notice, for it must be remembered that we are now considering the Son of God, in his divine, not his human nature. Even in the crucifix itself, we trace a remarkable progression of sadness. In the very earliest period the Cross only is given without the Divine sufferer.* Mention is made in the sixth century of a crucifix executed at Narbonne,† but this appears to be an unusual fact which is noticed as an innovation. In the tenth century crucifixes are occasionally seen, but the countenance of the crucified Lord is gentle and benevolent; he is also clad in a long robe with sleeves, the extremities of the arms and legs only being uncovered.‡

In the eleventh and twelfth centuries, the robe becomes

* The little image which placed itself miraculously upon the cross executed by Mark, an artist contemporary with Diocletian, represented not the crucified Saviour, but Emmanuel. Emmanuel, youthful and beardless, placed himself on the cross, between the archangels Michael and Gabriel, but he was not affixed to it. See Labbe, *Conciliorum Collectio maxima*, vol. vii., col. 768. Second Council of Nice.

† "Est et apud Narbonensem urbem, in ecclesia seniore quæ beati Genesii martyris reliquiis plaudit, pictura quæ Dominum nostrum quasi præcinctum linteo indicat crucifixum."—Greg. of Tours, *De Gloria Martyrum*, lib. i., cap. xxiii.

‡ Similar figures of Christ abound in the cabinets of Christian antiquaries. M. de Sommerard possesses several. The miraculous crucifix of Amiens, called St. Saulve, is completely covered by a robe with numerous folds.

shorter, the sleeves disappear, and the breast is already uncovered in some instances, the robe being scarcely more than a kind of tunic.* In the thirteenth the tunic is as short as possible; in the fourteenth it is nothing more than a piece of stuff, or rather linen, rolled round the loins: and up to the present time, the figure of Christ upon the cross, has been constantly thus represented. At this period when the countenance of the crucified Redeemer becomes more sorrowful, and the impress of physical suffering is stamped upon his divine form, he is at the same time divested of the robe, and the slight garment by which he had been protected. Some artists went even farther, and affixed to the cross an image of Jesus without any covering whatever; God, thus absolutely naked, is indeed a revolting spectacle. Still I must acknowledge that I am not aware of more than one instance in which Christ is figured completely naked; it is to be found in a manuscript in the Bibliothèque Royale.† It is possible, nay probable, that the deficiency is owing to an error of the miniaturist; still that error, while restricting our assertion, does not the less serve to confirm its truth.

It may then be affirmed, that from the sixth century down to the fifteenth, the figure of the crucified is successively divested of every kind of drapery, until reduced to a state of almost complete nudity. The Son of God, even though in heaven, even though reigning triumphant, after the Ascension had sealed His victory over death, is still represented with a crown of thorns on his head, and the cross in his hand. In the thirteenth century he was clad in a robe and mantle; after the fifteenth, he is often divested of the robe, and but partially covered by the mantle, which leaves

* Examples are too numerous to be particularly quoted.

† *Heures du Duc d'Anjou*, p. 162. I fancy I have seen a second example of this, in the *Biblia Sacra*, No. 6829. If I recollect rightly, a Christ, entirely naked, is placed opposite to the miniature representing Eleazer the High-priest sacrificing a red cow without the camp of the Hebrews. The association thus intimated between Christ and the red animal, which was slain to expiate the sins of the Israelites, has led to the representing of Christ with red hair and beard, notwithstanding the quotations made above, from which we learn that the complexion of the Saviour was brown. As a man, the hair of Jesus may have been brown, but it is represented red in his symbolic character.

exposed the arms, legs and breast, and the spear-wound in his side.*

Artists plunged lower and lower still into the depths of a miserable materiality, until the time of Michelangelo, by whom Christ is pourtrayed in the Last Judgment, under the aspect of a Jupiter Tonans, and appearing from his gesture as if prepared to chastise the human race with actual blows. How melancholy is such an aberration of the mind in a man of genius! degrading thus the entire Deity, and particularly that one of the three Divine persons, whose ineffable love to mankind makes him in very truth the most perfect type of gentleness and mercy. The Florentine painter went farther even than the text of Damascenus, and the Byzantine frescos, for his Christ is devoid of dignity, while that of the Greeks although harsh, is still noble. By comparing the paintings of Michelangelo with the sculptured sarcophagi, and the Christ on the tomb of Junius Bassus given above, we are most strikingly impressed with the difference of epochs and of ideas. How great is the difference between the inexorable Christ of Michelangelo, and the merciful God depicted on ancient sarcophagi. What centuries of misery and misfortune must have passed away in that same country before the type preserved in the frescos of the catacombs changed into that in the Sistine Chapel! but it was not possible to pass without transition from one extremity to the other, and these changes and transitions compose the archæological history of the Son of God. Michelangelo himself does but give the latest interpretation of an idea which had existed before his time, and it has been remarked with justice, that the Christ of Michelangelo originated in that which the painter Orcagna had placed in the Last Judgment in the Campo Santo of Pisa, an engraving of which is given below.

Michelangelo, it will be seen, copied the gesture of Orcagna, but without understanding it. The Christ of the Campo Santo is not in the act of menacing the guilty, he is showing them the wound in his side, which he uncovers with his left hand, and the point of the nail in his right

* On funereal monuments of that period Christ is nearly always thus represented.

Fig. 67.—THE SUPREME JUDGE.
Fresco of the Campo Santo of Pisa; XIV cent.

hand, which he raises and uncloses at the same moment. Michelangelo imagined, in his rude, barbarous judgment, that Christ was in the act of fulminating, when he is simply exhibiting his wounds. The Christ of Orcagna is seated, that of Michelangelo is standing, and that attitude imparts to his warrior God a character more terrible still. Finally, the figure of Christ at Pisa, crowned with a tiara, robed in sumptuous vestments, with the head flashing light, is a pope, a god, and for that very reason pacific, and even benevolent, but the Christ of the Sistine Chapel, bare-headed, and without either nimbus or aureole, is nothing more than a man, and a man of the lowest grade. Never has the image of God been more degraded than by the severe Florentine artist.

From the period of the Renaissance down to our own, men have sought to restore to the figure of Christ all its early sweetness, its ineffably gracious and benevolent expression, and artists have thus fallen into an error, the very reverse of that into which Michelangelo had been betrayed, so that they have produced tame and languishing images of the Saviour, with fair hair, blue eyes, and in expression sentimental, rather than serious or serene. Still it must be acknowledged, that many praiseworthy attempts are made to bring back the figure of Christ to the same beautiful type, under which he was represented in the twelfth and thirteenth centuries. One cannot but view with satisfaction this intelligent reaction, against the brutal materiality and ferocity of the fifteenth and sixteenth centuries.

We discover from what has been already said that types of various character, and not, as has been erroneously asserted, one single universal type, have been employed in representations of our Saviour. Still, all these varieties may be reduced under two heads: Christ is either youthful and beardless, or he is bearded and has attained the age of manhood. Figures of the Son of God from the first ages of Christianity down to the twelfth century are distinguished by youthfulness and grace, together with the absence of the beard. From the twelfth century down to our own time, the beard of Christ is more or less fine and short, his age about thirty or forty. But between the eleventh and sixteenth centuries we rarely meet with beardless figures of Christ, while from the fourth to the thirteenth and fourteenth, the beard is most usually seen. Beardless Christs are very rare during the second period, while that attribute is frequently given in the first, and even in the paintings found in the catacombs.

It will be well to take the present opportunity of examining that question concerning the beauty or ugliness of our Saviour, which was so warmly canvassed during the first ages of the Church.

Some among the early fathers, those of the African Church in particular, have understood certain expressions of St. Paul in an extended sense, such as they cannot properly bear. The Apostle, writing to the Philippians, says thus, "Jesus made himself of no reputation, and took upon him the form of a servant, and was made in the likeness of men."* A God, who becomes man, lays aside the Godhead, but he may nevertheless clothe himself in a glorious human form. The Christians of Africa, extreme in everything, exaggerated the idea suggested by Saint Paul. They applied to the human nature what by the Apostle had been intended only of the divine. It must also be remembered, that they attached much importance to the following text of the Prophet Isaiah, who, in speaking of the Messiah uses the following words: "He hath no form nor comeliness; and when we shall see him there is no beauty that we should desire him. He is despised and rejected of men, a man of sorrows and acquainted with grief, and we hid, as it were, our faces from him; he was despised and we esteemed him not. Surely he hath borne our griefs and carried our sorrows, yet we did esteem him stricken, smitten of God and afflicted. But he was wounded for our transgressions, he was bruised for our iniquities; the chastisement of our peace was upon him, and with his stripes we are healed."†

* "Semetipsum exinanivit (Jesus Christus), formam servi accipiens" . . . &c. (Phil. xi. 8.)

† In the 53rd chapter of Isaiah, verses 2, 3, 4, and 5, we find the following remarkable words: "Non est species ei neque decor; et vidimus eum, et non erat aspectus, et desideravimus eum; despectum et novissimum virorum, virum dolorum et scientem infirmitatem," &c. St. Peter (Epist. i. ii. 24) says also, "Qui peccata nostra ipse pertulit in corpore suo super lignum, ut

The African doctors understood these words literally, and, notwithstanding the description given above, in which Christ is said to have been a man of singular beauty, they maintained that the Word in entering the world, took upon himself the burden of all human wretchedness and misery, with intent to heal it, and concentrated also in his own person, all the hideousness of physical deformity, with intent to transfigure it.

According to this doctrine, diseases of the soul should have been outwardly typified by the deformity of the body, and our blessed Lord would have been the most hideous of the children of men. That body in which, according to this doctrine, circulated all the venom of human misery, must have become corrupted and disfigured; the discoloured skin, attenuated muscles, wasted form, and impoverished contour, would have visibly testified the self-sacrifice of the Redeemer. The Son of God would have been inoculated with ugliness, just as a man who sucks a poisoned wound becomes envenomed with the poison he imbibes.

Others, the fathers of the Latin Church in particular, declared Christ to have been the most beautiful of mankind. Though upon earth, he was still the Son of God, and God is himself supreme in beauty. God is infinite in beauty as he is in wisdom, goodness and power. The infirmities and vices which he came to expiate had no power to sully his glorious form, any more than a sunbeam that touches or shines through an impure object can be polluted by the contact. The apostles and saints who cured men of fevers, the plague, and leprosy, who made the lame to walk, and raised putrefying corpses to life, did not thereby contract either corruption, deformity, leprosy, pestilence, or fever; why then should Christ, whose mission it was to save man from damnation, and purify him from the taint of sin, have assumed the livery of the vicious, or the deformity of guilt? Jesus, on the contrary, killed death, and dispelled its accompanying horrors. By his incarnation, in the womb of a virgin, Christ assumed all the beauty and grace of humanity and divinity; divinity still shone resplendent through the material body.

peccatis mortui, justitiæ vivamus; cujus livore sanati estis." "Who his own self bare our sins, in his own body on the tree, that we, being dead to sins should live unto righteousness."

Perplexed by these two opinions, so diametrically opposed, antiquaries turned to the art itself to discover which side had been preferred. But in their endeavours to solve that interesting problem, books were consulted instead of monuments, people read instead of observing, and the conclusions thus drawn were irreconcilable with the evidence afforded by the monuments themselves. Christian artists cannot certainly have been ignorant of the controversy that existed relative to this question; it was impossible for them to avoid taking part in it either directly or indirectly; they were compelled to solve the problem, either in the one sense or the other; and writers and theologians being at variance, artists also divided themselves into at least two parties, one formed of the partisans of ugliness, the other of the friends of beauty. Consequently, in works of Christian art, we meet sometimes with beautiful, and sometimes with deformed figures of Christ.

The terms ugliness and beauty require no particular definition; everybody attaches to those words certain ideas of form, easily recognisable, and which it is impossible to confound. Now, in the strict sense of these words, no figure of Christ, in painting or sculpture, at whatever period it may have been executed, can be called absolutely perfect in beauty, but above all, none really ugly are to be found. In fact, these artistic representations of the Son of God are, strictly speaking, neither ugly nor beautiful. They are simply men, and as men, tolerably well proportioned, but not remarkable either for beauty or the reverse. Christ, when represented as we find him on the monuments of the catacombs, under the figure of a young and graceful youth, does not appear to surpass in beauty other young persons of that age. Any youth of from fifteen to twenty might equal in beauty the youthful figure of our Saviour, graceful as it may be; and when represented as aged and saddened, he is not more ugly than any man of thirty or forty years of age. On monuments of the thirteenth century, in the cathedral at Paris, for example, on the tympanum of the left door of the western porch, Jesus is seen with his apostles and disciples, attending at the deathbed of Mary, his mother, and receiving in his arms the departing soul of the Virgin, which takes its flight towards heaven.

The figure here sculptured is neither more ugly nor more beautiful than those of the attendant apostles, or of the kings and patriarchs of the vaulting, who are ranged in several cordons around the tympanum. What is more remarkable still, were it not for the nimbus with which the head of the Saviour is encircled, it would be impossible to distinguish him either from his apostles, or from his ancestors, the kings and patriarchs in the vaulting; but around his head is a cruciform nimbus, while the apostles have the plain nimbus; and the personages of the Old Testament are without any nimbus or ornament whatever. Jesus is a man, and as a man, like other men. At the Renaissance indeed, artists sought to idealise, to beautify Christ; but their most exquisite creations are not those of which he is the subject. The forerunner of Christ, St. John the Baptist, both as child and as man, is, in the works of Italian, German, and French masters, as beautiful as the Saviour, whether man or infant. St. John the Evangelist is often more beautiful than Christ, his divine master and friend.

If an ugly figure of Christ should accidentally occur, we can easily convince ourselves that it is not so much physiological, as arising from a want of skill in the workman. An artist of bad taste and feeble execution, would make a bad figure, simply because incapable of producing a good one, and ugliness in such a case, must be attributed not to an adherence to any particular doctrine, but to the defects of the execution.* Upon inferior medals the figure of Christ is ugly, on those which are valuable and finely worked, he is beautiful. In other words, the Son of God is ill executed on the former, and well executed on the latter; but strictly and philosophically speaking, he cannot be called beautiful nor the reverse.

Must it then be supposed that while the fathers of the Church disputed concerning the mystical beauty or deformity of our Saviour, artists were insensible to all that was passing around them? While some amongst the former warmly

* See a figure of Christ, enamelled upon copper, of the end of the eleventh century, now in the possession of M. du Sommerard. The workmanship is rude in the extreme, and the excessive ugliness of the face, is carried out in the remainder of the person, and even in the decoration. It is evident, at a glance that the figure of Christ is badly executed rather than ugly.

espoused the cause of beauty, and others, with equal vehemence, supported that of deformity, would the art, which seems in every epoch to have been the interpreter of men's ideas, have remained neutral? that such was not, and could not have been the case, proofs will immediately be given. Artists, it is true, attend to the slightest rumour that reaches their ears. Through the medium of dimension, line, colouring, sounds, syllables and gestures; by architecture, sculpture, painting, music, poetry, and dancing, they reflect all images, however vague, which pass before their eyes. They repeat, defining and enlarging, whatever they hear, see, or touch; but while repeating they at the same time make it their own, subjecting it to a series of transformations, by which it becomes purified and embellished. They had heard the audacious language of Tertullian: "Jesus Christ was mean in aspect, and his human form not worthy to be gazed upon; yet vulgar, ignoble, dishonoured as he is, he is still *my* Christ whom I adore." * They knew that St. Cyril of Alexandria, speaking of the Saviour, had declared him to be the most ugly of the children of men.†

Vulgar artists, espousing the side of ugliness, would have represented Christ as deformed, with exhausted organisation, worn muscles, and ignoble expression; but ancient traditions, perfected by the new sentiments introduced with Christianity, yet lived amongst them. They perfectly comprehended that a figure, though considered unworthy of the divinity, might still be very beautiful for a man; and consequently that a God, under human form, beautiful as he might be, would still be ugly as a God, provided the characters of humanity were distinctly impressed upon his person.

Now of these characteristics, the beard is unquestionably one of the most visible and striking; for its colour and form give to the physiognomy a peculiar stamp, revealing the age and temperament. Artists, therefore, when wishing to represent Christ, divested of his god-like beauty, depicted him

* "Ne aspectu quidem honestus." (*Adv. Jud.* cap. xiv.) "Nec humanæ honestatis fuit corpus ejus." (*De Carnat. Christi*, cap. ix.) "Si inglorius, si ignobilis, si inhonorabilis, meus erit Christus." *Adv. Marcian*, lib. iii. cap. xvii.

† Ἀλλὰ τὸ εἶδος αὐτοῦ ἄτιμον ἔκλιπον παρὰ πάντας τοὺς υἱοὺς τῶν ἀνθρώπων.—St. Cyril of Alexandria, *de Nudatione Noe*, lib. ii. vol. i. p. 13.

as a bearded man; their scrupulous intelligence figured literally the energetic language of Tertullian, interpreting it in the sense of humanity. Those on the other hand who rejected that interpretation, and who contended for the beauty of our Saviour's person, represented him without a beard,

Fig. 68.—CHRIST SUFFERING; BEARDED, HUMAN OR UGLY.
Carving on Ivory; XII cent. Bib. Royale.

and, consequently, as free as possible from the attributes of humanity. In short, by the first, the ugly Christ was regarded as a man; by the second, the beautiful Christ was a God. To the one he was a being, bearing the marks of age; to the others, the partisans of beauty, Christ was a God neither of yesterday, to-day, nor to-morrow: a God to whom no precise age could be assigned, because he has been for ever, and will exist to all eternity.* The bearded Jesus is the ugly Christ of the fathers of the Church in Asia and more especially in Africa; the beardless Jesus is the Christ of the fathers of the Latin Church, and of Western art in general.

Works of art are all in harmony with the explanation just given. Take, for instance, two subjects on the same monument; a manuscript with carved ivory covers, both of the same epoch. On the right cover, Jesus is seen on the cross, as in the preceding engraving.

The feet are resting on a chalice † into which the blood is

* "Jesus Christus, heri, hodie, et in sæcula."—Heb. iv. 8. "Jesus Christ, the same yesterday, to day, and for ever."

† It seems probable that this chalice is the Graal, so celebrated in mediæval romance; to the discovery of which Perceval consecrated his life, and exposed himself to a thousand strange adventures. The Graal, it is said, was used at the Last Supper, and in that very vessel the wine had been changed by Jesus into his blood. Lastly, Nicodemus the converted Jew, or rather Joseph of Arimathea, collected in that sacred chalice the blood that flowed from the Saviour's wounds. In the course of after events, the mysterious Graal passed into France, where it became the subject of numerous long epic poems. It is said that the fable of these poems, and the origin of the Graal, may both be traced to Bretagne, but there is no foundation for the opinion. The story of the Graal was derived from the apocryphal books, all of which are of Greek or Asiatic origin. In France, in Champagne, and at Troyes, the history of which it is the theme was first developed, and this fine subject was borrowed by the Bretons from the French. It is with the Graal, and all other epics of the middle ages, as with the ogive style of architecture. The Gothic style originated and developed itself in France, or, to speak more strictly, in Picardy, Champagne, and the Isle of France: thence it passed into England, Sweden, Germany, Italy, and Spain. With respect to the Graal, which was for some time in our possession at Paris, under Napoleon, from 1806 to 1815, it is now restored to Genoa, where it is carefully preserved in the treasury of the cathedral, under the name of "Sacro Catino." This precious chalice is of glass, and not emerald, of a hexagon form, and furnished with two handles; it is one mètre fifteen centimètres in circumference: it was broken in the transit from Paris to Genoa. In monuments with figures of the twelfth, thirteenth, and fourteenth centuries, Christianity, personified under the form of a queen, receives in a chalice, still the Graal, the blood flowing from the wounded side of Jesus on the cross. Gori (*Thes. Vet. Dipt.* vol. iii. p. 116) has had an

intended to flow. He seems to turn one last look upon his mother before giving up the ghost. Below, on earth, Mary and St. John bewail the death, the one of her Son, the other of his friend, and both of their God.* Above, in heaven, the sun, girt by a circular and wavy aureole, and represented under the form of a young man without a beard, and the moon in the form of a woman, bearing a crescent on her head, appear touched by the spectacle, and as if sympathising with the agonies of the Lord of nature. On the opposite cover, the left, the nimbus of Christ is cruciform, but unornamented; and, as if in contrast, the Son of God is seated in heaven, surrounded by an elliptical aureole, and adorned with a nimbus, the circumference of which is decorated with pearls. The four symbols of the evangelists, the angel, the eagle, the lion, and the ox, attend the divine hero of the Gospel. On

engraving made from an ancient cover of a psalter at Fréjus, on which this subject is represented. In this the Christian religion, standing below Jesus, who is on the cross, holds a cup to receive the blood flowing from his feet, and in addition to this, the blood from the hands is caught by the Archangels Michael and Gabriel, each of whom likewise presents a chalice. In this example we have three Graals instead of one. Besides Genoa, the cities of Auxerre and Angers each claimed the honour of possessing the true Graal: it is in fact possible that not one cup only, but several may have been employed at the Last Supper, for different purposes. In the Ladye Chapel, at the back of the apse in the Cathedral of Beauvais, is a stained glass window of the thirteenth century, in the central rose of which a crucifixion is depicted. Adam, who, according to the legend, was interred at the foot of the cross, rises entirely from the tomb: a greenish drapery is thrown over his head, and round the loins. In his left hand he holds a golden cup, to receive the blood flowing from the Saviour's feet. The attention of antiquaries is invited to these various cups: with them the Graal originated; they contain the germ of all those epics of which the Graal has been the subject. From the apocryphal books in the first instance, from sculptured monuments, and the epics of our Champenois and Picard poets, the Bretons have drawn with lavish hands what are improperly termed their inventions. In the engraving given above, the feet of Christ, instead of being crossed and fixed with one nail, are separate and pierced with two. Previous to the thirteenth century, Christ was attached to the cross, by three or four nails, indifferently. Gulielmus Durandus is in favour of four nails, as was Gregory of Tours, long before his time. After the thirteenth century the practice of putting only three nails was definitively in the ascendant.

* St. John is bearded, as he is constantly represented by the Greeks; while amongst us, he is a beautiful youth, still beardless. The ivory above mentioned is Latin, but the age of St. John, and the personification of the sun as Apollo, and the moon as Diana, betray a decided Byzantine influence.

the right Christ is suffering; on the left he is triumphant. Here he is attached to the cross, the infamous gibbet; there he is surrounded by the aureole, the badge of divine glory. Nature, personified by mankind and the planets, appears at

Fig. 69.—CHRIST TRIUMPHANT; BEARDLESS, DIVINE, OR BEAUTIFUL. Carved Ivory of the XI cent.; Bib. Royale.

the opening of the manuscript to compassionate the suffering and death of the Redeemer, and at the close the evangelists symbolised by their attributes, celebrate his triumph, and the lion of St. Mark roars with joy and happiness.*

In this plate, Jesus the Son of Man transformed into the Son of God, dispenses to the world grace and knowledge, grace with the right hand, which is raised in the act of benediction, knowledge from the books which he holds in his left hand and in his lap. Science is here represented in all its fulness by the square book and the roll or volumen; these two, the only form of books then known, were in use

* "Marcus frendens ore leonis," as say the symbolists of the thirteenth century. "Marcus ut alta fremit vox per deserta leonis," as we find it written in an *Evangeliaire* of the ninth century, preserved in the Bibliothèque de l'Arsenal. (*Quatuor Evangelia theol.*, lat 33.) These expressions fully justify the roaring of our lion. An *Evangeliaire* in folio, belonging to the Sainte Chapelle at Paris to which it was presented in 1379, by Charles V., contains the following verses, in explanation of the four attributes of the Evangelist:—

> "Quatuor hæc Dūm signant animalia $\overline{X\rho\mu}$:
> Est homo nascendo, vitulusque socer moriendo,
> Et leo surgendo, cœlos aquilaque petendo;
> Nec minus hos scribas animalia et ipsa figurant."

Consequently these four attributes refer at the same time to Christ and to his Apostles. As to the place which they occupy, and the books held by each of the four, Gulielmus Durandus, in the third chapter of the first book of his *Rationale divinorum Officiorum*, speaks of them as follows: "Quandoque etiam circumpinguntur quatuor animalia secundum visionem Ezechielis et ejusdem Johannis. Facies hominis et facies leonis a dextris, et facies bovis a sinistris, et facies aquilæ desuper ipsorum quatuor. Hi sunt quatuor evangelistæ. Unde pinguntur cum libris in pedibus, quia, quæ verbis et scriptura docuerunt, mente et opere compleverunt." Durandus confounds the tetramorph of Ezekiel with the four separate attributes. In the tetramorph the eagle is above, but the angel or the man is in the centre, and in this case the attributes have no books. Durandus did not fully understand his own meaning, or, perhaps, being ignorant of the actual representation, he wished to exaggerate the importance of the "cœlos aquila petendo." Durandus always loves to find an exaggerated symbolic meaning, even at the expense of reason. The place, which, except in cases of error, the attributes of the Evangelists do, and ought invariably to occupy, is the following: beginning with Christ as the point of departure, the angel is on the right, and the eagle on the left, above; the lion on the right, and the ox on the left, below; the nature of the attributes, and the meaning they are designed to convey, renders this arrangement indispensable. To begin with the ascending line; the ox, which is the heaviest and most rude, is placed below; the lion roars on the second step, the eagle flies upon the third, and the angel rises superior to all. This order is sometimes ignorantly inverted. Errors occasioned by ignorance are of no greater importance than those daily committed by modern artists and church restorers of the present day.

at the same period amongst the Roman people. Symbolists of the middle ages, Gulielmus Durandus, amongst others, declare that the roll signifies imperfect or partial knowledge, and the square book perfect intelligence. For this reason, he adds, the roll (volumen) is given by sculptors and painters to the prophets, because to them the truth was only partially revealed, seen through a parable as it were, or imaged in a mirror; but apostles and evangelists, to whom the truth had been clearly and fully unfolded, and who taught it perfectly, bear the book instead of the roll. Christ who came to complete what had already been begun, who comprises in himself both the Old Testament and the New, He whom prophets had foretold, and apostles gazed upon, He who is the very incarnation of light and truth, is properly represented as bearing at the same time, the book and the volumen.*

The meaning here is clearly evident,† the artist has intentionally delineated an ugly figure of Christ in the sufferer on the cross, and a beautiful figure in the Saviour triumphant on the throne of heaven. Now the first is bearded, the second not so; consequently, the question of beauty and ugliness, so long discussed by the fathers of the Church, is here interpreted by Christian art, as referring to the absence or presence of the beard. This circumstance is decisive; it accounts for the bearded and beardless heads of the Saviour, which are seen simultaneously on monu-

* G. Durandus. *Rat. div. Off.* lib. 1, cap. 3. Suger commanded the execution at St. Denis of a stained glass window, on which various subjects were painted, the description of which he himself supplied, and had written certain verses in explanation of their meaning. One of the subjects, which is still in existence, represents Christ, raising a veil, which concealed the personification of the synagogue; the following verses, of which a few letters only remain, explain this action.

"Quod Moyses velat, Christi doctrina revelat;
Denudant legem qui spoliant Moysen."

The Old Testament, the Law of Moses, is a veiled doctrine which Christ came to elucidate with the living light of truth; in Christ we see truth face to face. This action of unveiling Moses and the prophets has given rise to several compositions in painting; a manuscript in the Bibliothèque Royale has this same subject twelve times repeated.

† It is more fully expressed in words in an ivory triptych, in the Cabinet des Medailles, &c., in the centre compartment of which the same subject is drawn, with the following inscription beneath it in Greek characters, "Tu as souffert comme chair, comme Dieu tu delivres!"

ments analogous, both in style and period, to the frescos and sarcophagi of the catacombs of Rome, and of the Aliscamps at Arles.

Whenever we meet with a youthful, beardless, and smiling figure of the Saviour, his feet resting on the personification of earth or of heaven, or else standing on the mountain of Paradise, or in the waters of Jordan, working miracles, or appearing before Pilate, we may conclude that the artist, being a partisan on the side of beauty as in the question which has just occupied us, has made Christ beautiful, considering him both as human and as accomplishing his evangelic mission. Whenever, on the contrary, and this is frequently the case, we see a bearded Christ, even though the functions he performs are divine rather than human, when standing, for instance, on the mountain of the four symbolic rivers, he gives his parting instructions to his apostles; we may affirm the artist to have been a partisan of the humanity of Christ, and to have made him ugly, that is to say human.

The manuscript of the Bibliothèque Royale is far from being the only monument in support of the solution just given. In Saint Guillem-du-Désert, in Lower Languedoc, there is still an altar, the front of which is formed of a black and white mosaic, representing the crucifixion on one side, and on the other, Christ triumphant. The Christ upon the cross is bearded and aged; but triumphant, that is surrounded by the aureole, which is oval, as in the example just given he is beardless and young. This curious work dates probably from the eleventh century, and appears to have been the same altar of Saint Guillem, which was consecrated by a legate of Gregory VII.*

This discussion concerning the beauty and ugliness of the Son of Man—or to speak as artists rather than as the fathers, the question concerning Christ, regarded in his divine and in his human nature—was of no actual importance, nor had it any real influence, except during the first period of Christian art, or from the fifth century down to the twelfth. At that time a decisive part was taken, in favour

* *Découverte et Réstitution de l'Autel de S. Guillaume*, by M. R. Thomassy, in the fourteenth volume of the "Mémoires de la Société royale des Antiquaires de France."

either of ugliness or beauty, although the Church had itself given no decision on that point, and in works then executed, sometimes one system, sometimes the other, appears to have the ascendant. Still the cause of beauty or of the divine nature, which had in the commencement been the strongest, finally yielded altogether about the twelfth, and more especially the thirteenth century, which period was marked by the exclusive triumph of ugliness, or the human nature. A manuscript already cited,* which dates from the close of the fourteenth century, contains a miniature of the priest Eleazar sacrificing a red cow, without the camp of the Hebrews, to avert the wrath of God. Opposite to this miniature is one of Christ on the cross; "Jesus is entirely naked," says the commentary, "and his skin is ugly and discoloured, because he bore our sins in his own body: Christ is here not only bearded, but entirely naked, and the colour of his skin is red; he is human, poor and ugly."† We find in this an additional proof of the gloom and reality which then possessed the world, and passed from society into art. Jesus even when exercising his divine functions is almost invariably bearded. He has a beard when ascending to heaven after the resurrection; when seated at the right hand of his Father in Paradise; when from the highest heaven, shedding blessing upon the earth, and when descending from the clouds, to judge mankind at the end of the world. With still greater reason he is represented bearded when baptised by St. John, when carried away into the desert to be tempted by Satan, when preaching, entering Jerusalem, and when suffering death upon the cross. In the engraving below, Christ is carried by Satan to the summit of a mountain, whence the genius of evil shows him all the kingdoms of the world, and the glory of them. Satan tells Christ, that he will give him all

* *Biblia Sacra*, No. 6829.

† The red colour of the hair, skin, and beard, is considered to be a mark of ugliness. For the last three hundred years nearly, Christ has been drawn with reddish beard and hair, in the idea of thus adhering more closely to the Jewish type. The people are persuaded, in spite of early tradition and the writings of S. John Damascenus, that Jesus was red complexioned, and in a saying, very popular in Champagne and Picardy, the common people assert that "Dieu a fait plus beau que lui parce qu'il était roux, tandis qu'il a créé des hommes bruns, et des hommes blonds.

that he sees spread before his eyes, if he will fall down and worship him: and our Saviour replies—"Thou shalt worship the Lord thy God, and him only shalt thou serve." (St. Matt. iii. 10.)

Jesus, as in all the preceding plates, is bearded, and has a cruciform nimbus.*

Fig. 70.—CHRIST BEARDED, TEMPTED BY SATAN.
French Miniature of the XII cent.

It is still more surprising to find humanity, and the beard, by which it is symbolised, attributed even to God the

* This design is taken from a manuscript in the Bibl. Roy. (*Psalterium cum figuris*, suppl. fr. 1132), dating from the twelfth century. Satan, in order the more easily to force Christ to yield, is accompanied by an assistant, who clasps the Son of God round the waist. This demon, by the assistance of his two pairs of wings and great muscular power, evidenced by the two great horns on his forehead, appears to have transported our Lord to the mountain. The other, the chief Satan, with the tail of a viper, and a human face upon his

Father, and to the Holy Ghost, although neither had ever been incarnate. But as has been said, Jesus draws into his atmosphere, the other two persons; and as he is bearded, the Father and Holy Ghost must be so also. In respect of the Father, an additional reason has been given above, in his being styled the Ancient of Days, and the long existence of the Divinity is intimated by one of the marks of old age, a long and fine beard. The Holy Ghost is also represented with a beard, to signify his being equal to the Father and the Son, and that like them, he had eternity for his portion. We shall see further, as we proceed in his history, that the Holy Ghost was often figured by a youth, with but very slight appearance of a beard, and even sometimes appears in the form of a young child.

ARCHÆOLOGICAL SIGNS, CHARACTERISTIC OF OUR SAVIOUR.

Neither the age nor the countenance can be regarded as permanent characteristics of Christ, for, as has been seen, his age varies from fifteen to sixty. In the catacombs Christ is constantly represented as an adolescent; upon stained glass of the sixteenth century, he is often an aged man: a similar uncertainty exists with regard to the features and all the other external attributes by which Christ might be distinguished. The death of the Virgin is sculptured on the tympanum of the left door of the western porch of Notre-Dame de Paris, and it is impossible to distinguish the figure of Christ from the Apostles there present with him, either by the features, or the general expression. In several of our drawings, those more particularly of the thirteenth and fourteenth centuries, a similar degree of uncertainty prevails. The vesture will not be found to present a better characteristic; Christ is ordinarily clad, like his apostles, in a robe and mantle. The royal crown that covers his head is not peculiar

stomach, holds a scroll, on which is written, "Hæc omnia tibi dabo, si cadens adoraveris me." But Jesus, with an imperious gesture of command, declares to Satan, *Him* whom he ought to adore, as is shown by the words of the roll in his left hand, "Dūm Deū tuū adorabis."

to Christ; kings, certain virtues, certain liberal arts, as seen in the Cathedrals of Chartres and Clermont-Ferrand, are similarly crowned. The tiara is worn by him in common with the Father, with Melchizedech, Aaron, and St. Peter. The book, whether open or closed, which he holds in his left hand, is borne also by the Apostles. Not one of these characteristics will be found specially confined to Christ.

Still there are other attributes which distinguish him from the crowd, even if they do not separate him exclusively from all others. Bare feet are an unfailing characteristic of angels and divine persons, and sometimes given to prophets, invariably to apostles. I am of course speaking only of persons represented clothed; for Job upon his dunghill, the beggar Lazarus before the gate of the wicked rich man, the traveller stripped by robbers and attended by the good Samaritan, the prodigal son during a certain period of his existence, many saints suffering martyrdom, and others besides, are naturally drawn with bare feet, since they are otherwise almost entirely destitute of clothing. But whenever a figure is represented clothed, and certain characteristics recognisable as marks of holiness, as, for example, the nimbus supplied, if the feet are bare, we may confidently affirm that such a figure is intended to represent a prophet, an apostle, an angel, or some divine being. Still this attribute serves but very vaguely to distinguish Christ, being shared by him with so many other persons; it must be remembered besides, that on sarcophagi, in ancient frescos, and frequently in very old mosaics Jesus is represented with sandalled shoes attached to the feet by thongs passing round and over the ankle. Christ is in the Roman costume, even to the sandals. In the fifteenth century it is by no means unusual to see Him with his feet in rich shoes, especially when he is apparelled as high priest or pope, of whom he assumes the entire costume.

In the fourteenth century likewise, particularly when accompanying the pilgrims to Emmaus, Christ is often clad like a pilgrim with a broad-brimmed hat, the pilgrim's staff, wallet, and strong shoes.* The same exception is made in

* A large statue of Christ, as Pilgrim, at Notre Dame de Rheims, is sculptured with shoes, like an ordinary saint, and a pilgrim's hat with wide borders, to shelter the traveller from sun and rain: the nimbus stamped with a cross alone serves to indicate the Saviour. In our mediæval legends, Christ is

regard to St. James, the patron saint of pilgrims. The cold reality and materialism of the fourteenth and fifteenth centuries seemed to shrink from making St. James, who travelled from Asia into Europe, or from Jerusalem to Compostella, undertake the pilgrimage barefoot. Yet, between the sixth and the fifteenth century, bare feet is an almost unfailing characteristic, distinguishing Christ from confessors, martyrs, virgins, and allegorical personages.

The glory, aureole, and nimbus, employed in the glorification of divine and holy persons, ought to be considered more particularly as the attribute of Christ than of any others, on account of the pre-eminent honours which have always been paid to the second person of the Trinity. Early monuments, in fact, always present the Son of God adorned with the most resplendent nimbus, and the most luminous aureole. Even in the womb of his mother, the Incarnate Word is already surrounded with rays, as may be seen in the curious example preserved in the following engraving.*

frequently made to assume the disguise of a pilgrim; to give a particular instance, he may be seen crossing a stream in a boat, guided by St. Julian le Pauvre and his wife. In pictures of this event, Christ is generally clothed like the great Christ at Rheims. The cruciform nimbus is here the sole attribute which characterises him, for the broad hat and the usual loose robe give him the appearance of an ordinary pilgrim. (See a bas-relief, representing St. Julian, which belongs to the close of the thirteenth century; it is now at Paris, No. 42, Rue Galande. This interesting bas-relief was taken from the church of St. Julian in that neighbourhood.)

* This drawing is copied from a painted window of the sixteenth century, which may be seen in a small church at Jouy, a little village in the arrondissement of Rheims. I saw at Lyons, in the year 1836, in the house of the architect Pollet, who is since dead, two wooden shutters, on which was a painting of the Visitation, executed in the fifteenth century. The Virgin and St. Elizabeth, both with child, salute each other with affection. The painter has had the boldness to represent upon each of the two cousins a little human being, intended for Jesus and St. John the Baptist. The two infants also salute each other. The little St. John seems to thrill with emotion, and bends piously to receive the benediction bestowed by the scarcely perceptible fingers of the Saviour. Pollet, at his death, as I have been informed, presented to the city of Lyons these interesting pictures, which certainly have some affinity with the painted window at Jouy, and will not be the least valuable of the curiosities in the Musée at Lyons. Considered as works of art, independently of their archæological interest, these paintings are not without value. A subject, exactly similar to that of Jouy, may be seen on an ancient enamel of Limoges, now in the possession of M. l'Abbé Texier, curé of Auriat (Creuse), and cor-

This aureole, formed of rays alternately straight, and wavy, or flamboyant, resembles that given above (Fig. 43.), except, that in this the infant Jesus seems immersed alone in a luminous oval, which is more distinctly defined and accommodates itself more completely to the contour of the body.

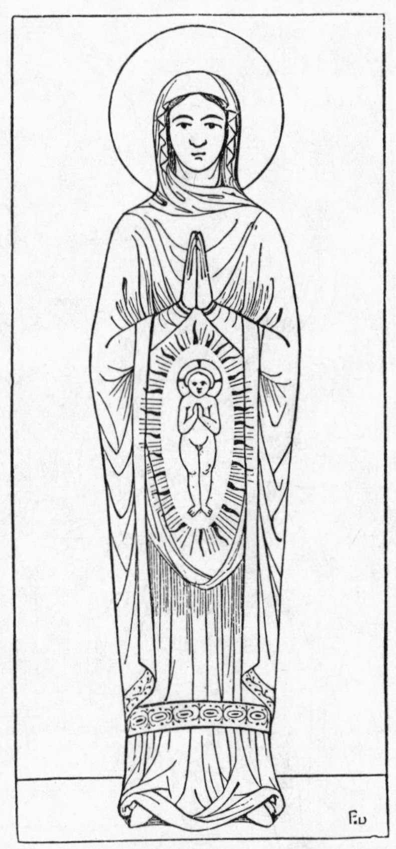

Fig. 71.—JESUS IN A FLAMBOYANT AUREOLE. Painted Window (French) of the XVI cent.

The form of the aureole, encircling the Divine Word, is extremely varied; elliptical, ovoïdal, circular, and quatrefoiled, as in several examples given above (see, amongst others, Figs. 36, 37, 38, 40); it takes the most ample, as well as the most simple, geometrical forms. The aureole being a material symbol of the divine honours paid to Christ, of the respect and admiration in which his atonement and doctrines were held, imagination, among the Greeks more especially, exerted itself to the utmost, in every sense, to

respondent of the Committee of Arts and Monuments. The Virgin is clad in a white robe, thrown partly back, and leaving exposed an under-robe of red and gold. God the Father, floating on the clouds of Heaven, blesses the mother of his Son. Upon the womb of the Virgin a little naked human being, with clasped hands, is represented, surrounded by a golden aureole. The figure of Mary stands out prominently from the background, which is blue. She is surrounded by the moon, a star, a tower, and a lily, &c., all attributes employed to distinguish her, especially in the fifteenth century.

Fig. 72.—JESUS AS AN ANGEL, IN AN AUREOLE COMPOSED OF TRIANGLES.*
Greek Painting of the xv cent.

* These representations of the assembled archangels (*ἡ σύναξις τῶν ἀρχαγγέλων*), presenting their youthful Lord to the adoration of the faithful,

invent and discover new forms of that attribute; seeking thus to testify to the world the infinite love which they bore to the Saviour. The triangle, as has been fully shown (History of the Nimbus, p. 58—63), is the symbol of Deity; two triangles indicate the Divinity even more strikingly, and several designate the absolute, infinite omnipotence of divine power.

Fig. 21 contains an example of a double triangle, but it is employed as a nimbus only, and not as an aureole: the bi-triangular attribute is given to the head only, not to the entire body.

In the figure annexed we have four triangles, not two simply intersecting each other, and from these four triangles emerges the body of the Son of God. The three great archangels, Raphaël, Michaël, and Gabriël, bear as if in triumph* the youthful God, who, with both hands extended, gives his benediction to the world. Jesus is represented with wings, like those of the archangels, because he was the messenger, the angel, "ἄγγελος," of the supreme will of God, to use the magnificent expression of the Greeks.

The Greeks frequently blunt the points of the triangles, or else connect them by a circular line of circumference; they thus restore the form of a perfect circle to the aureole, whence issues forth the youthful God. Fig. 38 contains a divine figure, probably intended for God the Son, or at least for God the Father, with the features and aspect of the Son. This figure is seated in the centre of two squares, with concave sides, having seven projecting triangular points; the

are very common among the Greeks. There is scarcely a church which does not possess a painting of that subject, either in fresco or on wood, placed on the division or iconostasis of the sanctuary. The three archangels, Michaël, Gabriël, and Raphaël, seem, in the ideas of the Greeks, to comprehend in their triple union, the military, civil, and religious power of the kingdom of heaven. Raphaël is regarded as, and attired in, the vestments of a priest; and in that character occupies the place of honour, being placed in the centre between Gabriël and Michaël. Michaël, always clad and armed as a warrior, is commissioned to combat demons and the enemies of God. Gabriël is the messenger of peace, and sent, for example, to announce to the Virgin Mary that she was to be the mother of our Lord. The difference of costume marks their separate functions.

* The name of each archangel is figured, according to the Greek custom, by the first letter of the name inscribed in the upper part of the nimbus.

extremities of these triangular points reach a circular line uniting all.

Here we again recur to the "imago clypeata" already more than once described, and of which several examples have been given.*

The Christ is blessing (Fig. 38) with one hand only, and sometimes, as in a painting in the Convent of Saint Laura, the hand, instead of blessing, is armed with a naked sword. The image, in such cases, is perfectly warrior-like, the circular aureole as well as the nimbus assimilating completely with the character of bucklers.

In the Manuscript of Herrade, we find the following description: "Light painted in the form of a circle round the head signifies that the saints invested with it are crowned with eternal light and radiance. For this reason, that it has the form of a round buckler, the saints being shielded by the divine protection as by a buckler: hence it happens, that they themselves sing 'Lord defend us with the buckler of thy will.'"† In the annexed design, the figure of Christ is more pacific in character; he holds a roll in the left hand, and the right gives the benediction. He has a circular aureole, contained within another, in which the Virgin is inclosed.

Fig. 73.—JESUS IN A CIRCULAR AUREOLE.‡
Silver Seal of Mount Athos.

* Especially Fig. 51.

† "Lumina quæ circa caput sanctorum in modum circuli depinguntur, designant quod lumine æterni splendoris coronati fruuntur. Idcirco vero secundum formam rotundi scuti pinguntur, quia divina protectione ut scuto muniuntur; unde ipsi cantant gratulabundi: Domine ut scuto voluntatis." . . . . (*Hortus Deliciarum.*)

‡ The above engraving is a copy of the seal affixed by the government of

The varied and splendid aureoles with which the person of the Saviour is adorned, are certainly remarkable for beauty; still they will not suffice to distinguish him from other divine persons. Thus, in a preceding engraving (Fig. 67) of Christ, taken from the Campo Santo, the Saviour was seen, encircled by an ovoïdal aureole, and sitting on a rainbow. The circumference of the aureole, and the interior of the nimbus, are striated with a number of lines, and embroidered like a rich garment.

Mount Athos to all laws and decrees. This government is called "épistasie;" it is composed of four monks, styled "épistates," elected every year in the month of May, by all the convents of the holy mountain. A perpetual secretary completes this annual authority. The deliberations of the elective power are not valid until the seal of the state has been affixed to them. The seal is of silver, and divided into four equal parts; one of these pieces is deposited in the hands of each épistate. When the deliberations are completed, each épistate places his quarter seal upon the table, so as to form a half-ball. The secretary takes the four quarters, and unites them by means of a key or a screw with a handle, which is deposited in his care; the seal thus recomposed is blackened by the smoke of a candle, and the paper, on which the act is written, is stamped with it. The secretary then divides the seal, returns to each of the deliberators his quarter, and retains the key himself. A letter delivered to me by the épistates was thus sealed; it was written in the month of October, 1839, to recommend me to the different monasteries which I purposed visiting. On the outer edge of the seal the following legend is engraved, in Greek and Turkish characters: "Seal of the épistate of the community of the Holy Mountain." The four épistates are considered, from the unanimity of their deliberations, as one single individual. The seal represents the Virgin and the Infant Jesus. The whole of Mount Athos is consecrated to Mary. Women, and even the female animals, are excluded from Mount Athos; it is, and always has been, inhabited by men, and men only. There are herds of goats, flocks of sheep, with horses and mules; and in some convents, turkeys and cocks abound; but neither she-goats nor ewes, mares, she-mules, hen turkeys, nor hens. Yet these very monks, notwithstanding their aversion to women, have placed their government under the protection of a woman, and nearly all their monasteries are either dedicated to the Virgin or commemorate some incident in her life. The two first convents are dedicated, one to the Nativity of the Virgin, the other to her Dedication in the Temple of Jerusalem. The last, which is at the bottom of the peninsular of Athos, is consecrated to the Death or the Assumption of Mary. Even in those convents which are not absolutely under the protection of Mary, one or more churches are consecrated to her. Mount Athos desired to throw off the dominion of women, and yet the entire mountain, the dwellings and churches, the monks and their acts, are governed and protected by a woman. Not one single festival in honour of the Virgin, from her nativity down to her death, and her coronation in heaven, is suffered to pass without being celebrated in every convent of Mount Athos. The worship of the Virgin Mary is carried to a much higher point in the Greek than in the Latin Church.

Fig. 74.—MARY, GLORIFIED LIKE JESUS CHRIST.
Italian Fresco of the XIV cent.

The head of Christ emits rays of so much power that they force themselves beyond the edge of the aureole; and yet, notwithstanding the care thus shown in specially honouring Christ, and showing forth his glory, the attributes above enumerated will not suffice to distinguish him from God the Father, nor even from his mother, a mere created being. In fact, in the very same fresco in the Campo Santo, in which the figure of Christ is thus brilliantly shown, the Virgin also is depicted, and with equal brilliancy. Mary is seated on a rainbow, and is surrounded by an ovoïdal aureole; the radiation from her head exactly resembles that of her Blessed Son. The field of the rainbow, the circumference of the aureole, the power and number of the rays, are equal to those seen in the figure of the Son of God.

The hands of Christ sometimes emit rays, as in the figure in Sainte Madeleine de Vezelay, at the door of the church properly so called;* but the Virgin is similarly represented, shedding from each of her fingers rays of grace upon those who invoke her assistance. A medal, recently struck in her honour, represents her thus shedding streams of grace and favour from each hand.

It has thus been shown that the various characteristics of age, feature, costume, or the aureole, are not sufficient to distinguish Christ, since his mother, and even ordinary saints, are often honoured in an equal degree; the nimbus is a more certain characteristic. Jesus, except in certain instances, mentioned in the history of that archæological ornament, always has a cruciform nimbus. As the transverse bars of this attribute are sometimes marked with the words ὁ ὤν, *Rex,* A and Ω, or A, M, Ω,† it is impossible to confound the Saviour to whom they refer with any other historical or allegorical persons. The three Divine Persons

* There are two buildings, the porch and the church; the statue alluded to is at the door of the church.

† In the poem of Rhaban Maur, *De Laudibus Sanctæ Crucis*, figura 1, Jesus is represented wearing a cruciform nimbus, on which the three letters A M Ω are inscribed; these three letters are the commencement, the middle, and the end of the Greek Alphabet, because Christ comprises in himself the past, the present, and the future. Rhaban conveys symbolically, what the Byzantines express literally by the three letters ὁ ὤν; but the same principle is at the root of both forms of expression. God is the Supreme Being (ὁ ὤν); he comprises, says Rhaban, the beginning, the middle, and the end of all; he

alone are entitled to a similar nimbus, and it pertains more especially to Jesus than to the others. We thus learn by degrees to distinguish Christ from others; we draw him gradually forth from the crowd around. With bare feet alone he might have been confounded with angels, apostles, and even prophets; now, and by the assistance of a nimbus thus characterised, we can pronounce the figure to be one of the three persons of the Trinity, and most probably the second.*

But when this person, thus decorated with the cruciform

was yesterday, he is to-day, he will be to-morrow. The poet Prudentius, in his ninth hymn, says:

"Alpha et Omega cognominatur ipse; fons et clausula,
Omnium quæ sunt, fuerunt, vel post futura sunt."

Upon the archevolt of an ancient church in the island of Barbe, near Lyons, is an inscription in bad Latin, but carved in beautiful characters, of the eleventh century:

"Alpha vel O, primus, finis michi convenit ergo."

Christ is supposed to be speaking; he holds a cross, with which he has overthrown a lion.

* The cruciform nimbus is indeed peculiarly applicable to Christ; the Father and the Holy Ghost seem, by adopting it, to pay homage to the Son, and to assume his livery. The following quotation, which is transcribed literally, will confirm all that has been said of the nimbus generally, and of the nimbus of Christ in particular: "Considerandum quoque est quod Jesus semper coronatus depingitur, quasi dicat; Egredimini filiæ Hierusalem, et videte regem Salomonem in diademite quo coronavit eum mater sua. Fuit enim Christus coronatus tripliciter. Primo a matre, corona misericordiæ, in die conceptionis; quæ corona duplex est propter naturalia et gratuita, ideoque et diadema vocatur, quod est duplex corona. Secundo a noverca, corona miseriæ, in die passionis. Tertio a patre, corona gloriæ in die resurrectionis. Unde: 'gloria et honore coronasti eum, Domine.' Demum coronabitur a familia corona potentiæ, in die ultimæ revelationis. Veniet enim cum senatoribus terræ, judicans orbem terræ in equitate. Sic et omnes sancti pinguntur coronati, quasi dicat filiæ Hierusalem: Venite et videte martyres cum coronis aureis quibus coronavit eos Dominus; et in libro Sapientiæ (Sap. v.): 'Justi accipient regnum decoris et diadema speciei de manu Domini.' Corona autem hujusmodi depingitur in forma scuti rotundi, quia sancti Dei protectione divina fruuntur. Unde cantant gratulabundi; 'Domine ut scuto bonæ voluntatis coronasti nos.' Verumtamen Christi corona per crucis figuram a sanctorum coronis distinguitur, quia per crucis vexillum sibi carnis glorificationem et nobis meruit a captivitate liberationem et vita fruitionem."—G. Durandus, *Rat. Div. Off.*, lib. i., cap. 3. It is plain that Durandus confounds the crown with the nimbus, or rather, he gives the same name to both. Besides, he declares that the cruciform "crown" distinguishes Christ from all the Saints.

nimbus, bears the great cross of the Passion, or the small Resurrection cross, and when from that cross there depends a standard, dipped in the blood of the Divine Victim; when the person has no robe, but a simple mantle, which leaves the arms and bosom bare, and is thrown open to show the wound in the right side; when the personage with a cruciform nimbus is clothed in the vestment of a Latin priest or a Greek archbishop, both as priest after the order of Melchizedech,* and because he is the great archbishop officiating in the Divine Liturgy;† when that person is surrounded by the evangelical attributes; when near his head we see the Latin monogram, I.C. or the Greek monogram, IC. XC.; when he is marked with the stigmata in the feet, the hands, and the side; when a crown of thorns is placed upon his head, and a book, either open or closed in his hand;‡ and when, upon the pages of the open book, either of the following texts are inscribed:—

Pax vobis: §
Ego sum via, veritas, et vita: ||

---

* "Tu es sacerdos in æternum, secundum ordinem Melchisedech." "Thou art a priest for ever after the order of Melchisedech." *Psalm*, cx., 4.

† Ὁ μέγας ἀρχιερεύς. Christ is thus depicted in the costume of an archbishop, receiving successively from the hands of a train of angels the different instruments used in the sacrifice of the mass, which the divine high priest is about to celebrate. The dome of the central cupola in the Greek churches is almost always adorned with that magnificent subject called the Holy Liturgy, "ἡ ἅγια λειτουργία."

‡ The book which Christ holds is sometimes closed, but more frequently open. These two different modes of representing the mysterious volume are thus explained by Durandus: "Divina majestas depingitur quandoque cum libro clauso in manibus, quia nemo inventus est dignus aperire illum nisi leo de tribu Juda. Et quandoque cum libro aperto, ut in illo quisque legat quod ipse est lux mundi, et via, veritas ac vita, et liber vitæ." (*Rat. div. Off.* lib. i. cap. iii.) See in the Apocalypse, v., 5, an allusion made to the Lion of the tribe of Judah.

§ This was the salutation usually addressed by Jesus to his apostles and disciples. In the triclinium of St. John Lateran, in the Mosaic in the apse, which was executed about the year 797, Christ is represented sending his apostles forth to baptise. He is standing upon a little hill or eminence whence flow the four mystical streams; he holds an open book, on which is inscribed *Pax vobis.* (Ciampini, *Vet. Mon.*, 2d pars., tab. 39, p. 128.) These words of love are also engraven upon the book which is in the hand of a figure of God, attended on the right by a cherub and on the left by a seraph, sculptured in marble in the church of St. Saturnin at Toulouse.

|| This is precisely the text quoted by Durandus, and taken from St. John the Evangelist.

Ego sum lux mundi : *
Ego sum resurrectio : †
Qui vidit me, vidit et Patrem : ‡
Ego et Pater unum sumus : §
In principio erat Verbum : ||
'Εγὼ εἰμὶ τὸ φῶς τοῦ κοσμοῦ : ¶

in such cases as the above, there is no room for doubt: the person of the Trinity thus represented must indeed be the Christ, for all the attributes, all the texts relate to him; and many of them could not possibly be considered as appropriate to any other. After the numerous portraits of Jesus Christ, given especially in the History of the Nimbus,** it seems unnecessary to repeat in this place, those representing the various characteristics which we have just enumerated.

A subject, very frequently repeated in the twelfth, thirteenth, and fourteenth centuries, leaves no room for uncertainty with regard to the person occupying the chief

* St. Lorenzo at Genoa, on the tympanum of the principal entrance.

† On a mosaic in the Church of St. Mark at Rome, the same from which the figure of Pope Gregory IV., with a square nimbus, given in the History of the Nimbus (Fig. 5), is taken. Christ is the central figure of the group; he holds an open book, on which is written, "Ego sum lux;" "Ego sum vita; Ego sum resurrectio." See Ciampini, *Vet. Mon.*, 2d pars., Fig. 37, p. 119.

‡ From a mosaic of the sixth century, in St. Michele, at Ravenna. St. Michele was built in 545.

§ The two latter inscriptions are given both together on a book held by a figure of Christ in mosaic, in the Church of St. Michele, at Ravenna; on the reverse is, "Qui vidit me, vidit et Patrem;" "Ego et Pater unum sumus" on the front. In addition to the book, Jesus holds a cross which is much taller than himself. See Ciamp., *Vet. Mon.*, pars. 1st, p. 80, tab. 24.

|| Monuments bearing this inscription are so common that it seems unnecessary to name them.

¶ Upon most of the books held by the Greek figures of Christ the Pantocrator. (See Fig. 49.) In the MS. of Panselinos all the inscriptions contained in the book held by Christ will be given: they are very numerous, and vary according to the place in which the Son of God is drawn, and the functions he is called upon to exercise. Thus, when he is "the Angel of the lofty will of God," we read either on the scroll, or on the book in his hands, "I came forth from the Father, and am come into the world: again I leave the world, and go unto the Father." (St. John, xvi., 28.) "Neither came I of myself, for he sent me." (Ibid. viii., 42.)

* * See particularly Figs. 7, 8, 15, and 17; other portraits yet remain to be given, which will complete the description of the person of Christ.

position therein. Upon stained glass and in illuminated manuscripts, executed more particularly during the three centuries just named, a person is seen sometimes standing, but more frequently sitting, around whom radiate seven little doves. This person has bare feet, and might perhaps, be taken for an apostle; but his nimbus is cruciform, and he is consequently one of the Holy Trinity. Now the doves are symbolic of the seven spirits of God, and, according to Isaiah,* the Apocalypse,† and the doctors of the Church,‡ the Son of God, Jesus the Saviour, was more especially endowed with the seven divine spirits. Thus, then, whenever we meet with a figure, whether youthful or aged, bearded or beardless, with or without the nimbus, surrounded by the seven doves, we may boldly affirm it to be intended for the Son of God. The subject may now be dismissed for the present, as it will be resumed in detail in the History of the Holy Ghost.§

One other indication may be mentioned, indirect it is true and drawn from history, but still serving almost invariably to point out the person of Christ. When, in any scene from Gospel history, a certain figure is represented, as performing the actions attributed to Christ by the Evangelists, such a person, even though divested of every peculiar characteristic hitherto pointed out, must be immediately recognised as in-

* *Isaiah* xi. 1-3. † *Rev.*, v. 6, 11, 12.

‡ Especially Rhaban Maur, "De Laudibus sanctæ Crucis." Fig. xvi., p. 312, first volume of his complete works.

§ In the Chapter on the Aureole, an engraving is given, Fig. 40, copied from a miniature in the "Psautier de Saint Louis" preserved in the Bibliothèque de l'Arsenal. Jesus, seated in the midst of an aureole-like oval of foliage, on the summit of the genealogical tree, is surrounded by seven divine doves. In the Church of St. Denis, upon the painted glass window given by the Abbé Suger to that Cathedral, the Son of God is twice represented guarded by a nimbus of the Seven Spirits. The same subject is painted on a window of the Sainte Chapelle at Paris, on the window of a village Church near Rheims, on the north Rose-window of the Cathedral of Chartres, &c. In the History of the Holy Ghost, two engravings are given, one taken from a manuscript, the other from some painted glass in Chartres Cathedral, representing the Seven Spirits mentioned by Isaiah in his prophecies. The Seven Spirits are also painted in the "Vergier de Solas," a curious manuscript in the possession of the Bibliothèque Royale; indeed so numerous are the monuments in which the Seven Spirits are shown animating and surrounding the Son of God, that it would be impossible to enumerate them.

tended for the Saviour. The present portion of this work on Christian Iconography is not, however, devoted to the Word in his human nature, but solely in his character of God. The history of the second Person of the Trinity here given, embraces his infinite and eternal existence before and after the incarnation; the question, therefore, must not be entered upon here, but will be more fully developed in the Evangelical History of Jesus. Besides, another subject, which is frequently the theme of representation, must be mentioned, as it appears to embrace the entire mortal existence of the Saviour. It is the Triumph of Christ after his Ascension. This apotheosis, so sublime in conception, and frequently admirable in treatment, crowns the acts of the Saviour's divine humanity. The gates of heaven had opened to give egress to the Word, who went forth to accomplish his mission upon earth; and three and thirty years later they again opened to admit the Son of Man, the Incarnate God, returning to take his place by the side of his Father, whither he is borne in triumph by saints and angels, the Redeemer of the first, the Sovereign of the last. Such is the subject, more or less rich in details and development, which is constantly seen either in painting or sculpture upon monuments of mediæval art.

THE TRIUMPH OF CHRIST.

When the full time appointed was accomplished, 4004 years after the creation of the world, God the Father sent his Son upon earth to live and die for men. God had promised that a Redeemer should be found to expiate the guilt of Adam, and when he judged that the fitting moment for fulfilling that promise had arrived, he summoned his Son, the Divine Word, to be both the organ and agent of his supreme will. According to prophecy, the second person of the blessed Trinity replied to this appeal in the words of David, "Then said I, Lo, I come." * The Son made himself immediately the messenger of the will of his Father; he offered himself as a sacrifice for the salvation of

* *Psalm*, xl., 7: "Tunc dixi: Ecce venio."

the world, and accepted with eagerness whatever sufferings were necessary to be endured in order to expiate the crimes of the human race.

This act of self-devotion which was first conceived in heaven, carried into effect upon earth, and finally completed where first it had originated, has been constantly delineated in works of art. What passed upon earth will be reserved for the history of the human life of our Saviour; but it is our intention at present to relate everything that preceded and followed the incarnation of the Son of God. Both in the Greek and in the Latin Church, that scene has frequently been depicted, in which the Word appears to say to the Father, "Lo, I come;" but in Greece where ancient traditions and early idealism are never lost sight of, the subject is treated with greater seriousness and beauty than with us. In the semi-cupolas surmounting the side chapels of their churches, a large beardless angel is often represented, either painted in fresco, or worked in mosaic, with his long wings unfolded to their fullest extent; the raiment of this beautiful creation is charged with gold and precious stones, and he holds in his hand a golden staff, as if prepared for a long journey. This angel, with wings outspread, preparing to descend from heaven to earth, is the Son of God. It is he who is to become the man Jesus Christ; he wears on his head a cruciform nimbus, like the persons of the blessed Trinity, and upon the arms of the cross which divides the nimbus, the following letters are written "*ὁ ὢν.*" He is represented as an angel, because he has become the messenger (*ἄγγελος*) of the Divine pleasure. Around his head, these solemn words are graven; "Ο ΑΓΓΕΛΟΣ ΤΗΣ ΜΕΓΑΛΗΣ ΒΟΥΛΗΣ." This angel of the supreme will is deeply impressive; it is, with the Pantocrator of the grand cupolas, the most remarkable figure ever conceived by Christian art in Greece. Pagan art certainly had nothing more beautiful, and the type might probably have borne comparison with the statue of Jupiter Olympus, which is now lost.*

* M. Paul Durand found it impossible, during our journey in Greece, to make a copy of one of these beautiful angels of the Supreme Will; I regret being consequently unable to offer any specimen of this type, which was invented by the Greeks, and has been executed by them only. Many of these glorious angels may be seen in Greece, particularly at Mistra,

The same theme has been treated amongst ourselves in a style less elevated but more human. The Word is no longer a celestial being, a Divine messenger, as with the Greeks, but a man, an infant, a poor human creature, naked, feeble, suffering. He descends to earth, less to publish the will of his Father, than to accomplish a painful pilgrimage; it is in fact, under the name of "a pilgrimage" that his mission is announced. He sets forth then, a poor pilgrim, taking a staff wherewith to support himself in his fatigues, and a scrip to contain the provision necessary for his journey. A manuscript of the fourteenth century, belonging to the Bibliothèque Sainte Geneviève, entitled, "Romant des trois Pélerinages," * gives an account in verse of the long and toilsome pilgrimage of Christ. The verses are interspersed with miniatures which interpret the text to the eye. Jesus, at the opening of the poem, is shown commencing his pilgrimage; he presents himself naked, under the form of a child of ten years old, to his Father, who addresses him in these words:—

En terre où iras l'aval
Auras assés poinne et traval,
Pour Adam de chartre getter
Et de ses peines délivrer.
Et plus de trente ans voyage
Feras et pelerinage
Avant que il soit la saison
De faire sa rédemption;
Car si homme très bien parfait
N'estoies quant feras le fait
De le racheter, complainte
En feroit justice enfrainte;

Meteora, Salonica, and Mount Athos. That in the convent of St. Barlaam, at Meteora, is one of the most beautiful; it fills the apse of the north aisle, and its pendant, in the south, is a figure of the Son of God, beardless, and which is entitled ὁ Ἐμμανουήλ (Emmanuel) *Isaiah*, vii., 14. In the *Guide de la Peinture,* that Byzantine manuscript from which I have quoted so freely, the following directions are given: "Without the sanctuary, in the vaulting of the transepts, represent the angel of the Supreme Will on a cloud, and supported by four angels. He holds a scroll, on which is written 'I came from God, and I return to him. I am not come of myself, but it is he that hath sent me.' Write also the following epigraph, 'Jesus Christ, the Angel of the Supreme Will.' In the second arm of the cross, let Emmanuel be represented in the vaulting on a cloud, saying from a scroll, 'The Spirit of God is upon me, because he hath anointed me to preach the Gospel to the poor.'"

* This Pilgrimage of human life was composed by Guillaume de Guilleville,

Si que pource que longuement
Tu feras pélerinement,
Bourdon et escherpe te fault
Dont au moins prendras cy en hault
Ma potence où t'appuieras
Et de quoy ton bourdon feras.*

These verses are accompanied by the drawing Fig. 75, which is to be found in folio 165 of the poem.

The little Jesus, previous to setting forth on his crusade, receives, from his Father, the scrip, or "escarcelle" (a large purse for money, in the original called "escherpe,") and the stick or staff, which is nothing more than the old man's staff or crutch of the Eternal Father. There is something touching in the idea of the Divine old man thus sending forth his youthful son, who had willingly devoted himself to death for the salvation of mankind, into a world where he would be constrained to wander long, and endure much labour and sorrow. It seems to flow from the heart, and reveals a deep sentiment of love towards man; but there is little of dignity either in the subject itself, or in the manner in which it is treated.† We here see an

monk of Chalis (no doubt Chaalis, a great Abbey in the department of the Oise, near Senlis). This work belongs to the second half of the fourteenth century, 1358; it contains 1st, *Le Pélerinage de la Vie;* 2nd, *Le Pélerinage dé l'Ame;* 3rd, *Le Pélerinage de Jésus Christ.*

* On earth, whither thou goest to descend,
Thou wilt have enough travail and suffering,
To free Adam from prison,
And deliver him from punishment.
And more than thirty years journey
Shalt thou make and pilgrimage
Before the season shall arrive,
To work out his redemption.
For if a very perfect man
Thou art not, when doing the deed
Of redeeming him, complaint
Will be made by offended justice.
And because for a long time
Thou wilt make pilgrimage,
A staff and scrip thou needest.
For which at least receive here above,
My crutch on which thou shalt lean,
And of which thou may'st make thy staff.

† The Father is here represented as a King; he is aged, adorned with the

instance of the fundamental difference between Christian art in the east and in the west. In the east, in Greece, it

Fig. 75.—THE WORD OF GOD; A CHILD, NAKED, RECEIVING FROM HIS FATHER THE STAFF AND SCRIP.
French Miniature of the XIV cent.

is colder, but more solemn; with us less severe, but more common-place. There is greater gentleness in our figures of Christ; he is not made, as in Greece, the bearer and executioner of his own sentence. The stream of fire which is to consume the condemned, does not flow from beneath the throne of the Son of God. Judaism and Islamism have not,

cruciform nimbus, and with bare feet. He is distinguished by the bare feet from all ordinary mortals, and the cruciform nimbus serves to distinguish him, as well as the Son, from all created beings whether earthly or celestial, from saints and angels. He is old, because the drawing is of the fourteenth century, a period at which he takes a distinct physiognomy; he is a king, perhaps, as has been already remarked, from being the work of a French artist.

as in Greece, frozen the ideas of the Latin Church by their harsh cruelty.

Jesus descends then upon earth, to perform his weary pilgrimage. We shall some day give a detailed account, by the aid of figured monuments, of that marvellous life of the Incarnate God; but at present we pass it over entirely, and hasten to the *dénouement*. Christ, by his powerful word and quenchless love, treads underfoot according to the prophecy of David, the lion and the dragon: he walks upon the asp and the basilisk: or, in other words, he tramples upon the most formidable and cruel passions, figured by four creatures chosen from the most terrible and gigantic of ferocious animals, and the most venomous of reptiles.—"Super aspidem et basiliscum ambulabis; et conculcabis leonem et draconem."*

The figure on the next page is taken from a beautiful Italian carving on ivory, supposed to be the work of the tenth century, from the age of the Son of God, his costume, and the form of the book which he carries in his hand.

The asp and the basilisk are here already dead, and Christ, a beautiful youth and beardless, crushes under his feet the lion and the dragon; † it is a modification of the sacred text. This subject is extremely frequent in our cathedrals, but it

* "Thou shalt tread upon the lion and adder: the young lion and the dragon shalt thou trample under feet." *Psalm*, xci. 13.

† With regard to the youth of Christ and his bare feet, Gori expresses himself thus (*Thes. vet. Dipty.* tom. iii., pp. 30, 31): "Quod vero Christus in prima juventæ suæ ætate sculptus exhibeatur, hanc formam ei tributam censent doctiores agiologi, quod hac specie cum humanitate clarius eluceat ejus divinitas, ex Davidis prophetico testimonio et oraculo. Quod profert Paulus ad Hebreos, i. 6. *Dominus dixit ad me, Filius meus es tu; ego hodie genui te.* Et paullo post, *Omnes*[1] *sicut vestimentum veterascent; tu autem idem ipse es, et anni tui non deficient.* Nudis quoque pedibus insistit, occultata divinitatis suæ majestate; sed statim aliis emblematibus quanta sit ejus virtus, fortitudo ac potentia ostenditur, dum nudis pedibus conculcat animalia quædam teterrima ac ferocissima." The figure fails, from inadvertence, to express the roaring of the lion, which is extremely well rendered on the carved ivory; the designer has omitted a characteristic which is rendered peculiarly necessary by the *circuit leo rugiens, quærens quem devoret.* Gori appears to consider the bare feet as exceptions merely, and marking in the species divine power; he is mistaken. This characteristic, as has been said, is an invariable adjunct, serving to distinguish apostles, angels, and divine persons, from all others figured in Christian art; it is a mystical symbol of the loftiest sanctity. The reasons will be given in the History of Angels.

Fig. 76.—JESUS TREADING UNDERFOOT THE SERPENT, THE BASILISK, THE LION, AND THE DRAGON.
Italian Ivory; x cent.*

is given with a host of variations. It is seldom that the four satanic beasts are represented at the same time. At

* This ivory is from the Musée du Vatican; it is engraved in Gori, *Thesaurus vet. Dipty.*, tom. iii. p. 33.

Notre Dame de Rheims, in the north porch, on the pier of the left door, is a superb statue of Christ, commonly known by the name of the "beautiful God," treading underfoot the dragon only. At Notre Dame de Chartres, in the south porch, on the pier of the central door, Christ treads under his naked feet the lion and the dragon; but the asp and the basilisk are not figured. In the western porch of Notre Dame d'Amiens, on the pier of the central door, is a figure of Christ resembling that at Chartres; but the dragon is more clearly defined.

In all the subjects above described the Saviour is crushing the powers of evil, the instruments and agents of Death; but in the following design, taken from the Missal of Worms,* he holds, enchained, the figure of Death itself. Death, under the form of a dirty man, with dishevelled hair, naked legs, and poor and scanty clothing, is chained by the hands and neck, with an iron collar (*carcan*) and handcuffs. To the iron collar is attached a chain, which Jesus holds firmly in his left hand. With the right, the beardless God threatens to thrust the end of the cross into the mouth of Death. The human beast foams, vomits forth flames, and writhes under the conquering feet, which trample on and hold him down.† Jesus is about to slay Death; he seems to address him, in those prophetic words from the Old Testament which are chanted during Holy Week in reference to the Passion of Jesus, and which purchased our redemption; "Oh Death I will be thy plagues,"‡ (Hos. xiii. 14), or rather, those words of St. Paul which are chanted on the same

* Manuscript in the Bibliothèque de l'Arsénal, *Theol. Lat.*, No. 192, in fol. This manuscript dates from the ninth or tenth century, according to the Cat. in the Bibliothèque de l'Arsénal. I should rather think it, of the eleventh.

† The figure of Jesus is as yet beardless, although the manuscript may be considered as belonging to the eleventh century; yet he is aged, and his brow seems wrinkled with years, rather than contracted by the exertion of his struggle with death. The nimbus is already cruciform, while in the preceding example it is still plain, or simply ornamented with a circle of arches alone. In Fig. 66, Jesus is also beardless, but his face is much more youthful; the Christ in the Worms Missal is rather shaven than beardless; that in the Vatican is beardless rather than shaven. The monument in the Vatican is further removed from the middle ages and approaches nearer to the primitive type than that of Worms.

‡ "De manu Mortis liberabo eos, de Morte redimam eos. Ero Mors tua, ô Mors; morsus tuus ero, inferne."

occasion, and seem to form their Gospel corollary, "O death, where is thy sting? O grave, where is thy victory!" (1 Cor. xv. 55.)*

Thus victorious, Christ re-ascends to heaven, and gives account to the Father of the mission which had been confided to him; which he had voluntarily imposed upon himself, and gloriously fulfilled. In the figure on the opposite page he is seen returning to Paradise, with the scrip and staff which he had taken at his departure. As a man, he has grown taller; he was an infant when he descended upon earth, and is now thirty or thirty-five years of age. He finds the Father seated by the side of the Holy Ghost, who is here in the form of a man, not as a dove. The Father is in the character of King; that is, crowned and holding the globe of power, the Spirit, in that of a doctor, or expounder of the Word, bearing the Book of Wisdom: both have their hands raised, conferring a

Fig. 77.—JESUS CHRIST CHAINS AND OVERPOWERS DEATH.
German Miniature of the XI cent.

* "Ubi est, Mors, victoria tua? Ubi est, Mors, stimulus tuus?" The subject painted in the Missal of Worms appears to be taken from this passage in the works of St. John Damascenus. "Quisnam est iste qui cruci affixus est? Quis hic qui resurgit ac SENIS illius caput calcat? Nonne, cum per imaginem erudiendo, respondes: Hic qui affixus est cruci, Dei filius est, qui ad tollenda mundi peccata eo fuit supplicio affectus. Hic qui resurgit, ipse est qui secum primum parentem Adam ob prævaricatonem lapsum mortuumque ressuscitat, quique infernum tot jam seculis vinctum, a quo ille insolubilibus vinculis ac vectibus in inferioribus terræ partibus tenebatur, proculcat." (*Opp. St. John Damascenus*, vol. i. p. 620.)

benediction according to the Latin form, on the third Person of the Trinity.

Fig. 78.—CHRIST RETURNING FROM HIS PILGRIMAGE.*
A French Miniature; XIV cent.

Christ bows his head, his frame is bent, he leans upon the staff, as if wearied with a mission which has cost him so much labour and toil. From this attitude and the expression

* This miniature is in folio, 225 verso. Observe that each of the three Persons has a cruciform nimbus; that of the Father, with a double line at the edge, appears richer than that of the other two; besides which the cross-branches in the nimbus of the Son approach more nearly to the outer line of the disk than those in the nimbus of the Holy Ghost. It is scarcely to be supposed that characteristics so trifling can have been intended to mark the different relations existing between those three Persons; besides, in the original miniature, the three nimbi are precisely similar. The difference is no doubt owing to the inattention of the copyist. The book carried by the Holy Ghost, and which is an attribute of intelligence, will serve to support an opinion to be hereafter developed in the history of the third person of the Trinity. The Father, drawing in a little on his seat, seems to make room for Christ, who will thus be seated on his right; while the Holy Ghost occupies the seat on the left.

of the countenance, it would appear indeed, as if the Saviour regretted having engaged in so heavy a task. In fact, the verses accompanying and interpreting this miniature, after the manner of those attached to the departure, leave no doubt as to the intention of the artist. The Son thus addresses himself to the Father :—

"'Père,' dist Jhésus, 'retourné
Suis à toy, et ai consummé
Ce que faire me commandas
Quant jus ou monde m'envoyas,
DONT BIEN JE M'EN FEUSSE PASSÉ.
Enseignes t'en ay aporté
Si com aultres pélerins font
Qui en estrange terre vont;
De tielx denrées com a là
Je t'ay fait venir par deça,
NON OBSTANT QUE GRANS COUSTEMENS
J'AYE MIS ET GRANS DESPENS.
* * * * *
Aussi,' dist Jhésus, 'mon bourdon
Ay aporté, et est raison,
Ce me semble, que mis il soit
Avec l'escherpe cy endroit,
Afin que ne soit oublié
Comment pélerin ay esté.'"*

The Father and the Holy Ghost consent to the request of Jesus, and the latter hangs the staff and scrip on a nail in

* "'Father,' said Jesus, 'returned
Am I to thee, and have fulfilled
What you commanded me to do
When to the world below you sent me,
Which I could well have dispensed with.
Tokens I have brought you,
As other pilgrims do
Who go into strange lands;
Of such wares as they have there
I have brought you some up here,
Notwithstanding that at great cost
I have procured them, and at great expense.
* * * *
Also,' said Jesus, 'my staff
I have brought back; and it were well,
It seems to me, that it should be put
With the scrip in this place,
So that it may never be forgotten
How a pilgrim I have been.'"

the wall, just as a warrior in time of peace hangs on the wall of his house his glorious arms:

> "Ainsi fu accordé. Là sont;
> Jamais remeus n'en seront."*

Nothing can be imagined more trivial than the entire scene. Christ is no more than an ordinary traveller; he regrets having wearied himself for little or nothing, and declares in the most common-place manner that he will never again commence such a journey. It has, as he avers, cost him dear, and he would gladly have avoided it.

While treating of the subject of the departure of the second person of the Divine Trinity for the earth, we believe we have already established at the same time the grandeur of Greek art and the puerile simplicity of art in the West. But in the Latin Church itself, though certainly between two distinct nations, we shall be called on to remark a similar irregularity and inequality in merit. French art was common-place; Italian art of the same period, had on the contrary, gained a remarkable degree of elevation, and it rose almost to sublimity. While in the "Pélerinage" of the Bibliothèque de Sainte Geneviève, Christ is made to give vent to a burst of ill-placed regret, expressed in ordinary language; in a manuscript executed in Italy and now in the Bibliothèque Royale, he conveys his meaning by a gesture only, without words. The Almighty Father is seen in the centre of an oval aureole traversed in every direction by jets of light, emanating from the person of the Deity. The Divinity displays itself in an universal radiance, emanating from every point of the circumference of the Divine figure. The rude bench seen in the preceding design, is here replaced by a kind of bluish rainbow, on which the Father is seated. The scene is not laid in a chamber, as above, but in the open air, on the summit of a mountain enamelled with flowers. Jesus, as the crucified, descending almost naked from the cross, (for he has no covering except the short garment with which he was clad upon the cross) appears in his Father's presence to render an account of the mission which had been confided to him;

* "Thus it was granted, there they remain,
And will never be removed."

Fig. 79.—JESUS SHOWING HIS BLEEDING WOUNDS TO THE FATHER.*
Italian Miniature of the XIV cent.

* This drawing recals to mind, although but imperfectly, the language of St. Anschaire, Archbishop of Hamburgh, who was carried up by the Spirit

the blood flows from his pierced feet, and his wounded side also weeps tears of blood. Jesus opens his hands, and, showing the blood flowing from the wounds that pierce them through and through, contents himself with saying, "See what I have done!" Thereupon God the Father forgives the sins of the world, and with the right hand bestows his blessing upon the Saviour. The drawing is given above.

The expression of the countenances is exalted, and worthy the sublimity of such a scene.*

Christ, after his return into heaven, still continues his intercession for man; he is at once both priest and victim, and Greek artists love to depict him in the costume of an archbishop, or a patriarch, treated with marked and honourable distinction by the other two persons of the Trinity, and receiving the adoration of a host of saints and angels. The Father Almighty, depicted as a Byzantine Emperor, holding in one hand the globe, and in the other the sceptre, appears amidst the clouds in the upper part of the frame; below him, in a luminous circle, shines the Holy Ghost under the form of a dove. The Archangels Michael and Gabriel, the Virgin, St. John the Baptist, and the famous Greek saints, St. George and St. Demetrius, bend reverentially before Christ, and are introduced to represent the various orders of saints and angels. Christ, like the

into heaven, and saw God, resplendent with light, sitting in the midst of the four-and-twenty elders of the Apocalypse: "Ab ipso (Deo) claritas immensa procedebat, ex quâ omnis longitudo et latitudo sanctorum illustrabatur . . . . Sed neque ita claritas talis erat quæ oculos contemplantium impediret, sed quæ oculos gratissime, satiaret. Et cum seniores sedentes dixerim, in Ipso quadammodo sedebant; nam nil corporeum erat tibi, sed erant cuncta incorporea, licet speciem corporum habentia, et ideo ineffabilia. Circa sedentes vero splendor, ab Ipso procedens, similis arcui nubium tenebatur." On the eastern rose-window of the Cathedral of Laon, the four-and-twenty elders are seated on a crescent or rainbow, of a luminous or yellowish tint. Vide *Act. SS. Ord. S. Bened.*, vol. vi., *Life of St. Anschaire,* who died in 864. This biography was written by St. Rembert, disciple and successor of St. Anschaire.

* Bibliothèque Royale, *Speculum humanæ Salvationis,* suppl. lat. 1041. A similar manuscript may be seen in the Bibliothèque de l'Arsénal (*Théol. Lat.*, 42 B), executed in Italy, in the fourteenth century. The miniatures, although less perfect than those in the MS. in the Bibliothèque Royale, are nevertheless remarkable. The paintings are said to be by Giotto himself, or Taddeo Gaddi, his pupil. They are probably the work of neither; but the school to which they belong was one of the best in Italy.

Fig. 80.—CHRIST, AS THE GRAND ARCHBISHOP.*
Greek Painting of the XVI cent.

Father, has a cruciform nimbus, bearing the letters "ὁ ὤν." The names of St. George and St. Demetrius are each written in full on the scrolls above their heads; those of the Mother of God, and of St. John the Precursor, are traced in

* The design is copied from one of the fresco paintings so numerous in Greece.

an abridged form within the field of the nimbus; those of the two archangels are indicated only by the first letter, M for Michael, and Γ for Gabriel.

Christ crowned with the archiepiscopal crown, and robed in the different ornaments worn by the Greek Pontiffs, is called the "Great Archbishop," "ὁ μέγας ἀρχιερεὺς."

He is thus represented in the great cupolas of the Byzantine churches, receiving from the hands of angels, who pass successively before him, everything necessary for the mystical sacrifice of the mass.* This is what the Greeks distinguish more particularly by the name of the "LITURGY." The Cathedral of Rheims—Greek in this point as well as in several others—presents an example of this Liturgy, in the angels occupying the niches of the contre-forts. These angels, each of whom is distinguished by a special attribute, defile, so to speak, before a figure of Christ affixed against the apse on the exterior, and censed by other angels. The Christ at Rheims does not wear the pontifical costume as amongst the Greeks, but the office he fills is almost the same.†

Christ, the conqueror of demons, the Saviour of mankind, and the Eternal Intercessor with God for men, is represented as approaching to seat himself on the right hand of the Father, who puts all earth under his feet, and assigns to him the place of honour. Then joy breaks forth in Paradise

* The following words are inscribed on the book held by Christ in the character of Chief Pontiff: "Lord, Lord, look down from heaven; behold and visit this vine, and the vineyard which thy right hand hath planted." See the manuscript of Panselinos. A lozenge-shaped ornament, attached to a thread, will be observed resting upon the knee of Christ; it is called by the Greeks the "epigonation," and is frequently adorned with embroidered figures. The white stole, worked with crosses, is called "omophoron;" it is a portion of the consular, and more especially of the imperial, costume. The vestment so richly ornamented is called "saccos," and the long robe, answering to the alb of our own priests, is named "sticharion." The stole of our priests is called by them "epitrachilion." The cap is called "mitra," as with us mitre.

† The *Manuscrit du Duc d'Anjou*, Lavall., 127, in the Bibliothèque Royale, contains (fol. 139) a picture of Christ officiating at the mass. The moment selected is that of the consecration, and an angel, performing the duty of one of the children of the choir, supports the chasuble of the divine priest; The motive is taken from the following text: "Tu es sacerdos in æternum secundum ordinem Melchisedech." "Thou art a priest for ever after the order of Melchisedech."

and Jesus, attended by the acclamations of saints and angels, visits in triumph all the courts of heaven. The triumph of Christ is, of all subjects, that which has excited the most enthusiasm amongst artists; it is seen in numerous monuments, and is represented both in painting and sculpture, but always with such remarkable modifications, as impart to it the character of a new work. The eastern portion of the crypt of the Cathedral of Auxerre contains, in the vaulting of that part which corresponds with the sanctuary, a fresco painting, executed about the end of the twelfth century, and representing, in the most simple form imaginable, the triumph of Christ. The background of the picture is intersected by a cross, which, if the transverse branches were a little longer, would be a perfect Greek cross. This cross is adorned with imitations of precious stones, round, oval, and lozenge shaped, disposed in quincunxes. In the centre is a figure of Christ, on a white horse with a saddle; he holds the bridle in his left hand, and in the right, the hand of power and authority, a black staff, the rod of iron by which he governs the nations. He advances thus, having his head adorned with an azure or bluish nimbus, intersected by a cross gules; his face is turned towards the spectator. In the four compartments formed by the square in which the cross is inclosed, are four angels who form the escort of Jesus; they are all on horseback, like their master, and with wings outspread; the right hand of each, which is free, is open and raised, in token of adoring admiration. "And I saw heaven opened, and behold a white horse; and he that sat upon him was called Faithful and True, and in righteousness he doth judge and make war. His eyes were as a flame of fire, and on his head were many crowns; and he had a name written, that no man knew but he himself. And he was clothed with a vesture dipped in blood; and his name is called the Word of God. And the armies which were in heaven followed him upon white horses, clothed in fine linen white and clean." Such is the language of the Apocalypse, and this the fresco at Auxerre interprets, although with some slight alterations, which it will be well to observe.*

* This mural painting is a little injured, but still one of the most curious now in existence. It gives an approximate translation of a beautiful passage

Fig. 81.—THE TRIUMPH OF JESUS CHRIST, ON HORSEBACK.
A French Fresco of the XII cent.

In this, however, we find but the germ of those admirable triumphs, one of which is painted on glass in Notre Dame

in the Apocalypse, xix. 11-17. The absence of stirrups will be remarked; but stirrups being frequently seen in a more remote period, their absence cannot be regarded as a proof of antiquity. Christ has yellowish hair, a red beard and eyebrows; his robe is red or rose colour, the mantle grey and lined with yellow. M. Amable Crapelet, a young designer of Auxerre, has had the

de Brou, and another, described in the "Divina Commedia." That at Brou is one of the most complete in our possession; and in order to enable the reader to recognise the numerous personages composing it, as well as all other triumphs which are analogous, a succinct description of the whole will be given.

In the left aisle of the church of Notre-Dame de Brou is a chapel called that of the "Retable," or of the "*Sept-Joies;** it is lighted by a large window of stained glass, on which the assumption and coronation of the Virgin Mary are painted. The scene is enframed within a triumphal arch of antique form, and circular. The triumph of Christ is displayed on the frieze of the monument, in five compartments, four of which are occupied by persons preceding or following the Son of God. The great army, marching to their conquests, are similarly arranged upon the Arc de l'Etoile, at Paris. At the head of all, advance Adam and Eve, a youthful and naked pair, about to enter Paradise, with hands clasped in gratitude. They are followed by Abel, the first martyr in the world, naked also like his father and mother; after them comes Noah, raising high in air the ark, in which, at the time of the Deluge, the last germs of men, animals, and plants were preserved. By accepting the doctrine of belief in one true God, and guarding it for his chosen people, Abraham saved the world intellectually, as Noah had done materially. He advances, accompanied by his son Isaac, whom he had been on the point of offering up in sacrifice to God, and who bears upon his shoulders, as did Jesus in later times, thé wood on which he was to be immolated. Moses next raises on high the tables of the law, as Noah does his ark; behind him is the prophet Jonah, swallowed up and vomited forth by a sea monster, as Jesus by the grave; Jonah bears on the

kindness to make me a very correct copy of this interesting painting. The divine figure is placed at the back, in the concha of the apse, contained within an aureole of quatre-foils, and accompanied by the attributes of the Evangelists and by the two candlesticks with seven branches, given above, Fig. 36. The nimbus of Christ is here rose-colour, and the cross green.

* This chapel takes its name from a beautiful alabaster, "retable," on which are sculptured the seven happy events of the Virgin Mary's life: the Annunciation, the Visitation, the Nativity, the Adoration of the Magi, the Appearance of Jesus, the Descent of the Holy Ghost, and the Assumption.

end of a pike the slain monster, resembling in form the "Death," whom the Son of Man is crushing beneath his feet (Fig. 77). Jonah is succeeded by David, who formerly danced before the ark, and is here represented singing and striking the harp, in presence of the cross, the ark of the new covenant. Here and there in the crowd succeeding, shine conspicuous Sampson, Gideon, Eli, Solomon, Hezekiah, that is to say, the principal judges and the most glorious kings. A group of men and women follow; they are the Sibyls, and others, filling up the number of the greater and lesser prophets. The prophets are represented by Isaiah, who had exclaimed, "There shall come forth a rod out of the stem of Jesse, and a branch shall grow out of his roots" (Isa. xi. 1); and "Behold, a Virgin shall conceive and bear a Son, and shall call his name Emmanuel."—(Isa. vii. 14.) The women are represented by the Persian Sibyl bearing a lantern in her hand, and announcing the advent of the Messiah; by the Lybian Sibyl, holding a lighted taper, and presiding at the birth of Christ, the light of the world;* by the Cumæan

* The attributes borne by the Sibyls cannot be very distinctly traced, owing to the distance at wnich the frieze is from the base. The Sibyls thus placed opposite to the Prophets is a favourite subject at the period in question. At Brou they are sculptured a second time in marble, on the tomb of Philibert-le-beau. The Sibyls are sculptured at Autun, on the reredos called "*noli me tangere*," in a chapel of the Cathedral. They are sculptured on the western porch of the Church of Clamecy (Nièvre), and painted on glass in Saint-Ouen, at Rouen, in the Cathedral of Beauvais, and the Cathedral of Auch. In the Cathedral of Sens, one of the Sibyls is announcing to the Emperor Augustus the birth of the Saviour. They are sculptured on the wooden stalls of St. Bertrand de Comminges and of the Cathedral of Auch; they are represented in inlaid work on the backs of the stalls belonging formerly to the ancient Chapel of Gaillon, and now in the church of St. Denis; and in several manuscripts we find them painted on parchment, particularly in the *Heures d'Anne de France*, daughter of Louis XI., which are in the Bibliothèque Royale, No. 920. A chapel, called that of the Sibyls, stands at the entrance of St. Jacques, at Dieppe: it has twelve niches, which ought to be filled by the statues of the twelve Sibyls. Chapels of that name are to be found in the apse of St. Etienne de Châlons (Marne). The above are all in France; there are some also in Germany, in the stalls of the Cathedral of Ulm, amongst others. Michael Angelo and Raphael, in Italy, have both employed themselves on this beautiful subject. The Iconography of the Sibyls would doubtless contain much highly interesting matter, and we may expect many curious details on that subject in a work now in preparation by M. Ferdinand de Guilhermy. The Sibyls are not seen on monuments earlier than the twelfth century; in writings they may be traced back to the earliest

Sibyl, who holds a manger in her hand, from her having predicted that Christ should be born in a stable; and the Phrygian Sibyl, bearing a standard, because she had prophesied of the resurrection and victory of Christ. Three standards or flames float in the air, tinged with the blood of Christ, the divine martyr. Trumpets, as potent as those at whose sound the walls of the city of Jericho fell prostrate, ring out the victory of the crucified. With these prophets and prophetesses, the ancient world, the world anterior to Christ, approaches to its close.

Then the new world, the Christian world, appears. The personages in it are arranged chronologically; they begin with the Apostles, and first of all with St. Peter, who holds in his hand two silver keys; that which opens, and that which closes, Paradise. Then follows St. Paul, with the sword with which he was beheaded, symbolic also of the sword of his piercing word. Then St. Andrew, bearing on his shoulders the cross on which he died; St. John with the poisoned chalice, whence Death flies away, in the form of a dragon. They are followed by the other Apostles, each according to his rank; Simon carries the saw with which he was sawn asunder; Matthew, the pike with which his heart was pierced; Thomas, the square or rule, which marks him as the patron of architects. The Apostles are succeeded by the Martyrs, who shed their blood for the faith, bearing witness by the sacrifice of their lives to the earnestness of their belief, and whose countless legions are represented by a few of their glorious chiefs. St. Stephen may be recognised by the stone, which wounded his forehead; St. Laurence, by the gridiron, which he raises in the air as a standard of triumph; the great St. Christopher, who is a head and shoulders taller than the tallest of those around him, bears the little Jesus upon his shoulders: he is nearly naked, like one of the ancient Athletæ, or like a Christian of the lower orders, of whom he is supposed to be the per-

period, to Lactantius, St. Augustine, and St. Jerome; they are spoken of in the apocryphal traditions. They seem afterwards to have been forgotten, throughout the middle ages properly so called, from the seventh to the fifteenth century; yet Vincent de Beauvais mentions them in the *Speculum Universale*, and they may be seen in sculptures belonging to the close of the twelfth century, in the Cathedral of Auxerre.

sonification. This colossus, bends beneath the little Jesus as beneath an enormous weight: he is leaning on the stem of a palm-tree, which he uses as a staff. Beside the Martyrs, appear the Confessors, St. Augustine, St. Ambrose, whom we believe to recognise by their mitres; the aged St. Jerome, in the robes of an ordinary priest, not of a cardinal, as it was then the favourite custom to represent him. Next, the brilliant Emperor Charlemagne, clad in full armour of wrought or forged iron, the crown upon his head * and the sceptre on his right shoulder: his left hand rests upon the guard of his sword, and he walks by the side of the poor Saint Roch, who, clad in pilgrim garments, appears utterly worn out by his long journeyings. Behind this crowd we discover, emerging from the gates of a city, the different religious orders; the Benedictines, the original

* The following description of Charlemagne's crown is taken from a book on Heraldry, Clark's, 1827:—

"This crown, which is divided into eight parts, is made of gold, weighing 14 pounds, and is still preserved (1827) at Nuremberg. (Now, I believe, at Vienna.) The fore-part of the crown is decorated with twelve jewels, all unpolished. On the *second* part, on the right hand, is our Saviour, sitting between two cherubs, with each four wings, whereof two are upward, two downward, and under this motto:

'PER ME REGES REGNANT.'

"The *third* part, on the same side, has only gems and pearls. On the *fourth* part is King Hezekiah sitting, holding his head with his right hand, and by his side Isaiah the Prophet with a scroll, whereon is this motto:

'ECCE ADJICIAM SUPER DIES TUOS 15 ANNOS.'

Also, over the head of these figures, 'ISAIAS PROPHETA,' 'EZECHIAS REX.'

"The *fifth* part, which is behind, contains jewels semé. The *sixth* part has the effigy of a king, crowned, and a scroll in his hand, with these words,

'HONOR REGIS JUDICIUM DILIGIT,

as also, over his head, 'REX DAVID.'

"The *seventh* part is only of gems; but the *eighth* has a king, sitting, with his crown upon his head, and on a scroll which he holds in both hands, is this motto:

'TIME DOMINUM,' and 'REGEM AMATE,'

as likewise over his head, 'REX SOLOMON.'

"On the top of this crown is a cross, whose fore-part contains seventeen jewels, and in the top of the cross are these words:

'IHS NAZARENUS REX JUDÆORUM,'

as also in the arch or semicircle, these:

'CHVONRADUS, DEI GRATIA ROMANORUM IMPERATOR AUG.'

which shows that the semicircle was added after Charlemagne's time by the Emperor Conrad.—Trans.

possessors of the Priory of Brou; the Augustines, into whose hands it subsequently passed; the preaching friars or Dominicans; the Minors, or Franciscans; the Carthusians or disciples of St. Bruno. All are clad in costumes fashioned according to the rules of their order and of its appropriate colour. These monks, like the martyrs and confessors preceding them, are represented by the chiefs of each order, St. Benedict, St. Dominic, St. Francis, St. Bruno; they are supposed to be followed by a crowd of persons, who have not as yet passed the walls of the city and who throng to the gates. This city represents the earth, which is constantly giving birth to a new race of saints.

But between these two worlds, the old and the new, between the prophets and the apostles, there is a break, a change, and it is precisely to point out the course, and illustrate the manner of that transition, that the entire procession is formed; for it is in honour of Christ, by whom the Old Testament is united to the New, that this multitude are thus ranged in order. Christ is placed between the crowd which precedes and that which follows; the place he holds is the geometrical centre; but he is not immediately reached after quitting the prophets, nor on quitting Christ do we come immediately to the apostles. After the prophets comes a "suite" or cortège, forming the close of the ancient world; before the apostles, there is an advanced body which is the commencement of the new.

In fact, after the prophets, the supporters of the old law, those Jews appear who foresaw the dawn of the new; they are the Christianising Jews, as they were styled by the school of Alexandria—the Cyrenian who assisted Jesus to bear his cross; Longinus, who pierced his side; Gamaliel, who interred his crucified body; the penitent thief, who was converted upon the cross, prayed that Christ would have him in remembrance, and on the very day of his death entered with Christ into the paradise of God (St. Luke, xxiii. 43). The penitent thief, who is naked, and almost as gigantic as St. Christopher, walks leaning on his cross, as St. Christopher on the palm-tree. It was a fine idea to convert the cross of the thief into a tree of salvation, a staff of support for the pilgrim whose steps are directed towards heaven. Lastly, below that gigantic personage, are seven little naked infants, hand in hand, and forming a circle like the antique "hours." They are meant to represent the Innocents who were the first of all Christian martys to shed their blood for Christ. The first of these little martyrs holds in his hand the sword by which he was pierced in the arms of his mother.* After Christ, but preceding the apostles, advances another martyr, St. John the Baptist; he carries, raised on the point of a pike, that Divine Lamb, whom in life he pointed out to his disciples, and of whom he was the forerunner; he bears the lamb as a legionary bears the Roman eagle at the head of the column. John the Baptist opens the march of the New World, and closes that of the ancient. A Jew by birth and a Christian in heart, he had received circumcision, the bloody baptismal rite of the Jews; yet he already performed the ceremony of baptism, the peaceful circumcision of Christianity. St. John the Baptist forms therefore the link, connecting the New Testament with the Old.

Finally, in the centre of all rises the Hero of the Triumph, Jesus Christ, who is seated in an open car with four wheels. He alone is adorned with a nimbus formed of rays, departing from each point of the head, and which illumines everything around. With one glance he embraces the past which precedes, and the future, which is to succeed him. His face resembles that drawn by Raphael and the masters of the period of Renaissance, agreeing with the description given by Lentulus and Damascenus; it is serious and gentle. In the centre of the chariot is placed a starry globe traversed by the ecliptic, on which the twelve signs of the zodiac are brilliantly figured. This globe is symbolic of the world, and forms a throne for Christ: the Son of God is seated on its summit. The car is placed upon four wheels, and drawn by the four attributes or symbols of the Evangelists. The angel of St. Matthew, and the eagle of St. John, are of celestial whiteness; the lion of St. Mark, and the ox of St. Luke, are of a reddish yellow, symbolising the earth on which they dwell. The eagle and angel do, in fact, fly; while

* It is probable that these seven children may be the seven brother Maccabees; the Latin Church honours them, like the Innocents, with a special worship. But, in either case, the motive is the same. (See the *Legenda aurea* "de septem Fratribus Machabeis.")

the lion and the ox walk. Yet upon the painted window all the four have wings. A rein of silver, passing round the neck of each of the four symbols, is attached to the pole of the chariot. The Church, represented by the four most elevated religious potentates; by the Pope, the Cardinal, the Archbishop, and Bishop, or, by the four chief Fathers, St. Gregory, St. Jerome, St. Ambrose, and St. Augustine, drives the four-wheeled car, and in conjunction with the Evangelists, urges it onward. Jesus guides his triumph, not holding reins, but shedding blessings from his right hand wherever he passes.

The entire assemblage of persons represented on the window, are seen marching onwards, singing with joy. Within the spaces, formed by the mullions which trellis the upper part of the window, forty-six angels are represented with long golden hair, white transparent robes, and wings of yellow, red, violet, and green; they are all painted on a background of azure, like the sky, and celebrate with blended voices, or with musical instruments, the glory of Christ. Some have in their hands instruments of different forms, others books of music. The four animals of the Evangelists seem with sonorous voice, to swell the acclamations of the hosts of saints; the ox with his bellowing, the lion with his roar, the eagle with his cry, and the angel with his song, accompany the songs of the forty-six angels who fill the upper part of the window. At the head of the procession is an angel who leads the entire company, and, with a little cross which he holds in his hand, points out to all the Paradise they are to enter. Finally, twelve other angels, blue as the heaven into which they melt, join in adoration before the triumph of Christ. They appear as if reading the monumental inscription, which is seen above the frieze, and immediately below the ovæ of the cornice:

TRIUMPHANTEM MORTIS CHRISTUM
ÆTERNA PACE TERRIS RESTITUTA, CÆLIQUE JANUA BONIS OMNIBUS ADAPERTA,
TANTI BENEFICII MEMORES DEDUCENTES DIVI, CANUNT ANGELI.

"Christ, triumphant over death, has given to the world eternal peace, and opened the gate of heaven to all righteous persons."

"Grateful for so great a benefit, saints * conduct, and angels glorify him."

* This is at the period of the Renaissance—when the epithet *Saint*, as

Dante has given a description of a similar triumph, but marked by some interesting differences. The Florentine poet formed his cortège of figures taken from the Apocalypse and Christian symbolism. At Brou, with the exception of the attributes of the Evangelists, everything is historical. In the sixteenth century, in fact, history began to predominate over symbolism, which in the thirteenth and fourteenth centuries had reigned supreme. Dante, who was a politic poet, drew the Triumph, not of Christ, but of the Church; the triumph of Catholicism rather than of Christianity. The chariot by which he represents the Church is widowed of Christ, whose figure is so important on the window of Brou; the chariot is empty, and Dante neither discovered this deficiency, nor was concerned to rectify it; for he was less anxious to celebrate Christ and his doctrine, for their own sake, than as connected with the organisation and administration of the Church. He described the car as drawn by a griffin, thereby representing the Pope, for the griffin unites in itself the characteristics of both eagle and lion. Now the Pope is also twofold in character; as priest, he is the eagle floating in the air; as king, he is a lion, walking upon the earth. The ultramontane poet regarded the Church, that is the papacy, in the light of an absolute monarchy; not a limited monarchy as with us, and still less a republic, as amongst the schismatics of Greece, and of the east. Consequently, while at Brou, the cardinal, the archbishop, and bishop, assist the Pope in guiding the car of the Church; in the "Divina Commedia," the Pope is alone, and accepts of no assistance from the other great ecclesiastical dignitaries. At Brou the car is guided by the Evangelists, or by their attributes; ecclesiastical power is content merely to lend its aid. According to the Italian poet, the Evangelists, although present at the Triumph, do not conduct it; the Pope is himself the sole guide of the Church, and permits neither the Evangelists to direct, nor ecclesiastics to assist him. The Pope seems to require no assistance; his eye

applied to men glorified, had been dropped and replaced by that of *divine*. This qualification is rather Pagan than Christian; it embraces the idea of apotheosis rather than canonisation. In fact the idea is so carried out; the *arc de triomph* on which it is painted is antique and not modern; Pagan, both in style and form, and not Christian.

and arm alone are sufficient for him. (Dante, *Purgatorio*, Cantos xxix—xxxii.)

Thus, then, it is proved necessary to study the smallest details in analogous representations; for, as we here see, these details may serve to determine, or at least may afford a clue, to the epoch, the country, and the artists, by whom they were imagined.*

JESUS CHRIST AS A LAMB.

Christ has hitherto been spoken of solely as represented under the figure of a man, either youthful or aged; but there is one symbolic form which has been given him from the very earliest period of Christianity, which has continued in use throughout the middle ages, and has endured even to our own day; it is that of the Lamb. Very frequently the four Evangelists are symbolised, and of this we have already seen examples; St. Matthew, by an angel; St. John, by an eagle; St. Mark, by a lion; St. Luke by an ox: and their master is quite as often represented by a lamb. In fact, St. John the Baptist, on beholding Jesus, had exclaimed, "Behold the Lamb of God." (St. John, i. 28.) Christ dying on the cross, is the symbolic lamb spoken of by the prophets, the lamb who meets death, and suffers himself to be slain without murmuring.† Christ, shedding His

* No mention is here made of other triumphs, resembling those on the window at Brou, and in the poem of Dante, because a special monography would be necessary, in order to treat fully of a series of similar representations. Instead of being elevated on a car, Jesus Christ is frequently represented on board a vessel, which he steers himself, and directs towards the port of Paradise. In this case the metaphor is changed, and we have the ship of the Church instead of the car; but the motive is the same; and the arrangement of the persons, or the passengers as they may be called, resembles that at Brou. A painted window in S. Etienne-du-mont, at Paris, contains one of these aquatic triumphs of Christ; but it is far less complete than the terrestrial. The procession at Brou may be compared to that of the Panathenæa, on one of the friezes in the Parthenon. The conception of that at Brou, the arrangement of the persons, the *tout ensemble* of the composition, in short, appears to us superior to the antique procession of Phidias. In point of execution, the window at Brou is of singular beauty.

† *Vide*, in different parts of the prophetical writings, the comparison of

blood for our redemption, is the lamb slain by the children of Israel, and with the blood of which the houses to be preserved from the wrath of God, were marked with the celestial "*tau.*" * The Paschal Lamb, eaten by the Israelites on the night preceding their departure from Egypt, is the type of that other divine lamb of whom Christians are to partake at Easter, in order thereby to free themselves from the bondage in which they are held by vice.† St. John, in the Apocalypse, saw Christ, under the form of a lamb, wounded in the throat, and opening the book with the seven seals. (Rev. vi., vii.) ‡

Jesus on the cross with the lamb under the knife of the butcher. The services appointed for Passion week are filled with similar comparisons, "Sicut ovis ad occisionem ducetur, et quasi agnus coram tondente se obmutescet et non aperiet os suum." "He is brought as a lamb to the slaughter, and as a sheep before his shearers is dumb, so he openeth not his mouth." Isaiah liii., 7.—Matth. xxvi., 5.—Acts viii., 32.

* Compare the Prophecy of Ezekiel, ix., 4, 6, with Exodus, xii., 7, 13.

† (Exodus, xii., 7, 13.) The Abbé Cahier has made some learned observations on the immolation of the prophetic lamb. This subject has been very frequently delineated by Christian artists, and it is painted on glass in the windows of the Cathedrals of Bourges and Chartres in particular. See the "*Vitraux peints de St. Etienne de Bourges,* par MM. Arthur Martin et Charles Cahier, prêtres, ch. i., plate i." In the same work may be seen, plate vii., a glass painting at Bourges, on which is delineated the mission given by Christ to his Apostles, to baptise and convert all nations. Quite at the top of the last-named picture, and opposite to that personification of the Church, in which Religion gives milk from her breast to two of the faithful, and crowns them with her two hands, a lamb is painted: it is of a blueish colour, upon a blue ground, and surrounded by a cloud or nebulous aureole of a golden hue. The lamb has a nimbus, the ground gules, crossed with gold: with the right fore-foot he supports a flame-coloured cross, from which floats a banner. The end of the banner is cut into two stripes or streamers, resembling the larger feathers of a wing, the form called by us swallow-tailed; the field of the banner is marked by a black cross, quartering the A, the Ω, and X, and another little cross. This latter quartering comprises in itself the three former, which clearly designate Christ and his attribute of eternity, the commencement and end of all things. The lamb turns with a look of animation towards the standard, which he bears with a lofty pride. These two medallions, representing the lamb who has redeemed us, and Religion, by whom we are nourished, crown this remarkable window with most sublime effect.

‡ "Et vidi . . . agnum stantem tanquem occisum, habentem cornua septem, et oculos septem." (*Apoc.* v.) We understand from this text how it is possible for the head of a lamb to be armed with horns even of large size, as will be seen in the examples below, Figs. 85

Finally, Christ is the Lamb, who offered himself as a victim to wash away in his own blood the pollution of our nature, and of our carnal actions;

"CARNALES ACTVS TVLIT AGNVS HIC HOSTIA FACTVS,"

as we read in the inscription, engraved around the circle within which the Lamb of God is inscribed in the annexed plate.

Fig. 82.—THE LAMB OF GOD; SYMBOLIC OF JESUS CRUCIFIED.
Engraving on copper, of the XI cent.

The monument from which this design is copied belongs to the eleventh century; it is a plate of copper chiselled and carved with open work. The plate was probably attached to the cover of a book of the Gospels; its form is square, with the lamb in the centre, and on the sides are personifications of the four rivers of Paradise, the Tigris, the Euphrates, the Pison, and Gihon.* The following lines, engraved upon the

and 88, for the horns are allegorical, not natural. Still seven appear to be the number required, as in Fig. 88; when there are two only, the explanation is not so easily given.

* This relic forms part of the collection of M. du Sommerard. The

sides of the plates, explain the allegorical meaning which the four streams are intended to convey:

> "Fons paradisiacus per flumina quatuor exit;
> Hec (*sic*) quadriga levis te $\overline{X\rho\epsilon}$ per omnia vexit."

The Lamb of God, thus surrounded by the mystic streams, or looking down from the summit of the mount whence the four springs issue, is of a date far earlier than the eleventh century; in Fig. 23 we have given an example taken from the catacombs, and which belongs to the fifth and sixth century of our era.* In our own day, the Lamb is frequently represented upon chasubles and altar-frontals, lying as if dead, upon the book with the seven seals, or standing, and holding with one of his feet, sometimes the fore-foot and sometimes the hinder one, the banner of the resurrection. This latter mode of representation is more popular and common than the former; it enters as an armorial bearing into the blazon of several towns and noble families; the city of Rouen bears gules, with a Paschal Lamb argent, and the family of Pascal also bears a lamb argent, but on an azure field.†

St. John the Baptist is often depicted carrying the Lamb of God; it is in fact, an attribute by which he is more particularly distinguished. The following plate gives a drawing taken from a colossal statue adorning the side walls

streams are called "Gyon," "Phishon," "Tygris" and Eufrates," and are represented after the antique manner; they are figures of men, nearly naked, wearing the Phrygian bonnet, and each bearing an urn, whence the streams escape. They are sculptured almost in the same manner on the western porch of the Cathedral of Rheims.

* In monuments, erected by the primitive Church, the Lamb is frequently represented standing on a mountain, whence flow the four rivers of the terrestrial Paradise, or else, encircled by the personifications of those rivers. The lamb is Christ—the rivers are the Evangelists. "Quatuor flumina, quatuor Evangelistæ," as say the doctors of the Church. The simile has been carried still further, and Gulielmus Durandus (*Rat. Div. Off.* lib. vii.) says that Gihon, is St. Matthew; Pison, St. John; Tigris, St. Mark; Euphrates, St. Luke. Durandus, and Pope Innocent III., find curious affinities between the qualities of each Evangelist, compared with those of his corresponding stream. "Per Physon Johannes, per Gion Mattheus, per Tigrim Marcus, per Eufratem Lucas designati sunt. Sic enim clare probat Innocentius III. de Evangelistis in sermone."

† *L'art héraldique*, par Baron; in 12. Paris, 1695.

of the north porch of the Cathedral at Chartres. St. John, with bare feet, as if he were an apostle of the New Testament, a nimbus like that of a saint, and clad in raiment of camel's hair,* points with his right hand to the Lamb which he holds in the left.

Fig. 83.—ST. JOHN THE BAPTIST CARRYING THE LAMB OF GOD.

Statue of the XIII cent.; in the Cathedral of Chartres.

The Lamb is inscribed within an aureole. He has not a cruciform nimbus, because sculpture had not yet adopted that attribute; but it ought, strictly speaking, to have been given. We find it in Fig. 82 preceding, and on a large statue of St. John the Baptist, which stands against the side wall, of the western porch of the Cathedral of Rheims.

In the fourteenth century, the Lamb, which by general consent, had been treated symbolically until that time, degenerated into reality and mere nature. The St. John subjoined, belonging to the same period, holds the lamb, no longer in a disk, or divine aureole, but precisely as a shepherd would carry any little lamb that happened to be weary, or which he was caressing.

In the fifteenth century, this naturalism becomes more

* "Ipse autem Johannes habebat vestimentum de pilis camelorum et

striking. At that period the Lamb loses his nimbus, he runs upon the ground, browses on the grass of the desert where St. John is reposing, supports himself on his two hinder feet, and places his fore-feet on the Precursor, whom he attempts to caress. Lastly, in a pretty tableau on wood of about the sixteenth century, which may be seen in a side chapel of Notre Dame de Brou at Bourg, the naturalism is carried even farther. St. John is there represented sitting on a green mound in a forest, on the bank of a little river. Under his left arm he holds the Lamb, which has entirely lost its hieratic character. With the right hand St. John offers him water, which he has dipped up in a shell. In the Lamb of God, sensible of thirst, and drinking to assuage it, how little is there of Divinity! How different this Lamb of Brou, which belongs to the sixteenth

Fig. 84.—A NATURAL LAMB, CARRIED BY ST. JOHN.
French Miniature of the XIV cent.*

zonam pelliceam circa lumbos ejus. . . ." (St. Matt. iii. 4.) The Greeks in their representations of St John the Baptist, constantly add to the raiment of camel's hair and leathern girdle, hair rough and uncombed. We have seen an example of this in Fig. 24.

* The above drawing is taken from the "Roman des trois Pélerinages," a manuscript in the Bib. de Sainte Geneviève. The miniature may be found at fol. 187, verso. The cathedral at Rheims, which is at least one hundred years in advance of the other cathedrals in France, both in statuary and ornamental sculpture, presents, as early as in the thirteenth century, a figure

century, from that decorating an ivory coffer, brought as we are told, from the Convent of St. Gall, and executed probably in the ninth or tenth century. On the lid of this coffer, a Lamb, bearing a cruciform nimbus, and placed upon a disk like an "imago clypeata," is adored by four angels, who prostrate themselves before him, and by the four-and-twenty elders of the Apocalypse, who extend their hands towards the Lamb, as if to receive the treasures of his grace. While these scenes are supposed to be passing in the lower heaven, above, in the highest, a hand, the hand of God the Father, issues from the clouds and darts forth five floods of light, which fall upon the Lamb, the symbol of his Son.*

Here the theme is treated with sublime gravity and mysticism; at Brou, the reality is almost common-place. However, at Brou, behind the St. John, is placed a little reed cross with a scroll, on which is written, "Ecce agnus Dei," which serves to remind the beholder of the severity of the symbol. This inscription is ordinarily annexed to representations of the Divine Lamb; it may be seen at Arles in the old church of the cemetery of the "Dames de Saint Césaire." Four flat ribs or mouldings in the vaulting of the apse, rise from foliated capitals or imposts, and meet at a keystone or boss on which the Lamb is sculptured, bearing the cross of the resurrection; the inscription, "DEI ECCE AHGNUS,"† upon two semicircular bands, is engraved around the lamb.

of St. John, holding in his arms, and caressing, a charming little lamb. This pretty group may be seen amongst the multitude of statues, which give animation to the interior wall of the western porch, and render that portion of the admirable building a chef-d'œuvre, unequalled by any other edifice in France.

* This curious coffer belongs to M. Michéli, who has had it modelled and put in circulation as an object of commerce.

† The *h* in *ahgnus* seems to indicate an aspiration which was then heard somewhat distinctly in the pronunciation of that word, at least in Provence. We have already shown that at Chartres a sculptor of the thirteenth century wrote *terrem* instead of *terram*. At the same period we see, almost universally, upon painted glass, enamels, and sculpture, *Solomon* or *Solomonem*, instead of *Salomon, Salomonem:* in manuscripts we frequently find *Salemons.* In the old church in the island of Barbe near Lyons, in the midst of an inscription relating to Christ, we see *michi* instead of *mihi: michi* is still used in Italy. These instances, and many others, may probably be considered as indicating peculiarities of pronunciation prevalent at certain periods and in certain localities, and should be carefully noted.

On sculptures and paintings on glass in which events or figures from the Old Testament history are depicted, in connexion with scenes taken from the New, a young man is seen killing a lamb, while an old man dips a pen or a stylus into the blood of the victim, and with it marks a tau (τ) upon the lintel of the doors of those houses which the wrath of God was to pass over.*

In all sculptures, and paintings on glass or on parchments, representing subjects taken from the Apocalypse, the Lamb with seven horns and seven eyes is represented breaking the seals of the mysterious volume.

Fig. 85.—THE LAMB OF GOD, UNDER THE FORM OF A RAM.
From a French Sculpture of the close of the XIII cent., in the Cathedral of Troyes.

It is invariably a lamb that is depicted; never a sheep nor a ram, for the words of Scripture are most explicit on

* Vide the large colossal statues ornamenting the western doors of the cathedrals of Amiens, Rheims, and Senlis. A similar statue is in the north porch of Notre-Dame de Chartres. See also a painted window in the Cathedral of Chartres, north side aisle, and a window in the apse of the Cathedral of Bourges. Both windows form part of the monography of the Cathedral of Bourges, a work, the drawings in which are by M. Arthur Martin or under his direction, and the text revised by M. Charles Cahier. On the painted window at Bourges we read, below the prophet who is writing, "*Scribe thau.*"

that point: "Ecce agnus; vidi agnum; agnus Dei; agnus qui tollis peccata mundi." Yet, by a most unaccountable anomaly, in the Cathedral at Troyes is a sculpture of the Lamb of God as a ram, on the boss, or "clef" of the vaulting. The peculiar form of the ram is very clearly marked, and in the drawing here given, on the preceding page, it will be seen that he has two horns, of considerable strength, and extremely well defined.

It is unquestionably a ram. On the other hand, it is, no less clearly, designed for the Lamb of God, since it bears the Cross of the resurrection, as does the Paschal Lamb, and has a cruciform nimbus like the persons of the divine Trinity. Up to the present time no other example of a similar peculiarity has been met with; the above was discovered in Champagne, where, as at Rheims and Troyes, the art may be considered as forming an exception to ordinary rules, and might almost be termed *schismatic* with respect to Christian art in other provinces of France. The drawing here given is strictly correct, and was not executed without a rigid examination of every part, even the most minute and seemingly imperceptible.* The horns are characteristic of physical strength; they may, perhaps, be intended to signify that the ram is symbolical of the divine power of the Son. In that case, the horns would be to the Lamb, what the double triangular nimbus is to the Father Almighty,† or the cruciform and double cruciform nimbus given to the Lamb, in the chapter treating of the nimbus (Fig. 13); both are indications of absolute power.

Art was not content, in the first ages of Christianity, with representing Jesus Christ only under the form of a lamb; other personages of the Old and New Testament were also figured under the form of lambs or of sheep; as, for instance, Abraham, Moses, St. John the Baptist, and the

* M. Fichot, an artist of Troyes, made the above drawing, after having decided with me, by the aid of an excellent magnifying glass, that the horns were real, and as distinctly marked in form and dimensions as the drawing indicates. This sculpture adorns the key-stone or boss of the vaulting, placed at the height of twelve mètres from the ground, in a chapel in the south aisle of the Cathedral of Troyes. It seems a singular circumstance that the lamb should be changed into a ram in the province of Champagne, which affords pasture to numerous flocks of sheep.

† Fig. 21.

Apostles. The Apostles are constantly seen under that form upon ancient sarcophagi, in the frescos of the cata-

Fig. 86.—CHRIST AND HIS APOSTLES, UNDER THE FORM OF LAMBS OR OF SHEEP. Latin Sculpture; first centuries of the Church.

combs, and on the ancient mosaics of the Roman basilicæ. The figure given above represents Jesus in human form, standing upon the mountain of Paradise, and giving his last instructions to his apostles. The divine person is accompanied by his symbol, the lamb, bearing a cross upon its head.*

* This figure of Christ, with seven lambs, is copied from a sarcophagus of

Below the mountain, and turning towards Jesus are six lambs representing the Apostles, there was not space sufficient for the sculptor to give all the twelve. None of these lambs, not even that of God, have any nimbus, because that mark of distinction had not then been adopted by Christians. Even the person of Christ himself has no nimbus. In this, we have seven lambs only, but several Latin mosaics, at Rome and at Ravenna in particular, present twelve lambs, issuing, six from Jerusalem, and six from Bethlehem, all advancing towards Jesus, who has the form of the Divine Lamb, and is standing near the Jordan. All Christianity thus seems to be tending towards that stream.*

In the "Rationale of the Divine Offices," Gulielmus Duradus says: "The Apostles are also sometimes painted under the form of twelve sheep, because they were slain like sheep for the Lord's sake; and sometimes the twelve tribes of Israel are so represented. When however, more or less sheep than twelve are painted, then another thing is signified, according to that saying of Matthew: 'When the Son of Man shall come in his glory—then shall he sit on the throne of his glory; and before him shall be gathered all nations, and he shall separate them one from the other, as a shepherd divideth the sheep from the goats.'" Thus

white marble, brought originally from the cemetery of the Vatiçan. The entire sarcophagus is engraved in Bosio. (*Roma Sotterr.*, p. 63 of the Italian edition, printed at Rome, 1632.) On the right and left of Christ rise two palm trees; upon that on the right is a bird, a dove, perhaps the Holy Ghost. If so, this, together with the little dove sculptured on the frieze of the tomb of Junius Bassus, would be the most ancient representations of the Holy Ghost.

* Vide Ciampini, *Veter. Monim.*, passim. In the *Rom. Sotterr*, p. 411, the twelve apostles, with Jesus as shepherd in the midst of them, are sculptured standing, upon a sarcophagus found near St. Lorenzo fuori delle Mura, at Rome. Each figure is attended by a lamb, and Jesus caresses the largest amongst them, that which figures as the Lamb of God. In addition to this, at the two extremities of the sarcophagus, two shepherds still denoting Christ, are accompanied by five lambs. The figure on the right has three, one of which he caresses with tenderness; that on the left two, which he blesses according to the Latin form. There are thus in this pretty scene, eighteen lambs. Read in the Gospel all those texts in which Christ compares himself to the good shepherd, and likens men to sheep; in which before his death he compares himself to the good shepherd who is smitten, and whose sheep are scattered abroad; and where he confides his beloved sheep to St. Peter, that they may be led into good pastures. (St. John x., St. Luke xv., St. Matth. xxvi.)

the Apostles, the tribes of Israel, and the faithful, were symbolised by the lamb and the sheep.* The same prac-

* "Pinguntur etiam quandoque (Apostoli) sub forma duodecim ovium, qui tanquam bidentes occisi sunt propter Dominum; sed et duodecim tribus Israël quandoque sub forma duodecim ovium pinguntur. Quandoque tamen plures, vel pauciores oves circa sedem majestatis pinguntur, sed tunc aliud figurant, juxta illud Matt.: cum venerit Filius hominis in majestate sua, tunc sedebit super sedem majestatis suæ, statuens oves a dextris, et hædos a sinistris." (Gulielmus Durandus, *Rat. Div. Off.*, lib. i., cap. 3., edition of Venice, 1572.) Durandus seems to intimate by this text, that in his time the Apostles, the tribes of Israel, and the righteous raised to life, were all painted under the form of sheep; but there still exist a crowd of monuments, all painted or carved, and belonging to the same epoch (the thirteenth century) in which Durandus lived and wrote. Now, in these monuments, which number amongst others the cathedrals of Rheims, of Amiens, of Paris, of Chartres, and Sens, not one single sheep is introduced, whether as an apostle, as one of the tribes, or as one of the elect near the throne of God. Long anterior to that period, from the fourth until about the ninth century, but almost exclusively in Italy, the figure of lambs or sheep was given to the persons of whom Durandus speaks, and the lambs which have been described as issuing from Bethlehem and Jerusalem, and going to drink the waters of Jordan, near which the Son is standing, may very possibly have been the tribes of Israel, rather than the Apostles. In a certain letter (the twelfth in the collection) addressed to Sulpicius Severus, bishop of Tours, St. Paulinus, bishop of Nola, mentions his having caused a mosaic to be executed in the apse of the basilica of Fondi. This was a mosaic representation of the Trinity. The cross was symbolic of Christ, and was placed upon a rock or eminence.

"Et quia celsa (crux) quasi judex de rupe superstat,
Bis geminæ pecudis discors agnis genus hædi
Circumstant solium; lavos avertitur hædos
Pastor et emeritos dextra complectitur agnos."

This is literally the flock of lambs and goats mentioned by Durandus. It must then be concluded, that our bishop of Mende spoke, not of French but of Italian art; and further, that he borrowed his opinions from the writings of preceding Liturgists, instead of forming it from the figured monuments of his own time. Besides numerous other circumstances authorise this conclusion: it will not do to accept without examination, and to regard as constant and contemporary with Durandus all the customs detailed with so much satisfaction by that Liturgist. Durandus was a compiler, and his book was made up of materials drawn from ancient works, frequently unknown in our country. Thus, in the same chapter, the third in the first book of the *Rationale*, he says that the square nimbus is awarded to every prelate and virtuous man, whose portrait is painted during his lifetime. But it has already been shown, in the History of the Nimbus (p. 31.), that the custom is peculiar to Italy, and was never adopted in France. The quotation from Durandus is given below: it completes all that has been already said of the nimbus. "Cum vero aliquis prælatus aut sanctus vivens pingitur, non in formam scuti rotundi, sed quadrati, corona ipsa depingitur, ut quatuor cardinalibus virtutibus

tice has been carried further still, as has been said; the personages of the Old Testament, and even common Hebrews, have been depicted under the symbolic figure of the lamb. Entire scenes from the Bible have been represented as performed by religious actors transformed into lambs. It seems as if ancient apologues, and the fables of La Fontaine were put in action, and performed by allegorical animals who become preachers of wisdom. The tomb of Junius Bassus, for example, which is of white marble, dating from the fourth century of our era, and is still to be seen in the Musée Chrétien of the Vatican, represents various subjects taken from the Old and New Testament: the Fall of Adam and Eve; the sacrifice of Abraham; Job, mocked by his wife; Daniel, between the lions; Jesus, entering Jerusalem, or standing before Pilate, or triumphant, and giving his instructions to St. Peter and St. Paul.

The various personages in these different scenes are all standing in flat frames, or in circular or triangular-shaped niches. But neither antiquaries nor engravers have ever examined the frieze or the pendentives by which the arcades of the lower compartment are connected with each other; or at least, they do not appear to have understood the plan of the decoration. Going from left to right as if reading, we discover first, three lambs in a furnace, then, a lamb holding a rod in its right fore-foot strikes a rock, from whence a spring of water descends, while two other lambs, one of which is lying down, and one preparing to drink, watch the performance of the action; next is a lamb raising his fore-foot, as if to receive a book presented to him by a hand extended from the clouds; then a little lamb plunged in the water while a larger lamb extends its left fore-foot

vigere monstretur, prout in legenda beati Gregorii habetur." Were we not constrained by the study of existing monuments to restrict the adoption of this practice to Italy, it might be imagined, from the expressions employed by Durandus, that square nimbi had also been seen in France. It is therefore necessary to qualify the above quotations by comparing them with works of art, and to ground our archæological principles rather on the monuments before our eyes, than the books in our hands. It will be observed that the name of *crown* or *buckler* is given by Durandus to the nimbus. This attribute is in fact a religious crown, and according to the mystical ideas prevalent in the middle ages, it formed a buckler for the head, a sort of casque protecting the saints, as we read in the *Hortus Deliciarum* of the Abbess Herrade.

above its head; then a lamb, touching with a rod three baskets full of bread; lastly, a lamb touching with a rod a corpse standing upright in the tomb. These scenes, in which lambs are the actors, are copies of similar scenes performed by men, and constantly sculptured upon ancient sarcophagi. They comprise the history of the Old and New Testament; the principal episodes being selected and figured by allegorical beings; by this plan of decoration the subjects represented by the human figures placed in the arcade are repeated and continued.

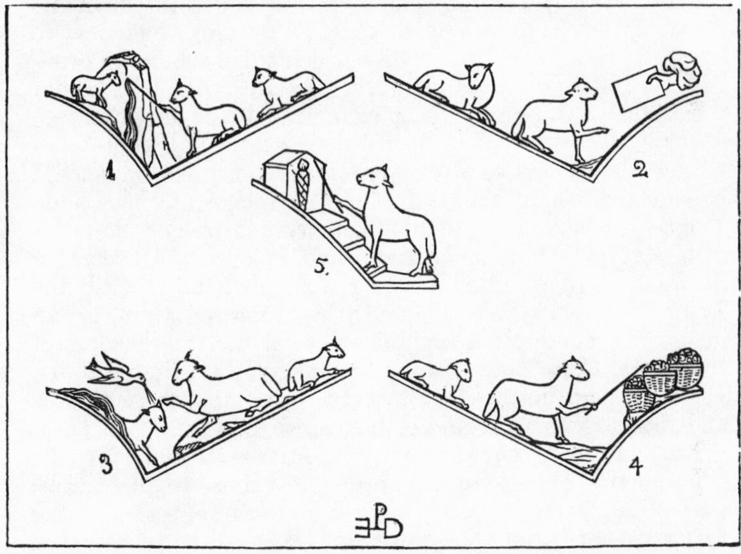

Fig. 87.—LAMBS, REPRESENTING SCENES FROM THE OLD AND NEW TESTAMENT.
Latin Sculpture of the IV cent.

The three lambs in the fire, are the three children whom Nebuchadnezzar caused to be thrown into the furnace.* In No. 1, Moses, as a lamb, strikes the rock and the water flows. In No. 2, Moses, under the same form, receives the tables of the law. No. 3, Jesus Christ repre-

* This subject, badly executed in Bosio (*Rom. Sotterr.*, p. 45), has been omitted here, the five remaining sufficing for the demonstration.

sented by a little lamb, is plunged into the water of Jordan; and while the Holy Ghost under the figure of a dove, breathes grace upon the little head of the Divine Lamb, St. John the Baptist, represented by a large lamb, pours upon the head of the same lamb the waters of baptism; Jesus, as a lamb, multiplies the loaves in No. 4, with the same rod which he employs in No. 5, for the resuscitation of Lazarus.

The favour in which the Lamb was at that time held was so great, that the human figure of Christ was almost entirely abandoned that the emblem might be substituted in its place. The Church was disquieted by this tendency to Idealism; she feared lest reality and history should be eventually swallowed up by allegory. In the year 692, under the Emperor Justinian II., a council, called Quini-Sextum, formally decreed that in future the historic figure of Jesus Christ, the human countenance of the Son of God, should be substituted in paintings for the image of the Lamb. The text, which is not without importance is as follows:—"In certain venerable pictures and images, the Precursor St. John, is represented pointing with his hand towards the Lamb of God. We adopted this representation as an image of grace; to our apprehension, it was the shadow of that lamb, Christ, our God, whom the law exhibited to us. Having then, in the first instance, accepted these figures and shadows, as signs and emblems, we now prefer to them grace and truth, that is to say, the fulness of the law. In consequence of this, and in order to expose to all regards, perfection, even in paintings, we determine that for the future, in images of Christ our God, He shall be represented in His human form, instead of in that of the Lamb, as in former time. We must contemplate all the sublimity of the Word through the veil of His humility. The painter must, as it were, lead us by the hand to the remembrance of Jesus, living in the flesh, suffering and dying for our salvation and thus obtaining the redemption of the world." *

* "In nonnullis venerabilium imaginum picturis, agnus qui digito Præcursoris monstratus, depingitur, qui ad gratiæ figuram assumptus est, verum nobis agnum, per legem Christum Deum nostrum, præmonstrans. Antiquas ergo figuras et umbras, ut veritatis signa et characteres Ecclesiæ traditas, amplexantes, gratiam et veritatem præponimus, eam ut legis implementum suscipientes. Ut ergo, quod

Notwithstanding this positive prohibition, so independent are artists, or so potent is ancient tradition, that we have never ceased to represent Jesus under the form of a lamb. It is still true, that since that period, the idea of the Lamb has not been so far abused as to travesty all the personages of the Old and New Testament as had been done by the sculptor on the tomb of Junius Bassus, but the Divine Lamb was painted and sculptured, quite as frequently as before.

At Bourg, in the sixteenth century, the Lamb of God was represented drinking water from a shell presented to him by St. John; in our own time, on the doors of the tabernacles of our churches, on the back of the chasubles worn by our priests, the Lamb is figured either sleeping, or lying slain, upon the book of the seven seals. In fact, Jesus is especially represented as a lamb, when St. John the Baptist points to him first, and when he breaks the seals of the Apocalyptic volume. In the first case, the lamb is natural; in the second, it is symbolic, ideal, and monstrous in respect to reality. Thus it has seven horns on its head, and seven eyes on the forehead and neck. The number is mystical, like that of the heads and horns of the infernal beast in the Apocalypse. It indicates, according to St. John, the seven spirits of God sent throughout all the world. The seven gifts of the Holy Spirit bestowed upon the Lamb, are called Virtue [*power*], Divinity [*riches*], Wisdom, Courage [*strength*], Honour, Glory and Benediction [*blessing*].*

perfectum est, vel colorum expressionibus omnium oculis subjiciatur, ejus qui tollit peccata mundi, Christi Dei nostri humana forma characterem etiam in imaginibus deinceps pro veteri agno erigi ac depingi jubemus, ut per ipsum Dei Verbi humiliationis celsitudinem mente comprehendentes, ad memoriam quoque ejus in carne conversationis, ejusque passionis et salutaris mortis deducamur, ejusque quæ ex eo facta est mundo redemptionis." See le Père Labbe, *Conciliorum Collectio maxima*, vol. vi., col. 1177, "Concilium Quini-Sextum." St. John Damascenus (Oratio iii., *De Imaginibus*) literally repeats the 82nd canon of this Council (Quini-Sextum) or *in Trullo*, which prohibits the representation of the Lamb. The council wished to substitute history entirely for symbolism; but the use of the symbolic figure was still uninterruptedly persisted in, particularly amongst us, even side by side with the historic.

* "Et vidi . . . AGNUM stantem tanquam occisum, habentem cornua septem et oculos septem, qui sunt septem spiritus Dei, missi in omnem terram

Thus each eye indicates a faculty, each horn is an emblem of the power which enlightens and fortifies the Divine lamb. Antiquaries ought to pay great attention to the position of the eyes and horns, no less than to their number. They are generally placed upon the head, but the throat frequently bristles with horns, as with a mane, and is pierced with seven eyes, as with ocellated* spots. As to the number, it ought to be invariable; but either from error, indifference, want of room, or inattention, sometimes six horns, or

Fig. 88.—THE LAMB OF GOD, WITH SEVEN EYES AND SEVEN HORNS.†

From a French Miniature of the XIII cent.

. . . Et audivi vocem angelorum . . . dicentium voce magna: Dignus est Agnus qui occisus est, accipere virtutem, et divinitatem, et sapientiam, et fortitudinem, et honorem, et gloriam, et benedictionem." "And I beheld, and lo in the midst of the throne and of the four beasts and in the midst of the elders stood a lamb as it had been newly slain, having seven horns and seven eyes, which are seven spirits of God sent into all the earth . . . And I heard the voice of many angels . . . saying with a loud voice: Worthy is the lamb that was slain to receive power, and riches, and wisdom, and strength, and honour, and glory, and blessing."—*Apocalypse,* v., 6, 11, 12. Rhaban Maur (*De Laudibus Sanctæ Crucis,* fig. 15) gives a drawing of a lamb armed with seven horns. On the horns is read "Septem spiritus," and on the body of the lamb, "Ecce agnus Dei, ecce qui tollit peccata mundi." This lamb has a cruciform nimbus, for he is the symbol of Deity; but he has neither the seven eyes nor the wound, as in our Fig. 88.

* *Ocellus,* Lat. little eye; the term "ocellated" is applied to marks on the skin of the Jaguar and the Ocelot, *Felis pardelis.—Translator.*

† This lamb with seven eyes and seven horns, is taken from a manuscript copy of the Apocalypse in the Bibliothèque de l'Arsénal (*Théol. Lat.*), dating from the thirteenth century. The work is of very indifferent execution, the Apocalyptic Lamb in particular; but I had no other specimen equally complete at hand. On a window in the Cathedral at Auxerre is a lamb of much more

five, or even four only are seen.* At other times, and this is very common, the Apocalyptic lamb is degraded to the condition of a natural lamb, and in consequence has merely the germ of horns not yet visible; in this case he has two eyes only. We are continually made sensible of the wilfulness and independence of the human mind; the artist interprets the sacred text according to his pleasure, and recals the mystic to the real, when peculiarity of character inclines him thereto. The following verses composed by Alcuin, may still be read in a Carlovingian manuscript, written and painted under Charlemagne :—

> " Omnia quæ præsens tellus producit alendo
> Et maris hæc facies limbo circumvenit amplo
> Agne, deum solio semper venerantur in alto.
> Sanguine qui fuso tersisti crimina secli,
> In cruce, tu Karoli detergas vulnera regis."

These lines were written under a miniature representing the Lamb, the four-and-twenty elders of the Apocalypse, the earth and sea. Under another miniature, in which the Lamb alone was painted, two other verses also composed by Alcuin, were inscribed—

> " Hunc Moyses agnum monstravi, lege futurum
> Cunctis pro populis perferri vulnera mortis."

The poet does not describe the Lamb referred to, either in the first or the second inscription: but it is probable that even the Lamb of the first subject, the Apocalyptic Lamb, was natural, and had two horns and two eyes only, like the Lamb still to be seen in the Bible of Charles le Chauve. The " Charles " named in the last verse of the first inscription, is Charlemagne.†

Thus, then, notwithstanding the decree of the Council Quini-Sextum, Christ still continued to be figured by the

careful execution. A painted window on the north side of the nave in the Church of St. Etienne du Mont, and bearing date 1614, presents a curious example of this mysterious lamb, and of the entire apocalyptic scene in which it is introduced.

* On a painted window in the Cathedral at Auxerre, I fancy I have remarked six horns only, on the head of an apocalyptic lamb, which is seen standing, with its feet upon the book with seven seals. This window, which belongs to the thirteenth century, is in the south aisle of the choir. In St. Etienne du Mont, the Apocalyptic Lamb has seven horns and seven eyes, but he has no nimbus, and is not wounded in the side.

† Baluze, *Miscellanea*, vol. iv., " Carmina Alcuini in fronte codicis."

lamb. That this fact should be true of the western or Latin Church, which had always shown a coolness towards the Greek, even at the time of the Council Quini-Sextum, does not seem surprising; and a decree emanating from Constantinople, may be safely looked upon as not accepted at Rome: yet even in Greece the canon of the council appears to have been unknown, or if known, certainly disregarded; the figure of the Lamb, substituted for that of Christ, is everywhere to be met with, both in mosaics and fresco paintings. I have read inscribed below that figure in the churches of Athens, of the Meteora, and Mount Athos: "ὁ ἀμνὸς τοῦ Θεοῦ."*

Besides this, in the eastern as well as in the western Church, it has always been customary to chant during the service of the mass; "O Lamb of God that takest away the sins of the world, have mercy upon us."† The Sacred Lamb has constantly been invoked in prayer, and represented in sculpture and painting, without any regard being paid to the Council Quini-Sextum. Lastly, in the thirteenth century, even at a period when history strove to gain the ascendancy over allegory, a method was discovered by means of which, the person of Christ and his symbol, were both represented at the same time. Before the thirteenth century, the symbol had the preference; after this, a prejudice arose in favour of reality. But in the time of Gulielmus Durandus, the happy medium was almost attained; the Lamb, although holding a secondary place, was not then too completely sacrificed to the person of Christ. The following quotation from Durandus will form a complement to the decision of the council. "Because John the Baptist pointed to him, saying, 'Behold the Lamb of God;' therefore some represented Christ under the form of a lamb; 'But forasmuch as the shadow hath passed away, and that Christ is very man; therefore,' saith Pope Adrian,‡ 'he ought to be represented in the form of a man.'

* In the Convent of Philothéou, on Mount Athos, is a Lamb of God of large size, with the following inscription: "ὁ ἀμνὸς τοῦ Θεοῦ."

† "Agnus Dei, qui tollis peccata mundi, miserere nobis."

‡ Adrian I., in the eighth century. It is singular that the pontiff of Rome, addressed himself to Barasius, patriarch of Constantinople, when expressing the above opinion.

The Lamb of God must not be depicted on the cross as a principal object: but there is no let, when Christ hath been represented as a man, to paint a lamb on an inferior part of the cross, or on the reverse."*

It must be confessed that the permission here given by the Bishop of Mende, to represent Christ and his symbol at the same time upon the cross, has been little used, for monuments of that kind are extremely rare, and any which may be discovered ought to be carefully noted. But if Christ and the Lamb have not been frequently represented together in the same subject, the Lamb of St. John the Baptist, or that of St. John the Evangelist, have never ceased to be represented separately.

JESUS, AS THE GOOD SHEPHERD.

Christ has then constantly been represented in the form of a lamb; but he is besides frequently drawn under that of the good shepherd, who guards the lamb. Jesus, as a lamb,

* "Sciendum autem est quod Salvatoris imago tribus modis convenientius in ecclesia depingitur, videlicet: aut residens in throno, aut pendens in crucis patibulo, aut ut residens in matris gremio. Quia vero Johannes Baptista Christum digito demonstravit dicens: 'Ecce agnus Dei,' ideo quidam dessignebant Christum sub specie agni. Quia vero tamen umbra transivit, et Christus verus est homo, dicit Adrianus papa (*De Consecratio. Distinct.* iii., cap. 6.) quod ipsum, in forma humana depingere debemus. Non enim agnus Dei in cruce principaliter depingi debet; sed, homine depicto, non obest agnum in parte inferiori vel posteriori depingi, cum ipse sit verus agnus qui tollit peccata mundi. His quidem et aliis diversis modis Salvatoris imago depingitur propter diversas significationes." (G. Durandus, *Rat. Div. Off.*, lib. i. cap. 3.) Durandus, as has been already said, takes all his examples from Italian art, or rather from Italian books. The French liturgist lived surrounded by the sculptors and painters, by whom our most celebrated cathedrals were then filled with statues and images, and yet he had never seen either images or statues. He closed his eyes to monumental art in his own country; he never studied it, except by reading, often without understanding them, the writings of foreign authors. Amongst us, we do not at the same time depict Jesus on the cross, and the Lamb at the foot of the cross; but in Italy, from the fourth to the fifth century, the cross was drawn, probably without any figure of Christ, but with the Divine Lamb at the foot. In fact, the following lines appear in the works of St. Paulinus, Bishop of Nola, in the middle of the twelfth Epistle, addressed by Paulinus to Sulpicius Severus:

"Sub cruce sanguinea niveo stat Christus in agno,
Agnus ut innocua injusto datus hostia leto."

yielded up his life without a murmur, and he also, like a shepherd filled with solicitude for his flock, came to seek lost man, and to lead him back to the bosom of his God. Jesus, as He has himself said, is the good shepherd who seeks and bears upon his shoulders the wandering sheep, the unfaithful soul, and brings it back to the fold. "I," said Jesus, by the mouth of St. John, "I am the good shepherd, and know my sheep, and am known of mine. As the Father knoweth me, even so know I the Father; and I lay down my life for the sheep. And other sheep I have which are not of this fold; them also I must bring, and they shall hear my voice, and there shall be one fold and one shepherd." (St. John, x. 14, 15, 16.) As we proceed, we shall find that Christ has been represented as the fish, and at the same time as the fisherman who takes the fish: in the former case he is both the lamb and the shepherd. On the door of the Church of St. Pudentiana, at Rome, is a Lamb of God in a medallion, with the following inscription,—"Dead and living, I am but one; I am at once the shepherd and the lamb."* The figured monuments in the catacombs, the sarcophagi, and more especially, paintings in fresco, constantly present the figure of a shepherd, youthful, beardless, clad in a short tunic striped with two longitudinal bands; he is standing, and bears upon his shoulders the sheep that had been lost, and that he loved. At his feet are the faithful sheep, browsing, or lying down. In the following design, taken from a fresco in the catacombs, the shepherd has in his right hand a pan-pipe, whilst with the left he holds the sheep securely on his shoulders.

These various representations have reference to those words of Jesus Christ—"What man of you, having an hundred sheep, if he lose one of them, doth not leave the ninety and nine in the wilderness, and go after that which is lost, until he find it? And when he hath found it he layeth it on his shoulders rejoicing. And when he cometh home, he calleth together his friends and neighbours, saying unto

* "Hic agnus mundum restaurat sanguine lapsum,
Mortuus et vivus idem sum, pastor et agnus."
(Ciampini, *Vet. Monim*, part 1, cap. iii. p. 23.)

St. Paulinus (*Epist.* iii., ad Florent.) says again: "Idem agnus et pastor reget nos in sæcula, qui nos de lupis agnos fecit; earumque nunc ovium pastor est ad custodiam, pro quibus fuit agnus in victimam."

them, Rejoice with me, for I have found my sheep which was lost" (St. Luke, xv. 4—7). St. Thomas Aquinas must have

Fig. 89.—JESUS, AS THE GOOD SHEPHERD.*
From a Fresco in the Catacombs, belonging to the first ages of the Church.

caught inspiration from these thrilling words, when engaged in composing his office of the Holy Sacrament. The great doctor and poet exclaims, in fact, in one of his hymns, "Good Shepherd, true bread, Jesus, have mercy on us.

* This drawing is copied from an engraving in Bosio. (*Rom. Sotterr.*, p. 351.) The Good Shepherd, bearing the sheep upon his shoulders and holding in his hand the Pandæan flute, is a very common subject in the earliest Christian era, at which time religion was wonderfully gentle in spirit. Bosio gives engravings of several such subjects. (See particularly, pages 339, 348, 349, 373, 383, 387.) Except the tunic, which in those examples is quite plain and simple, without the two longitudinal bands and without the mantle, the two latter figures precisely resemble the Shepherd in the above drawing. The shepherds hold the lost sheep more or less firmly on their shoulders, and seem more or less in fear, lest it should a second time escape. It is generally held by the four feet, with two hands, as in the examples given (pages 339, 383, 455, 461.) At other times, and more especially when, as in the present case, the right hand is occupied by a musical instrument, the sheep is retained by one hand only. Finally, in page 391 of *Rom. Sotterr.* the sheep is

Feed us, defend us, make us to see the goodness of the Lord, in the land of the living. Thou who knowest all and canst do all, thou who feedest us here as mortals, make us there above, co-partakers, co-heirs, and companions with the holy denizens of heaven."*

In conclusion, it has been affirmed, at least by Pagan antiquaries, that the subject of the Good Shepherd does

seated affectionately on the shoulder of the Good Shepherd, who fears not, so weary is it, and so rejoiced at returning to its fold, that it will again endeavour to escape. In page 373, the fold which the sheep is about to enter is shown in the picture, and the treatment of the subject is thus rendered more complete. The number of the faithful sheep lying on the turf, or browsing at the feet of the Good Shepherd, is also varied: they are generally only two in number; but at page 265 there are seven. The Good Shepherd himself seems sometimes more weary than at others, of the burden which he bears upon his shoulders, or with the journey he has made in order to recover his lost sheep, but ordinarily he appears unconscious either of the burden or the fatigue. Nevertheless, in the example given (p. 391), he leans upon a staff like a pilgrim at the end of his journey. This theme reminds us of those beautiful words of the *Dies Iræ*—" QUÆRENS ME SEDISTI LASSUS." Thus, in pages 269 and 273, we see the Good Shepherd sitting, actually overpowered with fatigue. At Ravenna, in the Church of Galla Placidia, is a mosaic, executed in the year 440; it represents Jesus, adorned with a plain nimbus, and sitting on a hillock, in the midst of a rich landscape. The Saviour holds in his left hand the Resurrection cross, and caresses a sheep with the right; five other sheep view with pleasure this display of affection towards one of their own race. (Ciampini, *Vet. Mon.*, part 1, tab. 57, p. 227.) These divine shepherds are sometimes without the musical instrument, like that at Ravenna, and those examples at pages 339, 343, 473 of the *Rom. Sott.* Figures of the Good Shepherd are usually placed in the most honourable part of the sarcophagi and paintings, in the catacombs; they occupy the centre of the tomb, or of the vaulting, and are placed in the middle of the archivaults and tympanum. In consequence of the multitude of similar representations existing, the method of treatment is equally various; all these varieties should be noticed, however apparently unimportant, for they rarely fail to establish some fact or impart some new idea.

* The beautiful words of St. Thomas are given below:

"Bone pastor, panis vere,
Jesu, nostri miserere,
Tu, nos pasce, nos tuere;
Tu, nos bona fac videre,
In terra viventium.
Tu, qui cuncta scis et vales,
Qui nos pascis hic mortales,
Tuos ibi commensales
Cohæredes et sodales,
Fac sanctorum civium."

not belong properly, and as an invention of its own, to Christianity; according to them, Christians borrowed that idea, as they had done the nimbus, from Pagan art.

Still, supposing their assertions to be well-founded, the subject was one of love, which had strayed into Paganism, and the religion of Christ, so emphatically that of love, was well entitled to claim it as its own. Consequently the heart and imagination of Christians have dwelt fondly upon this theme; it has been unceasingly repeated, under every possible aspect, and may be almost said to have been worn threadbare by Christian art. From the earliest ages Christianity completely made it her own. It was seen everywhere, even on the most ancient sacred vases, with which we are acquainted, those venerable chalices of glass, some fragments of which may still be seen in our museums.

Tertullian speaks of chalices, on which were paintings of the Good Shepherd and the lost sheep.*

JESUS CHRIST AS LION.

The lamb is not the only symbol of Christ; the lion presents another; still, the lion is infinitely more uncommon than the lamb on figured monuments. Jesus, for the reasons given in a former place, has frequently been assimilated with the lion, and sometimes, although at this moment I can recal but two instances of the fact, we meet with a lion bearing a cruciform nimbus.† Had the nimbus been merely plain, the lion would have been recognised as the symbol of the Evangelist St. Mark, as has been shown in several previous examples;‡ but the cross, stamped upon the nimbus, proves beyond doubt, that it is intended for the Lion of Judah, that

* "Patrocinabitur Pastor quem in calice depingitis.—A parabolis licebit incipias, ubi est ovis perdita, a Domino requisita et humeris ejus revecta. Procedant ipsæ picturæ calicum vestrorum, si vel in illis perlucebit interpretatio pecudis illius; utrumne christiano an ethnico peccatori de restitutione colliniat." (*De Pudicit.*, cap. ii. and x.) In great museums, many of these chalices with figures of the Good Shepherd, are to be seen.

† That in the bible of Charles le Chauve, and on the window of the Abbè Suger in St. Denis.

‡ Pages 56 and 57. With regard to the plain or cruciform nimbus attri-

Lion who, by his resurrection, conquered death, and who, in the tomb, slept with open eyes, and a heart awake. On Mount Athos, in the great church, (Catholicon) of the Convent of Philothéou, there is a fresco painting representing the slumbers of the Infant Jesus; Mary and two angels, contemplating in adoration the repose of the Divine infant, prostrate themselves in prayer before him. At the feet of the child is a young lion, sleeping also, like him of whom he is the symbol, and around whom is an inscription taken from the Sacred Scriptures.*

The lamb, the lion, and the cross, are the three sole symbols under which Christ is represented.† But before attempting to prove this proposition, it will be expedient to define the difference of meaning between the words SYMBOL and FGURT; a distinction which must be strictly observed in the application of those terms, as the two words are frequently confounded, thus giving rise to many errors and disputes.

By the words symbol and figure, we understand any sensible, or tangible design, employed to convey an idea; the circular nimbus surrounding the heads of saints, is the material sign of their holiness. Considered in this light, the symbol, and the figure, are precisely the same. They differ in the following points. A symbol is an exterior formula, the representation of some dogma of religious belief; it is, like the dogma itself, an article of faith. The lamb is the symbol of Jesus Christ; for the sacred texts relating to the Divine lamb, oblige us to receive it as the necessary and

buted to the lion, we have spoken of that animal as symbolical of Christ and of St. Mark. The reader is referred to the *Vitraux de Bourges*, pp. 78 and 82, where curious and ample details concerning the lion as the symbol of Christ will be found.

* "Ἀνάπεσων, ἠκοίμηθη ὡς λέων, καὶ τῆς δύναται ἐγειρεῖν αὐτὸν;" this text is taken from the Book of Genesis, xlix. 9, "Judah is a lion's whelp." Instead of *καὶ τῆς δύναται*, it ought to have been *τίς*. The modern Greeks, who give the same pronunciation to the êta and iôta, frequently commit faults of this description. In the western porch of Notre Dame de Paris, at the left door, a little lion is represented, sleeping on the pedestal of a statue of the Virgin Mary, who holds Jesus in her arms. It is the Greek motive executed in sculpture.

† I allude here to symbols purely iconographic. The Old Testament is filled with figures, of which Jesus Christ is the type; these figures are real symbols, but being *historical* do not properly belong to the present work.

dogmatical representative of Christ. The Lamb, indeed, is Christ himself, Christ in person, and under a visible aspect. A figure, on the other hand, is an arbitrary representation of any idea. The figure, is not imposed by sacred dogmas, or by the revealed word; but results simply from the free operation of the human mind. The figure is a variable creation of the imagination. We are required to receive a symbol, but may be persuaded to admit a figure; the first demands our faith, the second fascinates the mind. Christ is symbolised by a lion, and still more appropriately by a lamb; but he is merely figured by a pelican. The pelican, lacerating her breast that her young may be nourished with her blood, is an appropriate figure of Jesus, dying, and shedding his blood for the salvation of mankind. Still the pelican never has a nimbus, still less would it have a cruciform nimbus; neither is Christ ever represented by the pelican in the courts of heaven, nor does he take part under that form in any of the events there accomplished. The lamb on the contrary, wearing a nimbus divided by a cross, is constantly depicted in scenes both from the Apocalypse, and the Gospels; he is, indeed, Christ himself, under the form and appearance of a lamb. Lastly, the symbol, when fully developed, becomes a myth; but the figure unfolded in all its details, presents nothing more than an allegory. A myth is a belief, an assemblage of dogmas; an allegory is merely a combination of metaphors, and may be accepted or rejected at pleasure. A *myth* belongs to faith, an *allegory* rests only on opinion. The symbol is a divine creation, a revelation from God; the figure is of human invention and by man set forth. The water of baptism, the Eucharistic bread and wine, are signs, or symbols. It would not be possible in the Eucharist to substitute wine for water, nor in baptism to exchange water for wine, for those symbols are unchangeably, eternally the same. One figure may on the other hand be substituted for another, with perfect propriety; the vine, yielding its juice for the nourishment of man, may take the place of the pelican, which gives her blood to support her young. Finally, figures may be created by the imagination at pleasure; but not so symbols.*

* Vide in Baluze (*Missellanea*, vol. ii.), a work by St. Ildefonso, bishop

This being determined, we shall observe that the lamb primarily, and secondarily the lion and the cross are the sole symbols of Christ; but as figures of Christ, we have a host of objects offered to our view, drawn from the three natural kingdoms. We have the fish, the pelican, the eagle, the hen, the serpent, and many others amongst animals; the vegetable kingdom gives, together with a thousand others, the fig-tree, the vine, the olive, and the cedar. Amongst minerals, all precious stones either from their colour, their solidity, or their transparency, are employed as figures of Christ, as well as the mountains in their collected form. The principal constellations, the sun and moon in particular, have been regarded as reflecting the glory of the Son of God.*

When once launched into the domain of imagination, we enter upon an ocean of boundless expanse; it is not possible, nor would it be profitable, to enumerate the countless images under which Christ has been FIGURED. Still, since one amongst those images has attracted peculiar attention, and been an object of study with antiquaries, it will be well to notice it here, were it only with a view to removing such erroneous opinions as have been adopted on that subject. The image here alluded to is—the fish.

JESUS, FIGURED BY THE FISH.

The fish, in the opinion of antiquaries in general, is the symbol of Jesus Christ; we, however, should be inclined to consider it as nothing more than a figure. A fish is sculptured upon a number of Christian monuments, and

of Toledo, and disciple of Isidore of Seville. This work, entitled *Liber adnotationum*, gives an allegorical explanation of several plants, flowers, fruits, animals, and minerals, comparing them to Jesus Christ, and to the Church. St. Ildefonso died in 667; consequently this text is of great value from its antiquity. The symbolists of the middle ages, Durandus, Jean Beleth, Jean d'Avranches, and Hugues de Saint-Victor, drew much of their information from that work. These interpretations will be found in the second part of the *Lib. Adnot*, pp. 43 to 45 of the 2nd volume of Baluze.

* Vide, with regard to the sense in which the words symbol, figure, and myth, are to be taken, M. Guignaut's work on the *Réligions de l'Antiquité*,

more particularly upon the ancient sarcophagi; it is either single, or attended by other attributes, and is placed beneath funeral inscriptions. It is seen also upon medals bearing the effigy of our Saviour,* and upon engraved stones, cameos, and intaglios.† The fish is also to be remarked upon the amulets worn, suspended from the neck by children, and upon ancient glasses and sepulchral lamps.‡ Montfaucon mentions a mosaic in the Cathedral of Ravenna, in which the fish is introduced as symbolic of Christians. In the interior of a grotto in the necropolis of Cyrene, in Africa, is a fresco painting, in the centre of which the Good Shepherd is seen bearing a lamb upon his shoulders, which he holds firmly by all the four feet. At the feet of the Shepherd are six lambs, already armed with horns, and looking stedfastly at their master.

The Shepherd is clothed in a tunic as in the monuments of the catacombs, his head is, besides, adorned with a crown of leaves. But in addition to this, above the principal lamb, seven fishes are ranged in a circle, a valuable peculiarity which appears to blend the allegory of

tom. 1, part 1, p. 16, et suiv; tom. 1, part 2, p. 528, et suiv. M. J. J. Ampère, in a course of lectures at the College of France, in 1837, clearly established the respective value of the terms, symbol, figure, image, metaphor, emblem, myth, allegory. I have been chiefly guided by M. Ampère on the particular point here discussed.

* I am not myself acquainted with any instances of this, but merely repeat a fact generally admitted to be correct.

† M. le Marquis Fortia d'Urban possesses a white chalcedony, in the form of a truncated cone, which is pierced through, and might have been worn as an amulet. On the base of the cone is a figure of Christ, youthful, beardless, drawn in profile, with the name XPICTOY, and the image of the fish. This monument, according to M. Raoul Rochette, who has given an engraving from it (*Types du Christianisme*, frontispiece, and p. 21), must belong to the period of Alexander Severus. It appears that Christ—if the figure be indeed intended for Christ—has a radiated crown, resembling that worn by Roman emperors.

‡ M. de Belloc (*La vierge au Poisson de Raphael*, Lyon, 1833,) has caused lithographic drawings to be made of eight Christian monuments calculated to throw light upon the question under consideration. Amongst them are two cornelians, two engraved stones used as seals, one gold ring, an amethyst, and a sardonyx. Besides these, he has given us a sepulchral lamp, representing fishes, dolphins, cruciform anchors, and a man fishing with a line, with the allegorical cyphers ΙΧΘΥΣ, A. Ω., IH. XΘ., and even the word CΩTHP. All these various monuments are Italian, and belong apparently to a very remote period.

the Good Shepherd with that of the fish. The fish, and the Greek cross are also seen filling up branches of foliage painted on the wall of a Christian "hypogée" (subterranean tomb or crypt), situated near Aphrodisias in Africa.*

Baptismal fonts are more particularly ornamented with the fish. Thus at Gemona in Frioul, and Pirano in Istria, are two large baptismal urns bearing the fish.†

In a village church near Beigetad, in Denmark, around a baptistery, are three fish, intertwined in the form of a triangle.‡ France also contains a few similar examples. The fish is distinctly figured on the baptismal font at Boulogne sur Mer; it is said to be also on that of St. Jacques at Compiègne.§ In Saint Germain-des-Près, at the entrance of the western semicircular chapel, in which the baptismal font is placed, and where I imagine it has always been, a female Siren, and a male and bearded Siren, are to be seen on the capital of a column; both of these fabulous animals hold fishes in their arms, while other fishes play beneath the waters, which undulate around those fantastic personages.

Fishes are seen sometimes in other parts of the church, besides the baptisteries. In the nave of St.-Caprais-d'Agen three fishes are depicted.

A fish is sculptured upon a statue found in the cemetery of St. Jean, dep. de la Nièvre.

To conclude, in sculptured or painted monuments, representing the Lord's Supper, the last repast of Jesus Christ, the fish is figured amongst the meats; it accompanies the Paschal Lamb amongst others. On the gates of the parish church of Nantua, the second apostle standing on the left hand of Christ, carries a fish perfectly defined.|| In

* Vide the curious paintings in the work written by Pacho, *Voyaye dans la Marmorique et la Cyrénaïque,* Atlas, planches xiii., li. These paintings date probably from the earliest epoch of Christianity.

† P. Belloc, *Vierge au Poisson,* p. 78.

‡ It is in Münter (*Images Symboliques et Représentations Figurées des Anciens Chrétiens,* in-4°., en Allemand; Altona, 1835,) that this fact is mentioned. M. Cyprien Robert notices it, in his *Cours d' Hiéroglyphique Chrétienne,* and we repeat it here, but without attaching any peculiar importance to the circumstance.

§ *Bulletin du Comité Historique des Arts et des Monuments,* session of 1840-1841; notice de M. Charles Bazin, pp. 115-118.

|| *Vierge au Poisson,* p. 77.

manuscripts with miniatures,* on painted glass and enamels of the thirteenth and fourteenth centuries,† the fish is constantly exhibited, placed upon a dish in the middle of the table at the Last Supper, amongst the loaves, knives, and glasses, which are used at the repast.

Such is the evidence afforded by monuments; the written testimony of authors is as follows:—

Before the time of Constantine, the texts name the ΙΧΘΥΣ, but without giving any explanation of it; the mystery, if mystery there be, remained such during the entire period of persecution. It is simply a literary metaphor, or at least, it was the wish of the earlier Christians that it should be so considered. Christianity found it necessary to appropriate the images of Paganism, and to purify them with a Christian ideality, but they remained simple images still. "Let the dove and the fish, the vessel, flying before the breath of the wind, the harmonious lyre used by Polycrates, and the marine anchor sculptured by Seleucus, be signs unto you," says St. Clement of Alexandria.‡ Tertullian adds, "We are little fishes in Christ our great fish. For we are born in water, and can only be saved by continuing therein."§

But the metaphor aspired ere long to the elevation of the figure, and a similitude which had until that time been purely literary, became mystical. About the middle of the fourth century, Optatus, Bishop of Milesia, in Africa, declared that "the single name of fish, according to the Greek denomination, contained in the letters composing it, a host of sacred names, ΙΧΘΥΣ gives in the Latin, Jesus Christ, the Son of God, the Saviour.‖ In fact, by

* Vide several Latin MSS. in the Bibliothèque Royale.

† Painted windows of the Cathedral at Chartres, and the Sainte Chapelle, at Paris. M. du Sommerard (*Album des Arts au Moyen Age*) gives a drawing of an enamel belonging to him, and representing the repast of Jesus in the house of Simon the Pharisee. A fish is represented on a dish in the centre of the table, as forming the principal viand. This enamel is of the twelfth century.

‡ "Signa vobis sint columba, aut piscis, aut navis quæ celeri cursu fertur a vento, aut lyra musica qua usus est Polycrates, aut anchora nautica quam insculpebat Seleucus; et si quis piscator effictus fuerit, Apostoli meminerit et puerorum qui ex aqua extrahuntur." (Clem. Alex. *in Pœdag.*, lib. iii., cap. ii.)

§ "Nos, pisciculi secundum 'ΙΧΘΥΝ' nostrum Jesum Christum, in aqua nascimur, nec aliter quam in aqua manendo salvi sumus."—Tertullian, *Lib. de Baptis.*, cap. i., No. 2, *Adversus Quintil.*

‖ "Piscis nomen, secundum apellationem græcam, in uno nomine per

taking each letter of ΙΧΘΥΣ for the initial of a Greek word, we make "Ἰησοῦς Χριστὸς Θεοῦ Υἱὸς Σωτήρ." From that time forward, oriental subtlety, always prepared for a *jeu-de-mots* of that description, repeated almost to satiety, religious similitudes drawn from waves and navigation, from the seas and their inhabitants. Funeral inscriptions were preceded and accompanied by the ΙΧΘΥΣ.* The ΙΧΘΥΣ was even admitted into the internal composition of these inscriptions, of which a very remarkable and excellent example is supplied by the mysterious inscription at Autun; in that monument, ΙΧΘΥΣ is three times repeated, perhaps four times, and in different forms of application.† Jesus Christ was not only compared to the fish, which gives itself to be eaten, but also to the fisherman by whom the fish is taken, even as Christ takes souls in the net of his love.

Thus on the one hand, Julius Africanus calls Jesus Christ the great fish taken by the fish-hook of God, and whose flesh nourishes the whole world.‡ Saint Prosper of Aquitaine says, "the Saviour, the Son of God, is a fish prepared in his passion, and by whose entrails we are constantly and daily nourished and enlightened." § "ΙΧΘΥΣ is the mystical name of Christ," exclaims St. Augustine, "because he descended alive into the depths of this mortal life, as into the abyss of waters." ‖ "Christ," says the same father, "is the fish, which young Tobias took living from the stream;

singulas litteras turbam sanctorum nominum continet 'ΙΧΘΥΣ,' quod est latine, Jesus Christus Dei filius, Salvator." (*Optat. Milev.* in Bibl. Patrum, vol. iv., lib. iii.)

* Vide the Christian inscription, discovered by Boldetti in the cemetery of St. Epimaque, at Rome, and mentioned by Fabretti.

† This inscription, recently discovered at Autun, is in Greek, sculptured on white marble, and appears to date from the third century. A work is announced by M. Letronne on this monument, which has been examined by MM. Haze and Rochette, and which the Père Secchi, censor of the Pontifical Academy at Rome, has discussed in a special memoir.

‡ Julii Africani, *Narratio de iis quæ, Christo nato, in Perside acciderunt.*

§ "Dei filius salvator piscis in sua passione decoctus, cujus ex interioribus remediis quotidie illuminamur et pascimur."

‖ "Ichthus, in quo nomine mystice intelligitur Christus, eo quod in hujus mortalitatis abysso, velut in aquarum profunditate vivus, hoc est sine peccato, esse potuerit." (*Cité de Dieu.*)

whose heart (liver), consumed by passion, put the demon to flight and restored sight to the blind."* The name of piscina given to the baptismal font, of which the water, the atmosphere of fishes, purifies us from all stain and becomes the means of salvation, is derived from the fish, symbolising Him by whom we are nourished, healed, redeemed.†

On the other hand, Jesus was called "fisher of men," as he had himself given a similar appellation to St. Peter,‡ St. Gregory Nazianzen says that Jesus, the fisherman, descended into the stormy abyss of this world in order to draw men from it like fishes, and carry them up into heaven. M. Robert informs us, that on one of the sarcophagi in the Vatican,§ described by Bottari, Jesus is represented standing on the shore, a line in his hand, and a crowd of little aquatic beings nibbling at the bait. An engraving taken from a cornelian, and published by the Abbé Vallarsi, at Verona, in his notes on St. Jerome, represents a young fisherman, holding a little fish on his hook; against the fish is the word ΙΧΘΥΣ. But the most complete existing monument of this description, is furnished by a miniature in the manuscript of Herrade. God the Father is there represented holding in his hand a line, which he casts into the abyss of ocean. The line itself is formed of the busts of patriarchs, prophets, and kings, enchained one with the other, from Adam, who is nearest God, down to David who is next to the hook; the bait, in fact, is no other than Jesus the Saviour, attached to the cross.

Jesus, descends into the abyss, seeking Leviathan who

* "Est Christus piscis ille qui ad Tobiam ascendit de flumine vivus, cujus jecure per passionem assato fugatus est diabolus." *St. Augustine.*

† "Hic est piscis qui in baptismate per invocationem fontalibus undis inseritur ut quæ aqua fuerat a pisce etiam piscina vocitetur." (*Optatus Epis. Milevitanus.*)

‡ And St. Andrew also. St. Matt. iv. 18, 19; St. Mark. i. 16, 17.—*Trans.*

§ M. Cyprien Robert, has given a course of lectures on Christian hieroglyphics, printed in the "Université Catholique." Vol. vi., from p. 345 to p. 352, treats of the delicate question here discussed; we have borrowed considerably from the interesting work to which we refer, and shall continue to do so. Although compelled to lay considerable restrictions on the latitude allowed by M. Robert to symbolism, and to refuse our assent to certain conclusions at which he arrives, we are nevertheless disposed to render full justice to the real merits of that learned and ingenious work.

bites the cross by which he is to perish, while Christians cling to it as the means of their salvation.* The imagination of artists and poets, sculptors and fathers of the Church, painters and preachers, has never ceased to draw from this theme a thousand comparisons and metaphors, spun into tedious allegories. To the fathers already named, we may add St. Jerome, Origen, Bede, St. Ambrose, St. Eucharius, and others besides, all of whom have made allusion to the fish, the sea, the anchor, the vessel, and the bark, in speaking of Christ, of redemption, and of the Church. The bark of St. Peter, the ship of the Church, are images employed even in the fourth century in the Apostolical Constitutions.† Images which have continued in use in ecclesiastical language even to the present day, and which, as late as the close of the sixteenth century, supplied subjects for curious paintings on glass.‡

Finally, an ancient text, sufficiently comprehensive, appears to present a compendium of the scattered words of the primitive fathers, and to have been the source of the imagery subsequently adopted in the west, in treating of that subject; it is extracted from a Merovingian manuscript brought from St. Benoît-sur-Loire. The manuscript is a missal, and contains the following benediction:—

"Stand, my beloved brethren, on the borders of the crystal fountain. Bring hither the new men who carry on exchange and commerce from the interior to the coast. May all, rowing upon the water, strike the new sea, not with oars, but with the cross; not with the hand, but with the heart; not with the staff, but with the sacrament. The extent is small it is true, but replete with grace. The Holy Spirit has steered

* *Hortus deliciarum.*

† In the *Apostolical Constitutions*, published in 1578, by the Jesuit Turrianus, we read: "Sit ædes (he is speaking of the Church) oblonga, adorientem versus, navi similis." The orientation of churches is thus proved to have been formally prescribed in the earliest times.

‡ A painted window, brought from the cloisters and now placed in a chapel at the side of the choir, in the church of St. Etienne-du-Mont, and near to the tomb of Ste. Geneviève, presents a vessel steered by Jesus Christ, and filled with a crowd of passengers of every age and condition, amongst whom the portrait of Francis I. has, it is said, been recognised. The vessel of the Church, guided by Christ, whose hand is on the helm, flies with spreading sails, towards the eternal port.

like a good pilot. Let us pray to our God and Master that he will sanctify these waters."*

The concurrent testimony of facts, ancient authors and monuments, lead us to the conclusion, that the fish is emblematic of Christ; but the next point to define is, in what measure, it may thus be regarded as an emblem. Can we affirm with certain antiquaries, that the fish is a true symbol of Christ, or does it not rather appear, as if he were simply figured by it?

That the lion, and more especially the lamb, are symbols of Christ, is sufficiently proved by the Gospels and the Book of the Revelation, by councils, the liturgy, and the general practice of art. The archæologist sees Jesus, as completely incorporated in the lamb, as the theologian does in the bread and wine; in iconographic symbolism, the lamb is altogether annihilated that he may be replaced by the Son of God, as in a similar manner the material elements of bread and wine, are affirmed to disappear by consecration, and to become the body and blood of Christ. The lamb does not merely by his presence recal the Son of God to mind, but exhibits him, as if He had actually assumed that form. In short, the lamb is a symbol, demanding faith; but with the fish it is not so; the fish is merely a metaphor, rendered evident to the senses through the medium of a drawing. The sight of a fish may remind us of Jesus, to whom it makes allusion, but our Saviour cannot be personally visible in the fish, because He is not in him.

In regard to the Eucharist, the Church of Rome holds, that the bread and wine after consecration become the very body and blood of Christ; Protestants, on the contrary affirm, that in the consecrated elements, symbols only of the body and blood of Christ are to be recognised, and not our Saviour in person. Antiquaries too, are Protestants, in

* "Stantes, fratres carissimi, super ripam vitrigi fontes (*sic*). Novos homines adduc eis de terra littori mercatores sua commercia. Singuli navigantes pulsent mare novum, non virga sed cruce; non tactu sed sensu; non baculo, sed sacramento. Locus quidem parvus, sed gratia plenus. Bene gubernatus est Spiritus-Sanctus. Oremus ergo Dominum et Deum nostrum ut sanctificet hunc fontem." (Mabillon, *De Liturg. Gall.* Missale Gothicum, xxxvi. p. 247.) M. Michelet (*Origines du droit Français*) could not omit so poetical and invaluable a text; that profound historian has given a translation of it, accompanied by highly interesting reflections.

respect of the fish, and say that it is to be considered only as an emblematic figure, not as embodying the person of Christ.

In speaking of the lamb, however, we borrow the language of Christian orthodoxy, and declare that Jesus himself is hidden under the form of the lamb. For this reason, also, the nimbus of the lamb is stamped with a cross, and completely resembles that of Jesus, because indeed, Jesus is there present, although under the figure of a lamb. But on the other hand, the fish is never represented with a nimbus of any kind, either plain or cruciform.

It is in a word a simple image applied sometimes, and even frequently, to Christ; but in the same manner only, in which the vine is taken amongst vegetables, and the pelican among birds. The fish reminds us of Christ, but the lamb represents him; the latter is a serious symbol, taken from the Sacred Scriptures; the first, a mere figure, extracted from ecclesiastical books. We are required to recognise the lamb, but permitted to reject the fish.

The image of the fish is sometimes, and even frequently, applied to Christ; but not invariably. Indeed, we must guard against the extremes into which Italian antiquaries, and those among the French who follow their example, have been betrayed. These learned men assert, but without reason, that whenever a fish is seen represented upon a Christian monument, it must necessarily bear reference to Jesus Christ. But if it can be proved that even the lamb upon religious monuments, does not invariably figure Christ, with how much greater reason may the same be alleged concerning the fish? The lamb indeed, sometimes figures the Apostles, Christians in general, and even Jews; a palpable proof of which is afforded by the tomb of Junius Bassus, amongst others. Frequently also, the lamb has no particular personification; it enters as pure ornament into any work of art, in the same manner as the dove, or cock, a duck, or a sparrow. In such a case the lamb of course has neither a plain, nor a cruciform nimbus. Nor is the fish in general, of higher importance; it is an insignificant ornament, and does not, either immediately or remotely, apply to Christ. The fish, when seen upon coins even of Christian money, may, and in fact frequently is found, to be merely an attribute of the city in which the coin was issued; or a mark of the warden of the mint, and has no other meaning than the horse, the owl, or the fish, seen upon coins of different cities.

It may be remarked as a singular fact, that the mystical anagram, Jesus Christ, the Son of God, the Saviour, made by a Greek of Alexandria, from the word ΙΧΘΥΣ, produced no results in Greece. In that country we never meet with any fish, either in painting or in sculpture, which could have been intended to figure Christ. Fishes indeed there are in the mosaics, and especially in the frescos of Greece, but they are swimming in the open sea, and come at the time of the Last Judgment, to restore the human limbs which they have devoured. One brings an arm, another a leg; this dolphin, a man's head; that whale, a woman's bust.* Fishes are also seen gliding in the waters of Jordan at the moment of our Saviour's baptism. They are seen in the Red Sea, when the Hebrews pass through it dry-shod. But these fishes do not symbolise Christ any more than the figure of the ancient River Jordan, who is present leaning on his urn, at the baptism of Christ; or the abyss of the Red Sea, represented under the figure of a terrible Hercules, seizing and drowning Pharaoh. These fishes have no allegorical meaning; they are natural, and Jesus Christ is not signified by them. He must be sought for in the Latin monuments.

But even in those monuments, the fish, when it has any meaning whatever, usually has a completely different meaning to that attributed to it. Thus, the fish is frequently represented upon the ancient sarcophagi from the catacombs, collected in the Musée Chrétien of the Vatican; the carp,

* This singular and highly animated subject is represented in paintings where the Last Judgment is somewhat minutely detailed; it is particularly complete at Salamis, in the Church of the Panaghia phanéroméni, and the Monastery of Vatopédi on Mount Athos. The Manuscript of Herrade (*Hort. Delic.*), Byzantine in many respects, presents the same subject, with the accompanying legend: "Corpora et membra hominum a bestiis, et volucribus, et PISCIBUS olim devorata nutu Dei repræsentantur, ut ex integra humana massa resurgant, incorrupta corpora sanctorum quæ non tantum per bestias, ut depictum est, afferuntur, sed nutu Dei præsentabuntur." The Apocalypse (xx. 13) says: "Et dedit mare mortuos, qui in eo erant." "And the sea gave up the dead which were in it."

and the dolphin, alone, or accompanied by other creatures or objects, are represented on those tombs. It has been concluded that they bore, although under a different form, the same signification as the cross, or the monogram of Christ also engraved upon those tombs, and that they are symbolic, or at least emblematic of God the Saviour. The idea is most probably erroneous; for one instance in which such an intention is evident, fifty would be found to betray a different motive. In fact, it is customary amongst all nations, to represent upon the tomb of a deceased person, the attributes of the trade he had followed during his life. Even at present, in the cemetery of the Armenians, at Constantinople, all the sepulchral stones bear symbols of the profession exercised by the defunct person who lies beneath. For an Armenian tailor, scissors, thread, and needles are figured; for a mason, hammers and a trowel; a shoemaker has a last, leather, and a shoemaker's knife; a spice-merchant, scales; a banker, pieces of money. The same may be observed in other cases; amongst ourselves, in the middle ages, a pair of compasses, a rule, and a square, were graven upon the tomb of Hugh Libergier.* In the cemetery de l'Est, at Paris, a pallet marks the burying-place of a painter; a chisel and hammer that of a sculptor; animals, speaking and acting, masks, which grimace and smile, indicate, in the same inclosure, the tombs of La Fontaine and of Molière. It was just the same amongst the Romans; a fisherman had a boat upon his tomb: a shepherd, a sheep; a grave-digger, a mattock; a navigator, an anchor or a trident; a vine-dresser, a cask; an architect, the capital of a column, or the instruments of his art.

The opposite plate represents a sepulchral stone, decorated with a small house, a tomb, in which a corpse is placed erect at the top of a flight of steps, a candlestick with seven lamps or branches, and a balance. This was pro-

* This tomb is at present in the Cathedral of Rheims; it was brought from the Parish Church of St. Nicaise, built by Libergier in the same city. The architect of Rheims, like Michel le Papelart, architect of Châlons-sur-Marne, carries a model of a church, which he supports against his breast, next his heart. These two great men, one of whom erected the Church of St. Nicaise at Rheims, and the other, St. Etienne of Châlons, both belong to the thirteenth century. Libergier died in 1263, and Papelart in 1258.

bably the tomb of a spice-merchant, or a vender of oils and perfumes. The little house may probably have been the shop; there he weighed in his scales the perfumes necessary for embalming the dead, and oils to feed either funeral lamps, or those used by the living.

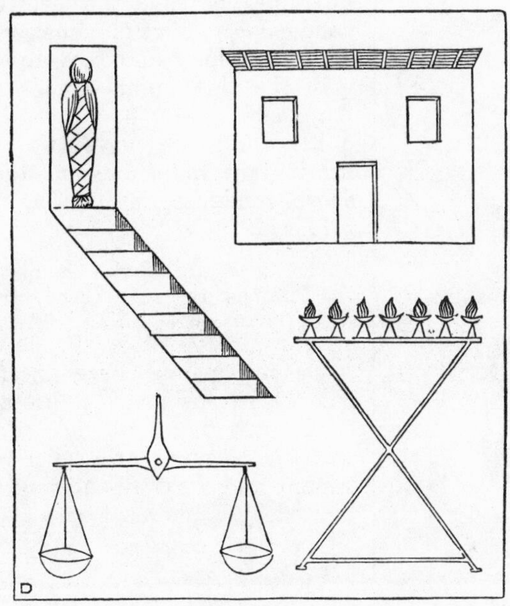

Fig. 90.—TOMB OF A VENDER OF OIL.*
Latin Sculpture; Intaglio of the earliest Christian era.

Another tomb is ornamented with two pairs of compasses, one with curved legs, another with straight legs; a square, a rule, a ball of twine, a plummet furnished with its line and lead, a hammer or pick, a chisel, and a gouge; it is evidently the tomb of an architect. With the first pair of compasses,

* An engraving of this stone is given in Bosio (*Rom. Sotter.*, p. 302); it has been supposed to belong to the fifth century, because Stilichon is named in the inscription occupying the upper part. Besides the four objects given in our plate, there is also a large fish, a kind of dolphin. From that fish was extracted the oil which was sold in the shop, weighed in the balances, and burned in the lamps kindled for the dead.

the architect tested thicknesses as with the modern calipers,* with the second he traced circles; with the square he drew right lines; he measures short distances with the rule, and employs the line in those which are more considerable; he finds the level or perpendicular with his plummet, chips the stone with his hammer, sculptures it with the chisel, and rounds it with the gouge.

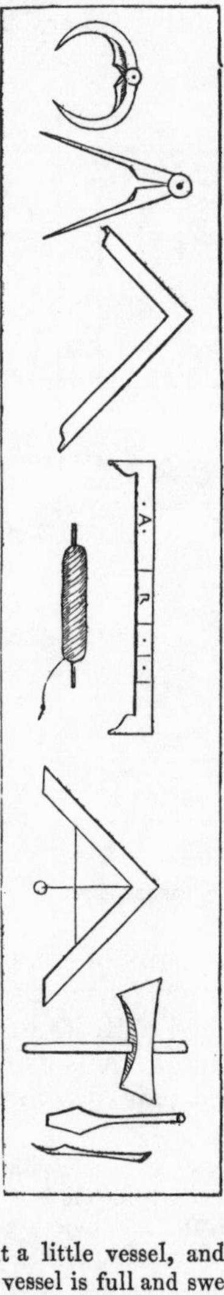

Fig. 91.—THE TOMB OF AN ARCHITECT.†
Latin Sculpture of the first ages of the Church.

Elsewhere we have a shepherd bearing on his shoulders the tired sheep, reminding us of that passage in Virgil.

. . . . . En ipse capellas
Protinus æger ago; hanc etiam vix,
Tityre, duco.‡

Or perhaps we have a carpenter who wished his axe to be preserved;§ or a gravedigger of the catacombs with his pickaxe; or a sailor with his trident and boat re-entering a port lighted by a pharos,|| or a fisherman

* *Calipers* (*Pistolet*, Fr.) Caliper—or caliper compasses—whence "calibre." A pair of compasses, with curved legs, used for measuring small diameters.—*Translator.*

† This funereal stone was found at Rome, in the vineyard of Sixtus the Fifth; an engraving of it is given in *Rom. Sotter.*, p. 505.

‡ Eclogue the First.

§ The axe, the famous *ascia*, so frequently figured on tombs by the Romans, and relating to which much may yet be said, probably has no other meaning than that here given. It seems very doubtful whether it be of such singular value as has generally been supposed.

|| Beneath the porch of St. Maria, in Trastevere, a tumular stone is preserved, bearing incised upon it a little vessel, and a lighthouse of three stories in height. The sail of the vessel is full and swelling, and the lighthouse illuminated. M. Tournal, to whom I am indebted for this information, believes the representations to be

with his fish; an architect with the Corinthian capital which he loved; a fowler with a dove; a baker with a loaf; a shoemaker with soles, or a last; one who sold by weight, with scales and a steel-yard; a labourer, a flail to thresh the corn; one who cut wood or stone with a saw, and so on with others. In Fig. 93, a few of these objects are represented; they are not mystical emblems, but simply the attributes or tools of artisans.

Fig. 92.—SARCOPHAGUS OF A MARINER, WHO AFTERWARDS BECAME A SHEPHERD.*
Sculpture of the earliest Christian period.

Formerly when an individual died he was interred together with the objects that he had loved during life,—his horse, his clothes, his valuable things, even his wife, a

symbolic. In the notes transmitted to me by that learned antiquary, descriptive of those tombs in the catacombs which he has studied, he affirms that the palm tree is the symbol of strength, durability, and virtue; that the footprints, and the snail, allude to our passage from this world to another, and to a modest and retired life; that the bushel signifies fulness of days, and that the horse is an emblem of death. We give the reasons which preclude our accepting these almost too ingenious explanations.

* This figure fills the centre of a sarcophagus of white marble, found in the vineyard of the Salviati College, at Rome. I have some difficulty in believing that any reference to the Good Shepherd is here intended, and imagine the sarcophagus to have been executed by the orders of a man, who was both a sailor and a proprietor of sheep; a rich fisherman perhaps, who afterwards became an opulent breeder of sheep. Without positively affirming this to be a fact, I believe that the objects sculptured make allusion to material life rather than to religious sentiments.

custom which prevails even now in India. At the same time these objects were figured upon his tomb; and in later periods, even after the custom of burying them with the dead had been discontinued, they still continued to be so represented upon the tombs.

It is in this fact, at least, according to my judgment, that we must seek an explanation of the greater number of objects represented on sarcophagi, or the frescos of the catacombs. We shall not, then, be induced to say, with Italian antiquaries, that the bark sailing into port by the light of a pharos, signifies the soul which has done with the storms of life, and enters heaven with spreading sails, guided by the light of faith, and warmed by the heat of charity;—that the dolphin in the water is our Saviour, the friend of man, who came down from heaven to bring redemption to man, and to withdraw him from the abyss;—that the dove, holding in its beak a branch or a crown, is Christ, coming to announce to men that God has dried up the deluge, and is ready to receive them into the verdant Gardens of Paradise. We shall not say, looking at the representation of a bunch of grapes, a loaf, an amphora, a flail, a balance, a lamp, the sole of a shoe, a horse, a ram, a peacock, a flower, a heart-shaped leaf, a rule, a level, or any of the numberless other objects engraven upon the sarcophagi, that the first symbolise Christ who gave his blood and his body for man; or that others symbolise God, who threshes the souls of the virtuous in his divine barn, who weighs them in the balance, and endows them with light; or the soul, which quitting earth, leaves only the impression of its steps, and flies, without a moment's pause to heaven; or that it is the soul which is powerful as the ram, always awake, like the eye-gemmed tail of the peacock; the soul perfumed by charity, ruling its life by, and bringing every feeling into subjection to, the law of justice. Instead of receiving such interpretations, which cannot be justified by reason, we shall rather, on seeing these various images, assert, that in one tomb rests a boatman, in another a fisherman, in the next a farmer; here sleeps a vinedresser, there a baker, a tavern-keeper, a thresher, a merchant selling goods by weight, a spice-merchant, a shoemaker, a knight, a shepherd, a poultry-keeper, a gardener, a mason, and so on. We know, in fact, that funeral inscriptions abound with errors, both of orthography and grammar,* and that most of these tombs were erected by the lower classes of society, and for themselves.

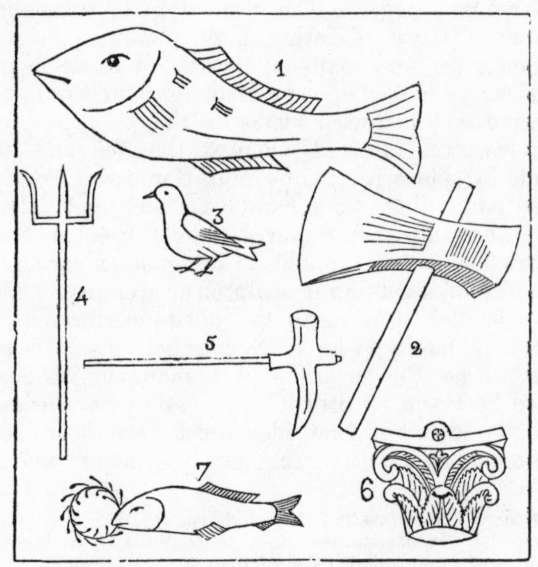

Fig. 93.—VARIOUS ATTRIBUTES, REPRESENTED ON THE TOMBS OF THE PRIMITIVE CHRISTIANS.
Sculpture and Painting in the Catacombs.

The above plate contains some of the numerous attributes sculptured in relief, or incised on the sarcophagi and funeral stones, erected in the primitive ages of Christianity. The sarcophagi found in the Aliscamps at Arles,† those which fill the crypts of the great churches in the south of France, those which may still be seen dispersed throughout Marseilles, St. Maximin and Toulouse: lastly, the sepulchral stones in the Musée at Lyons, present analogous attributes. Those in the preceding plate, Fig. 92, are collected from the monuments

* This observation was made by M. Tournal during a journey which he has lately made into Italy.

† The Cemetery at Arles is mentioned by Dante. *Inferno*, Canto ix., —*Translator*.

in Rome, and are all engraved in Bosio's great work.* The large fish indicates the fisherman by whom he was caught, or the workman by whom the oil was extracted from it. The trident announces the grave of a sailor, the mattock that of a grave-digger. The occupation of grave-digger in the catacombs, was of rather high standing; in primitive monuments we find many memorials of these men,† who, amongst us are looked upon as of an inferior class, but at that time, when they hollowed tombs for the Saints and Martyrs, were themselves interred amongst the rich and noble, or even side by side with Saints and Confessors; they were represented holding in one hand a mattock, and in the other a lamp; the lamp they required to light their subterranean labours. The hatchet ought to designate a carpenter, and the capital of a column, a sculptor or architect. The dove probably makes allusion to the duties performed by the mother of a family, who feeds her household birds; such appears to be the meaning of a monumental sculpture, engraved by Bosio.‡ Still it may possibly have arisen from a symbolic idea, but that idea must have been borrowed from profane rather than religious sentiment: and I could

* *Rom. Sotterr.* passim, particularly pp. 216, 505, 506, 508.

† Ciampini *Veter. Monim.* and Bosio, *Rom. Sotterr.* In Bosio, p. 373, two plates are given representing the paintings in the eleventh chamber of the cemetery of the Saints Marcellinus and Peter. Two grave-diggers are there painted in fresco, one holding a lamp, with which he lights the labours of his companion, who is digging with a mattock, almost exactly resembling that in our drawing, Fig. 93. (See Bosio, also, pages 305 and 335, four other grave-diggers using similar instruments: one of them is removing the earth with a shovel.) At page 529 (of Bosio), a grave-digger in a short tunic has his own name, and that of his occupation written above his head, FOSROTOFIMUS, which Bosio conceives to mean FOSSOR TROPHIMUS. Bosio expresses himself thus—"The annexed letters I believe to be intended for *Fossor Trophimus*, whose name may be read in the *Sinopse di Doroteo*, amongst those of the seventy disciples of the apostles; and he is also mentioned in an Epistle, written by St. Paul to Timothy (2nd Epistle to Timothy, iv., 20). The office of grave-diggers and of burying the dead was, as we are told by St. Girolamo, the first in the church."—St. Hieron. *De Septem Gradibus Ecclesiæ.* "Le lettere che sono appresso, credo che vogliano dire, *Fossor Trophimus.* Il cui nome si legge nella sinopse di Doroteo, trà i settenta discepoli degli apostoli; e si fà di esso mentione in un' Epistola, che St. Paolo scrive a Timoteo. Questo grado di fossori, che sepellivano li morti, era il primo nella chiesa, come afferma St. Girolamo."

‡ *Rom. Sotterr.*, p. 95.

willingly trace in it an allusion to the gentleness of the deceased, whether a man or a woman—the constancy of the husband or of the wife. At all events, supposing it to indicate the resurrection, like the dove, which returning to the ark after the deluge, announced that the waters had subsided, and that the dry land appeared,* we cannot thence infer positively, that the fish had filled an analogous position, nor above all, that it was the SYMBOL of Christ; the dove is named in the Old Testament, but the fish, most certainly is neither in the Old nor the New.

Whenever then a fish is seen upon a tomb, or on monuments of different kinds, its presence must not be too hastily interpreted in a mystical sense, but the most simple and natural explanation ought first to be adopted. For example, if the presence of one or more fish in any religious monument signified that Jesus were in the body of those animals, either symbolically or merely by a figure, it would, strictly speaking, be necessary to maintain that the same divine person is signified by the fish sculptured on the capitals in the Church of St. Germain des-Près. Now on one of these capitals we see a siren, male and bearded, holding a fish in his arms; and a female, beardless siren holding another fish; and besides these, two other fishes united by a thread of water. The first group ought then to be regarded as the Father Almighty holding his Son; the second, the Virgin Mary with the infant Christ; the third, the Father and Son linked together, and with whom, to complete the symbol, a third fish ought also to be connected.

It has indeed been imagined, that the Trinity was thus figured on a baptismal font, on which three fishes were represented. On the font of St. Jacques de Compiègne also are three monsters, which have been pronounced to be fishes; but in the latter case the fishes are nothing more than hideous apes, and there might as easily have been more of them, as three only.

With regard to the fish sometimes represented on the

* In Bosio (*Rom. Sotterr.*, p. 449 and others.) Noah receives in his hands the dove, which carries a branch in its beak (p. 411, ibid.) The dove is without the branch (*vide* Bosio, pp. 377, 381, and 531 also.) This subject is extremely common in the Catacombs. The example, p. 531, is one of the most curious on account of the singular form of the ark.

table at the Lord's Supper, placed before Jesus or the Apostles, for what reason should it be declared to be symbolic of Christ? As the table is equally loaded with viands, and with birds variously cooked, it would become necessary, reasoning from analogy, to discover in each of these dishes a symbol of the Son of God; so gross a conclusion cannot for a moment be admitted. Besides, had the fish been intended as a symbol of Christ, its head would have been decorated with a cruciform nimbus, as without that proof the assertion is gratuitous, and may with equal justice be either affirmed or denied. Now the nimbus is never on any monument found encircling the head of the fish; yet it would not be more extraordinary to place a nimbus on the head of a fish, than it is strange to see a hand, the head of a bird, a dove, or a lion, with a cruciform nimbus. The nimbus never having been given, it seems scarcely probable that symbolism, or even a figure, can have been involved in it.

The white marble ambo at Ravenna, called the throne of the Arian bishops, is divided in height, into six panels or pictures, and into ten in breadth. Each row of panels is occupied by a series of ten animals. Commencing at the top and going downwards, we find ten sheep, ten peacocks, ten doves, ten stags, ten ducks, and ten fishes. It is scarcely probable that these animals can have been thus disposed with any allegorical intention; they are arabesques, and purely ornamental. The sculptor drew the theme, not from his faith, but his imagination. An arabesque is a caprice, and not the expression of any idea connected with religion or philosophy. Assuredly, neither Raphael, nor Jean Goujon had any intention of expressing a religious dogma, when the one painted, and the other sculptured, those delicate arabesques, with which the eye of the beholder is still delighted.

Had Raphael been asked the historical meaning of the bouquets of filberts hanging from the barbels of three or four gudgeon, which may be seen in the Vatican, he would probably have disdained to reply; he would have laughed at any one, who solicited from him an explanation of those lovely naked forms, fishes in the lower part of the body, and women above, dancing upon branches of creeping plants, in the framework of his pictures. What mean those old Satyrs, those little loves, those chaplets of shells, those fantastic panoplies, birds suspended by the claw, sparrows pecking at bunches of grapes, the eagles and griffins moistening their beaks in cups, which decorate the pilasters and mullions of the screen enclosing the choir of Notre Dame de Chartres? They are placed there merely to amuse, not to instruct; to divert the eye, not to enlighten the mind. They are mere ornaments, produced by the chisel of the artist, at the suggestion of his own fancy and pleasure, not by the inspiration of faith. The same may probably be said of the arabesques sculptured in the eleventh century, on the throne of the Arian bishops.

If the sheep, instead of being placed at the summit of that monument, above the peacocks and doves, had been on a level with the stags, it might have been said that the animals were ranged in classes, two and two, according to the sphere in which they lived; peacocks and doves, which dwell in air where they support themselves by their wings, would then occupy the top of the throne; sheep and stags which graze upon the earth, would guard the middle of the monument; below them would be the ducks and fishes, which either love water, or inhabit it. The duck, of aquatic nature in the formation of its webbed feet, terrestrial from the weight of its body, aërial by the structure of its wings, would thus form a connecting link between the doves and the fishes. But, we repeat it, the place occupied by the sheep renders such an explanation impossible.*

Besides, were it even possible thus to explain the arrangement of the animals, the idea sought for in the fish and other animals, ten in number, would not even then have been attained, nor could they have reference to Christ. Here again, supposing those three classes of animals to be employed to represent all animated nature, the fish might be the sign of an idea; but other monuments on which the fish is figured, cannot bear the same interpretation. A funeral urn, in Notre-Dame de Grotta-Ferrata, has a representation of two young boys, both naked, and sitting upon rocks, from the top of which they are fishing with a line.

* I have been favoured by M. Tournal with a drawing of this singular monument at Ravenna.

Each has taken a little fish. Below, in the sea, are large fishes, swimming, and other fishes adorn the cover of the urn. There is no inscription to tell the names or condition of those in whose memory the urn was made; but it seems highly probable that some fisherman had it placed there, in memory of his sons, who probably followed the same profession as himself.* The Romans, in the sculptures of their tombs, made allusion to the condition, and even to the name of the person deceased. Some reference to the profession or trade is, as we have endeavoured to prove, of constant occurrence; one single example only of allusion to the name of the person interred shall be quoted. A child, named Porcella, had died, and on her tombstone is inscribed a little female pig, denoting the name of the young deceased.†

To resume: it is possible that the fish may have been intended, and occasionally employed, as an emblem of Christ; but to pretend that all fishes must necessarily bear that signification, is to ground a general theory upon a few rare exceptions. Lastly, the restrictions just imposed upon the mystical meaning of the fish, must I think be extended to all other figures, sculptured upon the tombs and earlier monuments of Christians.

In the opposite figure, with a short tunic, a vine-dresser may be recognised, standing near the cask which indicates his profession. He is starting for the fields with a mattock on

* This urn is at present used to contain the water given to fever patients to drink for their cure. It is engraved in Montfaucon's work, (*Ant. Expl.*, vol. xv., p. 115, Fig. 47.) A crystal urn, in the form of a fish, was found near Tongres in 1698; it bears the following inscription:—"Politicus Albiniæ karissimæ suæ." Bosio (*Rom. Sotterr.*) gives an engraving of an ancient Christian sarcophagus, on which is represented a man fishing with a line. P. Belloc (*Vierge au Poisson*) has had a lithograph made from an engraved cornelian, upon which is a fisherman holding a basket in one hand, and in the other a line from which a little fish is suspended: the word ΙΧΘΥΣ is written near the fish. It is very doubtful whether any of these bear reference to the actual presence of Christ, or can even be understood as applying figuratively to our Saviour.

† An engraving of the above-mentioned monument is given in Seroux d'Agincourt's work (*Hist. de l'Art par les Monum.*, section de Sculpture, planche 8). The following inscription is engraved upon it, and below the writing the emblematic animal is drawn:—

"PORCELLA HIC DORMIT IN P.
Q. VIXIT ANN. III., M. X. D. XIII."

his shoulder, and carrying in the left hand a wallet, containing his provision for the day. It would not perhaps, be difficult to give of this figure an allegorical interpretation,* since the butt, the clothing, and attitude, even to the wallet

Fig. 94.—GRAVE-STONE OF A VINE-DRESSER.
Sculpture of the Catacombs.

and the implement of labour, are all susceptible of a symbolic meaning; but it would be impossible to defend or justify such a system. In the cemetery of St. Agnese, at Rome, is a fresco painting, not of a single vine-dresser or wine-merchant, as in the above figure, but of eight persons, carrying on their shoulders a butt, no doubt filled with wine; two other butts are near. The fresco surmounted a tomb, in which were interred the eight individuals of different ages thereon represented; forming an entire family of wine-merchants.†

* An engraving of the above stone is given in Bosio (*Rom. Sotterr.*, p. 505). The design is accompanied by the following inscription :—

"D. M.,
GAVDENTIO FECERUM,
FRATRI QUI VICSIC ANNIS,
XXVIII. M. VIII. D. XVII."

The orthographical errors here remarked, may be easily accounted for by the station in life of the deceased; his brothers, by whom the monument was erected to his memory, were probably of the same trade. *Fecerum* written for *fecerunt*, *vicsic* for *vixit*, are curious examples of the numerous errors to be met with in the funeral inscriptions of the early Christians.

† Bosio (*Rom. Sotterr.*, p. 557,) gives a copy of this singular monument.

It is far from correct, to give invariably a mystical explanation of vases, canthari,* vials, caskets, casks, lamps, candlesticks, scales, weights, flails, hammers, scissors, hatchets, bushels, tesseræ, anchors, vessels, houses, chairs, loaves, grapes, dates, olives, roses, cypresses, palm-trees, palms, hearts, birds, fishes, and quadrupeds; or to explain, by the medium of symbol or allegory, all the instruments, the tools of various trades, the domestic utensils, natural flowers, fruits, or leaves, the objects of art, the human or animal representations, and fantastic beings with which those early monuments are covered. To do so would be to give a hypothetical and often unreasonable acceptation to objects, the meaning of which is evident, simple, and not figurative; but to go so far as to apply all these symbols to Christ, as some persons have been inclined to do, would be to pass beyond all due limits, and even to transgress the bounds of propriety.

Still, amidst all these innumerable symbols, there is one which predominates over all others, and which, by its presence only, defines the nature of the monuments on which it shines. It is the Cross. In this portion of the present work, which professes to be a history of the second Person of the Trinity, in his divine nature only, the cross, considered as the instrument of punishment on which the human nature of our blessed Lord expired, could not appropriately demand a place: as such, it belongs exclusively to his earthly life, and not to his divine existence. Still, the Cross, like the Lion and the Lamb, symbolises the second person in the Trinity. When, for example, the entire Trinity is represented, the Father, by the portrait of a man, and the Spirit, by the image of a dove, Christ is often figured by the Cross alone; † while He, in his own peculiar person, is

* "'Canthari,' 'Cantharus,' a goblet or drinking cup, of Greek invention. It was furnished with handles (*Virg. Ecl.*, vi. 17), and was the cup particularly sacred to Bacchus (*Macrob. Sat.*, v., 21), as the scyphus was to Hercules." —Rich's "Companion to Latin Dictionary."

† Vide the mosaic in St. John Lateran, at Rome. The Father, under the figure of a man about thirty years of age, is in the clouds, in heaven, whence half only of his body appears. From him the Holy Spirit seems to emanate. It is in the form of a dove, and descends fluttering upon a highly decorated cross. The cross, widowed of Christ, is planted on the summit of the mystic mountain, and bathed on every side by waters, which escaping, flow down the sides of

absent. He is embodied in the Cross, as He is in the Lamb,* or as the Holy Spirit in the Dove. Under that character, the Cross is here entitled to notice, and will accordingly be described.

THE CROSS, A SYMBOL OF CHRIST.

The cross is more than a mere figure of Christ; it is in Iconography either Christ himself or his symbol. A legend has, consequently, been invented giving the history of the cross, as if it had been a living being. It has been made the theme and hero of an epic poem, the germ of which may be discovered in books of Apocryphal tradition. This story is given at length in the Golden Legend, "*Legenda aurea,*" and is detailed and completed in works of painting and sculpture, from the fourteenth century down to the sixteenth. A short abridgment of the History of the Cross would not be useless here, since it would afford a guide to determine what signification ought properly to be attached to that symbol, and what interpretation should be given to the figures and numerous works of painting and sculpture with which our cathedrals are adorned; but to do this would lead us into details too comprehensive and extended, and the reader must therefore be referred to the work of Jacobus Voragine. The first part of this little poem on the Cross of Christ, will be found at the Feast of the Invention of the Cross, and the second, at that of its Exaltation. The Invention is celebrated on the 3rd of May, the Exaltation on the 14th of September. After the death of Adam, Seth planted on the tomb of his father a shoot from the Tree of Life, which grew in the terrestrial Paradise. From it sprang three little trees, united by one single trunk. Moses thence gathered the rod, with which he by his miracles astonished the people of Egypt, and the inhabitants of the desert. Solomon desired to convert that same tree, which

the mountain in four streams, to which stags and sheep repair, to slake their thirst. These streams afterwards fall into a river, as large as a lake, and symbolic of the Jordan.

* St. Paulinus, Bishop of Nola, wrote thus to Sulpicius Severus: "Sanctam fatentur Crux et Agnus victimam."—*Epist.* xii., ad Severum.

had become gigantic in size, into a column for his palace; being either too short or too long, it was rejected and served as a bridge over a torrent. The Queen of Sheba refused to pass over on that tree, declaring that it would one day occasion the destruction of the Jews. Solomon commanded that the predestined beam should be thrown into the probationary pool (Pool of Bethesda), and its virtues were immediately communicated to the waters. When Christ had been condemned to suffer the death of a malefactor, his cross was made of the wood of that very tree. It was buried on Golgotha, and afterwards discovered by St. Helena. It was carried into captivity by Chosroes, King of Persia, delivered, and brought back in triumph to Jerusalem, by the Emperor Heraclius.* Being afterwards dispersed in a

* The subjoined note is extracted from Curzon's "Monasteries of the Levant," a most interesting work :—

"It is related in the apocryphal Gospel of Nicodemus, that when Adam fell sick, he sent his son Seth to the gate of the terrestrial Paradise to ask the angel for some drops of the oil of mercy, which distilled from the Tree of Life, to cure him of his disease; but the angel answered that he could not receive this healing oil until 5500 years had passed away. He gave him, however, a branch of this tree, and it was planted upon Adam's grave. In after ages the tree flourished and waxed exceeding fair, fcr Adam was buried in Mount Lebanon, not very far from the place near Damascus, whence the red earth of which his body was formed by the Creator had been taken. When Balkis, Queen of Abyssinia, came to visit Solomon the king, she worshipped this tree, for she said that thereon should the Saviour of the world be hanged, and that from that time the kingdom of the Jews should cease. Upon hearing this, Solomon commanded that the tree should be cut down and buried in a certain place in Jerusalem, where the Pool of Bethesda was dug; and the angel that had charge of the mysterious tree troubled the water of the pool at certain seasons, and those who first dipped into it were cured of their ailments.

"As the time of the Passion of the Saviour approached, the wood floated on the surface of the water, and of that piece of timber, which was of cedar, the Jews made the upright part of the cross; the cross beam was made of cypress, the piece on which his feet rested was made of palm, and the other on which the superscription was written was of olive. After the crucifixion, the Holy Cross, and the crosses of the two thieves, were thrown into the town ditch, or, according to some, into an old vault which was near at hand, and they were covered with the refuse and ruins of the city. In her extreme old age, the Empress Helena, making a pilgrimage to Jerusalem, threatened all the Jewish inhabitants with torture and death if they did not produce the Holy Cross from the place where their ancestors had concealed it; and at last an old Jew, named Judas, who had been put into prison and was nearly famished, consented to reveal the secret; he accordingly petitioned Heaven, whereupon the earth trembled, and from the fissures in the ground a delicious aromatic

multitude of fragments throughout the Christian universe, countless miracles were performed by it: it restored the dead to life, and gave sight to the blind, cured the paralytic, cleansed lepers, put demons to flight, and dispelled various maladies with which whole nations were afflicted, extinguished conflagrations, and calmed the fury of the raging waves.

The wood of the cross was born with the world, in the terrestrial paradise; it will re-appear in heaven at the end of time, borne in the arms of Christ or of his angels, when the Lord descends to judge the world at the last day.

After reading this history, some conception may be formed of the important place held by the cross in Christian Iconography. The cross, as has been said, is not merely the instrument of the punishment of Jesus Christ, but is also the figure and symbol of the Saviour. Jesus, to an Iconologist, is present in the cross as well as in the lamb, or the lion. Chosroès flattered himself that in possessing the cross, he possessed the Son of God, and he had it enthroned on his right hand, just as the Son is enthroned by God the Father.* So also the earliest Christian artists, when making a representation of the Trinity, placed a cross beside the Father and the Holy Spirit; a cross only, without our crucified Lord. The cross did not only recal Christ to mind, but actually showed him. In Christian Iconography, Christ is actually present under the form and semblance of the cross.

The cross is our crucified Lord in person; "Where the cross is, there is the martyr," says St. Paulinus.† Conse-

odour issued forth, and on the soil being removed the three crosses were discovered; and near the crosses the superscription was also found, but it was not known to which of the three it belonged. However, Macarius, Bishop of Jerusalem, repairing with the Empress to the house of a noble lady who was afflicted with an incurable disease, she was immediately restored to health by touching the true cross, and the body of a young man, which was being carried out to burial, was brought to life on being laid upon the holy wood.

"At the sight of these miracles, Judas, the Jew, became a Christian, and was baptised by the name of Quiriacus, to the great indignation of the Devil, for, said he, 'By the first Judas I gained much profit, but by this one's conversion I shall lose many souls.'"—*Translator*.

* See the *Legenda Aurea*, "De Exaltatione Sancti Crucis."

† "Ubi crux est martyr ibi."—*Opp. Div. Paulini Episcopi Nolani.* Epist. xii., ad Severum.

quently it works miracles, as does Jesus himself: and the list of wonders operated by its power is in truth immense. By the simple sign of the cross traced upon the forehead or the breast, men have been delivered from the most imminent danger. It has constantly put demons to flight,* protected the virginity of women, and the faith of believers; it has restored men to life, or health, inspired them with hope or resignation.

Such is the virtue of the cross, that a mere allusion to that sacred sign, made even in the Old Testament, and long before the existence of the cross, saved the youthful Isaac from death, redeemed from destruction an entire people whose houses were marked by that symbol, healed the envenomed bites of those who looked at the serpent raised in the form of a "tau" upon a pole.† It called back the soul into the dead body of the son of that poor widow who had given bread to the prophet.

A beautiful painted window, belonging to the thirteenth century, in the Cathedral of Bourges, has a representation of Isaac, bearing on his shoulders the wood that was to be used in his sacrifice, arranged in the form of a cross; ‡ the Hebrews too, marked the lintel of their dwellings with the blood of the Paschal Lamb, in the form

* See in the Golden Legend a number of events of that description, chiefly at the Feasts of the Invention and of the Exaltation of the Cross. In St. Saturnin, at Toulouse, is an enamelled châsse belonging to the twelfth century, on which is represented the wonderful translation of a portion of the cross from the Abbey of Josaphat, in Palestine, to Toulouse. It is a national branch of that epic cycle styled by us the Legend of the Cross.

† The above-named subject is represented upon a painted window given by the Abbé Suger to the Cathedral of St. Denis, and which now fills a window in the apse. The brazen serpent, in form resembling a griffin, is suspended from a column (in most cases, it is in the form of a T). Upon the monster is planted the cross, on which Christ is nailed. The following inscription forms the legend of the subject:—

"Sic ut serpentes serpens, necat ereus oms;
Sic exaltatus necat hostes in cruce Xρs."

‡ According to certain commentators, it was the fact of Isaac's carrying the wood for his sacrifice in that form upon his shoulders, that prompted God the Father to send an angel to arrest the arm of Abraham. In numerous sculptures and paintings Isaac is thus represented, going to the place of sacrifice; more particularly in one piece of sculpture in the interior of the west porch of Notre Dame de Rheims, and on a painted window in the north aisle of Notre-Dame de Chartres.

of a "tau" or cross without a summit.* The widow of Sarepta picked up and held cross-wise two pieces of wood, with which she intended to bake her bread.† These figures, to which others also may be added, serve to exalt the triumph of the cross, and seem to flow from a grand central picture, which forms their source, and exhibits Jesus expiring on the cross. It is from that real cross indeed bearing the Saviour, that these subjects from the Old Testament derive all their virtue.‡

In the ninth century the praises of the cross were sung,

* The Hebrews were commanded, previous to their departure from Egypt, to mark all their houses with the blood of the Paschal lamb, in the form of a "tau," or cross with three branches. And when God, as we are told in the book of Exodus, saw that blood, he passed over their houses, and the plague that smote the Egyptians, touched not the Israelites. *Exodus*, xii., 7, 13, 29.

† When Elijah met the widow of Sarepta, that woman picked up two pieces of wood, which she held up in the form of a cross, and God, for that action, increased the quantity of meal and oil in her house, and afterwards permitted the Prophet to restore her son to life.—*Lib.* iii. *Reg.* xvii., 10, 16, 32. (In our version, 1 Kings, xvii., 10, 16, 22.) On most monuments, the two pieces of wood are placed either in the form of an ordinary cross, as in the windows of Bourges and Mans, or in that of an X, commonly called St. Andrew's Cross, as in the window at Chartres and on a sculpture at Rheims.

‡ The following text, relating to the subject of the cross and its anticipated virtue, is extracted from the writings of Gulielmus Durandus. It explains the subject of the painted window at Bourges, and of those at Chartres, and Mans; this interpretation being given by a cotemporary of the painting, it has been thought expedient to give the text unmutilated. It is necessary, in order to make progress in archæology, that books should be compared with, and corrected by the monuments of their time. "Numquid, ait (Stephanus papa) omnia chrismata, id est sacramenta, quæ cum chrismatis unctione præstantur, sacerdotalis hic ministerii crucis figura, id est signo, perficiuntur? Numquid baptismatis unda sine cruce sanctificata, peccata relaxat? Et, ut cætera prætereamus, sine crucis signaculo, quis sacerdotii gradus ascendit? Baptisandus quoque signo crucis signatur in fronte et in pectore . . . Sane crux Domini multipliciter fuit in Veteri Testamento præfigurata; legitur siquidem quod Moses ad mandatum Domini æneum serpentem erexit in palo, in deserto, pro signo; quem aspicientes, qui percussi fuerunt a serpentibus illico sanabantur. Quod ipse Christus exponens inquit, in Evangelio: 'Sicut Moses exaltavit serpentem in deserto, ita exaltari oportet filium hominis, ut omnis qui credit in ipsum non pereat, sed habeat vitam æternam.' Legitur etiam quod cum Joseph applicuisset Manassem et Effraim ad Jacob, statuens majorem ad dexteram et minorem ad sinistram, ut eis secundum ordinum benediceret, Jacob manus commutans, id est in modum crucis cancellans, dextram posuit super caput Effraim minoris, et sinistram super caput Manassæ majoris et dixit: 'Angelus, qui eruit me de cunctis malis benedicat pueris istis.' Item

as men sing those of a god or of a hero, and Rhaban Maur, who was Archbishop of Mayence in 847, wrote a poem in honour of the cross. Men of lively imagination, prompted by feelings of passionate attachment, exhaust their ingenuity in attempting to trace in clouds or mist, or in the strange forms with which natural objects are invested by the shades of night, the semblance of the cherished form of her they love. So too, Rhaban Maur detects the form of the cross in numbers, in geometrical lines, in supernatural beings, and in human creatures. Not content with what he discovers, he invents combinations of letters, which give him the cross; he makes his poetry subservient to the puerile design of representing the cross, under every possible form, with the syllables of which the verses are composed. Finally, these syllables, changed into acrostics bear a sense calculated to interpret the meaning of the images they are employed to form. Rhaban seems inspired with the most passionate love for the cross.*

Long before the time of Rhaban, the fathers of the

Moses ait: 'Die ac nocte erit vita nostra pendens, et videbitis et cognoscetis.' Christus enim nocte fuit in cruce pendens, quia tenebræ factæ sunt ab hora sexta usque ad nonam. Quod etiam fuerit pendens, certum est. Rursus legitur: 'Ezechiel audivit Dominum dicentem ad virum vestitum lineis, habentem attramentarium scriptoris ad renes: Transi per mediam civitatem et signa thau in frontibus virorum dolentium et gementium.' Et post hæc dixit vii. viris: 'Transite per mediam civitatem, et percutite omnem super quem non vidibitis thau, nemini parcet oculus vester.' Item Hierem: 'Congregabo omnes gentes, et erit eis in signum thau.' Item alibi: 'Et erit principatus ejus super humerum ejus.' Christus enim portavit super humeros crucem in qua triumphavit. Johannes quoque vidit angelum ascendentem ab ortu solis, habentem signum Dei vivi, et clamabat voce magna quatuor angelis, quibus datum est nocere terræ et mari, dicens: 'Nolite nocere terræ et mari, neque arboribus, quousque signemus servos Dei in frontibus eorum.' Item lignum missum in Marath, aquas dulcoravit amaras et ad lignum missum in Jordanem, ferrum quod inciderat enatavit, hoc est lignum vitæ et in medio paradisi de quo sapiens protestatur, benedictum lignum, per quod fit justitia, quoniam regnavit in ligno Deus. Hoc ergo crucis signo se armat Ecclesia, in pectore et in fronte, significans crucis mysterium esse corde credendum et manifeste ore confitendum. Per hoc enim signum confunditur civitas diaboli et triumphat Ecclesia, terribilis ut castrorum acies ordinata, juxta illud: 'Terribilis est locus iste, &c.' Et alibi: 'Vidi civitatem magnam sanctam, Hierusalem novam.' Et August. tamen dicit, undecima distinctione ecclesiasticarum, quod nulla scriptura Novi Testamenti vel veteris docet fideles crucis signaculo insigniri."—G. Durand., *Rat. Div. Off.*, lib. v., cap. 2.

* See the entire poem of Rhaban Maur, *De Laudibus Sanctæ Crucis*, in his complete works, in fol., Coloniæ Agrippinæ, 1626, vol. i., pp. 273—337.

Church had remarked, that the figure of the cross was engraven on the productions of nature, seen in the works of men, in the position of inanimate objects, and the gestures of the living.

The world is in the form of a cross; for the east shines above our heads, the north is on the right, the south at the the left, and the west stretches out beneath our feet. Birds, that they may rise in air, extend their wings in the form of a cross; men, when praying,* or when beating aside the water while swimming, assume the form of a cross. Man differs from the inferior animals, in his power of standing erect, and extending his arms.

A vessel, to fly upon the seas, displays her yard-arms in the form of a cross, and cannot cut the waves, unless her mast stands cross-like, erect in air; finally, the ground cannot be tilled without the sacred sign, and the *tau*, the cruciform letter, is the letter of salvation.†

The cross, it is thus seen, has been the object of a worship and adoration, resembling if not equal to, that offered to Christ. That sacred tree is adored almost as if it were equal with God himself;‡ a number of churches have been dedicated

* The primitive Christians always extended their arms in prayer, standing most frequently instead of kneeling, as may be seen in the earliest frescos of the catacombs.—*Translator.*

† St. Hieron. (*Comment. in Marcum*), "Ipsa species crucis quid est nisi forma quadrata mundi? Oriens de vertice, Arcton dextra tenet, Auster in læva consistit, Occidens sub plantis formatur .... Aves, quando volant, ad æthera formam crucis assumunt; homo, natans per aquas, vel orans, forma crucis vehitur. Navis per maria antenna crucis similata sufflatur. Thau, littera signum salutis et crucis describitur."—M. Cyprien Robert (*Cours d'Hieroglyphique Chrétienne*) quotes the above text, and adds, "Justin Martyr in his Apology bids us observe that the sign of the cross is stamped on everything; there is no labourer who may not find its figure among his implements, and man himself, by raising his arms, forms a cross. Minucius Felix, speaking to princes, exclaims, "the staffs of your trophies imitate the instrument of our salvation, and the armour which is hung upon them is the image of the crucified Redeemer." Tertullian (*De Oratione*) expresses the same feeling as St. Jerome and St. Ambrose (*Serm.* VI). The letter *tau*, the numerical value of which is 300, presented an immense field, in which the mystics of Alexandria laboured with unwearied diligence.

‡ The word "adore" is used to express the worship rendered to the cross, the symbol of Christ; still this worship is not the same as that called "Latria," or the "worship, which should be rendered only to God."

to it under the name of the Holy Cross.* In addition to this, most of our churches, the greatest as well as the smallest, cathedrals as well as chapels, present in their ground plan the form of a cross, and we are thus recalled more immediately to Iconography, and led to name the principal varieties of that figure.

THE VARIETIES OF THE CROSS.

There are four different sorts of crosses. The cross without a summit; the cross with a summit but with only one transverse bar; the cross with a summit and two transverse bars; the cross with a summit and three transverse bars.

The cross without a top has three branches or limbs only; it takes the form of the T or symbolic "tau," of which we have already spoken. Many ancient churches, particularly the Basilicas of Constantine, St. Peter, and St. Paul, at Rome, are built very nearly in the form of a *tau;* the Church of Bellaigue in Auvergne also offers the same combination.† The mystical virtues of the *tau* have already been mentioned, and need not be recapitulated here.

The cross, with a top and transverse bar is composed of four limbs, and possesses the greatest virtue; the cross, with three branches or limbs, is in fact the anticipatory cross, the typical cross, the cross of the Old Testament; that with four branches is the true cross, the cross of Christ, the cross of the Gospel. The virtue of the cross in *tau* was derived solely from the cross with four branches; it was like a planet, having no light in itself, but receiving all its splendour from the sun of the Gospel. The cross of Christ was formed of

* Sainte-Croix, the Cathedral of Orleans; Sainte-Croix, now St. Germain-des-Près, built by Childebert; Sainte-Croix, at Quimperlé (*Finisterre*), a church of singular form; Sainte-Croix, a charming church at Mont-majour, near Arles; Santa Croce at Florence, and many others besides. There are in France at least eighteen abbeys called Sainte-Croix. [To these may be added the church of Saint Cross at Winchester. *Saint* being the Latin "Sanctus, holy," the word is preserved, or rather translated in the name of *Holy*rood, in Edinburgh, which is also dedicated to the memory of the Holy Cross; the same observation will apply to the churches of "Saint Sepulchre, Saint Saviour."—*Translator*.]

† See M. Mallay, *Eglises Romano-Byzantines de l'Auvergne*.

one vertical shaft, and of a transverse beam, having the form of a gibbet or a hammer.* "And observe," says Gulielmus Durandus, "that the cross is divided into four parts; whether on account of the four elements, polluted through our sin and healed by the passion of Christ; or by reason of men; whom Christ draws to himself from the four parts of the world, according to the words of his own prophecy, 'And I, if I be lifted up from the earth will draw all men unto me' (John, xii. 32.) These four parts may relate to the human soul; the cross is lofty, long, large and deep. The depth is in the foot which is buried in the earth; the length is from the root to the arms; the breadth extends with the arms; the height is from the arms to the head. The depth signifies faith planted on a sure foundation; the height is hope, having its resting place in heaven; the breadth charity, extending even to the left, or our enemies; the length perseverance, which continues, or is without limit.†

The different forms of the cross with four branches, resolve themselves into two principal types, which are subdivided into several varieties. These are called, the Latin and the Greek cross, the first being favoured by Greek Christians and those of the East, the second by the Latin Christians of the West.

In each of these two types, the cross is composed of two parts, a shaft, and a transverse bar, cutting it across the stem. But in the Greek cross the transverse branch divides the upright shaft into equal parts, and the two arms of the cross are together equal to the upright. If a circle be

* "Habuit crux Christi lignum erectum in longitudinem, alterum transversum in latitudinem quasi in modum potentiæ seu martelli, quæ duo significata sunt per illa duo ligna quæ paupercula mulier in Sarepta collegit." (Gulielmus Durandus, *Rat. Div. Off.* Lib. vi. cap. 77, De Die Parasceves.)

† "Et adverte quoniam crucis figura quadripartita est, vel propter quatuor elementa quæ in nobis vitiata Christus sua passione curavit, vel propter homines quos ex quatuor partibus orbis ad se trahit juxta illud; si exaltatus fuero a terra omnia traham ad me ipsum. Vel et hæc quadratura pertinet ad mortalitatem; habet enim longitudinem, latitudinem, sublimitatem et profundum. Profundum est acumen quod terræ infigitur, longitudo est inde ad brachia, latitudo est in expansione, latitudo seu sublimitas est a brachiis usque ad caput. Profundum significat fidem quæ est posita in fundamento, altitudo spem quæ est reposita in cælo, latitudo charitatem quæ est ad sinistrum et ad inimicos extenditur, longitudo perseverantiam quæ sine fine concluditur." (Gulielmus Durandus, *Rat. Div. Off.* Lib. v. cap. 11.)

divided by two right lines, passing through the centre, those two lines will give you a perfect Greek cross; this it is which divides the nimbus worn by divine persons. The cross then, is composed of four parts, equal in themselves; viz., the foot, the top or summit, and two cross branches.

In a Roman cross, the foot is longer than the upper part, or the branches; it could not be contained within a circle, but would require a rectangular figure. In the Roman cross, the shaft is longer than the transverse branch, and the foot of the shaft longer than the upper part. The form is that of a man standing with arms extended. From the extremity of the left arm to that of the right, the interval is smaller than that from the head to the feet; the distance from the head to the shoulders is smaller than that from the shoulders to the feet. The extended arms form the transverse bar, from the head to the shoulders, the upper part of the shaft; from the shoulders to the feet, the lower part. The Latin cross resembles the actual cross of Christ, but the form of the Greek cross is ideal. The Latins, who were more material in sentiment than the Greeks, preferred the actual form; the Greeks, more spiritual than the Latins, idealised the reality, poetised and transfigured the cross of Calvary. The Greeks transformed the instrument of punishment into an ornament.

These types were not at first specially confined the one to the Greek, the other to the Latin Church; they were originally common to both countries, and were admitted indifferently by both. Thus it is said, in Procopius, that the Church of the Holy Apostles at Constantinople was constructed on the plan of a cross, and the foot of the church or the nave, was made longer than the upper part or choir, in order to give it more exactly the form of a cross.*

Still the most ancient Greek sculptures, at Athens, in the Morea, in Macedonia, and Constantinople, contain crosses

* "The text of Procopius (*De Ædificiis Just.* p. 13) is very explicit; "Hinc inde procurrentia transversi spatii latera inter se æqualia sunt; spatii vero in directum porrecti pars, illa quæ vergit ad occidentem, alteram superat quantum satis est ut figuram crucis efficiat." (*Πεποίετα μείζων ὅσον ἀπραξάσται τὸ τοῦ σταυροῦ χήμα.*) Thus the arms of the cross are equal in themselves; but the western nave is longer than the choir, by all the extent necessary to constitute a cross of crucifixion, or Latin cross.

with branches of unequal length. That primary type must therefore have been known and practised in Greece. As to the second, the Cross with equal branches, it is the most commonly adopted by the Greek Church.

The cross with four equal limbs was known and adopted in the West, as well as that with unequal branches. Thus sarcophagi, columns, pillars, and altar-stones were, and still are, marked with a cross of equal limbs;* but the other cross belongs more especially to us.

Both types were then originally common to both churches. In the sequel, the first type, that with branches of equal length, predominated in the east, and that form of cross was called the Greek cross; the second type, the cross with unequal branches, predominated with us, and was termed the Latin cross. In the Eastern Church I repeat, the Greek cross displays itself in the ensemble and details of religious monuments, in the architectural portion as well as in the decorative. In the ground-plan, many Eastern Churches have the form of a Greek cross, and the following drawing gives the plan of a church erected in the Holy Land, upon the site of the well to which the Samaritan woman whom Jesus converted, went to fetch water.† (St. John, iv., 6, 20.) The shaft of the cross given below seems, however, rather longer than the transept, but this is probably an error of the artist Arculfe. At all events, even supposing the form to be correct as here given, it is still a Greek, rather than a Latin cross.

The capitals of most Byzantine churches are marked with a Greek cross. In the Church of St. Demetrius at Salonica, in St. Sophia at Constantinople, St. Mark at Venice, and San Vitale at Ravenna, a monument purely Byzantine, the cross

* In the exterior wall, on the north side of the nave, in the Church of St. Maurice at Rheims, a funereal stone is inserted, on which is sculptured a Greek cross, formed like the Maltese cross. Engraved *en creux* (incised) on the limbs of the cross is this inscription: "Hic jacet Arma,—mater—matertera—neptis." The first part is at the top, the second in the left cross-bar, the third on the right arm; the last word, neptis, is at the foot (Fig. 108, no. 5), a design approximating closely to the cross of St. Maurice. The artist has here given only the general form or outline.

† Other analogous plans are given by the *Comité Historique des Arts et Monuments, dans les Instructions sur les Monuments fixés*, 1e cahier, pp. 108, 110.

with equal branches, either free or inscribed within a medallion, shines forth from the surrounding cable mouldings, interlacements, and acanthus leaves.*

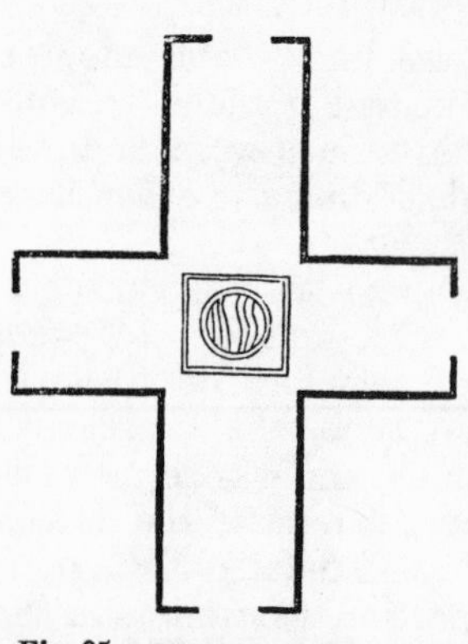

Fig. 95.—CHURCH, IN THE FORM OF A GREEK CROSS.‡
French engraving on a wax tablet; VII cent.

In paintings, the vestments of St. John Chrysostom are adorned with small Greek crosses, dividing circles into four equal parts; other Greek crosses, free, and multiplied to infinity, adorn the chasuble of St. Gregory Nazianzen. The nimbus of God is divided by a cross with branches of equal length;† that borne by the Knights of Malta, descendants of the Knights Hospitallers of St. John of Jerusalem as a distinctive decoration of their order, has the four branches equal.

Our churches in the West are generally disposed in the form of the Latin cross, with limbs of unequal length, the upper part, and cross beams, being shorter than the foot. The longitudinal nave is formed by the foot; the transepts, or transverse nave, by the cross-beams; the choir by the top.

The higher we ascend in the centuries of the middle ages,

* See the capital of a column from St. Vitale.—*Instructions du Comité Historique des Arts et Monuments.*

† See below, Figs. 101, 104, 108, several varieties of the Greek cross.

‡ The drawing here given is an outline, reduced from the original plan which was made in the seventh century by Arculfe, Bishop of France. That bishop traced upon tablets of wax the plans of the principal edifices in Palestine, of the Church of the Holy Sepulchre, of the Cénacle,[1] and the Church of the Ascension. When the *Act. SS. Ord. S. Bened.* were published, these tablets were still in existence, and the Benedictines had engravings made from them, and inserted in the second part of the third Benedictine century. The Church of the Well of the Woman of Samaria, was copied from one of those plates. In the centre is the well, bearing in the original the inscription "Fons Jacob."

[1] "Cénacle" is a term only used in French in the style of the Holy Scriptures (see *Dict. de l'Academie*); it signifies a refectory. "Jesus washed the feet of his disciples in the Cenaculum." (*John* xiii. 5.)—ED.

the shorter we find the choir, while the nave increases in length. In the basilica of Constantine, the transverse nave, called the "croisée" or transepts, cuts the longitudinal nave immediately near the apse, and consequently leaves no space for the choir.* After the thirteenth century the choir lengthens, and the transept descends further towards the west.† There are even some churches in which the transverse nave, or transept, is nearer to the porch than to the apse; so that the form of the Latin cross is still preserved, the branches being unequal in length to the shaft, and the transept cutting the nave into two parts of unequal length; but it is a Latin cross reversed, and the top is longer than the foot. The Church of St. Germain l'Auxerrois, at Paris, is of this description. The nave, from the porch to the transepts, is four compartments in length; from the transepts to the end of the church there are nine, an addition of five. The head, which ought to be shorter than the feet, is in fact longer. The cross-bars are short, as is fitting in a Latin cross, and not more than three compartments each in length.‡

* The ancient Church of St. Peter, built by Constantine, St. Paolo fuori delle Mura, and Sta. Maria Maggiore, are all built in that form. Even in the Pagan basilica of Vitruvius some indications of a transept may be discovered; and it has thence been imagined, erroneously, as it appears to me, that the form of the cross, apparent in our churches, was neither allegoric in its meaning nor peculiar to Christianity. The existence of Roman monuments more or less cruciform in design, cannot rob Christians of the honour of having been the first to attach a symbolic meaning to the form of the cross adopted in the building of churches. Besides, the transverse nave differs surprisingly both in size and position, from that of Vitruvius, which is not so much a nave as a double recessed passage for exit or entrance. Finally, the writings of Beleth, Durandus, Hugues de Saint-Victor, and other liturgists, assert that churches are built in the form of the cross in memory of our redemption. The Comité des Arts et Monuments (*Instructions sur les Monuments fixés,* 1e cahier, style Latin, pp. 92, 93, 94) have given various plans of basilicas, more particularly that of St. Paolo, which resembles a T with a short cross-bar. Independent of the apse, which projects outwards, the form of the *tau* is complete, and it is a perfect cross, but of three branches only.

† This may be observed in most of our cathedrals; in those of Amiens and Laon more particularly. See the plan of Notre-Dame de Paris in *Les Instructions sur les Monuments fixés,* 11e cahier, p. 11.

‡ The Comité Hist. des Arts et Monuments, in the *Instructions Monuments fixés,* 11e cahier, pp. 14, 15, give four different plans, one of which is that of a reversed cross.

But several of the English churches are built on a plan which is neither that of the Latin nor of the Greek cross properly so called, nor yet of the *tau*. These singular edifices are divided, not by one single transept, but by two. The first transept cuts the longitudinal nave in the centre; the lower or western portion forms the nave, properly so called; the upper part is the choir, retro-choir, or chancel (*chevet*) of the church. But the upper part is itself divided into two equal portions by a second transept not so long as the first. Below, that is to say, from the first to the second crossing, is the choir; above, or from the second crossing to the upper end of the church, is the retro-choir or sanctuary. The great churches of Lincoln, Beverley, Rochester and Worcester, are thus designed.* Imagine the form of the cross of Christ, against which was nailed a long, wide scroll, bearing the well-known inscription, "Jesus of Nazareth, the King of the Jews." The place on which this writing was affixed is shown in English churches, and forms the eastern crossing, that by which the upper end of the church is divided into two equal parts; the next is the usual transept, the cross-bar, on which the arms of the Saviour were extended.† The above form is that of the Cross of

* The Comité Historique des Arts et Monuments (*Instructions Monuments fixés*, 11e cahier, p. 14) have mentioned these plans and given diagrams of them. In the *Monasticon Anglicanum*, by Roger Dodsworth and William Dugdale, will be found engraved plans of these curious English churches. This work was printed in London; the first vol. in 1655, the second in 1671, and the third in 1673.

† The form just described is almost peculiar to English edifices; yet the great Church of Cluny had double transepts, and each of the four cross arms was crossed a second time. The Church of St. Quentin has two transepts, but one is of later date than the other, and does not belong to the primitive plan, but was constructed only to enlarge the building. The Abbey Church of St. Benoît sur Loire offers, though imperfectly, a form of church with a double transept. I know no other buildings in France with the same arrangement as the Churches of Cluny, St. Quentin, and St. Benoît. The celebrated window in the Church of St. Etienne de Bourges, already mentioned several times, and with which the work of MM. Martin and Cahier on the windows of that cathedral opens, presents, in a medallion of the Resurrection, Jesus Christ issuing from the tomb, and bearing in his left hand a little golden cross. This cross, by an irregularity which in our country is not unique, has a double crossing; a large double window in Notre Dame de Chartres affords another example of the same cross. The lower crossing is rather shorter than the upper. There can be no doubt of its being intended to represent the part on

Lorraine, of the Hospitallers of the Holy Spirit, and it belongs also to that, which at the present time, indicates the archiepiscopal dignity. It is called the cross with double branches, and probably originated in Greece; for it is constantly seen in Attica, in the Morea, and on Mount Athos. The following design represents one which decorates the western gate of a church at Athens.

The plan of cruciform churches was often revealed in visions; an angel appeared at night to a sleeping saint or bishop, and described to him the form of some building which God desired to have erected in his honour; people were then immediately set to work to build a church according to the model seen in the dream.* Or it happened that the outline of the church to be erected, was seen traced in luminous lines upon the clouds of heaven, and, following the example of Constantine, who had caused the labarum to be executed according to the form of that which he had seen marked by lines of fire in the air, so they built the edifice according to the luminous design which had appeared; or perhaps the site or form of the proposed basilica was seen delineated in lines of dew upon the perfectly dry ground; † on one occasion the snow extended hither and

which the writing was fixed. The lower crossing forms the transverse bar on which the arms of our Blessed Saviour were extended. The cross, however, here described, from its dimensions, which are very small, and its colour, which is of a golden yellow, presents a reduced image of the real cross; it is a cross in miniature, a Resurrection cross in short. The most interesting conclusions may be drawn from the great number of crosses with double cross-arms, to be found in Greece, most of them dating from a remote period, and the form of the double transverse cross assumed by several of the large churches in England. I have little doubt that an inquiry, conducted with care and intelligenee, and directed towards that object, would produce results which may indeed be anticipated, but are not therefore the less curious. Can it be possible that England has allowed herself to be influenced by Byzantine genius more than France? This remains to be proved.

* A remarkable instance is that of St. Martin-des-Champs, at Paris. It appears that the biblical text—"Fac secundum exemplar quod tibi monstratum est in monte," was applied more especially to the construction of churches, the plan of which was revealed in dreams, or by apparitions in the clouds.

† St. Gérémar, or Germer, the first Abbot of Flavigny, about 658, requested of St. Ouen a site for the erection of a monastery. The two saints, after three days of fasting and prayer, saw an angel, who announced to them that God had heard their petition, and that the spot destined for the future monastery was Flavigny

thither in lines marking where the walls were to be raised.

Lastly, the Abbey and Church of St. Michael in France, in the department de la Manche, and St. Michael in Italy, at Mount Gargano, were traced upon the earth by the footsteps of a bull.*

If an art so severe as that of architecture yet stooped to fashion its plans according to the various admitted forms of the cross, we may with good reason expect to find that in sculpture and painting, both fanciful and decorative arts, the cross would be designed after a still greater variety of models, presenting numerous, and sometimes most extraordinary, peculiarities. We have not only a cross with two cross-bars, but the number of the latter is sometimes increased to three. The cross thus made has therefore eight branches, each bar being divided into two, thus forming six, while the shaft brings two others, the foot and the summit. Crosses with one, two, or three transverse beams, become like the tiara, the hat, and the mitre, a medium of hierarchical distinction. The Pope alone was entitled to have borne before

a place in the midst of a great solitude. They went to that place. "Ubi cum pervenissent et multum dubitarent quid agerent, ecce nebula descendit de cœlo et circumdedit totum locum ubi construendum erat monasterium, et cum nebula superna vox dicens: Electi Dei, ecce iste locus metuendus est... cumque obtutus suos adspectum nebulæ defigerent (sancti), statim ab adspectibus eorum subtracta est. Ex eadem autem nebula in circuitu loci, quasi quædam virga geometricalis, ros totum locum circumdans remansit, ut daretur intelligi verum esse, quod superna vox cecinit. Tunc circumeuntes locum, repererunt signum cœlestis roris impressum. Beatus atem Audoenus certus de angelica visione et de superna voce, accipiens virgam in manu, per vestigia nebulæ mensus est plateam in circuitu, ubi ecclesia aedificaretur, ubi officinæ construerentur et cœtera monachorum vitæ utilia." (*Act. SS. Ord. St. Bened.*, vol. ii., "Vie de Saint Germer écrite par un anonyme contemporain.")

* See the *Golden Legend*, "De Sancto Michaele Archangelo." The Legend says, "In loco qui Tumba dicitur juxta mare, qui sex miliaribns ab urbe Abricensi distat, Michael episcopo prædictæ civitatis apparuit, dicens et jubens ut in prædicto loco ecclesiam construeret et sicut fit in Monte Gargano, ita et ibi in memoriam Sancti Michaelis Archangeli celebraret. Cum autem episcopus de loco, in quo ecclesiam construeret, dubitaret, ab ipso edocetur ut ibi construi eam faceret ubi thaurum (*sic*) a latronibus absconditum inveuiret. Iterumque de loci amplitudine dubitâns, jubetur modum in amplitudine, statuere quantum videret thaurum in circuitu pedibus intrivisse." Mount Gargano, now St. Angelo, is in the kingdom of Naples, province of Capitanate, in the ancient Apulia.

him the triple cross. Cardinals and archbishops were honoured with the double cross; the single cross was

Fig. 96.—GREEK CROSS, WITH DOUBLE BRANCHES.*
Athenian Sculpture of the XI cent.

* This cross is the complement to that which will be given in Fig. 99: it forms a pendant to it. Upon the cross, Fig. 99, appear the letters ĨC X̃C̃; upon the above, ÑĨ-K̃A, which completes the phrase, "Jesus Christ is conqueror." The eagle and the falcon at the foot of the cross must be allegorical, as will be remarked in speaking of Fig. 99.

relinquished to the bishop.* The capitals of columns, the coffers and lids of sarcophagi, mosaics and fresco paintings, painted windows and carved woodwork, present crosses innumerable, and in variety proportionate to their number. These crosses are either free, single, or intertwined with other subjects.

When the cross is free, and not loaded with attributes and ornaments, it requires to be distinguished from the Cross of Calvary, and the Resurrection Cross. The Cross of the Passion, the actual Cross, the wood on which Jesus died, is that square rough tree composed merely of a shaft and a cross-bar. It is a cross of that form that we generally see placed in the arms of the Father, when he holds the Cross with the effigy of the Saviour nailed upon it.† The same cross is placed in the centre of our churches, at the opening of the grand arch, which, as well as the cross, is called triumphal.‡ The same cross, also, is planted in our fields,

* It was in the fifteenth and sixteenth centuries principally that the cross was called on to fill the part which heraldic ornaments perform in blazonry. It is vexatious that that custom was not adopted at an earlier period, since it is extremely useful in distinguishing between an archbishop and a bishop. Let us suppose that a figure has disappeared entirely from a sculptured bas-relief or a painted picture: if the cross only be still remaining in the hand, it would be possible to determine, according to the form of the cross, whether the individual were a bishop, an archbishop, a cardinal, or a pope. (See at St. Denis, on the gates of wood brought from the chapel of Gaillon, Pope Gregory the Great holding in his hand a cross with a triple cross-bar.)

† A painted window in the apse of the Cathedral of St. Denis, dating from the time of Abbé Suger, has the representation of a four-yoked car (or quadriga), on which is placed a large green cross. This cross, although embossed with filagree ornaments, is a true cross, a Passion cross ; and our Saviour is attached to it. God the Father, adorned with a plain and not a cruciform nimbus (this nimbus appears to be modern), bears the cross in his arms. It is the earliest example which I know of that subject, which was a peculiar favourite in the fifteenth and sixteenth century. Although a period of five hundred years intervenes between the two, the window of St. Denis greatly resembles that at Troyes, a drawing of which is given, Fig. 63. Both at St. Denis and at Troyes the Holy Spirit, by a singular coincidence, is omitted in the representation of the Trinity. This circumstance will be noticed in the sequel.

‡ "Crux triumphalis, in plurisque locis, in medio ecclesiæ ponitur, ad notandum quod de medio corde Redemptorem nostrum diligimus, qui, juxta Salomonem, corpus suum media charitate constravit propter filias Hierusalem, et ut omnes signum victoriæ videntes, dicant ; Ave salus totius sæculi, arbor salutifera. Et ne unquam a nobis dilectio Dei oblivioni tradatur, qui, ut

at the place where four roads meet.* The Resurrection Cross is the symbol of the real cross; Christ springs from

Fig. 97.—CHRIST, ARMED WITH THE CROSS OF THE RESURRECTION, DESCENDING INTO LIMBO.
French Miniature of the XIII cent.

the tomb, and, holding it on high, mounts triumphantly to heaven. A banner, or a flame generally floats on the arms of the Cross of the Resurrection, for it is nothing more than a

servum redimeret, tradidit unicum filium, ut Crucifixum imitemur. Crux autem in altum dirigitur, per quod Christi victoria designatur."—Guill. Durandus. *Rat. Div. Off.*, lit. 1., cap. 1.

* Several examples are given above of the actual cross, of the instrument of punishment on which our Saviour was suspended.

standard, the shaft of which, instead of being sharpened into a spear or pike, terminates in a cross. The cross which the Paschal Lamb supports by one of his feet, and that usually carried at the head of religious processions, are crosses of the Resurrection and Ascension. We no longer have a tree, as in the Cross of the Passion, but a staff.

Christ is here represented descending into Limbo, and breaking the gates of hell with the Resurrection Cross. He draws from that place of suffering the souls of the first righteous, or those of the Old Testament saints, at the head of whom advance Adam and Eve. The devils howl and gnash their teeth at the sight of Christ, who is trampling one of them beneath his feet, and snatching from their demon grasp, those whom they imagined to be their prey.* Sometimes Christ in heaven, seated with the Father and the Holy Ghost, carries a Resurrection Cross, instead of the Cross of the Passion. The Passion Cross, the true cross, is that of suffering; the other, the Resurrection Cross, is triumphant. The second has the same general form as the first, but spiritualised; it is the cross of suffering transfigured.

Both of these crosses are historical, for both took part in the Crucifixion and Resurrection of Jesus Christ; but there are others which, being purely emblematic, present varieties even more numerous than the former. Several of these crosses have been adopted in the science of heraldry, and are distinguished by names denoting their form and nature. The fulminated or thunderbolt cross is composed of thunderbolts; the ringed, or linked cross, of rings or links; the cabled cross, of cables; the cross voided, is when the field is entirely open, with nothing but an edge to mark the form; the cross pierced, when it is perforated merely in the centre; and corded, when it is wound about with a cord. A cross, cut by a single traverse at each arm, is called crosslet (*recroisée*); and double-crosslet (*recroisetée*), when the traverse is doubled. If the extremities of each branch are

* It may be cursorily remarked that the entrance to hell is of triple form; first we have the gate of a fortified castle; then the jaws of a monster; lastly, the chimney of a furnace. The above drawing will appear again in the History of the Devil; it is taken from a MS., with miniatures of the thirteenth century, in the Bib. Roy.

terminated by one or by two serpents' heads, it is said to be *gringollée*, or *guivrée*;* by a crescent, crescented; by an anchor, anchored; by a dart, barbed, or *barbée*; by a cramp-iron, *cramponnée*; by a trefoil, trefled or *botoné*; by a *fleur-de-lis*, *fleury*, or *flory*; by one or more balls, *pommetty* or *bourdonnée*.† When from the point of each branch the descent is by steps or degrees, the cross is termed degraded (*perronnée*). When the end is sharp or rounded, it is pointed, or *moussée*; potent when each arm is surmounted by a traverse, like the head of a crutch; and *pattée*, when the extremities spread. The Maltese cross is *pattée*, but the extremity of each *pattée* is notched at a sharp angle.

Fig. 98.—GREEK CROSS; AS THE CROSS OF LORRAINE.‡

Sculpture of Mount Athos; first ages.

The above indications will be sufficient for our purpose; a more extended developement of the varieties would occupy too much time and space. It may, however, be mentioned as something remarkable, that nearly all these heraldic crosses are Greek and not Roman. Might not the form have originated in the East, at the epoch of the Crusades, or rather, as is not improbable, might it not have been necessitated by the form of the shield?

When the cross is intertwined and accompanied by ornaments and attributes, the varieties become so

* "*Guivré*, boa, serpent ou bisse qui parait dans l'écu avec un enfant à mi-corps issant de sa gueule." *Dict. Heraldique.* Tours, 1848.

† "*Bourdonnée*, une croix pommetée à la manière d'un bourdon de pélérin. (Les prieurs mettent un baton bourdonnée derrière l'écu de leurs armes.)" *Dict Heraldique.* Tours, 1848.

‡ This cross, with double arms, is sculptured on a slab of white marble, which serves as sustaining wall to the little rotunda called "πηγὴ," or

numerous that to attempt an enumeration would be completely useless. A few are given below.

In Greece, representations of the cross are usually attended with the inscription, IC̄ XC̄ NIKA (Jesus Christ is Conqueror). The preceding engraving gives the figure of a cross with double arms, called amongst us the Cross of Lorraine, and forming the plan of the several English churches, mentioned above, as well as of the three French churches.

The foot of the above cross is bifurcated, and cut into the form of acanthus leaves.* The whole inscription here accompanies a single cross. In other instances the inscription is divided into two parts; the first portion is engraved above a cross placed on the left, the second above another cross placed on the right hand. Below the first are two peacocks, standing face to face, animals which appear to be

"φιάλη," at the entrance of the large and ancient convent of St. Laura on Mount Athos. These fountains, ancient baptisteries, are at present used for giving and receiving holy water.

* The ornament from which the cross rises, as from a root, deserves to be studied with the greatest care. Foliated at its commencement, and having reverse curves on either side, it afterwards loses the upper curve and retains only the simple curve below: it forms a sort of crescent, but a foliated crescent. Later than this, in our own time, the foliage disappeared entirely, leaving the crescent still more strongly marked; for each curve or quarter circle unites and receives at its junction the foot of the cross. The cross of Christ is here triumphant and trampling on the crescent of Mahomet, as in our monuments St. Michael overthrows and tramples upon Satan. It is thus in fact that this figure of the rooted cross is interpreted by the partisans of the symbolic school; but the crescent is formed only by the gradual degradation of the double foliation in opposite curves, and has no reference either to Mahomet or the crescent. This opinion will receive full confirmation from the study of the Byzantine crosses of Mount Athos, Constantinople, and throughout Greece; for in those countries, crosses, entirely in the form of a crescent, existed before the birth of Mahomet, and even in the time of Justinian. With regard to certain medals of Maguelonne, on which the cross is seen fixed in a kind of crescent, we are told that the bishop, by whom this money was issued, had made alliance with the Mussulmans, and in token thereof united upon his coinage the crescent and the cross. In the first place it is highly improbable that any French bishop would make an alliance with the Mussulmans, it is still more unlikely that he would ever have united the symbol of Jesus with that of Mahomet; or that, had he done so, a Christian population would have submitted to a like insult. The cross upon the coins of Maguelonne exactly resembles the rooted crosses, a very ancient example of which is afforded by that of St. Laura on Mount Athos. A great analogy exists between the ancient rooted crosses and anchor crosses.

symbolic, since, in a certain manuscript,* and upon a monumental stone in the museum of Narbonne, peacocks are

Fig. 99.—GREEK CROSS, WITH DOUBLE CROSS ARMS.
Sculpture at Athens; XI cent.

represented, crowned like saints with a nimbus. In a medallion below the second cross there is an eagle with

* The MS. above mentioned was quoted in the chapter on the nimbus.

wings counter-crossed, and in another a falcon with wings abased. The falcon wears the collar, leash, and bell. The foot of the first cross is *pattée*, of the second degraded (*perronnée*); both are cut by a broad, double crossbeam, or traverse. The cross with peacocks is made of ribbons interlaced; that with the eagle and falcon is of narrower ribbons, plaited.

Both of these crosses adorn the western porch of a church at Athens, and are sculptured upon slabs of white marble. The cross with the eagle and falcon was given in Fig. 96. It was necessary therefore to complete the subject, by the addition of that with the two peacocks, the latter being placed on the left hand and supplying the first half of the inscription.

At the foot of the painted or sculptured crosses adorning the churches in Greece, animals are constantly represented face to face, contemplating, with a mixture of love and terror the symbol of redemption, before which they appear to bend in humiliation. The lion, the eagle, the falcon, and the peacock, are the animals most commonly seen; the eagle and the peacock are emblems of pride; the falcon and the lion remind us of barbarous violence and brutal cruelty, and all may well signify those evil passions which are constrained to bow beneath the yoke of the cross; the dove and the sheep, so frequently seen on the frescos of catacombs and ancient sarcophagi, might announce that virtues emanate from the cross, in the same manner in which vices are overwhelmed by its power. St. Paulinus, Bishop of Nola, sends to his friend Sulpicius Severus, the following distichs, which

M. Journal, who sent me a drawing of the stone at Narbonne, and one also from a sarcophagus in St. Etienne, at Bologna, representing two peacocks face to face, looking at a cross, writes as follows: "The peacock has frequently been employed as an emblem, from the fourth century down to our own time. We find it in mosaics decorating the vaulting of Sta. Costanza in Rome; on the pavement of St. Mark's at Venice, and the sarcophagi at Ravenna, and in the Vatican. The sarcophagus of Pope Zozimus (418) is preserved in St. Lorenzo fuori delle Mura at Rome, and that of Santa Costanza in the Vatican contains only genii employed in the vintage, peacocks and sheep." I do not myself imagine either the sheep or the genii to be invariably emblematic, and think the fancy of the artist had more influence in suggesting the style of decoration. Still it would be well for Christian antiquaries to devote some time to the study of this singular subject.

he had had written near two crosses painted red, cinctured with a crown of flowers, and attended by two doves:

"Ardua floriferæ CRUX cingitur orbe coronæ
Et Domini fuso tincta cruore rubet."

"Quæque super signum resident cœleste columbæ,
Simplicibus produnt regna patere Dei."

One would imagine these lines to have been composed for a cross thus figured on a marble sarcophagus, brought from the cemetery of the Vatican.* Saint Paulinus says again,

". . . . . . Tolle crucem qui vis auferre coronam."

If the allegorical intention of the preceding examples be uncertain, still it cannot be questioned in the following cross which is *pattée* inscribed within a circle, and quartered with four open books, each of which is surrounded by a circular aureole. Several designs have been already shown, in which Christ, inclosed in an aureole either elliptical or circular, is attended by the attributes of the four Evangelists. In the figure given below, Christ is symbolised by the Cross, and the four Evangelists by their Gospels.

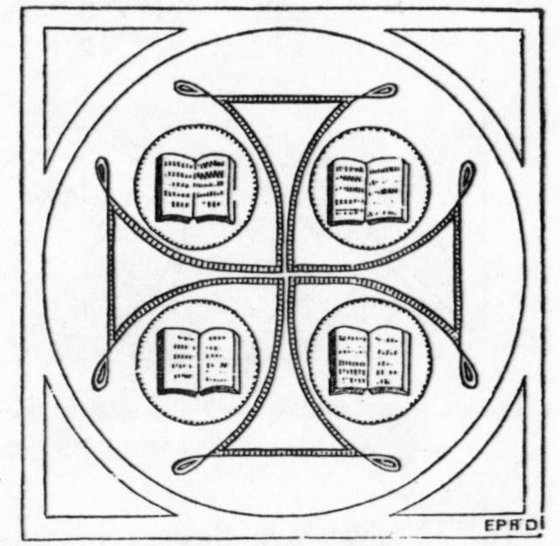

Fig. 100.—CROSS, QUARTERED WITH THE FOUR GOSPELS.

Fresco in the Catacombs; the earliest ages.

The cross is not merely accompanied by symbols and

* See the works of St. Paulinus (*Epistola*, xii., ad Severum), and Bosio (*Rom. Sotterr.*, p. 79). In treating of allegorical representations, an immense field is open to the imagination; we must therefore, pause here, and refer the reader for fuller details to the whole of the fourth part of *Rom. Sotter.*, beginning from the 41st chapter in particular. Although unable to accede to all the opinions elicited by Bosio, we are not the less inclined to recommend

ornaments, but it is, if we may so speak, interlaced with them. The monogram of Christ, the chi (X) and the rho (P) of Χριστὸς, the iota (I) of Ἰησοῦς, combine and produce Greek crosses, Roman crosses, and stars with six branches of equal or unequal lengths.

These crosses are either free, or else inscribed within circular or square medallions. In the following plate, composed of six cruciform monograms, the CHI is a St. Andrew's cross.

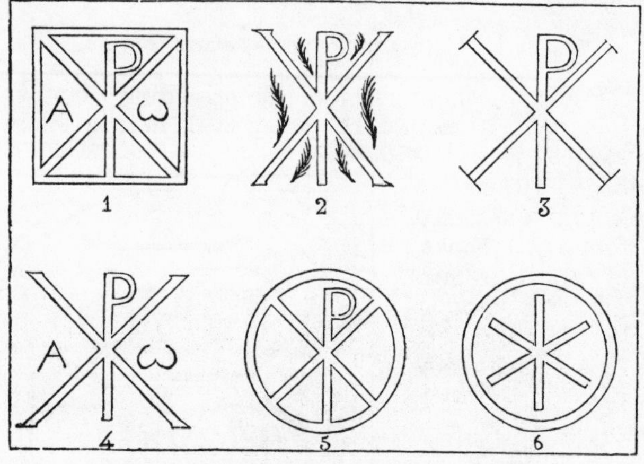

Fig. 101.—VARIOUS CROSSES OF THE GREEK FORM.

Sculpture of the ancient Sarcophagi; earliest epoch.

In the first five figures in this plate, the RHO cuts the CHI vertically at the point where the two branches intersect each other. We thus have the two first letters of ΧΡΙΣΤΟΣ. The monograms of Nos. 2, 3, and 4, are free; Nos. 1, 5, and 6 enclosed; No. 3 is composed of the X and P only; No. 2 is accompanied by palm branches, intended probably to designate triumph and glory; No. 4, like No. 1, is completed by the

that the most scrupulous attention should be paid to everything relating to symbolism. The question of Christian symbolism is of grave import, and one of the most delicate in our national archæology, and cannot be solved satisfactorily, unless our conclusions be supported, solely and entirely, by facts.

addition of the Greek letters A and Ω, signifying that Christ is the commencement and the end of all things. No. 5 is inscribed within a medallion, but the rays of this mystic wheel extend to the circumference, and are confounded with it, while those of No. 6 do not adhere to it, (this example is termed *couped* or *humetty*.) Besides, this last figure is no longer a RHO, but an IOTA, which is the first letter of Ἰησοῦς, as CHI is of Χριστὸς. The sixth monogram thus appears to be the most complete; the preceding examples express only CHRIST, the latter JESUS CHRIST.

Fig. 102.—A GREEK CROSS OR STAR, WITH SIX EQUAL BRANCHES.
Sculpture in S. Demetrius at Salonica. IV cent.

The engraving subjoined was taken from the capital of a column in the church of St. Demetrius, at Salonica; it would be exactly similar to No. 6, if the rays composing it were disengaged instead of touching the line of circumference.

In the above figure, the IOTA, not the RHO, cuts the CHI, but the six rays reach, and are circumscribed by a circle; in that given below, they are in a square, and with this variety: that the CHI does not divide the IOTA into equal parts: the foot of the IOTA is longer than the top.

Fig. 103.—GREEK CROSS, WITH SIX BRANCHES OF UNEQUAL LENGTHS.
Sculpture of Salonica; IV cent.

In the preceding examples the CHI preserves its natural form, that of a St. Andrew's cross, a cross saltire; in those which follow, on the contrary, the CHI becomes a true cross with a vertical shaft, and horizontal cross-bar. Besides, instead of six branches for the X and P, there are no longer more than four; the vertical shaft of the X curves and becomes RHO. The monogram is more and more contracted, and the lines forming it are economised.

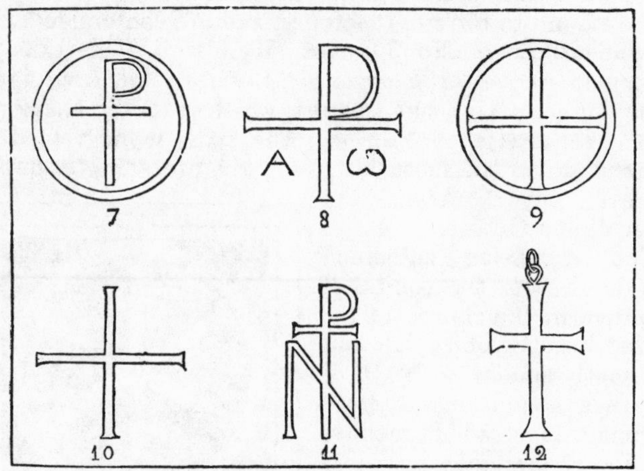

Fig. 104.—GREEK AND LATIN CROSSES, OF VARIOUS FORMS.
Monuments in the Catacombs; the earliest epoch.

No. 12 in the above plate is the same in form as the pectoral cross worn by bishops. Nos. 9 and 10 give the Greek cross, one disengaged, the other engaged in a circle; the disk of No. 9 thus stamped with the cross, exactly resembles a cruciform nimbus; in No. 7 the disk is also divided by a cross, but the branches of that cross do not reach to the circumference, and the vertical shaft is rounded into a Rho (P). In No. 8, as in Nos. 1 and 4., the A and Ω accompany the monogram. No. 11 presents in addition, an N, which, traversing the foot of the cross, is most probably the initial of noster, and gives to this monogram the meaning of " XRISTOS NOSTER,"*. With us the epithet is amplified into "Our Lord Jesus Christ."

* These monograms were of Greek origin, but the Latins did not abandon them, or modify them according to the form of the Roman letters, until a very late period. In the catacombs and early mosaics, the monograms of Christ and of the Virgin are in Greek letters—IC, XC and MP, ΘY. The alpha and omega have continued in use in this country down to the present day. The name of Christ was written in Latin at Chartres, in the thirteenth century; but

In the following example the monogram is given in combination with the cross, but the cross is borne like a standard by a young neophyte; it is, in fact, a kind of labarum.

Fig. 105.—MONOGRAM, UNITED WITH THE CROSS.
Sculpture of the Catacombs; of the earliest period.

Inscriptions and allegorical ornaments, in short, more numerous even than those which have just been seen, accompany the cross, and assist in developing the events and ideas which that symbol recals to our minds. A Christian seal, a design from which, magnified by the camera lucida and given below, is engraved with a cross, in the form of a TAU (T); the CHI (X) crosses the shaft of the TAU, which is rounded above into a RHO (P). The name of Christ and the figure of his cross are comprised in these lines. Christ the Son of God, is the commencement and the end of all; the A and Ω, the beginning and end of intellectual signs, and, by extension, of intelligence itself, and lastly, of the human soul, accompany the cross, on the right hand and on the left. The cross has crushed and conquered Satan the old serpent; a serpent, therefore, unrols and entwines himself around the foot of the cross. This enemy of the human race seeks above all things to destroy the soul, which is represented under the form of a dove; but the dove, although menaced by the serpent, looks stedfastly at the cross, whence she derives her strength, and by which she is rendered safe from the poison of Satan. The word SALUS, written below the ground

the first two letters are Greek, the third and fourth might be either Greek or Latin, and the two last are exclusively Latin, XPITVS. The first sigma is omitted. Here the monogram of Christ is Greek, while that of the adjective, *noster*, is Latin. In the Evangéliaire, in the Sainte Chapelle, at Paris, quoted above, p. 273, the first of the four verses transcribed has *Dominum* in the Latin, and *Christum* in Greek:—

. . . . "Quatuor D$\overline{\text{UM}}$ signant animalia $\overline{\text{XPM}}$."

on which the cross and doves are standing, is the song of triumph poured forth by faithful Christians in honour of Jesus and the cross.

The cross which follows on the next page, Fig. 107, is another triumphal cross. Placed amidst the stars of heaven, this cross stands upon the same inscription, SALUS, the sense of which is completed by the word MUNDI, and is surrounded by a resplendent circle of precious stones; the cross itself is starred with precious stones.* Three other inscriptions occupy respectively each of the other extremities, as Salus Mundi does the extremity of the foot. The arrangement is as follows:—Above the summit of the cross, that is, in heaven, we read, "I. M. D. V. C. These letters are interpreted, with greater or less propriety, by "Immolatio Domini Jesu Christi." But in this manner no account is given of the V. or the Y., if indeed it is a V. or a Y. and not an I.,† besides, two

Fig. 106.—MYSTIC CROSS.
Engraved stone of the earliest epoch.

* This is indeed the gemmed, the starry, the floriated cross, *crux gemmata, crux stellata, crux florida*, as it is called when richly decorated. (See, in *Rom. Sotterr.*, p. 131, a beautiful example of a gemmed and floriated cross, with the A and Ω suspended by little chains from the cross-beams.) Rhaban Maur says, interpreting the sixteenth figure, in reference to the cross: "Descripsi ergo hic FLORIGERAM crucem quatuor coloribus præcipuis, id est hyacinthino, purpureo, byssino et coccineo, ut floris illius jucundissimi decorem demonstrarem, quem prophetica locutio narrat de stirpe regia exortum, qui speciosus præ filiis hominum existens, omnium virtutum decorem in semetipso ultra omnes mirabiliter ostendit." Rhaban, it will be seen, formally asserts the beauty of Christ. The same passage is terminated by the following words: "Homo Christus Hiesus inter homines natus serenus resplendebat, quia totius decoris pulchritudine INTUS FORISQUE plenus erat." (See the works of Rhaban Maur, vol. i., p. 313, *De Laud. Sanctæ Crucis.*)

† This cross has been copied from an engraving, which may possibly, as there is great reason to fear, be incorrect, and not from the monument itself. Ciampini (*Vet. Mon.*, pars. 1[a]., tab. 24), who gives it, explains the five letters as above, and does not remark that the V and the Y contradict his explanation. Gori (*Thes. Vet. Dipty.*, vol. iii., p. 22,) has had an engraving made from the cross of Ravenna. He replaces the five Latin letters of Ciampini by the five

letters are here given for the first word, and one only for the other three. This inscription, bearing reference as it does, to the self-devotion of the Deity, is properly placed in heaven rather than on the earth. Upon the earth, that is to say, at the foot of the cross which descends towards our world, we read, "Salus mundi," because the world is saved through the Cross of Christ. Finally, Christ, whose comprehensive charity embraces the universe, the ancient world as well as the future, from the creation down to the end of time, —Christ, by whom patriarchs and apostles, prophets and saints are redeemed, the first man as well as the last, truly deserved that the cross on which his

Fig. 107.—STARRY CROSS.*
From a mosaic at Ravenna, in S. Appollinario in Classe; VI cent.

Greek letters ΙΧΘΥC, forming the celebrated word on which we have already dwelt so long. If Gori's reading be correct, this fact is of the highest importance. I regret extremely not having myself seen that curious monument. I requested M. l' Abbé Lacroix, the clerc-national and historical correspondent at Rome, to favour me with information respecting this mosaic. M. Lacroix, who has made the Church of St. Apollinaire in Classe, in which that mosaic is preserved, an object of especial study, has taken a most careful and exact copy of the cross. He informs me that the word is really ΙΧΘΥC, as Gori asserts. This fact is of great moment in determining the question whether Christ were actually symbolised by the fish or not. M. Lacroix has also sent me a drawing of a monument, recently discovered by himself, on the hill of the Vatican behind St. Peter's; it is a sepulchral marble, belonging to the earliest Christian era. Above two fishes, which are affronted, or looking towards each other, is inscribed "ΙΧΘΥC. ΖωΝΤωΝ," that is to say, "'Ιησοῦς Χριστὸς Θεοῦ Υιος Σωτὴρ Ζῶντων," "Jesus Christ, Son of God, Saviour of the living." After such facts as these, which completely set the question at rest, we are compelled to yield, and to acknowledge that the fish has most decidedly been employed as a figure, if not a symbol of Christ. M. Lacroix has counted 99 stars in the field of the cross of Ravenna; he thinks that that number may be intended to refer to the 99 just persons, in relation to whom there is less joy in Paradise than at the conversion of a single sinner. This interpretation could not, however, be adopted without some hesitation. The design in our possession contains 21 stars only; but copyists are seldom correct.

* It is to this cross surrounded with stars that the exclamation of the Emperor Heraclius might apply, "O crux splendidior cunctis astris!" This is still sung in the offices of the Church. (See the "Golden Legend," *De Exalt. St. Crucis.*)

arms were extended should be marked with an A and Ω, signifying the beginning and the end of all things.

The cross is unquestionably the symbol of Christ; it *is* Christ under the figure of the gibbet on which he suffered. Thus we see it spoken of as if it were Christ himself: Jesus, in the Gospel, said, "I am the light of the world;" (John, viii. 12.) "I am the way, the truth, and the life;" (John, xiv. 6;) and "Whosoever liveth and believeth in me shall never die. (John, xi. 26.) So also in the Church of St. Pierre du Dorat, on the top of a cross accompanied by the A and Ω, we read the four words, LVX. PAX. LEX. REX.* The cross gives light, in the same manner as Christ, who shone in the darkness; the cross calms and regulates the passions; governs and directs man in the path of duty; it is the torch, peace, law, and a guide.

The four words LVX. PAX. LEX. REX. are written in the form of a cross, as in No. 1 of the following design, but with one variation. In the field of the Greek cross, below, we read the following words, also disposed in the form of a cross: LVX. DVX. LEX. REX. Thus DVX is substituted for PAX. Finally, the tomb of St. Angilbert, son-in-law and peer of Charlemagne, seventh Abbot of St. Riquier, had the following four verses inscribed on the four sides of the slab: the lines begin and end with the four words sculptured at Dorat, and will serve to explain their meaning.

REX, requiem Angilberto da, Pater atque pius REX;
LEX legum, vitam æternam illi da, quia tu LEX.
LVX, lucem semper concede illi, bona qui es LVX;
PAX, pacem illi perpetuam dona, es quoniam PAX.†

Thus the cross, like Christ, or even God himself, lights and guides us, and we may apply to it the words, spoken by St. Paul, of God. "In it (him) we live, and move, and have our being." (Acts xvii. 28.)

* This inscription, communicated to me by M. de Guilhermy, is a work of the twelfth century. It is graven on the north wall of the church at Dorat, surmounting, as has been said, a Greek cross, with the A and Ω; but beneath the cross is a second inscription, in which the faithful commend themselves to the protection of God and the guardianship of his angels.

† *Act. SS. Ord. S. Bened.*, fourth Benedictine century, first part. "Life of St. Angilbert."

In this light it was regarded by Dante, when in Paradise he described the souls of the just as kneeling and praying

Fig. 108.—GREEK AND LATIN CROSSES, OF VARIOUS FORMS.*
From French monuments of different periods.

in the interior of a cross of fire, in which they breathe, where they dwell, and which forms their world.

* Numerous varieties of the cross are given in this plate, but a crowd of others exist, which it would be impossible to enumerate. It is necessary in treating subjects of this nature, to attend to the most trifling variety of form, for such varieties are generally characteristic of an epoch, a country, or an idea. No. 1 gives the cross of Dorat; No. 2 serves as an antefix or crown-work to the gable of the chevet of the Romanesque Church of Olizy, near Rheims; No. 3 is a cross pattée with the cross-beams re-crossed, and the top in the form of a tau; No. 4 is an open bay or embrasure in the eastern wall of the apse in the Church of Beine, arrondissement of Rheims. The chevet of the church at Beine is square, like that in the Cathedral of Laon; but the rose, which in the Cathedral of Laon is open in a full circle, at Beine assumes the form of a cross. No. 5 nearly resembles the design of a sepulchral stone inserted in the south wall of St. Maurice at Rheims. A funeral inscription, of a certain degree of archæological importance, is engraved

The subjoined figure is a picture of the inhabited Cross,

Fig. 109.—INHABITED CROSS.
Florentine engraving, 1491.

upon the four branches of the cross. On the upper part is written: "HIC JACET ARMA;" on the left, "MATER;" on the right, "MATERTERA;" below, "NEPTIS." No. 6 is the Maltese cross. The cross No. 7 is engraved upon the lintel of a chapel in Pont-Faverger, near Rheims. No. 8 gives the form of a pectoral cross, sculptured on the breast of a female statue of wood, in the clock tower of the rural church of Binson, where it was discovered by M. Hippolyte Durand and myself in 1837: it belongs to the Romanesque epoch, probably about the tenth century. This wooden figure is two inches in height, and the most ancient existing in France. The proprietor of the church would do well to preserve this curious effigy with greater care. No. 9, which is not here in its proper place, gives an example of the heart-shaped leaves so constantly seen on sarcophagi, and which accompany monumental inscriptions: it belongs to the paragraph where the various figures depicted upon tombs are described, and to which an allegorical meaning must, with moderation, be assigned. The eight varieties of the cross, given in the above plate, are, although exceptions, very common in France. Nos. 2, 3, 4, 5, and 7 all belong to the arrondissement of Rheims. It would be interesting employment

as described in the Divina Commedia, printed at Florence in 1491.*

This cross is resplendent with a glory far more radiant than the suns and constellations of every kind which blaze around it. Dante thus explains the subject. The poet, being arrived with Beatrice in the planet Mars, exclaims—

" M' apparverò splendor dentro a' duo raggi,
Ch' io dissi ; O Eliòs, che sì gli addobbi !
Come distinta da minori e maggi
Lumi biancheggia tra' poli del mondo
Galassia† sì, che fa dubbiar ben saggi,
Sì costellati facean nel profondo
Marte quei raggi il venerabil segno,‡
Che fan giunture di quadranti in tondo
Qui vince la memoria mia lo 'ngegno ;
Ch 'n quella croce lampeggiava Christo.

* * * *

Di corno in corno, e tra la cima e 'l basso,
Si movean lumi, scintillando forte
Nel congiungersi insieme e nel trapasso ;
Così si veggion qui diritte e torte,
Veloci e tarde, rinnovando vista,
Le minuzie de' corpi lunghe e corte
Muoversi per lo raggio, onde si lista.
Tal volta l'ombra, che per sua difesa
La gente con ingegno ed arte acquista.

---

to collect, from every department and arrondissement of France, the different varieties of the cross to be found in each. Nothing should ever be omitted or neglected in Iconography, particularly when relating to so important a figure as the cross of Christ. The form, the colour, and the ornaments decorating or accompanying the divine cross, ought to be studied with the minutest care. M. Tournal has lately sent me a drawing of a very ancient bas-relief, found recently at Narbonne, and on which two persons are figured, one sitting, the other erect, supporting a gemmed cross pattée. At the top are two doves drinking from a vase : the A and Ω depend from the cross-bars ; between the top and the transverse bar radiate two figures, either stars or expanded roses. A dragon appears to be expiring at the feet of the sitting person : a rose of eight petals, a square, and two circles are semés on the left of the cross. All these figures may, with much appearance of probability, be explained by symbolism, even to the satisfaction of those who, like ourselves, restrict the symbolism within comparatively narrow limits.

* *Paradiso*, Canto xiv., l. 94.

† The Galaxy, or Milky Way. ‡ The Cross.

E come giga ad arpa in tempra tesa
    Di molte corde, fan dolce tintinno
    A tal, da cui la nota, non è intesa;
Cosi da' lumi che lì m 'apparinno,
    S' accogliea per la croce una melode,
    Che mi rapiva senza intender l'inno."*

*   *   *   *

Qual per li seren tranquilli e puri
    Discorre ad ora ad or subito fuoco,
    Movendo gli occhi, che stavan sicuri,
E pare stella, che tramuti loco,
    Se non che dalla parte, onde s' accende
    Nulla sen perde, ed esso dura poco;
Tale dal corno, che 'n destro si stende,
    Al piè di quella croce corse un astro †
    Della costellazion, che lì risplende;

---

* With such mighty sheen,
And mantling crimson, in two listed rays
The splendors shot before me, that I cried,
"God of Sabaoth! that does prank them thus!"
As leads the Galaxy from pole to pole,
Distinguished into greater lights and less,
Its pathway, which the wisest fail to spell;
So thickly studded, in the depth of Mars,
Those rays described the venerable sign,
That quadrants in the round conjoining frame.
Here memory mocks the toil of genius. Christ
Beamed on that cross; and pattern fails me now.

*   *   *   *

From horn to horn,
And 'tween the summit and the base did move
Lights, scintillating, as they met and passed.
Thus oft are seen with ever changeful glance,
Straight or athwart, now rapid and now slow,
The atomies of bodies, long or short,
To move along the sunbeam, whose slant line
Checkers the shadow interposed by art
Against the noon-tide heat. And as the chime
Of minstrel music, dulcimer, and harp,
With many strings a pleasant dinning makes
To him, who heareth not distinct the note;
So from the lights, which there appeared to me
Gather'd along the cross a melody,
That, indistinctly heard, with ravishment
Possess'd me.

Cary's Dante, Paradise, Canto xiv., l. 86.

† The spirit of Cacciaguida. See note † next page.

Nè si partì la gemma dal suo nastro:
"Ma per la lista radial trascorse,
Che parve fuoco dietro ad alabastro."
* * * *
Ben supplico a te, vivo topazio,
Che questa gioia preziösa ingemmi,
Perchè mi facci del tuo nome sazio."*

This saintly splendour was the spirit of Cacciaguida.† He speaks at some length to Dante of his ancestors, and the future fate of the poet himself. He then adds in canto xviii.—

"In questa quinta soglia ‡
Dell' alvero che vive della cima,
E frutta sempre, e mai non perde foglia,
Spiriti son beati che giù, prima
Che venissero al cielo, fur di gran voce,
Sì ch' ogni Musa ne sarebbe opima.
Però mira ne' corni della Croce:
Quel, ch' io or numerò, li farà l'atto
Che fa in nube il suo fuoco veloce

---

* "As oft along the still and pure serene,
At nightfall, glides a sudden trail of fire,
Attracting with involuntary heed
The eye to follow it, erewhile at rest;
And seems some star that shifted place in heaven,
Only that, whence it kindles, none is lost,
And it is soon extinct; thus from the horn
That on the dexter of the cross extends,
Down to its foot, one luminary ran
From mid the cluster shone there; yét no gem
Dropp'd from its foil, and through the beamy list
Like flame in alabaster glow'd its course.
* * * *
"This, howe'er,
I pray thee, living topaz! that ingemm'st
This precious jewel; let me hear thy name."
Cary's Dante, Paradise, xv., l. 11 and 81.

† It is thus explained by annotators. Cacciaguida was the great great grandfather of the poet. It would have been better to translate the Italian by the French words "âme," or "lueur;" there are no "shades" (ombres) in the *Paradiso* of Dante, in which everything is fire or flame. In the Inferno the souls of the lost are darkness; those suffering in the Purgatorio are shades, and the glorified souls in Paradise are splendours. Such is the progression observed, and no doubt intentionally, by Dante.

‡ The planet Mars—the fifth division of Paradise.

Io vidi per la croce un lume tratto
Dal nomar Josuè ; com' ei si feo ;
Nè mi fu noto il dir, prima che il fatto.
Ed al nome dell' alto Maccabeo
Vidi muoversi un altro roteando ;
E letizia era ferza del paleo.
Così per Carlo Magno e per Pèr Orlando
Duo ne seguì lo mio attento sguardo,
Com' occhio segue suo falcon volando.
Poscia trasse Guglielmo, e Rinoardo
E'l duca Gottifredi la mia vista
Per quella Croce, e Roberto Guiscardo.
Indi tra l' altre luci mota e mista
Mostrommi l' alma, che m' avea parlato,
Qual era tra i cantor del Cielo artista."*

Thus amongst the twelve little naked beings inhabiting the cross given in our design, and representing the souls of valiant warriors, Dante mentions eight, who occupy the arms of the cross, beginning from left to right. In the left arm are Joshua, Judas Maccabæus, Charlemagne, and

* "'On this fifth lodgment of the tree, whose life
Is from its top, whose fruit is ever fair,
And, leaf unwithering, bless'd spirits abide,
That were below, ere they arrived in Heaven,
So mighty in renown, as every Muse
Might grace her triumph with them. On the horns
Look, therefore, of the Cross ; he whom I name
Shall there enact, as doth in summer cloud
Its nimble fire.' Along the cross I saw
At the repeated name of Joshua,
A splendour gliding ; nor, the word was said
Ere it was done ; then at the naming, saw,
Of the great Maccabee, another move
With whirling speed ; and gladness was the scourge
Unto that top. The next for Charlemain
And for the peer Orlando, two my gaze
Pursued, intently, as the eye pursues
A falcon flying. Last, along the cross
William, and Renard, and Duke Godfrey, drew
My ken, and Robert Guiscard. And the soul
Who, spake with me, among the other lights
Did move away and mix ; and with the choir
Of heavenly songsters proved his tuneful skill." *

Cary's Dante, Paradise, xviii., l. 25.

---

* The translation of Dante's *Divina Commedia,* used by M. Didron, was that of M. Brizeux, but it has been thought preferable to quote the original text with Cary's translation.—Ed.

Roland; in the right, William the Conqueror, Richard Cœur de Lion, Godfrey de Bouillon and Robert Guiscard.

Cacciaguida is one of the four souls, not named, who are kneeling in the stem, and upper part of the cross. This cross does not contain the crucified in person, and yet Dante in canto xiv., declares that Christ there shone resplendent; in fact, as has been said, the Cross is the symbol of Christ. Iconographically considered, the Son of God is in the Cross, as he is in the Lamb, and in the Lion; he is there hidden under the semblance of the instrument of punishment on which he died. To sum up therefore; the second person of the Trinity is *figured* by an infinite number of different objects; three alone, the Lamb, the Lion and the Cross, are *symbols* of our Lord. Even the Fish does not rise to the dignity of a divine symbol.

Fully to complete the history of the Cross would have required a special monography; the present notice is therefore limited, from necessity, to the essential points of this important subject. We shall conclude with a few words only on the making the sign of the cross, on the colour, and on the Triumph of the Cross.

THE SIGN OF THE CROSS.

The sign of the cross, made in token of recognition of its power, is common to all Christian antiquity: that symbolic gesture has from the earliest times preceded, attended and closed the actions and thoughts of Christians. The cross in which "the philosopher St. Paul gloried," says St. John Chrysostom, "every faithful Christian wears suspended round his neck; it was represented on the wearing apparel, chambers, beds, instruments, vases, books, cups, and even on animals." St. Cyril of Jerusalem, in his instructions to catechumens, desires them to trace the cross upon their foreheads, to alarm and drive away Satan, and he further adds—"Make that sign whenever you eat or drink, when you seat yourselves, when you lie down or rise up; in a word, let it accompany every action of your life." We read also in St. Augustine: "Si dixerimus catechumeno: Credis in Christum? respondit: Credo, et signat se cruce." The same father adds elsewhere: "As the hidden rite of circumcision was the appointed sign of the old covenant, so the cross on the uncovered brow is the token of the new."*

The sign of the cross is made either upon others or upon one's self; in the first it is an action of benediction, in the second an individual act.

God is the only source of all benediction. In several of the drawings previously given,† he is chiefly thus shown in the act of benediction.

The delegated representatives of God on earth, Popes and Bishops more especially, are also divinely commissioned to bestow benedictions on mankind. Angels, although the ministers of the Deity, are not his representatives by the same title as the Pope, or Bishops, who are his vicars by virtue of their apostolical descent. The functions of the priesthood can be exercised by men only; angels are not, and cannot be represented blessing.

The angel on the roof of the chevet of the cathedral at Chartres, which was destroyed by a conflagration, has in modern times been replaced by an angel in the act of blessing the city which lies outspread beneath him; but this is an offence against both our liturgy and iconography: God, and men alone, have the power to bless.‡

St. John the Baptist is usually represented by the Greeks in the act of blessing with the right hand, and holding in

* M. Cyprien Robert (*Cours d' Hierogl. Chrét.*) has quoted these various texts; we append that of Tertullian (*De Corona Militis*, cap. 111): "Ad omnem progressum atque promotum, ad omnem aditum et exitum, ad vestitum, ad calciatum, ad lavacrum, ad mensas, ad lumina, ad cubilia, ad sedilia, quacumque nos conversatio exercet, frontem crucis signaculo terimus." Tertullian says again (*De Oratione*, cap. xii.): "Nos vero non atollimus tantum manus, sed etiam expandimus e dominica passione modulatum, et orantes confitemur Christo."

† Particularly (to mention only the earliest engravings) at Figs. 2, 6, 17, 21.

‡ The error of which the sculptor of the angel at Chartres Cathedral is here guilty, combined with numerous others committed in the restoration of St. Denis, St. Germain-l' Auxerrois, the Cathedrals of Rheims and Avignon, ought to convince the civil and ecclesiastical administration of the necessity of appointing a council of liturgists and antiquaries, who having studied Christian archæology under every possible aspect, might be consulted on many delicate points. The

the left, his head, the reed cross, or the scroll, and calling men to repentance. St. John is a man, a minister of God, the precursor of Christ. To him all the power and prerogatives of the priesthood were delegated by God. He therefore gives the blessing by good authority.* Yet, amongst us, St. John the Baptist is always represented holding the Lamb of God in his left arm, the index of the right hand being engaged in pointing to it; that hand points but does not bless.†

The gesture of benediction is, as we have already said, either Greek or Latin; it is always given with the right hand, the hand of power. In the Greek Church it is performed with the forefinger entirely open, the middle finger slightly bent, the thumb crossed upon the third finger, and the little finger bent. This movement and position of the five fingers, form, more or less perfectly, the monogram of the Son of God.

The Greeks, who were well versed in the refinements of mysticism, naturally adopted that form of benediction.‡ The subjoined directions for depicting the Divine Hand in the act of blessing, are extracted from the "Guide for Painting," a Byzantine manuscript; they commence thus: "When you desire to represent a hand in the act of blessing, you must not join the three fingers together, but let the thumb be crossed on the third finger, so that the first, called the index, may remain open, and the second finger be slightly bent. Those two fingers form the name of Christ IησουC, I.C In fact, the first finger remaining open signifies an I (iôta), and the curvature of the second forms a C (sigma). The thumb is placed across the third finger, and the fourth, or little finger, is slightly bent, thus indicating the word XριστοC, X.C. The union of the thumb with the third finger makes a X (chi), and the curvature of the little finger

angel symbolising the Church of Soissons, in the painted window in Notre-Dame de Rheims, has the forefinger only of the hand open, and the angel of the metropolitan Church of Rheims has the entire hand open, but neither of those angels is giving a benediction.

* See above, Fig. 24. A St. John in the Byzantine style, brought from M. Hymettus. The precursor gives the benediction in the Greek manner.

† Sup., Figs. 83 and 84, two engravings of the precursor in the Latin style He points to the Divine Lamb, but without blessing.

‡ See above, Figs. 21, 49, 52. God the Father and the Son, giving the Greek benediction.

forms a C (sigma), and these two letters form the 'sigle,' or abridgment of Christos. Thus, through the divine providence of the Creator, the fingers of a man's hand, though more or less long or short, may be placed in such a manner as to figure the name of Christ."

The Latin benediction is given with the thumb and two first fingers open; the third and the little finger remaining closed.* This arrangement of the fingers appears to be symbolic. Gulielmus Durandus and Jean Beleth affirm that that manner of blessing symbolises the Trinity, and that the three open fingers signify the three Divine persons.† The two closed fingers are emblematic of the two natures of Christ, the human and divine. The Greeks, as will be seen, have developed this germ of symbolism, and have assigned each separate finger by name to one of the three persons. It may not be impossible to find a Greek benediction on some of the monuments of western iconography existing in our own country. Such a circumstance would deserve to be carefully noted, as affording an incontrovertible proof of the operation, either direct or indirect, of Byzantine influence. One fact of this nature, discovered in those edifices in our country which are now very gratuitously termed Byzantine, would close the discussion, and be of more value than all the dissertations which have been written on that point.

It appears that in former times priests as well as bishops gave the benediction with three fingers extended; but at a later period, when it was thought desirable to establish a more marked difference between the episcopal benediction and that of a simple priest, bishops reserved to themselves the right of blessing with three fingers; and priests no longer gave the benediction except with the hand entirely open. In addition to this, bishops gave their blessing as it were full face, priests only in profile, with the hand held sideways. Lastly, during the performance of ecclesiastical offices and prayers, in which bishops give three successive benedictions, and three times make the sign of the cross, priests give one blessing only, and make one single sign. The episcopal

* See above, Fig. 54. A most remarkable instance of the Latin benediction given by a divine hand.

† Gulielmus Durandus, *Rat. Div. Off.*, lib. v., cap. ii., J. Beleth. *Explicatio Divin. Off.*, cap. xxxix., de Evangelio.

benediction is then the same as that of the priest, but in its fullest amplification. It becomes, therefore, necessary, in the study of iconographic monuments, to examine carefully not merely the position of each finger but the direction of the hand. Christian archæology, to become a science, requires, like botany and other natural sciences, to be scrutinised even in its most minute and microscopic details; in fact, the true science exists only in those details.

An individual making the sign of the cross upon his own person uses the right hand, the thumb and first and second fingers open, and the third and fourth closed. There is in this respect no difference between the Greek and the Latin Church. Gulielmus Durandus says, that the sign of the cross is made with the three fingers to invoke the Trinity. The Greeks have the same opinion, but add that each finger symbolises one of the Divine persons. The Archbishop of Mistra, whom I interrogated on that subject,* told me that the thumb, from its strength, indicated the Creator, the Father Eternal, the Almighty; that the middle finger was consecrated to Jesus Christ, who has redeemed us, and is, therefore, in respect of men, the chief person of the Trinity; that the forefinger, standing between the middle finger and thumb figured the Holy Ghost, who unites the Father and Son, and in representations of the Trinity is placed between those two persons.

With the three fingers open, the body is marked with the form of a cross, beginning at the brow, and descending thence to the breast, crossing that vertical line by another or horizontal one drawn from the left shoulder to the right. The Greeks go from the right to the left, and it appears that with us also in the thirteenth century, at the time when Durandus wrote, the line was traced indifferently from either shoulder. The present chapter cannot be better closed, than by the translation of an extract from the writings of Durandus, which comprehends everything that remains to be said concerning the sign of the cross:—

"The sign of the cross should be made with three fingers, because while tracing it we invoke the Trinity. Hence the prophet exclaims, '*Quis appendit tribus digitis molem*

* During a visit to Greece, in the month of September, 1839.

terræ.' " (Isaiah, xl. 12, Editio Vulgatæ.)* Still the thumb has the pre-eminence, because we fix our whole faith upon God, one and three. Immediately after the invocation of the Trinity the following verse may be said, "Show me a token for good; that they which hate me may see it, and be ashamed; because thou, Lord, hast holpen me, and comforted me." (Psalm lxxxvi. 17.) But Jacobites and Eutychians, affirming that there was in Christ one single nature only, the divine nature, and at the same time, one single person only in the godhead, make "the sign of the cross, as we are told with one finger only. This error has been eradicated by the decision of the canons." (Distinction XII., ch. i. and ii., question 3rd; "*Some Eutychians,*" &c.)

Some persons sign themselves from the head even to the feet, to signify mystically that God, having bowed the heavens, descended upon earth. He did, indeed, descend, to raise us from earth to heaven. They next sign from right to left; first, to show that they prefer things eternal, signified by the right hand, to things temporal signified by the left; secondly, to remind us that Christ passed from the Jews to the Gentiles; and, thirdly, because Christ, coming from the right hand, that is to say, from the Father, conquered on the cross the Devil, typified by the left, whence the words, "I came forth from the Father and am come into the world." (John, xvi., 28.) But others signing themselves from left to right justify that formula by the text, "He came from the Father, he descended into hell, and returned to the throne of God." In fact, they commence by making the sign in the upper part, which designates the Father; then they descend below, meaning the earth; then they go to the left, which marks hell, and so re-ascend to the right, signifying to heaven; for Christ thus descended from heaven to earth, and afterwards re-ascended from hell to heaven, where he sits at the right hand of God the Father. Secondly, by doing thus they intimate that we must pass from misery to glory, and from vice, signified by the left, to virtue, whose

* The Latin vulgate of St. Jerome says, "Quis mensus est pugillo aquas, et cœlos palmo ponderavit? quis appendit tribus digitis molem terræ, et liberavit in pondere montes, et colles in statera?"—Edition 1564, Antwerp, *Plantini.* The English version, however, does not admit of this interpretation; it has it, "*and comprehended the dust of the earth in a measure.*"—Ed.

place is on the right, as we read in the Gospel of St. Matthew. Christ, in fact, had passed from death unto life. Thirdly, because Christ raises us, through faith in his cross from things which pass away, to things which endure for ever.*

In the present day, however, an individual making on his body the sign of the cross employs the right hand entirely open, instead of the three fingers only;† but, on the contrary, he uses one finger only, the thumb, to trace the sign of the cross on the forehead, the mouth, and the heart, when (before reading the Gospel, and as a response to the deacon who prepares to chant it,) homage is rendered to God by inclining the body and saying "*Gloria tibi, Domine!*"

These three little signs are made in the form of a Greek cross, and on three different parts of the body, to signify that we believe with the heart and the mind, and are ready to confess with the lips our faith in that divine word about to be spoken.

The thumb is also used by the bishop and priest in tracing the little Greek cross with which the faithful are signed upon the forehead, and other parts of the body, previous to the administration of the Holy Sacrament. And it is with the thumb more especially, and making the sign of the cross, that the priest places on our brow at the commencement of Lent, the ashes which are to remind us, that from dust we came, and to dust we shall return.

* G. Durandus, *Rat. Div. Off.*, lib. v., cap. ii. J. Beleth (*Explicatio Offic.*, cap. xxxix., de Evangelio,) uses almost the same language as Durandus. The translation here given is literal. It is easy to see that much in these explanations is puerile and laboured, but they prove that in the thirteenth century the sign of the cross was made from above to below, and from left to right, or from right to left indifferently. At present the Latin Church signs from left to right, and the Greek from right to left. The pre-eminence of the right over the left, alluded to in p. 181, is here fully developed.

† The early Christians, says M. Cyprien Robert (*Cours d' Hierogl. Chrét.* already quoted), did not sign themselves, as at the present time, with the entire hand, and in such a manner as to embrace half of the body, but simply with the first finger of the right hand, and (as is now done by Greeks and Russians) they traced that sign three times following, in the name of each of the three Divine persons. The Hebrews and Pagans gave the benediction with the three fingers extended: "Digitus tria thura tribus sub limine ponit." (*Ovid.*) For that reason a malediction was uttered with the hand closed.

THE COLOUR OF THE CROSS.

The cross is historical and symbolical, or real and ideal; on the one hand it is an instrument of punishment, on the other, an attribute of glory.

The historical cross, that which the Saviour bore upon his shoulders to Calvary, and upon which he was crucified, is a tree, and consequently its colour is green. On the painted window in St. Etienne de Bourges,* on those of Notre-Dame de Chartres, and of Rheims, on those in the Ste. Chapelle at Paris, and in the miniatures of our illuminated manuscripts, the cross is a tree with the branches lopped off, but still covered with a greenish bark. Sculptures themselves confirm this fact; the colouring now has generally disappeared from those which have been painted, but the round tree covered with bark, and stripped of its branches, is still very apparent, as in the west porch of Notre-Dame de Rheims. In the liturgy and the writings of the fathers, we meet continually with invocations to the cross as a divine tree, a noble tree, the likeness of which no earthly forest could produce, a brilliant and precious tree, a tree covered with leaves, sparkling with flowers and loaded with fruit.†

The green colour was retained even after the cross had been squared and stripped of its bark, in order to be transformed into an actual cross, by the axe of the carpenter. It was no longer a tree, but a thick plank or beam; and yet it is still green. Upon that squared beam, green or blackish branches were traced, making the cross appear like a support, or thick trellis to which the vine is attached, and over which it spreads itself. The grape which yields its juice to nourish man, is the perpetual symbol of Christ, who shed his blood to redeem the world. Vine branches are therefore represented clinging to, and spreading their tendrils over, the cross on which the Saviour is suspended, in the painted

* *Vitraux de St. Etienne de Bourges,* by MM. Martin and Cahier, pl. i., c. iii., &c.

† See the *Vexilla regis prodeunt,* and the *Pange lingua* of Good Friday, attributed to Fortunat and Claudius Mamert. See, the Poems of Prudentius; the works of Peter Damien, &c.

windows in our cathedrals. A window in the Abbey of St. Denis, executed by command of the Abbé Suger, and which bears the two verses transcribed below, is especially remarkable from the beauty of the verdant branches displayed upon the cross.

Probably, and in pursuance of the same metaphor, the little symbolic cross with which the nimbus of Christ is adorned, is occasionally tinged with green. On the painted windows at Bourges, in the subject of the Last Supper, the Washing of Feet, the Taking of Christ in the Garden of Olives, the Descent into Hell, &c., the cross of the nimbus is green. Still, that little cross being almost as frequently white, red, or yellow, the green probably has no symbolical meaning.

As the blood of Christ flowed over the tree of the cross, the green bark just described is frequently painted red: "The cross blushes, and is dyed in the blood of the Lord," writes St. Paulinus of Nola, addressing Sulpicius Severus, and he placed these words, as an inscription beside two crimson crosses.* The blood flowing from the body of Christ, the wine pressed from the grape of which Jesus is the deathless antitype, frequently stained the cross with red; examples of this, from the fourteenth century down to the present time, are much too numerous to be quoted here.†

In regard to the colours of the ideal cross, that also is ideal; red being that of the real cross by metaphorical extension; blue, because the cross is heavenly; white, because white is the most luminous of all colours, and light is the visible image of the invisible Divinity. It is to make the cross a centre of light that it is represented loaded with diamonds and flashing stones; it is to envelope it with

* See above, p. 391, the distich quoted by St. Paulinus. In the *Vexilla Regis*, St. Fortunat exclaims:—

> "Arbor decora et fulgida,
> Ornata regis purpura,
> Electa digno stipite
> Jam sancta membra tangere."

† Read several texts collected by M. Cahier (*Vitr. de S. E. de Bourges*, p. 49, 50), and in which a curious parallel is drawn between the blood and wine, the vine and body of Christ, the wine-press and Calvary.

flashing fire, that it is surrounded with stars as at Ravenna; but even then, the Cross itself is more radiant than the constellations around it, and the Church exclaims, "O Crux splendidior astris!"

THE TRIUMPH OF THE CROSS.

The Cross, like our blessed Saviour himself, is carried in triumph, and representations of that ceremony are very numerous in our religious monuments. We shall be content with mentioning in the first place, a piece of sculpture in the western porch of the Cathedral at Rheims, the Invention of the Cross by St. Helena; and secondly, the painted windows from four churches in the city of Troyes, which represent the legend mentioned in the beginning of this chapter. But in France, the History and Triumph of the Cross are treated in a very summary manner; in Italy they are figured with much greater detail.* In Greece, the triumph, or exaltation of the cross, is the object of a particular predilection. There is not a church in that country without some fresco or oil painting representing that subject. The prescribed arrangement of the Triumph is as follows:—

Below is the earth, above the sky; upon the earth is an immense city filled with palaces and churches, towers and domes; the city is intended for Constantinople, and in the midst of it extends a vast square, which is the hippodrome. Galleries with circular vaulted arcades, and balconies of carved wood, form a kind of framework round the square, which is thronged with people, who also crowd the balconies and galleries. In the centre of the hippodrome is a gigantic

* Pietro della Francesca, born at Borgo-San-Sepolcro, a Roman painter, painted at Arezzo, the Chapel of the High Altar of San Francesco, for Luigi Bacci, a citizen of that place. He there represented the History of the Cross, from the moment when the seed, which produced the tree of which the cross of Christ was made, was placed under the tongue of Adam by his son Seth, until that period when the Emperor Heraclius entered Jerusalem, walking bare-foot, and bearing on his shoulder the instrument of man's salvation. The works of Pietro are of the year 1458, about.—See his life in Vasari, *Lives of Painters.*

pedestal on which stands the Patriarch, wearing a dome-shaped crown, resembling that worn by the Byzantine Emperors, and with a circular nimbus like that of Saints. He is the Patriarch of Jerusalem, St. Macarius; he holds in his two hands a cross, twice the size of a man, which he presents to the adoration of the people. The multitude, composed of the three ranks of society, of soldiers, ecclesiastics, and the people, break forth into acclamations. The ecclesiastics, preceded by the Patriarch of Constantinople, who wears a nimbus like St. Macarius, surround the cross; the soldiers, headed by Constantine, and the Empress St. Helena, are on the right; * on the left is a crowd composed of men, women, children, and old men.

The foot of the cross rests upon earth; its summit reaches heaven. The skies are peopled by a countless crowd. On earth is the Church militant; in heaven shines the Church triumphant. The nine orders of angels are displayed on the left, ranged according to the disposition of St. Denys, the Areopagite. On the right are seen the saints divided into military, ecclesiastic and laic, properly so called. The heavens, by this triple division, have agreement with the earth, but it is with the earth transfigured. Each saint, standing on the clouds, presses against his bosom a little cross, the miniature of that which all adore. In the centre of heaven, but far above both saints and angels, the Trinity shines forth resplendent. The Father Almighty, an aged and venerable figure, crowned with a triangular nimbus, is on the left; on the right is Jesus Christ, adorned with a nimbus, on the cross arms of which is written Ο ΩΝ. In the centre, enveloping both the other Divine Persons, in a radiation of light that

* The Emperor has a nimbus like that of a saint, according to the Greek and Eastern custom, which has been mentioned in the chapter devoted to the History of the Nimbus, p. 131. Constantine is indeed regarded as a saint by the Orientals, equally with St. Helena. Even in the West several martyrologies honour him as a Saint, and keep his festival on the 22nd of May. The Greeks celebrate it on the 21st of that month. In some of the engravings which I brought with me from Mount Athos, St. Helena and Constantine are represented supporting, one on the right hand and the other on the left, a gemmed cross, planted on the globe of the world: both Helena and Constantine wear the nimbus, and bear around their heads one of the following inscriptions:—"Ἡ ἅγια Ἑλένη"—"Ὁ ἅγιος Κωνσταντῖνος."

seems to kindle Paradise, the Holy Spirit shines resplendent under the form of a dove.

Below, at the foot of the cross, is a youthful ecclesiastic, a deacon, bearing a torch with three branches upon one single stem, and which seems as if intended to reflect the glory of the three Divine Persons. Besides this, the heavens are united to the earth by different angels, who, bending towards the top of the cross, incline themselves reverentially before it. These celestial beings form a sort of nimbus to the cross, for they are ranged all around it like a crown. Each of them carries one of the instruments of the passion; one holds the lance, another the sponge, a third the hammer, a fourth the nails, and a fifth the crown of thorns; one exhibits the cord with which the hands of the Saviour had been bound, another the scourge with which his glorious body was torn. Rays of light, emanating from the Holy Spirit and the Trinity, from the nimbus of saints, and from the nimbus and bodies of the angels, direct their bright beams towards the grand cross, which in its turn reflects back their radiance.

Such is the Triumph of Christ; it is constantly painted in Greek churches, and forms one of their most precious ornaments.* The same subject is occasionally represented in the West, but with fewer details and less magnificence. It is not unusual, as in a sculptured example preserved in the Cathedral of Rheims,† to see the cross carried up to heaven by angels; but the *cortège* attending the triumphal tree is far less numerous and indeed less complete. Yet one painting, executed in the time of the Abbé Suger, and now adorning the apse of St. Denis, deserves notice.‡ The subject is simple in itself, but represents, at the same time, the Glorification of the Cross, and that of Christ. There is a green cross to which Christ is attached, historiated in filagree work. The Father holds this cross between his arms, and it

* On the pictures and engravings representing the triumph is written "Ἡ *παγκόσμιος ὕψωσις τοῦ τιμίου σταυροῦ*." I brought with me from Karès, the capital of Mount Athos, an engraving of this remarkable subject.

† In the western porch, above the Invention of the Cross, by St. Helena.

‡ P. 384, note 2, we have noticed this curious subject. MM. Arthur Martin and Charles Cahier mention the painted window of St. Denis, *Vitraux Peints de St. Etienne de Bourges*, as bearing comparison with it.

rests upon a car with four wheels, called in the inscription painted below, a "quadrige." This car is simply the Ark of the Covenant, upon which the cross seems to be planted, and within which are seen the Tables of the Law and the Rod of Aaron. One of the four attributes of the Evangelists appears as if harnessed near each wheel. This curious picture reminds us completely of the Triumph of Christ, in the Church of Notre-Dame de Brou; but the subject there is rather the triumph of the crucified. Besides the presence of the Father, the absence of the Holy Ghost, and the Ark of the Covenant, which forms the pedestal of the cross, give the theme, as here treated, an interest peculiar to itself. The following distich, composed by Suger himself, is appended as an explanatory legend:—

> Fæderis ex arca cruce Xρι sistitur ara;
> Federe majori wlt (*sic*) ibi vita mori.

To note all the triumphs of which the cross has been the object, it would be necessary to recapitulate the various crosses employed as marks of distinction or of reward by different religious, chivalrous, military, and even civil orders, all of which terminate, and are as it were comprehended in our cross of honour.

HISTORY OF THE HOLY GHOST.

The Holy Ghost is the third person in the Divine Trinity. God the Father meditating on himself, by that meditation God the Son was engendered. God the Father and God the Son love one another, and from that mutual love, the Holy Ghost proceeded. Such is the dogma, according to the relation by which the three persons individually are characterised and distinguished one from another, the Father would most properly possess memory, the Son intelligence, and the Holy Ghost love. This is the doctrine adopted by St. Augustine,* and most of the fathers, as will be seen in the subsequent chapter devoted to the Holy Trinity.

In the reciprocal relations of the Divine persons the Holy Spirit is the God of love, but in his relation with man, he

* *De Trinit.*, lib. ix., cap. 6.

appears rather to be the God of intelligence; as the Father is the God of strength and creative power, and Jesus Christ the God of self-devotion and of love. This subject, serious in itself, and of great importance in Iconography, must be treated at greater length.

DEFINITION OF THE HOLY GHOST.

It cannot be doubted that Jehovah, in his relation towards his creatures, is the God of omnipotence and strength. In history Jehovah is constantly described as exerting the divine attribute of power. The historical facts, narrated in the Old Testament seem to be created by the breath of His will, and to unfold themselves under the power of His sword; in the moral precepts of the ancient law, a spirit is heard threatening, which is not that of love. "The fear of the Lord is the beginning of wisdom," says the Psalmist, (Psalm cxi. 10.)* and Solomon echoes those words, adding, "The fear of the Lord is a crown of wisdom."† "Ye shall reverence my sanctuary," says the book of Leviticus, xxvi. 2.‡ The Prophet Isaiah, in enumerating the gifts poured out by the Holy Spirit into the human soul, places fear amongst the principal.§ "Whom the Lord loveth he chasteneth," as St. Paul repeats in the Epistle to the Hebrews.|| If, with the assistance of a concordance of the Old Testament, we were to seek all those texts in which fear is extolled or God declared to punish men by fear and terror, we should be almost terrified at their number.¶ Lastly, everything is

* Initium sapientiæ timor Domini.

† "Corona sapientiæ timor Domini." (*Ecclesiasticus*, i., 18.) These words are inscribed within the cupola surmounting the centre of the transept in the Chapel of Anet: they surround a crown, figured in relief. The cupola appears like the diadem of that elegant building.

‡ "Pavete ad sanctuarium meum."

§ *Isaiah* xi., 1, 2.

|| *Prov.* iii., 12; Epistle to the *Heb*. xii., 6.

¶ In the "Index Biblicus" of a Vulgate printed at Lyons in 1743, we read at the head of numerous paragraphs, in which the analogous texts are quoted, "Timendus est Deus;" "Timoris Dei fructus, utilitas et laus;" "Timoris Dei defectus, causa peccandi;" "Timore punit Deus et terrore." "Timoris Dei exempla." There are 119 texts, relating to fear, and in which terror is erected into a sovereign virtue.

condensed into the terror which the name of Jehovah alone ought to inspire,* and we also, struck with awe by those texts which to us, children of a religion of love, are less familiar than they were to the Hebrews, still exclaim, at compline, or evening prayer, at the termination of the offices for the day, "Lord, turn away thine anger from us."†

There is a wide difference between the spirit of the Jewish religion, which makes us tremble before God like timid children before a severe father, and that of the Christian, every word of which breathes on man the caressing spirit of love. Between Jehovah and Jesus stretches an entire world. The one employs the constrictive power of severity, the other the expansive agency of hope and love. The hand of the ancient law is upraised to punish the slightest fault; the new law is a mother weeping even while she reproves the errors of her children, and caressing while she reproaches them. "The Lord, let Him be your fear and your dread," cried the prophet Isaiah, (Is. viii. 13.) "Beloved, let us love one another," said the dying Apostle St. John (1 John, iv. 7); and in thus saying he repeated, perhaps for the thousandth time, the lesson he had learned when leaning on the heart of his divine friend and master. In fact, while Jehovah sings, "Enter my house in fear," the whole moral teaching of Jesus is comprehended in the following words: "Thou shalt love the Lord thy God with all thy heart, and with all thy soul, and with all thy strength, and with all thy mind; and thy neighbour as thyself."‡ Jesus Christ is love itself; before giving his life for man he said to his disciples, "A new commandment I give unto you, that ye love one another; as I have loved you that ye also love one another. By this shall all men know that ye are my disciples, if ye have love one to another."§ And the Evangelist St. John—he who so well understood the heart of

* "Sanctum et terribile nomen ejus." Psalm cxi., 9. "Holy and reverend is his name."

† "Averte iram tuam a nobis."

‡ St. Luke x., 27. There is in the ancient law a germ of love, but it is chilled by fear; the word of Christ was needed to warm and make it grow.

§ "Mandatum novum do vobis, ut diligatis invicem sicut dilexi vos, ut et vos diligatis invicem. In hoc cognoscent omnes quia discipuli mei estis, si dilectionem habueritis ad invicem." (St. John xiii., 34, 35.)

his adorable master—has left on record the following beautiful words: "When Jesus knew that his hour was come, that he should depart out of this world unto the Father, having loved his own which were in the world, he loved them unto the end."*

To us the Holy Ghost appears as the God of intelligence: he manifests himself to the world to instruct or to enlighten the mind of man. On the other hand, he is, as has been said, the God of love, because he proceeds from the mutual love of God the Father and God the Son. It becomes necessary, therefore, in order to escape the confusion, into which we should otherwise be led by the study of monumental figures and the works of early writers, to establish some well-marked distinction in regard to the Holy Ghost. It must be remembered that the Holy Ghost may be considered in his relation to the other Divine Persons, in which case he is the God of love, proceeding from, and uniting in bonds of love or charity, both the Father and the Son, or else, abstracted from the Trinity, he may be regarded only in his relation to men, and as God of intelligence alone. To study the nature of the Holy Ghost in his relation to the other Divine persons and apart from man, would be to enter the sphere of theology, but to inquire into his actions in respect of men, is the province of history. The theologian considers the Holy Ghost as the God of love; the historian as the God of intelligence.

It must here be observed, and will be more fully proved in the chapter on the Trinity, that the double attributes of love and intelligence, given to one and the same Divine Person, have brought confusion, both into thelogical dogmas, and historical narrative, into religious doctrines and the art, and lastly into argumentative discussion and Iconography. In history, Christ is the God of love, while in theology that character is assigned to the Holy Ghost.

Theology makes the Son of God, or the Word, the God of

* "Sciens Jesus quia venit hora ejus ut transeat ex hoc mundo ad Patrem, cum dilexisset suos qui erant in mundo, in finem dilexit eos" (St. John xiii., 1). Mahomet declared that every prophet had his own peculiar attribute; that the characteristic of Christ was gentleness; that his own was energy.

intelligence, while history attributes to the Holy Ghost every characteristic derived from that quality.

The attributes of the Son and of the Spirit are not therefore clearly defined, nor marked with sufficient exactitude; they float from one to the other; still intelligence appertains definitively to the Holy Ghost, as love does to the Son. When the Holy Ghost loves man, it is with a reasoning affection—a love born in the intellect rather than the heart. This character is sufficiently evident in the worship rendered by the Church to that Divine person.

The Holy Spirit is the God of intelligence always invoked when men would engage in any difficult or arduous undertaking, as in human affairs we consult a man of mature experience and calm reason, before entering upon any difficult or hazardous enterprise. When a judge is about to re-open his tribunal, or a professor to resume his chair, masses are addressed to the Holy Ghost, imploring him to enlighten and inform their minds, so that the one may not be wanting in justice and discernment, nor the other deviate from the truth in instructions. All councils—the grave œcumenical councils, in which are discussed, explained and determined all the tenets of the faith, and the principles of morality—place themselves under the protection of the Holy Ghost. The discussions are opened by a Mass addressed to the Holy Ghost, and the Holy Spirit, constantly present, hovers above the assembly during the conference, to direct their consultations and preserve them from error. The Holy Ghost is invoked at the commencement of all religious offices, and implored to bestow on devout worshippers intelligence to comprehend the offices in which they are about to engage. In the hymn composed in honour of the Holy Spirit, attributed to Charlemagne himself, and which is sung whenever divine enlightenment is especially desired, we find amongst others the following words:—

"Come Creative Spirit, visit the minds of thy faithful servants. Finger of the hand of God, thou dost enrich all lips with eloquence. Kindle light in our senses, that by you we may know the Father and acknowledge the Son, and that we may ever believe thee to be the Spirit of the one and of the other. By your breath the understanding is lighted up, and burns with divine fire."* From the language of these poetical prayers it is clearly seen that they are addressed to the God of intelligence, and would be far less appropriate either to the Father or to the Son. Still, as has been already stated, the Holy Ghost infringes upon the attributes of the Son, or upon love; for we read in the same hymn, and in connexion with the words just quoted,† "Fill with celestial grace the hearts that thou hast created. Thou who art a living spring, fire, and charity, pour love into our hearts."

But these may be considered as the words of an inflamed imagination, as uttered by the ardent souls of the middle ages. Profoundly Christian in faith, and deeply loving in heart, they could not refrain from lending to the coldness of reason something of the warmth of love. Other expressions in the same hymn attribute to the Holy Spirit strength, a quality which belongs incontestably to God the Father. The Holy Ghost is thus implored to give strength:—"Strengthen us by thy power, that we may learn to endure the infirmities of the body; drive back afar our enemies;

* "Veni Creator Spiritus,
Mentes tuorum visita.

* * *

Tu septiformis munere,
Dextræ Dei tu digitus,
Tu rite promissum Patris,
Sermone ditans guttura.

Accende lumen sensibus.

* * *

Per te sciamus da Patrem,
Noscamus atque Filium;
Te, utriusque Spiritum,
Credamus omne tempore.

* * *

Afflante quo, mentes sacris
Lucent et ardent ignibus."

The *septiformis munere* finds its explanation in a passage from Isaiah, of which we have already spoken, and which will be noticed presently with fuller details; it refers to the seven virtues, the gifts or properties of the Holy Ghost.

† "Fons vivus, ignis, caritas.

* * *

Infunde amorem cordibus."

give us forthwith peace; and thus preceding and guiding us, keep us from all error."* Still Charlemagne did not mean to assert absolutely, that power was the exclusive attribute of the third Person, nor did he intend, by the few words which describe him as "inflaming hearts," to imply that love appertained to him only. In his union with the Trinity the third person possesses, in common with the other two, love and strength; but considered in himself, he possesses first, and above all, intelligence. As early as the time of the ancient law, and amongst the Jews, the Holy Spirit is said to have directed and enlightened the mind; for Isaiah,† speaking of the seven spirits which constitute the Divine

* "Infirma nostri corporis
Virtute firmans perpeti.

Hostem repellas longius
PACEMque dones protinus
Ductore sic te prævio,
Vitemus omne noxium."

It is singular to find the warlike Charlemagne, whose life was one perpetual scene of warfare; who fought bloody battles in the north, south, and east of Europe, perhaps, also, in Asia, and the west, thus invoking peace. In the centre of the cupola of the Cathedral of Aix-la-Chapelle, above the tomb of Charlemagne, an enormous crown is suspended; a kind of gigantic luminary of chiselled, gilded and enamelled copper, presented by the Emperor Frederic Barbarossa. The Catholic Cæsar of the Romans (Cæsar Catholicus Romanorum Fridericus), as Barbarossa styles himself in that luminary, caused the eight beatitudes to be engraven below eight great lamps, by which the crown is supported; and we are astonished to find Barbarossa exclaiming, in conjunction with the inscriptions engraven beneath the lamps: "Beati mites, quoniam ipsi possidebunt terram"—"Beati PACIFICI, quoniam filii Dei vocabuntur." The terrible Barbarossa, albeit himself of no very pacific disposition, adds again, at the head of an inscription of eight verses, engraven on the upper part of the crown, and referring to the crown itself:—

"Celica Jherusalem signatur imagine tali;
Visio PACIS, certa quietis spes ibi nobis."

Charlemagne and Barbarossa, as is here seen, both wrote and acted alike.

† *Isaiah*, xi., 1, 2, 3. "Et egredietur virga de radice Jesse, et flos de radice ejus ascendet. Et requiescet super eum SPIRITUS Domini; spiritus sapientiæ et intellectus, spiritus consilii et fortitudinis, spiritus scientiæ et pietatis et replebit eum spiritus timoris Domini." And there shall come forth a rod out of the stem of Jesse, and a branch shall grow out of his roots: and the Spirit of the Lord shall rest upon him, the spirit of wisdom and understanding, the spirit of counsel and might, the spirit of knowledge and of the fear of the Lord.

essence, enumerates them under the following denominations:—

The Spirit of Wisdom,
The Spirit of Understanding,
The Spirit of Counsel,
The Spirit of Strength,
The Spirit of Knowledge,
The Spirit of Piety,
The Spirit of Fear.

All these spirits bear reference to reason, with the exception of the last two, which originate in feeling, and the fourth in strength: but the greater number, four out of the seven, and the first three among those four, the three chief, belong to reason. The evidence of history forcibly confirms the doctrine here set forth concerning the Holy Ghost; for in the most celebrated manifestation of the Spirit, at the Feast of Pentecost, he manifests himself to instruct the ignorant and to enable the apostles to speak and understand all the known languages of the world. Even in the present day the Feast of Pentecost is one of reason rather than of love; for it is the commemoration of the descent of that divine light, which, resting like a tongue of flame upon the heads of ignorant and uninstructed men, conferred on them in a moment the gifts of genius.

It would be easy to prove, by various facts, that it is the office of the Holy Ghost to enlighten the reason rather than to inflame the heart; it will be necessary to name a few, because the part filled by that Divine person in His intercourse with men, ought to be clearly stated and defined. Such matters are of high interest with regard both to archæology and modern art; the past and the future.

The Last Supper being ended, the Saviour, ready for his suffering and death, consoled his Apostles, and announced that he was about to be taken from them; he added, that he would not leave them fatherless, but would send them another protector.* "I will pray the Father and He shall

* "Et ego rogabo Patrem, et alium Paracletum dabit vobis, ut maneat vobiscum in æternum, Spiritum veritatis, quem mundus non potest accipere, quia non vidit eum, nec scit eum. Vos autem cognoscetis eum, quia apud vos manebit et in vobis erit."

give you another comforter, that he may abide with you for ever; even the SPIRIT OF TRUTH, whom the world cannot receive, because it seeth him not, neither knoweth him; but ye know him, for he dwelleth in you, and shall be in you." (St. John, xiv. 16, 17.) Thus Christ, the God of love, was on the point of quitting his Apostles, but the place he held among them was to be filled by the Holy Ghost, the Spirit of truth, the Spirit that teaches, and whom all men must learn to know.

Christ is a father about to part from children already arrived at maturity; and he confides them to the guardianship of an instructor who will enlighten their intelligence, even as he has himself informed their hearts. It was necessary at first, as with children, to open the minds of the Apostles and first disciples, and this Christ had done; now, as adolescent, it became necessary that their minds should be instructed; and to the third person of the Trinity that office was assigned. They are to receive the God of truth, in the place of the God of love, who is taken from them; the Spirit is to succeed to the Son. In fact, not long after the Holy Spirit, under the figure of light-dispensing rays, descended upon their heads, the seat of intelligence. The Spirit of truth, the rays of fire, the illumined heads, and the gift of languages instantaneously communicated, all bear allusion to the intellect; and in them the heart had little share. Having completed our examination of the Holy Scriptures, we turn next to history, both actual and legendary.

During the whole of the middle ages a belief prevailed that the Holy Ghost addressed his ministry more peculiarly to the intelligence, revealing himself to men to enlighten and inform their minds. Gregory of Tours, in the sixth century, asserts that the column of fire, which guided the Hebrews to the promised land, after their departure from Egypt, was the type or figure of the Holy Ghost.* Now the pillar of fire could not, in those burning deserts of Arabia, have been intended to communicate warmth, but was to give light. On the other hand, love is constantly compared to a fire dispensing warmth, and intelligence to a light-giving flame;

* *Hist. Eccl. Franc.*, lib. i.

thus, then, Gregory of Tours declared the Holy Ghost to be more properly the God of the intellect than of the heart—of intelligence rather than of love.

A dramatic and highly interesting legend recorded in the Life of St. Dunstan, archbishop of Canterbury, in the tenth century,* closely shows the nature of the Holy Ghost, and the definition which ought to be given of his attributes. Three men convicted of coining false money had been condemned to death. Immediately before the celebration of mass on the day of Pentecost, the festival of the Holy Ghost, St. Dunstan inquired whether justice had been done upon the three criminals: he was informed in reply, that the execution had been delayed on account of the solemn feast of Pentecost then in celebration. "It shall not be thus," cried the indignant archbishop, and gave orders for the immediate execution of the guilty men. Several of those who were present remonstrated against the cruelty of that order;† it was nevertheless obeyed.

After the execution of the criminals, Dunstan washed his face, and turned with a joyful countenance towards his oratory.‡ "I now hope," said he, "that God will be pleased to accept the sacrifice I am about to offer," and in fact, during the celebration of mass, at the moment when the Saint raised his hands to implore that God the Father would be pleased to give peace to his Church, to guide, guard, and keep it in unity throughout the world, "a dove, as white as snow, was seen to descend from heaven, and during the entire service remained with wings extended floating silently in air above the head of the archbishop."§ The mass being ended, the dove directed its flight towards the south part of the altar, where stood the tomb of the

* St. Dunstan died on the 19th of May, 988. See the *Act. SS. Ord. S. Bened.* vol. from the year 950 to 1000, for the life of that great artist, who was at the same time a famous archbishop. In that volume will be found the legend under consideration, and which were better omitted in the history of that illustrious man; still, the interest attaching to it may excuse its apparent severity.

† "Edictum nonnullis videbatur crudele," says the hagiographer.

‡ "Lota facie, ad oratorium, exhilarato vultu, abiit."

§ "Nivea columba, multis intuentibus, de cælo descendit et, donec sacrificium consumptum esset, super caput ejus [Dunstani] expansis alis et quasi immotis, sub silentio mansit."

blessed Odo, and bending, extended its wings around the two sides of the shrine and appeared to caress it with its beak. Dunstan marvelled at that prodigy. After the mass he retired alone, penetrated with emotion, and weeping at so clear a manifestation of the Divine favour. Having divested himself of the chasuble, and there being no attendant there to receive it, it remained suspended in air during divine pleasure, for fear, lest by falling to the ground it might disturb the meditations of the servant of God.

Thus then the sacred dove, personifying the Holy Ghost, marked in the most striking manner, his approbation of an act of cruelty, or at least of an action thus characterised by several of the clergy surrounding St. Dunstan. The cruelty, however, was, strictly speaking, merely an act of rigorous justice; but the approbation of the Holy Spirit, clearly proves that that Divine person presides over intelligence rather than sentiment. Men would probably have refused during the middle ages, to represent Jesus Christ performing the parts attributed to the Holy Ghost, in this legend, for Christ is the divine representation of love.

During the sixteenth century, in the year 1579, when Henry III. re-organised that order of knighthood which is called "Du Saint Esprit," that distinction was restricted solely to political men, and particularly to our magistrates, that is to say, men of intelligence. In so doing, he carried out the intention with which the order had originally been founded in the year 1352. The order of St. Michael the warrior archangel, was conferred on soldiers only; that of the Holy Ghost, the divine representative of intelligence, was restricted to the chief classes of the civil professions.*

Abelard was a man of intelligence, not of love; a dialectician, a philosopher. Abelard never exhibited any marks of attachment to Heloise; his replies to the letters of that impassioned woman, who had sacrificed herself for him, are cold and indifferent. Besides this, inasmuch as Abelard

* The order of St. Michael was founded in 1496. Three hundred years earlier, in 1163, the military order of the Wing of St. Michael had been founded; this latter was completely absorbed into the order of 1469. Although completely warlike at first, that order was afterwards, under the restoration, conferred on great artists more especially, thus completely reversing the original intention.

was devoted to the Holy Ghost, that he founded in his honour the Monastery of the Paraclete, and caused a figure of the Trinity to be sculptured, in which the Holy Ghost was identical with the Father and the Son, and more absorbed into the other two persons than is permitted by our creed; from these various facts we may conclude that the Holy Ghost is the God of intelligence, and Abelard honoured the third person of the Trinity as responding best to his own temperament and character.

Finally, the testimony of Art fully coincides with the preceding theory. When St. Stephen addressed the Jews that discourse in which the Christian religion is discussed and proved, and which is recorded in the Acts of the Apostles, the youthful preacher was "filled with the Holy Ghost."* There is in the Cathedral of Sens, a fine painted window, closing the open gallery, above which shines the rose window of the south transept, the subject of which is the first Martyr addressing the assembled Jews. The Holy Ghost is there represented under the figure of a white dove with a golden coloured nimbus, displaying its wings above the head of the young teacher. The dove sustains the intellectual power of St. Stephen, by overshadowing him, as it were, with his wings.

St. Catherine (of Alexandria), the daughter of a king, was learned in all the liberal arts; she wished to enter into a controversy with the Emperor Maxentius, disputing by the aid of every species of logic and mode of reasoning, and metaphorical, allegorical and mystical syllogisms, concerning the existence of a single God, the creator, disposer, and regulator of all beings, whether animate or inanimate, of stars, and men, and concerning also the incarnation of his Son Jesus Christ. Maxentius, who could not maintain his ground against a woman so highly gifted, sent into all countries in search of learned men, surpassing all others in worldly science, and capable of entering the lists with that royal lady. Fifty answered his summons and addressed a thousand questions to the saint, who gave them such decisive answers as filled them with mute astonishment and admiration. Catherine, said Jacobus de Voragine, knew every-

* "Cum esset plenus [Stephanus] Spiritu-sancto." (*Act. Apost.* vii. 55.)

thing, whether relating to theology, philosophy, natural science or historical records, and a reference to the legend will show the immense extent of that field of philosophy, which was filled by her science and intelligence.*

The Spirit of God did, in fact, speak in her. In the north aisle of the Cathedral of Freybourg in Brisgau, is a painted window representing a figure of St. Catherine wearing a golden nimbus and crown to mark her character as saint and the daughter of a king; she is sitting like the Virgin in the Cenaculum, in the midst of an assembly of doctors, who are disputing with her. The saint is triumphant in her argument, the doctors confess themselves vanquished, and the Holy Spirit is seen descending on the head of the powerful logician, under the semblance of a white dove, having a golden nimbus stamped with a red cross. Thus far we learn from art in France and Germany; Italy, in her turn, furnishes striking examples to confirm the truth of the preceding facts.

Vasari gives numerous descriptions of pictures in which the Holy Ghost is represented, and in every instance he is given as the Creator of science. Take, for example, a painting in one of the compartments of the vaulting of Santa-Maria-Novella, at Florence; it is the work of Taddeo Gaddi, and the subject, the Descent of the Holy Ghost: "Upon the partition the seven sciences are painted, and below each of them, one of the most celebrated professors, by whom they have been illustrated. The science of Grammar is personated by a woman instructing a child, and immediately below is the figure of Donato, the famous writer. Next comes Rhetoric, and at her feet is a figure with two hands resting upon books, while from beneath his mantle issues a third hand, approaching his mouth. Logic, armed with a serpent hidden beneath her veil, is attended by Zenon Eléate. Below the figure of Arithmetic holding the abacus tables, Abraham, the inventor of that science, is seated. Below

* *Legenda aurea*, "de Sancta Katherina, virgine et martyre." "Katherina, Costi regis filia, omnibus liberalium artium studiis erudita fuit. Per varias conclusiones syllogismorum allegorice et metaphorice, diserte et mystice multa cum Cesare disputavit. Hec autem puella, in qua Spiritus Dei loquitur, sic nos in admirationem convertet (say the learned men who disputed with her) ut contra Christum aliquid dicere aut omnino nesciamus aut penitus formidemus."

Music, who is surrounded by musical instruments, is Tubal-Cain, listening intently to the tones produced by striking an anvil with two hammers. Geometry, recognised by the square and compasses, is above Euclid; and Astrology, holding a celestial globe, above Atlas.

"On the other side, the seven theological sciences are connected with different personages, among whom we remark a pope, an emperor, a king, cardinals, dukes, bishops and marquises. The Pope is Clement V. The centre of this composition is occupied by St. Thomas Aquinas, who was learned in all sciences. At his feet are several heretics, Arius, Sabellius, and Averroës, and around him Moses, St. Paul, St. John the Evangelist, and other saints; the whole surmounted by personifications of the cardinal and theological virtues.*

"In the chapel of San-Domenico, in Santa Caterina de Pisa, Traini (the best scholar of Andrea Orcagna) represented St. Thomas Aquinas sitting, and holding books, from which luminous rays are transmitted to the Christian people surrounding him. A crowd of doctors, clerks, bishops, cardinals, and popes are kneeling near, amongst whom we remark particularly Urban VI. At his feet are Sabellius, Arius, Averroës, and other heretics and philosophers, with their books torn to pieces; while Plato and Aristotle point to the Timæus, and the Ethics. The Redeemer, surrounded by the four Evangelists, occupies the upper part of the picture, and bestows his blessing on St. Thomas, on whom he sends down the Holy Spirit." †

Hence it seems clearly apparent, that the Holy Ghost is the creator, inspirer, and director of science; but if any doubts still remained, they would speedily be removed by Herrade, abbess of Sainte Odile. In fact, a miniature in the beautiful manuscript, already so frequently mentioned,‡

* *Vies des Peintres;* Vasari, "Vie de Taddeo Gaddi." Translated into French by MM. Laclanché et Jeanron, vol. i. pp. 372, 373.

† Ibid. "Vie d'Andrea Orcagna," vol. i.s pp. 387, 388.

‡ *Hortus Deliciarum.* Philosophy is there represented as a human being with three heads, and one single body; the three heads signify Ethics, Logic, and Physics, which, at that period, constituted the grand elements of philosophy, the text runs thus, "Spiritus Sanctus inventor est septem liberalium artium," &c. In the "Bibliothèque communale" of Rheims, a manuscript Bible, of the

represents Philosophy, giving birth to the seven liberal arts, which comprehend every branch of science known in the middle ages. But the Holy Ghost is himself the inventor or creator of the Christian Muses, and he was so represented by Taddeo Gaddi, more than a hundred and fifty years after the time of Herrade.

Herrade says, first in a legend explaining those figures, and next in a running text developing the legend: "The Holy Spirit is the inventor of the seven liberal arts, which are: Grammar, Rhetoric, Dialectics, Music, Arithmetic, Geometry, and Astronomy." Thus then, in all his relations with men, and whenever the Holy Ghost appears, it is in order to give life by his breath, to the intelligence which perceives, to the knowledge flowing from that intelligence, and thence to the memory which is the handmaid of science, and retains what has been discerned by intelligence. It is proved therefore by reference to the concurring testimony of history, allegory, legends, morals, and the arts, writings and monuments, that the Holy Spirit in his relation to man, is indeed the God of reason, and not of feeling.

If in his connexion with the other Divine persons he can be regarded as the God of love, he is, as we see, in his relation to mankind, the God of intelligence; in his character of God, he enlightens and instructs; he does not give

eleventh century probably, presents a similar subject, forming a frontispiece to the Book of Ecclesiasticus. That book opens with the words "Omnis Sapientia." In the O of "omnis," is a miniature painting of the allegory of knowledge or wisdom, both which had the same meaning in the middle ages, as is still the case in our villages; in Champagne and Picardy any one who is *learned* is called *wise*. In the O majuscule, above mentioned, philosophy, (PHYLOSOPHYA) is seated on a throne; she is personified by a woman, wearing on her head a nimbus like that of a saint; she places her right hand on a semi-circle, occupied by Physics (PHISICA); the left on one containing Logic (LOGYCA); the feet on one filled by Ethics (ETHICA). The indiscriminate use in these manuscripts of Y and I is worthy of notice. These three daughters of Philosophy are three veiled women, without the nimbus, and drawn in bust merely. They have little medallions, in which are inscribed the names of the sciences derived from them. Grammar, geometry, and astronomy belong to physics; rhetoric and dialectics are derived from logic; justice, temperance, strength and prudence proceed from ethics. (Vide *Biblia Sacra*, in fol. A, pars 2.)

strength to the mind, nor warmth and tenderness to the heart.*

Fig. 110.—SPIRIT OF INTELLIGENCE, HOVERING ABOVE DAVID.
From a Greek Miniature of the x cent.

* Bibl. Roy., *Psalterium cum Figuris,* Greek, No. 139. On the open book in David's hand is written, "Ο Θϛ ΤΟ ΚΡΙΜΑ ϹΟΥ Τω ΒΑϹΙΛΕΙ ΔΟϹ ΚΑΙ ΤΗΝ ΔΙΚΑΙΟϹΥΝΗΝ ϹΟΥ Τω Υἱω ΤΟΥ ΒΑϹΙΛΕωϹ." It will be

The above plate is made from a miniature in a Greek manuscript; the same from which the miniature of the prophet Isaiah, standing between day and night, was extracted. (Fig. 52.)

David, attended by the Spirit of wisdom and of prophecy, is represented holding a book, on the open leaves of which is written, "O God, give wisdom to the king, and justice to the son of the king."* Both the text and the two personifications of wisdom and prophecy, supporting the throne, bear reference to intellect.

From the wisdom and uprightness of the Spirit, was to be obtained that wisdom (judgment or discernment), which David implored for himself, and the gift of righteousness (justice) which he asked for Solomon his son; the wisdom of whose well-known judgment is still an object of admiration. The prayer of David was graciously received by the Almighty, and the Holy Ghost is seen hovering above the head of the king whom he fills with his gifts. The nimbus surrounding the head of David and of the two allegorical figures, deserves to be remarked. This picture is in fact the apotheosis of intelligence sanctified by the Holy Spirit. The Holy Spirit is the God of reason.

Further, this dogma is found in the following passage from the 1 Corinthians, xii. 7—11, and is well worthy of careful consideration: "But the manifestation of the Spirit is given to every man to profit withal. For to one is given by the Spirit the word of wisdom; to another, the word of

remarked that the *sigma* has in every instance the form of C; the *epsilon* and *omega* are equally archaic. Observe the *fleurs-de-lis* of the tenth century, scattered, together with quatrefoils, over the mantle of David. This reminds me of a crown-fleury of white marble, sculptured on the south façade, outside the principal Church of Chilandari, in the great monastery of Mount Athos. The apse of the Church of Hecatompyli, at Mistra, is also decorated with *fleurs-de-lis.* The manuscript is acknowledged to belong to the tenth century, Hecatompyli appears to be of the thirteenth, and the crown of Chilandari of the fifteenth. I doubt whether, in France, any well-authenticated *fleurs-de-lis* are anterior to the eleventh century, and I believe them to have been an ornament selected accidentally from amongst many others, and adopted by the Kings of France as a blazon about the twelfth or thirteenth century.

* Psalm lxxiv., 1. "Give the King thy judgments O Lord, and thy righteousness to the King's son." The French Bible of Rochelle, 1616, says: "O Dieu donne les jugements au roy, et la justice au fils du roi!" M. Didron always quotes from the Latin Vulgate.—*Translator.*

knowledge by the same Spirit; to another, faith by the same Spirit; to another, the gifts of healing by the same Spirit; to another, the working of miracles; to another, prophecy; to another, discerning of spirits; to another, divers kinds of tongues; to another, the interpretation of tongues. But all these worketh that one and the self-same Spirit, dividing to every man severally as he will."* Moses had already said that the Spirit of God gave the gift of prophecy and the knowledge of the future;† and in the Acts of the Apostles, it had been said in addition, that the Holy Ghost spoke by the mouth of the prophets.‡ This agrees in every point with the text of St. Paul, and the design in the Greek manuscript. St. Peter had reproached Ananias with lying to the Holy Ghost; now falsehood is peculiarly a vice of the intellect. These scattered texts collected by modern science and reflection, group and multiply facts which have hitherto been isolated, and are still too rare; and placing them in a more striking light, enable us to determine that the reign of the Holy Spirit has commenced. What in the middle ages seemed doubtful is now beginning to be determinate, and each of the three Divine Persons, recovers his own peculiar attributes.§

Besides Christian art itself, sometimes pointedly, attri-

* In the same Epistle (Chap. ii., 10, 11) St. Paul says: "The Spirit searcheth all things, yea, the deep things of God." And again, "The things of God knoweth no man, but the spirit of God." This would perhaps be a fitting place to enter on the subject of the sin against the Holy Ghost, a sin which appears to be purely intellectual, unpardonable, and concerning which so much discussion has arisen; but to notice that serious question would entail a very long dissertation, in which monumental archæology has very little part. Besides, a Benedictine treatise, written in German by Martin Gerbert, may be consulted on that point; it was printed in 1767, and is entitled, *De Peccato in Spiritum Sanctum in hac et in altera vita irremissibili.*

† *Lib. Numerorum,* xi., 25, 29. Tertullian (*De Anima,* cap. ii.) says: "Sancti Spiritus vis operatrix prophetiæ."—Act. Apost., xviii., 25.

‡ Acts v., 3.

§ There are three persons in the Godhead. Power is the attribute of the Father, by whom all things were created; love of the Son, by whom all men are redeemed; intelligence of the Holy Ghost, who enlightens all. Such is the explanation given by M. Fabisch, a Lyonnais statuary, in his introduction to the history and philosophy of Christian art. (Vide *L'Institut Catholique,* vol. ii., p. 308, No. de Décembre, 1842.) "L'Institut" is a periodical collection; it is published under the patronage and inspection of M[sgr] de Bonald, Cardinal Archevêque.

butes intelligence to the Holy Ghost, while assigning strength to the Father, and love to the Son.

The following drawing offers an example of this fact, which is of high interest and importance.

Fig. 111.—THE HOLY GHOST, AS THE GOD OF INTELLIGENCE, CARRYING A BOOK. From a French Miniature of the XIV cent.*

God the Father, holding the globe, the attribute of omnipotence and of the creation—of which he is the divine author,—is placed in the centre of this Trinity. The Son, who, in accordance with the scriptures, is sitting on the

* French manuscript, Bibl. Roy., fonds Lavall.

right hand of the Father, holds the cross on which he died, and which is sometimes surmounted by a pelican tearing her breast, that she may supply her little ones with nourishment.* This cross is the symbol of love.

The Holy Ghost, on the left of the Father, is of equal age with the Father and Son, and all three are symbolically covered with the same mantle. The Holy Ghost holds an open book, the attribute of intelligence, and of the same form as the tables of the Law. The book is invariably used to symbolise intelligence, study and science. A quotation from Durandus, given above, leaves no room for doubt on this point. The roll signifies imperfect science, the book perfect knowledge. The book should be given to apostles, and the rouleau to prophets, to mark the degree of knowledge possessed by each.† Here the Holy Spirit is then the source and principle of intelligence, and thus it will henceforth be usually figured.

* See a remarkable drawing in black tints upon silk, in the possession of M. Jules Boilly. This piece of silk, which is 2 mètres 50 centimètres in length, and 70 centimètres in height, was brought from the environs of Narbonne, and must have been executed in Germany. It was no doubt employed as an altar decoration. In the centre, Christ is represented dying; around him stand his mother, St. John the Evangelist, the Christian religion personified, and Isaiah, the personification of the Jewish religion and David. At the foot, a king and queen are kneeling; they resemble the figures of Charles V. of France and his queen, now in St. Denis, and which have been taken, erroneously, for St. Louis and Blanche of Castile. The K of Karolus forms an ornament to the frame. On the right and left of the crucifix are representations of the arrest of Christ in the Garden of Olives, the scourging, the bearing the cross, the interment, the descent into hell, and the appearing to Mary Magdalene in the garden. At the top of the cross, the pelican is seen piercing her bosom. This work is of the fourteenth century, and the execution very remarkable. A pelican is also placed at the top of the cross in many crucifixions to be met with in illuminated manuscripts. The pelican accompanies the crucifixion as the symbol of absolute devotedness; it is seen on the painted windows of the thirteenth century, decorating the chapel at the end of the apse, in the ancient Abbey-church of Orbais (Marne, arrondissement d'Epernay.)

† Refer back to what is said on that subject, p. 274. The subjoined extract is from G. Durandus, and will be read with pleasure. "Ante Christi, adventum fides figurative ostendebatur, et quoad multa in se implicita erat. Ad quod ostendendum patriarchæ et prophetæ pinguntur cum rotulis, per quos quasi quædam imperfecta cognitio designatur. Quia vero Apostoli in Christo perfecte edocti sunt, ideo libris, per quos designatur congrue perfecta cognitio, uti possunt." (*Rat. Div. Off.* lib. i. cap. 3.) ["Because before the advent of

WORSHIP OF THE HOLY GHOST.

The external homage rendered to the Holy Ghost, although less profound than that paid to Christ, still far exceeds that attributed to God the Father. The Holy Spirit is represented by art less frequently than Jesus Christ, but more often than Jehovah.

Many churches and monasteries have been dedicated to the third person of the Trinity, under the name of the Holy Ghost, or that of Paraclete, or Comforter. In Italy, at Florence, we find a church and cloister, which were adorned with paintings by Cimabue.* At Rome, a church and hospital, built and sculptured by Marchione d'Arezzo, under Pope Innocent III.;† at Arezzo an oratory was dedicated

Christ the faith was set forth under figures, and many things were not yet made clear; to represent this, the patriarchs and prophets are painted with rolls, to signify that imperfect knowledge. But because the Apostles were perfectly taught of Christ, therefore books, which are the emblems of this perfect knowledge, are open." From the first book of Durandus, translated by two of the founders of the Cambridge Camden Society.]

* Vasari, *Vies des Peintres;* "Life of Cimabue." The church was rebuilt by Brunelleschi.

† Vasari, *Vies des Peintres;* "Life of Arnolfo di Lapo." This hospital and church (Santo-Spirito-in-Sassia) were in the Borgo Vecchio, (See the "Mémoires de la commission des Antiquités de la Côte d'or," in 4to, tom 1. pp. 3—99: "l'Histoire de la fondation des hôpitaux du Saint Esprit, de Rome et de Dijon," par M. G. Peignot.) The hospital of the Santo Spirito at Rome was built in 1198, by Pope Innocent III.; still this is merely a restoration, for its origin is traced back to the eighth century. On this model, a church, also dedicated to the Holy Ghost, was built at Dijon in 1204, by Eudes III., Duke of Burgundy. A bull of 1241 recapitulates the privileges granted by the popes to the order of the Knights Hospitallers of the Holy Ghost in general. In enumerating the countries, provinces, and towns in which that order possessed lands and hospitals, Dijon, Dôle, Tournus, Besançon and others are named. The Hospitallers of the Holy Ghost wore on their religious habits, as a distinctive mark, a cross of silver, with double branches, resembling the cross of Lorraine. Some examples of that cross are given above, Figs 96 and 98. The form of the double cross of the Hospitallers of the Holy Ghost was revealed by an angel to Pope Innocent III., the founder of the order. The robe worn by the fraternity was blue, the cloak black, and with the double cross. In the hospitals of Rome and Dijon, orphans, foundlings, the sick, poor, and pilgrims were received. The hospital existed as late

to the Holy Ghost, the high altar of which was painted in fresco by Taddeo Gaddi, the pupil of Giotto.* The church of Santo Spirito, at the entrance of Palermo, built in 1173,† is famous in the history of the country, from the event which occurred there and called forth the long meditated vengeance of John de Procida.‡ The Campo Santo of Palermo is a dependency of that church.

At Cobourg, in Germany, is a church named after the Holy Spirit. In France, in the department de la Somme, a chapel belonging to the parish church of Rue, is called Saint-Esprit; an abbey in the same department, founded in 1218, is called " Paraclet-des-Champs.§ The abbey of the Paraclete at Nogent-sur-Seine, is famous from having been founded by Abelard, and the fact that Heloise was its first abbess.||

Abbeys of the Holy Ghost, existed at Beziers and Luxem-

as 1790. In the library of the city of Troyes there is a curious manuscript, filled with drawings, executed by the hand; the text contains a history and description of the above-named hospital of the Holy Ghost, and the drawings present views of all parts of it. At Dijon is a similar manuscript, and the book of M. Peignot is copied from that beautiful work.

* Vasari, *Vies des Peintres,* " Life of Taddeo Gaddi."

† Fasellus says: " Gualterius Panormitanus cænobium S. Spiritus, Cisterciencis ordinis, condidit anno 1173."

‡ It was the custom at Palermo to attend mass in the church of Santo Spirito on Easter Tuesday. On the last day in the month of March, in the year 1282, the natives of Palermo were, as usual, assembled in great numbers in the church. A French soldier named Droet, who had entered the church with the worshippers, insulted a young lady of Palermo, distinguished by her virtues and beauty. Her relations assembled at her cries, and massacred the brutal soldier. The populace, by whom the French were held in detestation, fell upon all who were in the church, and butchered them. The news soon spread through the city, and then began the Sicilian Vespers.—Gally Knight, " Monumental Excursion in Sicily," and *Bulletin Monumental,* de M. de Caumont, vol. v., p. 198.

§ The Abbey above named was for women, and founded by Enguerraud, Lord of Boves: two of the daughters of Enguerraud were the first Abbesses. The Abbey belonged to the Order of Citeaux: it is at present a farm, and few remains of its ancient buildings have been preserved. I am indebted for this information to M. Goze, correspondent of the " Comité des Arts et Monuments," at Amiens. It will be observed that this Abbey of the Paraclete was of the Order of the Citeaux, like that of the Santo Spirito at Palermo.

|| Both the Paraclete of Picardy and that of Champagne Sens were convents of women. Perhaps it was so appointed on account of the name Paraclete, which signifies Comforter. Beneath the wings of the sacred dove Heloise took refuge in her grief and sought for consolation.

bourg; abbeys of the "Sainte Colombe," (the dove, *colombe*, is the symbol of the Holy Ghost) existed in the diocese of Limoges, in the territories of Ardres, near Vienne, in Dauphiné, near Sens, and in the diocese of Chartres.* Thus the third Person of the Holy Trinity, under his twofold appellation of the Holy Ghost and Paraclete, and also under that of "Santa-Colomba," possessed considerable establishments, and churches and chapels, cloisters and monasteries, were dedicated to him.

It will be sufficient to have mentioned the preceding facts, without noticing similar dedications either in England or Spain.† In France two little towns, one in Provence, and another in Gascony, are dedicated to the Holy Ghost.‡ In conclusion, in our Liturgy is an entire service devoted to the honour of the Holy Ghost. Hymns, prose, litanies, and prayers have been composed in his honour; one of the highest religious festivals of the year, Pentecost or Whitsuntide, is consecrated to him, and celebrated in May, the finest season of the year, and in the most beautiful month.

These honours are great, especially when compared with those paid to the Father Almighty, in whose honour no church has ever been raised, no festival instituted. §

* *Monastères de France*, by M. Louis de Mas-Latrie, in *L'Annuaire Historique* for the year 1838.

† M. Cyprien Robert (*Cours d'Hieroglyphique Chrétienne*, in *L'Université Catholique*, vol. vi., p. 266) says: "The first Basilicas, placed generally upon eminences, were called Domus Columbæ, dwellings of the dove, that is, of the Holy Ghost. They caught the first rays of the dawn, and the last beams of the setting sun." I have not been able to verify this fact, nor to discover on what the idea is founded. But if Basilicas built upon eminences were called dwellings of the dove, the name may possibly have been given because doves and wood-pigeons there found shelter, rather than from any reference to the Holy Ghost. This doubt is merely suggested, not affirmed, because, as I repeat, I am ignorant of the facts cited by M. Robert.

‡ The Pont St. Esprit is famous in Provence. The Island of St. Esprit is one of the largest of the New Hebrides.

§ Refer to Note, p. 236, in reference to the different honour paid to each of the three Divine persons. This difference may be explained and justified by history. The Father has never been seen; but the Son, by whom we are saved, and the Holy Ghost, through whom we are sanctified and enlightened, have both made themselves visibly manifest to men. They ought, therefore, to be more frequently represented and more tenderly adored than the Father; it is both more easy and more natural.

As has been already said, a well-known order of knighthood bears the name of the third Divine Person. The order of the Holy Ghost was a privileged order, and reserved to the highest families of the aristocracy; it was founded in 1352, re-organised in 1579, and was in existence as lately as 1830. Those above enumerated, comprise nearly all the honours, either civil or religious, paid to the Holy Ghost. The records of history, and the evidence of art, remain to be explored. Both in historical narratives, and in works of painting and sculpture, the part assigned to the third Person of the Holy Trinity, was unquestionably very glorious.

MANIFESTATIONS OF THE HOLY GHOST.

In sacred history we meet with frequent allusions to the Holy Ghost; he is sometimes mentioned by name, and has manifested himself on several occasions. Certain texts, in which, according to commentators, the Holy Spirit is more or less decisively revealed, will also claim our attention, for the act has seized upon those interpretations and carried out the expositions of the commentators by making the third person visibly present.

In the book of Genesis, God said, "Let us make man in our own image." The plural "let *us* make" here used, has been explained as bearing reference to the council held by the three Divine persons, and it has been asserted that the presence of the entire Trinity, and consequently of the Holy Ghost in person, was intimated by the employment of the plural number;* in the same manner the Trinity had been visibly revealed to Abraham, under the figure of those three young men, for whom the Patriarch prepared a repast, and before whom he afterwards prostrated himself (See Fig. 19). Socinians refuse to admit the plurality of the Divine persons implied in the "faciamus hominem ad similitudinem nostram." God, say they, merely used the plural as would an artist encouraging himself in his work, or a sovereign, who, speaking of himself, never employs the singular; besides, he may simply in thus speaking have

* See a drawing given above, Fig. 6.

addressed an angel, whom he intended to employ in the work of creation. The opinions held by Socinians, have been more or less forcibly refuted by theologians; the latter declared that the three persons of the Trinity were as distinctly revealed in the first chapter of Genesis, by the word "faciamus," as in the third, "Behold the man is become as one of us, to know good from evil;" * or as in the eleventh, where it is written, "Go to, let us go down and there confound their language." †

Whatever may be thought of these controversies, the Holy Ghost certainly appears by name in the third verse of the first chapter of Genesis. "The earth was without form and void; and darkness was upon the face of the deep; and the Spirit of God moved upon the face of the waters." ‡

When God the Father is described as receiving the Son, and placing him on his right hand, we frequently see, at the head of the Psalm cx. § in manuscripts with miniatures, the Holy Spirit hovering above the other two persons of the Trinity, or uniting them by the points of his extended wings; or placing himself by the side of the Father, on his left hand. The prophet Isaiah frequently names him, and even analyses the properties belonging to him; those seven spirits of God which shine around the Messiah, rest upon him, and fill him with their essence. ||

The archangel Gabriel, said to Mary, "The Holy Ghost shall come upon thee, and the power of the Highest shall overshadow thee." (Luke i., 35.)

Subsequently, at the baptism of Jesus Christ, the text is even more precise, for the Holy Ghost appears visibly under the figure of a dove.¶

* "Ecce Adam quasi unus ex nobis factus est." (*Gen.* iii., 22.)

† "Venite, descendamus et confundamus linguam ipsorum." (*Gen.* xi., 7.)

‡ "Spiritus Dei ferebatur super aquas." (*Gen.* i., 2.)

§ "Dixit Dominus Domino meo, sede a dextris meis," &c. "The Lord said unto my Lord, Sit thou at my right hand." See particularly Fig. 78. The Holy Spirit there represented holds a book, as in the preceding example, Fig. 111.

|| "Effundam spiritum meum super semen tuum." (*Isaiah*, xliv. 3.) "I will pour my spirit upon thy seed, and my blessing upon thy offspring." The seven attributes of the Spirit are enumerated in Isaiah xi. 2.

¶ St. Matthew, iii. 16, says: "Ecce aperti sunt ei (Jesu baptisato et oranti) cœli, et vidit spiritum Dei descendentem sicut columbam." (St. Luke adds,

Fig. 112.—THE HOLY SPIRIT AS A DOVE, "MOVING UPON THE FACE OF THE WATERS."
From a French Manuscript of the xv cent.*

"corporali specie" [bodily shape], iii. 22.) "The heavens were opened unto him, and he saw the Spirit of God descending like a dove, and lighting upon him." In looking through the preceding engravings and others to be given hereafter, several "Baptisms" will be found in which the Holy Ghost appears. See especially Fig. 53.

* The miniaturist, misled by a love for the picturesque, has been very

He appears to Jesus, settles upon him, fills him with virtue, and leads him to the desert, to be tempted of the devil. Before quitting the earth, Jesus promises his apostles to send them the Holy Ghost, the Paraclete, the Spirit of Truth.* In fact, "when the day of Pentecost was fully come, they were all with one accord in one place, and suddenly there came a sound from heaven as of a rushing mighty wind, and it filled all the house where they were sitting. And there appeared unto them cloven tongues like as of fire, and it sat upon each of them. And they were all filled with the Holy Ghost, and began to speak with other tongues, as the Spirit gave them utterance." (Acts ii. 1—4.) The above is the most important and complete of all the manifestations of the Holy Ghost; it seems like the Epiphany of the third divine person.

In addition to these historical manifestations there are others which pertain, at the same time, both to history and legends, and which art has been eager to adopt.

Jesus Christ, after having accomplished his mission upon earth and terminated his mournful pilgrimage, re-ascended to heaven, to give account to his Father of everything he had done; in the monuments representing that beautiful scene, the Holy Ghost is generally shown accompanying the Father Almighty in his reception of his Son.

In the history of God the Son we have given a drawing in which the Holy Ghost is sitting by the side of the Father, who gives his blessing to his Son on his return from his terrestrial pilgrimage. The Holy Ghost who holds a

unfaithful to the text. The earth, instead of being without form, void, and covered with darkness, as described in Genesis, is charming in aspect, clad with verdure, and brilliant with light. The little waves over which the Holy Spirit moves, and which in the engraving are rendered merely by little dry black lines, are in the original heightened by lights. The lights on the water of that beautiful stream are glazed with silver, and the water shines like crystal. The manuscript from which the drawing is taken is in the Bibliothèque de l' Arsenal; it is a book of the Hours, of the fifteenth century. *Théol. Fr.*, viii. f°. 3, verso.

* "Et ego rogabo Patrem, et alium Paracletum dabit vobis, ut maneat vobiscum in æternum, spiritum veritatis." "And I will pray the Father, and he shall give you another Comforter, that he may abide with you for ever; even the Spirit of Truth." (*St. John*, xiv. 16, 17.)

book, the attribute of intelligence, also gives his blessing to Jesus.*

After the Ascension comes the Assumption; after the Triumph of Christ, that of Mary: the Virgin Mary being dead, "the Apostles carried her body to the sepulchre, and sat near, as it had been commanded by the Lord. On the third day, Jesus came with a multitude of angels, and saluted the Apostles with that salutation which they knew so well, 'Peace be with you.' The Apostles answered, 'To you, oh Lord, who alone doest great marvels, to you be the glory.' 'What favour and dignity,' asked Jesus, 'ought at this moment to be given to my mother?' And they replied: 'It appears just to your servants, that you who have conquered death, and who reign throughout eternity, should raise up the dead body of your mother, and place her eternally at your right hand.' Jesus consented, and immediately the archangel Michael appeared, and presented to him the soul of Mary. Then the Saviour said these words: 'Rise, my mother, my dove, tabernacle of glory, vase of life, celestial temple, so that your body, which has never been polluted by the approach of man, may not suffer decay in the tomb.' Then the soul of Mary returned into her body, which rose glorified from the tomb. Thus the Virgin, accompanied by a throng of angels, was carried away into the azure abode.† Having ascended into heaven, Mary was there welcomed by the three persons of the Trinity; she knelt at their feet, and was crowned with the crown of a queen and empress." It is at her triumph that the Holy Ghost attends especially in the figured monuments of the fifteenth and sixteenth centuries.‡

* See *ante*, Fig. 78. This subject is extracted from the *Romant des Trois Pélerinages*, a manuscript in the Bibliothèque Sainte Geneviève.

† *Legenda Aurea*, "De assumptione beatæ virginis Mariæ."

‡ These monuments are very common; one of the most curious is that given in the following Figure, and in which the Trinity, as equal in every respect as possible, assist at the coronation of Mary. Is it, as seems probable, the Father, who crowns Mary his celestial daughter? The figure on the right of the Father does indeed appear to be the Son, and the Holy Ghost is on his left hand. It is only by comparison with other similar monuments of the same period, and in which the three Divine Persons are characterised by different attributes, that it is possible to decide that the Father is placing the crown upon the head of the Virgin. A coronation of Mary, in which the

Fig. 113.—THE HOLY GHOST, AS MAN, ASSISTING AT THE CORONATION OF THE VIRGIN. French carving on Wood, XVI cent.; stalls of the Cathedral of Amiens.

To these visible appearances of the Holy Ghost, partly historical, and partly legendary, others must be added bor-

Father, the Son, and the Spirit, are completely distinct, is given, Fig. 126. Were there no monument of that description now in existence, nothing could have been affirmed relative to the distinction of persons; for in the thirteenth, and even in the fourteenth centuries, the Son crowns his Mother, and neither

rowed solely from legends, which are more or less authentic, and have constantly been figured by art.

The first to be mentioned is that relating to St. Joseph. In the apocryphal history of the Nativity of the Virgin, we are told that the High Priest consulted God that he might learn for whom the young virgin, Mary, was destined in marriage. God commanded that rods belonging to all those of the tribe of Judah who were unmarried, should be shut up in the Holy of Holies; and that the designed husband should be known by a white dove's escaping from the staff and soaring towards heaven.

As Joseph extended his hand to receive the rod, a dove escaped from it, white and more brilliant than snow; then, after flying several times round the temple, it soared upwards to heaven.* In several fresco paintings, in various miniatures of manuscripts, and particularly amongst the Italians, a white dove, the Holy Ghost, is seen escaping from the flowering staff carried by St. Joseph, at the time of his marriage with the Virgin.

A sculpture illustrating the presence of the Holy Ghost, at the moment when the Blessed Virgin is giving birth to the Infant Saviour, may be seen on the tympanum of the door, in the north porch of the cathedral at Paris, but is not well authenticated. Probably the Holy Ghost, who resembles a little bird, a humble sparrow rather than a dove, was added in some recent restoration, dating from the Empire.

The Holy Ghost, the muse of truth, the muse of Christianity, has inspired poetry, love and truth, ideas and feelings. In the Greek manuscript it is seen† hovering above the head of David, whom he seems to protect with his two

the Father nor the Holy Ghost pay her that honour. Reasons drawn from the Old Testament may account for that circumstance; Jesus and Mary are compared to Solomon and Bathsheba, and we know that Bathsheba was crowned by her son. (See in the Bibliothèque Royale, Suppl. l. 638. In the third part of that MS. the Son blesses the Mother, whom two angels are about to crown.)

* *Codex Apocryphus Novi Testamenti,* by Fabricius. That subject has been represented on the fine Romanesque baptismal font, in a parish church in the environs of Saintes; antiquarians, being ignorant of the legend, have taken the staff of Joseph for a sceptre, and the dove for an eagle.—See the *Bulletin Monumental,* viii., p. 319.

† See *ante*, Fig. 110.

extended wings; David, whose head is illumined by a large nimbus, listens attentively to the breathings of the Holy Spirit, and collects new songs of praise while holding his psalter open with a verse inscribed upon it. The Holy Ghost is not content with giving inspiration himself to David; the prophet-king is also assisted on the left by the spirit of prophecy, on the right by that of wisdom; two genii, two young women each adorned with a nimbus, symbolic of power no less than of holiness,* one of them holding a roll, the other a large closed book. These two women between them possess the perfection of knowledge; figuratively expressed under its two principal forms by the roll or volumen, and the square book.

St. Stephen, as has been already said, derived his inspiration from the Holy Ghost, who by the mouth of the young deacon, pronounced the discourse recorded in the Acts of the Apostles. The Holy Ghost perches like a tame bird upon the right shoulder of Gregory the Great; the dove holds a discourse with the Pope and inspires him with those noble works which have placed him at the head of the four fathers of the church.†

* The above characteristic alone would suffice to prove the Byzantine origin of the manuscript, or, at least, of the tradition. Let the reader refer to what has been already said on that subject, more particularly at pages 84, 89, and 92.

† Paul Diacre, "Life of St. Gregory" (*Sancti Gregorii Opera*, in fol. Paris, 1705, vol. iv., pp. 14, 15), thus relates the curious legend which is frequently depicted at length in our churches, and is sculptured in the Cathedral of Chartres, on the pier of the confessors, in the arch on the right side of the south porch: "A fideli et religioso viro . . . " (he is speaking of Peter, the deacon of St. Gregory) "fideliter post obitum ejus (sancti Gregorii) nobis narratum didicimus, quod cum idem vas electionis et habitaculum Sancti Spiritus visionem ultimam prophetæ Ezechielis interpretaretur, obpansum velum inter ipsum et eumdem exceptorem tractatus sui, illo per intervalla prolixius reticente, idem minister ejus stilo perforaverit et, eventu per foramen conspiciens, vidit columbam nive candidiorem super ejus caput sedentem, rostrumque ipsius ori diu tenere appositum. Quæ cum se ab ore ejusdem amoveret, incipiebat sanctus pontifex loqui, et a notario graphium ceris imprimi. Cum vero reticebat Sancti Spiritus organum, minister ejus oculum foramini iterum applicabat, eumque, ac si in oratione levatis ad cœlum manibus simul et oculis, columbæ rostrum more solito conspicabatur ore suscipere." In figured representations, the dove is perched on the shoulder of St. Gregory; in the text of the biographer it rests upon the head of the pontiff. The difficulty of representing upon the head of the Pope the dove which lays the

The works of St. Jerome wére written by that saint under the immediate inspiration of the Holy Ghost. Thus, in very beautiful miniatures, a dove is depicted breathing into the ear of St. Jerome rays of intelligence, and the saint writes under the influence of that

gift of eloquence upon his lips, no doubt occasioned the alteration. For every other reason, the dove would be more fitly placed upon the head, the seat of intelligence, as is seen in Fig. 110. The dove whispering in the ear of St. Gregory the Great, reminds us of the text: "fides ex auditu."

* St. Gregory the Great was not the only man directly and visibly inspired by the Holy Ghost under the form of a dove; the incomparable Gregory VII. enjoyed the same distinction, and in his office at the head of the sixth lesson is written: "Dum missarum solemnia perageret, visa est viris piis columba e cœlo delapsa humero ejus dextro insidens, alis extensis caput ejus velare; quo significatum est Spiritus Sancti afflatu, non humanæ prudentiæ rationibus ipsum duci in Ecclesiæ regimine." Saint Ephrem of Syria declared that he had seen a shining white dove alight upon the shoulder of St. Basil the Great, and dictate to that Father the fine writings which are so familiar to us. All this is but an imitation, and ought to be regarded as such, of the Holy Ghost descending in the form of a dove upon the Apostles, assembled in the Cenaculum.

Fig. 114.—POPE GREGORY THE GREAT, INSPIRED BY THE HOLY SPIRIT.
French Statue of the XIII cent., in the Church of Notre-Dame de Chartres.*

inspiration.* It is a singular circumstance that this dove has no nimbus, but the omission must be accidental, as there can be no doubt that it is intended for the Holy Ghost.

Another saint, she who best loved God, but who at the same time best understood and reasoned on her love, was inspired by the Holy Ghost with deep intelligent tenderness, expressed in those fervent and highly intellectual effusions which will invest her with eternal glory. In engravings, therefore, St. Theresa is represented sitting holding the pen, which is to transcribe her immortal thoughts. The saint, whose head is surrounded by a radiating nimbus, raises her eyes to heaven, whence issue kindling rays. Upon one of these rays, the largest and longest of all, is written, "Spiritus intelligentiæ replevit illam;† and the Holy Ghost, descending from heaven behind her in a flamboyant aureole, explains by his visible presence the signification of these words.

Lastly—and in this an admirable task is assigned to the Holy Ghost—he directs the actions of kings. At the consecration of the kings and queens of England, a duke, even at the present day, bears before the sovereign, who is about to receive the sacred investiture, a sceptre surmounted with a dove.

In Montfaucon will be found a design representing Charlemagne carrying likewise a sceptre surmounted with a dove,

Mahomet himself, fully conscious of the credit with which a similar phenomenon would invest his doctrines, taught a pigeon to perch upon his shoulder, and the bird would remain there for several hours. The Arab prophet made that tame dove pass for a celestial messenger, commissioned to reveal to him the pleasure of the Almighty. The dove was regarded, even amongst Pagans, as a medium of instruction, an organ communicating the will of Deity. From the summit of the oaks of Dodona, doves prophesied of the future.

* MS. de la Bibl. Roy., *Biblia Sacra,* No. 6829,* close of the fourteenth century. The subject is engraved by Willemin in his *Monuments Inédits.*

† If the Holy Ghost had been the God of love, St. Theresa, the beloved of God, would undoubtedly have been the object of his inspiration. Yet the inscription intimates that he imparts intelligence, not love. The Holy Spirit enlightens and does not warm St. Theresa: "Accendit lumen sensibus."

---

* This is called the *Bible Moralisée:* for a full account of this beautiful MS. see *Les Manuscrits François de la Bib. Roy.*, by M. P. Paris, vol. ii. p. 18. No. 6829[2] Bibl. Roy. is of a similar character, and by the same hand, but the miniatures not so highly coloured.—*Editor.*

which is evidently intended to symbolise the Holy Ghost.* If the sceptre be regarded as a staff to assure the steps of the sovereign, the dove is a spirit to direct his course.

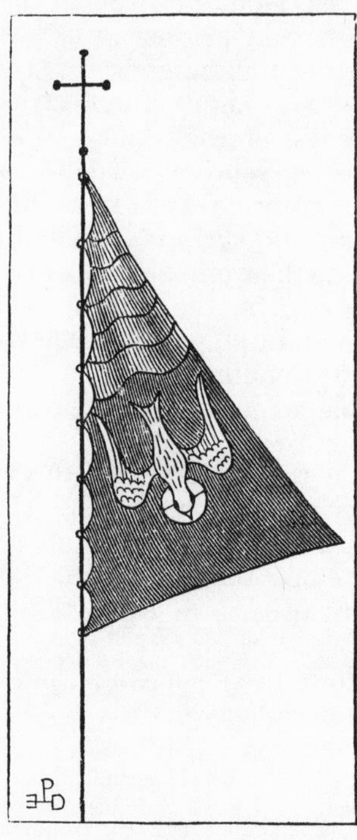

Fig. 115.—THE HOLY GHOST, AS A DOVE UPON A STANDARD.

French Miniature, xv cent.; Bibl. Roy., Heures du Duc de Berri.

Below is a divine dove embroidered on a standard, which is at the same time religious and military; religious from the cross, by which the shaft is terminated, and military in its form. The dove descends from heaven, which is figured by the embroidered undulations in the upper part of that warrior veil, and descending to earth hovers above the battalions, who are about to engage.

The above standard is in the hands of a personified figure of the Christian religion, or the church, preparing to subdue Paganism and the synagogue.

At the ceremony of the consecration of the kings of France, after the rite of unction, white doves were let loose in the Church, indicating, we are told, that as the captive birds regained their liberty, so the coronation of the king restored independence to the similarly captive people. This explanation, however, appears to me very unsatisfactory; the people did not, in fact, lose liberty by the sovereign's death, nor did they recover it through the consecration of his successor. I am rather disposed

* *Monum. de la Monarch. Franç.* I cannot affirm that this engraving is worthy of full credit; but in the tomb of Philippe le Bel, at St. Denis, violated in the year 1793, a golden sceptre was found, five feet in length, and terminated by a tuft of foliage, upon which was represented a bird, made of copper, and gilded like the sceptre. Vide M. de Chateaubriand, *Génie du Christianisme,* vol. iv., Notes et Éclaircisse, p. 442.

to view this custom as conveying an idea analogous to that of the sceptre on which the Holy Ghost rests. The Holy Ghost, the divine doves, took possession of the cathedral, as the king, after consecration, became gifted with understanding. The multitude of doves let loose in the church, signified, perhaps, that the king was just endowed with all the gifts of the Holy Spirit, and that if one or the other perished in him, so great was their number, that some must invariably be left. Each gift of the Holy Spirit is symbolised by a dove, as will be shown in several examples; the numerous doves at the ceremony of the consecration, may therefore be intended as images of the many virtues of royalty.*

THE HOLY SPIRIT AS A DOVE.

Spiritus in Latin, and Πνεῦμα in Greek, signifies breath and breathing; from the Latin *Spirare*, we have derived the word respire. The Spirit, therefore, is air put in motion; in nature, it is wind; in man, the soul; in both, life and movement.

Motion and rapidity are then the essential properties of the mind; when, therefore, men desired to represent under a visible form that divine and viewless spirit, by which all nature is animated, the mind, naturally reverted to that living being, which is in the highest degree endowed with velocity and activity of movement. The bird in one moment rises from the earth and soars upwards into the expanse of heaven, where it vanishes from our sight; it transports itself from country to country, with a facility equalled only by its speed; it traverses in a moment the largest tracts of space, in all their height and extent. The bird, in the organic kingdom, was necessarily selected as the image of mind, or the spirit, which is breath set in motion, rapidity vivified.

* At the consecration of Charles X. in 1825, after the enthronement, a large number of doves were let loose in the Cathedral of Rheims. Many of them burnt their wings in the numberless torches lighting the church; I received one which fell dead into my arms.

Ornithological forms have been employed by Christianity, not merely as expressive of swiftness and velocity, but of spiritual nature, and the incorporeal essence. The second idea is, however, correlative with the first, for the soul is as buoyant as the body is weighty. Angels, bodiless spirits, are represented with wings on their shoulders: they have always two, sometimes six, as is the case with the Cherubim and Seraphim.

Fig. 116.—ANGEL OR CELESTIAL SPIRIT, WITH SIX WINGS.
Painting on Wood, by Perugino.*

Not only are angels figured with wings on their shoulders, but sometimes placed on wheels figurative of swiftness, or upon wheels which are both winged and flamed, and thus made to express the extreme of velocity. Nothing is swifter than light. The following tetramorph (the four attributes of the Evangelists united in one single body) with its triple wings, of long, powerful, and numerous feathers, is the figure or type of unparalleled velocity, and still further heightened by the winged and fiery wheels on which that mysterious symbol is placed.

Acting on the same principle, but giving it a more extended application, artists have lent the wings and form of a bird to allegorical figures created by their imagination. By Pagans, as well as Christians, the wind has generally been personified by a head, blowing puffs of winds, and violently agitating a pair of wings joined to the neck. Air itself has been represented under the form of a young man, vigorous, naked, holding beneath his feet and in his arms the four winged winds, which belong to the four cardinal points; the Air has two powerful eagles' wings attached to his shoulders, signifying the swiftness with which it flies, and passes from calm to tempest.† Amongst the ancients as

* The picture containing the above seraph is at present in the Church of St. Gervais, at Paris; the subject of it is the Father, surrounded by celestial spirits.

† See at the head of a manuscript in the *Bibliothèque Communale* of Rheims (Exceptiones de Libro pontificali), a superb drawing on parchment

well as the moderns, wings are given to Fame, "that subtle evil of unparalleled rapidity, and which, swift alike by feet and wings, is nourished by movement, and gains strength on her course."* By virtue of the same symbolism, Victory, like Mercury, who is the celestial messenger, bears wings on her shoulders, and sometimes also on the head and feet; Victory without wings was an exception, consecrated by a temple existing in the city of Athens, on the summit of the Acropolis.

The middle ages, faithful to the ideas of paganism,

Fig. 117.—WINGED TETRAMORPH, BORNE ON WINGED AND FIERY WHEELS.
Byzantine Mosaic, of the XIII cent.†

representing the air winged, holding under his feet and in his hands the four heads, also winged, of Zephyr, Auster, Aquilon and Eurus. Outstretched and powerful wings are seen on the winds painted in the pastoral of St. Gregory, which in 1836 was preserved in the bishopric of Autun, where I had an opportunity of examining it. Upon the Lavatory, *lavabo*, brought from the Abbey of St. Denis, and now placed in the Ecole des Beaux-arts, Jupiter, Diana, and Aer are sculptured in high relief; each has two wings on the head, fixed near the ears. This curious monument is of the thirteenth century.

* Such is the language of Virgil (Æneid iv.) in his description of Fame, from which we shall borrow only the following:—

> "Fama, malum quo non aliud velocius ullum
> Mobilitate viget, viresque acquirit eundo."

The ancients also represent the thunderbolt with wings.

† This mosaic is at Vatopedi, one of the principal convents of Mount Athos.

which it completed and carried to perfection with singular felicity, always regarded wings and ornithological forms as attributes of rapidity. Consequently, the angel or SPIRIT of youth, whom nothing can fatigue, and whose course nothing can arrest, is properly represented winged. In fact he is thus seen in a manuscript from which several subjects have already been borrowed.*

Fig. 118.—THE SPIRIT OF YOUTH.
From a French Miniature of the XIV cent.

The Pilgrim, who is in the vigour of age, meets Youth, with green wings, the colour of hope, on his feet. Youth

* Romant des trois Pélerinages, in the *Bibliothèque de Sainte Geneviève*, p. 79.

has fair hair, a blue robe; he carries the pilgrim on his shoulders; and says to him while crossing the sea:

"J'ai nom Jeunesce la légière,
La gileresse, la coursière,
La sauterelle, la saillant,
Qui tout dengier ne prise un gant.
Je vois, je viens, je sail, je vole,
Je espringalle et carolle.
Mes piés me portent où je veuil
E eles ont; tu les vois bien à l'euil.
Bail çà la main, je veuil voler
Et par la mer te veuil porter." *

There is a surprising rapidity in this poetry of the fourteenth century.†

The Church, that abstract generalisation of all Christians, that society, animated by the Holy Ghost, has, like the Holy Ghost been assimilated to a dove. The Pope likewise, who is the vicar of God and director of the Church—the Pope who ought rather to be an angel than a man, and spiritual rather than material, has been allegorised and endowed, up to a certain point, with the form of a bird. A few observations on the symbolic figures of the Church and the Pope will complete all that remains to be said concerning the Holy Ghost.

In the Manuscript of Herrade, the Church is represented under the form of a dove, resembling the figure of the third Divine Person of the Trinity, but with some distinguishing

* "I am called Youth, the nimble,
The tumbler,[1] and the runner,
The grasshopper, the dasher,
Who cares not a glove for danger.
I see, I come, I bound, I fly,
I sport and caracole.
My feet they bear me whither I will,
They 've wings; your eyes may see them.
Give here thine hand, with thee I 'll fly
And carry thee over the sea."

† The French poem, in the *Bibliothèque de St. Geneviève,* is one of the most curious books extant, both as to text and miniature.

1 "Gileresse" means the active gentleman who plays the fool on a stage in a fair.—Edit.

features. The fore part of the body is silvered, the back part gilded. The dove has wings on its head, on its shoulders

Fig. 119.—THE CHURCH AS A DOVE WITH SIX WINGS.
A Franco-German Miniature of the XI cent.

and its feet; these triple wings, bear it as swiftly as thought or an uttered word, from one extremity of Christianity to another. Everything here is emblematic, and the text explaining the miniature is as follows: "This dove signifies the Church, which by its sacred eloquence is sonorous as silver; she is adorned with learning and wisdom, that she may impart those gifts to others. This dove is of gold, because she is radiant with charity; the pale or red gold with which the lower part of her back is covered, signifies the love of the faithful."*

* *Hortus Deliciarum.* "Hæc columba significat Ecclesiam, quæ per divinam eloquentiam quasi argentum est sonora et erudita, et sapientia exornata

Dante has represented, not the Church, but the Pope under the form of a bird. That bird, however, is not a dove, but a griffin, a fantastic creature half eagle and half lion. The griffin is an eagle in the upper part, a lion in the lower. Although Dante speaks of a griffin, not a dove, the fact deserves notice here from its connection both with the idea which assimilates the Church with a dove partly of gold and partly of silver, and also with that by which the Holy Spirit is figured as a dove, which is in colour nearly monochrome. The dove of the Church, in Herrade, forms a transition between the griffin of Dante and the dove of the Holy Ghost; the nature of the griffin is twofold, and the Church shines with a twofold colour; the dove of the Holy Ghost is winged like the griffin and the dove of the Church, but it has one single nature only, and is, therefore, of one colour.

The description given by Dante, in the Purgatorio, is as follows:—

The poet describes the triumph of the Church, arranged almost like that depicted in the church of Brou and described above. The candlestick with seven branches is at the head of the procession followed by the twenty-four elders of the Apocalypse, and the four attributes of the Evangelists. Next to them is a car with two wheels, symbolic of the Church rolling onwards, supported by the Old and New Testament. "On two wheels it came, drawn at a gryphon's neck," * and escorted on the right by the three theological, and on the left by the four cardinal virtues. Next in order, and behind the car, are the twelve apostles, preceded by St. Luke and St. Paul.

ut alios erudiat. Hæc et columba est aurea, id est caritate splendida; et posteriora dorsi ejus sunt in pallore vel rubore auri, id est caritas fidelium." These expressions seem to be taken from the 68th Psalm, 13. "Si dormiatis inter medios cleros, pennæ columbæ deargentatæ, et posteriora dorsi ejus in pallore auri." "Though ye have lien among the pots, yet shall ye be as the wings of a dove covered with silver, and her feathers with yellow gold."

* The gryphon, the "mystic shape that joins two natures in one form," as he is called by Dante, draws the car to which he is harnessed, and

"He above
Stretched either wing uplifted 'tween the midst
* * * *
And out of sight they rose. The members, far

The mystical bird of two colours is understood in the Manuscript of Herrade to mean the Church; in Dante, the bi-formed bird is the representative of the Church, the Pope. The Pope, in fact, is both priest and king; he directs the souls and governs the persons of men; he reigns over things in heaven. The Pope, then, is but one single person in two natures, and under two forms; he is both eagle and lion. In his character of pontiff, or as an eagle, he hovers in the heavens, and ascends even to the throne of God to receive his commands; as the lion or king he walks upon the earth in strength and power.*

As he was bird, were golden; white the rest,
With vermeil interveined."

He is "a mystic shape, that joins two natures in one form." And when the eyes of Beatrice

"Stood
Still, fix'd toward the gryphon, motionless.
As the sun strikes a mirror, even thus
Within those orbs the twyfold being shone;
For ever varying, in one figure now
Reflected now in other. Reader! muse
How wondrous in my sight it seem'd, to mark
A thing, albeit steadfast in itself,
Yet in its imaged semblance mutable."

Cary's Dante, *Purgatory*, c. xxix., l. 105, and xxxi., l. 119.

* Some commentators of Dante have supposed the griffin to be the emblem of Christ, who, in fact, is one single person, with two natures; of Christ, in whom God and man are combined. But in this they are mistaken; there is, in the first place, a manifest impropriety in describing the car as drawn by God as by a beast of burden. It is very doubtful even whether Dante can be altogether freed from the imputation of a want of reverence in harnessing the Pope to the car of the church. Finally, the Triumph painted on the window of Notre Dame de Brou, exhibits the Church personified by its four great dignitaries, the Pope, the Cardinal, the Archbishop, and the Bishop, who push on the wheels of the car of the Church. That motive is analogous in principle to the griffin of Dante. As to Christ, he is borne in triumph on the car; as one triumphant, he directs but does not draw. Lastly, in the manuscript of Herrade, the Church is symbolized by a bird of two colours, and the Pope is but the living representative of the Church: he is the incarnation of the Church. Between the bird of Herrade and the gryphon of Dante, the analogy is complete. Commentators have been misled by the twofold nature of the gryphon, but that difficulty is removed by recollecting that the Pope resembles the eagle in his spiritual character, and in his temporal authority the lion. The Pope is one person, but of two natures and two distinct forms. Thus considered, the allegory of Dante becomes clear and intelligible.

The dove, amongst birds, from its gentle and loving nature, in the first place, and in the second, from the purity of its plumage, has been preferably selected as the image of the Holy Ghost. Indeed, a white dove is regarded, both in historical narration and in works of art, as the impersonation of the Spirit of God—a divine breath, a brilliant and unsullied symbol of the Trinity. We are told in history that the Spirit of God descended, in the bodily shape of a dove, upon the head of the Saviour immediately after his baptism by St. John.* The Holy Ghost is almost invariably figured in works of art, under the semblance of a dove, as has already been shown in several examples given above,† and as will be seen in many to be hereafter given.

In particular legends the divine Spirit, or the Holy Ghost, is described as incarnate under the figure of a dove; the spirit of man, or the soul, appears also under that form. Abundant evidence may be found in our legends, of the Holy Spirit having made himself manifest under the semblance of a dove. The following are taken from writings of various epochs:—

In Gregory of Tours, we read,‡ "While the pupils were singing psalms in the Cathedral of Trèves, a dove descended from the vaulting, and flew sportively round the youthful Aredius, who was being brought up and educated by the Bishop Nicet. The dove rested upon his head, intimating thereby that he was already filled with the Spirit; she afterwards descended upon his shoulder. When Aredius returned into the bishop's cell, the dove followed and entered with him, and for several days refused to quit him. Aredius returned afterwards to Limoges, that he might console his mother, to whom he alone was left."

At the consecration of Clovis, the divine dove presided actually over the Christian destinies of France. Clovis and the bishop of Rheims, St. Remi, repaired in procession to the baptistery, where the chief of the Franks was to be consecrated king and made a Christian. "When they arrived

* Et descendit Spiritus Sanctus corporali specie, sicut columba in ipsum (St. Luke iii., 22.) "And the Holy Ghost descended in a bodily shape like a dove upon him."

† Figs. 21, 40, 53.

‡ *Hist. Eccl. Franç.*, vol. ii., p. 136, of M. Guizot's translation.

there, the priest, bearing the holy chrism, was stopped by the crowd, and could not reach the sacred font. But a dove, whiter than snow, brought thither in her beak the 'ampoule'* filled with chrism sent from heaven. St. Remi took the vessel and perfumed with chrism the baptismal water."† "In the same country, at the distance of twenty kilomètres from Rheims, stood the celebrated abbey of Hautvillers, rendered illustrious in modern times by Thierry Ruinart; it was built according to the plan which the Holy Spirit, assuming the form of a dove which was always as white as snow, traced in his flight."‡

With regard to the souls of the saints, the immortal spirits of men, they also ought to appear under the form of doves, for the soul is made in the image of God. In a monastery at Redon in Brittany, a child, dumb from its birth, implored God to heal its infirmity. One day when he was in the field, keeping the cattle of the monks, he was overpowered by sleep. "On a sudden he was enveloped in a wondrous light coming from the East. In the midst of that light there appeared to him a dove of snowy whiteness; it touched his lips, and caressed his face, saying to him, 'I am Marcellinus.' The child arose healed, and related with his own lips what he had seen and heard.§

One dove only is mentioned in the preceding legend: in that following we have a troop seeking a sister soul which is about to leave the earth. "Duke Louis of Thuringia, the husband of St. Elizabeth of Hungary, being on the point of expiring, said to those around him: 'Do you see those doves more white than snow?' His attendants supposed him to be a prey to visions; but a little while afterwards he said to them, 'I must fly away with those brilliant doves!' Having said thus, he fell asleep in peace. Then his almoner Berthold, perceived doves flying away to the East, and

* The "ampoule" is a *phial* of white glass; the original vessel was destroyed in 1793, An. 2 of the Republic.—Ed.

† *Flodoard.* History of the Church of Rheims, liv. i.

‡ *Act. SS. Ord. S. Bened.*, vol. ii., année 685. "Vie de S. Berchaire, Abbé d'Hautvillers.

§ *Act. SS. Ord. de S. Bened,*, IVe. siècle bénédictin, 11e part de 855 à 900, p. 216. "Et ecce repente circumfulsit eum lux immensæ claritatis ab oriente; et in medio luminis apparuit illi quasi columba niveo candore, tetigitque os ejus et protexit faciem, et dixit ei, Ego sum Marcellinus."

followed them a long time with his eyes."* An Englishman who was present at the death of Joan of Arc, declared in a written deposition to that effect, which is still preserved, that he had seen a dove fly from the mouth of Joan with her last sigh and rise to heaven.† The divine dove appeared at the baptism of Clovis, the founder of the monarchy, and a similar dove escaped from the heart of Joan of Arc, by whom the same monarchy was restored when on the verge of ruin.

THE COLOUR OF THE HOLY GHOST REPRESENTED AS A DOVE.

With regard to the colour of the divine dove, it is always that of snow, which (as is positively affirmed by the text) it surpasses in brilliancy and whiteness.

This dove being the symbol of God, we naturally expect

* M. le Comte de Montalembert, *Vie de Sainte Elisabeth.* The author quotes Berthold, MS. Life of the Duke Louis : "Videtis-ne columbas has super nivem candidas? Oportet me cum columbis istis splendissimis evolare. Vidit easdem columbas ad orientem evolare." The beautiful legend of St. Polycarp, who was burned alive, is well known, adds M. de Montalembert ; his blood extinguished the flames, and from his ashes there rose a white dove, which flew towards heaven. A dove was seen issuing in the same manner from the funeral pyre of Joan of Arc. M. Cyprien Robert (*Cours d'Hierogly. Chrét.*) says, in speaking of the dove : "This bird is an emblem most frequently met with upon primitive sarcophagi. It is there represented carrying in its beak a branch of palm or olive, or piercing grapes, figuring thereby the souls of the faithful, which fly away in their innocence, dropping blood like costly wine upon the earth. Thus the soul of St. Reparata, Virgin and Martyr, who had refused to offer sacrifice to idols, is seen rising in the form of a dove from her decapitated body. The same thing is related of St. Potitius, and the bishop St. Polycarp, both of whom were beheaded, and from their blood arose a bird as white as snow, which flew with rapid wing to heaven. The Acts of the Martyr St. Quentin say, with a suavity of language and an impulse of faith that is very charming : 'Visa est felix anima velut columbâ, candida sicut nix, de collo ejus exire et liberissimo volatu cœlum penetrare.' In those rude spirits, still shrouded in the darkness of idolatry, the immortality of the soul, and its surviving the body, was thus made intelligible ; and subsequently, when anthropomorphism crept into the art, the soul was sometimes figured by a little child, issuing from the mouth of the deceased." M. Robert might have said *very frequently*, and even *almost always*, instead of *sometimes*, so common during the middle ages was the custom of representing the soul under the form of a naked child.

† M. Michelet, *Histoire de France,* vol. v., p. 176.

to find it charged with that colour or tincture in which the hues of all the virtues are symbolically united.* The beak and claws are generally red; but this is natural with white doves.† The nimbus on its head is almost always of a golden yellow, and divided by a cross which is frequently red,‡ but sometimes black.§ In the Cathedral at Auxerre, the field of the nimbus is red, and the branches of the cross are of gold.|| But I do not believe that any archæological characteristic is to be gathered from the difference of colour; it can only be observed that the richest and most resplendent hues have been generally preferred.

It has been seen that light formed an integral part of all divine figures; and that God the Father, and the Son, being considered as the sources of light, were clad in radiance, and surrounded by an atmosphere of most dazzling brightness. It was therefore indispensable that the Holy Ghost, being God, co-equal with the Father and the Son, should be represented as equally resplendent in appearance. We are told by Ermold le Noir, the historian of Louis le Débonnaire,¶

* According to some early writers on symbolism, every virtue had its own emblematic colour, and white, the colour of light, being, as we are told by writers on optics, produced by the blending or combination of all the seven prismatic hues, is with peculiar propriety employed as symbolic of that union of every virtue with the most exalted intelligence, which exists in the person of the Holy Ghost.—*Translator.*

† M. le Docteur Comarmond, Librarian of the Palais Saint Pierre, at Lyons, is in possession of a Byzantine manuscript, dating from the tenth or eleventh century, and brought originally from the Grande Chartreuse. The manuscript is filled with beautiful miniatures, and covered with plates of ivory, curiously carved. In the scene representing the baptism of Christ, the Holy Ghost appears under the form of a white dove, with red beak and claws, and a few black spots on the back and wings.

‡ Instances of this are too frequent to be cited; it will suffice to observe that doves having a red nimbus with a golden cross are sometimes met with, but the reverse is most common.

§ Painted window of the fourteenth century, in the south aisle of the Cathedral of Freyburg, in Brisgau.

|| Painted window of the thirteenth century, in the passage behind the Sanctuary. The Holy Ghost is there seen hovering between the waters. An engraving of the Holy Spirit, taken from this window, is given at Fig. 129.

¶ Ermoldus Nigellus. (*Collection des Historiens de France,* by M. Guizot.) This divine dove, which was equal in size to an eagle, reminds me of an ivory coffer belonging to M. Michéli, and brought from the Abbey of St. Gall; the Holy Ghost is there carved under the form of his winged symbol. He has a cruciform nimbus, and is standing facing the spectator in the form of an eagle,

that "The guardianship of the church consecrated to the Virgin Mary* was formerly confided to Theutram . . . . One night he saw the temple filled with light like that of the sun, and resembling the beams shed forth by that luminary on the serenest days of summer. Springing from his bed he endeavoured to discover the source of those dazzling streams of light, which seemed to fill the sacred edifice. A bird of the size of an eagle was covering the altar with its extended wings, but that bird was not of terrestrial birth. His beak was of gold, his claws of some material more costly than precious stones; his wings emulated the azure of the sky, and his eyes sparkled with celestial light. The holy priest, seized with astonishment, dared not encounter the glance of the bird, but he contemplated with admiration his wings and body, and, above all, marvelled at his sparkling eyes. The bird remained upon the altar, until the moment when the three crowings of the cock were heard, summoning the monks to matins. Then he took flight, and the window opposite to the altar opened miraculously of itself, to give him space to pass, and quit the temple. Scarcely had the dove risen in his flight to heaven when the light disappeared, proving by its eclipse that that bird was an inhabitant of the kingdom of God."

This Spirit, which carried with it its own light, and revealed by that symbol his celestial, or perhaps even his divine origin, resembled those doves of enamelled or gilded copper, which were formerly suspended over altars, and attached by a little chain to the vaulting of the church. The interior of the dove was hollow, and the sacred elements were inclosed in it. The dove served for a tabernacle, and Jesus was contained within it, as he had been previously in the body of Mary, the bride of the

which it resembles also in size; the wings are extended, and droop abased upon a disk, which is slightly concave. A hand, extended from the clouds, points towards the gigantic dove. The hand is that of God, but instead of being placed on a cruciform nimbus, three rays or jets of light emanate from it. The dove is adored by four angels. This coffer belongs, undoubtedly, to the tenth century; the poem of Ermold was written in 826; and both in the poem and on the coffer the dove bears the form of an eagle. It appears to have diminished in size from century to century, and at the close of the middle ages is no larger than a large sparrow.

* The Cathedral of Strasbourg, dedicated to Notre Dame.

Holy Ghost, as she is called in sacred scripture. In cabinets of Christian antiquities similar divine doves, formed of metal, are sometimes found. The orbit of the eye is encrusted with rubies or other precious stones, the beak is of gold or copper, with gilded claws and feet, the head and breast are encrusted with red enamel, the blueish green and white enamel curves of the wings all remind us of the golden beak, the luminous eyes and azure wings of the celestial Spirit seen by Theutram.*

Except where the material of which the dove was formed was opposed to it, or where the imagination, as in the case of Theutram, suggested new forms and colouring, the divine doves were always white, lustrous, and differing very slightly from natural doves in size. Yet, at the moment when the heaven and the earth, having just been created, present still only a bare and formless chaos, the Holy Ghost, moving upon the face of the water, is as black as the darkness covering the face of the abyss. For God had not yet made the light, and the intense gloom of the darkness is well conveyed by the idea of its eclipsing even the light of the Holy Spirit.† The white colour assumed by the Holy Ghost bears yet higher import, from the fact of its being symbolic. In Persian antiquity two genii, the one good and the other evil. Ormuzd and Ahriman contend for and partition the world between them. One of these gods presides over virtue, and reigns during the day; the other one, over evil, and governs the night. Ormuzd, the good genius, is luminous, sparkling, resplendent, as pure as the light which is subject

* M. du Sommerard (*Atlas des Arts du Moyen Age*, c. xiv., pl. 3,) has given a drawing of one of these doves, of enamelled and gilded copper, belonging to M. le Colonel Bourgeois ; and M. l'Abbé J. Corblet, member of the Society of Antiquaries of Picardy, has published a liturgical memoir of the ciborium of the middle ages, at the end of which is a drawing of an enamelled dove deposited in the Musée at Amiens. This latter dove, which belongs to the twelfth century, appears to have been employed as a deposit for the consecrated elements. A shallow cavity, hollowed in the back between the wings, and closed by a lid, which was kept in its place by means of a moveable button, was used for that purpose. The dove here described was brought from the Abbey of Raincheval (Somme). See the *Mémoires de la Société des Antiquaires de Picardie*, vol. v.

† This sombre dove is from a manuscript of the thirteenth century, *Théol. Lat. et. Fr.* 8, Bibliothèque de l'Arsénal.

to him; Ahriman, on the contrary, is dark and funereal, as night and hell, over which he has dominion. The contest between those two principles is visibly interpreted by the alternate and continued struggle between light and darkness.

The good influence which, amongst Christians maintains a perpetual struggle against the power of evil, is the same spirit of light, combating with the spirit of darkness. The colour assigned to the Holy Ghost is therefore white, the most luminous colour, and indeed that in which all are

Fig. 120.—AN EVIL SPIRIT, BLACK.
From a Franco-German Miniature of the XI cent.*

combined; while that given to the spirit of evil is black, being the total absence of light. Hitherto mention has

* This design is taken from a miniature in the *Hortus Deliciarum.*

been made only of the white resplendent dove everywhere diffusing light; it creates day wherever it appears and leaves night in every spot which it abandons.

In the preceding plate, a bird, a malevolent spirit is seen breathing into the ear of a magician thoughts as dark and evil as himself.

This dark, cloudy, and sombre spirit, violent in its attitude and lean in body, stretches its meagre throat towards the ear of the wicked man, who transcribes the evil thoughts which it inspires. The word spirit is constantly interpreted in Christian art by the form of a bird. When the spirit is good the bird is white, and when evil, black; it is in fact the devil.*

Fig. 121.—SPIRIT OF EVIL, THE SOUL OF AN IDOL.

A French Miniature of the XVI cent.†

It is of the latter form and colour in the drawing subjoined. Satan is a kind of human gnat with bat-like wings, and flying with rapid motion towards the statue of a woman; a naked idol representing some pagan goddess, and standing upon a column on which her worshippers have placed her.

Besides the preceding examples, Christ, the Saints, and

* Hermas says, in the Pastor: "In autem crede Spiritui venienti a Deo, habenti virtutem. Spiritui autem terrestri vacuo, qui a diabolo est, in quo fides non est neque virtus, credere noli."—(*S. Hermæ Pastor*, lib. ii., mandata 9, apud Fabricium. Codex Apocryphus, Nov. Test., pars iii., p. 903.) "Believe the Spirit which comes from God, and has power as such. But believe not the earthly and empty spirit, which is from the Devil, in whom there is no faith nor virtue."—Hone. *Apocryphal New Test.*, Hermas II., Command. xi., 12.

† St. Augustine, *Cité de Dieu*, MS. de la Bibliothèque St. Geneviève, fol. 21.

the Apostles, are frequently seen on painted windows, manuscripts with miniatures and tapestries, expelling from demoniacs the evil spirits by which they were possessed, and the birds, one or many, representing those spirits, and which issue from the mouth of the possessed, are invariably black. In the History of the Devil a great number of texts will be given in which Satan is called an Ethiopian, black, smoky, and dark, while angels and good genii are white, and illumine every spot near which they pass almost equally with the Holy Ghost. To the Holy Ghost especially must be applied what Dante said of angels:

> "Poi, come più e più verso noi venne
> L'uccel divino, più chiaro appariva,
> Perchè l'orchio dappresso nol sostenne." *

THE HOLY GHOST AS MAN.

The Holy Ghost has at times taken a form less common and more singular than that of a bird; it is the human form. The dove, from the sixth and seventh century down to the present time, has been the constant representative of the Holy Ghost, but about the tenth century, as it appears, a rival symbol was introduced.

The new type, however, never seems to have gained much favour; its duration was far shorter than that of the dove, and its adoption much more limited. It was not till the tenth century that the idea of figuring the Holy Ghost as man was first put in practice; and towards the close of the sixteenth century it was, again, superseded exclusively by the dove, which indeed had never ceased to be the favourite symbol.

"As we approach our own time," says M. Cyprien Robert, "the genius of modern invention sought to represent the Holy Ghost as a beautiful young man, the immortal youth

* *Purgatorio,* Canto II., l. 37.

> "As more and more toward us came, more bright
> Appeared the bird of God, nor could the eye
> Endure his splendour near."—*Cary's Dante.*

by whom nature is captivated.* But the Pope, in a bull which will be quoted elsewhere, prohibited the use of that image, as contrary to tradition. Speaking strictly, the Word alone ought to be clothed in the human form, for every visible and external manifestation of the Divinity was made in his person: the Creator seen in the terrestrial paradise, and Jehovah appearing on Mount Sinai, were, in fact, the Word. Nevertheless, it is understood that on those occasions he appeared under the form of an aged man, and thence was confounded with the Father Eternal. With regard to the Holy Ghost, however, it was impossible to give him the human form, without becoming instantly involved in serious error. Thus the Pope was right in remaining firm, and upholding the ancient dove."†

One of the earliest and most celebrated examples of the Holy Ghost made man by the power of art, is mentioned in an English manuscript, attributed to St. Dunstan, who died in 988, and was Archbishop of Canterbury. In this curious volume, the three Divine Persons are all represented in the human form. The Father is drawn as an emperor, and aged, the Son as Christ, and holding his cross, is

* *Chronique de Strasbourg*, année 1404. The citation is made by M. Robert.

† *Cours d'Hiéroglyphique Chrétienne*, dans L'Université Catholique, vol. vi., p. 352. Representations of the Holy Ghost as man are more ancient than is supposed by M. Robert. One example, dating from the tenth century, is known to exist, and there are probably others, even of earlier date. The bull referred to by M. Robert is, no doubt, that published by Urban VIII., but his prohibition applies to the representing of the Trinity under the figure of a single head with three faces, or of one single body, and not to figures of the Holy Ghost in human form. However, from the moment in which it became allowable to represent the Father as man—he whom no man hath seen, or can see—one could not interdict the representing of the Holy Ghost himself under the same form. In iconography, as well as in theology, the three Divine Persons are not merely similar, but also co-equal; what is attributed to one is therefore equally appropriate to the others. It was well to represent the Holy Ghost in the likeness of a dove, but better still to give him the human form. The Council *in Trullo* raised its voice to oppose the custom of representing Christ as the Lamb, and decreed that he should be depicted in future as man; it were equally to be wished that the symbolic dove of the Holy Ghost should be superseded by the human type, and I sincerely wish that Christian artists would invest the third person of the Trinity, as frequently as possible, with the human form; that type, hitherto but lightly esteemed, would afford a thousand new and charming motives.

younger, and may be perhaps thirty years of age; the Holy Ghost, who has no distinguishing attribute, is young and almost beardless.*

In the twelfth century, in the year 1180, the Manuscript of Herrade gives the three Persons as perfectly equal in attitude, costume, and physiognomy. The Holy Ghost, like the other two persons is there represented as a man of between thirty and five-and-thirty years of age. A little while earlier, but at the commencement of the same century, Abelard, as it appears, had commanded a Trinity to be sculptured in stone, resembling that depicted by Herrade. It was executed for the Abbey of the Paraclete, at Nogent-sur-Seine, but is no longer in existence, having been destroyed at the time of the Revolution. But le Père Mabillon, who probably had seen it, mentions that the Holy Ghost, being in the human form, had his hands crossed upon his breast, and said, "I am the breath of both" (of the Father and the Son). The Divine Spirit wore a crown of olives, was clothed in a long robe, and shared with the Son, the mantle of the Father.†

Too great a propensity to confound the Spirit with the two other Persons of the Trinity, and the discussion raised on that point by the doctrines of Abelard, appear to have suspended, during one hundred or one hundred and fifty years, representations of the Holy Ghost in human form. They were, however, resumed in the fourteenth century; they became more numerous in the fifteenth and sixteenth, and were finally abandoned in 1560, under Francis I.

From the fourteenth century to the sixteenth, these representations abound, and considering the Holy Ghost, with reference to age alone, we find figures of him in the human form, varying from the tenderest infancy, some months only, or a few years of age, up to an advanced period of old age. In a manuscript ‡ of the fifteenth century, he is exhibited

* M. le Comte Auguste de Bastard (*Peintures et Ornements des Manuscrits*) gives a copy of the Trinity of St. Dunstan.

† *Annales Benedict,* vol. vi., p. 83, No. 14. The monument described by Mabillon is not certainly of the time of Abelard, but the close of the fifteenth century. It is vexatious that the learned Benedictine should have neglected to determine the age of the carving, which is not now in existence.

‡ MS. containing various services, Bibl. Roy., suppl. i., 638. The Creator

floating upon the waters, at the moment when God is creating the heaven and the earth. The Holy Ghost is extended upon the waves, which are slightly agitated; he is a naked infant just born.

Fig. 122.—THE HOLY GHOST, AS A CHILD, FLOATING ON THE WATERS
From a Miniature of the XIV cent.

One might imagine the figure to be intended for the little

has a golden nimbus, with numerous rose-coloured rays, but without any cross. The globe in his left hand is also without a cross. As to the Holy Ghost, he is entirely without a nimbus. This miniature is placed in the latter part, about three-fourths, of the manuscript, before the office "in Dominica in palmis." In spite of my repeated cautions, the copyist has introduced three characteristics not to be found in the original, and it became necessary to mention errors so serious, and which would have been expunged, had they been discovered earlier.

Moses, floating on the waves of the Nile, and picked up by Pharaoh's daughter. But in this miniature the Word of God is on the shore, separating the light from the darkness. In another manuscript the Holy Ghost is rather older; he is still a child, and carried in the arms of the Almighty Father, as an infant is carried by its mother, but he is already eight or ten years of age.

Fig. 123.—THE HOLY GHOST, AS A CHILD OF EIGHT OR TEN YEARS OLD, IN THE ARMS OF THE FATHER.
French Miniature of the XVI cent.*

In a picture of the Holy Trinity, drawn to illustrate Dante's Paradiso, the Holy Ghost is fifteen years of age.† He is only ten or twelve in a figure given above (Fig. 61).

In a manuscript in the Bibliothèque Royale,‡ the Holy Ghost has already a beard; he is aged twenty or five-and-

* In the Bibliothèque de Ste. Geneviève, *Heures Latines*, No. 464.

† Sixteenth century. The work containing this drawing belongs to M. Longueville Jones, English correspondent of the *Comité Historique des Arts et Monuments.*

‡ *L'Aiguillon de l'Amour Divin,* in 4to., No. 5094 or $\frac{7275}{3}$, fifteenth century.

twenty. On a bas-relief of the sixteenth century, decorating the tympanum of a village church,* he is about thirty. The Holy Spirit may there be recognised by the Divine dove, which he holds in his left hand, pressing it against his bosom. This beautiful youth appears like the brother of Jesus, whom he resembles in features, countenance, figure, and attitude. The length and colour of the hair are the same in both Divine Persons; but the Holy Ghost is younger than Jesus Christ, and much younger still than God the Father. Jesus Christ is the elder brother of the Divine family. The Dogma declares that the Word is the Son of God, and that the Holy Ghost proceedeth from the Father and the Son. All the three persons are co-eternal and of equal age. But Art desired to set forth that fact in her own manner, and to place materially and sensibly before our eyes the filiation of the Word, and the procession of the Holy Ghost. With that object they represented the Son as younger than the Father, and the Holy Ghost as still more youthful than either. Thence arise the differences of age which, theologically considered, would have been heretical, had it been designed to indicate any actual difference of age; but they may be received as orthodox, having been employed to characterise, although but in a rude manner, the difference of relationship subsisting between the Divine Persons.

The Holy Spirit, as represented on the stalls † in Amiens Cathedral, is three or four years older; he is of precisely the same age as Jesus Christ, who is sitting near him, and who assists, together with the Holy Ghost, at the coronation of the Virgin by the Eternal Father. Jesus Christ and the Holy Ghost are twin brothers, and the Father being of the same age, precludes in this group any idea of family or generations, and implies only the co-eternity and equality of the three Persons.

In the Manuscript of Herrade, the Holy Ghost might be said to be forty years of age, like the other Divine Persons. The expression of the countenance is more serious, more severe, and even sorrowful than in any of the preceding

* See below, Fig. 126.

† The left row, looking towards the high altar, and at the opposite extremity to the nave.

examples, in all of which the physiognomy is well marked, according to the difference of age. Joyous in the child and gay in the young man, it becomes serious and saddened in him who has numbered thirty years.

Lastly, in various monuments,* the Holy Ghost is represented as aged, with a long beard, gray or white hair, and a wrinkled forehead; he is fifty, sixty, seventy years of age, like the Father Eternal. At that time, that is, in the fifteenth century, the Father Eternal had recovered the authority, of which, during the middle ages, he had been deprived; he imposes his form and features on the Holy Ghost, and even on Jesus Christ; he creates the world in his likeness and image. The ideas of paternity, filiation and progression, then disappear, chased by the co-eternity and co-equality of the three persons.

These portraits of the Holy Ghost as man, although not uncommon, particularly in the fifteenth century, are however far less numerous than representations of him under the form of a dove; the proportion may be reckoned, probably, as one in a thousand. Besides, these deified human figures appear late and disappear at the time of the Renaissance. Now the symbol of the dove, pure and elevated though it be, is inferior to the human type, even as a bird is inferior to a man.

It becomes, then, a subject of rejoicing, when, after having so long and so continually seen the Holy Ghost degraded to the lowly condition of a dove, he appears at length transformed into man; just as we watch with pleasure the transformation of a rude insect, into a brilliant, elegant, and swift-winged butterfly.

We see an onward progress from the bird to the man. One who devotes a life to the study of archæology, and is weary of meeting with the Holy Ghost under the figure of a bird, at every step he takes in every century, or on every monument, will rejoice when accident presents to his view a beautiful young man, beardless, or with a fair and soft beard, with fresh and rosy cheeks, waving and golden hair, and a

* See especially the manuscripts in the Bibliothèque Royale, known by the titles of *Bréviare de Salisbury* and *Heures du Duc d'Anjou*, Lavall. 82 and 127.

gentle, benevolent smile. One would receive with open arms the Divine youth, as would a mother the son who left her in his childhood and after long years of absence returns to his home, having grown into a tall and handsome man, rendered himself illustrious and intelligent, gained opulence, and attained to manhood.

Although the practice of drawing the Holy Ghost as a young man was abandoned at the Renaissance, it should be our care to revive the idea and bring it to perfection. Christian artists do wrong to neglect so noble a theme, whether in depicting the entire Trinity, or the Holy Ghost singly.

The Spirit, as man, has not yet finished his career; it belongs to the future more especially, to do honour to intellectual gifts, and to cultivate reason in the person of the Holy Ghost, as in past ages power was venerated in God the Father, and love in God the Son.

QUALITIES PECULIAR TO THE HOLY GHOST.

The Holy Ghost has hitherto been considered as a single person, one and indivisible; but although an attempt has been made to define his qualities by exhibiting him as the God of intelligence, still these Divine qualities which are more especially his own, the Divine attributes of the Holy Ghost and the qualities which he peculiarly possesses, remain to be enumerated. We read in Isaiah* "And there shall come forth a rod out of the stem of Jesse, and a Branch shall grow out of his roots; and the Spirit of the Lord shall rest upon him,† the Spirit of wisdom and understanding, the Spirit of counsel and might, the Spirit of knowledge and of the fear of the Lord."

* Isaiah xi., 1, 2.

† In the *Speculum Humanæ Salvationis*, a MS of the fourteenth century preserved in the Bibliothèque de l'Arsénal (Théol. Lat. 42, B. fo. 6 recto), is a picture of David or Jesse sitting. From the bosom of the Patriarch issues a bush or rose-tree. At the top of that tree shines a rose of five petals, in the centre of which, as in a nest of flowers, a bird, a little dove, is seen. It is the Holy Ghost in fact reposing in that flower. "In the year 1007," says the reverend Father, Dom Guéranger, (*Institutions Liturgiques*, vol. i., p. 309),

These words were addressed to the Messiah, to Jesus, to Emanuel, whom a Virgin was to conceive and to bring forth; to that little child who was to bear the government upon his shoulder, and whose name was to be called Wonderful, Counsellor, the Mighty God, the Everlasting Father, the Prince of Peace.* The Divine child was therefore clothed in the Spirit of God, whose faculties are seven in number, for he possesses, as his peculiar gifts, wisdom, understanding, counsel, strength, knowledge, piety, and fear.

This subject has frequently been portrayed by Christian artists; a tree springs from the bowels, the breast, or the mouth of Jesse.† The symbolic trunk spreads to the left and right, throwing forth branches, bearing the kings of Judah, the ancestors of Christ; at the top, seated on a throne or in the chalice of a gigantic flower, is the Son of God. Surrounding the Saviour, and forming as it were an oval aureole, seven doves are ranged one above the other, three on the left, three on the right, and one at the top. Each dove inspires the Saviour with some property peculiar to itself; one with wisdom, another intelligence, the third counsel, and so on. These doves which are of snowy whiteness, like the Holy Ghost, and adorned like him with a cruciform nimbus, are simply living manifestations of the seven gifts of the Spirit. The Holy Ghost is drawn under the form of a dove; each of the seven energies distinguishing him, is also figured under the same type. They may be termed seven personifications of that God, who in one person, combines seven different attributes, as the absolute

"Fulbert, Bishop of Chartres, composed the following Introit for the nativity of the Virgin:—

"Stirps Jesse virgam produxit, virgoque florem,
Et super hunc florem requiescit Spiritus almus.
Virgo Dei genitrix virga est; flos, Filius ejus."

* Isaiah, vii. 14; ix. 6. From the concluding words is derived the Introit still sung at Christmas.

† At Rheims, the mystical tree rises from the mouth of David, that is to say, from the organ of intelligence, and not from the breast or bowels, the organs of material life; it bears on its summit a large flower, in which reposes the Messiah, Jesus, the Emmanuel of Isaiah. See in the Bibliothèque de Rheims, the manuscript entitled *Bible Historicale;* it is of the thirteenth century, and numbered $\frac{28}{18}$.

Divinity comprehends in one Supreme head three distinct persons.

We have given above (Fig. 40) a drawing taken from the Psalter of St. Louis, in which Christ is shown at the top of the genealogical tree, and surrounded by the Seven Spirits. In this last miniature, Jesus Christ is in the arms of his mother, and the seven little doves fly towards the child and seem to delight him with their mysterious song.

Fig. 124.—JESUS CHRIST SURROUNDED BY THE SEVEN GIFTS OF THE HOLY GHOST.

French Miniature of the XIV cent.*

It would be interesting to determine the place occupied by those doves in respect of Christ whom they surround as in a circle.

The spirit of Christian æsthetics and the principles of the reciprocal hierarchy of persons and things, have been explained in the chapter on the History of God the Father; it will therefore be sufficient for the present, to repeat, that the top is more honourable than the lower part, the left inferior to the right, and the circumference to the centre. The top is preferred to the base, and the right to the left, in the same way as that in which the focus or centre, predominates over the radiation. Now, in Isaiah the order given to the gifts of the Holy Spirit is as follows: wisdom, understanding, counsel, strength, knowledge, piety, the

* Manuscript in the Bibliothèque Royale, *Biblia Sacra*, 6829. Nothing is more common than to see doves thus surrounding the Saviour, whether as man or infant.—The same subject is twice repeated on the windows of the Cathedral of St. Denis, three times on those of Chartres, once upon the stained glass in the Collegiate of St. Quentin, in the Cathedrals of Amiens and Beauvais, and on those of the Church of Breuil, a village in the arrondissement of Rheims.

fear of God. If we ascend, beginning with the fear of God, wisdom will be at the summit; if on the contrary, wisdom be placed lowest in the series, the fear of God will hold the upper degree or highest rank; but in either case, strength and knowledge will occupy the centre. Isaiah, opening his list with wisdom and closing it with fear, has unfortunately omitted to say whether he was ascending or descending from one quality to another. We cannot therefore say which is the root or base, which is the summit, which the supreme virtue, and which on the contrary the lowliest. A wide field was open to the conjectures of mediæval artists and symbolists, and the place assigned to each quality ought probably to possess and contain the expression of some individual preference or antipathy. Influenced by an analogous order of ideas, we see that in depicting the three theological virtues, Faith, Hope, and Charity, an artist or moralist of compassionate and tender feelings places Charity at the summit; another, who was at the moment in sorrow or suffering, Hope; a third, racked by the pangs of doubt and scepticism, and feeling the inestimable value of belief, would elevate Faith above all. Fénelon and St. Vincent de Paul might have esteemed Charity above the two other virtues, but St. Jerome, Tertullian, and Bossuet, would unquestionably have preferred Faith to Charity. Thus the rank that may be assigned to either virtue, reveals to us some individual sympathy of the artist's mind, or occasionally some social feeling. What has been said of Fénelon, St. Vincent de Paul, Bossuet, St. Jerome, and Tertullian, applies equally to society in general. When in any epoch or century, Faith is the predominating influence, that virtue occupies the highest place; one crowns her as queen and seats her on the throne of state. When on the contrary the lessons of belief have been learned, and men are crushed by a weight of suffering of every kind; when wars, famine, and pestilence ravage a country, that country flies for refuge to Hope. Faith is brought down from her throne, and Hope elevated in her place. When again the moral feeling is blunted, when the sick and blinded heart is barren and dark, not knowing how to guide itself aright, then Charity stands forth, the pharos of the soul, and offers a remedy to Hope.

Such has in fact been the course pursued, and thus it may be traced in the progress of Christian art. In the primitive ages of Christianity to believe was the first imperative necessity; to believe and to confess the incarnation of the Word, the immortality of the soul, and the resurrection of the body; consequently, to stimulate Faith was the task imposed upon all early monuments. Ancient sarcophagi, the frescos in the catacombs, the mosaics in the Roman basilicas, all speak the same language, and constantly present to our view the birth, the actions, and resurrection of Christ. Life is constantly extracted from Death, to show that at the Final Judgment the reanimated body shall quit the tomb; thus Jonah is vomited forth by the whale; the three children of the Babylonish captivity are spared by the flames of the fiery furnace; Jesus raises Lazarus to life. To believe was then indispensably necessary; for the object to be achieved was the substituting of one religion for another; it was the reign of Faith. But when evil days came at the time of the invasion, first of the barbarians, next of the Normans, and especially after the time of Charlemagne, when the empire was torn by divisions in every quarter, when war spread from province to province, and from city to city; when feudalism was engendered, and all hearts distracted with apprehensions of the year 1000; then men turned to Hope, and she was placed at the head of the three great virtues. The world believed, and Faith was no longer in danger, but Hope was doubly needed, amidst the anguish of such terrible events as seemed to forbid all cheering anticipations from the future. In the twelfth century, everything assumed a firmer footing; the year 1000 had passed, and men marvelled to find themselves still among the living. The hand of royalty, beneficent and powerful, began to crush and subdue the petty tyrants of feudalism; far-sighted in its views, it re-established order, and reformed or rather invented laws and administration. Men were happy; but as is too often the case, happiness produced indifference, luxury, self-indulgence, and pleasure. Those effeminate and egotistical souls required therefore to be exalted and animated by the ardent devotedness of Charity.

It is possible, by close study, to discover in the sculptures of cathedrals, in painted glass windows, and the miniatures of illuminated manuscripts, variations of feeling, indicating a difference of period: a material difference—an individuality—may even be discovered in edifices of the same era, but erected in different countries.

Thus, in the Cathedral of Paris, as has been already remarked, confessors rank higher than martyrs, that is to say, intellect is more highly venerated than faith. At Chartres, on the contrary, faith takes precedence of intelligence, martyrs of confessors. In the church of Notre Dame de Brou, founded by a woman, the primal virtue is charity. During the Renaissance, when men were Pagan rather than Christian in sentiment, not one only of the theological virtues was neglected, but all three at once, and the four cardinal virtues were substituted in their place—Prudence, Justice, Temperance and Strength, moral virtues exalted in Pagan times far above all others. In short the personified virtues represented on Christian monuments, testify by their nature, their number, and the rank they occupy, the social condition of the period and country in which they were produced.

The places respectively assigned to the seven gifts or qualities of the Holy Ghost cannot, therefore, be a matter of indifference. It might have been sufficient merely to draw attention to that subject in order to prove its importance; but it will not be wholly useless to produce a few examples in support of the above remarks. Isaiah, as we have said, leaves undetermined the places to be assigned to wisdom and to fear.

In arranging, by ranks, the seven virtues, ought fear to be placed in the lowest, and wisdom in the highest? Probably it may be so; for Isaiah, naming wisdom first, and closing with fear, appears to have established a series, the component parts of which are all descending. Wisdom is at the head, like a chief, followed by his subordinates.

Besides, fear is a simple sentiment, while wisdom, on the contrary, is a complex virtue; wisdom, therefore, ranks higher than fear. Thus, indeed, it has been regarded by all civilised people, and in every religion. A man, acting under the influence of fear is inferior to one who is guided by wisdom. Lastly, a sacred text corresponding with that of

Isaiah, seems to offer the desired solution. We are told in the Psalms, that "The fear of the Lord is the beginning of wisdom."* Fear in its entirety, then, is but a member or part of wisdom, the great compendium of all virtues. From fear is born wisdom, as from the root springs an entire tree with its lofty summit.

Thus, then, the last of the gifts named by Isaiah is the weakest; the first, the most powerful. Fear is to be placed lowest. Rising from piety to knowledge, strength, counsel, and intelligence, we at length attain to wisdom, ascending, as from the lowest step of a ladder we gain the summit. Such ought to be the arrangement, in a vertical line; in a horizontal line wisdom should be at the head, and fear at the opposite extremity. Rhaban Maur, in the poem already quoted, has disposed the seven gifts of the Spirit.

He ranges them vertically in the form of a cross; and then distributes them horizontally in the manner just explained.† The figure formed by the above arrangement is nearly as follows:

Spiritus
Sapientiæ,
Spiritus
Intellectus,
Spiritus
spiritus spiritus spiritus consilii, spiritus spiritus spiritus
sapientiæ, intellectus, consilii, fortitudinis, scientiæ, pietatis, timoris.
Spiritus
Scientiæ,
Spiritus
Pietatis,
Spiritus
Timoris.

If the line be circular and uninterrupted, the virtues should be placed almost like the hours on a dial plate. Wisdom the first and most important, should be at the top, where the first hour is placed: fear at the hour of twelve. In a circular, or in an ogive arch, fear should be at the spring of the arch, on the left; piety in the same part on the right, and wisdom should be the key-stone of the archi-

* "Initium sapientiæ timor Domini."—Ps. cxi. 10.

† Rhaban Maur, *De Laudibus Sanctæ Crucis,* first volume of his collected works, p. 312, Fig. 16.

volt. Such would be the normal arrangement, made in accordance with the writing of the Prophet; but according to the reasoning given above, from preferences indulged at certain periods, and in different countries—from the different sympathies and temperament of individuals—we might expect many inversions to arise, and in fact they did so. These varieties require to be carefully noted, because from them historical deductions, and other important information may be drawn.

In the Apocalypse * the lamb is described as endowed with seven eyes and seven horns, which are the seven spirits of God; Christ the Lion of Judah, receives the seven gifts of the Divine Spirit. Now the gifts named in the Apocalypse differ in some respects from those enumerated by Isaiah, both in name and hierarchical arrangement. They are given below, both in the order in which they are placed by Isaiah, and in the Apocalypse:

Isaiah.	*Apocalypse.*
SAPIENTIA.	VIRTUS.
INTELLECTUS.	DIVINITAS.
CONSILIUM.	SAPIENTIA.
FORTITUDO.	FORTITUDO.
SCIENTIA.	HONOR.
PIETAS.	GLORIA.
TIMOR.	BENEDICTIO.

Strength and wisdom are the only names found common in both texts. Strength occupies the same place, the centre

* Revelation, v., 6, 12. "Vidi . . . Agnum stantem tanquam occisum, habentem cornua septem et oculos septem, qui sunt SEPTEM SPIRITUS Dei missi in omnem terram . . . Dignus est Agnus, qui occisus est, accipere virtutem, et divinitatem,[1] et sapientam, et fortitudinem, et honorem, et gloriam, et benedictionem." "And I beheld . . . a Lamb as it had been slain, having seven horns and seven eyes, which are the seven spirits of God sent forth into all the earth . . . Worthy is the Lamb that was slain to receive power and *riches*, and wisdom, and strength, and honour, and glory, and blessing."

[1] This gift, in the earliest Latin Biblia, and the Vulgate is as here quoted, "divinitatem;" but in later versions it is "divitias," which agrees with the Greek version, "πλοῦτον," and our own accepted version, "riches."—ED.

in both; but wisdom is in the first place in Isaiah, and the third in the Apocalypse. The other names differ so remarkably, that it is impossible to trace any analogy between them.

We understand that wisdom, placed by Isaiah at the head of the seven gifts, may be styled virtue, by pre-eminence, because it is its highest expression. But between fear and benediction, glory and piety, science and honour, it is not easy to seize the connection, unless it be that benediction may be the cause of fear, and that honour and glory are the consequence, the product or effect of science and piety. As to the intelligence named in Isaiah, it is called in the Apocalypse "divinity;" * this circumstance may be adduced in confirmation of those already given, proving the Holy Spirit to be the God of intelligence, not of love.

Whatever may be the cause, still if a discrepancy so remarkable can be traced between the prophecy of Isaiah and the Apocalypse of St. John, it must be expected that differences will also be found in paintings and sculpture representing the seven spirits, the seven doves encircling the Saviour. The subject of Christ, surrounded by the seven doves, is represented on the stained glass in the Sainte Chapelle, Paris, Notre Dame de Chartres, the church of Breuil, a village in the arrondissement of Rheims, and in the church of St. Denis. Manuscripts with miniatures, executed between the twelfth and sixteenth centuries, frequently display the same subject; but it very rarely happens that each dove bears its name attached, so that it cannot be said with certainty that the first is the Spirit of wisdom, the second that of intelligence, &c. &c.† One manuscript, however, belonging to the latter part of the thirteenth century,‡ gives the seven spirits, all of whom are named, and placed in a

* If "divinitatem" is a wrong reading (see note [1], p. 481) this analogy will not apply, but it must always be borne in mind that artists in the middle ages took their subjects from the Vulgate, and therefore must be tested by that version.—Ed.

† In the window on the right of the western porch of the Cathedral at Chartres, and at St. Denis, in a window of the apse, terminating the right-hand aisle, the names are inscribed around the medallions encircling each dove, but in characters either so delicate, or so much worn, that I was unable to decipher them, although I made several attempts, and studied them with the greatest attention.

‡ *Vergier de Solas,* Suppl. Fr. 11, in fol.

semicircle, forming an arch above the Saviour. On the left, ascending, are the spirits of counsel, intelligence, and wisdom; on the right, ascending, the spirits of strength, knowledge, and piety. The spirit of fear looks down upon the rest from the key-stone at the top of the arch. This spirit appears to be supported on the left by wisdom, and on the right by piety; while its feet appear to rest upon counsel and strength. Intelligence and science, facing one another, are in the centre. In this arrangement fear is the supreme virtue; an Hebraic disposition, quite in conformity with the spirit of the Jewish religion, by which the fear of God was inculcated, and imposed as a governing principle upon men, in the same manner in which love is made the fundamental law of Christianity. The subject above described is at the summit of a tree, bearing at the top the Virgin, with the infant Saviour in her arms.

Opposite to this tree, in the same manuscript, the Virgin is again represented, holding our blessed Lord, and here, also, seven doves encircle the infant God. The names accompany the doves, but the order in which they are arranged is different. Disposed in the form of an arch, like the voussoirs of an archivolt, the doves rise from the spring of the arch on the left, and ascend to the top, where the fourth dove, or virtue, is placed, and being thence continued they descend to the spring of the arch on the right. In this arrangement the order of Isaiah is observed; on the left, which is inferior to the right, and in the lower part, which is less honourable than the upper, the dove of fear is perched; then appear those of piety, science, strength, counsel, intelligence and wisdom.

It is to be regretted that wisdom should be placed last, but the arch was probably treated as a straight or horizontal line, and the arrangement would in that case be completely in accordance with that of Isaiah, who places wisdom at the top, and fear at the opposite extremity.

Finally, the same manuscript contains one curious miniature, a kind of moral wheel cut into seven rays and composed of several concentric cordons. The rays form seven compartments divided into as many cordons, containing in each cordon one of the seven petitions in the Lord's prayer, one of the seven sacraments, one of the seven spiritual arms of justice, one of the seven works of mercy, one of the seven virtues, one of the seven deadly sins, and one of the seven gifts of the Holy Ghost.* From the number of cordons in this wheel, it resembles a many coloured cockade plaited in seven folds; taking the cordon of the seven spirits of God separately, we have the dial of a clock; a dial divided into seven instead of twelve hours or degrees.

Following the order of the dial, in that miniature we find intelligence in the first division, fear in the sixth, and wisdom at the highest point. The other virtues occupy the intermediate spaces, and follow the order of Isaiah. In this, then, unlike the first picture, wisdom predominates, not fear, according to the prophet's intention; fear is completely subservient.

It were useless to dwell longer on this subject, although in itself curious and rich in historical deductions and moral inductions. It will, therefore, be sufficient to observe that to be consistent with the nature of the Holy Spirit, which is pure intellect, it would be necessary, in representing the seven doves, to place intelligence in the highest rank; fear and strength in the lowest division, piety and wisdom above fear and strength. Lastly, as approaching more closely to intelligence, and serving as its support, science should be on the left, and counsel on the right of that supreme virtue, which in itself comprises all. We should then, at the base, have the genius of strength, in the centre that of love, and

* Reiner, a Benedictine monk of the thirteenth century, composed seven hymns in honour of the Holy Ghost. The number seven was, in the middle ages, esteemed a sacred number. Authors of that period observed with infinite pleasure that there were seven gifts of the Holy Ghost, seven sacraments, seven planets, seven days in the week, seven branches on the candlestick of Moses, seven liberal arts, seven churches of Asia, seven mysterious seals, seven stars and seven symbolic trumpets, seven heads of the dragon, seven joys and seven sorrows of the Virgin, seven penitential psalms, seven deadly sins, seven canonical hours. The mystics gave explanations of all numbers, but more especially of the number seven; they form, by addition and subtraction, a most peculiar kind of arithmetic (see particularly Bede, Rhaban Maur, and G. Durandus). "Septenarius numerus est numerus universitatis," says Jacobus de Voragine, *Legenda Aurea*, "De Sanctis Machabæis. Mahomet himself says, in the Koran, c. ii., v. 27, "God visited the skies, and formed there seven heavens." God, according to Mahomet, divided the sky into seven heavens, or seven concentric layers, superimposed like the pellicules of an onion.

reason at the summit. Seven chapels are frequently seen to radiate from the semicircular absides of our cathedrals; as, for example, at Chartres, and at Rheims; let us suppose, then, the two first chapels, namely, the first on the left hand, and that on the right to be dedicated to fear and strength; the two following, the one on the left to piety, that on the right to wisdom; the two next to science and counsel, and lastly that called the Chapel of the Virgin (Lady Chapel), the largest and most magnificent, to be consecrated to intelligence. Such would be their proper logical distribution.

Still such an arrangement would deviate from that choser by Isaiah.

When the locality itself presents no impediment, and the space has been carefully distributed, the seven doves are all represented; but when the contrary is the case, two or three or even four of the doves are omitted without scruple, and five only represented, or possibly no more than four or three. Mediæval artists were not embarrassed by trifles; when they desired to represent the twelve principal virtues, the twelve months of the year, the twelve apostles, the four and twenty elders of the Apocalypse, and the space, from being ill-calculated was found to be insufficient, two-thirds, or one-half, or one-third only, according to circumstances, were carved or painted. On the other hand, when there was a superabundance of space, they represented thirty elders, fifteen months, or twenty virtues; the same cordon of patriarchs, kings, martyrs or virgins was two or three times repeated.* It was the same with the Holy Spirit. In the nave of the cathedral of Chartres, on the north side is a painted window representing Mary holding before her the Saviour, who is surrounded by a circular aureole; six white doves, not seven (space was wanting), converge towards the Divine child.

In the same cathedral in the rose window of the north

* In the Cathedral of Chartres, where space was abundant, particularly in the lateral porches, many of these repetitions are seen: the wise and foolish virgins are there represented twice; the virtues and vices are three times repeated; the kings, ancestors of the Virgin, are copied four times over. In the western porch, where there was a deficiency of space, two months are omitted in the zodiac sculptured on the left door, and they are carried over to the right door, where they have no signification, but merely fill up a vacancy.

transept, four only appear, each approaching to endow Jesus Christ with some special gift; but in the window on the

Fig. 125.—SIX DIVINE DOVES, INSTEAD OF SEVEN.
Painted Window of the XIII cent.; Cathedral of Chartres.

right side of the west porch, the seven doves were figured without exception. Similar examples may easily be found and multiplied.

It would be an interesting question to determine which of the spirits were sacrificed, and which on the contrary were preferred and there represented. Some curious information would doubtless be elicited from that fact. For example, if the painter of Chartres, suppressing the doves of fear, strength, and piety, had reserved only those of wisdom, science, counsel, and intelligence, should we not be obliged to conclude that he, being of an independent spirit, had made his own selection amongst the gifts named by Isaiah, and as a follower of reason had preferred that attribute to all others—to either love or power?

More yet remains to be said on this same subject. Abelard, who discoursed much concerning the Divine persons and discussed their nature, declared that Christ was devoid of the spirit of the fear of God. Such at least is the heavy accusation brought against him by Saint Bernard, his antagonist. A manuscript of the Abbé of Clairvaux, discovered by the PP. Martenne and Durand, in the abbey of Vigogne, contains, amongst other heretical propositions extracted from the works of Abelard and sent by S. Bernard to Pope Innocent II. the following: "Quod in Christo non fuerit spiritus timoris Domini."* Abelard, taking the expression in its rudest sense, could not understand that it was possible for Christ to fear the Father; still he does not deny that the other six spirits were all found in Christ. At Chartres too, we find that on the painted window in the nave, which was about seventy years later than the period in which Abelard wrote, there are six doves only instead of seven; the one suppressed is precisely that at the top, the same which in a miniature taken from a manuscript† in the Bibliothèque Royale, is called the spirit of the fear of God. Might it not then be possible that the doctrine written and preached by Abelard, was interpreted materially on the painted windows of Chartres? It seems not at all improbable, when we remember that in the same church, liberty is personified and placed in the middle amongst the virtues, and holding the highest rank; when the magician, elsewhere degraded, is then introduced amongst saints, and in a very honourable position; and when we see subjects taken from the most anathematised among the apocryphal legends painted as decorations for the apse. Whatever may have been the cause, the omission ought to be established as a fact: it would seem therefore expedient to direct the attention of antiquaries to the sure, or at least probable relation, existing throughout the middle ages, between the sculptured monuments and doctrines that were at least under the ban of suspicion, if not heretical; between theo-

* *Voyage Littéraire de deux Réligieux Bénédictins*, 11e partic, p. 213.

† *Le Vergier de Solas*, already quoted.

logians, philosophers, and artists. In the present case, unfortunately, and as regards this particular point, the question at issue cannot be determined, for two of the painted windows at Chartres bear no inscriptions, and on the third they are illegible in consequence of its height.

The seventh spirit, which is omitted, may be any other, and not that of fear; but, whichever spirit it may be that is thus forgotten or sacrificed, it is to be regretted, on account of the results which might have been deduced from it, that the name is unknown.

The seven doves, like the Holy Ghost himself, have a nimbus, and even a cruciform nimbus; for as attributes of God they also are divine, and for that reason entitled to wear the characteristic tokens of the persons of the Trinity.

In a manuscript in the Bibliothèque Royale,* each of the seven doves has a cruciform nimbus. At Chartres, the four doves in the rose window, which gives light to the north transept, have each a red nimbus with a white cross.

Still, as has been shown, the seven doves are not all of equal importance; one of them represents an inferior quality, that of fear; another, the supreme virtue, that of wisdom. These various gradations were sometimes fixed by the art after her own manner. The art has, it is true, figured the six doves symbolising fear, piety, science, strength, counsel, and intelligence, as holy doves, but merely celestial, not divine; they have a nimbus, but it is plain, like that worn by saints and angels. With respect to wisdom, however, that faculty has been deified by the art, the dove, by which it is represented, is alone endowed with the cruciform nimbus, worn exclusively by the Persons of the Trinity. The engraving given in Fig. 40, in the History of the Aureole, which is taken from the Psalter of St. Louis also treats the spirit of wisdom as of higher importance than the six others. The dove that represents wisdom is not only placed at the top of the tree of Jesse, in itself a special distinction, but it alone, amongst all the others, has a nimbus round the head. The nimbus is plain, it is true; still it indicates a peculiar distinction, which the other six do not enjoy. The seven doves are inclosed in an entirely circular aureole. The

* *Miroir de l'Humaine Salvacion,* already quoted.

glory, according to the definition already given, (the union of the nimbus and aureole), is here restricted to the dove of wisdom, the body of which is alone enveloped in an aureole, and the head in a nimbus.

Occasionally, also, we meet with a recurrence of the equality of the seven gifts, as the seven doves, wherein we find all alike destitute of the cruciform, or perhaps of any, nimbus, thus apparently depriving them of their divine or celestial nature.

When this happens in works of the sixteenth century, it must not be regarded as specially applicable to the spirits of God only; for at that period all saints, angels, the Virgin, and even the Persons of the Holy Trinity, were deprived of the nimbus. But if one has reason to remark the absence of the nimbus in the fourteenth century, it has been the result probably of forgetfulness. We have more than once had occasion to repeat that artists frequently committed errors in their designs, as copyists have done in their transcriptions. Thus, in an example previously given, taken from a manuscript of the fourteenth century,* the absence both of the cruciform and plain nimbus may have been an error of the artist, arising from neglect, not intention, and it would therefore have no significance. Besides, the nimbus must already have lost somewhat of its original value, since that of Jesus radiates from every side, and not, as would be strictly correct, from three points only, the brow and temples forming the three plumes of light which have been mentioned in the History of the Nimbus. (See above, Fig. 34.) On several monuments with figures, and particularly in the miniatures of manuscripts, the doves being necessarily of very small dimensions, it is difficult to determine whether the nimbus is, or is not, cruciform.

* *Biblia Sacra,* 6829, Bibl. Royale; the drawing is given above, Fig. 124. The Virgin holding Jesus Christ illumined by the seven spirits, is placed beneath the candlestick with seven branches; it is with a similar intent that the resurrection of Jesus is placed below Jonah, vomited forth alive by the whale, or that Christ shedding blood and water from his wounds, is placed immediately under the rock which Moses strikes, and which yields a spring of running water. The candlestick, lighted by seven fires, is the image of Jesus animated by the seven spirits; and this supplies an additional proof that the Holy Ghost is the God of intelligence, since even his special attributes are figured by torches, which give light but not warmth.

This is particularly the case with those in the "Vergier de Solas."

The seven doves, like the Holy Spirit, are white, with red beak and feet: like the Holy Ghost, too, they are the size of natural doves. Still, as the Holy Ghost appeared to Theutram, the guardian of the Cathedral at Strasbourg, under the form of a bird as large as an eagle, so also the doves, figuring his attributes, sometimes grew to the dimensions of the largest eagle. In general, however, the doves of the Holy Ghost are smaller than the Spirit himself, for the fraction ought to be less than the whole; and in such cases they are no larger than the doves of Virginia, which attain to the size only of a common sparrow. Occasionally the Holy Ghost himself is reduced to equally small dimensions, and his attributes ought, with still stronger reason, to contract themselves into proportionably diminutive size. It is necessary to guard carefully against mistaking a little bird, an humble sparrow, for the dove of the Holy Ghost.

The Holy Ghost, as has been said, does sometimes degenerate into the appearance of a sparrow; but the cruciform nimbus on its head immediately marks it to be the symbol of the third Divine Person. When, as frequently happens, the nimbus is absent, the subject in which the little dove is seen, and the place it occupies, preclude it from being confounded with any ordinary bird. In all subjects in which the two Persons are seen together, the dove, however small and unnimbed, forms the third.

Any bird, descending from heaven, and hovering about the head of the Virgin, at the moment when the angel announces to her that she is to be the mother of the Saviour, must be intended for the Holy Ghost; and any bird in the cenaculum—above the river Jordan—or extending its wings above the heads of the apostles, or that of Christ, can be no other than the divine symbol. A group frequently sculptured in our churches during the fourteenth and fifteenth centuries, and even at the close of the thirteenth, represents the Virgin either sitting or standing, and holding in her arms the Infant Jesus. With one hand the Divine Child caresses his mother, with the other he is playing with a little bird, which he holds by the wings, by the neck, and by the tail, pulling its feathers and gently caressing it. This bird is not the divine dove, or the Holy Ghost, but a sparrow, a chaffinch, a nightingale, a red-breast, which serves as a plaything for the Infant Saviour, as any object or animal might do.

We must not be deceived, nor imagine that bird to be a divine symbol. In the church of Vertus (Marne), a group carved in stone, about the end of the thirteenth century, represents the Infant Saviour thus sporting with a little bird; the sparrow, however, becomes impatient and angry, and pinches, with his beak, the fingers of the Divine Infant, who is tormenting it.*

The seven gifts of the Holy Spirit, or the seven doves, belong strictly to Jesus alone; yet in Germany, where woman is revered and honoured more than in any other country,† the Virgin Mary has almost been raised to an equal rank of divinity. On a painted window in the north aisle of the cathedral of Freybourg, in Brisgau, the Virgin is represented sitting, holding the infant Saviour, who is clothed in yellow, and standing on her left knee. Jesus has a cruciform nimbus; in the left hand he holds a beautiful red flower, which may possibly be a rose, but if so, a sweet-briar rose, simple, and with numerous yellow stamina. The right hand is extended to take a large red plum, presented him by his mother. Mary wears a green robe, a mantle of violet-colour lined with red, and on her head a white veil,

* A figure of the Virgin, of white marble, presented by Jeanne d'Evreux, wife of Charles Abel, to the Abbey Church of St. Denis, and at present belonging to the Church of St. Germain-des-Près, holds in her arms the infant Saviour, who is playing with a bird, but more gently than the little Jesus at Vertus. In the hospice at Rue (Somme) Jesus, in the arms of his mother, is amusing himself in a similar manner with a little bird, taken erroneously for the Holy Ghost. *Voyage Pittoresque dans l'Ancienne France*, province of Picardy, by M. Abaron Taylor. The same motive with trifling variations may be seen in several churches in the arrondissement de Rheims, more particularly in that of Courcy.

† Both before and after the introduction of Christianity, the Germans and Alemanni played an important part in religious history, both civil and political. The fact is attested by existing books and monuments. At Cologne, irrespective of St. Ursula and her eleven thousand companions, by whom that city and the entire country of Germany were protected, more than half the number of churches in that city are dedicated to female saints. In the Cathedral of Freybourg, in Brisgau, the whole series of painted windows are filled with subjects taken from the history of the Virgin and the lives of female saints.

confined by a golden crown. A red nimbus, edged with pearls, or diamonds set in gold, illumines her countenance. The costume of Mary is most splendid. Around her nimbus, and not round that of Jesus, a flight of seven little white doves descend, converging towards the centre of the Virgin's nimbus, not in any way tending towards that of the Saviour; Mary, therefore, must be a Divine being, for she is endowed like her Son with the seven gifts of the Holy Spirit. It may be asserted that the doves are represented only on account of Jesus; but the fact that they clap their wings and rejoice before Mary, not the Son, cannot be disputed.

Besides, not merely the attributes of the Spirit, but the Holy Ghost himself is represented with the young Virgin. In the south aisle of the same cathedral of Freybourg, is a painted window of the fourteenth century, the subject of which is St. Anna, teaching the Virgin Mary to read. St. Anna, like a queen—queen through her daughter—wears above her white veil a crown of gold; she has also the red nimbus of a saint. A violet-coloured robe, and a yellow mantle lined with red, complete her rich attire. St. Anna holds in her left hand a richly bound book, in a cover of blue; she holds the little Virgin Mary in her right. The Divine little girl wears on her otherwise uncovered head a crown of gold, and a violet-coloured nimbus; her hair, which is of a golden yellow, falls in two long German tresses upon her shoulders. She is about eight or ten years old, and is clad in a little green robe, fitting closely to her shape. She attempts with her right hand to open her mother's beautiful blue book, that she may learn to read; but with her left she presses to her bosom a better master even than the book and St. Anna combined; she clasps the Holy Spirit, who already begins to impart inspiration to her. The Holy Ghost is a little white dove, with a golden nimbus and black cross. The symbolic bird has just alighted on the little maiden's hand, and its wings are still trembling; he has descended from heaven to play with the Divine child. It is a charming picture, and could have been produced by the tender and graceful genius of Germany alone.

With these few exceptions, which are no doubt to be attributed to the character of the German nation, the seven doves are restricted entirely to the Son of God, the Immanuel of Isaiah.

CHRONOLOGICAL ICONOGRAPHY OF THE HOLY GHOST.

Although there is the greatest possible variety as to the form of the Holy Ghost, since he is figured both as a man, as a dove, and as a man of every age from infancy up to old age, he still presents us but few chronological variations. Thus, from the earliest period down to our own time, the dove has been almost constantly the same in form, dimensions, proportions, colour, and attributes.

The different characteristics to be observed belong less to the epoch than to the country or imagination of the artist; they rest rather on æsthetics, and geographical situation, than on chronological distinctions.

The variations observed in the representations of the Holy Ghost as man are purely physiological, not chronological. Judging by chronological periods, the Man-God representing the Holy Ghost, ought to be depicted as a little infant in the eleventh century, when he appears for the first time; in the twelfth as a child of ten or fifteen; a youth of fifteen or twenty in the thirteenth; a young man in the fourteenth; a man of from forty to fifty in the fifteenth; and an old man in the sixteenth; but it is not thus.

In the eleventh and twelfth centuries the Holy Ghost becomes, immediately upon the first appearance, thirty or forty years of age, while in the sixteenth he is a child of only some months or a few years old, and again becomes, on a sudden, an old man of sixty. In the fifteenth and sixteenth centuries he is of any or every age.

It must, however, be observed, that up to the eleventh century, the dove alone is the appointed symbol of the Holy Ghost, and that, after that period, the dove shares that honour with the man. In the fourteenth century, and as late as the sixteenth, not only are the dove and human figure employed almost indifferently, but both are sometimes shown together on the same monument. The dove rests upon the head of the human image of the Holy Ghost, one example of which will be given in the history of the Trinity, or it descends upon the hand of the same divine Being, as in the engraving given below.

Fig. 126.—THE HOLY GHOST AS MAN, AND IN THE FORM OF A DOVE ALSO. French Sculpture of the XVI cent.

The Holy Ghost may here be likened to a knight carrying a falcon on his wrist.* It must also be observed, that until the close of the fourteenth century the human

* The above design is copied from a sculpture in the Church of Verrières (département de l'Aube), of which we have already spoken. The figures in this cene, in which the Virgin Mary is represented crowned by the Trinity, are very inferior; but they have been engraved with scrupulous exactitude. The original drawing is by M. Fichot. In similar works, representing the coronation of the Virgin by God the Father and God the Son, the following verses of the Psalmist are frequently inscribed as a text:—"Posuisti in capite ejus coronam de lapide pretioso" (Psalm xxi., 3). "Thou settest a crown of pure gold on his head." "Gloriâ et honore coronasti eum (eam) (Psalm viii. 5). "Thou . . . . hast crowned him with glory and honour." The above texts apply also to God the Father when he crowns the Son after his resurrection and ascension into heaven.

type of the Holy Spirit was always thirty or forty years of age; but from the fifteenth up to the middle of the sixteenth he takes every age. Lastly, from about the year 1550 to our own time the dove resumes the exclusive right which it had previously enjoyed of representing the Holy Spirit, and the man thenceforth disappears. The idea of representing the Holy Ghost as man has been so completely neglected, in modern times especially, that many persons will doubtless be surprised to meet with any such representations in the present work.

The dove alone was the symbol of the Holy Ghost as long as men were guided exclusively by history; and before pure reason or argumentative philosophy had been admitted into theology, evangelical history positively declared that the Holy Ghost appeared at the baptism of Jesus, under the form of a dove, and as a dove he was therefore represented. But when reasoning, and arguments deduced from reason, and no longer from history alone, invaded theology; when theology, which had at first been pure, became scholastic, in the hands of Anselme de Laon, Guillaume de Champeaux, Abelard, and others who preceded and followed them, then the Holy Ghost was likened even in person to God the Father, and he, like the other two Divine Persons, became man. But this, it must be remembered, was the period when Jesus Christ drew everything into his own orbit, and constrained even the Father to adopt his image and resemblance. The Holy Ghost followed the same course with the rest, and was depicted as of the same age and with the actual features of Christ as a man of thirty-three or even forty years of age. At a subsequent period, when the influence of reason penetrated even more deeply, in respect of the Divine Persons, a distinct individuality was preferred to resemblance; and the Holy Ghost was therefore made to differ, by art, from the Son, as the Father himself had been previously similarly distinguished from the Son. But it was at that time, also, that the Father regained the iconographic power that His Son had previously absorbed. The Father, instead of being himself veiled under the age and features of Jesus Christ, imposes upon Christ his own age and countenance as an old man, the Ancient of Days The Holy Spirit also has never been possessed of any special authority, but has almost always submitted to the iconographic revolutions originating in the Father and the Son: the Holy Spirit also had to bear the age and physiognomy of the Father; and was made to assume the appearance of an aged man.

Other chronological varieties may be deduced from art, that is to say, from the manner in which the dove or the man figuring the Holy Ghost are drawn. But these characteristics are not confined to the third Divine Person; they belong to all personages represented during the middle ages, and are common to Christian Iconography in general. The manner of treatment was large in the Latin epochs, minute in the Romanesque period, simple in the thirteenth century, mannered in the fourteenth, dry in the fifteenth. The whole cycle of art must, therefore, be studied in order to determine the precise age of any particular man or dove figuring the Holy Ghost. These æsthetic varieties cannot therefore be discussed at present.

THE ATTRIBUTES OF THE HOLY GHOST.

The attributes of the Holy Ghost may afford certain chronological varieties and other distinctive characteristics, similar to those mentioned in the History of the Father and of the Son; but as they are of the same nature with those of the other two persons of the Trinity, it will suffice merely to name them, and refer to the paragraphs in which they have already been more fully detailed. The Holy Ghost, like the Father and the Son, was at first distinguished from ordinary beings by a nimbus, next from celestial and glorified creatures, or from angels and saints, by a cruciform nimbus. That nimbus, however, goes through the same phases as have been described in chapters devoted especially to that subject; at first indeed the Holy Ghost, as in the ancient mosaics, was destitute of a nimbus;* sometimes, too, the nimbus is

* See the Holy Spirit hovering above the head of David, copied from a miniature in a Greek Psalter of the tenth century, Fig. 110.

radiating, but not cruciform, an instance of which is afforded by an ancient mosaic at Rome. The Holy Ghost is there represented on a palm tree, and precisely resembles the phœnix engraved upon Roman medals ; that bird, the symbol of immortality or of eternity, is constantly figured with a radiating nimbus. The Holy Spirit subsequently has a nimbus, but it is plain or without the cross. Later still the nimbus is divided by transverse bars, intersecting each other at right angles.

Fig. 127.—THE DIVINE DOVE, WITH A CRUCIFORM NIMBUS.
From a French Miniature of the XIV cent.*

Shortly after this, the field of the nimbus disappears altogether, the transverse bars alone remain, and are transformed into clusters or luminous floriations, rising from the brow and temples of the Holy Ghost, whether represented in the form of a man or of a dove. Finally even the clusters and floriation disappear and the Holy Ghost returns to the second primitive period when he had no nimbus, except that at that time he was destitute of any kind of glory. But we have arrived at the epoch when aureoles, the nimbi of the body, were tolerably frequent, under the form of rays, and the Holy Ghost, who has already been shown (Fig. 21) in a fresco at Mount Athos, placed in the centre of a radiating aureole, encircling both the other Divine Persons, was often thus represented, in the following design.

At the period when the cruciform nimbus was constantly given to all the three Divine Persons, it was not unusual for the dove representing the Holy Ghost to be entirely destitute

* Bibliothèque Royale, MS. Lat. fonds Lavall.

of any. This may have been an error similar to those already pointed out in reference to other facts, both analogous and

Fig. 128.—THE DIVINE DOVE, IN A RADIATING AUREOLE
From a French Miniature of the xv cent.*

dissimilar; but it arose more frequently from the diminutive size of the dove. That type, whether single or in connection with the Trinity, occupies but a very confined space, and the head forming so small a part of the Divine bird is sometimes scarcely perceptible. It is easily seen that it would have been almost impossible to represent a nimbus encircling so very minute a point. In sculpture, too, it was often very difficult, if not impossible, to circle the head of the Divine symbol with a cruciform nimbus; and it is therefore by no means unusual tq find doves without that attribute. When the dove approaches the diminutive dimensions of a sparrow, which we frequently find, it is always without any nimbus, plain, or cruciform. In the picture of Christ, surrounded by the seven doves of Isaiah, extracted from the Psalter of St. Louis,† six of the number have no nimbus, and that of the seventh is merely a plain nimbus. Still, as this picture is a

* See, in the Bibliothèque Royale, most of the books of "Hours" of the fifteenth and sixteenth centuries.

† The manuscript mentioned above belongs to the Bibliothèque de l'Arsénal. The drawing alluded to is given above, Fig. 40.

miniature, and the doves of a certain size, a cruciform nimbus might easily have been represented, more easily than in sculpture.

The other characteristic attributes of the Holy Ghost will not be mentioned here, since they are unconnected with chronology, and they will more naturally find a place in the chapter devoted to the History of the Holy Trinity.

HERESIES AGAINST THE HOLY GHOST.

Remarkable honours, as has been seen, were rendered to the Holy Ghost; churches were dedicated to him, a service established in his honour, and an order of chivalry consecrated to him. From the first ages of the Church down to the present time, the Holy Ghost has never ceased to be represented under the form either of a dove or of a man. He was thus depicted on the tomb of Junius Bassus, as early as the fourth century, shedding a stream of light upon the head of Jesus Christ.* Henceforth his symbol is constantly found upon the tombs of the early Christians, and Bosio, in his grand work, "*Roma Sotterranea*," supplies us with several examples.† In the Baptistery of St. John at Ravenna, which was built by the bishop Néon, in 451, is a mosaic, representing the baptism of Christ, and the Holy Ghost is there seen hovering above the Saviour's head.‡

A mosaic, dating from 533, in the church of Santa Maria in Cosmedin, in the same city, likewise contains a representation of the Holy Ghost.§

The mosaics in the church of Santa Prassede, in Rome, executed in the year 818, present a dove with its head encircled by a plain nimbus; this dove is resting on the

* The Holy Ghost here referred to is given *ante*, Fig. 87. See Bosio, *Rom. Sotterr.*, p. 45.

† See particularly pp. 87, 99, 351. The figure of the Holy Ghost at p. 155 scarcely appears to be ancient, although it is without a nimbus: at p. 351 it has a plain nimbus, and surmounts a pastoral chair, a cathedra or throne.

‡ Ciampini, *Vet. Monim.*, pars 1, tab. 70, p. 235.

§ Idem, ibid, pars 2, tab. 23, p. 78.

summit of a palm tree, while Christ is seen below, walking on the waters of the Jordan, and the hand of the Father is extended from the clouds. The hand is closed, holding a roll, on which the following words ought to be inscribed; "This is my beloved Son, in whom I am well pleased." * In the tenth, eleventh, and twelfth centuries, the Divine Doves appear to be very abundant, and numerous examples, already given, may be recalled to mind. In the thirteenth century, monuments, in which the Holy Ghost is figured, become innumerable. There is not, it may be said, one single representation of the Creation, either in painting or sculpture, in which the dove is not shown brooding over and animating the waters, as illustrative of the text, "Spiritus Dei ferebatur super aquas." †

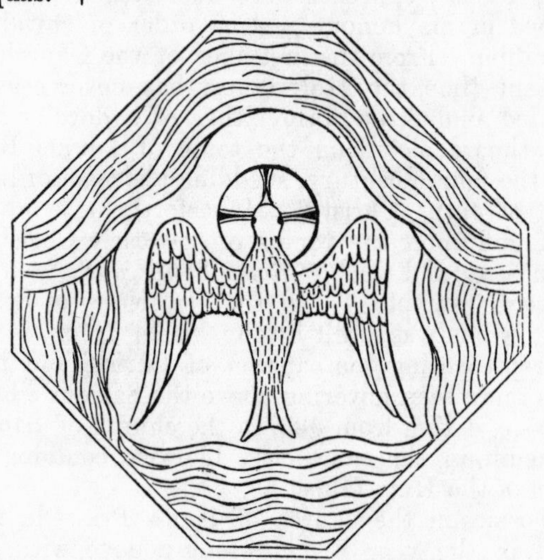

Fig. 129.—THE DIVINE DOVE, WITH A CRUCIFORM NIMBUS, FLOATING BETWEEN THE WATERS OF THE CREATION.
From a Painted Window of the XIII cent., in the Cathedral of Auxerre.

Both the art and the liturgy seem thus to have paid especial honour to the Holy Ghost, yet artists have fre-

* Ciampini, *Vet. Monim.*, vol. 2, Figs. 47, 52, pp. 148, 160.

† The dove here given, Fig. 129, is to be seen at Auxerre, in the Cathedral, on a painted window of the thirteenth century, in the side passage of the Sanctuary.

quently committed errors and have been guilty of omissions in respect of the Holy Ghost, to which Jesus Christ has never been exposed. Christ the most pre-eminently beloved of the three Divine Persons, lives constantly in the minds of Christians, and cannot under any circumstances be neglected or forgotten; but it is not thus with the Holy Ghost, who appears but very rarely in the Holy Scriptures, and who, in the devotional acts of the faithful takes a position inferior to Christ. Several instances of this tendency in the minds of men of the middle ages, are afforded by works of art. Thus it is not unusual for the Holy Ghost to be omitted even in pictures of Pentecost, a festival held peculiarly in honour of the Holy Ghost, and commemorating an event in which he was the most important personage. The scene is generally represented thus; the twelve Apostles (sometimes the Virgin is amongst them) are seated in the Cenaculum, and listening to the supernatural sounds heard above their heads. Above, descending from heaven, the Divine dove is seen, breathing rays or tongues of flame upon each of the Apostles' heads, and even on that of the Virgin, when the Virgin is present.

The Holy Spirit is, and ought to be, present; since, without him, it becomes difficult to explain the source of those rays of light descending from above. Still in a Spanish manuscript in the Bibliothèque of Amiens * twelve rays of red

The dove is white, with a red nimbus and yellow cross, the head raised, the wings extended, and the entire body surrounded by waves, which form a watery aureole of gold and azure: in spite of the text, the dove is not borne over the water, but is surrounded by it. The streams form an undulating frame-work round him, like the medallion encompassing a bust. In Fig. 112, the dove is seen literally borne upon the waters; in Fig. 122, the Holy Ghost is also borne upon the waters; but in the latter drawing, the figure is rather that of a little man or an infant, while in the other, and also in Fig. 129, here given, he has the figure of a dove.

* *Figuræ Bibliorum*, MS. in 4° of the year 1197. M. Dusevel, non-resident member of the "Comites Historiques," obligingly favoured me with an outline of this picture of the Descent of the Holy Ghost, from which the Holy Ghost himself is absent. In the grand cupola of the Church of St. Mark, at Venice, there is a mosaic, on a gold ground, representing the Apostles sitting and receiving the Holy Ghost, previous to their going forth to preach in all the world: a bluish ray descends upon each of them; at the extremity of each ray shines a tongue of fire, which rests upon the head of an Apostle. Here also, as in the Spanish manuscript, the Holy Ghost is absent; the flames

and yellow are seen issuing from heaven, and resting on the Apostles' heads; the Virgin is absent. The Holy Ghost is not apparent, and the rays seem to flow immediately from heaven; it is true that the heavens are opened, in the form of an inverted rainbow, and the Holy Spirit may be supposed to be concealed in those eternal depths, and thence to send forth his rays.

An enamelled triptych of the twelfth century in the Cathedral of Chartres (Chapelle Vendôme), exhibits a hand shedding upon the Apostles rays of fiery red; this subject is placed upon the wings of this singular monument of Romanesque workmanship.

The hand being in Iconography symbolic of God the Father, it must here be the Father who distributes the rays, and no longer the Holy Ghost, breathing them forth from his lips. Very different is the treatment of this subject in the cloister of St. Trophimus at Arles. There the twelve Apostles, but without the Virgin, are all assembled, all have the nimbus, and are clad in long garments, three without beards, and two much younger than the rest. The Apostles at St. Trophimus are not sitting, as they are usually represented, and as they are figured in the Spanish manuscript, and the triptych at Chartres amongst others; they are kneeling in order the more worthily to receive the Holy Ghost. In the upper part of the picture the entire body of the Divine dove is seen, and from its beak escape four cordons of flame, descending upon the heads of the Apostles. One ray, therefore, embraces three Apostles, unlike ordinary representations, in which a separate ray and tongue of fire descends upon each Apostle.

A painted window at Troyes, ventures even further than the triptych at Chartres.

The Trinity is painted on this little monument, which dates from the sixteenth century; the Father is there represented in papal robes, sitting on a rainbow, resting his

alone are seen. However, the Holy Spirit may possibly be symbolised even by those flames, and the third Divine person may be contained in a simple tongue of fire. He may be present in the form of a luminous ray as well as in that of a dove. I eagerly adopt this interpretation, for which I am indebted to M. l'Abbé Gaume.

feet on another rainbow, and holding in his hands the arms of the cross, on which his Son is nailed.

After the twelfth century, the Trinity is frequently thus represented; that manner of grouping the three Divine persons is one of the most common. In similar representations,* the Holy Ghost is always introduced in the form of a dove, either going from the Father to the Son, or from the Son to the Father; or placed at an equal distance between the two; or at the furthest placed upon one of the arms of the Cross. In this, however, the Holy Spirit is entirely forgotten, as is clearly shown in an engraving (Fig. 63) already given.

This drawing (Fig. 63) is minutely correct. The designer* has, at my request, accurately copied it even to the number of the rays, and of the undulating clouds, filling the field of the aureole; and to the exact number of crowns, encircling the tiara of the Father Almighty. The nimbi are both plain, the feet of the Father have shoes; the plate resembles in every point the painting on the window, and the figure of the Holy Ghost has never been introduced. Now the omission of one person out of three, and in a subject devoted more especially to the honour of the Trinity, is a fact of some moment, and proves the neglect to which artists were prone, in reference to the Holy Ghost.

This fact, extraordinary as it may appear, is not without a parallel in other epochs; in the sixteenth century, artists were equally careless, and scarcely less ignorant, in regard to religious subjects. The painted window in the Cathedral of Troyes, dating from that epoch, may not therefore be of any very great importance. But in the twelfth century, a learned and serious age, it was not thus. Still on one of the painted windows in St. Denis, executed by the command of Suger, windows which are still in existence, and the inscriptions for which were supplied by the learned Abbé himself, Christ is also seen attached to the cross, and supported in the hands of God the Father; it is the most ancient type with which I am acquainted of those representations so frequent during the thirteenth and fourteenth centuries.

* Several examples will be given in the chapter on the Trinity.

† M. Fichot, who has obligingly executed other designs for my Work

Now, in that Trinity also, the Holy Ghost is omitted, although a most convenient place might have been found for him at the summit of the Cross.* Such an instance of forgetfulness on the part of the pious Suger, could not have been intentional, and certainly demands explanation. Thus, the two extreme points in the history of our painting on glass, the twelfth and sixteenth centuries, present the same iconographic phenomena. In other countries, besides France, in the church of Vieux-Brissac, on the banks of the Rhine, for example, the stalls which were carved in the fourteenth century present a figure of the Father Almighty with bare head, a scarf upon his shoulders, and supporting the cross to which the Son is nailed. The Holy Spirit is omitted in that sculpture, as well as on the painted windows of St. Denis, and of Troyes.†

Thus too, in the catacombs, in scenes in which the Trinity ought to have been represented entire, in each of the three persons, the Father is in a measure suppressed, or at least does not appear.‡ At a subsequent period, the Father resumes, at the expense of the Holy Ghost, the place which the Holy Ghost had previously occupied, and in some few Trinities of the twelfth, fifteenth, and sixteenth centuries, one of the three Divine persons is still frequently absent, as in those of the fourth, fifth, and sixth; but it is not now the Father who is omitted, but the Holy Ghost. The Holy Ghost, therefore, has sometimes had reason to complain of artists.

Finally, the drawing already given, § in which the

* This painted window has already been noticed, p. 416, in the paragraph relating to the Triumphs of the Cross. It has been designed by M. L'Abbé Martin, *Vitraux de S. Etienne de Bourges*, Etude iv. F.

† It is just possible that the figure of the Holy Ghost may have been broken off; but I examined the stalls with extreme care, and could find no trace of any fracture. (Vide the *Missal of Poictiers*, Bibliothèque Royale, No. 873, for a Trinity without the Holy Ghost, folio 150.) It belongs to the sixteenth century.

‡ Not one single Trinity, actually complete, is to be found in the monuments of the Catacombs. In representations of the baptism of Christ, the Father is constantly omitted. In the Baptistery of San Giovanni, at Ravenna, fifth century, the Holy Ghost and Jesus Christ alone are depicted in the mosaic; the same thing occurs in a mosaic of the sixth century, in S. Maria in Cosmedin, also at Ravenna.

§ Fig. 60. This curious subject is taken from the Psalter of Jean, Duc de

Father and Son are represented with hands clasped in token of union, while the dove descends from heaven still further to unite them and himself with them by the extremities of his outstretched wings, appears to me to

Fig. 130.—THE HOLY GHOST IN THE UPPER PART OF THE CROSS; WITHOUT A NIMBUS, WITHOUT CRUCIFORM RAYS, WITHOUT ANY AUREOLE OR GLORY.
From a Painting on Panel, in the Church of St. Riquier; xv cent.

betray a strange want of reverence for the Holy Ghost. The celestial bird flies down from above, seeking to rejoin the two Divine persons, but an angel, whose body is seen issuing from the clouds of heaven, appears as if attempting to restrain the impetuosity of the bird by holding the tail between his two hands. The God thus kept in equilibrium between the two other Persons by the intervention of an

Berri, MS., in the Bibliothèque Royale, Suppl. Fr. 2015, and not, as has been erroneously stated, in the *Heures du Duc d'Anjou.* The miniature from which it was copied, is at the Psalm, "Dixit Dominus Domino meo."

angel, a being of his own creating, is indeed in a degraded and unworthy position. Little reverence can have been felt for the Holy Ghost, or such a subject could not have been thus grossly represented. We have already had occasion to remark the ill-feeling entertained by heretics and even by artists, in regard to the Father Almighty,* and the Holy Ghost appears to have been the victim of similar errors and passions.

The above observation is thrown out merely as suggesting matter for inquiry: the opinion expressed is merely submitted, not asserted as a positive fact. The figure last given, which will be followed by others of a similar character, is entitled to peculiar attention.

The above drawing, copied from a painting of the fifteenth century in the Abbey of Saint Riquier, is by no means reverential. The Father himself is treated with little respect, the Son is very poor, but the Holy Ghost is completely sacrificed. The bird with folded wings and claws, by which he is figured, is nailed on the upper part of the cross, instead of simply resting on it. The entire conception is wretched and undignified.

It is proper to remark in presence of such facts, that in the fourth century, Macedonius, patriarch of Constantinople, under Constantius, denied the divinity of the Holy Ghost: in the sixteenth century Socinius did the same. The Montanists did not deny the Holy Ghost, but made him double, thus equally lessening his dignity, and arriving almost at the same result with the Macedonians or followers of Macedonius. They considered the Holy Ghost to be distinct from the Paraclete.

Jesus having promised the Apostles, who were already endued with the gifts of the Holy Ghost that he would send them the Paraclete or Comforter, the Montanists imagined the one to be completely distinct from the other, and that the Paraclete was not the Holy Ghost. They therefore divided Christians into two bodies, the "πνευματικοί" who believed in the Paraclete, "a more perfect" form of the Spirit; and the "ψυχικοί" those who went not beyond the

* See the chapter on the History of God the Father, *passim*, and particularly p. 228.

first gifts of the Holy Ghost.* As the orthodoxy of Suger cannot be called in question, it seems the more astonishing that that great man should have suppressed the Divine dove in the above mentioned painted window, representing the Holy Trinity.

Severus, a heretic, who condemned the representing of the Holy Ghost under the form of a dove, was anathematised by the second Council of Nice, held in the eighth century. Arming himself with the pretext that the Holy Ghost ought not to be represented under the form of a bird, Severus carried away the doves of gold and silver that had been suspended above altars and baptismal fonts.† The interested heresy of Severus reminds us of the conduct of Dionysius the tyrant, who removed from the statues of Jupiter, the golden mantles with which they had been covered by the devotion of the pious, pretending that such a garment was too cold in winter and too warm in summer.

These facts are mentioned in order to direct the attention of antiquaries to the fact of the absence or presence of the Holy Ghost in representations of the Trinity, not with a view to drawing conclusions which may possibly be premature.‡

* The Holy Ghost had two names, "*ἅγιον πνεῦμα*," and "*ἅγια ψυχή*;" he was also called "*νοῦς*," and even "*λόγος*." The two first of these names indicate the soul, and seem to apply to the Spirit only in his attribute of love; the two others mean understanding, and are applicable to the spirit of intelligence.

† See the second Council of Nice. Consult an interesting work by M. L'Abbé J. Corblet, already quoted, and entitled, *Mémoires liturgiques sur les ciboires du moyen âge*, in 8vo, Amiens, 1842. M. Corblet writes thus:—"The fifth act of the second Council of Nice mentions the complaints made by the Monks of Antioch against the heretic Severus, who had appropriated to his own use the doves of gold and silver, suspended above baptismal fonts, under pretence that it was not right to represent the Holy Ghost under the figure of a dove." "Columbas aureas et argenteas, in figuram Spiritus-Sancti super divina lavacra et altaria appensas, una cum aliis sibi appropriavit, dicens non opportere in specie columbæ Spiritum-Sanctum nominare." The Fathers of the Councils of Nice and Constantinople condemned Xenara, who derided the custom of figuring the Holy Ghost by doves. (See *Duranti, de Rit. Eccl. Cath.* cap. v.)

‡ It may, perhaps, be possible to assign the absence of the Holy Ghost from the various painted and sculptured figures which have just been noticed, to a cause widely different either from forgetfulness or ill-will. Such representations, which, during the middle ages, were extremely frequent, are identical in every feature, excepting only the absence of the third Divine person, with those in which the three are united, and which we call Trinities. Still, when the

These outrages offered to the Holy Ghost were not confined to the earliest ages of Christianity alone; in the eleventh, twelfth, and thirteenth centuries men went so far as to question whether it could be right to raise churches in his honour, as had been done by Abelard.* The Holy Ghost, as has been shown, gave his name to many sacred edifices; but there was something insulting even in raising such a question.

Holy Ghost is absent, the artist may possibly have intended to depict, not a Trinity, but some other subject. The Father gives his Son to the world, and the Son offers himself for the salvation of mankind to die upon the cross; and it is the gift of the Father, and the sacrifice made by our Saviour, that the artist has sought to represent. Regarded in this light, the subject painted on the windows of S. Denis by the command of Suger, finds a very natural interpretation, and the same will serve also for the painted window at Troyes, the stall at Vieux Brissac, and the miniature in the Missal of Poictiers.

I am quite willing to restrict within these limits, the interpretation already given, and which might lead to the supposition that every instance of the Holy Ghost being omitted was an implied insult of that Divine person. Whatever may be the actual truth, great care is necessary in determining whether the person of the Holy Ghost is or is not figured in similar subjects. The chief advantage to be anticipated from the discussion now raised is, that it may excite persons interested in Christian Iconography to a more minute and scrupulous examination.

* Le Bœuf. *Etat des Sciences en France depuis le Roi Robert jusqu'à Philippe le Bel*, p. 149. Le Bœuf quotes the *Thesaurus Anecdotorum* and the *Amplissima Collectio*.

END OF VOL I.